THE ROUTLEDGE CO~
TO SCIENCE FIC~ ~

The Routledge Companion to Science Fiction is a comprehensive overview of the history and study of science fiction. It outlines major writers, movements, and texts in the genre, established critical approaches and areas for future study. Fifty-six entries by a team of renowned international contributors are divided into four parts which look, in turn, at:

- History – an integrated chronological narrative of the genre's development
- Theory – detailed accounts of major theoretical approaches including feminism, Marxism, psychoanalysis, cultural studies, postcolonialism, posthumanism, and utopian studies
- Issues and Challenges – anticipates future directions for study in areas as diverse as science studies, music, design, environmentalism, ethics, and alterity
- Subgenres – a prismatic view of the genre, tracing themes and developments within specific subgenres

Bringing into dialogue the many perspectives on the genre, *The Routledge Companion to Science Fiction* is essential reading for anyone interested in the history and the future of science fiction and the way it is taught and studied.

Mark Bould is Reader in Film and Literature at the University of the West of England. Co-editor of *Science Fiction Film and Television*, his books include *Film Noir* (2005), *Parietal Games* (2005), *The Cinema of John Sayles* (2008), *Neo-noir* (2009), and *Red Planets* (2009).

Andrew M. Butler is Senior Lecturer in Media and Cultural Studies at Canterbury Christ Church University. The editor of *An Unofficial Companion to the Novels of Terry Pratchett* (2007) and *Christopher Priest: the interaction* (2005), he has also written *Pocket Essentials* on *Philip K. Dick* (2000, 2007), *Cyberpunk* (2000), *Terry Pratchett* (2001), *Film Studies* (2002, 2005, 2008), and *Postmodernism* (2003). He co-edits *Extrapolation*.

Adam Roberts is Professor of Nineteenth-Century Literature at Royal Holloway, University of London, and the author of *Science Fiction* (2000) and *The History of Science Fiction* (2006). His most recent sf novels are *Gradisil* (2006), *Land of the Headless* (2007), *Splinter* (2007), and *Swiftly* (2008).

Sherryl Vint is Assistant Professor of English at Brock University. She is the author of *Bodies of Tomorrow* (2007) and is currently completing *Animal Alterity: science fiction and the question of the animal*. She co-edits *Extrapolation*, *Science Fiction Film and Television*, and *Humanimalia*.

THE
ROUTLEDGE COMPANION
TO SCIENCE FICTION

Edited by
Mark Bould, Andrew M. Butler,
Adam Roberts, and Sherryl Vint

LONDON AND NEW YORK

First published 2009 by Routledge

First published in paperback 2011
by Routledge
2 Park Square, Milton Park, Abingdon, Oxon OX14 4RN

Simultaneously published in the USA and Canada
by Routledge
270 Madison Ave, New York, NY 10016

Routledge is an imprint of the Taylor & Francis Group, an informa business

Typeset in Goudy Oldstyle Std 10.5/13pt by Fakenham Photosetting Ltd,
Fakenham, Norfolk
Printed and bound in Great Britain by TJ International Ltd, Padstow, Cornwall

British Library Cataloguing in Publication Data
A catalogue record for this book is available from the British Library

Library of Congress Cataloging in Publication Data
The Routledge companion to science fiction / edited by Mark Bould
... [et al.]. -- 1st ed.
p. cm. -- (Routledge literature companions)
Includes bibliographical references and index.
1. Science fiction--History and criticism. I. Bould, Mark.
PN3433.5.R69 2009
809.3'8762--dc22
2008028914

ISBN13: 978-0-415-45378-3 (hbk)
ISBN13: 978-0-415-45379-0 (pbk)

CONTENTS

CONTENTS

CONTRIBUTORS

Stacey Abbott is Senior Lecturer in Film and Television Studies at Roehampton and the author of *Celluloid Vampires* (2007). She is currently researching contemporary developments in cult television.

Mark Bould is Reader in Film and Literature at the University of the West of England. He is the author of *Film Noir: from Berlin to Sin City* (2005) and *The Cinema of John Sayles: lone star* (2008), and co-editor of *Parietal Games: critical writings by and on M. John Harrison* (2005), *Neo-noir* (2009), and *Red Planets: Marxism and science fiction* (2009). He co-edits *Science Fiction Film and Television*, and is an advisory editor for *Extrapolation*, *Historical Materialism*, *The Horror Journal*, *Paradoxa*, and *Science Fiction Studies*.

Piers D. Britton is Associate Professor of Visual Cultural Studies at the University of Redlands. His research is divided between sixteenth-century Florentine and Roman art, and the aesthetics of television and other popular culture. He is the co-author of *Reading Between Designs: visual imagery and the generation of meaning in The Avengers, The Prisoner and Doctor Who* (2003).

William J. Burling is Professor of English at Missouri State University, and the editor of *Mapping the Unimaginable: Kim Stanley Robinson and the critics* (2008). He has published on Robinson, Ursula Le Guin, China Miéville, and time-travel narratives.

Andrew M. Butler is Senior Lecturer in Media and Cultural Studies at Canterbury Christ Church University. The editor of *An Unofficial Companion to the Novels of Terry Pratchett* (2007) and *Christopher Priest: the interaction* (2005), he has also written *Pocket Essentials* on *Philip K. Dick* (2000, 2007), *Cyberpunk* (2000), *Terry Pratchett* (2001), *Film Studies* (2002, 2005, 2008), and *Postmodernism* (2003). He co-edits *Extrapolation*.

Jim Casey is Assistant Professor at High Point University. Primarily a Shakespearean scholar, he has also published on textual theory, performance theory, Chaucer, *Battlestar Galactica*, and comics artist David Mack.

Istvan Csicsery-Ronay Jr is Professor of English and World Literature at DePauw University. He is the author of *The Seven Beauties of Science Fiction* (forthcoming 2009) and co-editor of *Robot Ghosts and Wired Dreams: Japanese science fiction from origins to anime* (2007). He co-edits *Science Fiction Studies* and *Humanimalia*.

Victoria de Zwaan is Chair of the Cultural Studies Program at Trent University, and the author of *Interpreting Radical Metaphor in the Experimental Fictions of Donald Barthelme, Thomas Pynchon, and Kathy Acker* (2002).

Jane Donawerth is Professor of English and Affiliate in Women's Studies at the University of Maryland, and the author of *Frankenstein's Daughters: women writing science fiction* (1997) and co-editor of *Utopian and Science Fiction by Women: worlds of difference* (1994).

Neil Easterbrook is Associate Professor of Critical Theory and American Poetry at Texas Christian University. A consulting editor for *Science Fiction Studies* and *Extrapolation*, he has published on Søren Kierkegaard, William Carlos Williams, William Gibson, ancient Assyrian friezework, lexicography, and bad jokes.

Arthur B. Evans is Professor of French at DePauw University. The managing editor of *Science Fiction Studies*, he has published widely on Jules Verne and early French science fiction, including the award-winning *Jules Verne Rediscovered* (1988). He is general editor of Wesleyan University Press's "Early Classics of Science Fiction" book series.

Thomas Foster is Professor of English at the University of Washington. The author of *The Souls of Cyberfolk: posthumanism as vernacular theory* (2005), he is currently working on *Ethnicity and Technicity: nature, culture, and race in the cyberpunk archive*.

Lincoln Geraghty is Principal Lecturer in Film Studies at the University of Portsmouth. He is the author of *Living with Star Trek: American culture and the Star Trek universe* (2007) and *American Science Fiction Film and Television* (forthcoming), the editor of *The Influence of Star Trek on Television, Film and Culture* (2008) and *Future Visions: examining the look of science fiction and fantasy television* (forthcoming), and co-editor of *The Shifting Definitions of Genre: essays on labeling film, television shows, and media* (2008).

Joan Gordon is Professor of English at Nassau Community College, and Fulbright Distinguished Visiting Chair at the Maria Curie-Skłodowska University. A past president of the Science Fiction Research Association, she is the co-editor of *Blood Read: the vampire as metaphor in contemporary culture* (1997), *Edging into the Future: science fiction and contemporary cultural transformation* (2002), and *Queer Universes: sexualities in science fiction* (2008). She is currently working on a book triangulating among sociobiology, animal studies, and sf. She co-edits *Science Fiction Studies*.

Karen Hellekson is an independent scholar who works on sf, media studies, fan studies, and history. A founding editor of *Transformative Works and Culture*, she is a full-time freelance copyeditor in the scientific, technical, and medical market.

Matt Hills is Reader in Media and Cultural Studies at Cardiff University. The author of *Fan Cultures* (2002) and *The Pleasures of Horror* (2005), he is currently working on books on *Blade Runner* and *Doctor Who*.

Veronica Hollinger is Professor of Cultural Studies at Trent University, and co-editor of *Blood Read: the vampire as metaphor in contemporary culture* (1997), *Edging into the Future: science fiction and contemporary cultural transformation* (2002), and *Queer Universes: sexualities in science fiction* (2008). She co-edits *Science Fiction Studies*.

Mark Jancovich is Professor of Film and Television Studies at the University of East Anglia. His books include *Approaches to Popular Film* (1995), *Rational Fears: American horror in the 1950s* (1996), *Horror: the film reader* (2001), *Quality Popular Television: cult TV, the industry and fans* (2003), *Defining Cult Movies: the cultural politics of oppositional taste* (2003), *Film and Comic Books* (2007), and *The Shifting Definitions of Genre: essays on labeling film, television shows, and media* (2008). He founded *Scope: an online journal of film studies*.

Derek Johnston is a PhD candidate at the University of East Anglia, researching British television sf during the BBC monopoly.

Gwyneth Jones is a writer and critic of sf and fantasy, who also writes for teenagers as Ann Halam. She lives in Brighton, keeps a blog at <http://blog.boldaslove.co.uk/>, and a homepage at <http://homepage.ntlworld.com/gwynethann>. Her latest novels are *Rainbow Bridge* (2006) and, as Ann Halam, *Snakehead* (2007). A collection of short stories, *Grazing the Long Acre*, is forthcoming, and she has recently completed a space opera with the working title *The Princess of Bois Dormant*.

Darren Jorgensen is Lecturer in Art History at the University of Western Australia. He publishes on critical theory, Aboriginal studies, utopia, and new media. He is currently completing *Science Fiction and the Sublime*.

Abraham Kawa teaches Cultural Studies at the University of the Aegean. A novelist and scriptwriter, he has also published articles on comics and popular culture.

Paul Kincaid is the author of *What is it We Do When We Read Science Fiction* (2008) and co-editor of *The Arthur C. Clarke Award: a critical anthology* (2006). He was one of the founders of the Arthur C. Clarke Award, and administered it from 1996 to 2006.

James Kneale is Lecturer in Cultural and Historical Geography at University College, London, and co-editor of *Lost in Space: geographies of science fiction* (2002). He is currently writing about haunted London, and about counterfactual history and utopia.

Tanya Krzywinska is Chair in Screen Studies at Brunel University and President of the Digital Games Research Association. She is the author of *A Skin for Dancing In: possession, witchcraft and voodoo in cinema* (2000) and *Sex and the Cinema* (2006), co-author of *Science Fiction Cinema* (2000) and *Tomb Raiders and Space Invaders: videogame forms and contexts* (2006), and co-editor of *ScreenPlay: cinema/videogames/intertexts* (2002) and *Videogame/Player/Text* (2007).

Brooks Landon is Professor of English and Collegiate Fellow at the University of Iowa. He is the author of *The Aesthetics of Ambivalence: rethinking science fiction film in the age of electronic (re)production* (1992) and *Science Fiction after 1900: from the steam man to the stars* (1995).

Rob Latham is Associate Professor of English at the University of California at Riverside. The author of *Consuming Youth: vampires, cyborgs, and the culture of consumption* (2002), he is currently working on a book on New Wave sf. He co-edits *Science Fiction Studies*.

Isiah Lavender III is Assistant Professor of English and Director of the African and African American Studies Program at the University of Central Arkansas. He is currently completing *Blackgrounds of Science Fiction*.

Michael M. Levy is Professor of English and Chair of the English and Philosophy Department at the University of Wisconsin-Stout. A past president of both the Science Fiction Research Association and the International Association for the Fantastic in the Arts, he co-edits *Extrapolation*.

Roger Luckhurst is Professor of Modern Literature at Birkbeck College, University of London. He is the author of *The Angle Between Two Walls: the fiction of J. G. Ballard* (1997), *The Invention of Telepathy* (2002), and *Science Fiction* (2005).

Esther MacCallum-Stewart is a Research Fellow at SMARTlab, University of East London. She has written widely on the representation of history and warfare in sf. Her work examines the representation of history within digital game narratives, how players conflict, and how players interact socially, with an emphasis on MMORPGS.

Ken McLeod is Assistant Professor of Music History and Culture at the University of Toronto. He has published on identity politics in popular music, Chaos theory, popular music appropriations of art music, and the intersections between sf and rock music.

Farah Mendlesohn is Reader in Science Fiction and Fantasy Literature at Middlesex University. The editor of *Foundation: the international journal of science fiction* from 2001 to 2007, and co-editor of the Hugo Award-winning *The Cambridge Companion* *to Science Fiction* (2003), she is the author of *Diana Wynne Jones: children's literature and the fantastic tradition* (2005), *Rhetorics of Fantasy* (2008), and a forthcoming book on sf for children and teenagers.

Helen Merrick is Lecturer in the School of Media, Culture and Creative Arts at Curtin University of Technology. Her research focuses on feminist sf and feminist science studies. She is co-editor of *Women of Other Worlds: excursions through science fiction and feminism* (1999), and is on the editorial boards of *Extrapolation*, *Paradoxa*, and *Transformative Works and Cultures*.

China Miéville is the author of several novels, including *Perdido Street Station* (2000), *The Scar* (2002), and *Iron Council* (2004), a short-story collection, *Looking for Jake* (2005), and a novel for younger readers, *Un Lun Dun* (2007). His nonfiction includes *Between Equal Rights: a Marxist theory of international law* (2005). He is an honorary Research Fellow at Birkbeck School of Law, and Associate Professor of Creative Writing at the University of Warwick.

Aris Mousoutzanis is Visiting Lecturer in Media and Cultural Studies at Kingston University. He completed his Ph.D. on apocalypse, technoscience, and empire in 2007.

Graham J. Murphy teaches with Trent University's Cultural Studies Program and Department of English Literature and at Seneca College of Applied Arts and Technology. He is the co-author of *Ursula K. Le Guin: a critical companion* (2006), and is currently working on the intersections between utopian/speculative fiction, posthumanism, and insect discourse.

Patrick D. Murphy is Professor of English at the University of Central Florida and the founding editor of *ISLE: Interdisciplinary Studies in Literature and Environment*. He is the author of *Literature, Nature, and Other: ecofeminist critiques* (1995) and *Farther Afield in the Study of Nature-Oriented Literature* (2000), editor of *Literature of Nature: an international sourcebook* (1998) and co-editor of *Ecofeminist Literary Criticism: theory, interpretation, pedagogy* (1998).

Sharalyn Orbaugh is Associate Professor of Asian Studies and Women's and Gender Studies at the University of British Columbia. She specializes in modern Japanese cultural studies, particularly popular culture and sf.

Wendy Gay Pearson is Assistant Professor in Film Studies at the University of Western Ontario. She has published widely on discourses of sexuality, race, citizenship and belonging in both sf and contemporary Canadian film and literature. She is a co-editor of *Queer Universes: sexualities in science fiction* (2008).

Sean Redmond is Senior Lecturer in Film Studies at Victoria University of Wellington.

He is the editor of *Liquid Metal: the science fiction film reader* (2004), *Framing Celebrity: new directions in celebrity culture* (2006), and *The War Body on Screen* (2008). He is currently editing *Sounding Science Fiction* and *This is the Sea: the cinema of Takeshi Kitano*.

Michelle Reid is Research Officer for the LearnHigher CETL and a study adviser at the University of Reading. The assistant editor of *Foundation: The International Review of Science Fiction*, she co-edited *Parietal Games: critical writings by and on M. John Harrison* (2005) and has published articles on Damien Broderick, Nalo Hopkinson, and Charles de Lint.

Robin Anne Reid is Professor of Literature and Languages at Texas A&M University-Commerce. The author of *Arthur C. Clarke: a critical companion* (1997) and *Ray Bradbury: a critical companion* (2000), and the editor of *Women in Science Fiction and Fantasy* (2008), she is currently co-editing *Queering the Fantastic* and *The Fan Fiction Reader*.

John Rieder is Professor of English at the University of Hawai'i at Mānoa. The author of *Colonialism and the Emergence of Science Fiction* (2008) and editor of *Biography*'s special issue on "Life Writing and Science Fiction" (2007), he has also published on British Romanticism, children's literature, horror cinema, and Marxist theory.

Adam Roberts is Professor of Nineteenth-Century Literature at Royal Holloway, University of London, and the author of *Science Fiction* (2000) and *The History of Science Fiction* (2006). His most recent sf novels are *Gradisil* (2006), *Land of the Headless* (2007), *Splinter* (2007), and *Swiftly* (2008).

Alcena M.D. Rogan is Assistant Professor of English at Gordon College. She co-edited *Socialism and Democracy*'s special issue on sf (2006).

David N. Samuelson is Professor Emeritus at California State University, Long Beach. He has written on Gregory Benford, Arthur C. Clarke, Samuel Delany, Robert Heinlein, Ursula Le Guin, Walter Miller, and Frederik Pohl, and edited *Science Fiction Studies*' "Hard Science Fiction" special issue (1993).

Andy Sawyer is the librarian of the Science Fiction Foundation Collection at the University of Liverpool Library, and Director of their MA in Science Fiction Studies. He is Reviews Editor of *Foundation: The International Review of Science Fiction*. Recent publications include essays on Gwyneth Jones, Ramsey Campbell, Ursula K. Le Guin, and Terry Pratchett, and notes for new "Penguin Classics" editions of several H.G. Wells novels.

Joe Sutliff Sanders is Assistant Professor at California State University in San Bernardino. He is the International Conference on the Fantastic in the Arts'

Division Head for children's and young adult literature. Recent publications focus on girls' fiction, comic books, and metafiction for children.

J.P. Telotte is Professor of Film and Media Studies at Georgia Institute of Technology. Among his books are *Replications: a robotic history of the science fiction film* (1995), *A Distant Technology: science fiction film and the machine age* (1999), *The Science Fiction Film* (2001), *The Essential Science Fiction Television Reader* (2008), and *The Mouse Machine: Disney and technology* (2008). He co-edits *Post Script*.

Sherryl Vint is Assistant Professor of English at Brock University. She is the author of *Bodies of Tomorrow* (2007) and is currently completing *Animal Alterity: science fiction and the question of the animal*. She co-edits *Extrapolation, Science Fiction Film and Television*, and *Humanimalia*.

Marek Wasielewski is a Ph.D. candidate at the University of the West of England, researching early twentieth-century US comic strips.

Paul G. Williams is a Teaching Fellow in the Department of English at the University of Exeter. His research focuses on the ways in which the idea of race and colonialist assumptions resurface in the representation of modern and future war. He has published on Vietnam War films, *Mad Max Beyond Thunderdome*, *Hiroshima Mon Amour*, Langston Hughes, and the relationship between hip-hop culture and the War on Terror.

Peter Wright is Reader in English Literature and Film Studies at Edge Hill University. The author of *Attending Daedalus: Gene Wolfe, artifice and the reader* (2003), co-editor of *British Television Science Fiction* (2005), and editor of *Shadows of the New Sun: Gene Wolfe on readers, writers and writing*, he is currently co-editing *Critical Companion to Science Fiction Film Adaptations* (2009).

Lisa Yaszek is Associate Professor in Literature, Communication, and Culture at the Georgia Institute of Technology, and curator of the Bud Foote Science Fiction Collection. Vice-President of the Science Fiction Research Association, she is the author of *The Self Wired: technology and subjectivity in contemporary American narrative* (2002) and *Galactic Suburbia: recovering women's science fiction* (2008).

ACKNOWLEDGMENTS

In the shaping, commissioning, and editing of this volume, we have drawn upon conversations with and the knowledge, expertise, and support of more people than there is space to acknowledge. However, we would like to thank James Kneale, Jessica Langer, and Andy Sawyer for double-checking page references when our own resources were not sufficient.

INTRODUCTION

Mark Bould, Andrew M. Butler, Adam Roberts, and Sherryl Vint

Many different stories have been told about science fiction (sf), and this book retells, interrogates, contests, and revises some of them. For example, the origins of the genre have been argued about for decades. While some contend it was inaugurated by US pulp magazine editor Hugo Gernsback in 1926 (e.g., Westfahl 1998), others trace it back to writers from classical antiquity or the first century AD, such as Euripides, Cicero, Plutarch, Diogenes, and Lucian (e.g., Roberts 2006). Brian Aldiss (1973) influentially suggested Mary Shelley's *Frankenstein, or the Modern Prometheus* (1818) as the first ever sf text, while others have championed the fiction of Edgar Allan Poe in the 1830s and 1840s, Jules Verne from the 1860s onwards, and H.G. Wells from the 1890s onwards. A similar debate has raged over how to define the genre. The dozen main contenders identified by Clute and Nicholls (1993) and the 30 listed by Wikipedia represent a mere fraction of the attempts to delineate what sf is and to prescribe what it should be.

Such activities, while tremendously productive in some respects – including being a kind of phatic touchstone in fannish and academic circles – are incapable of producing definitive results or universal consensus. As John Rieder argues, "a genre consists of a web of resemblances established by repetition across a large number of texts" and therefore "the very notion of the founding instance or origin of a genre is self-contradictory, because the work in question is in an important way not an example of the genre it establishes, but rather a peculiarly influential violation of some pre-existing set of generic expectations" (Rieder 2008: 18–19). Moreover, genres do not have fixed identities. They "are not inert categories shared by all ... but discursive claims made by real speakers for particular purposes in specific situations" (Altman 1999: 101). They are ongoing, and by definition irresolvable, fields of contention between myriad discursive agents (between writers, readers, editors, directors, producers, viewers, players, fans, critics, detractors; between institutions of production, distribution, and consumption), many of whom may well be more interested in establishing, maintaining, and expanding markets for commodities and in promulgating ideologies than in the particular genre itself. And in an appropriately science-fictional manner, these discursive agents are not even necessarily human. Consequently, the origin stories, the bracketing off of ur-texts, prototypes, and precursors, the arguments over boundaries, margins, and hybrids, and definitions of any genre arise from myriad possible motivations and serve different purposes in an array of contexts. By their very nature, they emphasize certain people, texts, institutions and phenomena, and de-emphasize others. Decisions, conscious and otherwise, about what is central and what is peripheral, what is intrinsic and what extrinsic, shape and reshape any genre and our understanding of it.

Many of the first critical stories about sf, in both fan and academic discussions, argued that it was as worthy of attention as the rest of literature, while often also insisting on its unique qualities. In doing so, sf was effectively equated with prose fiction, and so other media – film, television, comics – and material practices – toys, games, environments – were omitted or marginalized as less serious, less valuable, less significant; and other genres were decried as inferior, particularly fantasy, which was typically treated as the feminized irrational Other to sf's masculine rigor and rationality.

Therefore, one principal aim of *The Routledge Companion to Science Fiction* is to bring into dialogue some of the many perspectives on the genre, without striving to resolve this multiplicity into a single image of sf or a single story of its history and meaning. For example, while the "History" section traces the development of sf in prose fiction from the seventeenth century to the present, more than half of its chapters are concerned with film, television, and comics, as well as material cultural practices, such as tourism, dime museums, and world's fairs; and the final section, on selected "Subgenres," offers a prismatic view of the kinds of stories sf tells across various media. The two central sections, "Theory" and "Issues and Challenges," situate these various historical understandings of the genre within an equally complex history of how the genre has been and is being studied, including some new approaches to it which are only now beginning to open up. *The Routledge Companion to Science Fiction* is thus designed to provide a survey not only of sf but also of the scholarship surrounding it.

The "History" section is divided by mode – prose fiction, film, television, comics, material culture – and organized by (rough) chronology so as to highlight a sense of the genre at specific historical conjunctures without sacrificing medium specificities. Some chapters do overlap slightly, but this is entirely appropriate as neither history nor media – nor our experience of them – are so neatly arranged. And although this is a substantial volume, we have not been able to include all that we would have liked – such as chapters on the longer history of sf, automata, radio, military planning, fashion, toys and games, UFOs and abduction narratives, futurology, the history of science, or sf art.

The "Theory" section examines the genre through the well-established perspectives and methodologies of sf scholarship. Some, such as Marxism, feminism, and utopian studies, laid the foundations for the academic study of the genre, while others played a dominant role in establishing media-specific critical approaches, such as the psycho-analytic theory underpinning much of the work on sf film. Some, such as nuclear criticism, are predominantly associated with a particular historical conjuncture, while others, such as postmodernism, played a significant role in bringing sf texts to wider attention, both popular and scholarly. Taken together, the chapters in this section situate sf within the major critical frameworks that have shaped its study.

The "Issues and Challenges" section proposes and explores elements of a future agenda for the study of sf. It provides an overview of theoretical approaches and methodologies that have not yet proven central to the study of sf, but which offer valuable tools for thinking about and understanding the genre. The chapters in this section are equally and simultaneously concerned with what sf can offer to scholars working within these paradigms. Some of the approaches highlighted in this section have recently been taken up in sf studies (e.g., music, environmentalism, science studies), and while some chapters draw attention to synergies between sf and well-established methodologies (e.g., young adult fiction, ethics and alterity), others introduce emergent areas of scholarship whose affinities with sf are promising (e.g., animal studies, digital games). In the next edition of this *Companion*, it may be that chapters currently in the third section will have moved to the second.

The "Subgenres" section focuses on different kinds of sf, each with its own distinct history and thematic concerns, and supplements the "History" section by identifying and elucidating techniques or themes that have developed and transformed across historical periods. Our selections are intended to cut across more than a century of sf, rather than being confined to a particular period. For example, while the New Wave and cyberpunk movements are dealt with in their specific historical contexts, by examining space opera as a subgenre it is easier to discern how such typically uncritical fantasies of imperialist expansion in the 1930s were reformulated in the 1990s as a vehicle for critiquing the politics of empire.

As this introduction hopefully indicates, we do not regard *The Routledge Companion to Science Fiction* as The One-and-Only True Account of Sf. In particular, we are conscious of its bias toward Anglophone sf from the US, the UK, and to a lesser extent Canada and Australia. Although some materials from other nations are discussed, these are mostly from northwestern Europe, the former Soviet Union, and Japan. One of the slowly emerging trends in sf scholarship is a sense of the genre as a global phenomenon, not merely in terms of the consumption of texts and practices produced in or by the First World, but also in its ability to express the experience of modernity among peoples excluded from the economic and geopolitical core. Sf has always been as much concerned with the past as with the future, and this volume stands at this moment in time, telling what has already passed in some of its richness, detail, and diversity, and looking forward into possible futures. No single book can tell the whole story of sf, but perhaps this one, in recognizing its own contingency, can open up a space for those voices still to be recovered and for those yet to come.

Bibliography

Aldiss, B. (1973) *Billion Year Spree*, London: Weidenfeld and Nicolson.
Altman, R. (1999) *Film/Genre*, London: BFI.
Clute, J. and Nicholls, P. (eds) (1993) *The Encyclopedia of Science Fiction*, London: Orbit.
Rieder, J. (2008) *Colonialism and the Emergence of Science Fiction*, Hanover, NH: Wesleyan University Press.
Roberts, A. (2006) *The History of Science Fiction*, London: Palgrave.

Westfahl, G. (1998) *Mechanics of Wonder: the creation of the idea of science fiction*, Liverpool: Liverpool University Press.

Wikipedia (n.d.) "History of Science Fiction." Online. Available HTTP: <http://en.wikipedia.org/wiki/History_of_science_fiction> (accessed 1 April 2008).

Part I
HISTORY

1

THE COPERNICAN REVOLUTION

Adam Roberts

This chapter is a small example of "long history" sf. The "long history" assumes, as its name might suggest, that sf is a cultural mode of relative antiquity, a view held by some commentators, though not, it should be noted, by most. The majority of critics are more comfortable with a "short history" model, seeing sf as a relatively *recent* development in human culture, beginning (according to some) with Gothic Romanticism – Mary Shelley's *Frankenstein, or the Modern Prometheus* (1818) is sometimes cited as the "first sf novel" – or (others say) beginning later still, with the work of Jules Verne and H.G. Wells in the later nineteenth century, or (according to yet others) even later than that, with Hugo Gernsback in the 1920s (see, respectively, Aldiss with Wingrove 1986; Luckhurst 2005; Westfahl 1998). These various accounts chime for many with the sense that sf is a characteristically modern phenomenon, one that does not truly flourish until the twentieth century.

But the "short history" leaves commentators with the problem of accounting for a large body of work of much greater antiquity that contains many of the features and tropes we all recognize as sf: travel to other planets, encounters with extraterrestrial lifeforms, utopian social speculation, and futuristic extrapolation. To call such works "proto-sf," "ur-sf," or "precursors to the genre" may be thought to beg the question (as if one decided that sculpture began with the work of Henry Moore, and so classified all earlier sculptural work as "proto-sculpture"). A simpler approach would be to note that if something walks like a cyberduck, and quacks like a cyberduck, then we might as well include it in our science-fictional aviary. That is a flippant way of putting it; but, as this chapter will try to show, there are in fact more important issues at stake in identifying the origins of sf with the Copernican revolution. To read the genre in that light is to see it as being determined by the forces present at its birth: the rapid and conceptually dizzying expansion of the cosmos, the encounter with alienness, a new way of thinking about time, and above all a cleavage between longstanding religious ways of understanding existence – which is, in essence, a magical apprehension of the cosmos – and the newer materialist, non-magical discourses of science.

Certainly it makes sense to separate out "*science* fiction" from "fantasy" on the grounds that the latter is magical; it always includes an excess that cannot be reconciled with or explained in terms of the world as we know it really to be. The consensus as to how the world actually works is called "science"; and just as "fantasy" exists in some sort of defining relationship with magic, so "sf" exists in some sort of defining relationship with science. This is true, even insofar as sf is in the business of exploring, and often transgressing, the boundary between what counts as science and what goes beyond (variously called "pseudoscience," "parascience," "mumbo jumbo," and so on). Of course, this boundary has not remained stable over the past few centuries; discourses now seen as pseudoscientific such as "mesmerism" or "spiritualism" were once counted as science but are no longer. But broadly speaking we can argue that sf begins at the time that science, as we understand the term today, begins. Copernicus has become emblematic of this sea-change in Western science. Howard Margolis (2002) lists nine "fundamental scientific discoveries" made around the year 1600 (including the laws of planetary motion, the magnetism of the Earth, and the distinction between magnetism and electricity) that together represent an unprecedented advance in scientific understanding. The title of his history of science sums up his thesis: It Started with Copernicus.

What was the Copernican revolution?

The second-century Alexandrian astronomer Claudius Ptolemy argued that the Earth lies at the center of the solar system, and that the Sun, Moon, five planets, and a sphere of fixed stars revolve diurnally about us, all of them embedded in transparent, crystalline, perfectly spherical shells. Medieval Europe found this model consonant both with people's common sense and with the biblical account of the cosmos. It is in this universe that early stories of interplanetary travel take place: for instance, Roman writer Cicero's Dream of Scipio (51 BC), in which the narrator dreams of roaming through the solar system, or Italian poet Dante Alighieri's epic poem Paradise (c. 1307–21), in which the narrator moves outwards from the Earth to the Moon, planets, and finally to the sphere of the fixed stars. Dante's poem makes plain that this Ptolemaic cosmos is a spiritual, and indeed theological, rather than a material place. Italian poet Ludovico Ariosto's poetical romance Orlando Furioso (1532) includes the journey of a chivalric hero to the Moon (helped up by John the Baptist) that makes no concessions to plausibility.

In fact the Ptolemaic model cannot explain all the observable astronomical data; but because this model was endorsed by the Church, challenging it was considered heresy. Mikołaj Kopernik, better known by his Latin name Nicolaus Copernicus, was a Catholic churchman and astronomer from Ermland (now part of Poland). His On the Revolution of the Celestial Orbs (1543) argued on the basis of careful astronomical observation that the Sun, not the Earth, is at the center of the cosmos. He was not the first to argue this – the medieval philosopher Nicholas of Cusa had suggested it in On Learned Ignorance (1440) – but Copernicus was the first to make the case on the back of properly collated scientific data, and it was his book that changed the way scientific culture conceptualized humanity's place in the universe.

Talk of a "Copernican revolution" is, perhaps, misleading; few "revolutions" in human affairs have been so cautious and, in some senses, conservative. Copernicus believed, for instance, that the planets moved in *circles* about the Sun, not because there was any observational evidence to this effect but because circles were assumed to be more "perfect" than any other shape, and Copernicus had not shaken off the medieval notion that idealized perfection was the true idiom of the heavens. Similarly, he believed like Ptolemy that the planets were embedded in crystalline spheres, rather than being bodies in ballistic motion. Again, where we might expect a *revolution* to happen rapidly, Copernicus's theories spread only very slowly, hampered by the Church's hostility, the small print run of his book and the inertia of the learned scholastic traditions. By the end of the sixteenth century most European scholars, whether they accepted or rejected it, knew about the theory, although the Catholic Church continued persecuting the theory well into the seventeenth century. So, for example, when Italian astronomer Galileo Galilei published a scientific work arguing in Copernicus's favor in 1632, he was condemned by the inquisition and compelled to recant. Johannes Kepler, as a Protestant, avoided the direct fury of the Catholic Church, although he faced other obstacles and hostility as he refined Copernicus's model, proving many things, not least (in *New Astronomy* (1609)) that planetary orbits follow ellipses rather than circles. By the end of the seventeenth century, English scientist Isaac Newton supplied, with his laws of motion and gravitation, the theoretical and mathematical necessities to make the fullest sense of Copernicus's cosmos. By Newton's time, science had become much more recognizably modern. In the words of A.R. Hall, Copernican science was "a growth, an intensification of the trend of medieval science, rather than a deflection from it. Almost everything that happens in the history of science in the 16th century has a medieval precedent, and would have been comprehensible, if repugnant, to earlier generations in a way that the science of the age of Newton was not" (Hall 1990: 449–50).

We might wonder, then, why it is conventional to talk of a Copernican revolution, rather than (say) a Keplerian or Newtonian one? In part, Copernicus gets credit as the first individual to advance heliocentrism on the basis of detailed research. But more importantly, it was Copernicus's theory that became the locus of opposition to the Church's domination of knowledge. The Copernican revolution is bound up with the ways in which science supplanted religion and myth in the imaginative economy of European thought; and sf emerges from, and is shaped by, precisely that struggle. Contemporaries certainly saw the new cosmology in these terms, and many of the earlier writers of sf were Protestants. John Donne's satirical work *Ignatius his Conclave* (1611) mocks the Pope for continuing to persecute the new science: Donne is surprised to meet Copernicus in Hell ("For though I had never heard ill of his life, and therefore might wonder to find him there; yet when I remembered, that the *Papists* have extended the name, & the punishment of Heresie, almost to every thing" (Donne 1969: 188)), but this is revealed to be a symptom of Ignatius Loyola's Jesuitical bigotry rather than Divine displeasure. Copernicus, on the other hand, is unfazed; when baited by Lucifer, he retorts that Lucifer is only a sort of alien lifeform ("I thought thee of the race of the starre *Lucifer*, with which I am so well acquainted" (Donne 1969: 188)). At the end of this satire Copernicus goes free and the Jesuits are all sent off to colonize the Moon, where, the narrator suggests, they can do less mischief.

Seventeeth-century interplanetary tales

Donne's speculative tale of lunar colonization was one of the earliest examples of what became a vigorous strand of seventeenth-century interplanetary romances (Marjorie Hope Nicolson (1960) lists some 200 of these, and hers is an incomplete list). Copernicus had opened up the cosmos, and writers rushed to fill the imaginative vista in radically new and materialist ways. The solidly science-based imaginative extrapolation of Johannes Kepler's *A Dream, or Lunar Astronomy* (1634; written c. 1600) captures exactly the shift in sensibility that enabled sf to come into being. It starts fantastically enough, with the narrator dreaming of meeting a witch, who in turn summons a demon to carry them both to the Moon; but once there, the story is given over to detailed scientific speculation about what life might actually be like in that place, where each day and each night lasts a fortnight. Kepler imagines weird utterly inhuman alien lifeforms, serpentine and estranging, forced to hide from the heat of the day in caves; and he backs up his speculation with detailed and carefully researched scientific appendices. Indeed, the appendices are four times the size of the brief prose narrative, a ratio which articulates a sense of the respective importance of the scientific and the imaginative in this work. This is the first genuine attempt at imagining alien life in terms of radical otherness, and some see *A Dream* as the first true sf novel (Roberts 2006: 42–5).

More commercially successful was Francis Godwin's space-journey adventure *The Man in the Moone or, a Discourse of a Voyage Thither by Domingo Gonsales, the Speedy Messenger* (1638). The first bestseller of this new sort of Copernican fantastic voyage, it went through 25 editions in the remainder of the century, and was translated into several languages. It is not hard to see why it was so successful, for it combines a solid narrative drive with a nicely handled apprehension of the marvelous. Godwin's Spanish protagonist flies up from the island of St Helena to the Moon by harnessing a flock of geese – no ordinary geese, these, but an unusual breed that migrates into outer space. On the Moon, he encounters a utopian society of humanoid creatures, before returning to Earth, landing in China. The whole thing is told with verve and a winning attention to detail, with enough verisimilitude that some contemporary readers believed it a true account.

Cyrano de Bergerac read the French translation of Godwin's book before writing his own sprightly and witty lunar voyage, *The Other World, or the States and Empires of the Moon* (1657). Cyrano's protagonist flies from France to Canada and thence to the Moon by employing a series of imaginative modes of transportation, including one craft powered by the evaporation of dew, and another by fireworks – this last device effectively a rocket that moves the logic of spaceflight from fantastical into plausibly *technical* idioms. Cyrano's lunarians, huge four-legged beings, refuse to believe that this tiny biped is a man (they eventually classify him as a kind of bird). In a sequel, *Comical History of Mr Cyrano Bergerac, Containing the States and Empires of the Sun* (1662), Cyrano builds yet another spaceship, this time using mirrors to focus the Sun's rays into hot blasts, and visits the Sun.

The Moon was a common destination. The anonymous Spanish work *Crotalón*

(1552) looks down upon the Earth from the Moon in order satirically to critique human stupidity. In the anonymous manuscript tale *Selenographia: the Lunarian* (1690), the Moon is reached with a giant kite. Daniel Defoe's *The Consolidator, or, Memoirs of Sundry Transactions from the World in the Moon* (1705) is similarly satirical. Other worlds were also approached. The female protagonist of Margaret Cavendish's *The Description of a New World, Called the Blazing-World* (1666) finds a new planet attached to the Earth at the North Pole, and, exploring it, is eventually made its empress. Edmund Spenser's epic poem *The Faerie Queene* (1590–6) is set in "Fairyland"; but the second book opens with a rebuke to those who had read the first book and claimed not to know where "Fairyland" is. Previously, Spenser insists, nobody had heard of Peru or America. Fairyland might be a similar case, perhaps located on the Moon or on another star ("What if within the Moones faire shining spheare? / What if in euery other starre vnseene?" (Spenser 1970: 71)). Imagining human travel to the Moon inevitably suggests reciprocation: lunar aliens coming to Earth. French writer Charles Sorel's novel *The True Comic History of Francion* (1623), perhaps the bestselling French novel of the century, wonders if there might be "a prince like Alexander the Great up there, planning to come down and subdue this world of ours," and speculates about the "engines for descending to our world" such an invader might be assembling (Sorel 1909: 425).

All the works so far mentioned are "scientific" romances in the sense that they try, with varying degrees of attention, to ground their speculation in the science of the day. But those very theories of science were deeply implicated in new theories of religion, such that the Renaissance (associated with the former) and the Reformation (associated with the latter) can be considered aspects of the same underlying cultural logic. This fact shapes the sf of the seventeenth century, just as it continues to shape the sf of the twenty-first. Certainly none of the earliest interplanetary stories were what we might call "secular." On arriving on the Moon and seeing its inhabitants, the hero of Godwin's *The Man in the Moone* cries out "Jesus Maria," which causes the lunarians to "fall all down upon their knees, at which I not a little rejoiced" (Godwin 1995: 96). John Wilkins's *The Discovery of a World in the Moone. Or, A Discourse Tending to Prove that 'tis Probable There May be Another Habitable World in that Planet* (1638) likewise discusses whether extraterrestrials "are the seed of Adam" and therefore "liable to the same misery [of original sin] with us, out of which, perhaps, they were delivered by the same means as we, the death of Christ" (Wilkins 1973: 186–92).

The problem for these authors was that imaginatively populating other planets with alien life undermined the uniqueness of Christ's atonement for original sin. The crucifixion was taken to be a unique event that saved the inhabitants of the Earth from damnation; but what about inhabitants of other planets? Either they had been abandoned by God, or else they each had their own individual Christ. Neither of these options appealed to seventeenth-century thinkers: the former implied an uncaring God, the latter degraded the uniqueness of Christ's sacrifice. Lambert Daneau's *The Wonderfull Woorkmanship of the World* (1578) rejects the idea that there could be "another world like unto ours" precisely because nobody can determine "what is their state, order, condition, fall, constancy, Saviour, and Jesus" or say "what likewise is their life everlasting, and from whence cometh the salvation of this second or third world" (qtd in Empson 1993: 201). Similarly, the first person Cyrano meets on the Moon is the biblical Elijah, who tells him "this land is indeed the same moon that you can see from your own globe, and this place in which you are walking is Paradise, but it is the Earthly Paradise" (Cyrano de Bergerac 1970: 44). Cyrano's Eden was high enough, as it were, to have avoided inundation by Noah's flood. Wilkins makes a similar case in *Discovery of a World in the Moone*, describing the Moon as a "celestiall earth, answerable, as I conceive, to the paradise of the Schoolemen … this place was not overflowed by the flood, since there were no sinners there which might draw the curse upon it" (Wilkins 1973: 203–5).

By the middle of the seventeenth century, this anxiety was, broadly, giving way to a belief that not only were there many other stars and worlds, but, as English philosopher James Howell put it in his *Epistolæ Ho-Elianæ* (1647), that "every Star in Heaven … is coloniz'd and replenish'd with Astrean Inhabitants" (Howell 2005: 530). But in fact this belief was just as theologically determined, based upon the idea that God would not create so vast a cosmic space to no purpose, and that therefore all planets *must* contain life. Two popular French works, Pierre Borel's *New Discourse Proving the Plurality of Worlds* (1657) and Bernard de Fontenelle's bestselling *Dialogue on the Plurality of Worlds* (1686), expatiated on this new idea, and Dutchman Christaan Huygens's *Cosmotheoros* (1698) zips around the Copernican universe to find not only that everywhere is inhabited but also that Justice, Honesty, Kindness, and Gratitude are omnipresent. These issues – the anxieties generated by Copernicus's undermining of our special place in the universe; questions of transcendence and atonement; and a sense of the purposiveness and profusion of cosmic life – still haunt sf. For instance, "savior" figures occur and reoccur in sf: the "chosen ones" of Robert A. Heinlein's *Stranger in a Strange Land* (1961), Frank Herbert's *Dune* (1965), the *Star Wars* trilogies (1977–83, 1999–2005), and the *Matrix* (1999–2003) trilogy, as well as superheroes like Superman and Spider-Man who carry the burden of having to "save" the world. I would argue that the reason why sf keeps returning to this figure concerns the forces that determined the origins of the genre. This is not, of course, to suggest that twentieth- and twenty-first-century sf is written in self-conscious dialogue with seventeenth-century theological debates of which few modern-day writers are even aware, but rather that these cultural forces, present at the birth of the genre, deter-mined and gave shape to sf as a whole, and indirectly affected those writers who took their places in the tradition of sf by following "generic" conventions. More to the point those questions are more than narrowly theological; they connect with broadly human-existential anxieties and uncertainties.

Time

Despite these and many other seventeenth-century stories about traveling into space, many critics remain unpersuaded that a "long history" is the best way of understanding sf's origins. To speak broadly, an important debate in sf criticism is whether the "voyage in space" is the genre's defining feature, or whether it is better to see sf as embodying a temporal imagination. This is not to say that sf novels must be "set in the future." Rather, what critics who see sf as temporally determined articulate is a sense that sf is a counterfactual literature: not things as they actually are, but as they might *be*, whether in the future, in an alternative past or present, or in a parallel dimension.

One of the axioms of sf criticism is that this "counterfactual" element enters the picture much later than Copernicus. For example, Paul Alkon insists that "the impossibility of writing stories about the future" was "widely taken for granted until the 18th-century" (Alkon 1987: 4), while Darko Suvin locates the "central watershed" of the development of sf as a specifically futuristic fiction "around 1800, when space loses its monopoly upon the location of estrangement and the alternative horizons shift from space to time" (Suvin 1979: 89). However, the case can be made that *time* was a determinant of sf long before this – that, in fact, the Copernican revolution unshackled the creative imagination from biblical rectitude in temporal, as well as spatial, terms. By opening up cosmological *spatial* scales, Copernican beliefs also challenged the chronological assumptions of European culture. The biblical Old Testament dates the creation a few thousand years ago (famously, Irish Archbishop James Ussher's *Annals of the World* (1650) calculated from biblical genealogies that the creation occurred at the sunset preceding Sunday 23 October 4004 BC); and the New Testament promises that the end of the universe is imminent. Neither claim is factually accurate. In the seventeenth and early eighteenth centuries, understanding of "long time" underwent a radical shift. French writer Jean de La Bruyère's *Characters* (1688) looks forward into enormous gulfs of time:

> Even if the world is only to last for a hundred million years, it is still in its first freshness and has barely begun; we ourselves are close to primitive man, and are likely to be confused with them in the remote future. But if one can judge of the future by the past, how much is still unknown to us in the arts, in the sciences, in nature and indeed in history! what discoveries are still to be made! what various revolutions will surely take place in States and Empires!
>
> (La Bruyère 1935: 107)

Benoit de Maillet's posthumously published *Telliamed* (1748) argues that humankind is half a billion years old, and much of its story is given over to a future extrapolation (of the world desiccating, flaring up to burn as a star, and then dying away to a dead and inert body) that takes billions of years more. Smaller-scale future extrapolations were commonplace. John Dryden's long poem *Annus Mirabilis* (1667) describes the Great Fire of London in detail and then ends with a lengthy future vision of the city that, he was sure, would rise from the ashes. Indeed, Alkon himself notes several seventeenth-century future histories, among them the anonymous *Aulicus his Dream of the Kings Sudden Comming to London* (1644), which narrates a possible political future, and French writer Jacques Guttin's popular *Epigone, the History of a Future Century* (1659); and it is easy enough to find even earlier counterfactuals than these. For example, the anonymous English play *A Larum for London* (1602) dramatizes the recent Spanish sack of Antwerp in order, explicitly, to present London with a possible future narrative of Spanish invasion. Time itself appears as a character on stage, exhorting the audience to consider how the future might play out and claiming that he "doth wish to see / No heavy or disastrous chaunce befall / The Sonnes of men, if they will warned be. " (Anon. 1913: 51)

Politics

By challenging the authority of scripture, Copernicus challenged the authority of the Church, and this, in an era when it was a prime axis of political power, makes the Copernican revolution a political phenomenon. This is reflected in the seventeenth-century flourishing of that more obviously political mode of speculative fiction, utopia. Thomas More inaugurated this subgenre with his short prose tale *Utopia* (1516), in which a traveler reports visiting a distant island upon which society is ordered in immeasurably better ways than in our corner of the world. The name "utopia" parses a double meaning (in Greek *eu-topia* means "good place" and *ou-topia* means "no-place" – a place both ideal and fictional). More's new genre caught on fairly quickly. Juan Luis Vives borrowed explicitly from More to plan a utopian welfare state in his native Spain in *Subventions for the Poor* (1526). Italian churchman Tommaso Campanella's *The City of the Sun* (1602) is closer to More's premise in imagining a fictional utopian city. Speaking broadly, it was this emphasis on *place* (good-place/no-place) that shaped imaginative engagement with utopian thought. Joseph Hall's *A World Other and the Same* (1605) and Charles Sorel's *The True Courier* (1632) both locate rather jolly utopias in an imaginary land to the south of Australia. Hans von Grimmelshausen's German picaresque novel *Simplicissimus* (1668) includes among its many adventures a sojourn in a utopia populated by sylphs in the middle of the Earth. As actual explorers mapped the globe, so writers found idealized worlds in all manner of places. French writer Gabriel de Foigny returned to the southern hemisphere for his utopia, *The Australian Land* (1676); Joshua Barnes's *Gerania* (1675) describes a kingdom of miniature humans "on the utmost Borders of India" (Barnes 1675: 1); Richard Head's *O-Brazile: or The Inchanted Island* (1675) is set in South America.

But this is not to say that utopia, any more than other seventeenth-century sf, was purely a spatial mode of writing. It is easy for utopia, insofar as it represents an ideal-izing commentary upon present-day concerns, to project its alternative into a notional future world. Englishman Samuel Hartlib dedicated his utopian fiction, *Description of Macaria* (1641), to the English Parliament as a model future development for the country as a whole ("Macaria was a kind of prismatic mirage which shone before the zealous projector to the end of his life" (Bush 1962: 266)). Some writers, like John Milton in his *The Ready and Easy Way to Establish a Free Commonwealth* (1660), preferred directly to address the actual possibilities of social change in the mode of political tract or polemic; but many others decided that their aspirations for the future of the country would be best embodied in fictional form. Samuel Gott's *Nova Solyma* (1648), imagining England's possible future as a religious republic (its title means "New Jerusalem"), and Gerard Winstanley's dry *Oceana* (1656), an account of a possible future-Britain, are two examples among many. Francis Harding's Latin poem,

On the Arts of Flying (1692), concerns an idealized future British Empire predicated upon the invention of flying machines: the rich leave Earth for the other planets, bequeathing their estates to the poor, with a new British aerial navy establishing peace on the Moon.

Conclusion

There is always the danger that an essay such as this will degenerate into a dry list of titles and dates. I have tried to show that whatever variety of sf it is that interests us (interplanetary travel, counterfactuals, alien encounters, utopias), there are many examples of it during the period immediately after Copernicus. I hope to have suggested, moreover, that this is no mere coincidence but rather a specific reaction to the imaginative expansion the Copernican revolution entailed. The continuing relevance of these tropes connects profoundly with the new ways of thinking about the world that came with the changes of the Copernican revolution. The seventeenth century was that period when science, as we understand the term, first began to impinge upon culture more generally; and the anxieties, and exhilarations, of that interaction, inflected through a number of religious discourses, are still shaping sf today.

Bibliography

Aldiss, B. with Wingrove, D. (1986) *Trillion Year Spree: the history of science fiction*, London: Gollancz.

Alkon, P.K. (1987) *Origins of Futuristic Fiction*, Athens: University of Georgia Press.

Anon. (1913) *A Larum for London, or the siedge of Antwerpe with the vertuous actes and valorous deedes of the lame soldier*, ed. W.W. Greg, London: Malone Society.

Barnes, J. (1675) *Gerania: a new discovery of a little sort of people anciently discoursed of, called Pygmies. With a lively description of their stature, habit, manners, buildings, knowledge, and government, being very delightful and profitable*, London: Obadiah Blagrave.

Bush, D. (1962) *The Oxford History of English Literature: the early 17th-century 1600–1660*, 2nd rev. edn, Oxford: Oxford University Press.

Cyrano de Bergerac, S. de (1970) *L'autre monde ou les etats et empires de la lune [Voyage dans la lune]*, 1657, ed. M. Laugaa, Paris: Garnier-Flammarion.

Donne, J. (1969) *Ignatius his Conclave*, ed. T. Healey, Oxford: Oxford University Press.

Empson, W. (1993) *Essays on Renaissance Literature*, vol. 1, ed. J. Haffenden, Cambridge: Cambridge University Press.

Godwin, W. (1995) *The Man in the Moone: or, a discourse of a voyage thither by Domingo Gonsales, the speedy messenger*, 1638, ed. J.A. Butler (Publications of the Barnaby Riche Society No. 3), Ottawa, Canada: Dovehouse Editions.

Hall, A.R. (1990) "Intellectual Tendencies: science," in G.E. Elton (ed.) *The New Cambridge Modern History: the Reformation 1520–1559*, Cambridge: Cambridge University Press.

Howell, J. (2005) *The Familiar Letters of James Howell*, 1647, ed. J. Jacobs, Whitefish, MT: Kessinger Publishing Company.

La Bruyère, J. de (1935) *Oeuvres complètes*, Paris: Gallimard, Édition Pleiade.

Luckhurst, R. (2005) *Science Fiction*, Cambridge: Polity.

Margolis, H. (2002) *It Started with Copernicus*, New York: McGraw-Hill.

Nicolson, M.H. (1960) *Voyages to the Moon*, 1948, New York: Macmillan.

Roberts, A. (2006) *The History of Science Fiction*, London: Palgrave.

Sorel, C. (1909) *La vraie histoire comique de Francion*, 1623, ed. E. Colombey, Paris: Garnier.

Spenser, E. (1970) *Poetical Works*, ed. E. de Selincourt and J.C. Smith, Oxford: Oxford University Press.

Suvin, D. (1979) *Metamorphoses of Science Fiction: on the poetics and history of a literary genre*, New Haven, CT: Yale University Press.

Westfahl, G. (1998) *The Mechanics of Wonder: the creation of the idea of science fiction*, Liverpool: Liverpool University Press.

Wilkins, J. (1973) *The Discovery of a World in the Moone. Or, A discourse tending to prove that 'tis probable there may be another habitable world in that planet*, 1638, intro. B. Shapiro, Delmar, NY: Scholar's Facsimiles and Reprints.

2
NINETEENTH-CENTURY SF

Arthur B. Evans

The sf genre obtained its name and social identity during the early decades of the twentieth century in the American pulp magazines. But a recognizable literary tradition was, according to many critics, conceived during the industrial revolution and born during the latter half of the nineteenth century in Jules Verne's *voyages extraordinaires* and H.G. Wells's *fin-de-siècle* "scientific romances." These two sf variants pioneered by Verne and Wells (hard/didactic versus speculative/fantastic) became the two major modes that have dominated the genre ever since.

The explosion of sf-type narratives during the nineteenth century can be understood only within the historical context of the industrial revolution and the transformative (and often alienating) social changes that accompanied it. The generally positive and positivist outlooks common in certain late-Enlightenment works such as Louis-Sébastien Mercier's futurist utopia *The Year 2440* (1771) and Marie Jean Antoine Nicolas de Caritat, Marquis de Condorcet's *Sketch for a Historical Picture of the Progress of the Human Mind* (1795) soon metamorphosed into their dark counterpart in works such as Mary Shelley's *Frankenstein, or the Modern Prometheus* (1818). Moving the source of terror from the supernatural to the scientific, Shelley's Gothic novel exemplified the Romantic rejection of the eighteenth-century Cartesian belief in the scientist as hero and in technology as inherently good. *Frankenstein* expressed the fears of an entire *mal-du-siècle* generation caught in a sudden paradigm shift between tradition and modernity. As such, the novel proved to be highly influential and popularized what was to become a standard nineteenth-century sf archetype: the mad scientist who, in his hubris-filled pursuit of knowledge and power, betrays basic human values. Notable works before and after *Frankenstein* that feature such Faustian scientists include E.T.A. Hoffman's "The Sandman" (1816), Honoré de Balzac's *The Centenarian* (1822) and *The Search for the Absolute* (1834), Nathaniel Hawthorne's "The Birthmark" (1843) and "Rappaccini's Daughter" (1846), Robert Louis Stevenson's *Strange Case of Dr Jekyll and Mr Hyde* (1886), Robert Cromie's *The Crack of Doom* (1895), H.G. Wells's *The Island of Doctor Moreau* (1896), and Jules Verne's *The Master of the World* (1904), among many others. Finally, although some sf historians have proclaimed Mary Shelley's novel the "ur-text" for the entire genre, others disagree, insisting that "SF is a literature of technologically saturated societies" and a "genre that can therefore emerge only relatively late in modernity ... a popular literature that concerns the impact of Mechanism (to use the older term for technology) on cultural life and human subjectivity" (Luckhurst 2005: 3).

As European society continued to mutate amid rapid industrial growth, the spread of new technologies, and various political upheavals, a new and radical idea began to take hold: that the future could be very different from the past. From this basic notion emerged a second sf thematic strand that proliferated throughout the nineteenth century: futuristic fiction. Félix Bodin's novel/manifesto *The Novel of the Future* (1834) argued for the importance of this new genre and described how such narratives, filled with the wonders of the scientific age, would constitute the epic literature of tomorrow (Alkon 1987: 245–89). About three decades earlier, in 1805, Jean-Baptiste Cousin de Grainville had already broken new cognitive ground in *The Last Man* by visualizing the Christian apocalypse in secular terms (an approach adopted by Mary Shelley in 1826 in a novel of the same name in which she imagines a plague wiping out the world's population). And, near the close of the century, Camille Flammarion's *Omega: the last days of the world* (1894) posited a kind of astronomical-cum-spiritualist apocalypse occasioned by the heat-death of our solar system. Other future-catastrophe (though not necessarily end-of-the-world) fictions from this period include Richard Jefferies's *After London* (1885), a post-holocaust novel in which England reverts to barbarism, and numerous cautionary future-war stories beginning with George Chesney's seminal invasion tale *The Battle of Dorking*, published in 1871, discussed in detail in I.F. Clarke (1992).

Much of the futuristic fiction of the nineteenth century sought to portray – either positively or negatively – humanity's social "progress" in the years to come. One imaginative and light-hearted example was Jane Webb-Loudon's *The Mummy! A tale of the twenty-second century* (1827), an elaborate science fantasy that pokes fun at her own society's foibles by means of an eccentric scientist's resuscitation of the mummy of Egyptian pharaoh Cheops who promptly travels to London (by dirigible) and begins to take an active role in the political affairs of the day. Other satiric works about the future include Émile Souvestre's comically dystopian *The World as it Shall Be* (1846) which depicts a world in the year 3000 that has air conditioning, designer drinking waters, steam-driven submarines, and phrenology-based education. Also full of humor and wonderfully illustrated by its author is Albert Robida's *The Twentieth Century* (1883), which recounts the adventures of a young woman named Hélène who is attempting to find a career in an extrapolated (and surprisingly feminist) Paris of 1952 where aircabs and high-tech pneumatic tubes transport citizens around the city, where each home contains a "telephotoscope" to broadcast the latest news and entertainment, and where the government is swept out of office every ten years in a planned "decennial revolution." Robida's other futuristic novels include *War in the Twentieth Century* (1887), *The Electric Life* (1892), and a unique time-reversal fantasy *The Clock of the Ages* (1902).

More serious utopias of the future were plentiful during the nineteenth century, but the role of scientific technology in their makeup differed greatly from one to the next. Consider, for example, Samuel Butler's *Erewhon* (1872), which visualized an anti-technology paradise in which machines have been banned from society for fear that they will evolve and eventually replace humans; or Edward Maitland's *By and By: an historical romance of the future* (1873), a Victorian "three-decker" novel that portrays an advanced pro-science society existing in a future Africa where, among its other technological feats, it has irrigated the Sahara Desert; or W.H. Hudson's *A Crystal Age* (1887), which depicts a futuristic ecological utopia whose citizens, organized as a matriarchal society, live in total harmony with nature. The most important example of this sf subgenre, Edward Bellamy's hugely popular *Looking Backward: 2000–1887* (1888), imagines a reason-based and technology-driven "socialist" utopia in Boston in the year 2000. Bellamy's novel quickly became an international bestseller, and "Bellamy Clubs" began to spring up across America to discuss Bellamy's political ideas. *Looking Backward* also sparked the publication of many other futuristic utopias and dystopias during the *fin-de-siècle* period of 1890–1900. Notable among these were William Morris's dreamily pastoral *News from Nowhere* (1890) and Ignatius Donnelly's grim vision of a capitalistic New York City that is destroyed from within by its disenfranchised and enraged lower classes in *Caesar's Column* (1890).

Not all later-century utopias were written in reaction to Bellamy, and in particular there was a strain of speculative fantasy written by women writers that inflected feminist aspirations, often dramatizing separatist versions of women-only futures: examples include Mary E. Bradley Lane's *Mizora: a world of women* (1880), Elizabeth Corbett's man-free *New Amazonia: a foretaste of the future* (1889), and Lady Florence Dixie's *Gloriana, or the Revolution of 1900* (1890), which maps a future revolution that leads to an England that achieves peace and prosperity under female rule.

Another important sf strain to emerge during the nineteenth century featured explorations of the distant past, and of ancient "lost" worlds. Edward Page Mitchell's protagonists travel back to a pivotal historical moment in sixteenth-century Holland in "The Clock that Went Backward" (1881), Mark Twain's *A Connecticut Yankee in King Arthur's Court* (1889) travels in time back to sixth-century Arthurian England in this satire on humanity's seemingly endless capacity for violence and folly, and in Grant Allen's *The British Barbarians* (1895) an anthropologist from the future travels back in time to study present-day England. Paleoanthropology is the main focus of the new emerging subgenre of prehistoric fiction which began with Pierre Boitard's *Paris before Man* (1861), was popularized in Jules Verne's *Journey to the Center of the Earth* (1864), and found its most elaborate expression in Stanley Waterloo's *The Story of Ab: a tale of the time of the cave men* (1897), and in the novels *Vamireh* (1892), *Eyrimah* (1896), and *Quest for Fire* (1911) by the prolific but mostly untranslated French writer J.-H. Rosny aîné. An entire civilization living within our hollow Earth is discovered by Captain Adam Seaborn in his *Symzonia: a voyage of discovery* (1820), the first of many nineteenth-century works to describe an unknown race, species, or culture existing within a hidden corner of our world. Others include Edward Bulwer-Lytton's subterranean Vril-ya in *The Coming Race* (1871), James DeMille's Antarctic race of Kosekin in *Strange Manuscript Found in a Copper Cylinder* (1888), William R. Bradshaw's hollow-Earth Plutusians and Calnogorians in *The Goddess of Atvatabar*

(1892), and several short stories on the lost-race theme by Rosny such as "Nymphea" (1893), "The Depths of Kyamo" (1896), and "The Prodigious Country of the Caverns" (1896). But it was the Victorian novelist H. Rider Haggard who would prove to be the master of this brand of lost-world fiction with his internationally bestselling adventure tales, including *King Solomon's Mines* (1885), *She* (1886), *Allan Quatermain* (1887), and *The People of the Mist* (1894).

The growing popularity of "hard science" sf – exemplified by the success of Jules Verne's novels during the latter half of the nineteenth century – may be traced (somewhat ironically given his reputation in his homeland) to the work of American poet, writer, and critic Edgar Allan Poe. Identified by Hugo Gernsback in the first issue of his *Amazing Stories* (1926–2005) as one of the three founders of what he called the genre of "scientifiction" (along with Verne and Wells), Poe pioneered the use of scientific detail to enhance the verisimilitude of his fantastic stories. His admittedly tongue-in-cheek note added to the lunar voyage of "The Unparalleled Adventure of One Hans Pfaal" (1835), for example, could almost stand as a first manifesto for hard sf as he urges "the application of scientific principles" to increase "the *plausibility* of the details of the voyage itself" (Poe 1978: 1001). The status of Poe's reputation as an early originator of the genre is directly proportional to the variety of sf themes and "narrative frameworks for bold scientific speculation" (Stableford 2003: 19) that he incorporated into his speculative tales: the mechanics of balloon flight in "The Balloon Hoax" (1844), the "science" of mesmerism in "A Tale of the Ragged Mountains" (1844) and "The Facts in the Case of M. Valdemar" (1845), the future destruction of Earth by a comet in "The Conversation of Eiros and Charmion" (1839), the discovery of lost worlds in "MS Found in a Bottle" (1833) and *The Narrative of Arthur Gordon Pym* (1838), and a futuristic utopia in "Mellonta Tauta" (1849). From his first published poems "Sonnet to Science" (1829) and "Al Aaraaf" (1829) to his last published philosophical essay called *Eureka* (1848), Poe repeatedly attempted to reconcile a scientific outlook with a sentimental religious mysticism – a *Weltanschauung* that, later in the century, would permeate the work of writers such as Flammarion and Rosny aîné.

Poe's influence on Jules Verne at the beginning of the latter's writing career was pivotal. After reading Baudelaire's translation of Poe's stories (titled, significantly, *Histoires extraordinaires*), Verne penned his only piece of literary criticism, an essay "Edgard Poë and his Works," published in the popular magazine *Musée des familles* (1833–1900) in 1864. Verne begins his article by praising Poe, explaining some aspects of Poe's life, and analyzing lengthy excerpts from Poe's stories. Verne then goes on to say: "they occupy an important place in the history of imaginative works because Poë created a distinct literary genre all his own" (Verne 1864: 194). It was not Poe's taste for the macabre, nor his odd penchant for hoax-humor, nor his technophobia that attracted Jules Verne to his imaginative fiction (Alkon 1994: 101–7). It was rather his attention to detail and his ability to make the bizarre believable and the extraordinary ordinary. In other words, it was Poe's use of scientific verisimilitude that impressed Verne. Although Verne went on to borrow extensively from Poe's oeuvre (balloons, cryptograms, maelstroms, mesmerism, even the entire narrative of *Arthur*

Gordon Pym), it was actually Poe's *style* that had the greatest impact on the future author of the *Extraordinary Voyages*.

Sometimes called the "Father of Science Fiction," Jules Verne popularized in the early 1860s a new hybrid fictional genre which he dubbed the *roman scientifique* (the scientific novel). Developed under the strict tutelage of his editor/publisher Pierre-Jules Hetzel, Verne's narrative recipe was as follows: an educational and fast-paced adventure tale heavily flavored with scientific didacticism, mixing equal parts of drama, humor, and "sense of wonder," and seasoned with a large pinch of positivistic Saint-Simonian ideology. After the publication and success of his first scientific novel about an aerial trek across darkest Africa called *Five Weeks in a Balloon* (1863), Verne told his friends at the Paris Stock Market where he had been working part-time to make ends meet: "My friends, I bid you adieu. I've had an idea … an idea that should make me rich. I've just written a novel in a new style … If it succeeds, it will be a gold mine" (Evans 1988a: 21). And a gold mine it soon proved to be, not only for Verne and his publisher but also for the history of speculative fiction. Verne went on to write more than sixty scientific novels from 1863 until his death in 1905. Most first appeared in serial format in Hetzel's family periodical the *Magasin d'éducation et de récréation* (1864–1916) and then were reprinted as luxury, fully illustrated octavo editions. Collectively, these novels were called the *voyages extraordinaires*, and they were published with a specific educative purpose: to help compensate for the lack of science instruction in France's Catholic-controlled schools. As Hetzel explained in his 1866 editorial preface to the collection: "The goal of this series is, in fact, to outline all the geographical, geological, physical, and astronomical knowledge amassed by modern science and to recount, in an entertaining and picturesque format that is his own, the history of the universe" (Evans 1988a: 30).

Marketing hyperbole aside, Hetzel's preface articulates an explicit goal for Verne's scientific novels: to teach the natural sciences through the imaginative medium of "armchair voyages." It was partly this social function that allowed Verne's hard/didactic sf to establish a successful "institutional 'landing point' and ideological model" for the genre (Angenot 1978: 64). From the geology and paleontology of *Journey to the Center of the Earth* to the physics of spaceflight in *From the Earth to the Moon* (1865) and from the oceanography and marine biology of *Twenty Thousand Leagues under the Seas* (1869) to the chemistry and applied engineering of *The Mysterious Island* (1875), Verne's narratives sought to teach science through fiction, not to develop fiction through science (or, in many instances, pseudoscience), as in the case of Wells, Rosny, and other early practitioners of speculative/fantastic sf. The difference between these two fundamental types of sf can be best illustrated by analyzing the role played by science itself in the discursive structure of these narratives – i.e., the manner in which a sustained scientific discourse is grafted onto a literary one. Verne's hard/didactic sf presumes a predominantly pedagogical function for such scientific discourse. In contrast, the primary goal of the science in speculative/fantastic sf is more expositional: to facilitate plot progression, to help create special effects and reader estrangement, and to build verisimilitude. That is to say, the "raison d'être of science in the narrative process itself shifts from primary position to secondary, from subject to context. It seeks no longer to address the reasoning intellect but rather the creative imagination" (Evans 1988b: 1).

Counterbalancing their sometimes heavy doses of scientific didacticism, three other aspects of Verne's *romans scientifiques* enhanced their appeal: their epic scope and visions of unlimited mobility, their quest-*Bildungsroman* and "initiatory" narrative structure, and their evocative portrayals of technology (especially vehicular). As exciting voyages to destinations "where no man had gone before," Verne's novels transported his readers to a host of geographical "supreme points" (Butor 1949: 3) – those impenetrable and richly mythic locales such as the North and South Poles in *The Adventures of Captain Hatteras* (1866) and *The Ice Sphinx* (1897), the Amazon jungles in *The Jangada* (1881), the hidden depths of the oceans in *Twenty Thousand Leagues under the Seas*, the dark side of the Moon in *Around the Moon* (1870), or even the distant planets of our solar system in *Hector Servadac* (1877). Most such fictional journeys in Verne's oeuvre are structured around a basic quest motif such as the search to find a missing father or husband as in *The Children of Captain Grant* (1867) and *Mistress Branican* (1891), mapping an unexplored region as in *The Adventures of Three Russians and Three English* (1872), or surviving as castaways on a deserted island as in *The Mysterious Island* or *A Two-Year Vacation* (1888). Most feature scientist/student or mentor/acolyte characters such as Lidenbrock/Axel of *Journey to the Center of the Earth* or Octave/Marcel of *The Begum's Millions* (1879) who serve to model growth and learning. And most include a truly memorable piece of technology – Verne's famous "dream machines." From Captain Nemo's spacious submarine *Nautilus*, to Barbicane's aluminum space-bullet (so similar to Apollo 11's), to Robur's powerful helicopter airship *Albatross*, to the steam-powered overland locomotive (fashioned to resemble an Indian elephant) of *The Steam House* (1880), to the many different modes of transport (both high-tech and low) used by Phileas Fogg in his circumnavigation of the globe in *Around the World in 80 Days* (1873), these fictional people-movers represented a new industrial-age utopian ideal: "facility of movement in a moving world – 'Mobilis in mobili' as Captain Nemo would say" (Evans 1999: 99).

It is important to note that Verne's post-1887 novels, written after Hetzel's death, sometimes reflect a dramatic change of tone when compared with his earlier and more celebrated *voyages extraordinaires*: the latter tend more often to be Romantic, pessimistic, nostalgic, and even fiercely anti-Progress (reminiscent of some of his pre-Hetzel short stories such as "Master Zacharius" (1854) or his "lost" novel, the dystopian *Paris in the Twentieth Century* (1994), rejected by Hetzel in 1863). As might be expected, the scientific pedagogy in these later texts appears severely abridged, watered down, or cut out altogether. Themes of environmental concern, human morality, and social responsibility grow more prevalent. Non-scientists are more often chosen as the stories' heroes, and what hero-scientists remain are increasingly portrayed as crazed megalomaniacs who use their special knowledge for purposes of world domination and/or unlimited riches. A striking example of these changes can be seen in the final volumes of Verne's "serial" novels: the trilogy of *From the Earth to the Moon, Around the Moon* (1870), and *Topsy-Turvy* (1889) and the two-novel series of *Robur the Conqueror* (1886) and *Master of the World* (1904). In *Topsy-Turvy* the heroic feats of ballistic engineering by Barbicane's Gun Club become (quite literally, at least in ambition) Earth-shaking when, instead of "shooting" a manned capsule around the Moon, they now seek to alter the angle of the planet's axis with the blast of a gigantic cannon. Wholly indifferent to the catastrophic environmental and human damage that would necessarily result from such a project, their scheme is to melt the Earth's polar ice cap in order to uncover vast mineral wealth for themselves. Similarly, in *Master of the World* the genius aviator Robur is brought back into the limelight, but it soon becomes evident that the once-heroic *Übermensch* of the skies has degenerated into a maniacal madman who now threatens global terrorism with his high-tech devices. Other post-1887 Verne novels target additional social and environmental issues: the cruel oppression of the Québécois people in Canada in *Family without a Name* (1889), the plague of politicians and missionaries destroying Polynesian island cultures in *Propeller Island* (1895), the environmental pollution caused by the oil industry in *The Last Will of an Eccentric* (1899), and the slaughter of elephants for their ivory in *The Village in the Treetops* (1901), among others.

Verne's imprint on the developing genre of sf during the nineteenth century was both deep and lasting. Because of his unprecedented success, writers from around the world soon began to imitate Verne's hard/didactic *romans scientifiques* and their emphasis on travel, science, and technology: in France, Louis Boussenard's *The Secrets of Mr Synthesis* (1888), Henry de Graffigny and Georges Le Faure's multi-volumed *Extraordinary Adventures of a Russian Scientist* (1889–96), and Paul d'Ivoi's action-packed series called the *Voyages excentriques* (1894–1914); in England and Germany, the many fictional works of Francis Henry Atkins (aka Frank Aubrey) and Robert Kraft; in Russia, the "geographic fantasies" of Vladimir Obruchev; in America, Edward S. Ellis's frontier sf western *The Steam Man of the Prairies* (1868), E.E. Hale's satellite story "The Brick Moon" (1869), Frank R. Stockton's *The Great War Syndicate* (1889), and the many Frank Reade Jr and Tom Edison Jr "invention" stories by Luis Senarens and other "dime-novel" writers who flourished toward the end of the century.

Since his death in 1905, Jules Verne's reputation within the French literary canon, among English-language readers and among contemporary sf scholars, has undergone many changes. In his native France, beginning in the 1960s and 1970s, Verne's oeuvre finally shed its stigma as paraliterature and joined the respectable literary mainstream; today his novels are taught in French universities. Verne's literary status in the UK and USA, however, continues to suffer from poor English translations, sensationalistic Hollywood adaptations, and a cultural mythology that persists in portraying him as an icon of "sci-fi" futurism. Fortunately, the past two decades have witnessed a growing renaissance of Anglophone interest in Verne that has resulted in many improved translations of his works, several new and accurate biographies, an online international fanbase, and a dramatic upsurge in the number of academic studies devoted to his fiction (Har'El; Evans 2008).

An important strand of non-Vernian speculative/fantastic sf that continued to develop throughout the nineteenth century – and surged after the publication of Charles Darwin's *On the Origin of Species* in 1859 – involves encounters with aliens and extraterrestrials. Imagining life on other worlds as a means for creating off-world utopias had been an important theme in sf at least since Francis Godwin's *The Man in the Moone or, a discourse of a voyage thither by Domingo Gonsales, the speedy messenger* (1638) and Cyrano de Bergerac's *The Other World, or the States and Empires of the Moon* (1657). Joseph Atterley (George Tucker) continued this rich tradition with his 1827 lunar romance *A Voyage to the Moon*. Charles Defontenay's *Star, or Psi Cassiopeia* (1854) is a much more ambitious work, which describes an entire "Starian" civilization inhabiting the planet Psi in the constellation of Cassiopeia. Percy Greg's *Across the Zodiac* (1880), Robert Cromie's *Plunge into Space* (1891), and Gustavus Pope's *Journey to Mars* (1894) all locate their alien societies on Mars (and also manage to find romance on the red planet) whereas in Kurd Lasswitz's *On Two Planets* (1897) a thriving Martian colony is discovered at the Earth's North Pole; finally, John Jacob Astor's *A Journey in Other Worlds* (1894) recounts an interplanetary tour of our solar system where the protagonists encounter, among other oddities, Earth-like dinosaurs on Jupiter and spirits of the dead on Saturn. In this latter vein of mystical alien encounters, special mention must be made of French astronomer Camille Flammarion whose oeuvre oscillates curiously between the solidly scientific (for instance his enormously successful *Popular Astronomy*, first published in 1875), the nonfictional but highly speculative (his 1862 *The Plurality of Inhabited Worlds*, which he describes the types of alien life that might exist on other planets in our solar system), and the profoundly spiritualist (his 1872 *Lumen*, which depicts conversations with a spirit who, traveling faster than the speed of light, encounters different alien lifeforms throughout the cosmos). Other sf tales about alien lifeforms who occupy the interstices of different dimensions include Fitz-James O'Brien's 1858 "The Diamond Lens" which describes a man's doomed love for a microscopic woman living in a drop of water, Edwin Abbott's delightful mathematical fable *Flatland* (1884) whose narrator, A. Square, lives in a two-dimensional world, and several *fin-de-siècle* sf stories by Rosny such as "Another World" (1895), where interdimensional alien species, wholly invisible to our limited senses, coexist with humanity on Earth. Also notable is Rosny's "The Xipéhuz" (1887), which chronicles an encounter between a nomadic tribe in Mesopotamia and a geometric-shaped and intelligent – yet totally inscrutable – race of alien energy-beings. Many years later, Rosny would transpose this xenobiological theme to an end-of-the-world narrative format in *The Death of the Earth* (1910), where the human species is finally superseded by a mineral-based alien species called the *ferromagnétaux*. Finally, Auguste Villiers de l'Isle-Adam's *Future Eve* (1886) initiated yet another – presciently postmodern – variant of "alien" sf with his wondrous android named Hadaly: a self-aware robot invented by Thomas Alva Edison as the "perfect" female but whose very existence raises a host of aesthetic and ontological questions about the "artificiality of contemporary existence" (Roberts 2006: 123) .Whether expressed as a utopian society on the Moon, as a nonhuman civilization inhabiting a distant planet or another dimension of space/time, or as a synthetic lifeform created as an exact simulacrum of ourselves, the recurring theme of the alien in nineteenth-century sf encapsulates one of the core values of the genre: the experience of alterity.

At the end of the nineteenth century, this developing mode of speculative/fantastic sf grew to full maturity with the "scientific romances" of H.G. Wells. Wells bridged the nineteenth and twentieth centuries both literally and symbolically. Although his writing career was long and prolific, the visionary novels that would inspire generations of sf writers after him were written during the brief period of 1895 to 1914. As mentioned, Wells's brand of sf is quite different from and extends beyond Verne's *roman scientifique* model in at least two fundamental ways. First, his fictions do not seek to teach science *per se* but rather to view the universe through scientific eyes. As Brian Stableford defined it, the Wellsian scientific romance "is a story which is built around something glimpsed through a window of possibility from which scientific discovery has drawn back the curtain" (Stableford 1985: 8). Second, Wells's fiction uses science more as an enabling *literary* device to enhance the verisimilitude and deepen the emotional impact of his fantastic visions. As the author himself explained, "Hitherto, except in exploration fantasies, the fantastic element was brought in by magic … It occurred to me that … an ingenious use of scientific patter might with advantage be substituted" (Wells 1934: viii). In other words, the science in Wells's scientific romances made his "thought experiments" more plausible, allowing readers to focus more fully on the *human* ramifications of the story: "So soon as the hypothesis is launched, the whole interest becomes the interest of looking at human feelings and human ways, from the new angle that has been acquired" (Wells 1934: viii).

Wells's creative genius was to breathe new life into the many sf topoi and tropes that he inherited from the sf tradition that preceded him, pushing them toward new cognitive and aesthetic frontiers. With his first novel, *The Time Machine* (1895), for example, Wells gave an innovative twist to the time-travel tale by offering a chilling portrayal of humanity evolving into Eloi and Morlocks by the year AD 802701 and, millions of years beyond that, of the end of the human species altogether on a dying planet Earth. Wells's next sf novel, *The Island of Doctor Moreau*, was a powerful reworking of the *Frankenstein* motif that dared to satirize organized religion (Wells later described it as an "exercise in youthful blasphemy"). Another moralistic mad-scientist tale followed, *The Invisible Man* (1897), where the physicist Griffin's discovery of the secret of invisibility transforms him into an insane megalomaniac who must be hunted down and killed. An ingenious interplanetary adaptation of the Chesney future-war novel, Wells's *The War of the Worlds* (1898) and its imagined Martian invasion took advantage of the public's heightened interest in the red planet following the publication of Percival Lowell's provocative book *Mars* in 1895. Wells also dabbled in the sf subgenres of prehistoric fiction, planetary disaster fiction, and lost-race fiction in "The Grisly Folk" (1896), "A Story of the Stone Age" (1897), "The Star" (1897), and "The Country of the Blind" (1904). He tried his hand at a Vernian lunar voyage in *The First Men in the Moon* (1901), using an anti-gravity substance called "Cavorite" (which prompted disapproving scolds from Verne). And finally, he produced several highly foresighted futuristic utopias such as *A Modern Utopia* (1905) and *In the Days of the Comet* (1906), as well as a number of prescient future-war fictions, such as *The War in the Air* (1908) and *The World Set Free* (1914).

H.G. Wells soon turned away from his early "scientific romances" toward more "realistic" novels and the (often estranging) world of international politics. But in his wake, an identifiable literary tradition had been established. Wells had taken Verne's

popular formula of scientific fiction, modernized its thematic repertoire and its herme-
neutic breadth, and had transformed it into a powerful instrument of speculation and
social critique. As the twentieth century dawned, this new literature had now earned
its *lettres de noblesse*, but it would still be years before it would receive its permanent
genre name of "science fiction."

BIBLIOGRAPHY

Aldiss, B. (1973) *Billion Year Spree: the history of science fiction*, London: Weidenfeld and Nicolson.
Alkon, P.K. (1987) *Origins of Futuristic Fiction*, Athens: University of Georgia Press.
—— (1994) *Science Fiction before 1900: imagination discovers technology*, New York: Twayne.
Angenot, M. (1978) "Science Fiction in France before Verne," *Science Fiction Studies*, 5(1): 58–66.
Butor, M. (1949) "Le point suprême et l'âge d'or à travers quelques oeuvres de Jules Verne," *Arts et Lettres*,
    15: 3–31; reprinted in (1960) *Répertoire I*, Paris: Éd. de Minuit.
Clarke, I.F. (1992) *Voices Prophesying War: future wars 1763–3749*, 1966, 2nd edn, New York: Oxford
    University Press.
Evans, A.B. (1988a) *Jules Verne Rediscovered: didacticism and the scientific novel*, Westport, CT: Greenwood
    Press.
—— (1988b) "Science Fiction vs Scientific Fiction in France from Jules Verne to J. Rosny Aîné," *Science
    Fiction Studies*, 15(1): 1–11.
—— (1999) "Vehicular Utopias of Jules Verne," in *Transformations of Utopia: changing views of the perfect
    society*, New York: AMS Press.
—— (2008) "Jules Verne in English: a bibliography of modern editions and scholarly studies," *Verniana*,
    1: 9–22.
Har'El, Z. "Zvi Har'El's Jules Verne Collection." Online. Available HTTP: <http://jv.gilead.org.il/>
    (accessed 1 April 2008).
Haynes, R.D. (1994) *From Faust to Strangelove: representations of the scientist in Western literature*, Baltimore,
    MD: Johns Hopkins University Press.
Luckhurst, R. (2005) *Science Fiction*, Cambridge: Polity.
Poe, E.A. (1978) *Poetry and Tales*, ed. Patrick F. Quinn, New York: Library of America.
Roberts, A. (2006) *The History of Science Fiction*, London: Palgrave.
Stableford, B. (1985) *Scientific Romance in Britain, 1890–1950*, London: Fourth Estate.
—— (2003) "Science Fiction before the Genre," in E. James and F. Mendlesohn (eds) *The Cambridge
    Companion to Science Fiction*, Cambridge: Cambridge University Press.
Verne, J. (1864) "Edgard Poë et ses oeuvres," *Musée des Familles*, April: 193–208.
Vernier, J.-P. (1975) "The SF of J.H. Rosny the Elder," *Science Fiction Studies*, 2(2): 156–64.
Wells, H.G. (1934) "Preface," in *Seven Famous Novels*, New York: Knopf.

3

FICTION, 1895–1926

John Rieder

The years 1895 and 1926 mark monumental events in the history of sf: the publication of *The Time Machine*, H.G. Wells's first important work of fiction, and the inauguration of *Amazing Stories* (1926–2005), edited by Hugo Gernsback, the first magazine devoted exclusively and explicitly to publishing sf (or "scientifiction," as Gernsback then called it). But there is no more than a loose connection between the two events, and certainly no developmental or progressive history that leads us from Wells's artistic achievement to Gernsback's entrepreneurship. In fact, Gernsback's pulp milieu bears only a slight resemblance to the publishing context in which Wells worked, and Gernsback's one novel-length piece of fiction, *Ralph 124C 41 +: a romance of the year 2660* (1911–12), entirely lacks the craft and thoughtfulness that make *The Time Machine* important. The history of sf in this period is diffuse, even if one simplifies the task by concentrating on English-language fiction, as I will do here. Writing that history involves the retrospective gathering together of scattered materials that find a clearly delineated focus and identity as early sf largely because of Gernsback's commercial project.

Nonetheless, Wells's importance is quite independent of Gernsback's. We would still be reading *The Time Machine* and assigning it some kind of special place in the history of generic innovation even if Gernsback's reprintings of Wells – and publication of Wells's many imitators – had not so thoroughly woven him into the fabric of pulp sf. The year 1895 marks a watershed in the history of sf not just because of *The Time Machine* itself, but because it inaugurates the most important phase of Wells's career. The major works that followed, including *The Island of Doctor Moreau* (1896), *The Invisible Man* (1897), "The Star" (1897), *The War of the Worlds* (1898), *When the Sleeper Wakes* (1899), *The First Men in the Moon* (1901), "The Land Ironclads" (1903), and "The Country of the Blind" (1904), comprise arguably the most important and influential body of fiction any writer has contributed to the genre. It is so impressive an achievement that it has sometimes inspired the exaggerated claim that Wells invented sf itself. In fact, he took up a range of devices and themes that were already being widely used, including time travel, future-war stories, contact with lost races, extraterrestrial journeys, scientific experiments gone awry, utopian speculation, and quasi-apocalyptic natural disaster. One of the distinctions of the fiction of Wells's great decade is that, more than any other writer, he gathered together in one place almost all of the disparate threads of what we now identify as early sf.

Even more compelling than the breadth of Wells's subject matter, however, is the depth of his exploration and transformation of it. In *The Time Machine*, for example, Wells seized upon and made his own a plot device that had enjoyed a great deal of popularity in the preceding decade. One of the most widely read and hotly discussed books of the period, Edward Bellamy's *Looking Backward: 2000–1887* (1888), narrates a contemporary New Englander's visit to the future where he observes a vastly more efficient and equitable society. Its famous and influential polemical counterpart, William Morris's *News from Nowhere* (1890), also uses time travel to promote a different vision of social improvement. Mark Twain's anti-clerical satire, *A Connecticut Yankee in King Arthur's Court* (1889), sends its time-traveler in the opposite direction, pitting a contemporary engineer's rationality and know-how against the brutality and superstition that rule Twain's imaginary sixth-century Arthurian England. It is sometimes said that Wells's key innovation upon the time-travel plot is his invention of the time machine itself, allowing him to replace the accidental time-travelers and Rip-Van-Winkle-like trances of these earlier stories with the deliberate exploratory journey of his scientist protagonist. Instead of the guided tours by which Bellamy's and Morris's visitors learn about the future, then, Wells's Time Traveller encounters the world of AD 802701 as a riddle that only gradually unfolds its secrets. The drama of interpretation, as the Time Traveller works through a series of hypotheses about the relationship between the surface-dwelling Eloi and the subterranean Morlocks who inhabit this far-future Thames Valley, makes for a fluent synthesis of the utopian and satirical material typical of earlier time-travel stories. And just as this plot's dynamism sets it apart from those of Bellamy and Morris, the clarity of Wells's exposition distinguishes his novel from the earlier, comparable, but somewhat opaque attempt at depicting a posthuman future in William Henry Hudson's *A Crystal Age* (1887).

Yet Wells's marvelous machine and streamlined plot development would be worth little more than a footnote in the history of sf were it not for the visionary power of the futures his Time Traveller visits. Sf, like the historical novel, is intimately bound up with ideas about historical change, especially the linked notions of progress, evolution, and modernity. For example, Grant Allen's time-travel novel, *The British Barbarians* (1895), exploits the widely shared assumption, which informed an entire generation of anthropologists, that contemporary Europe represented the fully developed phase of a history of civilization whose past developing phases were visible in non-European, savage societies. Allen (who, like Wells, was an advocate and popularizer of Darwinism) simply reverses the perspective of the ideology of progress by having an anthropologist from the future visit present-day England to study its savage rituals and superstitious beliefs. *The Time Machine* also reverses contemporary assumptions about progress, but, unlike Allen, Wells does not leave the ethnocentric framework of the ideology of progress intact. While Allen's future is simply and unquestionably superior to the present, Wells depicts a future in which humanity has degenerated into the subhuman Eloi and Morlocks, and then gives this degeneration a cosmic scale in the protagonist's brief, bleak glimpse of the entropic heat-death of life itself. Wells also attacks the identification of progress with industrialized Europe, by making the speciation of the Eloi and the Morlocks the ironic outcome of the triumph of technological rationality over scarcity. Furthermore, the future's technological triumph is undone in this manner not because its inhabitants lapse into the habits of "savage" societies, but because it perpetuates a form of savagery peculiar to contemporary "advanced" societies, the class division between capitalists and laborers. In the long run, the upper class's exploitation of the workers turns into dependence upon, and finally utter subjection to, them as the Eloi end up not only being tended to by the Morlocks but also becoming a staple item of their diet. Finally, this dialectical reversal of the capitalist masters into the slaves, or more precisely the cattle, of their machine-tending former servants obliterates the opposition between nature and culture itself, turning the man-made arrangement of class duties and responsibilities into a grotesque natural symbiosis. Thus Wells's tale challenges the entire framework of assumptions that bolster chauvinistic belief in the superior rationality of European industrial civilization. And Wells does so with a seamless weaving together of extravagant conjecture and realistic detail – as one of the Time Traveller's listeners comments, "the story was so fantastic and incredible, the telling so credible and sober" (Wells 1987: 89) – that would remain one of the benchmarks of stylistic achievement in the genre.

The Time Machine set a high standard that much of Wells's fiction lived up to in the years that followed. The depth and clarity he brought to the time-travel plot is typical of his handling of other popular types: invasion and the near-future war in *The War of the Worlds* and "The Land Ironclads"; the mad scientist whose experiments go disastrously wrong in *The Island of Doctor Moreau* and *The Invisible Man*; the extraterrestrial journey in *The First Men in the Moon*; the explorer's encounter with a lost race in "The Country of the Blind"; and apocalyptic natural disaster in "The Star." He made some remarkable innovations in these stories. For example, the Martians of *The War of the Worlds* are the prototype of all the cyborgs and the hyper-encephalic future humans and extraterrestrials of later sf, and in the Selenites of *First Men in the Moon* Wells pioneered the strategy of modeling alien anatomy and social organization on insects. But what characterizes Wells's great decade on the whole is not the novelty of his invention, but rather the way he breathes vitality into the commonplace plots and devices of an already thriving early sf.

What we now call early sf was perhaps nothing more than the loose aggregation of such commonplace devices. No one was consciously writing, publishing, or reading "sf" around 1900. Even the association of Wells's fiction with that of contemporaries like M.P. Shiel, George Griffith, and J.W. Beresford under the rubric of "scientific romance" (Stableford 1985) is more a way of identifying these writers' common tendencies and shared milieu than it is the delineation of an explicit, self-consciously employed generic category. Nonetheless, Gernsback and the American magazine writers did not invent sf out of nothing, and Gernsback himself was quite eager to identify a canon of earlier works that defined the sort of story his magazine was looking to publish. A generation of bibliographers has documented an almost exponential decade-by-decade proliferation, from the 1870s to the 1920s, of stories set in the future, or about marvelous inventions and heroic or mad scientists (the prototypes being Thomas Edison and Victor Frankenstein, respectively), or involving journeys into previously unexplored areas of the world (usually the poles or imaginary subterranean caverns, as the mapping of the world's inhabitable surface neared completion), or journeys into outer space, or into the past or the future, and so on. (The most comprehensive and informative of these bibliographies is Bleiler 1990; others, each of which has its strengths, include Clareson 1984, Clarke 1961, and Suvin 1983.) The ground for Wells's achievement was prepared by this steady growth, which was punctuated by more spectacular publishing phenomena such as Bellamy's utopia, or before that H. Rider Haggard's enormously successful lost-race romances (starting with *King Solomon's Mines* (1885) followed by *She* (1886) and *Allan Quatermain* (1887)), and the ongoing popularity of Jules Verne's *voyages extraordinaires*, all of which established a reading audience already attuned to a set of recognizable themes and expectations for Wells to exploit. The impact of Verne and Wells was crucial to the formation of sf, but the growing market for tales oriented toward the future, stories that extrapolated upon recent scientific and technological discoveries, and stories exploring utopian or merely exotic social formations was broader and more miscellaneous than can be accounted for by the influence of individual writers. Those increasing numbers who, during these decades, wrote and published early sf must have been responding to demands rooted in their society's collective experience of change and its collective investment in modernity.

First, these demands point toward an economic context. Surely the importance of technical innovation and scientific training to the growth and maintenance of a large-scale industrial capitalist economy has a great deal to do not only with the ongoing popularity of Verne's fiction, with its marvelous inventions and lengthy expositions of scientific fact, throughout this period, but also with the commercial success of the American dime novel's fictional adolescent hero-scientists, Frank Reade Jr (1892–8) and Tom Swift (1910–41). If Gernsback's vision of sf as an educational tool, his interest in amateur radio, and his other publishing ventures, like *Modern Electrics* (1908–13) and *Science and Invention* (1920–31), are any indication, the presence of a significant audience comprising young readers oriented toward engineering and fascinated by gadgetry was crucial to early sf.

Second, the social environment that attended the climax and crisis of imperialism nurtured the growing market for sf. The tensions of imperialist competition clearly underlie one of the most important and prolific veins of sf before the First World War, the invasion stories and forecasts of future war that Wells so decisively transformed in *The War of the Worlds* (on the future-war motif, see Clarke 1992). The vogue for such stories would seem not only to exploit popular identification with imperial projects and popular anxieties about becoming the victims rather than the wielders of imperial military power, but also to point once again to the economic backdrop of large-scale industrial production. The popularity of future-war stories coincides with the first great industrial arms race, from George Chesney's phenomenally successful, controversial and influential cautionary tale of a successful German invasion of England, *The Battle of Dorking* (1871), published in the aftermath of Germany's shockingly swift victory in the Franco-Prussian war, to the Great War itself, the horrors of which far exceeded its many fictional forecasts. The way in which Wells's Martian superweapons overwhelm earthly opponents echoes many an earlier fictional encounter involving new generations of armored ships or large artillery. Many tales of invasion and near-future war were strongly realistic, heavily concerned with extrapolating credible techno-logical advances, as exemplified by Wells's well-wrought and critically acute "The Land Ironclads." But the future-war plot on the whole steered steadily away from realistic prediction into ever more extravagant fantasy. Arthur Train and Robert Wood's *The Man Who Rocked the Earth* (1915) is typical, with its heady combination of imperialist politics, superweapons, mass destruction, and eccentric scientists – a mysterious and isolated one, who invents a flying machine and an incredibly powerful weapon with which he threatens to destroy the world unless national leaders put an end to their war; and a second, avuncular, absent-minded one, who saves the world from the first.

The general bellicosity of the milieu is impressive. British and American fanta-sists of war imagined their countries invading or being invaded by every possible national opponent (Germany was the most frequent choice) and many impossible ones. Xenophobia and racism were endemic. It is no coincidence that Wells's blood-drinking Martian invaders appeared in *Pearson's Magazine* in the same year that Bram Stoker's *Dracula* (1897) gave classic form to the plot of vampiric invasion. When the fantasy of international war expanded from domestic invasion to global conflict, the sides frequently were divided along racial lines. George Griffith's *The Angel of the Revolution* (1893) is an early example, M.P. Shiel's *The Yellow Danger* (1898) among the most extravagant. Shiel's plot involves a quasi-migratory Chinese invasion of Europe by an army of 400 million who simply walk across the countryside, laying it to waste like a plague of locusts. Carefully diagramed naval battles are a standard feature Shiel's novel shares with many future-war stories; his climactic battle is remarkable because it produces 20 million Chinese casualties. Shiel follows this with the most gruesome turn of all when the English deliberately unleash a cholera epidemic upon the Chinese swarm on the continent, killing some 150 million in the process. The theme of the Yellow Peril only grew more popular after Shiel, continuing unabated right into the interwar years, especially in the USA.

To some extent the scope of the disasters imagined in these racial fantasies partakes of a more generalized apocalypticism that manifested itself in stories of cataclysmic transformation, both natural and human-made – volcanic eruptions in Allen's "The Thames Valley Catastrophe" (1897) and Shiel's *The Purple Cloud* (1901); astral colli-sions in Wells's "The Star" (1897) and Arthur Conan Doyle's "The Poison Belt" (1915); a mad scientist's experiments in Frederick Turner Jane's *The Violet Flame* (1899); and all-out class warfare in Jack London's *The Iron Heel* (1908). Such stories vary considerably in the degree to which they perform secular transformation of enduring motifs in the Christian tradition, and the persistence of mythological motifs like flooding and cyclicality invites other forms of psychological and cultural inter-pretation as well. After the First World War, especially in England, this apocalyptic strain frequently blended with pessimism about the future of civilization in novels like Edward Shanks's *The People of the Ruins* (1920) and P. Anderson Graham's *The Collapse of Homo Sapiens* (1923).

Throughout the nineteenth century, colonial and imperialist expansion also provided an environment in which popular audiences avidly consumed both fictional and nonfictional accounts of exploration. By the early twentieth century, while the extent of Britain's empire (and of European imperialism in general) was reaching its peak, the still unexplored areas of the globe had become few and extremely remote. Stories of exploration became correspondingly more fantastic. Extraterrestrial adventure remained a relatively minor motif during most of this period; in the late nineteenth century extraterrestrial visitors were more often associated with occult wisdom and utopian speculation than with the earthly frontier. The great majority of imaginary exploration before Edgar Rice Burroughs's *Barsoom* stories (beginning with "Under the Moons of Mars" (serialized 1912, as book *A Princess of Mars* 1917)) occurred wherever on Earth the writers could still place an isolated enclave for earthly travelers to penetrate – in the African or South American interior, at the poles or under the Earth. But writers employed these options with impressive frequency. Historians of sf have had little to say about the lost-race and lost-world stories that make up several hundred of the more than 2,500 items in Bleiler (1990), but they are important precursors to the later development of adventure-oriented sf (see Rieder 2008).

Lost-race and lost-world narratives – the paradigm for lost-race fiction is set by Haggard's novels mentioned above; some typical, readable later examples are Frank Aubrey's *The Devil-Tree of El Dorado* (1897) and *The Queen of Atlantis* (1899), and Robert Ames Bennett's *Thyra: a romance of the polar pit* (1901); the lost-world romance is a variation pioneered by Conan Doyle's *The Lost World* (1912) – are on the whole formulaic and often relatively transparent fantasies of acquisition in which a small group of white men discovers an isolated civilization where they have exciting adventures finding treasure and love. The explorers frequently become embroiled in a civil war, allying themselves with a sympathetic princess against a perverse priesthood. Entry into the lost world is an ordeal, often involving a tortuous passage through an underground tunnel or river; this entrance is typically sealed upon the explorers' exit, making their journey a private and unrepeatable one rather than the vanguard of colonial penetration. These formulaic elements combine to construct a wish-fulfilling ideological distortion that casts colonial exploration and expropriation as a return to nature, a rediscovery of lost histories and properties, and salvation for the good natives (who embrace the white men as friends or lovers) against their true enemies, the bad natives (who regard the white men as invaders and sexual rivals). Yet in the best of such narratives, like Haggard's or Conan Doyle's, such fantasies are offered up for enjoyment and simultaneously exposed to critical examination, especially by enforcing some ironic distance between the narrator and the expeditionary leader.

Even in the hands of less expert writers, lost-race and lost-world narratives offer their readers a fascinating array of ideas about social and cultural possibilities. The stories tend to take an anthropological orientation that is ingenuously revealed in the subtitle of Thomas Janvier's *The Aztec Treasure House: a romance of contemporaneous antiquity* (1890). They often combine the idea that non-European societies represent moments in Europe's past with utopian speculation, as various lost races practice forms of communism, polygamy, nudity, vegetarianism, and eugenic discipline. Although most lost-race civilizations are based on savage, classical, or medieval societies, some are futuristic, as in Will Harben's *The Land of the Changing Sun* (1894). When combined with evolutionary theory, the scientific orientation of such fiction produces another entire subgenre about the relationship of human nature to culture, the narrative of human prehistory, such as Stanley Waterloo's *The Story of Ab* (1897), Wells's "A Story of the Stone Age" (1897), and London's *Before Adam* (1907). The same anthropological perspective, combined with a kind of vertiginous oscillation between the protagonist scientist's racist contempt for a contemporary savage society and his intellectual awe before what he takes to be a long-lost artifact of a super-advanced extraterrestrial visitor, characterizes London's "The Red One" (1918), one of the best pieces of sf from this period. But no one employed lost-race and lost-world geography with greater energy or a more spectacular proliferation of anachronistic materials than Burroughs (see, for example, *At the Earth's Core* (1914) or *The Land That Time Forgot* (1918)) and his one rival in terms of commercial domination of the pre-*Amazing* magazines, A. Merritt (see *The Moon Pool* (1919)). It is to a large extent Burroughs's combination of lost-race adventure formulas with an extraterrestrial, part-savage, part-medieval, part-futuristic setting in *A Princess of Mars* and its sequels that set the stage for the space operas of E.E. "Doc" Smith and Edmond Hamilton in the Gernsback magazines. (Sometimes Robert William Cole's dreary *The Struggle for Empire: a story of the year 2236* (1900) is cited as the first space opera, but this is no more than a piece of trivia; Burroughs and Merritt are the most significant figures.) Finally, in assessing the importance of lost-race fiction, we need to remember that its basic structure was often used as a vehicle of satire, both before Haggard's commercial breakthrough (Samuel Butler's *Erewhon* (1872)) and after (Wells's "The Country of the Blind"). In fact, two of the best pieces of feminist speculation in this period employ lost-race motifs: Inez Gillmore's very fine but little-known allegory *Angel Island* (1914), and Charlotte Perkins Gilman's deservedly famous parthenogenetic utopia *Herland* (1915).

Although we can plausibly identify several economic and social factors that encouraged the growing market for early sf, the coherence and the limits of the category itself remain open to debate. Perhaps the key question about this period is whether, and at what point, we can say that a new set of generic expectations had become sufficiently widespread and well enough defined to organize the production, distribution, and reception of the literature assembled in the bibliographies. Contemporaries' persistent association of Verne with Wells, to the annoyance of both, suggests the presence of some such recognition, because as individual artists they resemble one another so little that their association can only rest on some kind of generic common ground. This would imply that, decades before *Amazing Stories*, Verne and Wells were perceived to be staking out a new, if perhaps not very precise, position in the terrain of literary possibilities. And that terrain itself was rapidly changing. The emergent sf of 1895–1926 comes into visibility against the backdrop of the generic turmoil associated with the growth and increased diversity of reading audiences and with the marketing practices of what would soon come to be called mass culture. Sf attains the status of a recognizable genre within this mass-cultural transformation of the entire system of literary genres. In this connection, the somewhat inchoate state of early sf, compared with its relatively clearer status after the American magazines came to name and dominate the genre, makes the period all the more interesting and instructive.

One could well argue, in fact, that the loose boundaries, imprecise definition, and disparate audiences of 1895–1926 comprise a far more typical state of affairs for a literary genre than the one that has so often been the point of departure for discussions about sf, namely the highly self-conscious elaboration of the genre in the American magazines of the late 1930s through the 1950s, spearheaded by a powerful editor (John W. Campbell), featuring a highly visible group of writers strongly and sometimes exclusively associated with the genre, and attended by a self-identified, committed, and very vocal group of fans. The most serious attempt to come to terms with the differences between Wells's generic environment and that of sf's so-called "Golden Age" remains Stableford (1985), which describes a field of production strongly bifurcated along national lines, dominated by one-volume book publication in the UK, and by magazine publication, with a concomitant emphasis on the short story, in the US. The British "scientific romance," the tradition of Wells, flourished from the late nineteenth century into the 1950s, but from the 1940s on it was increasingly overshadowed and eventually displaced by American "sf," the tradition of Burroughs, Merritt, and Gernsback. But the opposition Stableford details could well be considered less a national than an endemic one developing between mass culture and the older literary practices that persisted alongside it, which were increasingly forced to redefine themselves in opposition to it.

Putting the divided field of early sf alongside the quasi-programmatic unities of the "Golden Age" helps remind us that sf itself is not merely a mass-market genre. Burroughs, with his tireless reiteration of a successful adventure formula, is certainly a prototypical mass-market writer, whose corpus resembles that of Zane Grey or Agatha Christie at least as closely as it does that of any other early sf writer. But Gernsback, in the first issue of *Amazing Stories*, would call upon Wells and Verne and Edgar Allan Poe, not Burroughs, as models; and the fact that Wells enjoyed success across a number of genres, including the realist novel, makes him anything but a special case, as witness the contributions to sf by Joseph Conrad (*The Inheritors* (1901)) and E.M. Forster (the important early dystopia, "The Machine Stops" (1908)). Outside of England, much of the best early sf was produced by writers with high prestige in other fields, such as the eminent French sociologist Gabriel Tarde, whose splendid satire *Underground Man* (1905) may have provided important inspiration for Forster's story; or John MacMillan Brown, chancellor of the University of New Zealand, whose *Riallora* (1897) and *Limanora* (1903) combine scathing satire against religious orthodoxy, racism, colonialism, and bureaucracy with one of the period's most ambitious and elaborately detailed futuristic utopias; or the great Czech writer Karel Čapek, who is most often remembered in sf history for inventing the word "robot" in *RUR (Rossum's Universal Robots)* (1920), but was also the most prominent writer of realist fiction in his country at the time of his death in 1938. Sometimes the affiliation of sf with older and more prestigious literary forms, such as the strong element of satire always present in the dystopia (for example, Yevgeny Zamyatin's *We* (written 1920, translated into English 1924)), has tended to isolate these strains of sf from the rest of the genre, but such hybrid products are arguably just as persistent and definitive a feature of the genre as the formulas of Burroughs or the marketing strategy of Gernsback.

Nonetheless, it is to the pulp magazines and their reconfiguration of fictional genres that we owe the dominant version of sf. The association between magazine publication and early sf goes back as far as the publication of Chesney's *The Battle of Dorking* in *Blackwood's* (1817–1980), or even, if one accepts Gernsback's claims, to Poe's magazine publications. But the crafting of magazines that pursued a sharply defined niche audience by publishing a very consistent genre of fiction becomes part of the history of sf when the success of Burroughs's "Under the Moons of Mars" and "Tarzan of the Apes" in *All-Story* (1905–20) in 1912 helped to focus and intensify the genre specialization of *All-Story* and its companion *Argosy* (1882–1978). Gernsback had already entered the publishing field in 1908 with *Modern Electrics*, which became *Electrical Experimenter* in 1913 and later *Science and Invention*. He began to make scientifically oriented fiction a regular part of *Modern Electrics* after publishing *Ralph 124C 41 +* there in 1911–12, and in 1923 he published a special "scientifiction" issue of *Science and Invention*, the year in which another important magazine, *Weird Tales* (1923–54), entered the field. In April 1926, when Gernsback published the first issue of *Amazing Stories*, *Weird Tales* featured on its cover a story by Robert E. Howard, the patriarch of sword-and-sorcery. Thus the mixture, in that first issue of *Amazing*, of reprinted stories by Poe, Verne, and Wells with three more recent magazine pieces (by George Allan England, Austin Hall, and G. Peyton Wertenbaker) suggestively combines an appeal to established, prestigious favorites with a selective endorsement of Gernsback's immediate milieu. Whatever we make of Gernsback's contribution to the development of modern sf, the magazines of 1912–26 offer a rich and still inadequately explored opportunity for research into its mass-cultural roots.

BIBLIOGRAPHY

Bleiler, E.F. with the assistance of Bleiler, R.J. (1990) *Science-Fiction: the early years*, Kent, OH: Kent State University Press.

Clareson, T.D. (1984) *Science Fiction in America, 1870s–1930s: an annotated bibliography of primary sources*, Westport, CT: Greenwood.

Clarke, I.F. (1961) *The Tale of the Future: from the beginning to the present day*, London: Library Association.

—— (1992) *Voices Prophesying War: future wars 1763–3749*, New York: Oxford University Press.

Rieder, J. (2008) *Colonialism and the Emergence of Science Fiction*, Middletown, CT: Wesleyan University Press.

Stableford, B. (1985) *Scientific Romance in Britain, 1890–1950*, New York: St Martin's Press.

Suvin, D. (1983) *Victorian Science Fiction in the UK: the discourses of knowledge and of power*, Boston: G.K. Hall.

Wells, H.G. (1987) *The Definitive Time Machine: a critical edition of H.G. Wells's scientific romance*, intro. and notes by H.M. Geduld, Bloomington: Indiana University Press.

4

SF TOURISM

Brooks Landon

From downtown Seattle's Westlake Center Mall station, it takes just two minutes by monorail to reach Seattle Center, in the shadow of the Space Needle and located within the strikingly odd Frank Gehry building that houses the Science Fiction Museum and Hall of Fame. Clock time, however, may not be the best way to measure the journey, as it not only takes riders to one of the obvious destinations for a tourist interested in sf, but also reminds us that something we might call "sf tourism" involves a matrix of locations, events, ideas, and technologically imbricated phenomena that promote and reinforce the attitude toward the world or free-floating epistemology of "sf thinking."

Of course, the Science Fiction Museum (SFM) deserves a prominent place in any discussion of sf tourism (as does the Maison d'Ailleurs in Yverdon-Les-Bains, Switzerland). The SFM, housing Microsoft billionaire Paul Allen's extensive collection of sf-related material and The Science Fiction and Fantasy Hall of Fame, is a nonprofit organization that features permanent and rotating galleries and exhibits designed to provide visitors with "thought-provoking ideas and experiences of science fiction … [It] promote[s] awareness and appreciation of science fiction literature and media … [and] pays homage to the most respected of science fiction practitioners – writers, artists, publishers and filmmakers" (EMPSFM n.d.). The SFM also offers traveling exhibits, hosts a range of SF-related events, sponsors a number of educational programs, and maintains an informative website. On a smaller scale, the Maison d'Ailleurs features exhibits and an extensive photo library, and houses a research center and archive. In the most literal way of thinking about sf tourism, these two museums would have to be primary destinations.

However, the concept of sf tourism is not just limited to these and other geographical destinations where sf is the announced subject or focus of an educational institution or commercial venture. That ride to the SFM reminds us of the longstanding iconic association of monorails not just with sf, but with the future in general, and world's fairs and amusement parks in particular, locations where countless people (over 5 million per summer at Coney Island during the early 1900s; over 20 million admissions to most of the large world's fairs) were introduced to the sensibility centered on change, progress, science, technology, and the future that sf ultimately codified in literature and film. Indeed, the Seattle monorail was built to carry visitors to the

1962 Seattle World's Fair, whose central iconic structure, the Space Needle, offered panoramic views from its observation deck 520 feet above the ground. Giant icons from earlier fairs include the 1,000-foot-tall Eiffel Tower constructed for the Paris Exposition of 1889 and the 260-foot-tall Ferris Wheel that was the centerpiece of the 1893 World's Columbian Exposition in Chicago. These most dramatic examples of the "technological sublime" (Nye 1994) had nothing directly to do with sf, but, alongside world's fairs, amusement parks such as Coney Island, dime museums, and related physical locations, promoted the kind of mindset about technology and the future that gave rise to sf literature.

Accordingly, this chapter will have more to do with what we might think of as material embodiments of sf's "sense of wonder," than with clearly self-identified destinations for the tourist interested in codified sf history or subject matter. I will focus on a number of formative elements in the emergence of mass culture (primarily in the US) that are not generally thought of as science-fictional, but whose obvious and influential affinity with sf thinking (Landon 2002: 2–10) is often noted. I will start with actual geographical destinations, whether historical or contemporary, ranging from world's fairs to Disney World, where a tourist could or can see sights that are inherently, but not necessarily, closely related to and supportive of the protocols of sf thinking. Smaller-scale but no less important destinations will include American dime museums, exemplified by P.T. Barnum's American Museum in New York. I will then turn to those virtual worlds created by technology, whether the world of the heavens constructed in planetariums, the hybrid world of motion-platform movie experiences, or the worlds of cyberspace, particularly as experienced in online multiplayer games. Finally, I will briefly consider some sf texts that feature fictional tourism in their plots, suggesting *sf about tourism* as yet another aspect of "sf tourism."

The case for a figurative construction of sf tourism (and for the construction of a material history of sf) rests on scholarship that explores the mechanisms by which technology has been constructed and represented in (largely American) mass culture in general and in literature in particular (see especially Tichi 1987; Nye 1994, 1997; Dery 1999). Most directly relevant to the conception of sf tourism are H. Bruce Franklin (1992) and Scott Bukatman (2003). Works such as these point toward and beyond the kind of cultural studies rethinking of sf history suggested by Roger Luckhurst (2005).

Franklin compellingly argues that the "principal form of science fiction in 1939" was the New York World's Fair (Franklin 1992: 108). Contrasting the fair's attractions, particularly its "Democracity" and the General Motors "Futurama," with representative stories in the 1939 volume of *Astounding*, he notes that "A fair billing itself as the World of Tomorrow may be considered just as much a work of science fiction as a short story or a novel, a comic book or a movie" (Franklin 1992: 119), while also offering a blistering critique of the corporate and automobile-centered future the fair promoted. Franklin was not alone in drawing this connection, as commentaries on the 1939 fair repeatedly invoke sf to explain its exciting appeal. Neil Harris describes all of the "Century of Progress" fairs of the 1930s as "Buck Rogers cities" (Harris 1990: 129), Morris Dickstein characterizes the World of Tomorrow as "a stunning piece of science fiction" (Dickstein 1989: 22), and memoirs of visits to the 1939 fair routinely describe it as "something out of Buck Rogers or Flash Gordon" (Rosenblum 1989: 12), or note that its vistas were strongly reminiscent of the view of the future offered in the movie *Things to Come* (Menzies 1936) (Appelbaum 1977: 5). Indeed, perhaps the strongest evidence of the science-fictional aspect of this and earlier fairs can be seen in the numerous photo books recording their transient wonders (see Appelbaum 1977, 1980).

Following Franklin, it is easy to enumerate ways in which previous world's fairs featured (starting with the London Crystal Palace Exhibition of 1851, but focusing most intently on the Paris Expositions of 1889 and 1900, the Chicago World's Columbian Exposition of 1893, the Buffalo Pan-American Exposition of 1901, and the St Louis Louisiana Purchase Exposition of 1904), both in their general utopian ambience and in their specific architecture and attractions, powerful inducements for imagining the future, celebrating change as the new constant of experience, constructing change as progress, and seeing science and technology as its driving force – all central aspects of sf thinking. In their time, these fairs were the greatest tourist attractions ever, as millions upon millions of visitors marveled at their wonders. Moreover, these earlier fairs were held during the period when sf was beginning to emerge from its various prototypes into the codified form it eventually assumed as a publishing category and mass-cultural phenomenon. At the heart of this process, at least in the US, were the dime-novel series featuring the exploits of boy inventors such as Frank Reade, Jack Wright, and Electric Bob, whose scaled-down *voyages extraordinaires* could be suggested by the "exotic" ethnographic and anthropological exhibits (and midway sideshows) that were prominent features of the great fairs and expositions, and whose amazing inventions could be easily imagined after a visit to the World's Columbian Exposition's Electricity Building, one of the premier attractions of the fabled White City, where Edison's and Tesla's actual inventions symbolically competed for the future.

Henry Adams (1973), drawing on his experiences at the Paris Exposition of 1900 and the Columbian Exposition in 1893, ironically observed that dynamos, emblems of the power and potential of electricity, were beginning to assume in the popular imagination a status previously accorded religion and its great icons. Robert W. Rydell has elaborated Adams's initial suggestion, detailing how American world's fairs became "symbolic universes" that resembled religious celebrations where the object of worship was change, relentlessly constructed as progress (Rydell 1984: 2). A striking component of these celebrations of progress through science and technology was a faith in notions of evolutionary hierarchy that elevated white races over those of color. As Rydell notes, "Scientific explanations about natural and social phenomena became increasingly authoritative, and the exposition planners enhanced and drew upon the prestige of science to make the presentation of America's progress more convincing" (Rydell 1984: 5). The authority of science and the application of evolutionary ideas to race produced a "sliding scale of humanity" (Rydell 1984: 65), with these fairs in general, and the great White City in particular, serving as "a utopian construct built upon racist assumptions" (Rydell 1984: 48). And sf inherited this aspect of the fairs just as surely as it inherited their focus on technological progress – including the unmistakable valorization of colonialism and empire by both European and American fairs.

The fairs were designed to serve an educational function, to be an "illustrated encyclopedia of civilization" that visitors could walk through (Rydell 1984: 45). Umberto Eco takes this idea a step closer to sf when he suggests that a world's fair cannot just be thought of as a "walk-in encyclopedia," but as a "teaching machine," an "enormous experimental laboratory," not one designed to produce immediate results but to offer "suggestions and ideas for architecture and design" (Eco 1983: 305–6). These and other characterizations of the nature and function of world's fairs will sound familiar to students of sf, where similar claims attended the emergence of the genre. So, while specific attractions at specific fairs (the Ferris Wheel and the Electricity Building in Chicago, the "Trip to the Moon" ride at the 1901 Pan-American Exposition, and exhibits of wondrous new technologies beyond number) made a trip to a world's fair a subtle endorsement of the scientific and technological change-and-progress-centered ethos of sf thinking, the great fairs at the turn of the nineteenth century into the twentieth may have had even greater influence on the development of sf at broader and more abstract levels, offering examples of "sf tourism" destinations *avant la lettre* while squarely endorsing the techno-enthusiasm of proto-sf dime novels.

World's fairs were temporary phenomena, rarely lasting beyond a couple of years, usually closed and torn down after only six months or so. However, precisely the aspects of these fairs that most obviously promoted the same ethos as did sf – exhibits featuring wild and exotic peoples from faraway lands and entertainment venues driven by new technologies – tended to live on in amusement parks. The most celebrated of these was Coney Island (see Kasson 1978; McCullough 2000; Register 2001), which, particularly between 1897 and 1911, was a kind of unruly successor to the World's Columbian Exposition of 1893 and the Buffalo Pan-American Exposition of 1901. It was the location of three legendary amusement parks: George Tilyou's Steeplechase Park, Frederic Thompson and Skip Dundy's Luna Park, and William H. Reynolds's Dreamland. Each prominently featured mechanical rides, disaster attractions, and fantastic architecture reminiscent at once of world's fairs and of Winsor McCay's imaginary landscapes for Little Nemo, and each offered a veritable orgy of electric lights at a time when they still signified the future. Tilyou, unsuccessful in his efforts to purchase the Columbian Exposition's Ferris Wheel for Steeplechase Park, constructed a scaled-down model and simply claimed that it was the world's largest. He also brought from the Pan-American Exposition the very successful "A Trip to the Moon" ride created there by Dundy and Thompson (who soon split from Tilyou to create their own Luna Park in 1903). This "dramatic cyclorama" cannot be described as anything other than one of the early destinations of sf tourism:

> Here visitors entered a spaceship in the middle of a large building for an imaginary ride to the moon. Peering out of portholes, they beheld a series of shifting images that gave the illusion of a flight into space, a sense reinforced by the rocking of the ship itself. After supposedly landing on the moon,

passengers left the spaceship to explore its caverns and grottoes, where they met giants and midgets in moon-men costumes, the Man in the Moon upon his throne, and dancing moon maidens, who pressed bits of green cheese upon them as souvenirs of the lunar voyage.

(Kasson 1978: 61)

Following the 17 April 1900 announcement that such a concession had been awarded to Thompson and Dundy, *The Buffalo Express* noted of the original attraction at the Pan-American Exposition:

The "trips" would be made at ten minute intervals and by a "combination of electrical mechanism and scenic and lighting effects ... to produce the sensation of leaving Earth and flying through space amidst stars, comets and planets to the Moon." The "airship" was to have huge wings and large propellers operated by powerful dynamos. It would also contain complicated mechanisms to provide the craft's "Anti-Gravitational Force." The building would be divided into three sections: "The Theater of the Planets," "The City of the Moon," and the "Palace of the Man in the Moon."

(Stanton 1998)

Several days before the ride opened at the Buffalo fair, ballyhoo for it included news reports that the spaceship had broken free of its moorings and broken through the roof of the building that housed it, and was only located three days later by the Lick Observatory in California. "A Trip to the Moon" is the obvious forerunner to a succession of increasingly realistic spaceflight simulations, best represented today by the "Star Tours" ride at Disneyland. Other more transient and less celebrated sf-themed attractions at Coney Island included "The War of the Worlds," "Twenty-Thousand Leagues under the Sea," and a ride to the center of the Earth.

As with the world's fairs, however, the ambience or experience of Coney Island was probably more important than individual rides or attractions in preparing mass audiences for sf. Coney Island was not just, as Kasson claims, a striking "harbinger of modernity" (Kasson 1978: 11–12), but one with striking similarities to what emerged as the early ethos of the genre. The appeal of Coney Island was transgressive, designed to liberate visitors from urban norms and from purely utilitarian concepts of technology. Its exotic architecture and unremitting emphasis on aspects of the grotesque offered entrance to what Luna Park co-owner Frederic Thompson described as "a different world – a dream world, perhaps a nightmare world – where all is bizarre and fantastic" (Kasson 1978: 66). Fiction requires suspension of disbelief, but sf requires a particular kind of suspension of disbelief, conceptually gerrymandered between rhetorics of realism and rhetorics of fantasy given "realistic" appearance by appeals to science and technology, and no spot on Earth better represented the broad contours of that science-fictional ethos than did Coney Island. While Luckhurst's "cultural history" of sf does not specifically mention Coney Island, it is the apotheosis of the phenomena he associates with the conditions for sf's emergence, most specifically those involving the extension or extrapolation of "aspects of Mechanism from the contemporary world" (Luckhurst 2005: 3).

Today, the obvious – but obviously not culturally transgressive – successors to Coney Island are Disneyland and Disney World, including Epcot Center, whose functional and symbolic ties to the 1939 and 1964 New York World's Fairs are also unmistakable. Just as surely as Disney's "Star Tours" and "A Trip to Mars" attractions update Dundy and Thompson's "A Trip to the Moon" (in fact, "A Trip to Mars" updates Disney's 1955 "A Trip to the Moon") and the various "Tomorrowlands" at Disney theme parks echo the futurist ethos of earlier world's fairs, the holistic experience of a Disney theme park clearly offers a frisson very similar to that of sf. Bukatman (2003) best suggests the interesting relationships between the Disney "worlds" and contemporary sf. While these destinations in sf tourism offer vestiges of the enthusiasm for technology and technocratic control associated with world's fairs, he notes the implications of the fact that these parks now offer what might be thought of as retro-futures more than the prospect of the future (a concept humorously explored in Cory Doctorow's *Down and Out in the Magic Kingdom* (2003)). Bukatman also discusses the new ways in which these parks narrativize experience ("We no longer feel that we penetrate the future; futures penetrate us"), and ways in which they, like considerable portions of recent sf (but with very different motivation), work to constitute "terminal identity" (Bukatman 2003: 15–18, 28–31). Accordingly, the Disney theme parks do not serve to promote the sf ethos in the way that Coney Island did so much as they emblemize the darker aspects of the technosphere that have become a persistent concern of contemporary sf.

Bukatman's use of the term "hypercinematic experience" reminds us of yet another way in which the material subjects of sf tourism have always been intertwined. World's fairs clearly promoted the rise of amusement parks like Coney Island; Coney Island and world's fairs obviously are the distant ancestors of the various Disney worlds; and all of these locations were important sites for the experience of various stages of film and television, as well as being prominently featured in both media. From its earliest days, film has aspired to kinds of "hypercinematic experience," as suggested by the never-realized plans by H.G. Wells and Robert Paul for a cinematic "time machine" (Landon 1992: xv) and the numerous American franchises for Hale's Tours, which in the early 1900s gave audiences the sensation of riding on a train while watching film shot from a moving train (Fielding 1970: 34–47). Coney Island at one time featured more nickelodeons than any other single location and was itself prominently featured in early Edison/Porter films; cinema desired to show motion and the kinetic attractions of Coney Island offered an obvious subject for the new medium (Musser 1991: 321). While one of Edison's first kinetoscopes may have been displayed in the Electricity Building at the Columbian Exposition in 1893, his machines and films were a major attraction at the St Louis Exposition in 1904. Cinema does not exactly lend itself to being a destination for sf tourism, but cinema technology has from the earliest days been associated with sf, as exemplified by Georges Méliès's celebrated *A Trip to the Moon* (1902), the first significant example of an sf film.

Cinema has been an important technological constant at each of the major historical destinations I have discussed, but there remains one early mass-culture phenomenon that may have been even more instrumental in preparing audiences for sf thinking: dime museums. Between roughly 1840 and 1900, dime museums, the American continuation and development of the European tradition of the "Cabinet of Wonders," introduced millions of people to a panoply of scientific information, exotic species, freaks, automatons, wax figures, and – possibly most important – to an aesthetic of fakery, hoax, or humbug very similar to that necessary for the success of sf. As popular in the latter half of the nineteenth century as movies are today, the dime museum "dazzled men, women, and children with its dioramas, panoramas, georamas, cosmoramas, paintings, relics, freaks, stuffed animals, menageries, waxworks, and theatrical performances" and "no previous amusement had ever appealed to such a diversified audience or integrated so many diversions under one roof" (Dennett 1997: 5). Dating from early in the century, dime museums experienced their heyday in the 1880s and 1890s as noteworthy examples appeared in St Louis, Baltimore, Boston, Chicago, Milwaukee, Cincinnati, Louisville, Cleveland, Minneapolis, St Paul, Detroit, Grand Rapids, and other cities. The most impressive museums had long been in Philadelphia (Charles Wilson Peale's Philadelphia museum operated from 1786 to 1845) and New York, the location of George Wood's Museum and Metropolitan Theatre, the Eden Musée, and the grandest of them all, P.T. Barnum's American Museum (see Vásquez 2004).

Barnum, America's legendary showman, mastered the combination of quasi-educational material with popular entertainment and was instrumental in codifying the "admiration of the perfection of the fake" as the "operational aesthetic" of the dime museum (Dennett 1997: 115). Barnum's attractions included the famed "Fejee Mermaid," the "Wooly Horse," "What Is It?" (which sensationalized Darwinian ideas by offering a possible "missing link"), numerous automata, such as the chess-playing Ajeeb and Herr Faber's Talking Machine, as well as a wide range of giants, midgets, human freaks – all contributing to the creation of an audience response quite similar to sf's "sense of wonder." More importantly, Barnum helped codify an aesthetic of hoaxing that constructed showmanship frauds as the positive side of "humbugging," an intellectual exercise that cultivated audiences who applauded the "many challenging and delightful aspects to a hoax" (Dennett 1997: 29–30). There are numerous examples of science-fictional hoaxes, including the great "Moon Hoax" of 1835, the "Newark Steam Man" of 1868, and the "Airship Hoax" of 1897, but dime-museums developed a much broader tradition of hoaxing, one not tied to any specific subject matter. A unique set of audience protocols emerged from the dime-museum experience, including self-conscious perfection of the fake, exemplified in waxwork exhibits, where the showman's goal was to make the palpably unreal as realistic as possible and the thrill for the viewer was actually in being deceived (Dennett 1997: 107). This new aesthetic for the suspension of disbelief in matters at once fantastic and "realistic" likely paved the way for the peculiarly conflicted aesthetic of sf.

There are, of course, many other physical locations – possible destinations, both historical and contemporary – of obvious potential interest and relevance to the sf tourist: planetariums, NASA facilities, Alabama's Space Camp, and transitory simulation amusement venues such as the Virtual Worlds Battletech Center sites. For a fee of $20 million or so, a tourist can visit the US/Russian International Space Station, and "space tourism" is an idea whose time seems to have arrived, at least for the very wealthy. In the summer of 2007, some 35,000 tourists attended the annual UFO Festival held in Roswell, New Mexico, the location of the International UFO Museum. And, for those who take cyberspace as a location and therefore a potential tourist destination, online worlds such as *Second Life*, with its claim of over 8 million "residents," and online multiplayer games, such as *World of Warcraft*, *The Game of Life*, and *Spore*, offer tourist destinations that might be thought of as hyper-sf, since they involve users in an inherently science-fictional interaction with computer technology, usually shaped by a narrative that is itself classically science-fictional. Indeed, one location that can be visited in *Second Life* is a world for sf fans, which features a virtual sf museum (Chosen 2005). And Bruce Sterling's "Dead Media" project is at once a virtual destination for sf tourism, and a stark reminder of the transitory nature of virtual tourism (Jennings n.d.).

Finally it is worth noting that the concept of "sf tourism" should also cover tourism as a subject in works of sf. And, not surprisingly, sf that takes tourism as a subject or plot device tends to include many of the "destinations" previously discussed in this essay: world's fairs, amusement parks, museums, virtual vacations. Robert Crossley discusses the importance of museums, particularly in British sf, arguing that they function as a kind of time machine as well as offering in the "spectacle of an observer examining an artifact and using it as a window onto nature, culture, and history" the "convergence of anthropological, prophetic, and elegiac tonalities that science fiction handles more powerfully than any other modern literary form" (Crossley 1992: 206–7). Crossley's approach to the function of museums in sf can be profitably extended to sf featuring fairs, such as Lewis Shiner's "White City" (1990) or Robert Silverberg's *World's Fair 1992* (1970), and amusement parks, such as Howard Waldrop's "Heirs of the Perisphere" (1999), George Saunders's "Pastoralia" (2000), and films such as *Westworld* (Crichton 1973), *Futureworld* (Heffron 1976), and *Jurassic Park* (Spielberg 1993). Other glimpses of sf tourism can be seen in Ray Bradbury's "A Sound of Thunder" (1952), Philip K. Dick's "We Can Remember it For You Wholesale" (1966), adapted as *Total Recall* (Verhoeven 1990). And no discussion of sf tourism would be complete without noting the obvious: the history of sf is the history of "going somewhere else to see the sights," whether through *voyages extraordinaires*, explicit time-travel narratives, or the implicit time travel of trips to the future. It should come as little surprise then that sf tourism is a concept that offers us new and valuable perspectives on the nature and function of sf.

Bibliography

Adams, H. (1973) "The Dynamo and the Virgin," in *The Education of Henry Adams*, Boston: Houghton Mifflin.

Anon. (1984) "Proposal for a *Diacritics* Colloquium on Nuclear Criticism," *Diacritics – A Review of Contemporary Criticism*, 14(2): 2–3.

Appelbaum, S. (1977) *The New York World's Fair 1939/1940 in 155 Photographs by Richard Wurts and Others*, New York: Dover.

—— (1980) *The Chicago World's Fair of 1893: a photographic record*, New York: Dover.

Buckland, W. (2001) "A Reply to Sellors's 'Mindless' Approach to Possible Worlds," *Screen*, 42(2): 222–6.

Bukatman, S. (2003) "There's Always ... Tomorrowland: Disney and the hypercinematic experience," in *Matters of Gravity: special effects and supermen in the 20th century*, Durham, NC: Duke University Press.

Chosen (2005) *Scifigeeks.net*. Online. Available HTTP: <http://www.scifigeeks.net> (accessed 1 April 2008).

Crossley, R. (1992) "In the Palace of the Green Porcelain: artifacts from the museums of science fiction," in G. Slusser and E.S. Rabkin (eds) *Styles of Creation: aesthetic technique and the creation of fictional worlds*, Athens: University of Georgia Press.

Dennett, A.S. (1997) *Weird & Wonderful: the dime museum in America*, New York: New York University Press.

Dery, M. (1999) *The Pyrotechnic Insanitarium: American culture on the brink of the millennium*, New York: Grove.

Dickstein, M. (1989) "From the Thirties to the Sixties: the World's Fair in its own time," in *Remembering the Future: the New York world's fair from 1939 to 1964*, New York: Rizzoli International Publications.

Eco, U. (1983) "A Theory of Expositions," in *Travels in Hyperreality: essays*, San Diego: Harcourt Brace.

EMPSFM (n.d.) "About EMPSFM". Online. Available HTTP: <http://www.empsfm.org/aboutEMPSFM/index.asp> (accessed 1 April 2008).

Fielding, R. (1970) "Hale's Tours: ultrarealism in the pre-1910 motion picture," *Cinema Journal*, 10(1): 34–47.

Franklin, H.B. (1992) "America as Science Fiction: 1939," in G.E. Slusser, E.S. Rabkin, and R. Scholes (eds) *Coordinates: placing science fiction and fantasy*, Carbondale and Edwardsville: Southern Illinois Press.

Harris, N. (1990) "Great American Fairs and American Cities: the role of Chicago's Columbian Exposition," in *Cultural Excursions: marketing appetites and cultural tastes in modern America*, Chicago: University of Chicago Press.

Jennings, T. (n.d.) *The Dead Media Project*. Online. Available HTTP: <http://www.deadmedia.org> (accessed 1 April 2008).

Kasson, J.F. (1978) *Amusing the Million: Coney Island at the turn of the century*, New York: Hill & Wang.

Landon, B. (1992) *The Aesthetics of Ambivalence: rethinking science fiction in the age of electronic (re)production*, Westport, CT: Greenwood.

—— (2002) *Science Fiction after 1900: from the steam man to the stars*, New York: Routledge.

Luckhurst, R. (2005) *Science Fiction*, Cambridge: Polity.

McCullough, E. (2000) *Good Old Coney Island: a sentimental journey into the past*, New York: Fordham University Press.

Maison d'Ailleurs Homepage. Online. Available HTTP: <http://www.ailleurs.ch/uk/index.php> (accessed 1 April 2008).

Musser, C. (1991) *Before the Nickelodeon: Edwin S. Porter and the Edison Manufacturing Company*, Berkeley: University of California Press.

Nye, D.E. (1994) *The American Technological Sublime*, Cambridge, MA: MIT Press.

—— (1997) *Narratives and Spaces: technology and the construction of American culture*, New York: Columbia University Press.

Register, W. (2001) *The Kid of Coney Island: Fred Thompson and the rise of American amusements*, New York: Oxford University Press.

Rosenblum, R. (1989) "Remembrances of Fairs Past," in *Remembering the Future: the New York world's fair from 1939 to 1964*, New York: Rizzoli International Publications.

Rydell, R.W. (1984) *All the World's a Fair: visions of empire at American international expositions, 1876–1916*, Chicago: University of Chicago Press.

Second Life (n.d.) Online. Available HTTP: <http://secondlife.com> (accessed 1 April 2008).

Stanton, J. (1998) "Coney Island – Thompson & Dundy." Online. Available HTTP: <http://www.westland.net/coneyisland/articles/thompson&dundy.htm> (accessed 1 April 2008).

Tichi, C. (1987) *Shifting Gears: technology, literature, culture in modernist America*, Chapel Hill: University of North Carolina Press.

Vásquez, A.A. (2004) "The Lost Museum," American Social History Project/Center for Media and Learning, The Graduate Center, City University of New York. Online. Available HTTP: <http://www.lostmuseum.cuny.edu/home.html> (accessed 1 April 2008).

5
FILM, 1895–1950

J.P. Telotte

While the history of sf cinema practically coincides with that of the cinema itself, most commentary on the genre begins with its spectacular explosion of popularity in the 1950s. It then tracks through the development of specific themes and concerns, particularly in the last decades of the twentieth century, that have a particularly cinematic resonance – concerns with the reproducible being (robots, androids), with the construction of reality (virtual worlds, virtual selves), with spectacular threats to our fragile world (an environment on the brink). Susan Sontag staked out this critical perspective, suggesting that cinematic sf was born out of those films of alien invasion and threatened apocalypse that dominated the 1950s and early 1960s, films that fashioned, as their narrative core, elaborate visions of disaster, that capitalized on the visual potential of such spectacles, and that claimed such elements as a kind of generic essence. Indeed, Sontag claimed that sf films "are not about science" but "disaster" (Sontag 1966: 213). However, sf's earlier history, leading up to that apocalyptic upwelling, attests that it has been very much about science, along with the technology it produces and the reason that drives both – which sometimes, through humanity's missteps, generate the ruinous consequences she observes. In sketching a history of sf film, then, we need to account for those elements that emphasize our potential for conception, construction, and projection, as well as those that confront us with the cautionary, even frightening, images that flow from this same spring. In fact, the flexibility to speak both positively and negatively about science and technology is one of the genre's most telling characteristics.

But rather than suggesting that sf is fundamentally concerned with science, I want to emphasize how this early period reflects a dynamic character, as sf cinema begins to establish its specific identity. Sf film might be understood through the prism of fantasy, a mode that, despite its dreamlike, often unsettling, and even frightening images, remains, at its deepest level, in constant dialogue with the real, with the way we operate upon it through reason, science, and technology, and thus with their potentials and pitfalls (see Telotte 2001: 10–16). Partly because of this dialogic stance the form also seems consistently self-conscious, as if intent on interrogating its own reality, including the technology involved in its creation.

This point echoes the observation that "science fiction in the cinema often turns out to be ... the fictional or fictive science of the cinema itself" (Stewart 1985:

159). While almost from its origins sf cinema has produced amazing and sometimes disconcerting icons and actions, they are usually not so much "an *inadequate response*" (Sontag 1966: 224) to cultural conditions as a generically specific response, an effort to situate that triad of reason–science–technology within the cultural order and help us gauge how they promise both to construct and destroy our world. That effort produces spectacles that are by turns disturbing and affirmative, yet also aware of their curiously double nature. This pattern can be traced even in the form's earliest examples, those pre-narrative or ur-sf texts of the "cinema of attraction" (Gunning 1986: 63) that dominated early film. For throughout the late 1890s and early 1900s numerous films appear that point toward the genre, as they emphasize astonishing machinery that, like the cinema, produces entertaining illusions, seeming transformations, or impossible shifts in time and place: mechanisms that transform animals, people, and objects, or that enable fantastic travels. For example, *The Sausage Machine* (no director credited 1897) displays a wondrous invention that turns dogs into sausages and sausages back into dogs; *Dr Skinum* (McCutcheon 1907) depicts a device that changes humans from ugly to beautiful; and *The Lion's Breath* (Davey 1916) offers a machine for transferring minds and personalities. If only with some difficulty recognized as sf, such works do reflect the genre's spirit. Evoking Machine Age attitudes toward science and technology, they center on the amazing properties (and humorous products) of various devices or machines, all of which trade upon the similarly amazing "attractions" that the cinema itself created.

These largely comic efforts take much of their inspiration from and help frame the work of Georges Méliès, typically seen as the father of the cinematic genre and best remembered for *A Trip to the Moon* (1902). With the cinematic apparatus's ability to create a new sense of time and space, Méliès created amazing appearances and disappearances, animated practically anything, and sent his characters on fantastic journeys and explorations in, for example, *The Impossible Voyage* (1904), *20,000 Leagues Under the Sea* (1907), and *The Conquest of the Pole* (1912). Influenced by Jules Verne's *voyages extraordinaires*, Méliès eschewed their emphasis on exposition and explanation, on the play of reason and science, in favor of fantastic images and events: exploding moon men, a flying train, undersea monsters, interplanetary travel. Yet more than simply spectacles, these efforts demonstrate his contribution to an evolving relationship between the new genre and the cinema's own technology. For to create his worlds of wonder, Méliès contributed to a growing arsenal of special effects (the stop-action camera, model work, use of miniatures, double exposures, primitive matting, and filtered photography), establishing a pattern that continues to inform sf film inasmuch as these advances led him not to develop more complex *narratives*, but to fashion new and more fantastic *visions*, while allowing his audience to experience things impossible in their far less fantastic reality. In short, with Méliès we see how the development of film technology would inspire both the imagery and techniques of sf.

Consequently, some have downplayed the science-fictional aspect of his work, arguing that, for example, "the fantasy powers of [his] trick films overrode any real interest in a technological future" (La Valley 1985: 146). Lewis Jacobs, retrospectively emphasizing "the complexity of his tricks, his resourcefulness with mechanical contrivances" (Jacobs 1979: 18), supports this argument. Yet such views miss the role of Méliès in establishing some of sf's key iconography and many of its primary plot concerns, including rockets, submarines (even flying submarines), automata, aliens, scientists and slightly mad inventors, interplanetary travel, monsters both terrestrial and extraterrestrial, and the technologically aided conquest of various physical and intellectual challenges. So while he never saw himself as a creator of sf in the manner of H.G. Wells, and while his films typically envisioned their various "attractions" with tongue in cheek, Méliès did sketch out a look and a manner for early sf cinema. Where his works fell short was in their exaggerated flourishes trumpeting the artifice of his worlds, often straining at the science and technology they depict and champion.

The more ambitious films that followed Méliès's lead would do little more than exploit some of the icons and circumstances he established. Thus, the 1910s and early 1920s saw various films import sf elements into narratives that draw just as strongly from the horror, melodramatic, and comic forms that the early cinema popularized. In the horrific vein, for example, we can see the kinship of works like the German *Homunculus* (Rippert 1916) and *Der Januskopf* (Murnau 1920), and the American *Frankenstein* (Dawley 1910), *Dr Jekyll and Mr Hyde* (Robertson 1920), and *A Blind Bargain* (Worsley 1922), the first film adaptation of Wells's *The Island of Doctor Moreau* (1896). While science is clearly at the core of their narratives, these films also emphasize a kind of *unreason* involved in scientific work, resulting in monstrous creations and horrific consequences and producing in the audience a kind of recoil from the scientific.

Films such as *The House of Mystery* (no director credited 1912), *The Automatic House* (no director credited 1915), and the Harry Houdini serial *The Master Mystery* (Grossman and King 1919) give a melodramatic inflection to those same elements by putting robots, inventors, and criminal scientists at cross-purposes with society. Downplaying the actual work of science, they focus on solving mysteries or crimes, either with the aid of or in opposition to the work of science and technology, in order to restore the social status quo. Tellingly, the same unhinged inventors and amazing inventions prove central to such comedies as *A Clever Dummy* (Hartman, Kerr, Raymaker, and Sennett 1917), in which Ben Turpin competes with a robot model of himself; *The Electric House* (Cline and Keaton 1922), wherein Buster Keaton creates an electrified home of tomorrow, only to suffer when his creations go haywire; *The Crazy Ray* (Clair 1922), about a device that can stop time and freeze motion; and *A Wild Roomer* (Bowers and Muller 1926), which centers on the creation of a utopian machine, a gargantuan device that frees the individual from labor by performing practically any household task, while also wrecking the house and, like the Turpin and Keaton films, holding technology hostage to laughter. While these film types place at the center of their narratives the play of reason, the discoveries of science, and astonishing technologies, they also stylize or exaggerate those elements, never integrating them into a coherent sf narrative. Rather, with the exception of Keaton, they generally continue to treat their sf elements as little more than "attractions," as narrative ploys that derive their real "sense" from the genre in which they have been granted a liminal status.

Yet that very liminality helps to isolate the functional nature of their sf elements, making the various man-made monsters, robots, electrified houses, and wondrous machines stand out, as if they were the real attractions or reasons for these films. It also helps them to point to another order of narrative that stands, as an absence, just outside the narrative world of these films. Certainly, in *A Wild Roomer*, one quickly senses this tension, as Charlie Bowers constructs his mammoth miracle machine in a tiny room in a boarding house, leaving him with no room to move around. It is a telling analogy for the dilemma facing many of these partially science-fictional works that evoke powerful icons or situations, only to find that they threaten to bulk beyond more familiar narrative structures or mundane plot concerns, to burst the seams of their rather conventional containers.

Providing a definitive break with this pattern and insisting on a specific identity for the new genre is a series of films, epic in scope, resources, and intentions, that appeared in the late silent and early sound period. Produced by various national cinemas, films such as *Aelita* (Protazanov 1924), *Metropolis* (Lang 1927), *The Mysterious Island* (Hubbard 1929), *End of the World* (Gance 1931), and *Things to Come* (Menzies 1936) drew on preexisting and increasingly popular sf literature, reached out to an international audience, and provided plot models for a variety of offspring and imitations. These elaborate films demonstrate the rapid, international flowering of sf, whose various icons, plot devices, and themes seem already well understood by filmmakers and audiences.

Aelita is a curious product of the early Soviet film system, directed by a successful pre-First World War filmmaker who had originally fled the Bolshevik revolution, and based on a novel by Alexei Tolstoy, a revolutionary and champion of technological progress. It is a film at odds with itself, yet it marshals soon-to-be familiar generic materials into a coherent, even ambitious narrative about an engineer, Los, who constructs a rocket, flies it to Mars, instigates a Soviet-style revolution, and becomes the consort of the queen, Aelita. This strange extension of the revolutionary spirit, however, turns out to be an elaborate daydream distilled from a combination of Los's ambitions, personal troubles, and his inability to focus on the everyday work of the revolution. While the "dream" undermines Tolstoy's revolutionary thrust, it ultimately gives the story a realistic ground, suggesting that there is no magical solution – not even technological magic – for personal and cultural difficulties, and leaving Los committed to the hard work of addressing such problems.

In its retreat from the scientific and technological fantasies of spaceflight and Martian culture, *Aelita* offers a sober view of the power of the reason–science–technology triad increasingly central to the genre. This partly results from Protazanov's conception of the film as unconventional social satire rather than sf. Moreover, he invests the sf imagery with the aura of those early film "attractions," presenting the futuristic Martian world in the stylized manner of constructivism, which drew on a perceived machine beauty and set a dynamic mix of different materials, opposed lines, and clashing shapes in opposition to the natural. The resulting world calls attention not only to its fundamentally constructed nature, but also to the possibility for (re)construction of human society, to an inherently revolutionary potential.

Simultaneously, these unrealistic sequences lend the film a reflexive dimension, suggesting an alluring dream, *constructed* from the ill-matching elements of a troubled psyche and consumerist yearnings, that all-too-easily distracts the individual from the realities of communist life. It thus results in a kind of allegorical commentary on the nature of capitalist cinema, which one might read as Protazanov's apologia for that period when he exiled himself to direct films in the West.

Metropolis may well have been influenced by *Aelita*, which was among "the most popular films exported to Germany" in this era and shows similarities in plot and style (Youngblood 1992: 60). However, the German film is more ambitious and polished, its depiction of a dystopian society proving a far more recognizable touchstone for post-First World War social frustrations. Co-scripted by director Lang and his wife Thea von Harbou, and based on her novel, *Metropolis* depicts a society given over to the powers of science and technology and ruled in a coldly rational manner. The wealthy live in skyscrapers and enjoy a life of play and leisure, while the workers, enslaved to the machines that make the upper world work, inhabit a dreary underground. When they revolt, only the intervention of the Master of Metropolis's son restores some hope. He kills the mad scientist Rotwang, exposes the robot created to mislead the workers, and intercedes with his father in their favor, offering, as a concluding title card puts it, a "heart" – or compassion – to help direct "the head and hands" of society. This formula pointedly addresses the reason–science–technology triad upon which the genre depends, suggesting both its implicit weakness and a cause – a fundamental imbalance, a lack of human feeling – that in following years would underlie sf's increasingly calamitous visions.

While that formula ill addresses the era's social unrest, the film's iconography was more effective and influential. *Metropolis* conjured two of the most significant images in the genre's history. The city of Metropolis, characterized by 200-story skyscrapers, vaulted roadways, and aircraft weaving among the giant buildings, reflects some of the era's key visions of urban development, such as the German Bauhaus (which engendered the International Style in architecture), the visionary buildings of Hugh Ferris in America, and Le Corbusier's urban reconceptualization in France. This impressive, if also disturbing, monumentalist urban vision, in which humanity itself practically disappears, was described by one reviewer as "the chill mechanized world of the future" (Gerstein 1972: 187). It quickly became fundamental to sf's futuristic vision, as *Just Imagine* (Butler 1930) and *Things to Come* illustrate. Just as influential was *Metropolis*'s formulation of arguably the genre's most important icon, the robot, a figure that readily resonated with Karel Čapek's celebrated play on the subject, *RUR* (1920). Lang's image of a robotic Maria embodies a duality that attaches to much of technology in this period: on the one hand, an alluring, gleaming image, its seductive power played out in its dance before the city's elite, and the ease with which it lures the workers into rebellion; on the other, a force of destruction and, striking a note that would increasingly figure in manifestations of the robot, a potential human replacement (Rotwang proclaims that with such machines "we have no further use for living workers"). This dual image of technology's attractions and subversions may well be *Metropolis*'s most important legacy to both sf and modern culture.

The film's visual style also bears mention, since it too deploys an avant-garde method to both support and critique its futuristic vision. Lang drew on the expressionist look that had singularly marked post-First World War German cinema. Its emphasis on unbalanced compositions, irregular spatial arrangements, the play of shadows, oblique and vertical rather than horizontal lines, stylized acting, and a fascination with reflective surfaces, shows especially in Lang's depiction of the workers' underworld, where it underscores the precarious nature of this future and the sinister forces that preserve its cultural imbalances. Moreover, in concert with the robot's foregrounding of the powerfully seductive play of images, that expressionist aesthetic subverts our conventional cinematic reality, reflexively challenging audiences to see their world in a radically different way.

While less challenging stylistically, the American *The Mysterious Island* similarly provides a double vision of science and technology, and a sense of the period's social restiveness. Ostensibly based on Jules Verne's novel, it retains much of the Verne spirit, emphasizing the technologically driven explorations typical of his work and modeling the sort of fantastic machines – here, twin submarines – that would become the centerpiece of a succession of sf films in following years (including the interplanetary rocket ship of *Just Imagine*, the life-restoring apparatus of *Six Hours to Live* (Dieterle 1932), the atomic gold-producing machine of *Gold* (Hartl 1934), and the radium-powered machine of *The Invisible Ray* (Hillyer 1935) that both cures blindness and destroys matter). The submarines have been developed by reclusive scientist Count Dakkar, who wishes to explore the oceans' mysteries, while ruling benevolently over the peasants inhabiting his island. But the leader of a Russian-styled revolution on the mainland seizes the submarines, intending to use them to solidify his power and "rule the world," suggesting widespread suspicions of both communism and technology itself. Dakkar sinks his submarines and kills himself rather than "be remembered as one who brought into this world an instrument of death and destruction."

Yet prior to that abjuring of the fantastic machine, *The Mysterious Island* presents a seductive array of spectacular images and events that for much of the narrative crowd out its warnings against social upheaval. Dakkar discovers a fully realized underwater society, complete with an aquatic version of *Metropolis*'s skyscrapers; his submarines engage in battles both above and below the sea; there are fights with a giant octopus and a horned sea serpent; one submarine destroys an entire fleet of warships; and there are scenes of revolution and counterrevolution, complete with close-ups of the revolutionary forces torturing captives. Making possible such fantastic imagery is state-of-the-art technology, as the film was shot in the new two-strip Technicolor process, included several expository "talkie" scenes, demonstrated early underwater photography techniques, and combined elaborate model work with live action. Its narrative of a scientist and his fantastic technology is powered by the cinema's own cutting-edge technology. Consequently, while it ends on a cautionary note, its attitude toward science and technology – including film technology – remains ambiguous. Its conclusion suggests the sort of tunnel vision our technology might foster, as seen in Dakkar's isolationist attitude, and the destructive potential that, in the wrong hands, it might unleash, but the film also champions technology's ability to help us penetrate the world's unexplored "depths," extend our knowledge, and show us things we have never seen before. And its emphasis on naturalistically presented fantastic images suggests that they are real possibilities. This double attitude evidences the sort of cultural ambiguity about the work of science and technology that would, throughout the next decade, result in films that increasingly drew the nascent sf cinema into the orbit of the horror genre, such as *Frankenstein* (Whale 1931), *Dr X* (Curtiz 1932), *Island of Lost Souls* (Kenton 1933), and *The Invisible Ray*.

Appearing shortly after *Mysterious Island*, *End of the World* is far less ambiguous in its attitude toward science and technology. Its narrative about a comet set to collide with Earth, based on a Camille Flammarion novel, underscores the power of science and technology to detect such calamitous events – to plot out their trajectory, and to predict their results – but it also points up how powerless we are and how little use our technology is in dealing with them. In fact, long sequences simply depict the panic that follows from this sobering recognition, as reason practically disappears and people descend into acts of desperation and despair, of looting and orgiastic behavior. When the Earth avoids destruction as the comet at the last moment deviates from its calculated path, the world's scientists convene, form a new government, and promise to "refashion this world on the basis of a new law" rooted in a thoroughly rational and scientific understanding and dedicated to ideals of "peace and brotherhood." This conclusion recalls the sort of balance that the end of *Metropolis* tries to strike and further underscores the political exigencies that crept into all of the era's major sf films. The recognition of science and technology's inability to avert disaster or solve the seemingly more manageable problems haunting this period helps explain an upsurge in apocalyptic-themed sf, including *High Treason* (Elvey 1929), *Deluge* (Feist 1933), and *SOS Tidal Wave* (Auer 1939).

Lending an extra complexity to *End of the World*'s dissection of scientific attitudes is its framing of much of the action through the mass media, thereby implicitly critiquing the work of film. In order to depict the various ways in which the world reacts to this impending calamity (and to capitalize on its special effects scenes of flooding, earthquakes, and crumbling human structures), the film emphasizes the work of the newspapers, radio, and newsreel cameras. Instead of simply reporting and mobilizing people to deal with the effects of the approaching comet, the media seize on another story, one that people will more readily accept, as they suggest an international conspiracy hoping to profit from false rumors of catastrophe by manipulating the stock market and the world's governments. *End of the World* thereby sounds a note of caution about technology and technological attitudes, pointing up the power of the mass media, including film, in an increasingly technologized world, and warning against investing too much authority in that mass voice.

A similar combination of apocalyptic destruction and eventual salvation – at the hands of both science and technology – structures the most famous British sf effort of this period, *Things to Come* (1936). The only film scripted by H.G. Wells, and the most expensive British film to that date, it brought together a number of visionary influences to shape its view of where human culture was heading. Reflecting the era's international tensions, more than half of the narrative presciently details a catastrophic world war that wreaks physical destruction like that seen in *End of the World* and introduces a plague that wipes out much of humanity. However, a significant portion of the film describes how, from the old world's ruins, a new one, with a distinctly futuristic look, arises. Following Wells's injunction that it "must not seem contemporary" but be "constructed differently" (Frayling 1995: 50), the film brought together various avant-garde influences: the Bauhaus's László Moholy-Nagy designed some sets, the surrealist Fernand Léger provided concept sketches and costume ideas, the schemes of the city planner Le Corbusier figured in the design of the new Everytown, and the industrial designer Norman Bel Geddes's plans for a futuristic airliner provided the model for the air force of the new order of "engineers and mechanics," united in order "to salvage the world." The resulting "great white world," as one character styles it, visually attests to the power of the science and technology these engineers and mechanics wield, as they overcome humanity's most destructive tendencies, concentrate humanity's powers on reconstruction, and produce a culture in which the divisions between workers and elite, so central to *Aelita*, *Metropolis*, and *The Mysterious Island*, seem to disappear.

Yet even with reason recovered and a society ruled by science and technology firmly established, the new world of *Things to Come* suggests an abiding suspicion of these powers and thus the fragility of the film's utopian promise. The monumental design scheme – massive buildings, outsized statuary and monuments, multistory television screens, the great space gun – produces a sense of awe in both the citizenry and the audience. But that design also signifies the *repressive* forces at work, as these monumental elements increasingly make the people feel like "such little creatures … so fragile, so weak," and help inspire new unrest. When the people rise up to smash the giant space gun, Everytown's leader orders the use of the sometimes deadly "gas of peace" against them. While *Things to Come* leaves us with an image of human aspiration, as the space gun fires a capsule of astronauts on an exploratory mission, the climate of resentment and revolt surrounding that mission qualifies its achievement and calls into question this world's technical trajectory.

Things to Come is one of a number of films in this vein during the 1930s, all of which emphasize these monumental hopes that were increasingly attached to the forces of science and technology – and that would produce their dark reflection in the outsized architecture ambitions of Nazi Germany. Both the German and British films of *The Tunnel* (Bernhardt 1933; Elvey 1935) recount the monumental effort to construct a transatlantic tunnel and ring in a new era of international trade and cooperation. Similarly, the multinational *FP1 Does not Answer* (1933) describes a plan to build a floating airbase in the middle of the ocean, thereby allowing planes to easily move from continent to continent and enhancing the potential for peace and commerce. Yet all of these films also suggest that such technology's very *monumental* impact might also diminish the human role, leaving us more open to manipulation, demagoguery, and ideological exploitation – a point *Things to Come* makes particularly explicit when a giant television screen proves the primary tool for fomenting revolt against the very technological accomplishments it represents.

With the advent of the Second World War and in its immediate aftermath, we find little to match these monumental images or the genre's earlier epic visions.

Instead, the sf banner is carried by what might almost be described as minimalist works – movie serials, typically produced by small American studios, working with limited budgets, driven by simple formulas, yet deploying much the same iconography that the major works described above had so elaborately developed: robots, rockets, fantastic machines, alien civilizations, even monumental cities. *Buck Rogers* (Beebe and Goodkind 1939) and the *Flash Gordon* serials (Stephani 1936; Beebe and Hill 1938; Beebe and Taylor 1940) further exploited the new science of rocketry and the fascination with possible space travel, already glimpsed in features like *Aelita*, *Woman in the Moon* (Lang 1929), and *Just Imagine*. Several serials emphasized the looming menace of the robot, seen in an earlier serial like *The Phantom Empire* (Brower and Eason 1935), but now given narrative prominence in *The Phantom Creeps* (Beebe and Goodkind 1939) and *Mysterious Doctor Satan* (Witney and English 1940), both of which anticipate the vogue for this menacing figure in the 1950s. In the immediate postwar period, a host of serials reflect Cold War fears by introducing a new concern with invading aliens, typically aided by weapons capable of mass destruction. Examples include *The Purple Monster Strikes* (Bennet and Brannon 1945), with its Martian invader wielding an Atomic Ray Machine; *Brick Bradford* (Bennet 1947), wherein the comic-book hero battles moon men armed with an Interceptor Ray; and *King of the Rocket Men* (Brannon 1949), *Radar Men from the Moon* (Brannon 1952), and *Zombies of the Stratosphere* (Brannon 1952), in all of which a scientist, aided by a rocket belt, fights off invaders armed with fantastic weapons. While foregrounding science and technology, these films link them to new sorts of weapons, reflecting widespread cultural anxieties about the Cold War and atomic power, and a new international consciousness.

Just as significant is the way in which these serials made their impact felt. Their effectiveness lies in their common formula, in which deadly menaces are revealed, death or destruction seems imminent, yet the narrative's hero or heroine fortuitously escapes and eventually, after many such incidents, triumphs. It is a machine-like pattern, marked by speed, narrative efficiency, and predictability, and its ultimate aim is to catch the audience up in its machine-like workings, bringing them back to the theater each week to re-experience the form's expected thrills and reassuring escapes. So while most serials never afford the level of self-consciousness of the sf features discussed above, their systematicity serves a similar function, practically foregrounding their narrative workings and acknowledging ("Don't miss the next thrilling episode . . ." they repeatedly enjoin) their desire for audience mastery. Moreover, they made this point not sporadically, whenever a new film was released, but *every week*, for the 12–15 weeks over which the action unreeled. They thereby constantly offered viewers dramatic encounters with the wonders of science and technology – depicted both as a menace and as a potential deliverance from that menace – and helped to work out the conflicted attitudes toward those elements that, in the postwar world, increasingly bulked into everyday life.

The serials also significantly contributed to this early history of cinematic sf in another way. For with their repeated stories of rocket flights and interplanetary travel and constant suggestions that something new was to be found "out there," they helped to accustom audiences to the work of the genre and even mapped a path for the first significant postwar sf features, the closely linked *Destination Moon* (Pichel 1950) and *Rocketship* X-M (Neumann 1950). With its adaptation of Robert Heinlein's *Rocket Ship Galileo* (1947), the former, produced by special effects expert and "Puppetoon" creator George Pal, helped establish a link to hard-sf literature, while it also assured a new level of authenticity thanks to its technical consultant, rocket pioneer Hermann Oberth, and noted space illustrator Chesley Bonestell's convincing matte paintings. Its documentary-style narrative effectively placed science and technology in the "starring" role, and used those elements to stake out a positive trajectory, as the exploration of space becomes a great adventure, much as *Woman in the Moon* had projected. Lacking the technical support (and budget) of *Destination Moon*, *Rocketship* X-M similarly draws much of its impact from its straightforward detailing of the science of spaceflight. The discovery of a nearly extinct Martian civilization, destroyed by nuclear conflict, allows the film to strike an important political warning for the Cold War world, while its concluding note, that the rocket's builders will create another ship to continue the important work of exploration, underscores the necessity for properly – rationally – directing the new powers of science and technology along a positive and peaceful path. Of course, over the next few years the genre would swerve in a rather different direction, with a proliferation of films in another, more threatening vein. Those films about alien invasion, atomic apocalypse, and mutant monsters, all suggesting how our technology might control and even destroy us, would prompt Sontag's famous, if somewhat misguided, assessment of the genre. But coming in the wake of *Destination Moon* and *Rocketship* X-M, they also further underscore the dual potential that marks the historical path of early sf cinema

Bibliography

Frayling, C. (1995) *Things to Come*, London: BFI.

Gerstein, E. (1972) "Metropolis," in S. Kauffmann and B. Henstell (eds) *American Film Criticism*, New York: Liveright; first published in *The Nation*, 23 March 1927.

Gunning, T. (1986) "The Cinema of Attraction: early film, its spectator and the avant-garde," *Wide Angle: A Quarterly Journal of Film History Theory Criticism and Practice*, 8(3–4): 63–70.

Jacobs, L. (1979) "Georges Méliès: artificially arranged scenes," in *The Emergence of Film Art*, 2nd edn, New York: Norton.

La Valley, A.J. (1985) "Traditions of Trickery: the role of special effects in the science fiction film," in G. Slusser and E.S. Rabkin (eds) *Shadows of the Magic Lamp*, Carbondale: Southern Illinois University Press.

Sontag, S. (1966) "The Imagination of Disaster," in *Against Interpretation and Other Essays*, New York: Farrar, Straus and Giroux.

Stewart, G. (1985) "The 'Videology' of Science Fiction," in G. Slusser and E.S. Rabkin (eds) *Shadows of the Magic Lamp*, Carbondale: Southern Illinois University Press.

Suvin, D. (1979) *Metamorphoses of Science Fiction: on the poetics and history of a literary genre*, New Haven, CT: Yale University Press.

Telotte, J.P. (2001) *Science Fiction Film*, Cambridge: Cambridge University Press.

Youngblood, D.J. (1992) *Movies for the Masses: popular cinema and Soviet society in the 1920s*, Cambridge: Cambridge University Press.

6
FICTION, 1926–1949
Farah Mendlesohn

When Hugo Gernsback founded *Amazing Stories* in 1926 he had reason to believe there was an existing market for stories like those by H.G. Wells and Jules Verne. In his other magazines, particularly *The Electrical Experimenter* (1913–20), Gernsback had discovered a receptive audience with a fondness for both the engineering stories he would champion (and which allied him with Verne) and the more lyrical scientific romances descended from Wells (a contemporary of Gernsback and of many of his readers). Wells and Verne were recorded as staple reading matter by many correspondents of the pulps (if only as complaints about Gernsback's use of reprints to fill out the early magazines). The "pulp" element of the new sf came not from Gernsback directly (who disapproved of it) but from the nature of the commercial market in the 1920s, and sf's habit of borrowing, begging, and stealing its clothes from every other popular genre developing contemporaneously. In addition, it came from a change in the market and a wider understanding of what constituted proper literature for adults.

Gernsback launched *Amazing Stories* (1926–2005) at a moment when magazine publications in the US were proliferating, and plummeting in price. As Susan Strasser (1999) notes, the high cost of paper – the US was a net importer of linen rags for papermaking – had hampered the expansion of publishing until the invention of cheap wood pulp paper made it possible to publish far more for far less. At the same time, the expansion of the railways and new ideas such as the Book of the Month club and cheap mail for publications, made it possible to send reading material to places without bookshops or libraries. For many, the main stockist of reading material was the local drugstore or hardware store.

Proliferation in any industry tends to lead to speciation. In the 1920s, general magazines such as *Argosy* (1882–1978) gave way to publications aiming to provide readers with more of what they liked. The "general" magazines continued be "general," but with a narrowing idea of what that meant. The marginal fiction found a home in specialized, genre-specific venues. The expansion of markets, however, did not mean an automatic expansion of material to fill those markets, and one can trace the careers of many of the early "hack" writers across magazines and genres. (One consequence of this highly active and demanding market and the role of hack writers was the "science-fictionalizing" of other forms, most prominently the detective story. Locked-room mysteries – popular at the end of the nineteenth century, and sharing many of the rationalistic values that attracted sf's often engineering-educated audience – were quickly combined in the early sf magazines with incredible invention stories.) The 1930s and 1940s saw "genre" fiction of all kinds pushed out of the literary magazines, and (for a short period) out of hardback publishing. This meant that the pulp magazines specializing in westerns, science fiction, horror, and romance might publish some very real dross, but they also had access to many of the best writers in America who could not get certain types of stories published in their regular markets.

The period 1926–49 was initially dominated by Hugo Gernsback, as influence if not as an editor. For the first year of *Amazing*, Gernsback filled up the pages with reprints, co-opting the works of Verne, Wells, Edward Bulwer-Lytton, Mark Twain, Rudyard Kipling, and Edgar Allan Poe into a de facto prehistory of sf. But he also published the likes of E.E. "Doc" Smith, the progenitor of the space opera, and by the time he lost control of *Amazing* in 1929, he was nurturing a range of new writers. *Amazing* carried on, under the editorship of T. O'Conor Sloane, who has been much maligned for "old-fashioned" ideas about science but who published some quite politically radical material. Sloane was succeeded by Raymond Palmer, who also started *Fantastic Adventures* (1939–52), a magazine at the pulpiest end of the spectrum. Gernsback launched *Science Wonder Stories* and *Air Wonder Stories*, under editor David Lasser, in 1929 (they merged in 1930 as *Wonder Stories* – retitled *Thrilling Wonder Stories* in 1936 – which ran under various editors until 1955). Other magazines, each with slightly different slants, included: Malcolm Reiss's *Planet Stories* (1939–55), which specialized in space opera; Mary Gnaedinger's *Famous Fantastic Mysteries* (1940–53), which was produced to reprint Munsey's magazine back catalog and thus introduced readers to older classics by A. Merritt, Ray Cummings, and others; and *Astounding Stories* (now *Analog*; 1930–), whose first editor, Harry Bates, favored "fast paced adventure in exotic settings" (Wolfe 2003: 98).

The sf published by Gernsback was rapidly superseded by the editorial contributions of Bates's successors at *Astounding Stories*. F. Orlin Tremaine introduced and advocated the now taken-for-granted "thought-experiment" story, such as Murray Leinster's "Sidewise in Time" (1934), in which consequence rather than awe was the key. Launched by Clayton Publications, *Astounding* survived a buyout by Street and Smith in 1932, and John W. Campbell was installed as editor in 1937. If Gernsback began the period, John W. Campbell was indisputably the editor who took sf into its own future. Campbell's editorial policy was very much in line with Tremaine's ambitions, but his liking for argument, his very hands-on editorship, and his clear desire to develop young writers – in some cases, it appears, to write up his own ideas – combined with a simple ability to pay more, quickly propelled *Astounding Science-Fiction* (as it was from 1938) to the front of the field. For the next 30 years, it was the leading magazine, offering a mixture of hard sf, social thought-experiments, and space opera. However, Campbell was a political conservative and left-wing writers were frequently forced to publish elsewhere, such as in the short-lived *Astonishing Stories* (1940–3). Edited by the young Frederik Pohl (like Campbell, an editor but one who continued to write), it published stories which were, politically, far more the inheritors of the Gernsback tradition than those in *Astounding*.

Although Gernsback was not, by the end of the period, the editor of the most successful magazine, and nobody now considers him to be the best of the early editors, he established the parameters within which the field's critical debates took place, and hosted the community of highly vocal readers and writers that we now call "fandom." This community created what we now understand as the language and ideological rhetoric of sf, although in the period under examination it was a cobbled-together pidgin. Only toward the end of the 1940s do writers who had grown up with the genre begin to handle its possibilities with grace and genuine invention.

Gernsback's stated purpose for sf was scientific popularization and education (see Westfahl 1998). The editorial page of his second magazine, *Science Wonder Stories*, contained the endorsement of scientifically educated associate editors. However, the degree to which he succeeded in generating a literary vehicle for scientific education, and even how desirable a goal it is for a literary form, is contested. Gernsback struggled to secure the kinds of stories he wanted, but they were scarce: many of the stories in his magazines function predominantly as vehicles for action and adventure, with the science only a thin gloss, so that Gernsback's editorials, which picked out whatever scientific value existed, were the crucial element in the formation of the ideology of what would become the sf community. In turn, readers were clearly "on-message," writing in to complain about scientific mistakes and inaccuracies, or to argue about the plausibility of certain speculations. However, as Westfahl (1996) makes clear, Gernsback's desire for scientific veracity and for sf's educational potential cannot be equated with what we now call "hard sf." Gernsback believed that sf should be grounded in what we know and what can be extrapolated from it. As the field developed, however, authors stretched this concept, taking on board the speculative "what if" of science (e.g., "What if a planet had seasons five hundred years long?"). These "what if" stories frequently use invented science and invent data in order to play a complex scientific game. They are Gernsback's descendants, but it is not clear that he would have approved.

The three basic plots of sf in the 1930s were the invasion story, the exploration/ first-contact story, and the invention story. The first of these descended from the future-war story (see Clarke 1992). In the nineteenth century, these posited invasions of various parts of Europe by other parts of Europe. In the twentieth century, Japan and "Asiatics" became the enemy of choice, and the victim country, America. True "alien invasion" stories – it is almost superfluous to mention that the humans always won – only began to materialize in the 1930s pulps, and many authors' imaginations do not seem to have extended beyond intelligent insects. The classic Bug-Eyed Monster is a creature of the cover artists and, later, the 1950s movies.

The second plot emerged from tales of imperial adventure by authors such as Joseph Conrad, H. Rider Haggard, and Edgar Rice Burroughs. In the pulp form, they resolved into exotic travelogs. Early pulp versions frequently involved the discovery of a lost race or hidden utopia through a telekinetic jewel, or some other means, and almost always involved the "loss" of the pathway to enchantment. Again, we have to wait for the genuinely alien: two stand-out stories of the period are Stanley Weinbaum's "A Martian Odyssey" (1934), in which humans get to meet an alien with an agenda of its own, and Murray Leinster's "First Contact" (1945), in which humans and aliens meet in space and have to figure out how to get home without giving away their home worlds' locations.

The invention story and its offshoot, the scientific mystery, can be seen as the taproot for sf as we understand it now. Heavily influenced by the technological utopians of the previous century and the acclamation of that unsurpassed self-publicist Thomas Alva Edison, invention stories assume that technological innovation is either for the good of humanity, or for evil. They are technocratic means of either introducing efficiency (e.g., a psychometric test, a time machine, a new airplane), or creating tyranny (the same set of inventions works just as well). But each and every invention is intended for one job, and any speculation within the tale focuses on that one job. The inventions typically exist as an interruption in an otherwise recognizable world and, except for trades directly affected by it, there are no unexpected consequences. Despite the example of Edward Bellamy's *Looking Backward: 2000–1887* (1888) and Gernsback's own *Ralph 124C 41+: a romance of the year 2660* (1911–12), invention fiction of the 1930s and early 1940s rarely attempted to create futuristic worlds for its new objects of desire (sometimes apparently "other" worlds, such as the far distant planet of Isaac Asimov's "Nightfall" (1941), remained so remarkably like ours that lengthy passages were required to explain why, really, they were not). Inventions and discoveries tended to be large and world-shattering, and authors rarely attempted to conceive of the large effect of a small change. Most of these stories in the 1930s, and well into the 1940s, end badly, frequently with the demise of both inventor and invention. What seems clear to me is that these stories do not, as some have argued, distrust science and technology – indeed, the disastrous outcome of "Nightfall" is an evangelical pamphlet for science – but they fail to understand both science and consequence.

Conditioned by Edison's self-promotion, most sf of this period (and well into the 1950s) was tied to the notion of the lone inventor whose inventions would be lost with his death. There is little sense that knowledge survives both because it is held in common, and because once the possibility is known, the science or technology is replicable. With the teaching of history locked into a Whiggish mentality of inevitable, linear progress – supported by the actions of Great Men who "foresaw" the outcome of their decisions – the "butterfly effect" or consequence was poorly understood. Until Robert A. Heinlein's *Beyond this Horizon* (serialized 1942, book 1948), with its complex and complicated future, *consequence*, which I consider the hallmark of full sf, remains missing. Its arrival may well relate to the very dramatic, visible changes which took place in the world between 1940 and 1949.

In addition to the major plots of 1926–49, we must also consider the concerns and anxieties authors expressed. Throughout the 1920s and 1930s, future-war fiction continued to emerge from the pens of Bulwer-Lytton, P.G. Chadwick, Dennis Wheatley, and Philip Francis Nowlan. However, the "generalized visions of doom" (Dowling 1987: 3), such as Phillip Wylie and Edwin Balmer's *When Worlds Collide* (1933), began to pall, perhaps because they inherently strip humans of control over their own lives. As the magazines developed in the 1930s, admonitory myths were temporarily consigned to the wastebasket and the rise of technocracy influenced even the disaster story. The ethos of the new American sf was to persuade the post-Darwin readership that the real consequence of human evolution was in human endeavor as a whole. Consequently, we begin to see disasters which humans can either avert or rise from, and more specific analyses of the consequence of economic or technological projects. Superweapons were more likely to be contributors to world peace than disasters in the making. H. Bruce Franklin (1988) points to a clear division between British (and European) and US understandings of the superweapon. George Griffith's *Lord of Labour* (1911) undermined the idea that any weapon could be so awful that humans would desist from war, and Wells's *The World Set Free* (1914) understood that technological sophistication would fuel rather than end warfare; but, in the US, many were convinced of the possibility of an "ultimate" weapon. Serialized in *Wonder Stories*, Carl W. Spohor's *The Final War* (1932), a tale of total war and mutually assured destruction, is rather an exception. Its sensitive political extrapolation is typical of the fiction preferred by Gernsback, but this was not the trend of American sf in the 1930s and 1940s. By the mid-1940s, many writers assumed atomic (or other super) weaponry was necessary, so tacitly accepted the consequences of nuclear war for America and the world – consequences smarter writers properly feared. Heinlein's "Solution Unsatisfactory" (1941), in which America forces universal disarmament under American dictatorship, is exemplary of this tension. In the related juvenile novel *Space Cadet* (1948), Heinlein mitigates this by transforming the Peace Patrol who control the weapons into a multinational agency, but the sense of an American Peace remains strong. In both texts, doubt is expressed, but swept away.

Among all this doom were pointillist utopias (see Westfahl 2007), works which offered moments of utopian imagining. Gernsback's *Ralph 124C 41+*, reissued in book form in 1925, set the tone. Whether under Gernsback and his emulators, or Campbell and his, the future could only be worse than the present if its purpose was to emphasize how excellent humans were *now*. One new element that emerged, however, was the very notion of utopia as a form of disaster in Karel Čapek's *RUR* (1920), Yevgeny Zamyatin's *We* (written 1920, publication in English 1924), and Aldous Huxley's *Brave New World* (1932), all of which demonstrated a suspicion of the machinery of civilization. However, among the writers for the pulps, the general assumption was onward and upward, whether to technocratic heaven or the stars.

Common to much disaster fiction of this period is the notion of racial disaster, as in Nowlan's *Buck Rogers* stories (1928, 1929). Typically, a weakened US is invaded by "Asiatics," who are ultimately the victims of genocide (Blacks are rarely mentioned, and are invisible as either invader or invaded until the 1950s). Such stories were ubiquitous enough for Gernsback to protest that readers and writers seemed to assume that *Air Wonder Stories* was desperate for such tales (James 1990: 29). Early Australian sf is also redolent of fear of both "Asiatics" and indigenous peoples. The best-known Australian story of this kind from the 1930s is probably A.J. Pullar's *Celestalia: a fantasy AD 1975* (1933) (see Webb and Enstice 1998), in which Australians and Asian Australians compete over definitions of nationality and ownership, while, as in so many Australian "yellow peril" stories, the aboriginal inhabitants are silently erased from the literary map. That this paradigm was already being challenged can be seen in Heinlein's *Sixth Column* (1941). Although full of familiar racist rhetoric, Heinlein castigates the Asiatic political system: he does not assume an *inherent* mindless will to obey, but sees the invasion as a result of ideological conditioning.

Of course, one element of the portrayal of "race" was in the conceptualization of aliens. At least in the first ten years, the magazines' aliens – represented most enthusiastically in Burroughs's *Barsoom* series (1912–43) – tended to be either utterly beautiful, vilely ugly, or insects, but gradually, with most credit going to Weinbaum's "A Martian Odyssey," aliens began to emerge as individuals. However, for the entirety of this period, it is impossible to escape the notion of hierarchy or human norms. Furthermore, efforts to stretch the envelope are too obviously allegorical: for example, Asimov's "Half-Breed" (1940) is an unsubtle, if moving, attack on the concept of miscegenation, but in its conclusion – that the half-breeds/tweenies are smarter than humans – falls back on notions of racial hierarchy.

Outside of the US, futuristic speculation, not tied to the demands and ideological frameworks of the magazines, was plentiful. The market for sf in the UK was predominantly in book form and linked to the desire for uplifting and educative political fiction, hence the popularity of speculative futurological essays, and of satires such as *Brave New World*, George Bernard Shaw's *Back to Methuselah* (1921), and Katherine Burdekin's *Swastika Night* (1937). Others sought to respond to the religious uncertainty and concern which flowered in the wake of the psychological trauma of the First World War: the serious scientific speculation of Wells's *The Shape of Things to Come* (1933); the mystical and theosophical space romance of David Lindsay's *Voyage to Arcturus* (1920); the Christian apologetics of C.S. Lewis's *Out of the Silent Planet* (1938) and its sequels; and the philosophical speculations of Olaf Stapledon's *Last and First Men* (1930) and *Star Maker* (1937). While earlier writers of the scientific romance such as M.P. Shiel and S. Fowler Wright survived into the 1920s, the hardback was not a mass-market form (see Stableford 1985), and there were few magazine markets for the sf short story, prompting new writers such as John Benyon Harris (John Wyndham) and Eric Frank Russell to turn to the US pulps.

In France, the influence of Verne supported the reputation of the genre. Distinguished writers such as André Maurois were comfortable publishing scientific romances, as was the Belgian J.H. Rosny aîné. In Germany, in the 1930s, Paul Alfred Muller wrote 150 issues of *Sun Koh, der Erbe von Atlantis* (1933–9), and 120 issues of *Jan Mayen* (1935–9), under the name Lok Myler. Both series featured eponymous charismatic heroes who raise Atlantis and transform Greenland to create more land for Germany and other white peoples and which were revived after the Second World War (1945–53 and 1949–50 respectively) (see Nagl 1974). Distinguished novelists such as Bernard Kellerman and Alfred Döblin experimented with sf, while Hans Dominik published popular sf throughout the 1920s and 1930s, becoming increasingly influenced by racial politics. Otto Willi Gail's *The Shot into Infinity* (1925) demonstrates the growing interest in space travel among German rocket scientists. Thea von Harbou's *Metropolis* (1926) and *Woman in the Moon* (1928) were connected to the screenplays she co-authored with Fritz Lang for his films. In Sweden, there was enough interest to publish the weekly *Jules Verne-Magasinet* (1940–7; retitled *Veckans Äventyr* in 1941, it soon began to favor other adventure genres), but in Italy, Romania, and Japan, sf continued to be published only sporadically in mainstream magazines.

One reason why American genre sf remained generally "American" was the sheer difficulty of submitting material from elsewhere, and getting paid for it. Early Australian writers, such as Joe Czynski, Alan Connell, and Phil Collas, had stories published in *Amazing*, but only Joe Czynski managed anything like a career, and that only while stationed in the US; on returning to Australia, the difficulty of ensuring safe mailing of manuscripts defeated him. Wynne Whiteford, who published several sf stories in Australia, only entered the American market when he traveled overseas in the 1950s. Other writers who published in Australia and the UK, in book form, included James Morgan Walsh, M. Lynn Hamilton, William Pengreep, and Helen Simpson. Walsh wrote space opera, Hamilton a hidden-world romance, Pengreep a classic invention story of an unconsciousness ray, and Simpson an evangelical novel of the future, not unlike the well-known *Left Behind* series (1995–). Blackford *et al.* (1999) estimate that perhaps two dozen books and novellas were published by Australian writers in this period: Arthur Russell continued the "invention story" tradition, complete with mad scientist; John Winton Hemming opted for the fabulous journey, this time a tour of Mars; Val Molesworth, one of Australia's early fans, produced both juvenile and adult space opera; and mainstream author Damien Healy also wrote some sf. The one exception to the generally poor quality of this fiction Blackford *et al.* note is *Tomorrow and Tomorrow and Tomorrow* (1947) by M. Barnard Eldershaw, the pseudonym of Marjorie Barnard and Flora Eldershaw. Set in a socialist twenty-fourth century, it fell foul of political censorship, and the full text was not published until 1983.

In the USSR, 15 to 30 or so prose sf stories and novels were published every year between 1923 and 1940, at which point the exigencies of war reduced publishing opportunities (see McGuire 1985). Pre-revolutionary Russian sf followed the model of scientific romance inherited from Wells and Verne, and in that form seems to have remained fairly acceptable at first. Its mildly utopian tinge initially suited the new Soviet Union, and seems to have been supported by both private magazines and the state markets – the state-owned magazine *World Pathfinder* (1925–31) even had as its subtitle, "Travel, adventure, science fiction." Invention and detective stories, such as those written by Alexei Tolstoy, seem to have been very popular, as were the future-war stories of Alexander Belyaev. By 1931, however, sf was criticized for its failure to conform to the ideological demands of socialist realism. The Russian Association of Proletarian Writers was particularly hostile to sf, and when the Union of Soviet Writers was formed in 1932 it absorbed RAPP's hostility: sf was idealist and hence time-wasting.

What we know of the US magazines, we know primarily through the eyes of scholars shaped by the 1970s and 1980s, such as Mike Ashley (2000). Our knowledge of important authors is channeled through hindsight, and often runs counter to the criticism in the magazines themselves. It is becoming increasingly clear that the period surveyed above is ripe for revision.

Recent years have witnessed a growing interest in the role of women in the magazines, as readers, writers, and subject matter. Brian Attebery (2002, 2006), Justine

Larbalestier (2002, 2006), Helen Merrick (1999), and Batya Weinbaum (1998) have all sought to question the long-held understandings of this period (sometimes perpetuated by the feminist writers and scholars of the 1970s) that there were no women writing for the early magazines, and that the field was both hostile to women and attached to stereotypical portrayals of them as sisters, mothers, and daughters. While I am not trying to suggest that the late 1920s and early 1930s were overburdened with women writers or enlightened portrayals of women, the period was considerably more women-friendly than the next 15 years. As Larbalestier, Weinbaum, and Eric Leif Davin (2006) show, Hugo Gernsback actively welcomed women writers. Davin lists many female writers in the period leading up to 1926 who published in the *All-Story Magazine* (1905–20) and *The Strand* (1891–1950), and there is no indication that anything about the new genre was intended to repulse them. Robin Roberts (1993) cites magazine covers featuring nubile young women and tentacled monsters as potentially alienating, but refers primarily to examples from the least popular of the magazines (*Planet Stories* and *Fantastic Adventure*). *Amazing*'s cover illustrations during this period were mostly of engines and exotic machinery (a brief flirtation with romantic photographic covers in the late 1930s was rejected by readers of both sexes). Most readers disliked "romance," but this should not be misunderstood as a euphemism for women (although younger readers clearly did see women in this role, as is evident in the fiction their generation went on to write in the 1940s).

Clare Winger Harris, one of the best known and admired of the early women authors, was published first in *Weird Tales*, in 1926, and won third place – and publication – in a 1927 *Amazing* competition. Although Gernsback expressed surprise, he attributed it to the lack of scientific education among women rather than their innate inadequacy. She went on to specialize in female-oriented utopias. Leslie F. Stone published 18 stories between 1929 and 1940 (see Weinbaum 1998), while C.L. Moore published over 50 stories within the period. These stories were well received by male readers, and the sex of the writer, often flagged by the editors, does not seem to have aroused much comment. Davin details at least 65 female authors writing before 1965, but while the generally evangelistic Gernsback was positively enthusiastic about female writers, there is some evidence that Campbell was not so keen. Stone reported a chilly reception from him, and even if he was not consciously attempting to exclude women, his ideas about sf did exclude many older writers and he does not seem to have made particular efforts to welcome female writers (Attebery 2006: 62).

In terms of *Amazing*'s content, Gernsback's writers were drawn from other (also young) genres, and were generally in their 20s and 30s when they began writing for the nascent sf magazines. Writers such as Harl Vincent and David M. Keller understood that in order for the human race to reproduce, it needed women. This understanding evaporated within a decade, and by the late 1940s, there were very few female characters in sf. Most of the early writers envisaged a future in which women's roles would be greater – Keller, for example, wrote about women who were doctors and engineers – but all of this period's authors assumed that women's primary interest was in rearing the next generation. What is not always noted is that they made the same assumption about men. In most sf of this period, marriage, or the availability for marriage, signals a man's sanity as it does a woman's: the professor's daughter is there as much to indicate his place in the world as she is to provide a love interest. In contrast, mad professors and overly driven inventors are almost always without female companionship. Masculinity is conferred in many of these fictions in terms of knowledge. Psychological authority, the ability to analyze and to convince others, is one of the dominating gender markers of sf in the 1930s and 1940s. Technocracy did not dispose of the physical man, represented for many by Kimball Kinnison in E.E. "Doc" Smith's *Lensman* series (1934–48), but it did co-opt it to offer many male readers a less physical alternative. Finally, Attebery (2002) has pointed to the feminization of the alien other in stories of this period: the language of superiority and inferiority is almost always couched as "hard" or "soft." This may be used to trick the reader, as in "Forgetfulness" (1937), written by Campbell under his Don A. Stuart pseudonym, in which "soft" aliens blaze with ferocity when they finally eject the humans, but the gender divide is rigid. Soft equals feminine, equals (in the end) inferior.

BIBLIOGRAPHY

Ashley, M. (2000) *The Time Machines: the story of the science-fiction pulp magazines from the beginning to 1950*, Liverpool: Liverpool University Press.

Attebery, B. (2002) *Decoding Gender in Science Fiction*, New York and London: Routledge.

—— (2006) "The Conquest of Gernsback: Leslie F. Stone and the subversion of science fiction tropes," in J. Larbalestier (ed.) *Daughters of Earth: feminist science fiction in the twentieth century*, Middletown, CT: Wesleyan University Press.

Blackford, R., Ikin, V., and McMullen, S. (eds) (1999) *Strange Constellations: a history of Australian science fiction*, Westport, CT and London: Greenwood Press.

Clarke, I.F. (1992) *Voices Prophesying War: future wars 1763–3749*, New York: Oxford University Press.

Davin, E.L. (2006) *Partners in Wonder: women and the birth of science fiction, 1926–1965*, Lanham, MD: Lexington Books.

Dowling, D. (1987) *Fictions of Nuclear Disaster*, Iowa City: University of Iowa Press.

Franklin, H.B. (1988) *War Stars: the superweapon and the American imagination*, New York: Oxford University Press.

James, E. (1990) "Yellow, Black, Metal, and Tentacled: the race question in American science fiction," in P.J. Davies (ed.) *Science Fiction, Social Conflict, and War*, Manchester: Manchester University Press.

Larbalestier, J. (2002) *The Battle of the Sexes in Science Fiction*, Middletown, CT: Wesleyan University Press.

——(ed.) (2006) *Daughters of the Earth: feminist science fiction in the twentieth century*, Middletown, CT: Wesleyan University Press.

McGuire, P. (1985) *Political Aspects of Soviet Science Fiction*, Ann Arbor, MI: UMI Research Press.

Merrick, H. (1999) "From Female Man to Feminist Fan: uncovering 'herstory' in the annals of sf fandom," in H. Merrick and T. Williams (eds) *Women of Other Worlds: excursions through science fiction and fantasy*, Nedlands: University of Western Australia Press.

Nagl, M. (1974) "SF, Occult Sciences, and Nazi Myths," *Science Fiction Studies*, 1(3): 185–97.

Roberts, R. (1993) *A New Species: gender and science in science fiction*, Urbana: University of Illinois Press.

Stableford, B. (1985) *Scientific Romance in Britain, 1890–1950*, London: Fourth Estate.

Strasser, S. (1999) *Waste and Want: a social history of trash*, New York: Metropolitan Books.

Webb, J. and Enstice, A. (1998) *Aliens and Savages: fiction, politics and prejudice in Australia*, Sydney: HarperCollins.

Weinbaum, B. (1998) "Leslie F. Stone's 'Men with Wings' and 'Women with Wings': a woman's view of war between the wars," *Extrapolation*, 39(4): 299–313.

Westfahl, G. (1996) *Cosmic Engineers: a study of hard science fiction*, Westport, CT: Greenwood Press.

—— (1998) *The Mechanics of Wonder: the creation of the idea of science fiction*, Liverpool: Liverpool University Press.

—— (2007) *Hugo Gernsback and the Century of Science Fiction*, Jefferson, NC and London: McFarland.

Wolfe, G.K. (2003) "Sf and its Editors," in E. James and F. Mendlesohn (eds) *The Cambridge Companion to Science Fiction*, Cambridge: Cambridge University Press.

7

GOLDEN AGE COMICS

Marek Wasielewski

There is a general consensus that the "Golden Age of Comics" began with the publication of the first complete Superman story in *Action Comics* no. 1 (June 1938). This DC comic book was phenomenally successful; by its third issue it had sold 900,000 copies, and this was largely due to the popularity of the Man of Steel (Jones 2004: 155). Superman, created by sf fans Jerry Siegel and Joe Shuster, epitomized a number of motifs that came to dominate the creation of superheroes and which demonstrate their deep connection to modernity: authoritarianism, the body, industrialization, eugenics, technologies of war, and the utopianism of the 1939 World's Fair.

The initial success of the Superman franchise owes much to DC's marketing campaign, which embedded the character within the American technological sublime. David Nye notes that US industrialization facilitated the development of a distinctly technological sublime that "reinvest[s] the landscape and the works of men with transcendent significance" (Nye 1994: xiii). The extended origin story printed in *Superman* (summer 1939) captures this intermixing of the everyday with the technological sublime. In the introductory panel, a streamlined rocket ship blasts away from an exploding Krypton; the intergalactic exodus is juxtaposed, in the next panel, with an elderly couple, the Kents, discovering the infant Superman. The second page features a dazzling sequence in which Superman discovers his unique abilities as he grows up. The top left and right panels show him learning to leap across the cityscape, his trajectory diagrammatically indicated by a curve of broken lines over a cross-section of a grid-like city. His superhuman strength and speed are signified in relation to icons of industrial modernity: he lifts an automobile, runs "faster than a streamlined train." Finally, the Man of Steel's invulnerability is demonstrated by a doctor's inability to break his flesh with a needle – "nothing less than a bursting shell could penetrate his skin."

Prior to the Golden Age, American sequential art was already implicated in the propagation of the technological sublime. Richard Outcault's *Yellow Kid* (1894–c.1898), possibly the first mass-produced comic strip, charted the political impact of industrialization in New York City. Winsor McCay's extraordinary *Little Nemo in Slumberland* strip (1905–13) cast industrial-era middle-class life as an Art Nouveau dream in which his sleepwalking protagonist found bizarre adventure and a menagerie of characters, twisted and distorted by fantastical mechanism, who embodied the impact of mechanization on modern urban subjectivities. McCay's engagement with Machine Age body politics set an important precedent in the representation of technology in comics culture; technology began to be depicted as an invasive force, sculpting and shaping the human in its own image.

This is especially striking in the superheroes whose exploits formed the basis of the Golden Age of the late 1930s to mid-1940s, notably Superman, the Batman, Captain America, and Wonder Woman. Roger Luckhurst notes that the development of comic books corresponds with the "moment that starts that perennial difficulty of constraining analysis of SF to a single aesthetic mode" as "pulp stories became strips became radio serials became single-reel film adventures" (Luckhust 2005: 66). In *Flash Gordon* (1934–), created by Alex Raymond, vivid depictions of streamlined cities and tear-drop rocket ships were part of a remarkable convergence in which sf "or at least its machinery, bled into the architecture and design of 1930s Art Deco" (Luckhurst 2005: 66). *Flash Gordon* corresponded with the publishing development of binding comic strips together to form complete comic books, and was central to the establishment of the action-adventure genre, which elsewhere featured such hard-boiled characters as Lee Falk's costumed hero, the Phantom (1936–), battling physically grotesque villains, notably the misshapen gangsters of Chester Gould's *Dick Tracy* strip (1931–).

The Golden Age was further defined by a change in the mass-marketing, which saw comic-book superheroes become strategically marketed commodities. For example, Superman was not just a crime-fighting alien from Krypton but also the power behind such 1940s products as "Force Toasted Wheat Flakes" and "Superman the Super Bubble Gum" (Daniels 1998). DC's control of Superman under trademark rather than copyright law initiated a new phase in the commercial exploitation of characters: "Once DC recognised Superman's status as a commodity, they defined him and sold him as a product in all his incarnations. By 1941 Superman was not so much a character who helped sell comic books as a product that comic books sold" (Gordon 1998: 134). With the establishment of Superman Inc. in 1939, DC pioneered the practice of a subsidiary company exclusively involved in licensing "the name and image" of a character "to various manufacturers" (Daniels 1998: 47). The commodification of the superhero was underpinned by the standardized cost-cutting Golden Age comic-book format of left-to-right linear sequences of panels. Artist and writer Will Eisner remarked that "We have made comic book features pretty much the way Ford made cars … I would write and design the characters, somebody else would pencil them in, somebody else would ink, somebody else would letter" (qtd in Wright 2003: 6). Such working practices, exacerbated by wartime paper shortages and accompanying pressures to follow a stripped-down and standardized layout, "contributed to visual sameness and formulaic stories of many early comic books" (Wright 2003: 6).

Such production methods had profound ideological effects. Scott McCloud notes that the budget four-color process, and the limited number of hues it could create, ensured that "costumed heroes were clad in bright, primary colors and fought in bright primary worlds" (McCloud 1994: 188). As a consequence, Golden Age superheroes were imprinted "with a new iconic power. Because costume colors remained exactly the same, panel after panel, they came to symbolize characters in the mind of the reader" (McCloud 1994: 188). For example, the cover of *Captain America Comics* no. 1 (March 1941) depicts the superhero punching Adolf Hitler in the face. The four-color inking process generates a jarring series of brightly colored contrasts: the striking red, white, and blue of Captain America dominates the recoiling fascistic browns of Hitler, an effect accentuated by the gaudy, bright yellow background. Indeed, the coloring of the page is central to the projection of the punch.

The authoritarianism of the Golden Age superhero comic was exacerbated by the influence of American pulp fictions on the development of the genre. This is readily apparent in Bill Finger and Bob Kane's the Bat-Man, who first appeared in *Detective Comics* no. 27 (May 1939). He combined the darkness and rage of Walter B. Gibson's the Shadow, a crime-fighter who debuted on radio in 1930 and had his own pulp from 1931, with the "idealized combination of brains and brawn" (Luckhurst 2005: 65) of Richard Seaton, the protagonist of E.E. "Doc" Smith's *Skylark* series of pulp space operas (1928–34). Batman's first adventures were heavily influenced by the uncanny – "the hero of these first episodes [roamed] the older worlds of Paris and Hungary in addition to New York on his grim pursuit of vampires, monks and other Gothic horrors" (Brooker 2001: 58) – and this points to the dialectic of technocratic "scientifiction," as advocated by editor Hugo Gernsback, and the weird fiction, such as the racialized nightmares of H.P. Lovecraft's *Cthulhu* fiction (Luckhurst 2005: 64). Batman's origin sequence, published in *Detective Comics* no. 33 (November 1939), conjoins scientifiction with the biological uncanny. After witnessing the death of his parents, young Bruce Wayne prays for vengeance in a panel whose Gothic qualities emerge in the heavy shading that obscures half of his face and in the flickering candlelight next to his bed, unusual in an age obsessed with electricity. Brooker notes that Bruce "is not turning to God for comfort in his loss, but vowing on the 'spirits'" (Brooker 2001: 53). The next panel dramatically changes the mood of the sequence: an adult Bruce "becomes a master scientist" in a laboratory, the room dark and wreathed with smoke, illuminated only by one harsh electric light. The following panel depicts him training his body to physical perfection, "able to perform amazing athletic feats," his explosive strength accentuated by the yellow nimbus surrounding him as he lifts weights. The transition between these panels reveals that the chemicals Bruce uses to train his mind catalyze the physical transformation of his body; bubbling test tubes explode into the upward lift of the barbell. Bruce becomes the Batman through practising physical culture, the sort of regimes expounded by such popular muscular titans as Eugen Sandow and Bernarr Macfadden. They aimed to energize the fatigued muscles of modern man by the appliance of industrial technology, while Bruce transforms himself by an act of alchemy, conducting experiments in the Gothic shadows.

Another Golden Age superhero, Captain America, created by Joe Simon and Jack Kirby, displays his national identity on his body. Bradford W. Wright notes his importance as a symbol of the war effort "with his instantly recognizable, red, white and blue costume, his shield of stars and stripes" (Wright 2003: 30). As a result of the strong anti-Nazi sentiment in Golden Age comic-book culture – "Many of the young artists creating comic books were Jewish and liberal" (Wright 2003: 35) – Captain America began his one-man war against the Axis powers almost a year before America entered the conflict. His adventures span the transitional moment in which comic-book culture was recalibrated to sell total war. His is a masculine birth, powered by a racialized dialectic of legitimate and deviant bodies. In *Captain America Comics* no. 1, in response to Axis sabotage, the US military transforms Steve Rogers – who had been rejected as unfit for military service – into a genetically engineered super soldier called Captain America. In a sterile laboratory, Professor Reinstein injects him with a serum, a "seething liquid" alive with energy. Rogers rapidly gains muscle mass, a white glowing aura around his body. Reinstein formally introduces his creation as "The first of a corps of super-agents whose mental and physical ability will make them a terror to spies and saboteurs." Initially an example of biological deviance, Rogers is purified by military-industrial technology and attains the heights of "mental and physical ability" exclusively reserved for white men.

Wonder Woman's creation was rather different. Psychologist William Moulton Marston, a consultant on DC's editorial board and a frequent contributor to *Family Circle* (1932–), was critical of the Golden Age superheroes' "blood curdling masculinity" (Jones 2004: 207). Asked by DC to counter these representations, Marston created Wonder Woman, who first appeared in *All Star Comics* no. 8 (December 1941). She embodied Marston's belief in an authoritarian, yet matriarchal, body utopia: Wonder Woman "is psychological propaganda for the new type of woman who should, I believe, rule the world" (Marston qtd in Jones 2004: 208). He believed that "Woman's body contains twice as many love generating organs and endocrine mechanisms as the male. What woman lacks is the dominance or self-assertive power to put over and enforce her love desires" (Jones 2004: 207). He thought she could propagate a vision of femininity that would counteract the sexism so prevalent in American society. However, his conception propagated the chauvinism of the comic-book industry by promoting a distinctly masculine representation of feminine power and beauty from within a framework of Machine Age sadomasochism. Marston had developed the technology for the lie detector, and Wonder Woman expresses the conjunction of sadomasochism, authoritarianism, and Machine Age technologies implicit in such a device. Her bullet-deflecting bracelets and lasso of truth were a play on industrialized authoritarianism. The lasso – anyone bound within its silky ropes would become her pet – was based on Marston's belief in "Love Allure," which was generated by "the subconscious, elaborately disguised desire of males to be mastered by a woman who loves them" (qtd in Jones 2004: 209). Stories often featured the binding of scantily clad women. In one story, Wonder Woman is "electrocuted and manacled to a wall – at ankles, wrists, arms and throat" (Jones 2004: 209), while a panel from *Wonder Woman* no. 5 shows the uniformed male villain tying Marva in a chair, assisted by Wonder Woman, who notes "Why, that isn't half tight enough!" (qtd in Jones 2004: 209). Furthermore, Wonder Woman's curvaceous body and skimpy, yet patriotic, costume were projected from hegemonic depictions of feminine beauty and, despite Marston's wishes, she was perhaps the most misogynistic superhero of them all, further reinforcing the gender division that was an integral aspect of the masculine birth paradigm.

The Golden Age's entanglement with industrial modernity is also evident in DC's campaign to embed their superheroes within the New York World's Fair. Christina Cogdell notes that its architects "created the fair's exhibits to be more than mere models of future probabilities. Because they were backed by organizations with social and political power and prestige, economic resources, and vision, the exhibits seemingly foretold future probabilities" (Cogdell 2004: 190). As a consequence, "the very space of the Fair was science-fictional, with boundaries blurred between futuristic exhibits, promotional films (with titles like *Rhapsody in Steel* and *The Birth of Industry*), and the site itself" (Luckhurst 2005: 66). Superman Inc. organized Superman Day with a guest appearance of the character as well as two specially commissioned comic books, *World's Fair 1939* and *World's Fair 1940*. In the latter, Superman's connection with the ethos of the fairs is made explicit. Jack Burnley's introductory panel shows Superman in midair soaring over the Trylon and Perisphere, while his depiction of the fair captures the flowing, evanescent quality of the streamlined exhibits – heavy shading accentuates the dynamic curves and fins of the structures, imbuing the architecture with a kinetic potential as if they were permanently in a state of flight. Indeed, flight was a central theme of the fair because, as Nye notes, "The airplane violated the natural order, defying gravity, and hurling a man so high he became little more than a speck in the sky" (Nye 1994: 202). Furthermore, flight sanitized the horrors of ground-based industrial warfare by emphasizing the agency and freedom of fighter pilots dueling in the air (Nye 1994: 202–3). Superman's flight pattern over the fair – his arms and legs stretch out in a parachutist's formation, while motion lines behind him accentuate his velocity – help to position him within the cultural axis of the fair. He embodies the vision of an efficient and clean corporate utopia, and heralds a militarized future in which technology enables combatants to perfect and transcend the horrors of total war through self-propelled flight.

Superman's exploits at the fair show how deeply connected the superhero genre was to modernity's veneration of speed and glorification of industrialized violence. In this, the ideological superstructure of the Golden Age comic-book industry bears striking resemblances to Italian futurism's attempts "to imagine the body's boundaries – as both permeable, shifting, and open to fusion with the environment, and as rigid, closed, and resistant to penetration" (Poggi 1997: 20). Golden Age superhero comics similarly oscillate between depictions of titanic strength or speed and fleeting sequences of panels which fragment and reconstruct these solid bodies in order to generate narrative. Italian futurism was concerned with the question of "how to create an immortal man/machine hybrid, a body already posited in the future tense" (Poggi 1997: 20), while the superhero "possesse[d] a new kind of body – only the Man of Steel has the constitution, organs and abilities equal to the rigors of the Machine Age" (Bukatman 2003: 53). Cecilia Tichi notes that as a consequence of industrial culture, Machine Age subjectivities were subsumed under a mechanized paradigm – "to be alive in the twentieth century is to see the world for what it is, a complex of mechanized systems" (Tichi 1987: 37) – and Siegel and Shuster projected this mechanized paradigm to its utopian conclusion: a Man of Steel in complete synergy with industrial technology; the technological sublime in human form.

There are other parallels between Golden Age superheroes and futurist art (and other right-wing interwar representations of masculinity), exemplified by Filippo Tommaso Marinetti's cyborg in *Mafarka le futuriste* (1909). Mafarka is a being of extraordinary power because, as the product of his creator's technological genius, he is "generated without the aid of what the novel calls a 'vulva'" (Poggi 1997: 27) – indeed, he is "beautiful and pure of all defects that come from the maleficent vulva and that predispose one to decrepitude and death" (Marinetti qtd in Poggi 1997: 27). Like Mafarka, Golden Age superheroes predominantly share a masculine birth, especially Superman, who is transported to Earth in the steel womb of his father's rocket ship. Superman's and Batman's violence is generated through a negation of the feminine: Superman keeps himself aloof from Lois Lane, while Batman and Robin form a homosocial fraternity, defining their actions through patriarchal displays of violence. Indeed the authoritarian nature of the Golden Age super-body seems to be implicitly grounded in misogyny.

Scott Bukatman positions the superhero as an act of rebellion against New York's grid system: "Through the superhero, we gain a freedom of movement not constrained by the ground-level order imposed by the urban grid" (Bukatman 2003: 188). However, this takes on a militaristic edge in *World's Finest Comics* no. 6 (summer 1942), which features Superman battling Metallo. Representative of the "totalitarian man" – "superbly armed, deliberately destructive and dominant" (Gleason 1995: 51) – this powerful "Man of Metal" ultimately has no chance against the completely machined body of Superman. Beneath his suit of advanced armor, he is merely flesh and blood, but the Man of Steel, like Marinetti's superman, is remorseless, pure, metallic surfaces. As such a story suggests, the Golden Age comic industry was uniquely attuned to the propaganda war against the Axis powers, helping to generate Manichean narratives through color in which the division between villain and hero, Axis and Ally, could be signified by a brushstroke. This is strikingly conveyed in a Human Torch story by Carl Burgos in *All Winners Comics* no. 1 (summer 1941), in which the android Torch and his flaming sidekick, Toro, paint kinetic war propaganda in the skies with flame, fiery depictions of Uncle Sam, Roosevelt, and Japanese atrocities.

A significant proportion of wartime research was directed toward the fashioning of the cybernetic American soldier in complete technological synergy with the industrialized killing spaces of the Second World War (see Galison 1994). Prototype computers were developed which fused human operators with their machines so as to maximize their killing capacity, such as Norbert Wiener's Anti-Aircraft predictor, which constructed a mathematical map of the space through which the enemy aircraft would travel and then calculated its next location. Devices such as this had a strong resonance with wartime comic-book superheroes, who were created through a violent mapping of industrialized bodies through gridded urban/textual spaces. As the industry was calibrated for war, this practice reached its logical conclusion in a deliberately militarized mapping of space through the trajectories of brightly clad cybernetic weapon systems. For example, *Marvel Mystery Comics* nos. 8–10 (June–October 1940) features a titanic showdown between the Human Torch and Namor, the Sub-Mariner, in New York City. Namor, at the time a villain, begins his onslaught by unleashing a "depth bomb" that floods the Hudson Tunnel, initiating a city-wide battle between the water-driven powers of Namor and the automated, self-combustion of the Torch. The battle is a dogfight as the two superheroes unleash their respective elements, destroying the George Washington Bridge and toppling the pinnacle of the Empire State Building. Namor and the Torch manipulate Machine Age New York to gain the advantage, resulting in crumpled tramways and melted steel girders.

Although the early Golden Age Superman fought the villains of the New Deal, such as war profiteers and slum landlords, the ideological core of the superhero comic, as the connections to futurism and military technology suggest, was deeply authoritarian. Superman's arrival on Earth in a streamlined rocket ship was not just a spatial transition. In effect, he came from a streamlined future. Dubbed "Man of Tomorrow," he resonated with the theme of the World's Fair, "Building the World of Tomorrow," which "rested" on the twin "ideological girders" of design euthenics and biological eugenics (Cogdell 2004: 191). Since the late 1920s, "newspaper headlines had proclaimed that geneticists were on the verge of being able to produce 'supermen' or different human 'types' at will," while "Industrial designers had reformed 'degenerate' products into their 'civilized,' 'cleanlined' counterparts" (Cogdell 2004: 190). In this context, the last son of Krypton represented a eugenically engineered race of white, future supermen.

This eugenic hierarchy is evident throughout Golden Age comics. Batman's enemies are signified by corpulent physiques and the slouched postures of inferior genetic stock. The Joker's white face and raving eyes accentuate his purple zoot suit, indicating that he embodies a racial and biological other (as Andrew Ross notes, he also "speaks in rappish rhymes and moves his body in shapeless jive" (qtd in Brooker 2001: 27)). In "Professor Hugo Strange and the Monster," from *Batman* no. 1 (spring 1940), the eponymous scientist escapes from prison and injects inmates of the Metropolis insane asylum with a serum which turns them into frenzied, but controllable, giants. The introductory panel depicts a dazzling, electrified cityscape with a physically degenerate monster looming in the moonlight and, in a set of extraordinary sequences, the monsters infect the city with their madness, using the very *mise en scène* of urban modernity – cars, street lamps – as projectiles and clubs to cause mass panic. Batman's response is utterly ruthless. A genetic crusader, he embodies Anglo-Saxon technology and physical prowess rescuing the city from a racial apocalypse: in one sequence, he machine-guns the monsters – "Much as I hate to take human life, I'm afraid this time it's necessary" – and in another, he lynches one of them beneath the Batgyro. In a similar vein, "The Case of the Hollow Men" (*All Winners Comics* no. 1 (summer 1941)) sees Captain America battle zombie hoboes reanimated by a necromancer in the pay of Hitler. In a dark and moody cityscape, the grayish putrescence of the undead bodies of the homeless contrasts with the seemingly alive and dynamic bodies of the superhero and his sidekick, Bucky. In a full-page layout, the zombies terrorize a city with their deviant yet extremely tough bodies, throwing automobiles from bridges, derailing subway trains and butchering the occupants. In the center of the page, the fanged necromancer laughs maniacally. In the showdown sequence, Captain America and Bucky infiltrate his lair, where he gloats about how he replaces the blood of his victims with "di-namo fluid." Displaying a body encased with futuristic technology, he explains, "This liquid of my own invention, will give his body super-vitality for twenty-four hours! During that period he cannot die." Such stories show how attuned the comic-book industry was to the wartime racialized hierarchy of bodies, from the seemingly vital, legitimate white bodies of American superheroes down to the undead, malformed, and deviant bodies of the opposition.

The overt violence and authoritarianism of the first comic-book superheroes provoked a moral panic, based on fears that the form was corrupting American youth with its aggressive approach to crime control. This was encapsulated in a 1940 *Chicago Daily News* editorial by Sterling North called "A National Disgrace": "Badly drawn, badly written, and badly printed – a strain on the young eyes and young nervous systems – the effects of these pulp-paper nightmares is that of a violent stimulant. Their crude blacks and reds spoil a child's natural sense of color; their hypodermic injection of sex and murder make the child impatient with better, though quieter stories" (qtd in Jones 2004: 168). North helped to catalyze a campaign in the early 1940s against superhero comic books (which set a precedent for the more substantial moral panic in the 1950s, exemplified – and fueled – by Dr Fredric Wertham's *Seduction of the Innocent* (1954)). In response, DC established an "advisory editorial board of child psychologists, educators, and welfare workers," and by curbing the violent excesses of their superheroes, DC finally cemented the identity and universes of their flagship character, "enact[ing] standards for Superman stories that prohibited – among other things – the destruction of private property other than that belonging to a villain. By mid-1941 villains were no longer auto plant owners but mad scientists and or common criminals" (Gordon 1998: 136). The effects of the anti-comic book campaign on Batman can be traced through the transformation of his horns, from menacingly long and pointy, to softened stubs. Toward the end of 1941 "Batman's moral code was firmly in place," with *Batman* no. 4 proclaiming that "The Batman never kills or carries a gun!" (Brooker 2001: 57). The character "was subtly modified to suit his new role as father protector rather than lone avenger" (Brooker 2001: 58).

These comic-book superheroes burned out remarkably quickly: "no successful superhero characters were introduced after 1944, and poor sales compelled publishers to cancel most superhero titles by the end of the decade" (Wright 2003: 57). In the end, their nemesis was not Hitler, but Archie comics, which had abandoned their own superhero lines to become "the leading publisher specializing in light-hearted teenage humor" (Wright 2003: 72) as a key readership for superhero comics, American GIs, were demobilized and "the end of wartime production controls opened the door for new publishers and a flood of new titles" (Wright 2003: 57). More fundamentally, Golden Age superhero comics declined because they had been expressions of a fleeting moment in American cultural history. The first superheroes, like the acidic paper they were printed on, were swiftly dissipating cultural artifacts. Like streamlined commodities, they were not built to last, but in the brief flowering of Golden Age superhero culture, characters such as Superman, Batman, Captain America, and Wonder Woman revealed the unique potential of comic books to convey technological and historical change.

BIBLIOGRAPHY

Brooker, W. (2001) *Batman Unmasked: analyzing a cultural icon*, London and New York: Continuum.

Bukatman, S. (2003) *Matters of Gravity: special effects and supermen in the 20th century*, Durham, NC and London: Duke University Press.

Cogdell, C. (2004) *Eugenic Design: streamlining America in the 1930s*, Philadelphia: University of Pennsylvania Press.

Daniels, L. (1998) *Superman, the Complete History: the life and times of the Man of Steel*, Hong Kong: DC Comics.

Galison, P. (1994) "The Ontology of the Enemy: Norbert Wiener and the cybernetic vision," *Critical Inquiry*, 21(1): 228–66.

Gleason, Abbott (1995) *Totalitarianism: the inner history of the Cold War*, New York: Oxford University Press.

Gordon, Ian (1998) *Comic Strips and Consumer Culture, 1890–1945*, Washington, DC: Smithsonian Institution Press.

Jones, G. (2004) *Men of Tomorrow: geeks, gangsters and the birth of the comic book*, New York: Basic Books.

Luckhurst, R. (2005) *Science Fiction*, Cambridge: Polity.

McCloud, S. (1994) *Understanding Comics: the invisible art*, New York: HarperCollins.

Nye, D.E. (1994) *The American Technological Sublime*, Cambridge, MA: MIT Press.

Poggi, C. (1997) "Metallized Flesh: Futurism and the masculine body," *Modernism/Modernity* 4(3): 19–43

Tichi, C. (1987) *Shifting Gears: technology, literature, culture in modernist America*, Chapel Hill: University of North Carolina Press.

Wright, B.W. (2003) *Comic Book Nation: the transformation of youth culture in America*, Baltimore, MD: Johns Hopkins University Press.

8
FILM AND TELEVISION, THE 1950s

Mark Jancovich and Derek Johnston

Accounts of 1950s sf film and television often present it as dominated by alien invasion narratives, in which monsters from outer space seek to subjugate or exterminate humanity. What is more, these narratives are commonly presented as rather simplistic products of Cold War tensions in which the alien is merely a thin disguise for Soviet aggression (see Biskind 1983; Lucanio 1987; Warren 1997). But there are a number of problems with such accounts. For example, as Jancovich (1996) argues, the alien invader was used in a number of different ways and often explicitly articulated anxieties about developments *within* American society, rather than simply fears of threat from outside. In films such as *The Thing from Another World* (Nyby 1951) and *Invasion of the Body Snatchers* (Siegel 1956), for example, the alien is associated with new forms of rational bureaucratic management at least as much as it is with communist expansionism. The first of these films concerns an isolated group of scientific and military personnel at the North Pole who discover an alien creature frozen in the ice. When the creature thaws out, it becomes clear that it feeds on human blood and can reproduce itself at an alarming rate, a situation that threatens human life on the planet. However, while the Thing is clearly presented as an aggressive threat that sees humanity as little more than food, the film also concerns a tension between the human characters. While the military personnel recognize the nature of the threat, the scientists want to preserve the alien for study, a strategy that proves to be as impractical as it is dangerous.

However, the opposition is presented as one not simply between the army and scientists, but between subordinates and authority. The scientists are presented as major authorities, with high-level Washington contacts, while the military personnel that oppose them are of low rank. As a result, not only are the scientists supported by the military high command – which is presented as inefficient and out of touch – but the scientists value the alien because its lack of emotions is seen as making it "our superior in every way." The scientists equate the alien's lack of emotions with their ideal of rationality and, like the alien, see ordinary people as being of no value other than to serve their own ends. As the chief scientist puts it, "knowledge is more important than life." In other words, *The Thing from Another World* is at least as anxious about the elite of experts that was emerging in postwar America as it was about any external threat from the Soviet Union or outer space.

Furthermore, alien invasion narratives were not simply a product of the Cold War period but had been a key element in the pulp magazines and comic books of the 1930s and 1940s, so much so that by the 1950s writers such as Ray Bradbury were parodying the form in stories such as "The Concrete Mixer" (1949). In other words, different media had very different understandings of sf as a genre and, in sf literature, the alien invader was already regarded as old-fashioned.

If understandings of sf within literature were very different from those in film and television, it is also a mistake to assume that film and television were the same, and there is now a growing body of work that demonstrates that genres work very differently in different media (Creeber 2001; Feuer 1992; Mittel 2004). As a result, the generic categories in operation in one medium are not necessarily operative in the other, and even when both media use the same generic term, it may be understood differently.

Furthermore, it is not simply that film and television are different from one another, but also that American sf films and television programs of the 1950s were fundamentally different from those made in Britain in the same period. Indeed, while most writing on the American context has tended to concentrate on the cinema, which is generally seen as far more creative than television in the period, the case was very different in Britain, where television is often seen as the more creative form.

In the United States, the cycle of sf films was initiated by the success of two space-exploration films, *Destination Moon* (Pichel 1950) and *Rocketship X-M* (Neumann 1950), the first of which was a colorful special effects extravaganza, in which a team of American industrial scientists beat the Russians to the Moon, while the second was a low-budget exploitation film, in which explorers land on Mars and encounter the savage remnants of a once advanced civilization that had destroyed itself in nuclear warfare. These two films set the terms for the 1950s fascination with sf exploration but they also revealed one of its problems. While *Rocketship X-M* is often seen as an inferior film, undermined by a small budget and a reliance on comic-book sensationalism (H.H.T. 1950), it actually achieves much greater narrative interest than *Destination Moon*, for which the main attraction was its groundbreaking special effects. As a result, producer George Pal, who had made *Destination Moon*, and became a key figure in 1950s sf and fantasy, recognized that he needed a stronger narrative for his next film of space exploration, *When Worlds Collide* (Maté 1951). In this film, a group of scientists discover that the Earth is doomed to destruction and rush to build a futuristic Noah's Ark that will transport a specially selected group of men and women to safety on another world. However, it is not only the narrative motivation that is stronger here, but also the personal and political conflicts that afflict the mission, particularly the fascistic schemes of its chief financial backer.

Pal continued his more "realist" approach to sf with a film about an expedition to Mars, *Conquest of Space* (Haskin 1955), but it proved a financial disaster and effectively put an end to this strand of filmmaking. A more enduring development was the strand which followed *Rocketship X-M* in featuring more fantastic stories that made little attempt to be "realistic" or "scientifically feasible," with films such as *Cat-Women of the Moon* (Hilton 1953), *Forbidden Planet* (Wilcox 1956), and *Queen of Outer Space* (Bernds 1958), all featuring explorers who travel to new worlds where they are menaced by the presence or the legacy of its alien civilizations. Similarly films such as *Lost Continent* (Newfield 1951) and *Creature from the Black Lagoon* (Arnold 1954) involved earthbound encounters with prehistoric worlds.

However, while *Conquest of Space* spelled the end of one aspect of the period, the previous year also saw the phenomenal success of Disney's *20,000 Leagues under the Sea* (Fleischer 1954), which would start a trend for tales of scientific exploration that were set in the Victorian era and included *From the Earth to the Moon* (Haskin 1958), *Journey to the Center of the Earth* (Levin 1959), and even George Pal's *The Time Machine* (1960).

As we have seen, though, the best remembered sf trend in the 1950s is not about human travel into outer space but rather alien visitations to Earth. While *20,000 Leagues under the Sea* demonstrated that a market existed for big-budget, prestige family films, these films were both costly and risky. However, following *The Thing from Another World*, a cycle of alien invasion movies, which were cheaper to produce, was also underway. While the market became flooded with sf films by the mid- to late 1950s, most of these were not from the major studios but from companies such as American International Pictures and Allied Artists that specialized in low-budget exploitation films.

Furthermore, many of these films were actually referred to in reviews as horror rather than sf, and it is important to acknowledge that they were as much a product of a new cycle of horror production in the late 1950s. Many of these films explicitly blur genre boundaries, for not only were sf films increasingly horror-oriented but there was also a renewed vogue for classic monsters of Gothic horror, which were given "a pseudo-scientific treatment" (Anon. 1957: 117). For example, Jack Arnold, who directed some of the best-loved sf films in the 1950s, including *It Came from Outer Space* (1953), *Creature from the Black Lagoon*, and *The Incredible Shrinking Man* (1957), also made *Monster on the Campus* (1959), a "variation on the Jekyll-and-Hyde theme" that was given an sf spin (Anon. 1959: 61).

In the first half of the 1950s, however, the stories of alien visitation were not necessarily horror stories about invading monsters, and many alien visitors were actually saviors of humanity. For example, during the 1940s and 1950s, Superman appeared in comics and films, and on radio and television. Not only was he an alien who protected the Earth from nuclear weapons in *Atom Man Versus Superman* (Bennet 1950), but *Superman and the Mole Men* (Sholem 1951), in which Superman defends a benign, subterranean species from "an unthinking, violent mob" of humans, was even seen as "a subtle plea for tolerance" (Gros. 1951: 6).

The best-remembered sympathetic alien is Klaatu in *The Day the Earth Stood Still* (Wise 1951), a dignified figure who visits Earth to warn us of the dangers of nuclear aggression. However, while many critics have seen this as a positive alternative to the alien invasion movies (e.g., Biskind 1983), it can be interpreted quite differently. If *The Thing from Another World* displayed anxieties about the new elite of experts, *The*

Day the Earth Stood Still was actually a highly authoritarian film, in which Klaatu's warning is also a threat: humanity is too irresponsible to handle nuclear power, and must surrender itself to a robot police force which will punish aggression with global extinction. If *The Thing from Another World* saw the rational as potentially repressive and the irrational emotions as the core of human identity, *The Day the Earth Stood Still* celebrates the rational and presents irrational emotions as simply negative: they are the cause of selfishness, greed, and fear, and must be repressed or transcended.

Alien aggressors also came in a number of other guises, and while some used brute force, others sought more insidious means of colonization. In *Invasion of the Body Snatchers*, for example, the people of Santa Mira are slowly being replaced by replicas that look and act like those they have replaced, but are really an alien fifth column infiltrating society. Again, however, it is unclear how much these aliens are simply meant to be associated with Soviet aggression, and the film has often been read as an attack on the *anti*-communist witch-hunts of the period. Furthermore, like *The Thing from Another World*, the film makes it clear that the authorities are implicated in the process: the aliens seem to replace them first and, even when they have not been replaced, they are incapable of either identifying or combating the problem. Even the process of being transformed from a human being into a blank, unemotional alien is claimed simply to accelerate a process that happens more slowly within American society anyhow.

Not all movie monsters were hostile alien invaders – some were manifestations of humanity's own destructive urges. For example, in *Them!* (Douglas 1954), nuclear testing in the desert turns insignificant ants into massive monsters that threaten to wipe out humanity, while, in *The Beast from 20,000 Fathoms* (Lourie 1953), a prehistoric monster devastates New York City after nuclear tests awaken it from an icy grave. In other films, the devastating effects of scientific progress were more personal: in *The Incredible Shrinking Man*, the hero gradually shrinks into nothingness; in *The Fly* (Neumann 1958), the hero's experiments accidentally fuse his body with that of a housefly.

Finally, when radiation was not causing wildlife to grow to frightening proportions, a number of films featured the grim aftermath of nuclear war. In some, the survivors were menaced by monstrous mutations, while others focused on internal struggles between the survivors. *The World, the Flesh and the Devil* (MacDougall 1959) even centered on racial tensions, suggesting that racial intolerance may not only have been responsible for humanity's destruction in the first place, but also promises to be a snake in the post-apocalyptic Eden.

American television sf followed a very different path. With the exception of Superman, 1950s feature films avoided comic-book heroes; but television sf was initially dominated by stories that emulated the heroes of comic books and film serials during the 1930s and 1940s. In addition to the long-running *The Adventures of Superman* (1952–8), for example, *Buck Rogers* (1950–1), *Captain Video and his Video Rangers* (1949–55), *Flash Gordon* (1954–5), *Rocky Jones, Space Ranger* (1954), and *Tom Corbett, Space Cadet* (1950–5), among others, battled evil masterminds with sf technology, and found adventure in space. Critics tended to be dismissive of these shows, which were seen as puerile entertainment and little more than crude devices to promote the sponsors' products to children. These shows also attracted other complaints, with *Captain Video* being cited in the debates around television violence during the period (Hill 1954: 29) and being accused of failing "to integrate sound educational material" into its format (Anon. 1951: 36).

However, television sf began to break out of the confines of children's programming and, as it did so, it sought to validate itself through a series of devices. *Science Fiction Theatre* (1955–7) claimed that "every story in the series will be based on scientific facts," while *Tales of Tomorrow* (1951–3) stressed it would rely on sf literature for its content (Adams 1951: 44, 119). These shows also sought to distinguish themselves by the nature of their format. During the 1950s, the single play had more prestige than the supposedly formulaic serial. As a result, by using the anthology format, shows such as *Out There* (1951–2), *Tales of Tomorrow*, and *Science Fiction Theatre* sought to establish a sense of balance between these two extremes. As weekly shows, rather than single plays, they could build audience loyalty, and by presenting a different story each week they avoided being seen as standardized and low quality.

This cycle of television sf ran from the late 1940s into the mid-1950s, and it is only in 1958 that signs of a new cycle start to emerge in the aftermath of Sputnik, although *The New York Times* was highly critical of television for its slow response to this event (Gobout 1958: X9). However, by the end of the decade, television sf finally achieved respectability with Rod Serling's *The Twilight Zone* (1959–64). Serling already had a strong reputation as the writer of several highly regarded single plays, particularly *Requiem for a Heavyweight* (1956), which often caused a stir with their controversial social commentary. He was well known "for his public protests against what he has described as 'interference of non-artistic people in an artistic medium'" (Shanley 1959: X19), and his decision to co-produce the show was therefore seen as a significant move. As executive producer he had greater control over his scripts, while the show's fantasy format enabled him to handle materials that had proved controversial in his earlier and more "realistic" scripts (see Buhle and Wagner 2003; Sconce 1997). As Serling himself said of his earlier work: "I was not permitted to have Senators discuss any current or pressing problem … In retrospect, I probably would have had a much more adult play had I made it science fiction, put it in the year 2057, and peopled the Senate with robots" (qtd in Engelhardt 1998: 153). The show was therefore one of the first instances in which television sf started to be taken seriously, with *The New York Times* not only identifying Serling as "one of television's abler writers" but also claiming that, in "the desultory field of filmed half-hour drama … Serling should not have trouble in making his mark. At least his series promises to be different" (Gould 1959: 39).

Despite this belated respectability, sf films had more prestige in the US during the period than television sf, and many films have acquired classic status since the 1950s. However, in Britain, the situation was significantly different, and it is television sf that is often seen as the more creative medium during the 1950s. Many British sf films were even based on television and radio series, although this is not to claim that there were no significant and well-regarded film projects, particularly in the first half of the decade. The Boulting brothers' *Seven Days to Noon* (1950), for example, sees a scientist threaten that, "unless atomic bomb production ceases by noon the following Sunday ... he will, himself, blow up all of London with a bomb he has stolen" (Myro. 1950: 20). In the process, the film deals with the responsibilities of scientists for the impact of their discoveries, a theme also present in *The Man in the White Suit* (Mackendrick 1951). Although this is a dark comedy, in which a young man invents an indestructible clothing material that never gets dirty, it also charts the shocking implications of this apparently benign discovery, implications that threaten to destroy the fabric of society.

Of the many 1950s British sf films adapted directly from television, the most significant were taken from the first two *Quatermass* serials. Such adaptations did not simply transfer material from one medium to another, but also involved substantial changes in conceptualization. This was often due to an attempt to negotiate two different audiences. On the one hand, the filmmakers clearly wanted to exploit the established interest in these stories among television audiences and, on the other, they also wanted to extend these pretested materials to new audiences, particularly in the hope of selling films to the American market. Indeed, the bid for the American market often required substantial changes so that, for example, Hollywood stars often had to be cast in leading roles to secure distribution deals in the US. As a result, while the changes were not necessarily "bad," there were often complaints about these adaptations, most famously from Nigel Kneale, the creator of the *Quatermass* serials, who complained about the way the Hammer studio "turned my troubled professor into a bawling bully" (Kneale 1979: 6).

The key cinematic innovation of the period was clearly from Hammer, which achieved phenomenal success with *The Curse of Frankenstein* (Fisher 1957). More than just another sf film, it was a formative influence on later production in Britain, America, and beyond. At one level, it too was a hybrid that combined two key elements of American production in the period to create something new and different. If American productions had modernized the Gothic horror monsters with sf, or reinvented sf by dressing it with Victorian settings and décor, *Curse of Frankenstein* took the Gothic and placed it back into a period setting. Furthermore, Frankenstein in this film was not a melodramatic mad scientist but a cold, hard rationalist with little concern for the consequences of his actions, and if the film is now remembered largely as a straight horror film, this is partly because its success encouraged Hammer to launch a number of horror series that have obscured its sf credentials.

While sf was still largely associated with pulp magazines and comic books in the US, and was only beginning to break free of its lowbrow image, the BBC was not burdened by such preconceptions due to the well-established European traditions of the literary scientific romance and of science-fictional themes and forms in legitimate theater. These more respectable forms of sf had been employed as early as 1938, when the BBC Television Service had staged a version of Karel Čapek's *RUR* (*Rossum's Universal Robots*) (1920), an influential play from which the term "robot" entered cultural consciousness. Similarly, in 1949, the BBC broadcast a version of H.G. Wells's classic, *The Time Machine* (1895). If these materials were not understood as sf at the time, they would become so later, and would provide a firm basis for those planning to develop television sf.

Another important aspect of these early shows was that they were not aimed predominantly at children, and even when the BBC began to produce sf for children in the 1950s, it was markedly different from that produced in the US. For example, *Stranger from Space* (1951–3) was not only developed with a strong educational agenda, but it also refused to limit its didactic aspects to the presentation of information. On the contrary, the show revolved around a series of serious moral problems and dilemmas as its young hero encounters alien life. *The Lost Planet* (1954) and *Return to the Lost Planet* (1955) were somewhat nearer to the comic-book adventures produced in the US, but they were adaptations of already-successful radio series transferred to television in the period immediately preceding the introduction of the first rival to the BBC monopoly, the new commercial Independent Television (ITV). In other words, they were produced at precisely the point at which the BBC was becoming aware that it could no longer be complacent about audiences but needed to produce more popular programming to compete for a viewing public.

Much the same was also true of the most important sf program of the decade, *The Quatermass Experiment* (1953). Indeed, it is often discussed as a television event whose importance in Britain during the period was second only to that of the live broadcast of Queen Elizabeth II's Coronation (see Barr 1986). Furthermore, although it was billed not as an sf story, but as a "thriller," the program is now firmly established within the canon of television sf. The story concerns an astronaut who returns to earth infected by an alien lifeform, and who gradually metamorphoses into a monster that threatens to absorb all life on the earth.

As should be clear from Kneale's description of his protagonist, Bernard Quatermass, as a "troubled professor," the serial was as much about its scientist's sense of guilt and responsibility as about the agony of its victim or the threat to the Earth. Kneale had already explored similar issues in an earlier play, *Number Three* (1953), and they would be central to his later work, including his 1954 adaptation of George Orwell's *Nineteen Eighty-four* (1949) and his examination of the tensions between science and exploitation in *The Creature* (1955).

If *Nineteen Eighty-four* transferred these questions to the context of a totalitarian dystopia, both *Quatermass II* (1955) and *Quatermass and the Pit* (1958) would continue these themes while suggesting that the roots of a totalitarian future were already firmly established in Britain. In *Quatermass II*, the country is governed by a cold bureaucracy that conceals an alien invasion, and even those who have not been mentally and physically contaminated by the alien species have surrendered their liberty for high wages. In *Quatermass and the Pit*, human intelligence is revealed to be the product of alien experimentation by a dying Martian race in the prehistoric past, and it is this biological engineering that is claimed to be responsible for the racial intolerance that motivates many human conflicts today. The serial also concerns Quatermass's attempt to resist the acquisition of his space research by the military, and the two strands of this plot come together in his final impassioned plea to camera: "Every war crisis, witch-hunt, race riot, and purge is a reminder and a warning … We are the Martians now. If we cannot control the inheritance within us, this will be their second dead planet."

The troubled scientist was also a feature of television programs such as *The Burning Glass* (1956) and *I Can Destroy the Sun* (1958). Anti-nuclear campaigner J.B. Priestley also wrote *Doomsday for Dyson* (1958), in which an ordinary man is held responsible for the nuclear destruction of the planet on the grounds that it is the apathy and complacency of people like himself that permits the proliferation of nuclear weapons. Both *Underground* (1958) and *The Offshore Island* (1959) featured grim stories of Britain in the aftermath of nuclear war.

Certainly, it could be argued that, after the introduction of commercial television in 1955, the majority of sf programming was developed by the new ITV with a populist agenda. However, alongside shows such as *The Invisible Man* (1958–9), which emulated the American adventure series and was clearly designed to be sold to the US, several of the challenging and controversial shows mentioned above were produced by ITV as part of its prestigious and influential *Armchair Theatre* (1956–68).

While the above discussion has provided an account of those American and British films and television programs that are often identified as examples of sf today, it is necessary to remember that generic terms do not simply describe a coherent and unitary body of texts; rather, generic definitions are bound up with complex social processes of classification that are subject to intense debate and conflict (see Jancovich 2000; Mittel 2004; Naremore 1998; Neale 2000). It is not simply that the boundaries of sf as a generic category were continually being contested during the period, but that these conflicts were due to fundamentally different conceptions of what the genre was and how it operated; and that they persist. Even today, when 1950s film and television sf is increasingly available in all its diversity and complexity, it is still often remembered as being simply concerned with alien invasions. Our account is not merely a corrective to that perception, but part of an ongoing, contingent, and irresolvable debate about the nature of the genre.

BIBLIOGRAPHY

Adams, V. (1951) "The World of the Future Comes to Television – Producers of 'Tales of Tomorrow' Mix Reality with Fantasy in Drama," *The New York Times*, 23 September: 119.

Anon. (1951) "Tele Followup Comment," *Variety*, 25 April: 36.

Anon. (1957) Review of *The Vampire*, *The Monthly Film Bulletin*, August: 117.

Anon. (1959) *The Monthly Film Bulletin*, April: 61.

Barr, C. (1986) "Broadcasting and Cinema 2: screens within screens," in C. Barr (ed.) *All Our Yesterdays: 90 years of British cinema*, London: BFI.

Biskind, P. (1983) *Seeing is Believing: how I learned to stop worrying and love the fifties*, New York: Pantheon.

Buhle, P. and Wagner, D. (2003) *Hide in Plain Sight: the Hollywood blacklistees in film and television, 1950–2002*, New York: Palgrave.

Creeber, G. (ed.) (2001) *The Television Genre Book*, London: BFI.

Engelhardt, T. (1998) *The End of Victory Culture: Cold War America and the disillusioning of a generation*, Amherst: University of Massachusetts Press.

Feuer, J. (1992) "Genre Study and Television," in R.C. Allen (ed.) *Channels of Discourse, Reassembled*, London: Routledge.

Gobout, O. (1958) "TV Blast-Off: A Slow Start," *The New York Times*, 3 August: X9.

Gould, J. (1959) "Rod Serling Series," *The New York Times*, 3 October: 39.

Gros. (1951) "Film Reviews," *Variety*, 12 December: 6.

H.H.T. (1950) "Love in a Spaceship at Criterion," *The New York Times*, 27 May: 23.

Hill, G. (1954) "Crime Themes Get More Time on TV – Los Angeles Report Reveals Increase in the Programs Offered to Children – 'Objectionable' is the Rating for Content of 27 Hours of the 60 Studied," *The New York Times*, 15 July: 29.

Jancovich, M. (1996) *Rational Fears: American horror in the 1950s*, Manchester: Manchester University Press.

——(2000) "'A Real Shocker': authenticity, genre, and the struggle for distinction," *Continuum: Journal of Media and Cultural Studies*, 14(1): 23–35.

——(2007) "An Unidentified Species: horror, the body and early television," *Intensities: a Journal of Cult Media*, 4. Online. Available HTTP: <http://intensities.org/Essays/Jancovich_Species.pdf> (accessed 1 April 2008).

Kneale, N. (1979) *Quatermass II*, London: Arrow.

Lucanio, P. (1987) *Them or Us: archetypal interpretations of fifties alien invasion films*, Bloomington: Indiana University Press.

Mittel, J. (2004) *Genre and Television: from cop shows to cartoons in American culture*, New York: Routledge.

Myro. (1950) "Film Reviews," *Variety*, 23 August: 20.

Naremore, J. (1998) *More than Night: film noir and its contexts*, Berkeley: University of California Press.

Neale, S. (2000) *Genre and Hollywood*, London: Routledge.

Sconce, J. (1997) "Science Fiction Programmes," in H. Newcomb (ed.) *Encyclopedia of Television*, Chicago: Fitzroy Dearborn.

Shanley, J.P. (1959) "A Playwright at the Controls," *The New York Times*, 20 September: X19.

Warren, B. (1997) *Keep Watching the Skies: American science fiction movies of the fifties*, Jefferson, NC: McFarland.

9

FICTION, 1950–1963

Rob Latham

A case can be made that the 1950s were the most consequential decade in the history of sf. The pulp magazines, whose ragged pages and gaudy covers had defined the genre for over two decades, were gone by 1958, supplanted by digest publications whose trimmer, less seedy appearance indicated an appeal to a more adult readership. The magazine culture itself was steadily giving ground to a burgeoning book market, from specialty presses run by sf fans to major lines at mainstream houses. Newer writers like John Wyndham and Ray Bradbury were soon household names, and works originally published in genre magazines (e.g., Walter M. Miller Jr's *A Canticle for Leibowitz* (1959)) became bestsellers when released in book form. Sf was thriving not only in film and television, but also in general-circulation periodicals, reaching a broad postwar audience primed to receive its vision of a world transformed by powerful new technologies. Ideas and inventions long championed within the field – space exploration, atomic energy – were imminent realities, which contemporary sf treated with growing sophistication as pulp styles of writing gave way to more polished and even experimental techniques. By the close of the decade, sf stood poised to achieve a cultural visibility, commercial success, and literary acclaim of which the pulp era could only have dreamed.

Yet, despite this great promise, the 1950s ended with setbacks that made many anxious about the genre's future. The US magazine market, long subject to boom and bust cycles, came perilously close to collapse, declining from a total of 23 titles in the summer of 1957 to only six by the end of 1960. As a result, numerous authors were either driven out of the field or forced to expand their output into other forms of writing. The early 1960s was a fallow period during which the genre, rather than consolidating its gains, lost markets and shed talent. With a few notable exceptions, sf writers seemed content to reprocess established themes and storylines that had grown stale with use. It was only with the advent of the "New Wave" later in the decade that the vast potential of the 1950s came to be fully realized.

Prose and pros: an evolving marketplace

John Campbell's *Astounding* (1930–), the dominant venue for serious sf during the previous decade, began to acquire competition in the form of ambitious new magazines that challenged not just its market share but its very vision of the genre. The two most important were *The Magazine of Fantasy and Science Fiction* (*F&SF*, 1949–) and *Galaxy* (1950–80, 1994–5). A stylish and erudite publication, *F&SF* took a catholic view of the field, mixing sf with fantasy and horror, and reprinting classic stories by Lord Dunsany and Robert Louis Stevenson alongside innovative work by younger writers such as Alfred Bester, Richard Matheson, and Philip K. Dick. The goal of the co-editors, J. Francis McComas and Anthony Boucher, was to publish "intelligent adult" sf, eschewing the "routine gadget-type story … or the Interplanetary Horse Opera" that prevailed in the pulps, while exploring the hazy "borderline between science-fiction … and fantasy" that Campbell's *Astounding*, committed to a purer hard-sf aesthetic, tended to avoid (McComas 1982: 12–13). Horace L. Gold, editor of *Galaxy*, was equally determined to strike out in fresh directions, shunning "the old pulp kind of interplanetary shoot-em-up" (Rosheim 1986: 10) in favor of sharply satirical, character-driven tales of dystopian near futures. Celebrated novels such as Bester's *The Demolished Man* (1953) and Frederik Pohl and C.M. Kornbluth's *The Space Merchants* (1953) appeared first as serials in *Galaxy*'s pages in 1952.

With *F&SF* and *Galaxy* soon joining *Astounding* as top-tier journals, a host of new titles arose in their wake. Some, such as *Fantastic* (1952–80) and *If* (1952–74, 1986), were destined for long-term success, while others (e.g., *Imagination* (1950–8), *Fantastic Universe* (1953–60)) did not outlast the decade. Sf pulps, many of which had been around since the 1930s (e.g., *Planet Stories* (1939–55), *Thrilling Wonder Stories* (1929–55)), were shouldered aside, either forced, like *Amazing Stories* in 1953, to convert to a digest format or else perishing in one of the routine culls the market suffered. Boom years included 1957 and especially 1953, when a record 181 issues of 38 different sf titles were published in the US and Britain; the mid- and late 1950s, by contrast, were shakeout phases in which assorted problems – rising production costs, the bankruptcy of a major distributor – conspired to wipe out marginal publications. The collapse at the end of the decade was particularly severe: "Fourteen magazines vanished within little more than 28 months" (Ashley 2005: 188), and the six survivors were far from financially secure. Many of the fatalities were "ripe for obliteration, put together in a hurry by people who knew nothing of science fiction, printing derivative yard goods and living off the reputations of their better brethren. But some of the good ones fell, too" (Pohl 1978: 216–17).

In contrast to this unnerving pattern of expansion and contraction, the sf book market displayed an impressively steady growth. During the late 1940s, a handful of prominent fans realized that over the years the genre had produced a sizeable backlog of stories, and developed a sufficient readership, to sustain presses dedicated to reprinting the best of this material in book form. Small publishing houses like Gnome and Shasta brought the work of authors who had made names for themselves in the pulps to a new generation of readers, their enterprising example eventually luring mainstream firms into the field. The first professional publisher to launch a hardcover sf line was Doubleday in 1950, its early releases including such classics as Bradbury's *The Martian Chronicles* (1950) and Robert A. Heinlein's *The Puppet Masters* (1951). Paperback houses such as Bantam, Ballantine, and Ace soon followed suit, flooding the market with fiction initially featured in the magazines but also, increasingly, with original work written expressly for book publication. In Britain, there was a similar mushrooming of sf lists among established presses like Weidenfeld & Nicolson and Michael Joseph, the latter making a small fortune from Wyndham's popular catastrophe stories (e.g., *The Day of the Triffids* (1951)).

The rise of a book market impacted the field in a number of important ways. The 1950s was the first decade during which the masterpieces of sf literature, which had appeared over time in ephemeral journals, were simultaneously available in durable editions, giving readers access not only to current work but also to the cream of the pulp archive. The range of formal techniques available to writers also expanded since a freestanding book was, at least potentially, a more aesthetically autonomous work than a novel or story cycle written with the exigencies of serialization in mind. Some authors, in collecting magazine stories, stitched them together with newly written passages into "fix-up" novels (e.g., Isaac Asimov's *I, Robot* (1950)) that, while still episodic, possessed a fresh structural coherence.

Above all, rather than catering to magazine editors who often demanded a specific ideological or stylistic slant (and who would sometimes, as in the case of Gold at *Galaxy*, revise submissions without consultation in order to achieve them), authors could begin to imagine themselves as independent professionals with their own unique artistic visions. Heinlein, for instance, grew so frustrated with editorial meddling (Heinlein 1989: 6, 163) that he began to write more or less exclusively for mainstream book publishers like Doubleday, Scribner's, and especially Putnam, for whom *Stranger in a Strange Land* (1961) was a surprise bestseller. During the boom years of the 1950s, it was actually possible for the first time to make a living as an sf writer; as Barry N. Malzberg has calculated, an average output of 1,000 words per day would produce an annual income of around $6,000 (nearly twice the national median), although, as he acknowledges, the disintegration of the magazine market at the end of the decade eroded these gains considerably (Malzberg 1982: 39–46).

One offshoot of sf's increasing professionalization was the 1956 founding of the Milford Writers' Conference, an annual workshop co-sponsored by James Blish, Judith Merril, and Damon Knight. At these gatherings, which brought together established authors and aspiring novices, unpublished manuscripts were exchanged and assessed, tactics for dealing with pesky editors hammered out, and the benefits and drawbacks of specific markets debated. An outgrowth of the first conference was *Science Fiction Forum*, a short-lived publication edited by Knight and Lester del Rey, designed to maintain the supportive shoptalk cultivated at Milford. Starting in 1959, a newsletter edited by Theodore R. Cogswell, *Proceedings for the Institute of Twenty-First Century Studies*, built on this foundation, providing a venue for wide-ranging and sometimes testy conversations regarding the exigencies of the sf marketplace. Complaints about tin-eared or intrusive editors were front and center; there was even consideration of a strike for higher word rates. The camaraderie fostered at Milford and in these published forums laid the groundwork for a writers' union, the Science Fiction Writers of America, which Knight would eventually found in 1965.

This movement toward professional status was not without its critics. Some authors who had entered sf via fandom worried that crucial links might be lost with this network of nonprofessionals, who could feel excluded from the presumed elite. The influence of fan culture has always been more pronounced within sf than other popular genres, and during the 1950s, as major meetings such as the World Science Fiction Convention grew in size and complexity, longtime fans began complaining about the "creeping professionalism" (Warner and Lynch 1992: 336) that was turning their close-knit, casual gatherings into a regimented assembly of self-interested cliques. Another concern was the literary pretension of the Milford crowd, their claim that authorial autonomy was essential if one were to be, in Merril's words, "an artist rather than an artisan" (qtd in Cogswell 1992: 48). The various writers' conferences and newsletters of the period were designed to promote not only higher occupational standards, but also a sense of sf as serious literature, a posture that drew grumblings from authors with a less exalted view of their craft. As del Rey observes, some became so disaffected with the emerging "consensus of taste" that they began to speak of a "Milford Mafia" whose growing influence was potentially pernicious (del Rey 1979: 223). These sorts of divisions would only become more pointed during the 1960s, providing fodder for the ferocious debates surrounding the "New Wave" movement.

Raising the bar: sf and/as literature

While the New Wave is generally seen as the moment when sf decisively shed its pulp heritage and began to adopt the aesthetic modalities of "mainstream" literature, this trend was actually set in motion during the 1950s. Indeed, Campbell's *Astounding* had, in the 1940s, already begun to curtail the worst excesses of pulp super-science in favor of more disciplined extrapolation rendered in cleaner, less breathlessly purple prose. Yet what counted most for Campbell was not aesthetic ambition or stylistic flair, but scientific accuracy (three of his chief contributors – Asimov, Heinlein, and L. Sprague de Camp – had trained as scientists and engineers). The most self-consciously literary, humanistically inclined author in Campbell's stable, Theodore Sturgeon, had so many run-ins with the intransigent editor that, once the new markets opened after 1950, he published only one story in *Astounding* during the subsequent decade, compared with scores in other magazines. Campbell had proven that a serious-minded alternative to pulp plots and styles could prosper in the genre, and the new digests of the 1950s, especially *Galaxy* and *F&SF*, set out to show that the field could now accommodate ironic satire, allusive wordplay, and ambitious character studies – in short, the kinds of writing that prevailed in the literary mainstream. Their success was an inspiration to those who had faith in sf's potential as a significant art form.

These true believers included the three founders of the Milford Conference, whose multifarious efforts throughout the decade – less as writers than as editors, critics, and propagandists – laid the groundwork for a vindication of sf as art that younger writers would embrace in the 1960s. Merril, who would herself emerge as a vigorous advocate of New Wave sf, kicked off, in 1956, a series of "year's best" anthologies that gathered work not only by genre authors but also by literary luminaries ranging from John Steinbeck to Eugène Ionesco. She justified this eclecticism in editorial summations that argued for a more expansive definition of sf as "science fantasy" or "speculative fiction": "fables of our time" that deploy "the frivolities of space-ships and ... robots" in order to "add emotional urgency and dramatic power to what are basically problems in philosophy and morality" (Merril 1956: 10). In the seventh annual volume, Merril declared that the "specialized cult of science fiction" was in the process of disappearing, as its "essential quality is absorbed into the main body of literature" (Merril 1963: 391) – a bold claim seemingly proven by the series' publication history: debuting with a specialty press, Gnome, it was soon picked up by a prestigious house, Simon and Schuster, running until 1967.

Blish and Knight made abortive attempts to pilot new magazines into the turbulent market (*Vanguard* (1958) and *Worlds Beyond* (1950–1), respectively), but these managed a total of only four issues. Their more lasting contribution to sf's new literary consciousness was their critical writing for a range of professional and fan magazines. Blish's pieces, printed under the pseudonym William Atheling Jr, were, like Merril's summations, geared to spur sf into the broader mainstream; his first essay, published in 1952, argued that this leap could only be achieved if the genre embraced standards of writing that included not simply "technical competence," but "[f]reshness of idea, acuity of observation, [and] depth of emotional penetration" (Blish 1973: 7). Failing this, sf could never hope to transcend "the little ghettos reserved for us in the Sunday book sections of daily newspapers" (Blish 1973: 17). Knight's reviews – appearing in a number of journals over the course of the decade, under the general title "The Dissecting Table" – were similarly uncompromising in their demand that sf adhere to elevated norms of writing in order to become "a field of literature worth taking seriously" (Knight 1967: 1). What is aesthetically pleasing in the best sf, he claimed, "is not different from the thing that makes mainstream stories rewarding, but only expressed differently ... not in small, everyday symbols, but in the big ones of space and time" (Knight 1967: 4). Both he and Blish could be scathing if specific authors or texts failed to live up to this ideal; the reputation of Golden Age titan A.E. van Vogt suffered a crippling blow when Knight lambasted him as a "Cosmic Jerrybuilder" (Knight 1967: 47–62).

Knight's trail-blazing reviews were gathered in book form as *In Search of Wonder* (1956) and Blish's criticism as *The Issue at Hand* (1964), both published by Advent, a small firm in Chicago that was, essentially, the first scholarly imprint in the field. (Fantasy Press, another fan-based enterprise, had released the first anthology of critical writing about the genre, Arthur Eshbach's *Of Worlds Beyond* (1947), in which Heinlein pioneered the term "speculative fiction" as an alternative connotation for sf.) Throughout the late 1950s and 1960s, Advent published a raft of nonfiction titles – critical studies, memoirs, bibliographies, encyclopedias – that helped generate a sense of the field as a cohesive topic of inquiry with its own hallowed history and textual canon. Their 1959 collection, *The Science Fiction Novel: imagination and social criticism*, edited by Basil Davenport, featured four substantial essays on the art of sf by Heinlein, Bester, Kornbluth, and Robert Bloch, with Kornbluth's "The Failure of the Science Fiction Novel as Social Criticism" unapologetically making use of "the methods of modern literary criticism" to address his subject (Davenport 1959: 49). Soon, mainstream authors were turning gazes of critical approbation toward the genre: British novelist Kingsley Amis's *New Maps of Hell* (1960), based on a series of lectures given the previous year at Princeton University, warmly defended sf against charges of escapism, celebrating it as a satirical "medium in which our society can criticize itself" (Amis 1960: 134). Meanwhile, sf was making its way into the classroom as a legitimate object of study, with Sam Moskowitz's 1953 course at New York City College leading the way, and talks by sf authors were becoming regular fixtures on college campuses (the essays in Davenport's volume being the fruits of a 1957 symposium at the University of Chicago).

Sf was also reaching a broader audience via general-circulation magazines, ranging from old stalwarts like *Collier's* (1888–1957) to upstart titles such as *Playboy* (1953–). The latter, whose fiction editor during the mid- to late 1950s was fantasy author Ray Russell, published stories by Arthur C. Clarke, Charles Beaumont, Robert Sheckley, Fredric Brown, and numerous other sf authors, paying rates that beggared the pennies-per-word of the genre magazines. In this colonization of prestigious venues, Heinlein was, as in so many areas, the pioneer, having placed his story of the capitalist conquest of space, "The Man Who Sold the Moon," with *The Saturday Evening Post* (1921–69) in 1947, thus paving the way for Ray Bradbury, who not only found a comfortable home in that journal during the early 1950s, but also set up shop in other mainstream outlets like *Esquire* (1933–) and *McCall's* (1897–2002). The venerable *Collier's* had long been a welcoming venue for fantasy, having featured Sax Rohmer's Fu Manchu stories in the 1930s, but in the 1950s its remit expanded to include sf, running several early tales by Kurt Vonnegut and serializing Jack Finney's classic novel of alien invasion, *The Body Snatchers*, in 1954. Vonnegut's crossover success during this period was proof of sf's growing acceptance: while his second and third novels, *The Sirens of Titan* (1959) and *Mother Night* (1962), were released as paperback originals, they were so well reviewed and sold so strongly that his next book, *Cat's Cradle* (1963), was brought out by a major hardcover house, Holt, Rinehart, and Winston. A triumphant career such as Vonnegut's simply would not have been possible for a US writer treating sf themes at any time prior to the 1950s.

Dystopia and apocalypse: sf in the postwar world

What accounts for this rising popularity and cultural visibility of sf? Most obviously, the technological revolution that accompanied the Second World War in a host of inventions, from atomic bombs to television, whose existence had been foreseen in 1920s and 1930s pulps. The accelerated tempo of scientific development in the postwar period, with all manner of new devices conspiring to transform or threaten people's lives, made sf seem not only prescient but uniquely relevant, since one of the genre's key themes has always been the inescapable reality of technosocial change. While sf in the mass media was more broadly popular than print sf (indeed, the 1950s were a boom period for sf film), the fact that the market could sustain, during its peak years, dozens of magazines and paperback lines, indicated that the field was growing not just as a specialized market but as a general consumer taste. The escalation of the US space program following the 1957 launch of the Soviet satellite Sputnik only increased sf's crossover appeal, priming the market for the bestsellers that would emerge from the genre during the 1960s. By this point, iconography whose appeal had been largely confined to a genre readership for over three decades – from rocket ships to rayguns, aliens to robots – pervaded British and American popular culture.

Two well-received novels by mainstream authors published on the cusp of the 1950s, George Orwell's *Nineteen Eighty-Four* (1949) and George R. Stewart's *Earth Abides* (1949), had shown how open a general audience could be to seriously purposed sf. Moreover, the specific scenarios treated in these texts – near-future dystopia and global apocalypse, respectively – were to become the genre's two most prevalent themes during the coming decade. The latter should not be surprising given that the USSR had tested its first atomic device in August 1949, leading to widespread anxieties about superpower competition and the imminent likelihood of global destruction. While the catastrophe depicted in Stewart's novel was precipitated by plague, the genre was soon generating, as Paul Brians (1987: 353–7) exhaustively shows, waves of stories dealing with nuclear holocaust specifically, with the decade bookended by Bradbury's *The Martian Chronicles*, where civilization begins afresh on Mars following the extinction of life on Earth, and Miller's *A Canticle for Leibowitz*, where a post-holocaust society rediscovers the secrets of atomic power and commences a fresh cycle of annihilation. Both books sold quite well, as did mainstream versions of the theme, such as Nevil Shute's *On the Beach* (1957) and Pat Frank's *Alas, Babylon* (1959), suggesting that sf held a substantial crossover appeal for readers seeking visionary treatments of the major looming terror in their lives. As Paul Boyer comments, "the status of the genre rose" during the atomic age, when its pulp fantasies became everyday realities; "for all its exotic trappings, science fiction is best understood as a commentary on contemporary issues" (Boyer 1985: 257–8), as a growing popular audience appreciated.

Indeed, postwar sf was more inclined to tackle topical, even politically contro-versial, issues than previous work in the field had been. While tales of disaster were always a staple of the genre, British and American authors now took up not only the risks of atomic devastation, but other man-made perils such as ecological catastrophe (John Christopher's *The Death of Grass* (1956)), industrial pollution (Kornbluth's "Shark Ship" (1958)), and overpopulation (J.G. Ballard's "Billenium" (1961)). Hot-button topics addressed during the period included runaway consum-erism (Pohl and Kornbluth's *The Space Merchants*, Fritz Leiber's "A Bad Day for Sales" (1953)), suburban conformity (Sheckley's "Cost of Living" (1952)), the dangers of McCarthyism (Asimov's "The Martian Way" (1952)), the brutal policing of dissent (Bradbury's *Fahrenheit 451* (1953)), and the homogenizing effects of modern mass media (Vonnegut's "Harrison Bergeron" (1961)). Much of this work was published in *Galaxy*, which specialized in hard-edged, satirical dystopias that were thinly veiled commentaries on the contemporary scene, as critics at the time perceived. In *New Maps of Hell*, Amis coined the term "comic inferno" to describe stories, especially by Sheckley and Pohl, that playfully proliferated technological novelties while maintaining a ruthlessly sardonic "connection with observable features of our own society" (Amis 1960: 104). Kornbluth's attack on the genre's perennial failure as social criticism indicates how important the political dimension of the field was to

1950s writers, with sf "among the very few mass markets where, sufficiently masked, an antiauthoritarian statement could be published" (Malzberg 1982: 34). The aggressive political consciousness of the 1960s New Wave was simply a more militant recrudescence of this 1950s strain of satirical critique.

Similarly, 1950s sf prefigured the New Wave's heightened attention to issues of gender and sexuality, topics the genre had always tended to treat with elliptical discretion if not to skirt outright. The explosion of magazine markets, and the consequent pressure for material to fill them, made editors less cautious in their choices than they might otherwise have been: Philip José Farmer's debut story, "The Lovers" (1952), a path-breaking tale of human–alien miscegenation, appeared in a struggling pulp (*Startling Stories* (1939–55)) that was desperate for new readers, as did his creepy Freudian 1953 follow-up, "Mother" (*Thrilling Wonder Stories*). Throughout the decade, Sturgeon specialized in bold explorations of formerly taboo subjects, ranging from multiple-partner relationships ("The Sex Opposite" (1952)) to homosexuality ("The World Well Lost" (1953)) to utopian gender-blending (*Venus Plus X* (1960)). The more open climate for such material may in part have been due to the growing diversity of sf authorship: whereas the number of women writers in the genre prior to 1950 did not exceed a small handful (with most of these, such as C.L. Moore and Leigh Brackett, publishing under ambiguous bylines), the subsequent decade saw the flowering of unapologetically female-authored, if not exactly feminist, sf, with Merril, Marion Zimmer Bradley, Mildred Clingerman, Miriam Allen de Ford, Zenna Henderson, Margaret St Clair, Katherine MacLean, and Kate Wilhelm enjoying thriving careers. Merril's *Shadow on the Hearth* (1950) showed what a female viewpoint could bring to the genre, tackling the theme of atomic conflict from the perspective of a suburban housewife struggling to cope with the burgeoning crisis.

By the early 1960s, sf had a broader-based appeal and an ampler thematic repertoire than ever before. The conviction that it was steadily becoming a more sophisticated form of literature was widespread, and not just among the Milford crowd. The demise of the pulps closed an era of interplanetary adventures geared largely toward young adults, making way for a more mature and cosmopolitan kind of fiction. Several classic novels of the period capture a sense of evolving maturity not only in their themes but also in their titles – Sturgeon's *More Than Human* (1953), Clarke's *Childhood's End* (1953). In its attention to character as well as concept, to stylistic panache as well as scientific precision, 1950s sf achieved historically unprecedented levels of literary success and critical acclaim.

Collapse and renewal: on the eve of the New Wave

And then the bottom fell out. Malzberg claims that the epic die-off of magazine titles at the end of the decade proves that "overextension inevitably hit the wall imposed by a readership which would not expand" (Malzberg 1982: 41); yet it is worthwhile to remember that, even amid the seismic contraction that afflicted the genre from 1958 to 1962, novels like *A Canticle for Leibowitz* and *Stranger in a Strange Land* were still selling tens of thousands of copies. The transition from a specialized (sub) culture centered on periodicals to a more general market oriented around hardcover and paperback books could not occur without some growing pains, although this is not to downplay the heartbreaking price paid by many writers and fans who lived through the resultant fallout. This price was evident in the host of authors who fled the field during these troubled years (Bester, Miller, Sturgeon, Algis J. Budrys, Ward Moore, Robert Silverberg, William Tenn), their places taken by competent but largely second-rank talents (e.g., Lloyd Biggle Jr, Keith Laumer, Fred Saberhagen) who, rather than continuing the trend of innovation, seemed content to retread familiar ground. What is unquestionable is that the genre failed, at the dawn of the 1960s, to capitalize on the favorable position it had attained during the previous decade, leading many to echo the plaintive query of Earl Kemp's 1961 Hugo-winning fanzine, *Who Killed Science Fiction?*

Yet heralds of sf's death were premature, since the forces that would revitalize the genre in the coming years had already taken root. While the magazines languished, the book market grew, gradually nurturing a generation of authors whose work would define the new decade. The program of aesthetic ambition and steady professionalism spawned by the Milford Conferences continued to supply an agenda for writers eager to push themselves creatively, to transcend prevailing orthodoxies. And Merril's "year's best" anthologies, in addition to showing that excellent work was still being done even amid the current doldrums, kept up the editor's calls for a newly relevant speculative fiction that would radically transform the field. These institutional structures provided the scaffolding for the New Wave that would emerge, first in Britain and then the US, during the mid-1960s. When J.G. Ballard rhetorically inquired, in a 1962 guest editorial in the British magazine *New Worlds*, "Which Way to Inner Space?," there were some, at least, who were prepared to give an answer.

BIBLIOGRAPHY

Amis, K. (1960) *New Maps of Hell*, New York: Ballantine.

Ashley, M. (2005) *Transformations: the story of the science-fiction magazines from 1950 to 1970*, Liverpool: Liverpool University Press.

Blish, J., as W. Atheling Jr (1973) *The Issue at Hand: studies in contemporary magazine science fiction*, 1964, Chicago: Advent.

Boyer, P. (1985) *By the Bomb's Early Light: American thought and culture at the dawn of the atomic age*, New York: Pantheon.

Brians, P. (1987) *Nuclear Holocausts: atomic war in fiction, 1895–1984*, Kent, OH: Kent State University Press.

Cogswell, T.R. (ed.) (1992) *PITFCS: Proceedings of the Institute for Twenty-First Century Studies*, Chicago: Advent.

Davenport, B. (ed.) (1959) *The Science Fiction Novel: imagination and social criticism*, Chicago: Advent.

del Rey, L. (1979) *The World of Science Fiction: 1926–1976: the history of a subculture*, New York: Ballantine.

Heinlein, R.A. (1989) *Grumbles from the Grave*, ed. V. Heinlein, New York: Ballantine.

Knight, D. (1967) *In Search of Wonder: essays on modern science fiction*, 1956, Chicago: Advent.

McComas, A.P. (ed.) (1982) *The Eureka Years: Boucher and McComas's The Magazine of Fantasy and Science Fiction 1949–54*, New York: Bantam.

Malzberg, B.N. (1982) *The Engines of the Night: science fiction in the eighties*, New York: Bluejay.

Merril, J. (ed.) (1956) *S-F: the year's greatest science-fiction and fantasy*, New York: Dell.

—— (1963) *7th Annual Edition: the year's best s-f*, New York: Dell.

Pohl, F. (1978) *The Way the Future Was: a memoir*, New York: Ballantine.

Rosheim, D.L. (1986) *Galaxy Magazine: the dark and light years*, Chicago: Advent.

Warner, H. and Lynch, D. (1992) *A Wealth of Fable: an informal history of science fiction fandom in the 1950s*, Van Nuys, CA: SCIFI Press.

10
FILM AND TELEVISION, 1960–1980

Peter Wright

Between 1960 and 1980, screen sf achieved a remarkable diversity, particularly in America, Britain, and Europe. Nevertheless, it remained socioculturally embedded, offering reflections both on and of its contexts. For such a reflective form, two turbulent decades of varying political and cultural tensions and changes in film and television consumption provided a rich set of stimuli. It would be misleading to argue, however, that screen sf was transformed in 1960; many of the themes and tropes found in 1950s productions influenced subsequent narratives.

In America, the concepts that enlivened 1950s sf cinema continued to appear in derivative poverty-row revisions of alien incursion narratives, monster movies, and mutant attacks, and even the mad-scientist films of the 1930s reemerged. The political ambiguity of many 1950s films was lost from fervent anticommunist narratives like *Cape Canaveral Monsters* (Tucker 1960) and *The Beast of Yucca Flats* (Francis 1961). Their xenophobic stance anticipated that of the anti-Chinese *Dimension 5* (Adreon 1966) and *Battle Beneath the Earth* (Tully 1967), which reflected Western anxieties following Mao's Cultural Revolution.

Fortunately, Hollywood's propensity for generic hybridizing prevented complete stagnation. Sf comedies appeared, including several self-conscious parodies drawn from literature (notably *The Nutty Professor* (Lewis 1963), *Sleeper* (Allen 1973), and *Young Frankenstein* (Brooks 1974)). *Frankenstein* (1818) was also the source for *Kiss Me Quick!* (Bukalew 1964), which established the sf-sexploitation subgenre popular in the 1970s (*Flesh Gordon* (Benveniste 1974) is a noteworthy example). With technology influencing Western culture more extensively, Hollywood infused the thriller with sf tropes to ensure contemporary relevance in *The Satan Bug* (Sturges 1965), *Capricorn One* (Hyams 1977), and *Coma* (Crichton 1978).

As America's social order was contested throughout the 1960s, the conventions of the 1950s sf film (see Sontag 1966: 209–12; Bould 2003: 85–6) were displaced by less metaphoric and more sober meditations on political and social uncertainties. Although John F. Kennedy came to office having proclaimed the 1960s "A New Frontier ... of unknown opportunities and perils," it was the perils – concerns over nuclear war, racial conflict, overpopulation and pollution – that often preoccupied American sf cinema following his assassination.

In terms of the nuclear threat, prestigious and low-budget productions rejected the metaphors of the 1950s in favor of the directness of *On the Beach* (Kramer 1959) and *The World, the Flesh and the Devil* (MacDougall 1959). The nuclear narratives of the 1960s can be divided into those situated in contemporary settings and those located in post-holocaust futures. George Pal's *The Time Machine* (1960) unites both categories, reinventing Wells's 1895 novel as a critique of Cold War politics. More interesting was Roger Corman's *The Last Woman on Earth* (1960), which explored the erotic and thanatotic drives impelling human self-destruction. Favoring pragmatism over psychoanalysis, Ray Milland's seminal survivalist text, *Panic in Year Zero!* (1962), presented an uncompromising study of post-nuclear expediencies. Where Milland's film was informed by contemporary survival rhetoric, the Cuban Missile Crisis cast its shadow over Sidney Lumet's austere *Fail-Safe* (1964) and Stanley Kubrick's satiric *Dr Strangelove or: How I Learned to Stop Worrying and Love the Bomb* (1964). Kubrick's blackly comic treatment of Armageddon exposed the absurdity of Mutually Assured Destruction as a defense policy and condemned the "lunacy of politicians and military men who can so easily come to terms with the unthinkable and the unspeakable" (Brosnan 1991: 116). The strength of the film's political critique lies in its juxtapositions. Objective information contrasts with farcical scenes, satirically exaggerated characters are inserted into a realistic *mise en scène*, and comedic episodes occur amid catastrophic events. In the film, US fears of a "doomsday gap" and a post-attack "mineshaft gap" satirize the arms race while reflecting genuine American fears of Soviet military superiority.

Such contemporary-set nuclear narratives faded from American cinema between 1964 and the early 1980s. Paul Boyer attributes this to "the illusion of diminished risk ... the loss of immediacy ... the promise of a world transformed by atomic energy ... the complexity and comfort of deterrence theory ... the Vietnam War" (Boyer 1985: 355). Films that explored the post-holocaust future did emerge, however, though they were less indicative of nuclear anxiety than of opportunistic filmmaking. Between 1964 and 1975, most films set in atomic wastelands were low-budget productions using cost-effective desert settings for convincing nuclear landscapes. Of these, *A Boy and his Dog* (Jones 1975) was the most provocative. Faithfully adapted from Harlan Ellison's 1969 novella, the film attributes the violence and misogyny of the post-nuclear world to middle-class self-interest and the pre-nuclear entertainment industry. As such, it can be interpreted as a dramatic statement on the cultural construction of masculine and feminine roles, which are played out disturbingly in a lawless landscape. After 1975, the atomic specter returned to haunt mainstream cinema only after the Three Mile Island incident, which almost coincided with *The China Syndrome* (Bridges 1979), and the Soviet invasion of Afghanistan.

Rising racial tensions, the Civil Rights movement, the Vietnam War, anxieties over environmental damage, and the space race all superseded the Bomb as the subject matter of sf film. *Planet of the Apes* (Schaffner 1968) and its sequels charted this shift. Collectively, they constitute a "liberal allegory of racial conflict" (Greene 1998: 1) that became consistently less allegorical. They were also significant as the first major sf film series and for their extensive and influential cross-marketing. With a *Zeitgeist* shaped by Vietnam and, later, Watergate, American sf cinema embraced the *Apes* cycle's apocalyptic sensibility throughout the early 1970s. Fears of biological weapons, which Richard Nixon renounced in 1969, affected *The Andromeda Strain* (Wise 1971), *The Omega Man* (Sagal 1971), and *The Crazies* (Romero 1973); concerns over overpopulation were expressed in *Soylent Green* (Fleischer 1973); and the recognition of ecological damage informed *Silent Running* (Trumbull 1971) and the "revenge of nature" cycle that followed Hitchcock's *The Birds* (1963) (e.g., *Frogs* (McCowan 1972), *Phase IV* (Bass 1973), and *Squirm* (Lieberman 1976)). Viewed through the pessimistic lens of the 1970s, America's continued technological development inspired a series of technophobic films, including *Seconds* (Frankenheimer 1966), *Colossus: The Forbin Project* (Sargent 1970), and *Westworld* (Crichton 1973). Consumerism was satirized in the dystopian *THX 1138* (Lucas 1971) and critiques of capitalism characterized *Death Race 2000* (Bartel 1975) and *Rollerball* (Jewison 1975).

By the mid-1970s, the Vietnam War had ended, Jimmy Carter was President and US–Soviet relations were improving. America's new optimism, growing steadily since Gerald Ford's declaration that "Our long nightmare is over," was reflected in what Vivian Sobchack terms "sf's second 'Golden Age'" (Sobchack 2005: 267). A year after America's bicentennial, Steven Spielberg's *Close Encounters of the Third Kind* (1977) and George Lucas's resonantly titled *Star Wars: Episode IV – A New Hope* (1977) moved American sf cinema away from the political critiques of the 1970s toward a special effects-driven cinema of attractions. Together, they confirmed the commercial viability of the big-budget blockbuster suggested first by *Jaws* (Spielberg 1975). More importantly, both films offered a salve in the form of compensatory myths for an America wounded by war and self-doubt.

Close Encounters inverts the alien incursion narratives of the 1950s to promise humanity incorporation into an apparently egalitarian universe, dissolving old divisions in the dawn of new possibilities. Its optimism, viewed in retrospect, is naïve and its politics conservative. *Star Wars* is a space opera bricolage of literary and visual sources ranging from 1930s chapter serials, to western and samurai films and Frank Herbert's *Dune* (1965). Populated with archetypal characters, the narrative self-consciously unites Eastern mysticism with the monomythic structure identified in Joseph Campbell's *The Hero with a Thousand Faces* (1949). It is unrelentingly nostalgic, morally unsophisticated, and wholly reassuring to an America looking for "new hope." Its unparalleled popularity, sustained by sequels, prequels, and an expanding universe of ancillary merchandise, confirms the West's continuing readiness to accept affirmative mythologies, particularly at times of national crises. Only Philip Kaufman's remake, *The Invasion of the Body Snatchers* (1978), countered such exuberance with an abiding sense of post-Watergate paranoia and distrust.

Star Wars's optimism was not unique, however. Conventionally, space-travel narratives represented Kennedy's New Frontier by supplying the rare positive futures found in American sf film of the period. *Robinson Crusoe on Mars* (Haskin 1964) celebrated humanity's ability to endure adversity; *2001: A Space Odyssey* (Kubrick 1968) showed humanity evolving ambiguously under alien influence; and *Marooned* (Sturges 1969) welcomed American endeavors in space and the possibility of US–Soviet cooperation. Kubrick's film is a technical masterpiece, showcasing the meticulous work of special effects engineers, model makers and matte artists. As a consequence, it is one of the few sf films to engender a genuine sense of wonder in the audience. Unfortunately, its evocation of the marvelous depends largely on these astounding visuals. With a slender narrative and a ponderous pace, *2001* is less successful at communicating its speculative themes. Its commentary on the relative primitiveness of humanity, its treatment of stagnation and transcendence, and its darkly humorous meditations on artificial intelligence are often too pedestrian to engage an audience intellectually. Nevertheless *2001*, like *Marooned* and *Robinson Crusoe on Mars*, evoked the hopefulness engendered by the space race and affirmed space as a place of adventure and either literal or metaphoric rebirth. Only John Carpenter's slyly amusing *Dark Star* (1974) suggested that space travel would become a dehumanizing chore.

Star Wars inspired several imitators, including Mike Hodges's camp *Flash Gordon* (1980) and Disney's *The Black Hole* (Nelson 1979), which also drew on *2001*. Although *Star Wars* was the catalyst for *Star Trek: The Motion Picture* (1979), director Robert Wise distanced his film from Lucas's kinetics by mimicking *2001*'s aesthetic. The result was a pedestrian film preoccupied almost lasciviously with smoothly curved starships and docking arrays. Its central plot – a highly evolved Voyager probe returning to Earth in existential crisis – is rendered incompatible with the cozy inter-relationships of the characters and by a superfluity of expansive, yet turgid, special effects sequences.

At the turn of the decade, two films anticipated the direction of American sf cinema. Though superior to and tonally darker than its predecessor, *Star Wars: Episode V–The Empire Strikes Back* (Kershner 1980) affirmed its simple morality and secured an audience for the now familiar high-concept, lowbrow special effects-driven fantasies that include the *Star Wars* prequels and most superhero films. Conversely, Ridley Scott's Anglo-American co-production *Alien* (1979) provided an altogether bleaker vision of the cosmos. Despite its derivative plot, the film is an intelligent meditation on the nature of power relationships under capitalism, the commercial expendability of the individual, and the alienating consequences of functional specialization. However, it complicates this critique by adopting a compromised feminist perspective that appears initially progressive yet becomes reassuringly conservative at its climax. This conservatism is also apparent in the film's employment of vaginal, penile, anal, and womblike imagery as a source of horror and disgust. H.R. Giger's startling alien designs, a fusion of the Freudian and the Lovecraftian, are the film's most influential element, although its critique of capitalist exploitation later characterized 1980s tech-noir.

Coterminous American television sf is aligned with *Star Wars* and the elementary television sf productions of the 1950s, which subjugated "science to a blend of adventure, soap opera, topicality (sometimes even seriousness) and moralizing" (Bould 2003: 89). During the1960s, television sf instituted the subjunctive premises that shaped it for the next 40 years. *My Favorite Martian* (1963–6), for example, introduced the alien visitor to Earth for culture-clash comedy, anticipating *Mork and Mindy* (1978–82) and *ALF* (1986–90).

The seminal nature of 1960s US television sf is attributable to three individuals: Rod Serling, Irwin Allen, and Gene Roddenberry. The sf stories in Serling's disquieting, yet moral, anthology series *The Twilight Zone* (1959–64) shaped *The Outer Limits* (1963–5; 1995–2002) and *Steven Spielberg's Amazing Stories* (1985–6). In contrast, Allen's light entertainments expressed few intellectual aspirations. His series, especially *Voyage to the Bottom of the Sea* (1964–8), a spin-off from his 1961 film, and *Lost in Space* (1965–8) championed conservative and family values. Although his productions were rudimentary, they shaped, directly or indirectly, much of the television sf that followed. Culturally, Roddenberry's *Star Trek* (1966–9) was more influential. It inspired television sf's first fandom, defined most space-adventure series that followed, and envisioned a liberal humanist future that contrasted sharply with its contemporary American context. As most critical commentators have observed, this contrast enabled writers to comment metaphorically and explicitly on civil rights, racism, sexism, the Cold War, and American imperialism. However, *Star Trek* is a paradoxical text. While it was often critical of American foreign and domestic policy (e.g., "Balance of Terror" (1966), "The Doomsday Machine" (1967), and "A Private Little War" (1968)), it frequently affirmed American values (e.g., "The Omega Glory" (1968)) or adopted a liberal stance that overlooked the resistance and conflict required to construct a genuine egalitarian utopia. Indeed, its treatment of women and alien cultures often exposed cultural prejudices and compromised its progressive aspirations for the future.

Looking back rather than forward, *The Invaders* (1967–8) was a retrograde alien infiltration narrative. Its influence on *The X-Files* (1993–2002) and *Dark Skies* (1996–7) is readily apparent. Less earnest were two series that exploited the popularity of the Bond films by uniting espionage with sf: the parodic *Get Smart* (1965–70) and *The Wild, Wild West* (1965–9), a steampunk series that affirmed American exceptionalism.

Between 1970 and the beginning of 1973, no new or significant sf series appeared on American television. Whether this was attributable to Allen's move from television to film projects, the cancellation of *Star Trek* and what that suggested about television sf to other companies, or cultural factors which oscillated between confidence (the moon landings) and disaffection (the Kent State killings, continued civil unrest, Vietnam) is unclear. American TV sf simply seemed incapable of affirming its customary faith in American institutions and, unable or unwilling to adopt an oppositional stance, remained almost silent. Apolitical productions like *The Fantastic Journey* (1973) and *The Starlost* (1972–3) were cancelled after less than a season. Only *The Six Million Dollar Man* (1973, 1974–8) proved commercially viable.

From 1974, American television sf adopted a restorative function, assisting audience recuperation from the vicissitudes of Vietnam and Watergate through the activities of superhuman protagonists. *The Six Million Dollar Man* and *The Bionic Woman* (1976–8) both patriotically revalidate the "military–scientific collaboration" evident in the 1950s American sf film (Bould 2003: 85). Other series adopted different though no less therapeutic strategies. *The Planet of the Apes* (1974) restated the core American values of liberty and freedom while *Logan's Run* (1977–8) shifted incoherently from conservatism to a problematic feminism.

The restoration of American pride was united with feminist discourse more successfully in *The New Original Wonder Woman* (1975–6) and *The New Adventures of Wonder Woman* (1977–9), which provided nationalistic balm. Wonder Woman was not only the embodiment of idealized American values, she was also a pop-camp feminist icon that questioned patriarchal authority, problematized the tenets of masculine performance, and encouraged female independence. The success of *Wonder Woman* inspired other superhero series, among them the popular *The Incredible Hulk* (1977–82). Somber and melancholic, *Hulk* was unlike other American television sf. Its protagonist, Dr David Banner, was a scientist who transformed into a monster when under duress. This Banner/Hulk dyad symbolized a country divided against itself; his identity crisis was metonymic for the crises that had riven America for two decades. The constant deferral of his curative reunification, while a requirement of episodic television, formed a bleak meditation on the possibility of American social and psychical integration at the turn of the decade.

This unique introspection contrasts with Glen A. Larson's opportunistic post-*Star Wars* space operas *Battlestar Galactica* (1978) and the camp *Buck Rogers in the Twenty-Fifth Century* (1979–81). Only *The Martian Chronicles* (1980), directed by Michael Anderson, distinguished itself at this point, maintaining the elegiac tone of Ray Bradbury's 1950 novel and evoking an appropriately otherworldly environment despite slack direction and unconvincing special effects. Richard Matheson's script sharpened Bradbury's critique of colonial expansion, but the series' true strength lay in its intermittently striking imagery.

Such expansionist views were limited in British sf cinema. After the 1956 Suez Crisis, Britain's influence waned and it abandoned pretensions to spaceflight. As I.Q. Hunter (1999b) observes, excluding characters in *Spaceflight IC-1* (Knowles 1965) and *Doppelganger* (Parrish 1969), only kidnapped Britons would journey into space in *They Came from Beyond Space* (Francis 1967), *The Terrornauts* (Tully 1967), and the sexploitative *Zeta One* (Cort 1969). Lacking a positive vision, British sf cinema at this time was principally one of anxiety. Cultural apprehensions were expressed through traditional sf tropes given particular contextual resonance. Ian Conrich argues, for example, that the derivative monster movies *Behemoth the Sea Monster* (Lourié 1959), *Gorgo* (Lourié 1961), and *Konga* (Lemont 1960) articulated "tensions created by a crisis in hegemony" (Conrich 1999: 88) originating from Britain's decline as an imperialist power. Providing compensatory myths, they repositioned Britain as central to world events and championed Britain's questionable military prowess.

Less reassuring are the Cold War narratives of the 1960s. *Village of the Damned* (Rilla 1960) and *Children of the Damned* (Leader 1963) – both adapted from John Wyndham's *The Midwich Cuckoos* (1957) – along with *The Damned* (Losey 1961) and *The Day the Earth Caught Fire* (Guest 1961), constituted a high point in British sf cinema. They addressed variously fears of infiltration, subversion, and radiation. Additionally, they denoted nervousness regarding the generation gap that would impel the counterculture in their problematic adult–child/youth relationships (see Hunter 1999a: 108–9). Means of controlling Britain's youth was the subject of Peter Watkins's *Privilege* (1967) and Kubrick's controversial 1971 adaptation of Anthony Burgess's dystopian *A Clockwork Orange* (1962). Kubrick's cinematic sensibility renders Burgess's critique of delinquent youth culture and draconian government a striking and disturbing cinematic experience. Although the film was widely criticized for its lurid, stylized violence, it is an intelligent, morally complex work that preserves Burgess's interrogation of the interrelationships between aggression, liberty, identity, and the state.

Throughout the 1960s Britain's growing intimacy with America and the Bomb was a source of equal concern. Watkins's docudrama *The War Game* responded partly to Labour's U-turn on unilateral disarmament, and partly to its silence on the consequences of nuclear attack. The BBC banned the film in 1965; following a theatrical release in 1966, it won the Oscar for Best Documentary. Unfortunately, Watkins's later films, the muddled *Gladiatorena* (1969) and the anti-Vietnam *Punishment Park* (1971), lacked its chilling urgency. Following the suppression of Watkins's film, the Bomb remained largely absent from British screens until the 1980s. Richard Lester's surreal *The Bed Sitting Room* (1969) was a rare exception. As its ironically stalwart survivors mutate absurdly into bed-sitting rooms and parrots, it is clear that Lester, like Kubrick, could not conceive of the unimaginable in realist terms, and provides a satire as critical – if not as coherent – as *Dr Strangelove*. In contrast, the visually captivating *Zardoz* (Boorman 1974) was a mystical exploration of the world after the Bomb, its pretentiousness mitigated by Geoffrey Unsworth's remarkable cinematography. Equally arresting is Nicolas Roeg's *The Man Who Fell to Earth* (1976), an elliptical, haunting metaphor for the loss of selfhood to capitalism.

Few British sf films were as inventive as those of Lester or Roeg. When it disengaged from popular anxieties, or adopted American models, it faltered. Alien invasion narratives were particularly bland. *The Day of the Triffids* (Sekeley 1962) and *Night of the Big Heat* (Fisher 1967) are clichéd and workmanlike, and Hammer's belated adaptation of *Quatermass and the Pit* (Baker 1967) dissipated the atmosphere of the original. Equally disappointing, and symptomatic of Hammer's continued decline throughout the early 1970s, is *Frankenstein and the Monster from Hell* (Fisher 1974), the final ignominious coda to the studio's *Frankenstein* series. Novelty also eluded British generic hybrids, which were less accomplished than American endeavors, with only the exuberantly camp *The Rocky Horror Picture Show* (Sharman 1975) successfully synthesizing a diverse generic heritage in its celebration of polymorphous sexuality. Nevertheless, British cinema was enlivened throughout the 1960s by the Bond films. *Dr No* (Young 1962), *Goldfinger* (Hamilton 1964), and *Thunderball* (Young 1965) all featured nuclear terrorism to maintain their pulp plotting but rendered no serious commentary on the Bomb. In the 1970s, *Moonraker* (Gilbert 1979) centralized Bond's previously ornamental sf elements to capitalize on the success of *Star Wars*. Bond's popularity inspired several American parodies (*Our Man Flint* (Mann 1966), *The Silencers* (Karlson 1966)) while Italy co-produced colorful parodies like *Operazione Goldman* (Margheriti 1966).

At the end of the 1970s, the quantitative decline of British film production left British sf cinema moribund. The derivative *Saturn 3* (Donen 1980) and exploitative *Inseminoid* (Warren 1981) indicated its qualitative deterioration. This was not true of British television sf, however, which flourished during the 1960s and 1970s. Throughout these two decades, it was more critical of its milieu than either British sf cinema or American television sf. The means of this critique – the figure of the scientist and the theme of nuclear conflict – derived from British television sf in the 1950s, albeit differently dramatized. The implicit or personalized disapproval of the establishment in Nigel Kneale's *Quatermass* trilogy (1953–9) became direct censure as scientists adopted dissident positions characteristic of the 1960s. *A for Andromeda* (1961), for example, denounced the political and military conscription of science and Europe's position as America's frontline in the Cold War. The sequel, *The Andromeda Breakthrough* (1962), condemned scientists complicit with capitalism and concluded by promising a renaissance led by a Wellsian scientific technocracy.

The conception of the scientist as sociopolitical redeemer achieved its apotheosis in the itinerant and eccentric protagonist of the original *Doctor Who* (1963–89). The Doctor "consistently adopted that liberal populist role in criticising 'sectionalist' forces of 'Left' and 'Right', and in rebuking the 'official' and the powerful in big business, the military, government or militant unions" (Tulloch and Alvarado 1984: 54). In short, *Doctor Who* continued the work begun in the *Andromeda* dramas. As a liberal, the Doctor occupied a neutral position from which he could criticize the mores of his contemporary audience. His critical role is never more apparent, nor as concerned with the state of contemporary Britain, than during the early 1970s. Where the first six seasons of *Doctor Who* offered historical adventures, alien worlds, and temporal voyages, seasons 7 to 11 (1970–4) dealt with more politically and socially pertinent material. Although part of the establishment, the third incarnation of the Doctor, played by Jon Pertwee, was notably more critical of his contemporary context than either of his predecessors. Indeed, he was unfailingly disparaging of the establishment, its representatives, and its metaphorical substitutes, commenting on racial and ecological tensions ("Doctor Who and the Silurians" (1970)), Britain's entry into the Common Market ("The Curse of Peladon" (1972)), industrial pollution ("The Green Death" (1973)), and difficult industrial relations ("The Monster of Peladon" (1974)). Additionally, it promoted "a liberal discourse of 'tolerance' and 'balance' against the militaristic tendencies of the Bug Eyed Monster (BEM) syndrome" (Tulloch and Alvarado 1984: 41–2). Unfortunately, when the series was adapted for the cinema to exploit the Daleks' popularity, neither *Dr Who and the Daleks* (Flemyng 1965) nor *Daleks – Invasion Earth 2150* (Flemyng 1966) retained the social conscience of the television series.

Sydney Newman, the instigator of *Doctor Who*, was also the motivator behind *Out of this World* (1962), which, together with *Out of the Unknown* (1966–71) and a number of single dramas, formed a high proportion of British television sf in the 1960s. Notable single plays addressed nuclear politics (*The Poisoned Earth* (1961)), the space race (*Campaign for One* (1965)), and reality TV (Kneale's contentious *The Year of the Sex Olympics* (1968)). The quality of such dramas made many contemporary serials retrograde by comparison, including the invasion scenario, *The Monsters* (1962), the alien subversion story, *Undermind* (1963), and the reactionary *Adam Adamant Lives* (1966–7). The latter contrasted with *The Prisoner* (1967–8), which used conflicting conservative and libertarian perspectives to document the difficulty of preserving one's identity in an intrusive modern state.

In the early 1970s, the rejection of the anthology series by both BBC and ITV precipitated the decline of the sf play. Exceptions included the hoax *Alternative Three* (1977) and the environmentally attuned *Stargazy on Zummerdown* (1978). Indeed, environmental damage was a recurring theme of the period. *Doomwatch* (1970–2), for example, followed a government department's work to prevent and expose scientific, military, and corporate negligence. Although similar to *R3* (1964–5), *Doomwatch* articulated a general mistrust of politicians and bureaucrats and was more disquieting in its emphasis on government complicity in conspiracies of silence.

Throughout the 1970s, British television sf showed disenchantment with domestic politics and an increasing parochialism that reflected Britain's dwindling international influence, its economic fragility, and a denial of the repercussions of its entry into the EEC in 1973. *The Guardians* (1971) is a disquieting, prophetic dystopian vision of a Britain suffering mass unemployment, a general strike, and raging inflation. More critical is the Orwellian dystopian thriller *1990* (1977–8). Such inwardness explains, in part, why Gerry Anderson's *UFO* (1970–3) and *Space: 1999* (1975–8) proved unpopular, unlike his puppet series (e.g., *Stingray* (1964–5), *Thunderbirds* (1965–6), and *Captain Scarlet* (1967–8)), which captured the 1960s qualified technophilia. His American-modeled live-action shows were simply too abstracted from British cultural life to succeed.

Alternatively, *Moonbase 3* (1973) was palpably claustrophobic; its sense of isolation undermined its optimistic premise and captured the mood of insularity felt (and often desired) in 1970s Britain (see Morgan 2001: 342). An equivalent insularity was found in *Survivors* (1975–7) and *Blakes 7* (1977–81). Written by Terry Nation, both advocated traditional values over the amoral mechanics of bureaucracy as industrial confrontation threatened cultural stability and government attachment to Brussels effected a "greater detachment of the community from the processes of administration" (Morgan 2001: 353–5). When *Quatermass* returned in 1979, Kneale provided an apocalyptic treatment of Britain's contemporary ills. However, although it reflected the sullen national mood, it was deeply conservative. By advocating self-sacrifice as the only means of rescuing society from ruin, Kneale attempted to reinstate nobility in an act that, for many, had already proved unacceptable. After the economic "sacrifices" expected by James Callaghan's government had given rise to the Winter of Discontent, Kneale's sentiment was as anachronistic as the serial's vagrant hippies traveling Britain's blighted landscape.

The Conservative victory in May 1979 provoked contrary responses from British television sf that continued into the 1980s. However, at the end of the 1970s, P.J. Hammond's somber and symbolic *Sapphire and Steel* (1979–82) presents Margaret Thatcher's election as the triumph of Conservative order over social chaos. The eponymous Thatcherite protagonists defend the temporal order against metaphorical versions of the perceived contemporary social malaise: ineffective politicians, immigrants, faceless bureaucracy. After the Winter of Discontent, it was not surprising that Sapphire and Steel were greeted as heroic figures despite their misanthropy.

After America and Britain, Japan was the largest producer of screen sf between 1960 and 1980. Predictably, Japanese sf cinema remained preoccupied with nuclear weapons and radiation. Such cultural anxieties were expressed in anti-nuclear films, including *The Final War* (Hidaka 1960); in transformation films, such as *Attack of the Mushroom People* (Honda 1963); and in the *kaiju eiga* (monster movie), which retained the dominance secured by Toho Studio's *Gojira* (Honda 1954). *Invasion of the Astro Monster* (Honda 1965) marked a shift in the genre as the creatures that once threatened civilization were enlisted for its protection. The film, together with *Atoragon, the Flying Supersub* (Honda 1964), presented a more positive perspective on nuclear weapons and acknowledged the economic revivification of Japan following the 1964 Olympics and the election of the pro-nationalist Liberal-Democratic Party.

In 1966, Daiei Studios instituted a series of *kaiju eiga* featuring Gamera, a giant turtle, to capitalize on the success of *Gojira*. Throughout the late 1960s, Toho and Daiei produced formulaic *kaiju eiga* for children and adolescents. Noriaki Yuasa's *Gamera Versus Zigra* (Yuasa 1971) gave the genre new relevance by introducing pollution as a key theme and articulated the growing global awareness of the ecological damage caused by industrialization. *Godzilla Versus the Smog Monster* (Banno 1971) centralizes pollution narratively and visually in the form of Hedora, a monster composed of industrial waste and animated by cosmic particles. Pollution gradually displaced radiation as the key theme in Japanese sf cinema. Notable films include *Godzilla Versus Megalon* (Fukuda 1972) and *Prophecies of Nostradamus* (Masuda 1974), which combines pollution with the disaster narrative then popular in both East (*The Submersion of Japan* (Moritani 1973)) and West (*Earthquake* (Robson 1974)).

In terms of Japanese sf's global influence, the emergence of animated series based on the highly cinematic *manga* or Japanese comic book is more significant (see Drazen 2002: 5). Japan's first *anime* series, *Astro Boy*, based on Tezuka Osamu's manga *Tetsuwan Atomu*, debuted in 1963. Following its success in Japan, Tezuka and others populated Japanese television with manga series. Matsumoto Reiji's *Uchû Senkan Yamato* (1974–5), which was later reedited into five feature films, remains one of the most influential.

In the wake of *Star Wars*, American popular interest in space opera was at its height. After expressing only a transient interest in anime during the 1960s, American audiences were now more receptive to Japanese imports. *Star Blazers*, the Anglicized version of *Uchû Senkan Yamato*, was purchased for American television to exploit the success of *Star Wars*. It garnered a significant US audience in 1979 and laid the foundation for anime consumption in the West. Occidental interest in anime was later consolidated with the release of Ôtomo Katsuhiro's highly successful *Akira* (1988).

Perhaps surprisingly Mexico followed Japan as the most active producer of sf-related cinema. Federico Curiel's mad-doctor films (e.g., *Los Autómatas de la Muerte* (1962)), *Frankenstein*-derived sf-horrors (e.g., *The Incredible Invasion* (Hill and González de León 1971) and children's space operas (e.g., *Gigantes Planetarios* (Crevenna 1965)) were overwhelmed by the juvenile exploits of masked wrestlers Santo and the Blue Demon, whose adventures span two decades from 1952. In the most bizarre entry in an admittedly bizarre subgenre, *Santo and the Blue Demon Versus the Monsters* (Solares 1968), the wrestlers are pitted opportunistically against *Gojira*-derived creatures.

The subgenre of medical sf begun in Mexico during the 1950s reemerged in Argentina's *The Curious Dr Humpp* (Vieyra 1971), Spain's *The Face of Terror* (Ferry 1962), and *Cries in the Night* (Franco 1962), and in the work of Canada's master of body-horror, David Cronenberg (e.g. *Shivers* (1974), *The Brood* (1975), *Scanners* (1980)). In Italy, the visually opulent space operas of Antonio Margheriti (e.g., *Battle of the Worlds* (1961), *The Wild, Wild Planet* (1965)), Mario Bava (*Planet of the Vampires* (1965)), and Roger Vadim (*Barbarella* (1968)) influenced both *Flash Gordon* and *Dune* (Lynch 1984). Where style took precedence over content in many Italian sf films, French sf cinema was more intellectual. Several cineastes associated with *Cahiers du cinéma* and the *nouvelle vague* produced intelligent sf films, including *La Jetée* (Marker 1963), *Alphaville* (Godard 1965), and *Je t'Aime, Je t'Aime* (Resnais 1968).

In Eastern Europe, Karel Zeman's Jules Verne adaptations, which constitute the high point of Czech sf cinema, continued with *The Stolen Airship* (1967) and *On the Comet* (1970). Other notable films include Hungary's post-apocalyptic *Windows of Time* (Fejér 1969) and Yugoslavia's visceral and ambiguously symbolic critique of fascism, *The Rat Savior* (Papic 1977). *The Golem* (Szulkin 1979), a rare Polish sf film, unites Kafkaesque paranoia with a surreal *mise en scène* to critique media control (a quality it shares with Finland's *A Time of Roses* (Jarva 1969)) and psychological dislocation in a post-nuclear landscape. *The Golem* is comparable thematically if not stylistically to Andrei Tarkovsky's *Stalker* (1979) which, together with *Solaris* (Tarkovsky 1972), form the pinnacle of Soviet sf cinema. *Solaris* follows a tradition of Soviet space-adventure films, including *The Andromeda Nebula* (Sherstibitov 1968). However, like *Stalker*, *Solaris* is conceptually more profound than the majority of screen sf between 1960 and 1980. One interpretation would suggest that where *Solaris* comments on the limits of human emotional maturity, *Stalker* posits the boundlessness of human imagination. At its best, the sf film and television of the period demonstrate something similar: the confirmation of the human capacity to visualize imaginative thought that, ultimately, reveals the limitations of our emotional development.

BIBLIOGRAPHY

Bould, M. (2003) "Film and Television," in E. James and F. Mendlesohn (eds) *The Cambridge Companion to Science Fiction*, Cambridge: Cambridge University Press.

Boyer, P. (1985) *By the Bomb's Early Light: American thought and culture at the dawn of the atomic age*, New York: Pantheon.

Brosnan, J. (1991) *The Primal Screen: a history of science fiction film*, London: Orbit.

Conrich, I. (1999) "Trashing London: the British colossal creature film and fantasies of mass destruction," in I.Q. Hunter (ed.) *British Science Fiction Cinema*, London: Routledge.

Drazen, P. (2002) *Anime Explosion! The what? why? & wow! of Japanese animation*, Berkeley, CA: Stone Bridge Press.

Greene, E. (1998) *Planet of the Apes as American Myth: race, politics and popular culture*, Hanover, NH: Wesleyan University Press.

Hunter, I.Q. (1999a) "The Day the Earth Caught Fire," in *British Science Fiction Cinema*, London: Routledge.

—— (1999b) "Introduction," in *British Science Fiction Cinema*, London: Routledge.

Morgan, K.O. (2001) *Britain Since 1945: the people's peace*, Oxford: Oxford University Press.

Sobchack, V. (2005) "American Science Fiction Film: an overview," in D. Seed (ed.) *A Companion to Science Fiction*, Oxford: Blackwell.

Sontag, S. (1966) "The Imagination of Disaster," in *Against Interpretation and Other Essays*, New York: Farrar, Straus and Giroux.

Tulloch, J. and Alvarado, M. (1984) *Doctor Who: the unfolding text*, London: Macmillan Press.

11
FICTION, 1964–1979
Helen Merrick

The year 1964 signals the advent of Michael Moorcock's editorship of *New Worlds* (1946–76, 1978–9, 1991–4, 1996–7), the British magazine at the heart of the "New Wave" – a "movement" that dominates most accounts of sf in the 1960s. Perhaps coincidentally, it was also the year that Leigh Brackett became the first female Guest of Honor at the World Science Fiction Convention. In terms of the broader cultural milieu, it is tempting to see sf of this period as overdetermined by the "swinging sixties," by the ferment of the counterculture, sexual revolution, the radical politics of the Civil Rights movement, Vietnam, Haight-Ashbury, Carnaby Street, the Beatles, and rock 'n' roll. In contrast, the 1970s appears a strangely under-determined decade in many accounts: a stale, holding period until the next new wave, cyberpunk, arrives in the mid-1980s to renew the vigor of sf. And although it has been a recurrent theme since at least the 1950s, the notion that one was "living in science-fictional times" had particular resonance in the 1960s and 1970s. This was a time of highly visible technological change, a playing out of many science-fictional hopes and fears: from nuclear power to computers, space-flight, moon landings, and the inexorable growth of entertainment technologies fueling the mass media (Levy 1995: 222–4).

The New Wave both dominates and complicates histories of this period, with a multitude of contradictory claims made for its influence (Latham 2005: 202). For some it is "the single most important development in science fiction" (Priest 1978: 164), an era that "transformed the science fiction landscape" (Silverberg 2001: 4), but others suggest that it is a meaningless generalization (Delany and Russ 1984: 31) or that it never really existed (Dozois 1983: 12; Ellison 1974: 40, 42). Even this brief sample suggests "an era of generational dissent, crisis and rebellion" (Luckhurst 2005: 141), leading to representations of the New Wave as absolute rupture, at the expense of important continuities both before and after (Latham 2006: 252–3).

While this period certainly saw a broadening of the style, themes, and tropes typical of sf, fears about the demise of "old style" sf were by the 1970s already shown to be unfounded. In retrospect, what the "battle" of the New Wave most obviously highlighted was an ongoing professional and critical anxiety over the cultural positioning of the genre. The differences between the New Wave and old guard were most commonly drawn (by both sides) as being a divide over sf's relation to the mainstream. The threat or promise of an escape from the "ghetto" looms large in this period, as sf seemed to gain a new respectability or at least visibility. This was the era of the first sf bestsellers: following Robert A. Heinlein's *Stranger in a Strange Land* (1961) were Frank Herbert's *Dune* (1965) and the US paperback editions of J.R.R. Tolkien's *Lord of the Rings*, which totaled more than a quarter of a million sales in 1965 (Levy 1995: 228). The biggest impact came with what many derogatorily referred to as "sci-fi" – the growing popularity of *Star Trek* (1966–9) when syndicated on US television and the astonishing success of the blockbusters *Star Wars: Episode IV – A New Hope* (Lucas 1977) and *Close Encounters of the Third Kind* (Spielberg 1977) – which heralded sf's transformation "from a primarily written literature of ideas into a primarily visual idiom" (Roberts 2006: 279). Sf also began to infiltrate the academy. The Science Fiction Research Association was founded in 1970, followed by the academic journals *Foundation* (1972–) and *Science Fiction Studies* (1973–) and the appearance of major critical works by Darko Suvin, Samuel Delany, and Brian Aldiss. The impact of fantasy and media sf was often figured as a threat to "genre" sf, signaling an anxiety that also colored responses to another "invasion," that of women as subjects, readers, and writers of sf.

New Worlds

The New Wave is most closely associated with the magazine *New Worlds* in its "swinging sixties" incarnation from 1964 to 1970 (see Greenland 1983, 2005; Priest 1978). The 23-year-old Moorcock was suggested as a successor by retiring editor John Carnell (who had already published J.G. Ballard, Aldiss, and Moorcock). During this relatively brief and financially turbulent period, *New Worlds* set out to transform what counted as sf, introducing new authors and providing a venue for the more experimental work of older writers such as Ballard and Aldiss. Kept alive in part by an Arts Council grant secured by Aldiss and others in 1966, its new approach was mirrored by a visual transformation to a new large format in July 1967, with M.C. Escher's "Relativity" (1953) as the cover (Priest 1978: 171). Moorcock himself funded a large portion of the magazine's costs, including author payments, through the relentless production of his popular fantasy novels.

Moorcock created a distinctively British space for writers, untrammeled by the restrictions of the US magazine market, inspired by the literary and artistic avant garde which looked more to William S. Burroughs and Jorge Luis Borges than traditional sf (Moorcock 1979: 11). In his first editorial, he declared Burroughs's work as "the SF we've all been waiting for," whose "desperate and cynical mood mirrors exactly the mood of our ad-saturated, Bomb-dominated, power-corrupted times" (Moorcock 1964: 2–3). Moorcock published stories which would become synonymous with the New Wave: radical in style and content, often explicit in terms of language and sexual references, and more concerned with "inner" than outer space. An exemplary moment of *New Worlds*'s history was the serialization of Norman Spinrad's *Bug Jack Barron* (1969). Featuring a media-saturated future of legalized cannabis, its explicit language led to W.H. Smith, a major newsagent chain, refusing to distribute the issue and to a parliamentary question on why public money was being spent on "filth" (Moorcock 1979: 14).

New Worlds featured most of the authors central to the British movement, including Aldiss, Christopher Priest, M. John Harrison, Hilary Bailey, Josephine Saxton, Charles Platt, and the Americans Pamela Zoline, Thomas Disch, and John Sladek. Moorcock himself contributed the countercultural antihero Jerry Cornelius, who featured in such novels as *The Final Programme* (1968) and *A Cure for Cancer* (1971) and was borrowed by other authors. Early on, Moorcock proclaimed Ballard as the "voice" of the movement, the harbinger of a "genuinely speculative and introspective" sf (Moorcock 1966: 2). Ballard had been publishing sf since the 1950s, and his explorations of "inner space" (a phrase from his 1962 *New Worlds* guest editorial) had begun independently of Moorcock's movement. However, Moorcock was to publish many of Ballard's more radical stylistic pieces, including such "condensed novels" as "The Terminal Beach" (1964), and the article "Myth Maker of the 20th Century," which promoted Burroughs as "an object lesson" for sf writers (Ballard 1964: 127). Moorcock's hype was reinforced by Ballard's many detractors, who saw work such as *The Drought* (1964) and *The Crystal World* (1966) as exemplifying the New Wave's pessimistic turn away from science and its hero-engineers. However, Ballard's importance lay not just in his uniquely shocking collage-style juxtaposition of artifacts, technologies, and bodies in mass-media landscapes, but in his conception of the utility of sf. Notwithstanding his critics (or the belief of some New Wavers that they needed to "outgrow" the genre and its readers), Ballard "remained committed to science fiction as the only literature capable of recording the transformation of human subjectivity by the technological revolution of the 1960s" (Luckhurst 2005: 151).

Although it could be viewed by opponents as a direct attack on "Golden Age" sf, the concerns of the *New Worlds* writers reflected a broader artistic refusal of "the shiny promise of technological modernity" (Luckhurst 2005: 143). Thus it is not surprising that a fascination with entropy characterizes many New Wave works, including Aldiss's *Greybeard* (1964) and *Barefoot in the Head* (1969), and Disch's *Camp Concentration* (1968). The theme is most famously rendered in Zoline's "The Heat Death of the Universe" (1967), significant for being a key text of both New Wave and feminist sf canons, and repeatedly anthologized as representative of both. Narrating the particularly feminized pressures of technologized domestic drudgery through the "hard" discourses of physics, entropy, and cybernetics, it crucially "opened up swathes of experience ignored by much of the New Wave" (Luckhurst 2005: 159).

An American New Wave?

Critics are divided as to whether there was an "American New Wave," or to what extent developments there and in the UK can be amalgamated into a singular "movement." The assignment of certain writers to a US "New Wave" obscures or ignores the continuities of tradition with both Campbellian sf and a decade of more counter-traditional works from the 1940s and 1950s, such as those by Frederik Pohl and Theodore Sturgeon. For Gardner Dozois, the American "New Wave" was already "set in its own distinct aesthetic direction," defined as much by the *Galaxy*-style sf of the 1950s as by the more historically remote Campbellian tradition (Dozois 1983: 11).

While many writers assigned to an American New Wave have resoundingly denied such membership, most critics nevertheless identify a core group of authors, including Delany, Disch, and Harlan Ellison, who all published early work in *New Worlds*, as well as Roger Zelazny, Robert Silverberg, and often Ursula Le Guin and Joanna Russ. A more controversial inclusion, but one whose influence on sf is inescapable, is Philip K. Dick. Some of his work in this period – *Do Androids Dream of Electric Sheep?* (1968) and *Ubik* (1969) – exhibits similar preoccupations with the mechanization of subjectivity and psychological experiments. Praised by critics and authors alike (despite a mixed and uneven oeuvre), Dick was distinguished by his attention to the "political and metaphysical implications" of science-fictional icons (Landon 2002: 113).

A key figure in promoting the New Wave to American audiences was author and editor Judith Merril. While wryly acknowledging her conferred status as "prophetess" for the New Wave, Merril's promotion of the British developments was not simply reactive (Merril 1967: 28). Rather, the work she collected in *England Swings SF* (1968) and praised in her *Magazine of Fantasy & Science Fiction* columns were exemplars of the "speculative fiction" she had been promoting through her *Year's Best* anthology series since 1956 (Latham 2005: 209). Significantly, Merril was one of the few contemporary observers to discuss the New Wave's relation to science in terms other than pessimistic rejection. In her 1966 essay "What Do You Mean: Science? Fiction?" she argued: "The literature of the mid-20th century can be meaningful only in so far as it perceives, and relates itself to, the central reality of our culture: the revolution in scientific thought which has replaced mechanics with dynamics, classification with integration, positivism with relativity, certainties with statistical probabilities, dualism with parity" (Merril 1966: 54). In this account, many of the "head shifts" associated with New Wave sensibilities are framed not as a rejection of scientific underpinnings of sf, but rather as a contemporaneous and realistic reflection of the state of scientific discourse in a post-Heisenberg age (Merril 1967: 30; Cummins 1995).

Also crucial to formulations of an American New Wave were Ellison's influential collections, *Dangerous Visions* (1967) and *Again, Dangerous Visions* (1972). Ellison brashly self-promoted the first as "a revolution," although one he was later at pains to distinguish from the New Wave. *Dangerous Visions* was certainly successful, selling 50,000 copies in hardback. It presented 33 stories by newer writers such as Ballard, Delany, Sladek, Carol Emshwiller, and Sonya Dorman, alongside those of established authors such as Pohl, Sturgeon, and Lester del Rey, suggesting "an exercise in reanimating American science fiction rather than a new breakthrough" (Luckhurst 2005: 164).

Dangerous Visions also marked a shift in the way sf was produced and consumed, part of an increasing trend away from magazines and toward original anthologies, such as Damon Knight's *Orbit* series (1966–76), Terry Carr's *Universe* series (1971–87), and Silverberg's *New Dimensions* (1971–80), and new paperback imprints such as Carr's Ace SF specials (publishing Keith Roberts's *Pavane* (1968) and Le Guin's *The Left Hand of Darkness* (1969)). By the mid-1970s paperbacks dominated, with almost 900 titles published in 1975 in an sf market estimated to be worth $40 million (Sutherland 1979: 163). This economic change was mirrored by a generational shift which brought a different kind of reader and writer to sf. Most new writers had not "come up through the ranks" as fans, and many had literary, rather than technical or scientific, college backgrounds. By the late 1970s, the dominance of the paperback and the increasing presence of sf in college courses meant that the genre was primarily "written by human-ities graduates for humanities graduates" (Sutherland 1979: 164). Increasingly, authors were not just writing sf "on the side," but were deliberately choosing to become writers of sf: they were "literally and demographically, new people" (Dozois 1983: 12).

It is tempting to characterize the New Wave/old guard schisms as one of genera-tional division, with the new generation as liberated, left-leaning radicals (Bainbridge 1986: 109–10). This picture is partially supported by the most public confrontation between old and new guards – the infamous "Vietnam" adverts in the June 1968 *Galaxy*. Supporting the war were Campbell, Heinlein, Poul Anderson, Larry Niven, and Jerry Pournelle, while their opponents included Le Guin, Dick, Russ, and Ellison, but also "Golden age doves" like Sturgeon, Asimov, and Ray Bradbury (Latham 2005: 213). Similarly, even those who expressed open opposition to the New Wave influence, such as Donald Wollheim, themselves helped to foster new writers: as Ace's sf editor, Wollheim was chiefly responsible for publishing Delany, Le Guin, and Russ (Latham 2005: 210–11).

In reviewing 1960s sf, it is easy to let the "war of the New Wave" distract one from the fact that many older writers continued to produce popular, award-winning work. Both the popular and the critical vote, represented respectively by the Hugo and Nebula awards, are a mix of New Wave authors, older writers, and new heirs of the "old guard," such as Niven, with his debut novel *Ringworld* (1970). Other doubly awarded stories from established writers included Fritz Leiber's "Gonna Roll the Bones" (1967), Sturgeon's "Slow Sculpture" (1970), and Anderson's "The Queen of Air and Darkness" (1971). Of the newer writers (not all identifiably New Wave), Herbert's *Dune* won both awards, as did Le Guin's *The Left Hand of Darkness*, and Delany's "Time Considered as a Helix of Semi-Precious Stones" (1969).

A perusal of awards listings also makes clear the other major development of the 1960s: the increasing visibility of women writers. Until recently the prevailing critical and popular view was held that – apart from very rare exceptions (such as C.L. Moore and Brackett) – women writers were absent from sf until a sudden breakthrough in the 1960s, brought about by the "softening" of the genre and an increase in women readers attracted by influences such as *Star Trek*. This is too simplistic a picture, but the 1960s certainly saw an increasing number of women writers emerge to both critical and popular acclaim. Authors who would make their strongest mark over the next decade began publishing and winning awards, with Russ's first story appearing in 1959, followed by Le Guin, Kate Wilhelm, and James Tiptree Jr. Some who had begun their careers in the 1950s or earlier became better known, including Emshwiller, Marion Zimmer Bradley, and Anne McCaffrey, who won the 1968 Nebula for her "Dragonrider" (1967) and a Hugo for "Weyr Search" (1967), the beginnings of her enormously successful *Pern* series.

The stale 1970s

The 1970s get short shrift in many critical accounts, its sf dismissed as "confused, self-involved, and stale" (Sterling 1986: 9), and depicted as a period of increasing insularity despite, or perhaps because of, the diversification of the genre into other forms (Roberts 2006: 298; Luckhurst 2005: 167). Some mourned the petering out of the New Wave as it was "absorbed into the system," accompanied by noisy (if premature) announcements of departure from the genre by Ellison, Silverberg, and Barry Malzberg in the mid-1970s (Priest 1978: 173; Luckhurst 2005: 168). Historically, the period can easily be cast as an "interregnum" between New Wave and cyberpunk movements, representing "either the dying fall of a failed avant-garde or an era of marking time" (Luckhurst 2005: 169). Yet, as Luckhurst argues, such flat accounts fail to reflect the sense of "structural crisis" infecting the decade, prefaced by Alvin Toffler's *Future Shock* (1970), evident in the global economic recession, and growing disaffection with advanced industrialization, and marked by increasing environmental activism, the growth of the women's movement, the perceived failure of left-wing politics, and the advent of terrorism and racial violence (Luckhurst 2005: 169–71).

Such concerns were certainly reflected in many of the works awarded both the Hugo and Nebula: Le Guin's "ambiguous utopia," *The Dispossessed* (1974); Joe Haldeman's powerful reflection on Vietnam, *The Forever War* (1974); Tiptree's "Houston, Houston, Do You Read?" (1976); Vonda McIntyre's *Dreamsnake* (1978); and John Varley's "The Persistence of Vision" (1978). Environmental concerns surfacing earlier in Ballard's disaster novels and John Brunner's overpopulation novel *Stand on Zanzibar* (1968) continued with the latter's *The Sheep Look Up* (1972), Le Guin's *The Word for World is Forest* (1972), and environmentalist Ernest Callenbach's *Ecotopia* (1975). Many writers associated with the New Wave produced some of their more powerful work, including Disch's grim near-future *334* (1972), Priest's *Fugue for a Darkening Island* (1972), Silverberg's *Dying Inside* (1972), Ballard's *Crash* (1973), and Moorcock's *The Condition of Muzak* (1977). Following his heady explorations of race, sexuality, language, and subjectivity in *Babel-17* (1966), *The Einstein Intersection* (1967), and *Nova* (1968), Delany returned with the epic, challenging masterpiece (and surprise cult classic) *Dhalgren* (1975), followed by *Triton* (1976), with its "heterotopic" excesses of gender and sexuality. Similar challenges emerged in Varley's body-swapping, sex-changing short stories and *Titan* (1979), while Zimmer Bradley's long-running *Darkover* series (1958–94) began to explore sexual politics in *The Heritage of Hastur* (1975) and *The Shattered Chain* (1976). Nevertheless, still winning awards throughout the decade were familiar names such as Isaac Asimov with *The Gods Themselves* (1972) and "Bicentennial Man" (1976), Pohl with *Man Plus* (1976) and *Gateway* (1977), and Arthur C. Clarke with *Rendezvous with Rama* (1973) and *The Fountains of Paradise* (1979).

The "feminine" invasion

The 1970s were seen by some observers to herald a new revolution – a fight between hard sf and "soft" sf, the latter mostly attributed to the influence of women in the genre (Aldiss with Wingrove 1986: 368). On the whole, the sf establishment apparently viewed the incursion of women positively, although reviews of books such as Russ's challenging *The Female Man* (1975) were often less than favorable and a number of heated and sometimes vitriolic debates about feminism raged in fandom (see Merrick 2009). Many critics noted with pleasure the increasing number of women writers: Peter Nicholl's *Encyclopedia of Science Fiction* listed over 60 female writers in the "women" entry (Nicholls 1979: 662), while Aldiss concurred with Ellison that "the best writers in SF today are the women" (Aldiss 1973: 306; Ellison 1974: 230). Even stalwarts like Asimov appeared to welcome this "invasion," although given the ongoing anxieties about the mainstreaming of sf, it was for him a double-edged sword: "It is the feminization of science fiction that has broadened and deepened the field to the point where science fiction novels can now appear on the bestseller lists" (Asimov 1982: 608).

What is not apparent in these critical narratives are the links between New Wave and the impact of the women's movement on sf. But it was the apparent "exhaustion" of the genre identified by New Wave challenges that, according to Luckhurst, helped reveal the possibilities for turning sf's vaunted potential for cognitive experiments back upon itself (Luckhust 2005: 182). Rather than rejecting sf's tools and tropes, feminist writers in particular reconceptualized the newly contested sf megatext as a space for alternative ways of thinking about gender, sexuality, and, less often, race. An obvious example lies in the ways in which feminist writers extended and reconfigured the aesthetic freedoms attendant on the (male) sexual revolution embraced by the New Wave, whereby "feminist SF served as a kind of conscience for the New Wave movement" (Latham 2006: 262).

Critiques of sf's normative approach to gender roles had already appeared from writers in the 1960s, such as Le Guin's *The Left Hand of Darkness* and Russ's *Picnic on Paradise* (1968). In different ways, both authors became more overt in their opposition to traditional sf narratives throughout the 1970s. The central text of feminist sf, Russ's *The Female Man*, finally achieved publication in 1975, with her other key works including "When it Changed" (1972), *And Chaos Died* (1970), *Alyx* (1976), and the wonderfully subversive *We Who Are About to . . .* (1977). Le Guin continued to develop her less radical, humanist critique of sf through novels such as *The Dispossessed*. Both also made important contributions to a burgeoning feminist sf criticism through essays such as Russ's "The Image of Women in Science Fiction" (1974) and Le Guin's "American SF and the Other" (1975).

The works of Tiptree, whose first story was published in 1968, were central to the 1970s, as were the complex responses to the author's persona, when in 1976 "he" was revealed to be Alice Sheldon. Notwithstanding the impact this revelation had on Tiptree's status as one of the field's most respected writers, stories such as "The Women Men Don't See" (1973), in which women prefer to abscond with aliens rather than continue living in patriarchal society, "Houston, Houston, Do You Read?," and the chilling "The Screwfly Solution" (1977) offered powerful critiques of feminine and masculine "nature." Also receiving critical and popular acclaim was McIntyre, who won a Nebula for her early story "Of Mist, and Grass, and Sand" (1973) and both Nebula and Hugo for *Dreamsnake*.

These texts – and others such as Suzy McKee Charnas's *Walk to the End of the World* (1974) and its sequel *Motherlines* (1978), Marge Piercy's *Woman on the Edge of Time* (1976), and Sally Miller Gearhart's *The Wanderground* (1979) – would come to form the central canon of feminist sf. In Britain in particular, a number of mainstream authors also explored gender and feminist concerns through sf, including Angela Carter, with *Heroes and Villains* (1969) and *The Passion of New Eve* (1979), and Zoe Fairbairns, with *Benefits* (1979).

Although not directly associated with this group of feminist authors, a significant new voice emerging at this time was Octavia E. Butler. Recognized as the first female African-American sf author, Butler joined Delany in demonstrating the genre's potential to interrogate race. From her debut novel *Patternmaster* (1976), the first volume of her *Patternist* series (1976–84), Butler's strong, black, female characters were central to her meditations on race, gender, power, and biology. With *Kindred* (1979), she brought the horrors of slavery vividly into the present through the figure of Dana who is thrown back in time to become a slave in the early 1800s.

Beyond the impact of the texts themselves, the sf community in the 1970s experienced a surge of feminist activity that amounted to a full-scale consciousness-raising, encompassing the reclamation of earlier writers, the development of a distinctly feminist sf criticism, and the consolidation of a feminist fan community. A sense of "herstory" was first advanced by Pamela Sargent's three *Women of Wonder* collections (1975, 1976, 1978), whose introductions offered comprehensive and informed analyses of the images and role of women in sf. Perhaps the first collection of feminist sf was McIntyre and Susan J. Anderson's *Aurora: beyond equality* (1976). Beginning with essays by Russ, Le Guin, and other authors and fans, a feminist sf criticism began to emerge, with articles appearing in the academic journals *Extrapolation* and *Science Fiction Studies*. The sophistication of feminist critical debate outside academe was demonstrated by the fascinating "Women in Sf" Symposium (published in *Khatru*), involving forthright and at times heated exchanges about gender and writing between Russ, Le Guin, Charnas, McIntyre, Wilhelm, Tiptree, Delany, and others (Smith 1975). In 1974, the first Worldcon panel to address women's issues was convened by Susan Wood. There followed a flurry of similar activities such as the Women's APA, the establishment of women-only "Rooms of our Own" at conventions, and the emergence of feminist fanzines such as *The Witch and the Chameleon* and *Janus* (later *Aurora*). This activity culminated in the establishment of the feminist convention Wiscon in 1976, which passed its thirtieth anniversary in 2006.

In attempting to summarize developments in the genre over this period, it is instructive to sample some of the more distinctive texts appearing in 1979. Alongside Butler's *Kindred* and Varley's *Titan*, we might find Italo Calvino's *If On a Winter's*

Night a Traveler, Douglas Adams's *The Hitchhiker's Guide to the Galaxy*, Darko Suvin's theoretical *Metamorphoses of Science Fiction: on the poetics and history of a literary genre*, Robert Wise's *Star Trek: The Motion Picture*, and Ridley Scott's *Alien*. Whether attributed to revolution, deterioration, or the changing forms of popular entertainment, such a list clearly signals that what counted as sf had changed significantly since the early 1960s. No matter what judgments are made about the revolutionary nature of the New Wave or feminism, this period solidified many of the facets of the genre as we know it today. We could, along with Brooks Landon, couch the change in terms of the triumph of what he terms "soft agenda SF," where attention is not so much on the scientific novum but on "ideological, political, and social issues" (Landon 2002: 175). Such a trend can be traced back at least to the 1940s, but it was certainly consolidated and intensified by the impact of the New Wave and the "mainstream" avant garde, feminist, and ecological movements. Ultimately this constitutes a "counter-tradition" which interrogates sf itself, "its confidence in a knowable and objective reality, and ... its ostensible confidence in the immutability of gender relations" (and, increasingly of race and heterosexism) (Landon 2002: 110). And, despite claims to the contrary, it has been the ongoing evolution and assimilation of such counter-traditions that has sustained the complex, perverse, and ever-adaptable organism that is sf.

Bibliography

Aldiss, B. (1973) *Billion Year Spree: the history of science fiction*, London: Weidenfeld and Nicolson.

Aldiss, B. with Wingrove, D. (1986) *Trillion Year Spree: the history of science fiction*, London: Gollancz.

Asimov, I. (1982) "The Feminization of Sci-Fi," *Vogue*: 555 and 608.

Bainbridge, W.S. (1986) *Dimensions of Science Fiction*, Cambridge, MA and London: Harvard University Press.

Ballard, J.G. (1964) "Myth Maker of the 20th Century," *New Worlds*, 142: 121–7.

Cummins, E. (1995) "Judith Merril: a link with the New Wave – then and now," *Extrapolation*, 36(3): 198–209.

Delany, S.R. and Russ, J. (1984) "A Dialogue: Samuel Delany and Joanna Russ on science fiction," *Callaloo*, 22: 27–35.

Dozois, G. (1983) "Beyond the Golden Age, Part II: the New Wave years," *Thrust*, 19: 10–14.

Ellison, H. (1974) "A Few (Hopefully Final) Words about the New Wave," in W.E. McNelly (ed.) *Science Fiction: the academic awakening*, Shreveport, CA: CEA.

Greenland, C. (1983) *The Entropy Exhibition: Michael Moorcock and the British "New Wave" in science fiction*, London: Routledge and Kegan Paul.

—— (2005) "The Field and the Wave: the history of *New Worlds*," in J. Gunn and M. Candelaria (eds) *Speculations on Speculation*, Lanham, MD: Scarecrow Press.

Landon, B. (2002) *Science Fiction After 1900: from the steam man to the stars*, London and New York: Routledge.

Latham, R. (2005) "The New Wave," in D. Seed (ed.) *A Companion to Science Fiction*, Oxford: Blackwell.

—— (2006) "Sextrapolation in New Wave Science Fiction," *Science Fiction Studies*, 33(2): 251–74.

Levy, M.M. (1995) "The New Wave, Cyberpunk, and Beyond: 1963–1994," in N. Barron (ed.) *Anatomy of Wonder 4*, New York: Bowker.

Luckhurst, R. (2005) *Science Fiction*, Cambridge: Polity.

Merrick, H. (2009) "The Female 'Atlas' of Science Fiction? Russ, feminism and the sf community," in F. Mendlesohn (ed.) *On Joanna Russ*, Middletown, CT: Wesleyan University Press.

Merril, J. (1966) "What Do You Mean: Science? Fiction?," *Extrapolation*, 7(2): 30–46.

—— (1967) "Books," *Fantasy and Science Fiction*, 33(5): 28–36.

Moorcock, M. (1964) "A New Literature for the Space Age," *New Worlds*, 142: 2–3.

—— (1966) "Ballard: the voice," *New Worlds*, 167: 2–3, 151.

—— (1979) "New Worlds: a personal history," *Foundation*, 15: 5–18.

Nicholls, P. (ed.) (1979) *The Encyclopedia of Science Fiction*, London: Granada.

Priest, C. (1978) "New Wave: a radical change in the 1960s," in R. Holdstock (ed.) *Encyclopedia of Science Fiction*, London: Octopus.

Roberts, A. (2006) *The History of Science Fiction*, London: Palgrave.

Russ, J. (1974) "The Image of Women in Science Fiction," *Vertex*, 1: 53–7.

Silverberg, R. (2001) "Reflections: the new wave," *Isaac Asimov's Science Fiction Magazine*, March: 4–8.

Smith, J.D. (ed.) (1975) *Symposium: women in science fiction, Khatru 3 & 4*, Baltimore, MD: Phantasmicon Press.

Sterling, B. (1986) "Introduction," in W. Gibson, *Burning Chrome*, London: Gollancz.

Sutherland, J.A. (1979) "American Science Fiction since 1960," in P. Parrinder (ed.) *Science Fiction: a critical guide*, London: Longman.

12
MANGA AND ANIME
Sharalyn Orbaugh

In both economic and cultural terms, manga and anime have become Japan's most significant artistic exports. Popular manga are translated into dozens of languages, and are available in bookshops throughout the developed world. Feature-length anime by well-known directors are commonly released worldwide, with Miyazaki Hayao's *Howl's Moving Castle* (2004), for example, grossing 27.5 billion yen (US$24 million) in 36 countries. Lesser-known anime films and television serials are downloaded and translated into local languages by a global network of fans, many being later commercially distributed on video or DVD with professional dubbing or subtitling. In 2005, the global market for anime reached 233.9 billion yen (US$2.1 billion). More significant, however, is the *cultural* impact of exported Japanese popular culture.

Since about 2000, the Japanese government has actively promoted the export of popular culture, in the belief that the "soft power" (Nye 2004) of cultural products might offset the consequences of over a decade of economic recession. (For example, manga and anime's popularity in East and Southeast Asia has brought large numbers of international students into Japanese universities just as decreasing domestic birthrates were threatening the survival of many institutions.) Given the contemporary global popularity and influence of manga and anime, it is significant that, from their first iterations, both media have frequently featured sf and fantasy themes; in fact, manga and anime have been fundamentally linked with the development of sf as a genre in Japan.

From the Meiji restoration to the Second World War: the beginnings of manga, anime and Japanese sf

The mid-nineteenth century marked the height of attempts by already modernized nations – Britain, the US, France, Russia – to colonize East Asia. In 1868, after nearly 250 years of isolation from the rest of the world under the *sakoku* (closed country) policy, Japan reopened to cultural and economic trade. Under Emperor Meiji, politicians and intellectuals began an intensive effort to modernize all aspects of society so as to avoid colonization. Key elements of modernity – including a strong military supported by the latest discoveries in medicine, discipline, and weaponry, and sophisticated transportation and communication systems to unite all parts of the nation

– were introduced. The Japanese government sent young men to Europe and the US to study the most cutting-edge technologies and the best systems for government and education. In just 50 years, Japan managed to equal and, in some areas, surpass the Anglo-European level of modernity. Two successful wars – against its huge neighbor China (1894–5), and against the even more powerful "European" nation of Russia (1904–5) – led to the beginnings of Japan's own empire: Taiwan (1895) and the Korean peninsula (1910). This display of military prowess saw Japan invited to join the Allied nations in the First World War, capturing and patrolling Micronesia and the small area of China previously colonized by Germany. This led, in turn, to an invitation to join the other victor nations as a founding member of the League of Nations in 1920 – a signal that, in the eyes of the West, Japan had achieved truly modern status. However, the League's refusal to consider Japan's proposal that the charter contain a statement of basic racial equality also clearly signaled that, as a "non-white" nation, Japan was still not considered an equal. This reminder of racial and ethnic prejudice had an enormous influence on the development of narrative culture, particularly in sf.

Another modernization tactic promoted in the Meiji period (1868–1912) was the translation of foreign books – works of fiction, as well as science and philosophy – into Japanese, which the *sakoku* policy had prohibited. One of the first foreign authors to become popular was Jules Verne (*Around the World in 80 Days* (1873) was translated in 1879, to great acclaim, followed by at least six more of his novels in the early 1880s). His science-based adventures appealed to a country trying to imagine its way into modernity, and the technological know-how and confident insouciance of his protagonists were soon replicated in Japanese popular fiction, such as Oshikawa Shunrô's 1900 *Undersea Warship* (*Kaitei gunkan*), which featured a submarine even more high-tech than Nemo's *Nautilus*.

Undersea Warship was typical of an important stream of pre-Second World War Japanese narrative, the adventure novel (*bôken shôsetsu*), which combined hardware technophilia with plots that usually involved patriotic, even jingoistic, actions to further Japan's power and reputation in the colonizing world. Titles such as Oshikawa's *Giant Flying Airship in the War Against Europe* (*Nichi-ô sensô kûchû daihikôtei*) suggest the tenor of the genre. A few decades later, as Japan began its military expansion into China and other regions of Asia, futuristic battle machines proliferated, in nationalistic-sounding adventure novels such as Yamanaka Minetarô's 1931 *Asian Dawn* (*Ajia no akebono*) and *Iron Men of the Great East* (*Daitô no tetsujin*). Many of these prewar adventure novels combined elements familiar to Western sf of the period, such as superweapons, with more romantic themes of Japanese men's unparalleled courage, purity, and gallantry.

Adventure novels were often serialized in the magazines for boys that arose in the first decades of the twentieth century, where they vied for space with the new popular medium of manga. The push for modernization had resulted in mass education and mass literacy, which in turn produced an audience for daily newspapers and magazines, which were increasingly aimed at specific demographic targets. In the late nineteenth century, national newspapers adopted the one- or two-frame political cartoons found in Western news media, but newer papers, aimed at working-class readers and children, soon began to include serialized manga, with a four-panel installment each day. Middle- and upper-class children enjoyed adventure-story manga in the magazines to which their families subscribed, such as *Boys' Club* (*Shônen kurabu*, launched in 1914) and *Girls' Club* (*Shôjo kurabu*, from 1923).

The word "manga" is made up of two *kanji* (ideographs) that mean "whimsical" and "picture." Although some trace the origins of manga to the twelfth century, the term itself was not coined until 1814, by Katsushika Hokusai, the woodblock print artist whose most famous work – a giant wave with Mt Fuji in the background – is well known internationally. Hokusai's manga, playful caricature prints, bear little resemblance to the current medium, but many of the print media in Hokusai's day did resemble today's manga in their vibrant combination of words and picture on one page. Susan Napier attributes manga's tremendous popularity in modern Japan to a longstanding cultural affinity for pictorial narrative (Napier 2005: 21). In the modern period, the label "manga" refers to a variety of printed genres that combine dialogue and pictures to produce a narrative. In fact, but unlike the similar comic strips, comic books, and graphic novels of other countries, manga sometimes include few or no words at all.

After the introduction of cartoon-type manga in the early twentieth century, the medium exploded in breadth and popularity. Manga serials were included in all types of print media, for all ages and classes. Although still (mis)identified with children and the lower classes, manga soon covered such a range of genres and degrees of seriousness that virtually any reader's taste could be satisfied. In the 1930s, popular manga serials were collected into book form, and these *akabon* (literally "red book") manga allowed fans to read large doses of their favorite narratives at one time instead of waiting for daily, weekly, or monthly installments. The 1930s also saw significant connections drawn between science and manga in the increasingly popular technology and engineering magazines for children and teenagers. Despite their serious educational (and militarist) tone, they invariably included manga pages, blurring the distinction between the scientific/practical and the entertaining/unproductive. In this pre-television age, manga were rivaled in mass-market popularity only by the movies, but were far more accessible to a wide range of ages and classes.

The rapid rise of print media was paralleled by the rapid importation and promotion of film: less than two years after the 1894 unveiling of Edison's Kinetoscope in New York, it had made its way to the city of Kobe; in 1897, two years after its premiere in Paris, the Lumière Brothers' Cinématographe exhibited films in Osaka; and in 1899, the first Japanese film was made (Ritchie 2001: 17). The first Japanese film company, Nikkatsu, was started in 1912, followed by Shôchiku in 1920. In 1921, urban Japanese listed the movies as their favorite form of entertainment.

From about 1914, short animated films were also imported to Japan. These included Russian and East European puppet animation and US cel animation (Tsugata 2004: 210–11). The origins of anime can be traced to 1917, when the first domestically produced animated film – Shimokawa Hekoten's five-minute *Imokawa Mukuzô, The Doorman* (*Imokawa Mukuzô genkanban no maki*), drawn with ink directly on the film

– was shown. Later that year at least three other animated films – by Shimokawa, Kitayama Seitarô, and Kouchi Jun'ichi – were released. In 1918 Kitayama's *The Tale of the Peach Boy* (*Momotarô*), based on a folktale, became Japan's first commercially successful animated film and the first animated film to be shown abroad, in France (Kusanagi 2003: 31). By the early 1930s, Japanese animators were working in a variety of forms – puppet, cut-paper, cel animation – and production standards were high. An increasing number of feature-length fiction narratives were produced, in many cases echoing the adventure stories for boys that included technophilic sf elements.

Manga, film animation, and sf thus all had roots in the Meiji period's drive for modernity, military power, and empire. It is not surprising, therefore, that both manga and animation were used extensively for propaganda purposes from the mid-1930s until 1945. In fact, with the intensification of Japan's war in China in the late 1930s, strict censorship made it impossible for manga artists or film directors to produce anything that was not explicitly supportive of government policy.

From the Second World War to the present: the manga boom, the sf boom, and the transformation of "Japanimation" into "anime"

In 1942, following Japan's bombing of Pearl Harbor and the US entry into the Pacific war, a group of Japanese intellectuals from various disciplines met in Kyoto to debate how best to overcome such a vast and well-equipped enemy: were science and technology inherently Western, and therefore not suited for use in a sacred imperial war? Or were the science and technology, so successfully imported and adapted since 1868, Japan's only hope? While the majority argued that it was the *Yamato damashii* (the "unique" Japanese spirit) that would save the nation, some contended that science was beneficial, and not in conflict with the Japanese spirit. The basic elements of this debate have configured Japanese sf ever since.

By the end of the war, militarized science had devastated Japan. At least 66 cities had been repeatedly bombed by Allied planes: more than 65 percent of Tokyo residences were destroyed by incendiary bombs; Osaka had lost 57 percent of its buildings; and Nagoya, 89 percent. On 9 March 1945, 2,000 tons of incendiaries leveled 16 square miles of Tokyo and killed at least 80,000 people. In the next 10 days, more than 1,500 sorties saw over 9,000 tons of bombs (2 million bombs) dropped on Tokyo, Osaka, Nagoya, and Kobe. Relentless further sorties eventually killed about 500,000 civilians and left roughly 15 million more homeless. Finally, on 6 August, the atomic bomb dropped on Hiroshima killed approximately 100,000 civilians; and, three days later, the Nagasaki bomb killed a further 70,000. The emperor's surrender speech referred to these new mysterious weapons, capable of destroying all humanity.

One result of this massive destruction was a reservoir of hideous images of what long-range technology could do to the human body. It is not surprising that so much of postwar Japanese culture addresses issues of science and its long-term effects. What is surprising, however, is that so much Japanese sf depicts technology with nuance and complexity, noting its favorable aspects as well as its dangers.

In the first few years after the war, as people struggled simply to find enough to eat and to rebuild their cities, popular cultural products such as print media and film were hard to come by. But in 1947, in Osaka, Tezuka Osamu published his long short story *New Treasure Island* (*Shin-Takarajima*) in manga form. It was an instant hit. Tezuka moved to Tokyo and the postwar manga boom – which favored long narratives published in single, cheaply bound volumes over the short strip of a few panels – began. By January 1949, 6,000 such single-volume stories had been produced.

By the mid-1950s, with the economy recovering, large publishers in Tokyo created a new genre of boys' and girls' magazines devoted exclusively to manga, including several stories by different artists in each issue. As manga stories grew longer, they had to be serialized, as in the monthly *Ribbon* for girls, launched in 1955, which is also representative of other significant developments of the 1950s – the demographic segmentation of the market for popular culture products. Those children who had grown up reading manga wanted to continue doing so as teenagers and adults, and new manga magazines emerged to fill those niches. Also in the 1950s a new genre of narrative comic for adults appeared, called *gekiga* (literally "dramatic pictures"). *Gekiga* featured more realistic drawing styles and complex narratives, often including violent or explicitly erotic content. Initially, *gekiga* were rarely available for sale, but could be found at *kashihon'ya*, stores that lent books to patrons for a fee. Citizen's groups voiced concern about the brutality and immorality of some *gekiga* stories, but with little real effect as the *kashihon'ya* system ensured that they were generally accessible only to older teenagers and adults.

In the 1960s, double-digit economic growth, relative social stability, and the postwar baby-boom population supported a surge in all popular culture media: television, magazines, comic books, and film. A number of weekly (rather than monthly) manga magazines were launched, such as *Boys' Jump* (*Shônen Jump*, from 1968), and found a ready audience. With people of all ages regularly reading manga, the distinction between manga for adults and for children blurred. *Gekiga* started to appear in mainstream manga magazines for adolescents and adults, and some children's manga took on *gegika*'s more realistic visual style and graphic storylines.

From a Western perspective, one of the remarkable aspects of contemporary manga is the extraordinary range of themes, genres, and drawing styles, a phenomenon that began in the 1960s. And as this variety proliferated, sf manga also flourished. In 1949, for example, one of the first great stars of manga, Tezuka Osamu, released a multi-volume manga, based on what he had heard about *Metropolis* (Lang 1927), which he claimed never to have seen. Like the film, Tezuka's *Metropolis* featured a feminine-looking robot created by a mad scientist deep in the heart of a multilayered city, but because of its length Tezuka's manga became much more complex, exploring issues of gender (and gender-switching, since the robot has a built-in sex-change button), class, the instability and injustice of the line that divides organic from artificial creatures, and – echoing Japan's recent wartime experience – the teleology of utter destruction. (In 2001, Rintarô adapted it as an anime movie.)

As the economy went into overdrive in the 1960s and 1970s, media technologies such as television began to enter every home. Animation techniques perfected in the film industry were transposed to the high-pressure, low-budget realities of television production, resulting in a recognizable style known outside Japan as "Japanimation." Tezuka was one of the first masters of "Japanimation," often turning his own manga into animated films or television shows. Arguably his most influential sf creation was *Astro Boy* (*Tetsuwan atomu*), who originally appeared in a manga serial that began in 1951 and ran in the boy's manga magazine *Young Man* (*Shônen*) for 18 years. In 1963 Tezuka turned *Astro Boy* into Japan's first animated television series; in the following year it became the first Japanese television series shown in the US.

Created by a mad scientist grieving for his dead son, Astro Boy had a fission reactor for a "heart" and machine guns in his hips. Nonetheless, he embodied innocence, bravery, and morality. He battled evil robots, saving the earth weekly in increasingly violent confrontations, before finally flying into the sun to save humanity. Like Godzilla, who debuted in the live-action *Gojira* (Honda 1954), Astro Boy presents a complex mix of the good and the bad ramifications of scientific progress. "Bad" science – US nuclear testing in the South Pacific – produced Godzilla and sent him on his destructive rampage, but only "good" science – made benevolent and pure by the self-immolation of the Japanese scientist – can defeat him. Similarly, Astro Boy's creation appears to be for "good" reasons – to soothe a grieving father – but turns out to be "bad" science intended merely to satisfy the father's emotional greed. When Astro Boy proves not to be an exact replica of the lost son and his creator–father sells him to a circus, science would seem to be producing "bad" results, but Astro Boy's generous and courageous character leads him to use his technological powers for "good," further purified by his eventual self-immolation.

The tensions here are between technoscience as a useful servant or the source of humanity's destruction; between the weak and fallible human spirit and the self-sacrificing human spirit which can turn science to good ends. These tensions drive a huge number of sf plots in postwar Japan, especially in the "techno-animist" subgenre. Similar to the jingoistic prewar narrative mix of hardware and the Japanese spirit, techno-animism incorporates mythical, often mystical, elements from Japan's traditional culture into futuristic narratives. Generally more ideologically complex than its prewar precursor, it still sometimes serves as a vehicle for neo-nationalist stories.

The fact that Tezuka worked in both manga and animation calls attention to a remarkable aspect of postwar popular culture in Japan: media working together rather than competing. The most common path is for a narrative to start out as a serialized manga and, after proving its popularity, to be remade into an animated television series, and later remade again into one or more feature films, or released in the popular OAV ("original animated video") for purchase or rental. For example, the 26-episode sf series *Neon Genesis Evangelion* was broadcast every Wednesday night from October 1995 to March 1996 on Tokyo TV Channel 12; later it was condensed into a theatrically released feature-length film. Some popular anime television shows release a theatrical film each year; other feature-length films are based on original stories that did not previously air on television. In many cases, the animated versions do not supplant the manga, which continues publication, and occasionally a story may be launched simultaneously in manga and animated versions.

Media scholars have pointed out the "cinematic" aspects of manga visuals, which incorporate a great deal of frame deformation or pictures that break out of their frames altogether, spilling across the page. Similarly, animation is a medium that allows for the depiction of things that do not and cannot actually exist. Long before the current masterpieces of cinematic special effects were possible, the "morphotic" aspect of animation allowed for the integration of radically transformed bodies and landscapes, making it especially suitable as a vehicle for sf and other fantasy or speculative narrative (Wells 2002: 15). It is therefore unsurprising that in Japan, where the "morphotic" media of manga and animation achieved such popularity, sf narratives should have reached levels of great sophistication and depth.

While television Japanimation of the 1960s and 1970s attained a measure of recognition in North America and Europe, it was not until the 1980s that Japanese animation began to claim a global audience. The sophistication and appeal of Japanese animated narrative products, regardless of media form, inspired a new respect, marked by the worldwide adoption of the Japanese term for these products: anime.

The word "anime" (a Japanese contraction of the English word "animation") currently refers to animated films, videos, and television shows associated with and usually produced in Japan. In these days of global anime fandom, an increasing number of non-Japanese animators have begun producing anime-style animations, so that the word may eventually lose its cultural exclusivity. Anime is distinguished from non-Japanese animation largely through its distinctive visual style. It is generally "flatter" than standard Disney or Pixar animation. To some extent a function of low budgets and tight production schedules, this two-dimensionality can also be seen in sophisticated stories with lushly detailed background scenes. For example, Oshii Mamoru's *Ghost in the Shell* (1995) is a complex, challenging sf film about cyborg subjectivity, aimed at an adult audience. The animation is dense and the production quality very high, but the visual depiction of the characters is flat, especially when compared with recent computer-generated films, such as *Shrek* (Adamson and Jenson 2001). Rather than a shortcoming of Japanese animation techniques, scholars and fans argue that this aesthetic is intentional, that it underscores the links between manga and anime and is a fundamental part of anime's appeal.

Major works and themes in sf manga and anime

Japanese sf shares many elements, themes, and narrative tropes with sf from other cultures – time travel, robots/androids/cyborgs, genetic mutations, spaceships, extra-terrestrials, imagined alternative presents or futures, high-tech weaponry, and so on – but national and cultural particularity has also led to a preference for some themes or genres that may be comparatively rare elsewhere. The following is a sketch of some of the most characteristic elements of sf manga and anime. (In many instances, the same story will be revived numerous times in its original medium, remade into films or OAVs, inspire a new spin-off manga, and so on. For example, the basic narrative universe of *Gundam* has been made into at least 14 television series and two feature-length films, and has inspired videogames, manga series, and novels. The dates listed, therefore, denote only the first appearance of a particular narrative in a particular medium.)

One conspicuous subgenre of Japanese sf is the romantic or slapstick comedy, often incorporating elements for both children and adults. The perennial favorite, *Dr Slump* (manga 1980, anime 1981), for example, features the child-oriented look of "gag" manga/anime, plus wacky stories, silly puns, and lots of slapstick, but also includes a female android, Arale-chan, and incessant scientific experimentation (such as cloning), as well as many sexual references aimed at adults. Another television anime, popular all over Asia, is *Doraemon* (anime 1973), featuring a robot cat who is sent back from the future to help a dweebish boy, Nobi Nobita, pull himself together so that his future descendants will have a better life. While marketed primarily to children, adults from Japan and elsewhere confess a continuing devotion to the show because of its sympathy toward weakness and failure.

Other comedic manga/anime feature a campy tone and girls in skimpy outfits to appeal to a teenage and young adult (mostly male) audience, including some of the series that have achieved the greatest popularity outside Japan: *Cutey Honey* (manga and anime 1973), featuring a voluptuous female-shaped android who is constantly changing clothes (allowing glimpses of nudity) in order to take on the appropriate fighting persona for the situation (always, not coincidentally, a persona with a sexy outfit – cowgirl, go-go dancer, etc.); *Urusei Yatsura* (manga 1978, anime 1981), about a gorgeous alien girl dressed only in a bikini chasing a hapless teenaged boy distinguished primarily by his lechery; *Dirty Pair* (anime 1985) starring two female officers in the Galactic Government's police force, who also dress only in bikinis as they chase down miscreants; and the more recent *Catgirl Nukunuku* (anime 1992) and *Sailor Moon* (manga 1991, anime 1992). Despite the inclusion of elements explicitly intended to appeal to heterosexual boys and young men, all of the above-mentioned stories were also popular among young women. One of the sources of Japanese popular culture's appeal outside Japan lies in the complexity and frequent dark tones included in even the silliest or most charming of stories. As Susan Napier points out, anime is a medium of "de-assurance" rather than reassurance, and this is no doubt one of the reasons for Japanese sf romantic comedy's global success (Napier 2005: 33).

There are also an enormous number of sf stories with challenging, adult-oriented themes. One motif that has persisted since the Meiji period adventure novels is an obsession with fighting, often giant robots and "mecha-suits" – robot-shaped suits of high-tech armor worn by, or piloted by, humans. Nuclear-powered Astro Boy was one of the first of these benevolent fighting robots, followed closely by *Gigantor* (*Tetsujin 28-go*, literally *Iron Man no. 28*; manga 1956, anime 1963), a huge intelligent flying robot directed by remote control. Gigantor was built during the Second World War to help Japan defeat the Allies, but was never used. Hidden away, Gigantor is discovered by the son of its late inventor, a detective who decides to use it to defend peace. Like Astro Boy, Gigantor's backstory has close ties to the issues debated most passionately during the war: the proper place of science/technology in a society devoted to humanist values. This is very appropriate, as Yokoyama Mitsuteru credits his inspiration for the manga to the sight of an enemy warplane flying across the Japanese sky in the Second World War. Both Tezuka and Yokoyama took frightening US-associated wartime images and transformed them into powerful Japanese warriors for peace and justice.

Astro Boy and Gigantor were two of the earliest manga/anime to showcase robots, but the subgenre became more adult-oriented in later years, in stories featuring mecha-suits and battle armor such as *Gundam* (anime 1979), *Macross* (anime 1982), *Dangaiô* (anime 1987), *Appleseed* (1988), *Patlabor I* and *II* (anime films (Oshii 1990 and 1993)), *Detonator Organ* (anime 1991), and *Evangelion* (anime 1995). This subgenre frequently emphasizes the importance of teamwork over individual heroics, and often depicts the necessity for the protagonist to let go of his or her ego-autonomy or body boundaries in order to synchronize properly with the mecha-suit or battle armor. In *Dangaiô*, for example, four pilots must perfectly synchronize with their planes and with each other in order to combine to create a huge fighting machine. Throughout the history of modern Japan, teamwork and the willingness to sacrifice some of one's individuality to mesh with others have been touted as important values, particularly since the 1960s, when hard work and self-sacrifice for the sake of the (national) team was said to be necessary for Japan's economic success.

In some later works, however, the ability to synchronize with one's suit goes too far, and is depicted as terrifying, reflecting increasing social discomfort with the oppressive nature of the drive for economic success that consumed the nation in the 1960s and 1970s. In *Guyver* (manga 1985, anime 1989), for example, the protagonist's body is physically invaded by alien body armor – tentacles penetrate his skin and orifices – which then turns him into a benevolent, powerful cyborg able to save his friends. Nonetheless, he is distraught at this body-invasion and his inability to expel the invading component, which retreats into a small area of his back most of the time, but takes over his whole body again when he is provoked to fight. *Rôjin Z* (anime film (Kitakubo 1991)), *Detonator Organ*, and *Evangelion* depict equally disturbing examples of bodies penetrated by or completely absorbed into body armor or other machines. Significantly, in each of these cases, the human in question is male. The fear of one's body or ego being violently penetrated is no doubt universal, but it is notable that many narratives in the postwar period feature machine–human hybrids without underscoring the horror of such a state. In these cases, the human body is almost always female (or female-shaped), and the interpenetration of body and machine is depicted as inevitable, an already accomplished state.

Donna Haraway (1991) and N. Katherine Hayles (1999) declare that we are all already posthuman cyborgs. Japanese sf, especially in anime, explores the anxieties and hopes accompanying the recognition that humans are transitioning inexorably into a new state of being. Anime that try to imagine the ramifications of our increasing fusion with machines include *Cyborg 009* (manga 1964, anime film (Serikawa 1966), anime 1968), *Bubblegum Crisis* (anime 1987), *AD Police* (anime 1990), *Appleseed*, *Battle Angel* (*Gunmu*, anime 1993), *Evangelion*, *Cyber Six* (anime 1999), and a series of films by critically acclaimed director Oshii Mamoru: *Patlabor I*, *Patlabor II*, *Ghost in the Shell* (manga 1991, anime film 1995), and *Ghost in the Shell 2: Innocence* (anime film 2004). These narratives play out various issues at the heart of cyborg subjectivity:

how much organic material is necessary to consider a being "human"? What are the juridical ramifications of bodies that incorporate less and less organic material? Do cyborgs reproduce or are they replicated, and what are the implications for human understandings of our own ontology? What does it mean to be male or female in a world in which body parts are interchangeable? Is human emotion possible in a world in which bodies are no longer containers for the mind/soul? Because of the huge number of narratives that address such questions, it could be argued that the nature and consequences of our transformation from the human to the cyborg is explored more thoroughly in Japanese popular culture than in any other venue. And it is significant to note again that the subjectivity of the cyborg is most often explored from a sympathetic, interior view. Rather than a frightening and disgusting monster, the human/technology hybrid is usually depicted as a being whose "monstrosity" is a function of its difference from intolerant others – a situation not unlike the one in which Japanese people found themselves after the 1920 League of Nations incident.

Many cyborg narratives include an element of gender-bending, questioning or simply dispensing with the differences in sexed bodies that are thought to divide male from female. For example, *Cyber Six*'s protagonist is a genetically enhanced warrior, who has a voluptuously feminine body in her fighting persona, but a male body when s/he returns to her Clark Kentish incognito persona. In *Ghost in the Shell*, the protagonist, Kusanagi Motoko, opens the narrative by complaining about her period but, as we soon discover, her body is completely artificial, and certainly does not bleed. Manufactured to serve the needs of the special government police force that employs her, her body is therefore not equipped with physical mechanisms to provide either the pain (such as in menstruation) or pleasure of the sexed body.

Gender-bending and/or the depiction of alternative sexualities is an important element of a number of sf narratives that do not feature cyborgs, such as *Metropolis*, *Sailor Moon*, and *Battle Angel*. While this is a time-honored and well-accepted aspect of Japanese popular culture, it is often considered too controversial or weird in a North American context, and is edited out of anime imported for television broadcast.

Finally, one of the most prevalent themes of Japanese sf is a fascination with apocalypse, which is, in some cases, narrowly averted – *Nadesico* (manga and anime 1996), *Astro Boy* – and in others features as the culmination of the narrative – *Metropolis*, *X* (anime film (Rintarô 1996)), *Hi no Tori* (*The Phoenix*, manga 1967), *Akira* (manga 1982, anime film (Ôtomo 1988)), and *Evangelion*. Other stories explore the dystopic aftermaths of apocalypse, such as *Nausicaa of the Valley of the Wind* (manga 1982, anime film (Miyazaki 1984)) and *To Terra* (manga 1977, anime film (Onchi 1980)). Like many of the aforementioned themes of postwar popular culture, a concern with apocalypse derives in large measure from Japan's experience of the Second World War and the atomic bombings. The morphotic nature of manga and anime makes them the perfect media vehicles for sf narratives in which the unthinkable, almost unrepresentable, event of total destruction is depicted.

Japanese sf manga and anime share many elements with sf from other media and cultures. However, Japanese sf also includes thematic and ideological elements, or particular points of view, that derive from the specific history of modern Japan and its relations with other nations in an explicitly international context, a fact that may explain its ever-growing popularity in an increasingly globalized world.

Bibliography

Haraway, D.J. (1991) "A Cyborg Manifesto: science, technology, and socialist-feminism in the late twentieth century," in *Simians, Cyborgs and Women: the reinvention of nature*, London: Free Association.

Hayles, N.K. (1999) *How We Became Posthuman: virtual bodies in cybernetics, literature and informatics*, Chicago and London: University of Chicago Press.

Kusanagi Satoshi (2003) *Amerika de Nihon no anime wa dou mirarete kita ka? (How Has Japanese Anime Been Seen in America?)*, Tokyo: Tokuma shoten.

Napier, S. (2005) *Anime: from Akira to Howl's Moving Castle*, New York: Palgrave.

Nye, J. (2004) *Soft Power: the means to success in world politics*, New York: Public Affairs.

Ritchie, D. (2001) *A Hundred Years of Japanese Film*, Tokyo, New York, and London: Kodansha International.

Tsugata Nobuyuki (2004) *Nihon anime no chikara (The Power of Japanese Anime)*, Tokyo: NTT shuppan.

Wells, P. (2002) *Animation: genre and authorship*, London: Wallflower Press.

13
SILVER AGE COMICS

Jim Casey

Michael Uslan traces the phrase "Silver Age of Comics" back to the letters column of *Justice League of America* no. 42 (February 1966), in which Scott Taylor of Westport, Connecticut wrote, "If you guys keep bringing back the heroes from the Golden Age, people 20 years from now will be calling this decade the Silver Sixties!":

> Fans immediately glommed onto this, refining it more directly into a Silver Age version of the Golden Age. Very soon, it was in our vernacular, replacing such expressions as Jerry Bails' ponderous "Second Heroic Age of Comics" or "The Modern Age" of comics. It wasn't too long before dealers were differentiating their sale of, say, *Green Lantern* #3 by specifying it was a Golden Age comic for sale or a Silver Age comic for sale.
>
> (Uslan 2005: 79)

Although other developments in the comic world, such as the work of Moebius (Jean Giraud) in France or Britain's *2000 AD* (1977–), intersect with those of the period, the Silver Age was primarily an American phenomenon, marked by a dramatic resurgence of superhero comics. Old heroes were revamped, sf origins were added, and more "realistic" characters and storytelling became the standard. To understand the Silver Age (and the reemergence of the superhero), however, one must go back more than 10 years before the term was first used.

In 1954, psychiatrist Dr Fredric Wertham published his scathing denunciation of the comics industry. Relying on undocumented, mostly anecdotal, evidence and Wertham's own expert opinion, *Seduction of the Innocent* stated that "chronic stimulation, temptation and seduction by comic books, both their content and their alluring advertisements of knives and guns, are contributing factors to many children's maladjustment" (Wertham 1972: 10). As he had done at numerous public appearances and governmental hearings, Wertham asserted that comic books were damaging the "mental hygiene" of the nation's youth, turning children and adolescents into violent, delinquent, illiterate, "sex-maniacs." Although "academically unsound," prompting numerous contemporary psychiatrists to dispute its claims, "its sensationalism ... and its author's evangelical zeal" were nevertheless "enough to inspire widespread moral panic" (Sabin 1996: 68).

To avoid government censorship, comic-book publishers opted for self-regulation. In 1954, the Comics Magazine Association of America created the Comics Code Authority, headed by former New York magistrate Charles F. Murphy. The CCA established and enforced stringent industry regulations, including prohibitions forbidding references to sex, challenges to authority, depictions of criminal methods, or representations of blood and gore, torture, physical agony, gruesome crime, or the walking dead, such as vampires, ghouls, or werewolves. It "was a setback for the art of comics, which was forced into essentially infantile patterns when its potential for maturity had only begun to be explored" (McAllister 1990: 62).

With the CCA's curtailment of acceptable subjects, the diversity of American comics narrowed and narrowed, until many publishers were driven out of business. Of the roughly 500 different titles vying for the public's attention in 1952, barely 300 remained by 1955 (Goulart 1991: 217). Crime and horror comics, Wertham's primary targets, were particularly affected by CCA restrictions, such as the specific ban on the use of "weird," "crime," "horror," or "terror" in a comic's title. For many publishers, this proscription impacted a significant proportion of their output; for example, "The monthly sales of Lev Gleason's [primarily crime comics] titles fell from 2,700,000 in 1952 to around 800,000 in 1956" (Goulart 1991: 217). Many publishers abandoned comics altogether, instead printing their magazines in the larger, black-and-white format not governed by the Code. EC Comics (Entertaining Comics, formerly Educational Comics), for instance, garnered pre-Silver Age success primarily through their horror and crime stories, although owner William Gaines claimed in 1969 that "EC was proudest of its science fiction comics," which freely borrowed and adapted (often without crediting their sources) from the works of mystery, sf, and fantasy authors such as Edgar Allan Poe, John Collier, Nelson Bond, Anthony Boucher, Fredric Brown, Otto Binder, and Ray Bradbury (Inge 1990: 118–20). After the creation of the CCA, however, EC eventually discontinued crime, horror, and sf comics and concentrated on the satirical comedy of its *Mad* magazine (1952–). Its tremendous popularity saved EC, but many companies were not so lucky: "By 1962, less than a dozen publishers accounted for a total annual industry output of 350 million comic books, a drop of over 50 percent from the previous decade" (Wright 2001: 182).

Of course, the Comics Code and the difficulties created by self-regulation were not the only factors leading to the comic-book recession. Serious distribution problems followed the collapse of the American News Company (half of all US homes had a television set by 1953) and posed a "serious and long-term problem" (Wright 2001: 181). Ironically, though, television may be credited with aiding the survival of comic books, specifically superhero comics. DC (at the time "Detective Comics" and published by National Periodical Publications) "weathered the challenge ... better than its competitors, primarily because of the popular *Adventures of Superman* television show [1952–8], which kept DC's flagship character highly visible and caused an entire generation to associate Superman with actor George Reeves. The Superman comic books seemed immune from recession, consistently selling around a million copies per issue" (Wright 2001: 182). Other than Superman, however, superhero comics had languished since the end of the Golden Age. Before the 1950s were over, Timely Comics had cancelled publication of even their most popular superhero comics, discontinuing *Captain America Comics* at issue no. 75 (February 1950), *Marvel Mystery Comics*, starring the Human Torch, at no. 92 (June 1949), and *Sub-Mariner Comics* at no. 32 (1949). When Atlas Comics (previously Timely, soon to be Marvel) attempted to revive the heroes in *Young Men* nos. 24–8 (December 1953–June 1954), *Captain America* nos. 76–8 (May–September 1954), and *The Human Torch* nos. 36–8 (April–August 1953), these Golden Age characters were too old-fashioned to survive more than a few issues each.

In 1956, DC editor Julius Schwartz reinvigorated superhero comics with his reintroduction of the Flash in *Showcase* no. 4 (October 1956). Rather than simply reinstate the old hero, he completely revamped the 1940s character. The Golden Age Flash, Jay Garrick, was a college student who had accidentally inhaled hard water vapors (later retconned – that is, altered to create a "retroactive continuity" – to heavy water vapors). He wore a red shirt emblazoned with a lightning bolt and sported a First World War Brodie helmet with wings (based on Hermes/Mercury's winged petasos helmet). The new Flash was police scientist Barry Allen, who acquired super-speed after he was simultaneously struck by lightning and doused with a mysterious chemical combination. His costume consisted of a red tights-and-cowl bodysuit, with a small lightning bolt on his chest and no helmet.

DC attempted to replicate the new *Flash* comic's success by reimagining other Golden Age characters. In 1959, Schwartz reinvented the Green Lantern, turning him into test pilot Hal Jordan, who became a member of the Green Lantern Corps (an intergalactic police force) after receiving a power ring from a dying extraterrestrial. New versions followed of Hawkman and his wife, Hawkgirl, winged police officers from planet Thanagar, and the Atom, a shrinkable scientist named Ray Palmer. In *The Brave and the Bold* no. 28 (February–March 1960), DC first featured these new superheroes alongside their Golden Age teammates – Batman, Superman, Wonder Woman – as the Justice League of America. Despite their new origins, however, they were not particularly revolutionary, mostly mirroring the attributes of their Golden Age counterparts. As Wright notes, "DC's comics were the image of affluent America. Handsome superheroes resided in clean, green suburbs and modern, even futuristic, cities with shimmering glass skyscrapers, no slums, and populations of uniformly well-dressed white people. There was nothing ambiguous about the hero's character, cause, or inevitable triumph"; this remarkably homogenous and unambiguous world was at odds with the real 1960s (Wright 2001: 184). Like Dell or Charlton Publishing, DC's "condescending perspective on young people" presented comics as reinforcing "appropriate values" *in loco parentis* – they were "slipping behind the times," failing "to speak to the social and emotional disorientation of young people. For an audience that demanded the empathy of peers, these comic books offered only the measured explanations of elders" (Wright 2001: 199, 201).

Gilberton Publishing already offered comics designed to deal with the concerns of adults rather than the issues and anxieties of young adults. The popularity of their Comics Code-exempt *Classics Illustrated*, which adapted literary classics into a comic-book format, peaked during the immediate post-code period (Sabin 1996: 76), yet many of these comics were purchased by parents rather than children. The market begged for stories and heroes more relevant to young readers. Superman was great, but what boy or girl could truly relate to him?

At Atlas Comics (soon to be Marvel), publisher Martin Goodman, noting the success of *Justice League of America*, directed comics editor Stan Lee to create a similar superhero team. Rather than simply duplicate DC's formula, he set out to create "realistic fantasy" (Lee 1974: 16, 73). Assisted by artist Jack Kirby, he transformed the superhero and the comics industry with the publication of *The Fantastic Four* no. 1 (November 1961). Beginning with its third issue, Marvel promoted *The Fantastic Four* as "The World's Greatest Comic Book" – and "for almost a decade during the 1960s it might well have been true" (Bettley 2001: 131). Unlike other superheroes, the Fantastic Four were unique, fallible, and human. Whereas DC superheroes all arguably had "essentially the same personality" (Wright 2001: 185), the Fantastic Four were individuals, each with differing values, goals, and objectives. Famously, the team fought themselves as often as they faced supervillains. In issue no. 3 (March 1962), Mr Fantastic asks, "Why must we always fight among ourselves? What's wrong with us?" Unlike their DC counterparts, the Marvel team faced real-world challenges: they bickered with one another, had difficulty shopping for clothes, had problems controlling their powers, and even had trouble paying the bills. In issue no. 9 (December 1962), after losing all their money when the stock market falls, Mr Fantastic laments, "If only we could be like the super heroes in some of these comic magazines, Sue! They never seem to worry about money! Life is a breeze for them!" The implication was clear: DC's characters were neither a part of nor relevant to the real world.

In contrast, not only did Marvel superheroes live in real US cities and interact with real people – in *The Fantastic Four* no. 10 (January 1963), Lee and Kirby appear in their own comic, speaking with both the team and the supervillain, Dr Doom – they also faced real problems and dealt with real issues. Unlike the confident, righteous, logical DC heroes, the Fantastic Four were not perfect. In fact, the very existence of their superpowers resulted from the miscalculations of their leader, Reed Richards. Had he conducted the necessary tests, he might have known that the shielding on the team's rocket was insufficient, but he rushed its launch so as to beat the communists into space. Consequently, the crew-members were bombarded by cosmic rays which altered their atomic structure, turning Richards into the elastic Mr Fantastic, Susan Storm into the Invisible Girl, Johnny Storm into the Human Torch, and Ben Grimm into the Thing. Grimm's anger and Richards's guilt regarding the accident continued to surface in the early issues, and combined with Johnny Storm's impetuousness and Sue Storm's romantic confusion over the Sub-Mariner to produce continual interpersonal conflict.

The essentially flawed nature of Marvel's superheroes was fundamental to Lee and Kirby's vision. "Perfect heroes are boring to the reader," Kirby explains, "they've got to have human frailties to keep the story interesting" (Wyman 1992: 106). Perhaps the most interesting of these new heroes was the Thing (see Figure 13.1). Orange-

Figure 13.1   The Thing (FANTASTIC FOUR: TM & © 2008 Marvel Characters, Inc. Used with permission.)

skinned and covered with rock-like scales, he was called "gruesome," "freak," even "monster" by friend and foe alike. In issue no. 3, Richards tells him, "Fate has been good to us, Ben! We've been able to use our powers to help mankind ... to fight evil and injustice!" To which Grimm responds, "Sure! It's been great for you! But what about me! I'm just a walkin' fright! An ugly, gruesome Thing!" The self-pitying creature's greatest desire was to be not a superhero but rather a normal human being. Although part of the team, he was an outsider, relegated to the fringe of society by his inhuman appearance. The pathos of the Thing's alienation struck a chord with readers, and Marvel quickly capitalized on their surprise hit with a string of reluctant heroes.

Lee and Kirby's next title, *The Incredible Hulk* no. 1 (May 1962), continued the themes of monstrosity and social ostracism, while demonstrating the creativity and adaptability that was integral to Marvel's success. As with *The Fantastic Four*, the publication co-opted various sf elements of the late Golden Age, exploiting the interests of its creators, especially Kirby, who boasted, "I've been a student of science fiction for a long, long time, and I can tell you that I'm very well-versed in science fact and science fiction" (Groth 1990: 92). But Hulk's origin story, like that of the Fantastic Four, also exemplified Marvel's wary exploration of scientific advancement. Rather than celebrating the wonders of technology, the comic warned of its concomitant dangers, telling the story of physicist Dr Bruce Banner, who became a modern-day Jekyll and Hyde after being exposed to the blast of his own gamma bomb. As Wright observes, this cautionary attitude toward science was unique to Marvel: "While DC used sci-fi to exalt the virtues of scientific progress and the certainty of peace through technology, Marvel spoke to the anxieties of the atomic age" (Wright 2001: 202). This ambivalence manifested itself again in Marvel's next hero, Spider-Man.

Robert Harvey believes Marvel's Silver Age heroes, particularly the Fantastic Four, were "more likely Kirby's creations than Lee's" (Harvey 1996: 45) and Kirby himself has claimed he invented Spider-Man (an assertion that Lee flatly denies (Salicrup *et al.* 1983: 37)). Certainly Kirby's artwork and plotting greatly contributed to the popularity of Silver Age Marvel comics, and Lee was well known for having artists work from the roughest of outlines, only later adding the dialogue to the finished product (a process now called the "Marvel Method"). But Lee's dynamic prose, creative input, and overall direction dramatically shaped each of Marvel's new super-heroes, and this is nowhere more apparent than with Spider-Man, Marvel's all-time most popular character. Lee began with the intention of fashioning a superhero specif-ically designed to appeal to Marvel's burgeoning teen audience, imagining a young man who "would lose out as often as he'd win – in fact, more often" (Lee 1974: 133). Lee obtained Goodman's permission to debut the character in *Amazing Fantasy* no. 15 (August 1962), the last issue of that scheduled-for-cancellation title. He then met with Kirby, who suggested adapting the Silver Spider, an unused character he and Joe Simon had developed in the 1950s. Lee approved, but when Kirby presented the first six sample pages he was displeased. Instead of a "skinny young kid with spider powers," Kirby had created "Captain America with cobwebs" (Simon with Simon 2003: 203). Kirby's Spider-Man was not normal enough for Lee: "I hated the way he was doing it. Not that he did it badly – it just wasn't the character I wanted; it was too heroic" (Theakston 2002: n.p.); he handed the assignment to Steve Ditko, who had originally been slated to ink the issue. Ditko completely reworked the character, abandoning Kirby's plot and the Silver Spider-based persona. He dropped the ideas for a magic ring, goggles, and web-gun, and added the costume, web-shooters, and spider symbol. Most importantly, he retained Lee's concept of a teenaged superhero who looked normal, perhaps even a bit scrawny. Teenagers had long been popular as sidekicks or comic relief, but it was a stroke of genius to turn one of them into the main hero. Whereas very few readers could identify with a flying alien, an Amazon princess, or a millionaire, all of them could, or soon would, identify with the teenager, Peter Parker. Misunderstood by his peers and persecuted by authorities, Parker, both as Spider-Man and in normal life, wrestled with issues confronted by the readers themselves – he had trouble getting dates, making money, and finding his purpose in the world – and possessed more believable goals and motivations. Unlike DC's "impossibly altruistic" superheroes (Wright 2001: 185), Spider-Man initially cared only for his family and himself, stating in the first issue that "the rest of the world can go hang." It was only after Uncle Ben died as a result of Parker's non-action that Spider-Man came to the famous realization that "in this world, with great power there must also come – great responsibility." The line was later retconned into Uncle Ben's mouth, but even from the beginning, it worked as a kind of Marvel code or mantra.

The impact of Spider-Man cannot be overstated. The young, brooding, antihero became the most widely imitated superhero archetype since Superman. Unlike his superpowered comrades, Spider-Man was often much weaker than his adversaries. As a result, he (and his comic) had to be smarter, craftier. Thomas Inge argues that "Given his anti-social attitudes and introspective insecurities, Spider-Man belongs to the trickster tradition among folk heroes" (Inge 1990: 142). This seems appropriate: the trickster acts as "interpreter, storyteller, and transformer"; he is "a master of borders and exchange, injecting multiple perspectives to challenge all that is stultifying, stratified, bland, or prescriptive" (Smith 1997: xiii). Trickster stories are "important in terms of creation, and in terms of creative community nurturing. They motivate … change, development, growth, and careful regard for behavioral mores of the community" (Doty 2001: 11).

Following Spider-Man, Marvel introduced more unlikely superheroes, including the Norse god Thor in *Journey into Mystery* no. 83 (August 1962), the mystical sorcerer Dr Strange in *Strange Tales* no. 110 (July 1963), the industrialist Tony Stark/Iron Man in *Tales of Suspense* no. 39 (March 1963), and the mutant team of X-Men in *The X-Men* no. 1 (September 1963). These titles helped to usher in the "Marvel Age of Comics." Part of what Lee later describes as "a big advertising campaign" (Salicrup *et al.* 1983: 45), the playfully self-congratulatory hype was carefully calculated to contribute to the publisher's larger agenda: "For the first ten to fifteen years of Marvel's existence, Lee and his company were selling more than just comic books. They were selling a participatory world for readers, a way of life for true believers" (Pustz 1999: 56). Lee integrated countless clever metafictional moments into the comics, such as the scene where Johnny Storm, reading *The Incredible Hulk*, compares the comic-book monster to the Thing (*The Fantastic Four* no. 5 (July 1962)). More than just witty metatextual flourishes, these instances hologrammed the fantasy of reader/character interaction, a fantasy Lee actively encouraged in his letters pages and in his informal, we're-all-buddies-here style. For the fans,

> the philosophy of a comics creating/comics reading brotherhood or club was very seductive, and inclusion in the Marvel family often began with Lee's hyperbole-filled prose, which was displayed in credit boxes, letter pages, and "Bullpen Bulletins," a regular feature filled with gossip about writers, artists, and new titles, all of which, according to Lee, were the greatest thing to come along since the debut of Spider-Man.
>
> (Pustz 1999: 48–9)

Lee cultivated the impression of the Marvel community as an ultra-hip, cutting-edge, insider's club, making fans feel knowledgeable and cool, part of the "in" thing. Wright confirms the efficacy of this approach when he reports that "From 1962 to 1967, Marvel's average sales figures doubled while those of its competition remained steady or declined" (Wright 2001: 223). Perhaps more impressive than the circulation numbers, however, was Marvel's incursion into new markets, including college students and ethnic minorities. It is probably an overstatement to claim that Lee "very likely saved comic books from an untimely death" (Braun 1971: 47), but he undoubtedly infused the industry with new life.

Lee often represented producers and consumers of the comics as part of a larger "Marvel family," affectionately referring to his team of writers, pencilers, and inkers as "The Bullpen," assigning colorful nicknames to the main contributors and, unusually for the time, including them in the credits for each issue. All of these things were done "with the intention of creating a sense of family" (Jacobs and Jones 1985: 70), but, as had been the case with Golden Age Superman-creators

Jerry Siegel and Joe Shuster, most Silver Age work-for-hire arrangements offered artists and writers no rights or royalties. In later years, this provoked major disputes between artists and Marvel over the provenance of certain characters and attendant copyright issues.

DC ultimately counteracted Marvel's success, once again through the influence of television. On 12 January 1966, ABC premiered its *Batman* television series (1966–8). The campy, star-studded show aired twice a week and featured the (in)famous catchphrase, "Tune in tomorrow – same Bat-time, same Bat-channel." The US went "bat-crazy" as comic-book sales rose, peaking at nearly 900,000 copies, the largest circulation of superhero comics since the 1950s (Bongco 2000: 98–9). By 1969, Batman and Superman titles represented nine of the top-10 bestselling comics in the US (Benton 1993: 177). However,

> DC Comics and, to a lesser extent, its competition benefited in the short term from the trendy preoccupation with superheroes that the show generated, but in the long run the show probably did more harm than good for the comic book industry. Watched by millions at the time, and millions more over subsequent years in syndication, the show reinforced in the public's mind the silliness and irrelevance of superheroes – and, by implication, comic books – in contemporary culture.
>
> (Wright 2001: 225)

Of course, the publishers themselves were partly responsible for this perception of comics as silly or irrelevant. Although they had begun to explore the myriad issues affecting their characters' personal lives, they largely ignored the most pressing social issues of the day, including gender equity, race-relations, and the conflict in Vietnam.

Despite the growing number of female superheroes, few offered new or interesting depictions of women, mostly conforming to damsel-in-distress or romantic interest stereotypes. Although many Silver Age superhero teams

> had at least one integral female member, they were always subordinate to the male superheroes. While the men of the Fantastic Four did the hard fighting, the Invisible Girl tended to overexert herself and faint often. The X-Men's Marvel Girl possessed the formidable power of telekinesis, but she too proved prone to fainting spells ... A founding female member of the Avengers, the Wasp, was an annoying airhead who spent most of her time panicking, fainting, and worrying about smudging her makeup in the heat of battle.
>
> (Wright 2001: 219–20)

Women in general were "relegated to minor roles in superhero texts, and presented in ways that give priority to men and the idea of adventure; women have their assigned places in the men's lives and are made secondary to what passes between a man and other men" (Bongco 2000: 111). Naming strategies further marginalized and infantilized superheroines. Teenage males, such as Spider-Man or Ice Man, were not referred to as "Boys," but superpowered women were constantly interpellated as "Girls." Despite getting married, having a child, and suffering through the stillborn death of her second child, Sue Storm, the Invisible Girl of the Fantastic Four, did not become the Invisible Woman until the 1980s.

Silver Age depictions of racial minorities similarly offered little innovation. Writers either "blackwashed" their otherwise conventional characters or created heroes who embraced rather than challenged (white) American cultural stereotypes. Earlier comics stories, such as EC's "Judgment Day" (*Weird Fantasy*, March–April 1952) – which, in defiance of the CCA (Diehl 1996: 95), featured a black astronaut in an allegorical tale of racism and segregation – had entered the Civil Rights debate, but Silver Age comics were peculiarly silent. In 1965, Dell Comics published *Lobo*, a western featuring an eponymous black gunfighter, but it lasted only two issues before being canceled due to lack of sales and resistance from individual sellers. As for superheroes, "Marvel comic books at this time rarely mention the civil rights movement, yet Marvel was the first publisher to integrate African Americans into comic books" (Wright 2001: 219). The Black Panther, the first black superhero in comics, debuted in *The Fantastic Four* no. 52 (July 1966) and joined the Avengers in *The Avengers* no. 52 (May 1967), but T'Challa was an African prince, and his life seemed far-removed from the everyday racial tension plaguing the US. Similarly, Luke Cage, the first African-American to star in his own series (*Hero for Hire*, from June 1972), seemed to have more to do with the successful blaxploitation films of the early 1970s than with pressing contemporary social issues.

More surprising perhaps, was the industry's near total blindness to the war in Vietnam. Virtually all 1960s war comics featured Second World War heroes, such as DC's Sgt Rock or Marvel's *Sgt Fury and his Howling Commandos* (1963–81). The few comics based in Vietnam were commercial failures: DC's "Captain Hunter" in *Our Fighting Forces* no. 102 (August 1966) and Millson Publishing Company's ridiculous *Super Green Beret* no. 1 (April 1967) are the most notable examples. Coverage of Vietnam was mostly left to the smaller companies, like Dell or Charleton Publications, which may have been the result of a lack of demand. In 1966, *Newsweek* suggested that the public was tired of reading about the conflict, and looked to the comics for relief rather than reality: "The truth is that some Viet comics are having much the same kind of trouble holding reader support for their war that the Administration is having rallying support for the real war" (Anon. 1966: 66). Whatever the reason, comic-book publishers disregarded the war and the social unrest that accompanied it. Even Marvel, after working so hard to represent its superheroes as real-world characters, lost touch with the issues and events most pertinent to the nation. And, as happened with the *Adventures of Superman* in the 1950s, comic book sales declined once again after the short-lived surge in popularity prompted by the *Batman* television series. The Silver Age was coming to an end.

The conclusion of the Silver Age cannot be pinpointed precisely, but the era's demise is apparent in various events during the early 1970s, culminating in the revision of the Comics Code Authority and the advent of darker, more disturbing stories. In 1970, the Nixon administration's Department of Health, Education, and Welfare asked Lee to run an anti-drug message in one of Marvel's top-selling titles. Lee complied, designing a tale that explored the dangerous and unattractive world of drug addiction. It was immediately rejected by the CCA because of its drug-related content, but Lee published it in *The Amazing Spider-Man* nos. 96–8 (May–July 1971) without their seal of approval. The ensuing controversy highlighted the regulation's inability to account for context and resulted in the 1971 revised Comics Code, which allowed for moral ambiguity, the depiction of corrupt public officials, and the inclusion of "narcotics or drug addiction" if presented "as a vicious habit"; vampires, ghouls, and werewolves were also permitted when presented within a "literary" framework associated with traditional texts and authors, but zombies, having no literary credentials, were still taboo (Nyberg 1998: 170–4). The more permissive Code allowed for greater latitude in storylines and subject matter, inaugurating a period of creativity and growth. Superhero stories became more serious, often more pessimistic. One of the very first of these stories, and arguably the most influential, concluded with the shocking death of Peter Parker's girlfriend (*The Amazing Spider-Man* nos. 121–2 (June–July 1973)). Entitled "The Night Gwen Stacy Died," it marked the beginning of a grittier, darker, more adult kind of story. It might as well have been called The Night the Silver Age Died.

Bibliography

Anon. (1966) "Pop Goes the War," *Newsweek*, 12 September: 66–71.

Benton, M. (1993) *The Comic Book in America: an illustrated history*, Dallas: Taylor.

Bettley, J. (ed.) (2001) *The Art of the Book: from medieval manuscript to graphic novel*, London: V&A.

Bongco, M. (2000) *Reading Comics: language, culture, and the concept of the superhero in comic books*, New York: Garland.

Braun, S. (1971) "Shazam! Here Comes Captain Relevant!" *New York Times Magazine*, 2 May: 32, 36–50, 55.

Diehl, D. (1996) *Tales from the Crypt: the official archives*, New York: St Martin's Press.

Doty, W.G. (2001) "Native American Tricksters: literary figures of community transformers," in J.C. Reesman (ed.) *Trickster Lives: culture and myth in American fiction*, Athens: University of Georgia Press.

Goulart, R. (1991) *Over 50 Years of American Comic Books*, Lincolnwood, IL.: Mallard Press.

Groth, G. (1990), "Jack Kirby Interview with Gary Groth," *The Comics Journal* 134: 58–99.

Harvey, R.C. (1996) *The Art of the Comic Book: an aesthetic history*, Jackson: University of Mississippi Press.

Inge, M.T. (1990) *Comics as Culture*, Jackson: University of Mississippi Press.

Jacobs, W. and Jones, G. (1985) *The Comic Book Heroes from the Silver Age to the Present*, New York: Crown.

Lee, S. (1974) *Origins of Marvel Comics*, New York: Fireside.

McAllister, M.P. (1990) "Cultural Argument and Organizational Constraint in the Comic Book Industry," *Journal of Communication* 40(1): 55–70.

Nyberg, A.K. (1998) *Seal of Approval: the history of the Comics Code*, Jackson: University of Mississippi Press.

Pustz, M. (1999) *Comic Book Culture: fanboys and true believers*, Jackson: University of Mississippi Press.

Sabin, R. (1996) *Comics, Comix & Graphic Novels: a history of comic art*, London: Phaidon Press.

Salicrup, J., Kraft, D.A., and Hagen, D. (1983) "[Interview of] Stan Lee," *Comics Interview*, 5: 35–48.

Simon, J., with J. Simon (2003) *The Comic Book Makers*, Somerset, NJ: Vanguard Prod.

Smith, J.R. (1997) *Writing Tricksters: mythic gambols in American ethnic literature*, Berkeley: University of California Press.

Theakston, G. (2002) *The Steve Ditko Reader*, Brooklyn: NY Pure Imagination.

Uslan, M. (2005) reprinted letter to *Comics Buyer's Guide* co-editor M. Thompson, *Alter Ego*, 3(54): 78–9.

Wertham, F. (1972) *Seduction of the Innocent*, 1954, New York: Kennikat Press.

Wright, B.W. (2001) *Comic Book Nation: the transformation of youth culture in America*, Baltimore, MD: Johns Hopkins University Press.

Wyman, R. Jr. (1992) *The Art of Jack Kirby*, Orange, CA: Blue Rose Press.

14

FILM SINCE 1980

Sean Redmond

Since 1980 sf film has taken hold of the cinematic imaginary. Key to New Hollywood synergistic practices, sf films often herald the "event" season, and according to the Internet Movie Database 30 percent of the All-Time Worldwide Box Office Top 100 are post-1980 sf films, a number of which are theme-park/game/film franchises. Able to offer seductive visions of the future and an affecting, spectacular sense of apocalypse, and to engage with the most important political and social issues of the day, sf film affects us in our bodies and makes sense of major social events and catastrophes.

The 1980s

Throughout the 1980s sf film continued to demonstrate a "doubling" (Telotte 1990) attitude to science and technology, embracing and celebrating invention (including the display of its own wondrously crafted special effects), yet identifying techno-science as responsible for any number of social ills. For example, in *Altered States* (Russell 1980) research scientist Eddie Jessup is driven by a portentous, godlike desire to find the ultimate state of human consciousness, one that has been set free from time, space, and embodiment. He immerses himself in a sensory-deprivation tank and ingests a drug made from the sacred hallucinatory mushrooms of a primitive tribe. Removing himself from the social world, from the familial and the domestic, he abandons his mind to the axis of infinity, to the breathtaking journeying sequences that take him to the point of creation. However, to survive this borderless rebirth, he must reconnect with the human, reentering the world and uniting with his wife. Science, the film suggests, needs a human, reproductive component if it is not to lead to self/species annihilation.

The diabolical power of technoscience is often aligned with corporate/government control. In *Alien* (Scott 1979), *Outland* (Hyams 1981), *Blade Runner* (Scott 1982), and *The Terminator* (Cameron 1984), science is conjoined with greedy, autocratic, self-interested corporations, and military-industrial complexes, with dire consequences for civilization. In *Blade Runner*, cities have become gigantic filth and commodity machines: the air is thick with pollution, and renegade killer replicants run amok; Western fears of Asia's growing influence are played out through a *mise en scène* populated with objects, adverts, and people of the "yellow peril"; and, with the natural largely extinguished or replaced by the synthetic and the manufactured, one can no longer easily tell what it is to be human.

Sf films' paradoxical technophobia/technophilia can take particular local forms. For example, in *The Quiet Earth* (Murphy 1985) issues of Pakeha/Maori racial and sexual identity, pacifism, anti-nuclear feelings, and cultural and geographical isolation resound as peculiarly New Zealand concerns. The three survivors of Armageddon – researcher Zac Hobson, idealized young white woman Joanne, and Maori tribesman Api – struggle to come to terms with their otherness and need to find solace in the absented world. Having cheated death because they were close to death, *The Quiet Earth* exemplifies what Sam Neill has labeled New Zealand's *Cinema of Unease* (Neill and Rymer 1995) in his eponymous documentary, or its quiet dislike of its cultural place in the world. Similarly, in the anime *Akira* (Ôtomo 1988), the fear of nuclear annihilation, and the collision between modernity and tradition, corporate-military science and individual free will, are played out within ritualized situations that are distinctly Japanese. Its largely positive representation of the Bosozoku rebel motorcycle gang gives contemporary Japan's disaffected and alienated youth a degree of cultural legitimacy. American independent sf films also address cultural issues with a particular resonance. For example, in Lizzie Borden's future-set feminist *Born in Flames* (1983), a male-led democratic socialist revolution continues to perpetuate class, race, and gender inequalities. Facing such continued oppression, a coalition of female activists (a "Women's Army") leads a second revolution, bombing the antenna on top of the World Trade Center so as to interrupt the circulation of patriarchal ideas through male-controlled mass media.

Sf film of the 1980s developed a range of (competing) aesthetic styles and utilized the art of special effects in newly self-reflexive and spectacular ways. *Flash Gordon* (Hodges 1980) reintroduced the delicious qualities of camp. Its exaggerated costumes, settings, actions, and character relationships are as frivolous, excessive, and potentially queer as its fetishized pinup protagonist who adores being looked at. The filthy, downbeat, post-industrial, Gothic pretensions of cyberpunk fill sf films with a contrasting aesthetic of moral decay and individual, historical, and cultural confusion. In *Blade Runner*, past, present, and future collide in an architectural maelstrom, with Mayan, Egyptian, and modernist surfaces vying for dominance. The world-weary Deckard, unsure of his own human identity, employs (fake?) photographs to confirm the authenticity of his own personal past. In *Tetsuo* (Tsukamoto 1989), a metallic, industrial-laden soundtrack scores traumatic man-to-machine transformations, primal scene fantasies, and sexual terror. Shot in 16mm black-and-white, with a heavy grunge aesthetic, rapid anti-realist editing, and stop-motion effects, this Japanese film is one of the exemplary cyberpunk texts.

In the 1980s special effects began to create a stream of awe-and-wonder moments that have since come to define the genre's pleasurable appeal. Whether it is a bejeweled spaceship soaring across the skies (*The Voyage Home: Star Trek IV* (Nimoy 1986)), a prosthetic alien ascending in a grid of white light (*E.T.: The Extra-Terrestrial* (Spielberg 1982)), or an intergalactic encounter between sentient beings (*Star Wars: Episode VI – Return of the Jedi* (Marquand 1983)), one is often addressed as a "wide-eyed child" (Grant 1999: 25), marveling at the specialness of the "creation" as it first comes into living, narrative being. At times, the self-reflexive nature of the special effect connects film, filmmaker, and audience in a complicit fan-like exchange. In *The Thing* (Carpenter 1982), for example, after a series of jaw-dropping moments revealing the alien's shapeshifting abilities, a character finally directly addresses the audience with the line "you've got to be fucking kidding," providing an extra-textual language for the unbelievable transformations (see Neale 1990).

The 1980s saw digital effects begin to replace traditional special effects such as stop-motion photography, optical printing, puppetry, and matting. *Tron* (Lisberger 1982) was one of the first films to use computer-generated graphics to create a 3D world. *Star Trek II: Wrath of Khan* (Meyer 1982) constructed the "Genesis sequence" with 3D computer graphics rather than traditional models and matte effects. In *The Abyss* (Cameron 1989), morphing software created the liquid-like transformations of the pseudopod water alien, a technique further developed in *Terminator 2: Judgment Day* (Cameron 1991). By the end of the decade, increasingly photorealistic digital effects were central to US sf cinema, ensuring the effects industry's development into a multi-billion dollar enterprise.

The international box-office success of George Lucas's first *Star Wars* trilogy (1977–1983) extended the range and type of product tie-ins and merchandising to accompany a Hollywood film and developed a substantial fandom. Lucas's visual effects company, Industrial Light and Magic (ILM), led the way in cutting-edge post-production visual effects services, providing unequaled artistry in model-making, matte-painting, computer-generated imagery, and digital animation, and winning nine Academy Awards in the 1980s, including one for *E.T.: The Extra-Terrestrial*. Directed by Lucas's friend and colleague Steven Spielberg, this suburban narrative features a cuddly alien messiah who heals the dysfunctional family who have taken him in, providing a solution for American familial and domestic crises.

In contrast, James Cameron and Paul Verhoeven are the "dark auteurs" of 1980s US sf cinema. Cameron's *The Terminator* (1984) utilizes the corporeal hulk of Arnold Schwarzenegger to play out its human/machine dichotomy. In the future, sentient machines are intent on wiping out humankind, so a warrior travels back to the present in order to assure the birth of the leader of the human resistance movement. This Oedipal journey culminates in a consummated primal scene in which Son, Mother, and Father engage in reproduction fantasies where they make good their own genealogical trajectory (the warrior becomes his own father). Verhoeven's *RoboCop* (1987) savagely critiques the relationship between law and order, bureaucracy and big business in crime-ridden near-future Detroit. Left for dead, his memories erased, Officer Alex Murphy is resurrected as RoboCop, the fascistic future of law enforcement, in this satire on the Reagan era.

Sf films were pivotal to the continued commodification of the cinema-going experience. The ride aesthetic – spectacular, effects-filled action sequences – began to dominate sf aesthetics, with sf films becoming display windows for the relay of "commodity intertexts" (Meehan 1991) – products, services, merchandising and other spin-offs. For example, *Back to the Future* (Zemeckis 1985) spawned two sequels, *Back* to the Future Part II (Zemeckis 1989) and Back to the Future Part III (Zemeckis 1990); CBS aired Back to the Future: The Animated Series (1991–3); Harvey Comics released Back to the Future comic books (1991–3); and in 1991, Universal Studios Theme Parks opened the simulator ride Back to the Future: The Ride. In contrast, fandom can be seen to reverse this process, with fans taking ownership of their favorite text, extending its life, developing its characters and contributing to public forums on its pleasures and purpose. In the 1980s, the Star Trek franchise continued to garner such responses, with "Trekkers" starting up fan clubs such as STARFLEET International and the International Federation of Trekkers, and organizing and attending conventions.

The 1990s

Culturally and politically, the 1990s were dominated by a sense of the coming millennium. Sf films were similarly haunted by an apocalypticism that suggested humankind was rapidly approaching its own termination point. In The Handmaid's Tale (Schlöndorff 1990), Gattaca (Niccol 1997), and Alien: Resurrection (Jeunet 1997), genetic engineering, cloning, and the failure of humans to reproduce represent the overriding threat to human survival and to what constitutes humanity. In Gattaca, life chances are fixed at birth. The "bioformed," the product of gene selection and engineering, are genetically perfect and destined therefore for life-success, while naturally born humans are essentially defective, second-class citizens. This posthuman hierarchy of power goes beyond the usual race, class, and gender binaries. The protagonist, one of the last citizens to be "humanly" born, should be condemned by his congenital heart condition to menial work and reduced life-expectancy. Adopting the identity of a genetically perfect athlete, he overcomes genetic imperfection and joins a mission to Mars. In an age of moral panics, Gattaca offers a powerful critique of a genetic science that would allow one to choose the physical and cognitive capabilities of one's offspring.

In Total Recall (Verhoeven 1990), Ghost in the Shell (Oshii 1995), and Virtuosity (Leonard 1995), the movement into the posthuman, the psycho-cybernetic, and the virtual throw the ontologically secure "real" self into doubt. A memory implant inputed into Total Recall's protagonist results in the splitting of his "self" and a desperate search for the real "me." In the anime Ghost in the Shell, "ghosts" or individual identities can move freely from one body, organic or inorganic, to the next. In Virtuosity, SID, a Sadistic, Intelligent, and Dangerous virtual reality entity created from the personalities of more than 150 serial killers, manages to escape into the real world, his diabolical powers magnified. In these posthuman films, then, one exists in multiple forms and such identity slippage is often suggested to be pathological and/or existentially or spiritually liberating.

The sf invasion narrative emerges in times of crisis. While such 1950s American films responded to, and informed, a prevailing set of fears (the Cold War; the Cuban missile crisis; an emergent, stifling bureaucracy; rapid consumerism; the racial Other who had begun to move into white neighborhoods), the reemergence of invasion narratives in the 1990s can be seen to speak to the fear of terrorism and to "wish for" terrorist acts. In *Species* (Donaldson 1995) and *Independence Day* (Emmerich 1996), the enemy Other comes to annihilate, even if this appetite for destruction is played for satirical laughs, as in *Mars Attacks!* (Burton 1996) and *Starship Troopers* (Verhoeven 1997). According to Jean Baudrillard, invasion films such as *Independence Day*, in which the White House is razed to the ground by alien firepower, are equivalent to the audience dreaming (witnessing) America's demise as a superpower. Baudrillard suggests that when the planes crashed into the World Trade Center on 9/11 viewers had not only seen this scene spectacularly played out before, but they had desired it: they were accomplices in it; and they therefore brought the invasion home (Baudrillard 2002: 14).

The 1990s ended with two major postmodern texts. In Andy and Larry Wachowski's homage to Baudrillard's theory of simulacra and the hyperreal, *The Matrix* (1999) liquefies the real and destabilizes the self. Thomas Anderson/Neo is a messianic computer hacker prophesied to lead humanity out of its subordination to sentient machines. Two alternate worlds exist: the soporific virtual world and the ruined real world. In the film's interior hallucinatory dreaming/waking state, the virtual–real Neo must lead humanity out of false reality and into self-governance. As such, *The Matrix* is a home-based terrorist allegory, with Neo leading disgruntled militants who want to overthrow the dominant power bases, even as its religious overtones suggest a longing for spiritual renewal in a post-God world. Simultaneously, the adulation of Neo also points to the celebrification of contemporary culture: he is the One, the star image "Keanu Reeves." In *eXistenZ* (Cronenberg 1999), the distinctions between real and virtual, organic and electronic, and mind and body are also collapsed, but here the erosion of hitherto discrete human borders and boundaries is a potentially liberating fusion. eXistenZ is a new virtual-reality game that one plays inside oneself: the player connects to it via an organic bioport into which is plugged the game pod's umbrycord. When one is playing, the virtual is the real since at neurological and psychological levels one has been invaded by the game and one lives in and through the gaming experience. Cronenberg violently sexualizes these interfaces: phallic, anal, vaginal, and reproductive imagery populate the film. Allegra, eXistenZ's designer, holds her pulsating game pod as if it were a newborn baby wrenched from her womb. When she is shot at by a would-be assassin, the gun is made of flesh and blood, and the bullets are made of human bone. Like much of Cronenberg's work, eXistenZ revels in abjection and bodily transgression, offering viewers the chance to vicariously experience the body compromised, the body that exists outside of gender norms.

In the 1990s, a depthless sense of space and of infinite spatial relationships pervaded sf film. This aesthetic of the limitless and the borderless, of groundless life, saw vertical and horizontal axes merge and conjoin in crowded, dizzying locations. For example, *The Fifth Element* (Besson 1997) envisions mid-twenty-third-century New York as a liquid metropolis with every "moment" of space in flux. Cabdriver Korben Dallas flies across New York City, but because beginning and end, first and second, high and low are not in linear or spatial order, the high-speed aerial chase is rendered positionless, or vortex-like.

A number of films adopted a retro-futurist style or entirely emptied their *mise en scène* of the shimmer of the future. For example, in its use of elaborate ornamentation and curving forms, *The Fifth Element* has a number of Baroque characteristics that contribute to its sensuous sense of movement. In *Gattaca*, early twentieth-century Bauhaus is indicated in the clean and sparse lines of furniture, buildings, and clothing, its rationalist, high-modern aesthetic perfectly symbolizing its future of cold genetic rationalism. In *Pi* (Aronofsky 1998), in which an obsessive mathematician searches for numerical patterns that will unlock the nature of the universe, a grungy, low-tech, present–past aesthetic dominates. Shot in high-contrast black-and-white, the *mise en scène* is filled with screens, phones, wires, and cables that are past-tense configurations, old patterns in a chaotic universe.

In Hollywood sf, computer-generated imagery (CGI) became increasingly central, offering "viewers the opportunity to participate in a popular cultural event that put the display of the digital artifact – or computer-generated image – at the centre of the entertainment experience" (Pierson 1999: 158). In many cases, the breakthrough CGI technique became the "must-see" narrative image of the film, reproduced in posters and trailers. For example, *Terminator 2*'s morphing technique, enabling "live" actor Robert Patrick and T-1000 liquid metal Terminator seamlessly to merge and blend, was marketed as the central experiential pull of the film. Warren Buckland (1999) considers CGI effects central to the development of a new aesthetic realism in cinema. The digital dinosaurs of *Jurassic Park* (Spielberg 1993) introduced CGI "live" animals with realistic movements, and believably textured muscles and skin. The photorealisitic digital elements were intercut with animatronic dinosaurs creating three-dimensional creatures that were as "real" as the live actors who also populated the screen. The 1990s ended with *The Matrix*'s breathtaking bullet-time sequences, which allowed for an infinite variation in time and space coordinates so that super-quick action could be slowed down, paused, or extended in a setting in which the camera could take up any number of positions and trajectories. The bullet-time technique has since been extensively used in computer games (*Requiem: Avenging Angel* (1999)) and music videos (Korn's "Freak on a Leash" (1998)).

Kathryn Bigelow's *Strange Days* (1995), set during the last two crime-ridden days of 1999, is a remarkable examination of millennium hysteria and virtual paranoia (see Jermyn and Redmond 2004). Lenny Nero, formerly an LAPD vice cop, deals in illegal, fully immersive "SQUID" memory recordings taken directly from the cerebral cortex. Jacked-in "tapeheads" feel everything the participant experienced at the moment the memory was recorded. The SQUID sequences, filmed with Bigelow's trademark hyperkineticism from the relentless point of view of the (male) tapehead, align the viewer with the memory hijacker. *Strange Days* explores the consequences of such carnal trafficking, in which transgendered immersion is possible, suggesting that the power binaries between men and women are in the process of disintegration or, possibly, renewal. In *Mars Attacks!*, Tim Burton's loving lampoon of the 1950s invasion narrative, bug-eyed monsters from Mars land on Earth to lay waste to human civilization. When scientists, politicians, and the military disagree on how to meet and treat the invader, it is left to a band of misfits and outsiders to save the day. Inspired by a series of old Topps bubble-gum cards that Burton had collected as a child, the film is permeated by an overriding sense of nostalgia for the (cinematic) past. Burton's signature reversal of dominant insider/outsider dichotomies is also in evidence, so it is in the glitzy, kitsch consumption palaces of Las Vegas that the Martians meet their hilarious end.

The relationship between film companies and fans is not always supportive. The former often bar the latter from creative engagements with the text. For example, Paramount Pictures actively litigate against fans who try to produce their own *Star Trek* films or products. However, film companies began to realize the economic and cultural worth of working with fans in extending the remit of the "original" film(s). For example, Lucasfilm and AtomFilms established the annual *The Official Star Wars Fan Film Awards* to showcase and reward the growing genre of fan films made by, for, and about *Star Wars* fans. There was an exponential rise in the number and quality of fan films made in the 1990s, thanks to the domestication of digital filmmaking and special effects in terms of affordability, accessibility and rendering power, and the development of internet distribution. For example, *The Blade Runner Chronicles* is a series of short fan films created for the internet: "what we are attempting to do is invoke the mood, and dark imagery of the film, and make something entertaining that has characters you want to follow" (Kennedy 2004).

Sf fans have themselves become the object of fascination and some ridicule. *Trekkies* (Nygard 1997) explores the influence of the series/films on the day-to-day life of fans: a dentist designs his surgery in *Star Trek* regalia; Barbara Adams of Little Rock, Arkansas, turns up as a juror dressed as the Commanding Officer of the USS *Artemis*, the Little Rock unit of the Federation Alliance. We learn that Klingon is taught as a second language to devotees; that marriages and unions take place in *Star Trek* scenarios and settings; and that *Star Trek* conventions are populated by people who dress, walk, talk, and sound like the characters with whom they so identify. *Galaxy Quest* (Parisot 1999) lampoons both the actors who play in such "cultish" sf series, and the fans who worship them, even as it gives fantastical legitimacy to this para-social intimacy.

The 2000s

The overriding concern of sf films of the new millennium has been with the security and viability of bodies and states. In films such as *Ever Since the World Ended* (Grant and Litle 2001), *28 Days Later* (Boyle 2002), *Resident Evil* (Anderson 2002), and *Ultraviolet* (Wimmer 2006), individual and social bodies are threatened by viruses and viral mutations that render them diseased, infected, pathological, or an incubator for Armageddon. In *A.I.: Artificial Intelligence* (Spielberg 2001), *I, Robot* (Proyas 2004), *Sky Captain and the World of Tomorrow* (Conran 2004), and *Transformers* (Bay 2007), cyborg machines and machine monsters threaten the supremacy of the fleshed Nation, and of what constitutes a human being. In *The 6th Day* (Spottiswoode 2000), *The One* (Wong 2001), *Natural City* (Byung-Chun 2003), and *The Island* (Bay 2005), cloning and genetic engineering results in corporeal inequalities, the blurring of the human/machine dichotomy, and a trade in human bodies. In *Matrubhoomi: A Nation without*

Women (Jha 2003), *Æon Flux* (Kusama 2005), and *Children of Men* (Cuarón 2006), bodies are rendered infertile or barren, and human civilization is therefore on the verge of extinction. In films such as *Signs* (Shyamalan 2002) and *War of the Worlds* (Spielberg 2005), despicable alien invaders attack and destroy the institutional, political, and cultural organs of society. In *The Day after Tomorrow* (Emmerich 2004) and *Sunshine* (Boyle 2007) ecological disaster threatens to wipe out the human race. And in films such as *Minority Report* (Spielberg 2002), *Equilibrium* (Wimmer 2002), *District 13* (Morel 2004), and *V for Vendetta* (McTeigue 2005), totalitarian regimes will the body into docile submission and compliance. This concern to "do to" the body may be a result of the cultural hysteria accompanying the War on Terror. Such films suggest that danger is everywhere in, on, and through the body. At a discursive level, they instruct the viewer to be vigilant, to self-survey their bodies for signs of infection or contamination, and to survey others (their neighbors) for the same. They respond to, fuel, and contribute to a conspiratorial surveillance culture. Viewers are told that their bodies must be ready for the danger, or else they will be taken over, infected, cloned, dehumanized, erased, or disappeared.

The imagery of 9/11 and the leitmotifs of the War on Terror recur. In *Ever Since the World Ended*, an attack that leaves a character mortally wounded is shot in the style of combat photography, while the torching and prosthetic remaking of Anakin Skywalker's body in *Star Wars: Episode III – Revenge of the Sith* (Lucas 2005) conjures up battlefield operations. In *28 Days Later* and *Children of Men*, military units patrol the streets, set up roadblocks and curfews, establishing a clear echo to the Gulf War and the siege situation in Iraq. In *War of the Worlds*, a blue-collar worker from New Jersey, estranged from his family, proves his worth as a father/heroic male. Not quite the mythic firefighter of 9/11, he nonetheless crawls through rubble, twisted metal, and burning fires to keep his children alive. Burning planes fall out of the sky; military missiles slice through the air; the alien enemy, intent on harvesting humankind for their own survival and domination, emerge fully armored from underneath, from within the borders of New York City. Human blood soaks the screen, the entire *mise en scène*, as if the social body of America is being bled to death.

The relationship between sf gaming and film has became increasingly close, with successful games adapted as films (e.g., *Final Fantasy: The Spirits Within* (Sakaguchi 2001), the *Resident Evil* (2002–) and *AVP* franchises (2004–), and *Doom* (Bartkowiak 2005)). Such adaptations brought the aesthetics of gaming to the form and content of the film. For example, *Doom*'s first-person shooter viewpoint is "translated" from the 1993 game, with the audience occupying the sightline of the protagonist's gun as he shoots at a never-ending number of zombies. Game-like aesthetics can also be found in the episodic, investigative, and "interactive" qualities of such films as *Star Wars: Episode II – Attack of the Clones* (Lucas 2002) and *Paycheck* (Woo 2003), which seem to have been designed as if they were (also) to be played.

Concurrently, sf films have become increasingly CGI-driven, arguably at the expense of storytelling. In *The Day after Tomorrow*, lengthy sequences were constructed from CGI alone, while *Star Wars: Episode III – Revenge of the Sith* contains a record 2,151 special effects. This "turn" to the "specially" virtual has had consequences for perception as the effect becomes the affective real. Stephen Prince (1996) argues that film theory itself needs to rethink the relationship between the viewer and the text, employing the term "perceptual realism" to understand how CGI has affected vision and belief. In *Final Fantasy: The Spirits Within*, CGI created photorealistic human actors, while *Avatar* (Cameron 2009) will "present characters designed on the computer, but played by human actors. Their bodies will be filmed using the latest evolution of motion-capture technology – markers placed on the actor and tracked by a camera – while the facial expressions will be tracked by tiny cameras on headsets that will record their performances to insert them into a virtual world" (Waxman 2007). While these two films aim for photorealism, the rotoscoping technique used in *A Scanner Darkly* (Linklater 2006) tried to capture the drug-induced paranoia of the source novel.

Danny Boyle's *28 Days Later* and *Sunshine* are exquisite examples of doomsday sf. The former, set in early twenty-first-century England, depicts the breakdown of society after the accidental release of a highly contagious virus. The infected crave for the flesh of the clean. Largely shot on a domestic Canon XL1 digital video camera, on a budget of under £5 million, the film has guerrilla-like qualities. Although *28 Days Later* was filmed earlier it resonates strongly with 9/11. In *Sunshine*, Earth is close to extinction as the sun fails. The spaceship *Icarus II* is launched, carrying a thermo-nuclear bomb with which to reignite the sun. Shot with a mixture of claustrophobic angles, shot lengths, and interiors, and expansive, radiant images of the sun and the cosmos, an overriding sense of self-sacrifice and destruction haunts the film, under-mining its upbeat ending. In contrast, Michael Bay's high-octane, ride-like sf films are light on philosophy, story, and characterization, but *The Island* and *Transformers* are nonetheless wonderfully stylish, kinetic, and cardio-affective.

Sf films are now produced or co-produced by almost every country with a film industry, with notable successes emerging in Europe (*Vortex* (Pohl, Germany, 2003), *Immortel, ad vitam* (Bilal, France/Italy/UK, 2004), *Renaissance* (Volckman, France/UK/Luxembourg, 2006)), Japan (*Gojira ni-sen mireniamu* (Okawara 2000), *Casshern* (Kiriya 2004)), South Korea (*The Host* (Bong 2006)), Australia (*Subterano* (Storm Australia/Germany 2003)), Hong Kong, Canada, Russia, and India, with many of these countries seeing a significant increase in the number and variety of sf produc-tions. For example, in India, *Koi . . . Mil Gaya* (Roshan 2003) shows an extraterrestrial bringing hope and salvation to a disabled child; *Matrubhoomi: A Nation without Women* shows a drastic countrywide shortage of women because too many infant girls are being killed at birth by families not wanting to pay dowries; and the eponymous superhero protagonist of *Krrish* (Roshan 2006) must save the universe from a scientist who has invented a computer that can predict the future.

The cult appeal of sf film has developed into whole communities, lifestyles, and associations coming together to pay and play homage to its imaginings. Blogs, video diaries, chatrooms, fan fiction, creative productions, clubs, books, conferences, conventions, meetings, gatherings, letters, magazines, journals, and confessionals have all expanded to gigantic proportions over the past few years. There are, for example, over 3,000 web-written *Matrix* fan fictions. The online *Sci-Fi Studio Magazine*, defined as "Fan Powered Entertainment," is run and written by sf fans. One can argue that identification and a sense of personal worth and belonging are increasingly navigated through such cultish affiliations and associations (and of course academics are not outside this pleasure dome of personal investment and identification).

Sf film since the 1980s is a feast of innovation and transformation. It has produced immeasurable moments of delight and wonder, terror and loathing, and it has spoken about the most important issues of the day. It *is* film history.

Bibliography

Baudrillard, J. (2002) "L'esprit du terrorisme," *Harper's*, trans. D. Hohn, February: 13–18.

Buckland, W. (1999) "Between Science Fact and Science Fiction: Spielberg's digital dinosaurs, possible worlds, and the new aesthetic realism," *Screen*, 40(2): 177–92.

Grant, B.K. (1999) "Sensuous Elaboration: reason and the visible in the science fiction film," in A. Kuhn (ed.) *Alien Zone II: cultural theory and contemporary science fiction cinema*, London and New York: Verso.

Jermyn, D. and Redmond, S. (2004) *The Cinema of Kathryn Bigelow: Hollywood transgressor*, London: Wallflower Press.

Kennedy, S. (2004) "FAQ," *The Blade Runner Chronicles*. Online. Available HTTP: <http://www.seans gallery.com/pages/brfaq.htm> (accessed 1 April 2008).

Meehan, E. (1991) "'Holy Commodity Fetish Batman!' The political economy of a commercial intertext," in R.A. Pearson and W. Uricchio (eds) *The Many Lives of the Batman: critical approaches to a superhero and his media*, London: Routledge/BFI.

Neale, S. (1990) "'You've Got to be Fucking Kidding!': knowledge, belief and judgement in science fiction," in A. Kuhn (ed.) *Alien Zone: cultural theory and contemporary science fiction cinema*, London and New York: Verso.

Pierson, M. (1999) "CGI Effects in Hollywood Science Fiction Cinema 1989–95: the wonder years," *Screen*, 40(1): 158–76.

Prince, S. (1996) "True Lies: perceptual realism, digital images and film theory," *Film Quarterly*, 49(3): 27–37.

Telotte, J.P. (1990) "The Doubles of Fantasy and the Space of Desire," in A. Kuhn (ed.) *Alien Zone: cultural theory and contemporary science fiction cinema*, London and New York: Verso.

Waxman, S. (2007) "Computers Join Actors in Hybrids on Screen," *The New York Times*, 9 January: 9. Online. Available HTTP: <http://www.nytimes.com/2007/01/09/movies/09came.html> (accessed 1 April 2008).

15

TELEVISION SINCE 1980

Lincoln Geraghty

Television sf has undergone tremendous change since the 1980s. In the face of challenges from cinema, the internet, and computer games, sf has been at the forefront of television's attempts to maintain a regular and devoted audience. From what is usually considered a lean period in Britain and the US during the 1980s, the genre has developed two distinct popular forms through which it continues to attract viewers in an overcrowded, diverse multi-channel climate: the cult series and the quality series. In the competition between established networks and new cable channels for revenue and audiences, in which inexpensive reality television shows have proved invaluable, more expensive dramatic formats, such as the series, serial, and miniseries, have combined with popular genres, such as sf, crime, horror, and medical drama, to produce programs that either maintain a small but hardcore fanbase over several seasons or attract millions of casual viewers through hype and marketing in a relatively short period of one or two seasons.

The cult television series and the quality series – both of which have roots in such 1960s series as *Star Trek* (1966–9) and *Doctor Who* (1963–89), which attracted devoted fans through reruns and fan conventions – have evolved dramatically during the past twenty-five years. Sf from the late 1980s is representative of the "Third Generation," in which "TV has become the principal medium" through which the genre is consumed by fans (Stableford 1996: 322). Through the merging of niche media, such as sf novels and magazines, with television, the "cultish" – in that it was produced for and consumed by a small fan community – was transferred to a widespread medium. The formula of the long-running, potentially infinite television series proved a highly suitable vehicle through which stories based on common sf narratives (e.g., space travel, time travel, alien invasion, alternate worlds) could be screened. The potential to attract devoted followers increases as series grow in narrative complexity and introduce more characters: "Seriality, textual density, and, perhaps most especially, the nonlinearity of multiple time frames and settings that create the potentially infinitely large metatext of a cult television text create the space for fans to revel" (Gwenllian-Jones and Pearson 2004: xvii). Alongside this development in cult television is the networks' need to attract new viewers as series that lacked longevity were replaced. The term "quality television" is, in the American context, bound up with the notion of nonhabitual viewing. Series that cannot rely on established audiences attract viewers through their concentration on high production values, compact narratives, and intense marketing to produce a sense of "essential viewing" or "must-see television" that ensures audiences tune in over a shorter period of time: "These programmes have also been referred to as 'date' or 'appointment' television, and they are distinguished by the compulsive viewing practices of dedicated audiences who organise their schedules around these shows" (Jancovich and Lyons 2003: 2).

The cult and the quality series appear to share similar characteristics, in that they attract a certain kind of viewer who interacts with the series passionately and regularly. In both cases, sf is very often the genre that audiences return to again and again, through either watching reruns of past series or getting engrossed in the latest high-concept, glossy serial. The following history will offer an overview of those series that not only offered intriguing sf but also changed the face of television.

From bust to boom – *Star Trek: The Next Generation*

Following a decade which gave us *The Six Million Dollar Man* (1974–8), *The Bionic Woman* (1976–8), *Space: 1999* (1975–8), *Battlestar Galactica* (1978–9), *Blakes 7* (1978–81), and *Buck Rogers in the 25th Century* (1979–81), the 1980s can be seen as a turning point in the growth and popularization of the genre. Although the long-running *Doctor Who* would eventually die a slow death in 1989, partly due to the fact that British television was experiencing huge financial cutbacks and industrial change, American sf was resurgent. *Star Trek*, no longer just a television phenomenon thanks to a series of successful blockbuster movies, reappeared on television with a new ship, cast, and crew in *Star Trek: The Next Generation* (1987–94). Renewed popularity for a long-cancelled cult series signaled a change in both television production and sf viewing practices. Gene Roddenberry's experiment of not first broadcasting on a network but rather distributing the series through syndication proved an important stimulus for other writers and producers to pitch their ideas for new genre television that had a clear popular following.

The restructuring of the established American television industry in the late 1970s and early 1980s as independent cable and satellite channels joined the major networks meant that stations could offer a wide and diverse range of programming for an increasingly media-savvy and genre-hungry audience (Johnson 2005: 95). Competition meant that networks had to invest in new technologies and new television formats to counter cable and satellite channels that could afford to cater to niche audiences: "New cable and satellite systems mean that general 'broadcasting' is not the norm, now we also have niche service 'narrowcasting', with special interest groups served by specialist channels" (Johnson-Smith 2005: 3). Furthermore, traditional formats such as the series and the serial merged, taking on characteristics familiar from BBC historical dramas and distinctive network serials like ABC's *Roots* (1977), and rebranded itself as the miniseries (Creeber 2004: 9). The 1980s saw epic-genre miniseries – historical dramas, such as *The Thorn Birds* (1983) and *North and South* (1985); prime-time soap operas, such as *Dallas* (1978–91) and *Dynasty* (1981–9) – growing in popularity. Such ratings-grabbing series not only influenced the format in which sf began to be made but also primed viewers for the repeated pleasures of formula television (see Gripsrud 1995).

V (1983) and its sequel, V: The Final Battle (1984), are symptomatic of the new format of sf television. While more a miniseries than a series, V developed a massive following outside of regular sf circles. The story was based on familiar sf B-movie narratives. Aliens in huge flying saucers set out to conquer the Earth. These lizard-like "Visitors" disguise themselves as humans and infiltrate the governments and the media. Clear parallels are drawn with the Nazis as the jackbooted Visitors round up humans and intern them in concentration camps (Booker 2004: 91). A human resistance continue to outwit and uncover the Visitors through a series of attacks and counter-propaganda that prompts a number of Visitors to swap sides and join the humans. High-budget effects, sets, and location shoots combined with a large cast helped make V popular with prime-time audiences. Backstories started to develop (the birth of an alien/human hybrid for example) that enabled audiences to interact with characters on a weekly basis, becoming more sympathetic with the minutiae of their daily lives and not just with the overall invasion narrative. A seemingly direct influence on the epic miniseries was Dynasty: the Visitors were commanded by power-hungry, super-bitch Diana, who was the spitting image in both demeanor and attitude to the villainous, manipulative Alexis Carrington.

British sf television at this time was not experiencing the same level of investment. However, the genre was still a favorite with audiences, as were imports such as Dallas, Dynasty, and V. Doctor Who producer Graham Williams had to comply with the BBC's tight budgetary requirements and entertain an audience increasingly familiar with and attracted to big-budget cinema and television from across the Atlantic (Chapman 2006: 123). The BBC's adaptation of John Christopher's trilogy The Tripods (1984–5) is seen as a relative failure in the corporation's long history of producing sf television for British audiences. Offered as replacement for Doctor Who, which underwent significant changes to its format in an attempt to bolster flagging audience ratings, The Tripods seemed set to fill the traditional Saturday teatime slot. With a generous mix of location shooting, special effects, alien invasion, and boys-own adventure, it was promoted as epic sf television that would ensure audiences tuned in week after week to watch the narrative unfold. However, it was axed after only two of its intended three seasons, having failed to gain a popular following.

While reasons for The Tripods' early demise are linked to its production contexts – BBC budgetary constraints meant that expensive series were a gamble – its visual imagery also played a part in its failure to attract an audience. Set in a post-apocalyptic future, in which humans lead a pre-industrial, almost medieval, existence, the dystopian narrative's earthbound landscape belied its high production values. It looked like it was set in the past rather than the future, and thus did not appeal to a teatime audience accustomed to high-action space adventure. While evincing the dichotomy between "prediction and nostalgia" (Roberts 2000: 30) at the heart of sf, its mediocre reception during the austere Thatcher era (with economic recession and rioting in the inner cities) intimates that 1980s British sf television needed to look upon a future where life was going to be better than the present. BBC series such as *The Hitchhiker's Guide to the Galaxy* (1981) and *Red Dwarf* (1988–99) perhaps succeeded because they offered humorous visions of space and space travel. Unable to compete with the special effects and futuristic look of expensive American series "the only option left for British science fiction TV was to have a laugh at itself" (Cook and Wright 2006: 15) and poke fun at the narrative tropes of sf and the cheap sets and effects epitomized by *Doctor Who*.

Star Trek: The Next Generation (*TNG*) was the embodiment of glossy American sf. New ships, sets, uniforms, and alien characters breathed life into a well-loved yet marginalized franchise. Its success in maintaining a mainstream audience without the backing of a major network intimated that audiences wanted more series that offered weekly snapshots of distant worlds and intergalactic exploration. The new series differed in many ways from the original, which was entirely located in a Cold War context and influenced by a distinctive 1960s visual aesthetic. Whereas the original replicated the New Frontier philosophy of John F. Kennedy through the figure of Captain Kirk, *TNG*'s Captain Jean-Luc Picard represented a more reserved kind of cosmopolitan diplomacy. Rather than shooting first and asking questions later, Picard preferred to talk through problems and the Federation acted as benevolent peacekeepers. Most episodes focused on the relationships between crew-members. Over seven seasons, this meant the audience became very familiar with and attached to individuals, with characters such as Troi, Riker, Crusher, and Worf also having their families introduced so as to help flesh out their backstories. The android Data offered huge scope in stories dealing with humanity and notions of mortality; episodes devoted to his character mirrored attempts by Gene Roddenberry to discuss the human condition through Spock, albeit in greater detail: "The series went from strength to strength as the characters were allowed to develop and interact with others in ways which were denied to the original crew" (Geraghty 2007: 4).

The Borg, a deadly cyborg race that assimilates people and their technology, were introduced in the two-part season-ending cliff-hanger "The Best of Both Worlds" (1990). Seen as a departure for the franchise, these new alien villains proved extremely popular with audiences and helped secure *TNG*'s renewal after dwindling ratings during the first two seasons. Lynette Russell and Nathan Wolski (2001) argue that they were *Star Trek*'s first attempt at questioning its own narrative, a prism through which ideas of "self and other, difference and sameness" were "explored and critiqued," and "a post-colonial mirror held up to reflect the nature of colonisation and assimilation" and in which the Federation's colonialist mission was "reflected and intensified." Where the Federation colonizes other worlds by implanting their values and laws through trade and political union under the distracting rubric of non-interference, the Borg "colonize from within, by injecting microscopic nanoprobes into the body of their prey." The Borg's popularity and their importance in flagging up issues relating to identity, our relationship with technology, and the historical consequences of imperialism and colonialism meant that *TNG* continues to attract critical attention twenty years after it first aired. Their influence can still be seen in the rejuvenated Cybermen of the new *Doctor Who* (2005–).

From the positive to the paranoid – *The X-Files*

The success of *TNG* in reminding networks and television audiences that sf was still a marketable genre on the small screen led to an "Age of Plenty" (Booker 2004: 111): *Quantum Leap* (1989–93), *Star Trek: Deep Space Nine* (1993–9), *Star Trek: Voyager* (1995–2001), *The X-Files* (1993–2002), *Babylon 5* (1994–8) and *Crusade* (1999), *Sliders* (1995–2000), *Alien Nation* (1989–90), *Space: Above and Beyond* (1995–6), *Stargate SG-1* (1997–2007) and *Stargate: Atlantis* (2004–), *Lexx* (1997–2002), Roddenberry's *Earth: Final Conflict* (1997–2002) and *Andromeda* (2000–5), a new version of *The Outer Limits* (1995–2002) that followed the new *The Twilight Zone* (1985–9), and one might also include genre hybrids like the teen sf/horror series *Roswell* (1999–2002), *Buffy the Vampire Slayer* (1997–2003), and *Angel* (1999–2004).

The impact of these series meant that the concept of prime-time "quality television" was firmly established by the mid-1990s, and their episodic formats also encouraged cable networks such as the Sci-Fi Channel (founded in 1992) to continue investment since they attracted a loyal and relatively affluent audience that could afford to buy into the ever-growing merchandising market. For Derek Kompare, cable networks "function as television *boutiques*: venues offering a limited array of products for specialized audiences" (Kompare 2005: 172). Series that started on the major networks would also end up on cable through syndication, adding to the pleasure of the rerun marathon which had become a staple cable marketing tool to attract sf fans. Genre hybrids, such as *Roswell*, which brought "in a variety of niche audiences with [its] blend of science fiction, action-adventure, young romance and melodrama" (Banks 2004: 17), signaled a shift in sf programming and its intended audiences, combining elements from the popular teen melodrama, epitomized by *Dawson's Creek* (1998–2003), and the invasion/conspiracy narratives fundamental to *The X-Files*. It also redefined models of teen masculinity through the characterization of its sympathetic and sensitive young hero.

Episodic series such as *Babylon 5* (*B5*) and *Deep Space Nine* (*DS9*) created long story arcs that both fed the audiences' expectations of sf and provided a stable and continuous world in which characters, plots, and personal histories could develop. These series not only manipulated generic tropes – the space station, intergalactic conflict – but also borrowed heavily from soap opera and serious television drama to help maintain their fictional worlds. For example, *DS9*'s "stories are linked by continuing 'soap opera'-type subplots such as Bashir's ineffectual attempts to romance Jadzia, Sisko's difficulties with his adolescent son, Jake, and Odo's continual pursuit of Quark. It is emphasised that *DS9* is a multicultural community in which … relationships between characters will be less bound by their rank and position" (Gregory 2000: 74). Subsequently, the increasingly complex storylines and character arcs helped perpetuate the cult audience's desire and passion for trivia and history. *DS9* resembled contemporary television series of the 1990s such as *Friends* (1994–2004) and *B5* as it increasingly emphasized relationships between friends, family, husbands, and wives (see Geraghty 2003). Entire seasons focused on the continuing war between the Federation and Dominion, the long story arc eventually culminating in the disappearance of Captain Sisko and the dividing up of the crew – their futures unknown. Viewers who would miss certain episodes risked not knowing what was going on and episodes often ended on a down note with little sign of resolution. As Creeber notes of this form of series, while it "is still continuous and never-ending, storylines now often develop from one episode to another (even introducing cliffhangers). This produces a cumulative narrative of sorts that does not exactly prevent viewers watching episodes in any order but which can be (and often are) watched in sequence" (Creeber 2004: 11). The week-in-week-out nature of *B5* and *DS9* ensured a popular following for both. However, their narratives saw a marked contrast in outlook for the future of Earth. *DS9* kept to the utopian blueprint offered in previous *Star Trek* series. The location of the space station on the edge of a newly discovered wormhole and in the middle of a tense political situation between the occupying and occupied worlds of Cardassia and Bajor emphasized the positive nature of the series, with the bonds among the Starfleet crew growing stronger as they faced further peril together. *B5*, on the other hand, was set in a future where Earth had "deteriorated relative to the late twentieth century in which the show was produced" (Booker 2004: 133) into a dystopian world where corrupt government after corrupt government had destroyed people's faith in authority and politics. Humans had seen hardship and death in brutal wars with the alien Minbari and the only way they could ensure survival was to create a space station which would act as intermediate neutral ground, "our last, best hope for peace." *B5*'s more pessimistic tone was shared by most of the series that would follow in the mid- to late 1990s. Out on its own, *Quantum Leap*, the story of Dr Sam Beckett's whimsical time-traveling tour of the twentieth century, was a rather more warmhearted series that focused on the potentials of individuals to enact change that, however small, could improve other people's lives forever. The series stands in marked contrast to the epic space operas just mentioned yet still garnered a devoted fanbase that showed sf's continuing capacity to attract a family audience in this period of change and pessimism. After its cancellation, the genre witnessed a bleak turn to paranoia.

Chris Carter's *The X-Files* was a mix of detective thriller and science-fiction horror, with a dash of postmodern pastiche added for fun. Each week, the protagonists, FBI Agents Mulder and Scully, would investigate the strange, the paranormal, and the "alien." In the first few seasons, these cases would often lead them to uncover strange human mutations and freaks of nature; rarely would the prospect of full-scale alien visitation be explored. After the release of *The X-Files* movie (Bowman 1998), the alien invasion motif was unashamedly used to drive the overall narrative of subsequent television seasons. Insectile aliens reappeared throughout the remaining four years, depicted as having a sinister interest in human anatomy and often in cahoots with the US government and FBI. Here, the archetypal alien figure of fear and mystery is shown to have invaded Earth with the purpose of exploiting human biology, propagating their race by using unsuspecting humans as incubators. The alien abduction narrative, established by extensive media coverage of the Roswell incident and other UFO stories, reflects "both our fear of being enslaved by technology and bureaucracy and our hope that, in some inscrutable way, technology may be our salvation" (Terry Matheson qtd in French 2001: 115). *The X-Files* achieved its cult status by creating a certain style that emphasized a sense of lack, reflected in the dark and moody sets, the "use of darkness and bright lights to obscure rather than reveal," and the series's metanarrative of secrets and concealment (Johnson 2005: 102).

This sat oddly in opposition to the contemporary political climate. The Cold War was over, America was undergoing an economic boom, and the optimism of Bill Clinton's administration was influencing both domestic and foreign policy. That *The X-Files* – and other postmodern series, such as *Wild Palms* (1993), *Twin Peaks* (1990–1), *Dark Skies* (1996–7), and *Millennium* (1996–9) – projected a dark vision of the near future is testimony to what Booker (2004) sees as a rejection of the national optimism at that time. Obvious connections to the impending new millennium, including the Y2K threat to global information systems, can be drawn. However, the paranoid invasion narrative of *The X-Files* was more than just a response to such fears. The "outsider" or alien "other" so often depicted in this period was representative of the growing poorer classes in society, a result of the widening poverty gap between the middle class who were indeed profiting from the economic boom and deprived workers worldwide. General mistrust of government and politicians was a mechanism through which the have-nots could manifest their resistance to the haves: "Thus, the richer Americans became, the more threatened and embattled they felt, and the paranoia of *The X-Files* responded perfectly to this mind-set" (Booker 2004: 147).

Reflections and revisions

Perhaps the relative failure of *The X-Files* spin-off *The Lone Gunmen* (2001) signaled a shift in attitudes at the end of television's period of paranoia; specific reference to conspiracy and political intrigue directly relating to government coverups and corruption proved unpalatable for audiences already on edge at the turn of the millennium. For example, the pilot episode of *The Lone Gunmen* sees the trio of computer hackers first introduced in *The X-Files* uncover a plot to plant a bomb on a commercial airplane and fly it into the World Trade Center. Such parallels to real-life events ultimately proved too hard to watch and the series was cancelled after 13 episodes.

Although British sf television seemed to have disappeared in the 1990s, American series continued to keep foreign audiences entertained. British sf comedy, however, was a favorite, with *Red Dwarf* producing some of its best material in the mid-1990s alongside US series *3rd Rock from the Sun* (1996–2001). The success of the sf–comedy hybrid has inspired more recent UK series like *Spaced* (1999–2001) and *Hyperdrive* (2006–), as well as films such as *Shaun of the Dead* (Wright 2004). The trend for knowing, postmodern self-parody is demonstrated in *Futurama* (1999–2003), where no holds are barred in Matt Groening's affectionate animated take on sf's tropes and icons. What these recent series all illustrate is the trend in self-reflexivity, in both Britain and America. After 9/11, visual media have undergone a shift in perspective as film and television increasingly look back on the past for a sense of familiarity and reassurance – to an age where political enemies and national threats were clearly identifiable. In today's climate of hysteria around violent terrorist acts perpetrated by a faceless enemy targeting civilians as well as the military, audiences are drawn to film and television that offer recognizable visions of the past, present, and future.

Star Trek: Enterprise (2001–5), *Firefly* (2002–3), *Smallville* (2001–), *Heroes* (2006–), *Battlestar Galactica* (2003–), *Mutant X* (2001–4), *Dark Angel* (2000–2), the animated *Captain Scarlet* (2005), *Doctor Who*, *Primeval* (2007–), *Life on Mars* (2006–7), *Ashes to Ashes* (2008–), and, to a certain extent *Farscape* (1999–2003), have all used the notion of the past or revised the narrative history of their predecessors to establish new stories and timelines – reworking familiar cultural myths and implanting them in a post-9/11 landscape. "Unreality TV" has become "the defining trend in television today" where established rules of small-screen drama have been "replaced by flights of fancy, leaps of imagination and a collective suspension of disbelief" (Naughton 2007: 14). Aspects of these new series are familiar, they either are based on established franchises or follow recognizable formats like those of the superhero comic book (*Heroes*) or the alien invasion narrative (*Invasion* (2005–6)), yet they are infused with a sense of unease – the audience does not know and cannot guess the outcome of stories, and it is as if the writers and producers do not really know either. *Lost* (2004–), with twists and turns that keep fans awake all night blogging on the internet, maintains a feeling beyond the simple paranoia of *The X-Files*. Sf has entwined itself further with fantasy to produce television that "has never been more now ... never more real" (McLean 2007).

Reimagined series like *Doctor Who* and *Battlestar Galactica* (BSG) are far grittier than their forebears. BSG, a prime example of new-style television programming that emphasizes the seriality of a compact plot (a fleet of humans search for Earth while being pursued and infiltrated by Cylons that look human), does not hide its allusions to the events of 9/11 and America's continued War on Terror and military occupation of Iraq. However, its design and *mise en scène* borrow heavily from today with characters opening hinged doors, listening to popular music on radios, and talking on phones with cords. These visual clues to the series' real-life production contexts are central to its engagement with current political, social, and philosophical issues (see Pank and Caro forthcoming). Similarly, *Doctor Who* has undergone changes to its traditional narrative that both acknowledge its roots in the old series and reflect developments in British television drama inspired by series like *24* (2001–) and *CSI: Crime Scene Investigation* (2000–), as well as *Buffy* and *The X-Files*, that "were notable for their self-consciousness, visual stylishness and re-imagining of established genres for a postmodern popular culture" (Chapman 2006: 185). Clearly, writer–producer Russell T. Davies had to maintain the cult audience by following established norms and keeping favorites such as the TARDIS, but the new Doctor has been fleshed out with a concentration on emotions and heroism that has never been seen before (Newman 2005: 115): "The back story of [the new Doctor] thus locates him within a particular archetype of masculinity: the traumatised war veteran ... racked by guilt over his inability to prevent the destruction of the Time Lords and holds himself responsible for what happened to them" (Chapman 2006: 190).

Through the ever-developing television market, fixed on niche audiences and quality, short-run productions, sf has a solid future. New viewing technologies such as digital television, On Demand, TIVO, and Sky Plus where *your* television can record programs it feels *you* like, in addition to the fan-oriented DVD box-set market where cult series can be bought and kept by enthusiasts and completists, ensure that the genre has an evolving, cross-generational audience that revels in current and old sf. With technology that allows viewers to revisit and relive childhood series, as well as watch new series that consistently refer back to the classics, sf television continues to do what the genre does best: picture the future by questioning the past.

Bibliography

Banks, M. (2004) "A Boy for All Planets: *Roswell, Smallville* and the teen male melodrama," in G. Davis and K. Dickinson (eds) *Teen TV: genre, consumption and identity*, London: BFI.

Booker, M.K. (2004) *Science Fiction Television*, Westport, CT: Praeger.

Chapman, J. (2006) *Inside the TARDIS: the worlds of Doctor Who*, London: IB Tauris.

Cook, J.R. and Wright, P. (2006) "'Futures past': an introduction to and brief survey of British science fiction television," *British Science Fiction Television: a hitchhiker's guide*, London: IB Tauris.

Creeber, G. (2004) *Serial television: big drama on the small screen*, London: BFI.

French, C.C. (2001) "Alien Abductions," in R. Roberts and D. Groome (eds) *Parapsychology: the science of unusual experience*, London: Arnold.

Geraghty, L. (2003) "Homosocial Desire on the Final Frontier: kinship, the American romance, and *Deep Space Nine's* 'Erotic Triangles,'" *Journal of Popular Culture*, 36(3): 441–65.

—— (2007) *Living with Star Trek: American culture and the Star Trek universe*, London: IB Tauris.

Gregory, C. (2000) *Star Trek Parallel Narratives*, London: Macmillan Press.

Gripsrud, J. (1995) *The Dynasty Years: Hollywood television and critical media studies*, London: Routledge.

Gwenllian-Jones, S. and Pearson, R.E. (2004) "Introduction," in *Cult Television*, Minneapolis: University of Minnesota Press.

Jancovich, M. and Lyons, J. (2003) "Introduction," in *Quality Popular Television*, London: BFI.

Johnson, C. (2005) *Telefantasy*, London: BFI.

Johnson-Smith, J. (2005) *American Science Fiction TV: Star Trek, Stargate and beyond*, London: IB Tauris.

Kompare, D. (2005) *Rerun Nation: how repeats invented American television*, New York: Routledge.

McLean, G. (2007) "The New Sci-Fi," *The Guardian*, Online. Available HTTP: <http://www.guardian.co.uk/media/2007/jun/27/broadcasting.comment> (accessed 1 April 2008).

Naughton, J. (2007) "Unreality TV," *Radio Times*, 21–27 July: 12–16.

Newman, K. (2005) *Doctor Who*, London: BFI.

Pank, D. and Caro, J. (forthcoming) "'Haven't You Heard? They Look Like Us Now!': realism and metaphor in *Battlestar Galactica*," in L. Geraghty (ed.) *Future Visions: examining the look of science fiction and fantasy television*, Lanham, MD: Scarecrow Press.

Roberts, A. (2000) *Science Fiction*, London: Routledge.

Russell, L. and Wolski, N. (2001) "Beyond the Final Frontier: *Star Trek*, the Borg, and the post–colonial," *Intensities: The Journal of Cult Media*, 1 (spring/summer). Online. Available HTTP: <http://intensities.org/Essays/Russell_Wolski.pdf> (accessed 1 April 2008).

Stableford, B. (1996) "The Third Generation of Genre SF," *Science Fiction Studies*, 23(3): 321–30.

16
FICTION, 1980–1992
Michael Levy

Here is the standard line: in the early 1980s sf was drifting in the doldrums and nothing much new was happening. The dinosaurs and traditionalists were receiving Hugos and Nebulas for work that was often culturally passé and nowhere near their best, with multiple nominations for writers Arthur C. Clarke (*The Fountains of Paradise* (1979), *2010: Odyssey Two* (1982)), Frederik Pohl (*JEM: the making of a utopia* (1979), *Beyond the Blue Event Horizon* (1980), "Fermi and Frost" (1985)), Isaac Asimov (*Foundation's Edge* (1982), *The Robots of Dawn* (1983)), Robert A. Heinlein (*Friday* (1982)), Clifford Simak ("Grotto of the Dancing Deer" (1980), *Project Pope* (1981)), Gordon Dickson ("Lost Dorsai" (1980), "The Cloak and the Staff" (1980)), Larry Niven (*Ringworld Engineers* (1979)), and Anne McCaffrey (*Moreta: Dragonlady of Pern* (1983)).

And then came the cyberpunks – William Gibson, Bruce Sterling, and the lesser lights who moved in their orbit. Gibson's *Neuromancer* (1984) took the Hugo and Nebula, defeating Heinlein and Niven, and the sf world was changed forever. That is the story and everyone who thinks that they are familiar with the history of sf knows it.

Well, maybe.

The cyberpunks were indeed the biggest thing to hit sf since the New Wave, and they did change the field significantly. Within a very few years, even though Gibson and Sterling were declaring the Movement dead, many of their favorite tropes – the disaffected, inevitably cool computer cowboy hero; the brain-modifying wetware and input jacks; the polluted future dominated by evil corporations – had become the standard coin of the genre, used even by veterans like Pohl and Poul Anderson, who had their roots in the 1940s. It is worth noting, however, that, although some of the veterans may have received award nominations largely on the strength of reputation (particularly Heinlein and Asimov), others (notably Clarke and Pohl) were in fact still writing at the top of their form, producing fiction that was indeed worthy of nomination. It is also worth taking note of the other nominees in those years. Some of them were traditionalists, who wrote extremely good traditional sf. Others, although not cyberpunks, were nonetheless experimenting in significant and useful ways.

For example, 1980 alone saw the publication of three particularly memorable novels, each of which may still be rated its author's finest work: Joan D. Vinge's

Hugo-winning *The Snow Queen*, Gene Wolfe's *The Shadow of the Torturer*, and Gregory Benford's Nebula-winning *Timescape*. *The Snow Queen*, which borrows from both Hans Christian Andersen's fairy tale and Robert Graves's *The White Goddess* (1947), tells a morally complex and beautifully written tale of lost love and political machinations set against a well-conceived alien landscape with distinct fantasy undertones. Comparable in both quality and feel to Frank Herbert's *Dune* (1965), it too was followed by a series of less memorable sequels. Gene Wolfe's *The Shadow of the Torturer* is also the opening salvo in what eventually grew to be a multi-volume megatext, although Wolfe somehow managed to make each title in the series noteworthy. Moving into territory previously explored by William Hope Hodgson's *The Night Land* (1912) and Jack Vance's *The Dying Earth* (1950), *Torturer* takes place in the unimaginably distant future, a time so remote from ours that our own far future has become the novel's prehistoric past. Set on an exhausted world whose sun is dying, it concerns Severian, a disgraced professional torturer who embarks on a religious pilgrimage of sorts. The novel's language is baroque, as is its multilayered, intensely allegorical plot, and like *The Snow Queen* it often feels closer to fantasy than sf. Severian's story continues in three further volumes (1981–3) of *The Book of the New Sun*, with *The Urth of the New Sun* (1987) clearing up loose ends. Two further sequences of novels, *The Book of the Long Sun* (1993–6) and *The Book of the Short Sun* (1999–2001), continue Wolfe's story, each from a radically different perspective. Taken as a whole, the series clearly qualifies as one of the masterpieces of genre fiction.

As Helen Merrick notes in her chapter above, a common fear among many long-term sf readers at this time was that, possibly due to the increased presence of women writers in the field (although Tolkien's success was arguably a bigger influence), true sf was being diluted by the work of writers who, like Vinge and Wolfe, were comfortable using fantasy tropes. However, physicist Gregory Benford, who famously defined writing hard sf as "playing with the net up" (Benford 1994: 16), produced a clear counterbalance to this tendency with *Timescape*, which is often considered to be the most accurate genre portrayal ever published of how real science is done. Set in a badly polluted and near-collapse 1998, it concerns a desperate attempt by scientists to use tachyons to send a warning message about the fate of the world to their counterparts in 1962. Avoiding much in the way of sf's usual pyrotechnics and sleight of hand, Benford nonetheless created a riveting tale of suspense that is simultaneously a serious exploration of the paradoxes involved in any attempt to communicate or travel through time.

Regardless of avant-garde movements such as the New Wave and cyberpunk, sf's bread-and-butter has largely always been tales of wondrous adventure set in outer space. Whether called space opera, space fiction, or planetary romance, the early 1980s produced several superior examples, with John Varley, David Brin, and C.J. Cherryh arguably the most talented authors involved. All three worked within future histories of their own creation. Varley's *Gaea* trilogy (*Titan* (1979), *Wizard* (1980), *Demon* (1984)), which has been praised for its innovative exploration of gender and sexuality, takes place within the body of an intelligent, planetary-sized alien being, Gaea, who has constructed a series of habitats, peopled by quirky, artificially constructed intelligent species, essentially for its own enjoyment. Brin's *Uplift* series, starting with *Sundiver* (1980), came to prominence with the Hugo- and Nebula-winning *Startide Rising* (1983) and Hugo-winning *The Uplift War* (1987). It sends humanity (accompanied by uplifted dolphins and chimps) out into a complex universe peopled by hundreds of not particularly friendly alien species, many of them enormously more ancient and intelligent than ourselves. (Three more volumes followed in the 1990s.) The prolific C.J. Cherryh's complex Alliance-Union Universe, with its many subseries, includes the Hugo-winning *Downbelow Station* (1981) and *Cyteen* (1988). Perhaps the finest creator of realistic, lived-in futures in outer space to grace the genre, Cherryh centers her stories on the men and women who actually run the space stations and haul cargo between star systems. Her dramatic, often painful novels feature complex characters and believable environments. All three writers also produced outstanding short fiction, with Varley doing his best shorter work of the period in "Beatnik Bayou" (1980), "The Pusher" (1981), and "Press Enter □" (1984).

The early 1980s also saw the publication of a number of odd and wonderful novels that do not fit into easy categories. Future Nobel Prize-winner Doris Lessing produced the extraordinary but very difficult *Canopus in Argos* series (1979–83). Alasdair Gray's *Lanark: a life in 4 books* (1981) combines intensely realistic, autobiographical sections in contemporary Glasgow with surreal chapters located in the futuristic city of Unthank to create a powerful work of dystopian fiction widely considered to be one of the most important modern Scottish novels. Christopher Priest's dream-like *The Affirmation* (1981) also moves back and forth between the contemporary world and a strange alternate universe. Brian Aldiss's *Helliconia* trilogy (1982–5) is a superb example of large-scale world building which chronicles one "great year" in the life of a planet whose eccentric orbit takes hundreds of Earth years to complete, allowing the author space for a wide-ranging, satirical, but at the same time deadly serious, critique of Western culture. The protagonist of Michael Bishop's Nebula-winning tale of time travel and evolution, *No Enemy But Time* (1982), appears to have true dreams about our Pleistocene ancestors. Norman Spinrad's *The Void Captain's Tale* (1983) uses Freudian psychology, explicit sexual content, and witty prose to reexamine many of the basic tropes of sf. These and other fine and original works may not always have won the major awards, but they demonstrate that, contrary to the simplistic standard-line, many exciting and innovative sf novels appeared in the early 1980s.

But then came cyberpunk. It was, of course, never the complete break from earlier sf that it claimed to be, with clear roots in the work of Alfred Bester, Samuel Delany, Philip K. Dick, and others. Bruce Bethke, not generally considered a cyberpunk, invented the term for the title of a 1980 short story (published 1983), but the label was popularized by Gardner Dozois, the editor of *Isaac Asimov's Science Fiction Magazine* (1977–), to describe the work of writers like Sterling, Gibson, and Lewis Shiner. In the early 1980s, Sterling, who had been publishing since the mid-1970s, used the pseudonym Vincent Omniaveritas in his newsletter *Cheap Truth* to push the fiction he valued and rant against what he saw as the complacency of most contemporary sf, singling out older writers like Heinlein but also such well-regarded contemporaries as Brin, Kim Stanley Robinson, and Michael Swanwick for withering and largely undeserved scorn.

Although as Omniaveritas he claimed to be skeptical of the various labels – including "punk," "the Movement," "neuromantic," and "cyberpunk" – that were being applied to the fiction he favored, Sterling nonetheless realized their value as a marketing ploy and, with tongue firmly planted in cheek, pushed cyberpunk as the next big thing in sf. This culminated in his landmark *Mirrorshades: a cyberpunk anthology* (1986), which featured superb fiction by not only the writers normally associated with the Movement, but also Greg Bear, James Patrick Kelly, and others. From there, of course, cyberpunk took off as a cultural meme employed by a variety of technophilic groups having little or no direct connection to the literary movement itself. By then, however, Sterling and company had already (prematurely, it turned out) proclaimed cyberpunk dead.

Key cyberpunk texts include: Sterling's *Shaper/Mechanist* stories (including "Swarm" (1982) and culminating in *Schismatrix* (1985), which combined ideas about cyber- and biologically-induced posthumanity with well-done space opera), his theoretically post-cyberpunk *Islands in the Net* (1988), and stories collected in *Crystal Express* (1989); Rudy Rucker's *Software* (1982), and its sequels, which explore the possibility of sloughing off this mortal coil and depositing our minds in software; Lewis Shiner's *Frontera* (1984), which concerns the grim fate of an abandoned NASA colony on Mars; John Shirley's influential proto-cyberpunk *City Come A-Walkin'* (1980) as well as *Eclipse* (1985), and its sequels, in which punks and rockers lead a revolt against the right-wing domination of the West; and various short stories by Pat Cadigan, such as "Rock On" (1984) and "Pretty Boy Crossover" (1986), eventually collected in *Patterns* (1989). Two other texts deserving mention here are Vernor Vinge's "True Names" (1981) and Greg Bear's "Blood Music" (1983; novel, 1985). Although not formally a cyberpunk story, Vinge's novella was one of the first pieces of fiction to explore the concept of what eventually came to be known as "cyberspace." Bear was as fascinated as Sterling with the possibilities inherent in the posthuman body. In "Blood Music," in which a scientist creates intelligent microorganisms that eventually transform him into something more than human, he almost single-handedly jumpstarted sf's ongoing love affair with nanotechnology.

The most important work of cyberpunk fiction, however, and one of most influential sf novels ever written, was Gibson's *Neuromancer*. Gibson's apprenticeship as a short-story writer produced such startlingly polished pieces as "The Gernsback Continuum" (1981) and "Johnny Mnemonic" (1981) (both collected in *Burning Chrome* (1986)), but *Neuromancer* was an instant wake-up call to the sf community. It has its flaws – the plot is at times a tad incoherent, the language occasionally overwrought, and Gibson's debts to Bester, William Burroughs, Raymond Chandler, and others has been widely analyzed – but its importance was instantly recognized. It remains the only novel ever to win the Hugo, Nebula, and Philip K. Dick awards. This dark, intensely metaphoric caper-tale of psychologically tortured and surgically altered computer hackers and street samurai working a dangerous heist for an unknown employer, set in a corrupt, garbage-filled and intensely urban near future, where soulless mega-corporations and enigmatic Artificial Intelligences run everything, became a new template for the field. Its immediate sequels, *Count Zero* (1986) and *Mona Lisa Overdrive* (1988), although perforce less startlingly original, were even more polished in their prose style and plotting. Gibson's later novels, beginning with *Virtual Light* (1993), fall outside the purview of this chapter, but represent (Sterling's proclamation of the death of cyberpunk not withstanding) a continuing refinement of his techniques and methods.

Michael Swanwick's controversial "A User's Guide to the Postmoderns" (1986), written partly in reply to Sterling's carryings-on in his fanzine *Cheap Truth* and which he later claimed was taken more seriously than he intended, argued that the most important contemporary (or "postmodern") sf writers neatly divided into two groups – the cyberpunks, consisting primarily of writers discussed above, and the humanists, including Connie Willis, Kim Stanley Robinson, John Kessel, and James Patrick Kelly (Swanwick later added Lucius Shepard and Nancy Kress to the humanist camp). Another writer Swanwick failed to mention, but who definitely belonged among the humanists, was Octavia E. Butler. Conveniently, Swanwick had a foot in both camps, having co-authored the cyberpunk "Dogfight" (1985) with Gibson, as well as writing the more obviously humanist *In the Drift* (1984). Indeed, his early career was marked by repeated movement back and forth across the divide, following the cyberpunk *Vacuum Flowers* (1987) with the Nebula-winning *Stations of the Tide* (1991), which feels much closer to Aldiss's *Helliconia* novels than anything by Sterling or Gibson.

But what exactly was "humanist" sf? Swanwick defined it as "literate, often consciously literary fiction, focusing on human characters who are generally seen as frail and fallible, using the genre to explore large philosophical questions, sometimes religious in nature" (Swanwick 1986: 7). It should be immediately obvious to any reader of the sf of this period that virtually all of these characteristics can also be found in cyberpunk (Gibson is among the most self-consciously literary writers in the field and Sterling is often philosophical). Still, it is clear that, despite the satiric overstatement (he describes Robinson as a gunslinger and compares Gibson to Elvis Costello), Swanwick had a point. In a transformation somewhat more subtle than that worked by the cyberpunks but equally important, sf was being remade in the fiction of Willis ("Firewatch" (1982), "The Last of the Winnebagos" (1988), "At the Realto" (1989)), Robinson ("Black Air" (1983), *The Blind Geometer* (1986)), Kessel ("Another Orphan" (1982)), Kelly ("Rat" (1986)), Kress ("Out of All Them Bright Stars" (1985), *Beggars in Spain* (1991)), Butler ("Speech Sounds" (1983), "Bloodchild" (1984)), Shepard ("Salvador" (1984), "R&R" (1986)), and Swanwick himself ("Mummer Kiss" (1981), "The Edge of the World" (1989)). The so-called humanists did not issue manifestos or shout from the rooftops about the differences between their work and earlier sf, but their short stories regularly achieved a level of literary quality previously reached by a very limited number of genre writers. They also produced superb fiction at novel length. Of particular note are Robinson's quietly understated post-apocalyptic *The Wild Shore* (1984), which was widely seen as standing in direct contrast to Gibson's more pyrotechnic *Neuromancer*, and Shepard's sf zombie novel *Green Eyes*, which three volumes, along with Swanwick's *Into the Drift*, constituted the spectacular 1984 relaunch of the much-praised Ace Specials series of uniformly packaged paperback originals. Other fine novels by the humanists include Robinson's *The Memory of Whiteness* (1985) and *The Gold Coast* (1988),

Willis's *Lincoln's Dreams* (1987) and *Doomsday Book* (1992), Kessel's *Good News from Outer Space* (1989), Butler's *Xenogenesis* trilogy (1987–9), and Shepard's *Life During Wartime* (1987). Of course, a number of writers who might easily have fallen under the humanist umbrella, but who had begun publication rather earlier, were still producing quality work in the 1980s, such as James Tiptree Jr's "The Only Neat Thing to Do" (1985) and *Brightness Falls from the Air* (1985), Roger Zelazny's "Unicorn Variation" (1981) and "Permafrost" (1986), Ursula K. Le Guin's "Sur" (1982), George R.R. Martin's "Nightflyers" (1980) and "One-Wing" (1980; with Lisa Tuttle), and any number of short stories by Harlan Ellison.

Another important writer who stands apart from the cyberpunks and the humanists, but who shares with the former a talent for controversy and with the latter an interest in religious issues, is Orson Scott Card, whose Hugo- and Nebula-winning *Ender's Game* (1985) became one of the bestselling sf novels of all time. *Ender's Game* tells the story of a military genius who, while still a child, is manipulated into exterminating what is believed to be a hostile alien species. At the end of the novel, however, it is discovered that the whole war was a tragic misunderstanding. In the first sequel, *Speaker for the Dead* (1986), which also won the Hugo and the Nebula, a grown-up Ender is shown, Christ-like, devoting his life to atonement for his crime. The controversy surrounding *Ender's Game* and Card's subsequent work stems from his willingness to espouse controversial political and social opinions, and the generally implicit use in his fiction of his Mormon beliefs. Together these practices made Card the field's foremost lightning rod as well as a major writer.

Between 1980 and 1992, no single political event polarized the field in the way the Vietnam War had in the 1970s, although the aftershocks from that international debacle continued to be felt in the fiction of, among others, David Drake, whose *Hammers Slammers* series of military sf (1979–), appeared to stem from a sincere belief that the US armed forces had been betrayed by the American government itself. Shepard's *Life During Wartime*, Geoff Ryman's *The Unconquered Country* (1986), and Bruce McAllister's *Dream Baby* (1989) considered the war from a leftist perspective. Reactions to the Reagan/Thatcher era's lessening of liberal social expectations and increased empowerment of large corporations were also common on both sides of the political spectrum. The cyberpunks, of course, were partially writing in response to the increasingly conservative times in which they found themselves, and Gwyneth Jones's *Divine Endurance* (1984), although set in the far future, is chock-full of veiled leftist political commentary. The libertarian right, a consistent element in sf, found its strongest voice during the 1980s in the work of Niven (*Oath of Fealty* (1981), with Jerry Pournelle, and *Fallen Angels* (1991), with Pournelle and Michael Flynn). Robinson's work had a powerful leftist perspective in *Pacific Edge* (1990) and the Nebula-winning *Red Mars* (1992), the first volume of his *Mars* trilogy, with its visions of ecologically sound leftist utopias. More pessimistic, George Turner, in the powerful but depressing *The Sea and Summer* (1987), portrayed a dying, overpopulated future Australia lacking the political will to do anything to improve its state. Another powerful warning about global warming and ecological catastrophe was Brin's *Earth* (1990). Ian McDonald's *Hearts, Hands and Voices* (1992) presents a beautiful but heartbreaking allegory for the troubles, both political and religious, in contemporary Ireland.

Joanna Russ had largely fallen silent by the 1980s, except for the fine "Souls" (1982) and "The Little Dirty Girl" (1982), and Suzy McKee Charnas had mostly turned to young adult fiction, except for her memorable werewolf tale "Boobs" (1989), but significant feminist sf did appear throughout this period. Suzette Haden Elgin's *Native Tongue* (1984), and its sequels, present an angry dystopia in which women, having lost most of their rights, create a secret language to aid in their attempt to undermine patriarchy. Le Guin's magnificent experiment in speculative anthropology, *Always Coming Home* (1985), postulates the development of the Kesh, a post-patriarchal society in a post-industrial future California. More influential, and among the most talked about speculative novels of the period, was Margaret Atwood's ferocious *The Handmaid's Tale* (1985), which envisions a genuinely sick, fundamentalist patriarchy in which women are little more than slaves, prized only for their ability to conceive. In Joan Slonczewski's novel of pacifism and deep-ecology, *A Door into Ocean* (1986), the all-female society of the planet Shora deals successfully with an invasion by an intensely patriarchal and militaristic culture. Josephine Saxton's *Queen of the States* (1986) concerns a woman who may be mad or who may be the subject of an alien interrogation. In Sheri S. Tepper's angry, post-nuclear holocaust *The Gate to Women's Country* (1988), modeled in part on Aristophanes' *Lysistrata*, women have taken control of society and fool the men into leading useless lives devoted to game-playing and carefully controlled military skirmishes. Jones's *White Queen* (1991), and its sequels, presented an unusually sophisticated analysis of gender roles, portraying the difficult interactions between humanity and an alien race whose concept of gender differs considerably from our own. Pamela Sargent's *The Shore of Women* (1986), Eleanor Arnason's *A Woman of the Iron People* (1991), and Nicola Griffith's *Ammonite* (1993) also successfully examine the implications of gender-segregated societies. During the 1980s, men also began to write seriously on gender issues. Varley has already been mentioned. Delany's difficult but rewarding *Stars in My Pocket Like Grains of Sand* (1984) explored the topics of desire and personal freedom with great moral seriousness and, along with Ryman's *The Child Garden* (1988) and Maureen McHugh's *China Mountain Zhang* (1992), dealt with homosexuality with significant intelligence.

The mid-1980s was a time for manifestos. Getting the jump on both Sterling and Swanwick were David Pringle and Colin Greenland, whose editorial in the spring 1984 issue of the British magazine *Interzone* called for a new radical hard sf that would, unlike the inward-turning New Wave, take on not just politics but also cutting-edge science. In the mid- to late 1980s, *Interzone* published a wide range of outstanding fiction by veterans such as M. John Harrison, Thomas Disch, and Ian Watson, and talented new authors, such as Ryman, Griffith, Kim Newman, and Mary Gentle (and Sterling and Gibson). It also published a number of writers who specifically came to be associated with radical hard sf, including Paul J. McAuley, Stephen Baxter, Charles Stross, and Australian Greg Egan, each of whom went on to write important hard-sf novels, including McAuley's *Four Hundred Billion Stars* (1988) and *Eternal Light*

(1991), Baxter's *Raft* (1991) and *Timelike Infinity* (1992), Stross's *Accelerando* (2005), and Egan's *Quarantine* (1992).

Throughout its history, people have repeatedly proclaimed the death of sf or insisted that changes in the publishing industry were making it harder and harder for genuinely good work to find an outlet. Nonetheless fine novels and short stories continue to appear, with the late 1980s and early 1990s a particularly fertile period. Two particular trends stand out: "second-generation" cyberpunk and the "new space opera."

Of course, trying to decide which authors are first- and which are second-generation cyberpunks (or post-cyberpunks) is largely a waste of time, in part because some of the original cyberpunks never really stopped writing the stuff, and in part because so many people tried it once or twice in careers devoted primarily to other sorts of fiction. Cadigan, whose contributions to the movement during its supposed heyday were limited to well-crafted short stories, went on to produce (and is in fact still writing) significant cyberpunk novels, including *Synners* (1991) and *Fools* (1992). Other successful continuations of the subgenre include Walter Jon Williams's *Hardwired* (1986), Spinrad's *Little Heroes* (1987), George Alec Effinger's *When Gravity Fails* (1987) and its sequels, Newman's *The Night Mayor* (1989), and even literary novelist Marge Piercy's *He, She, and It* (1991). Cyberpunk-influenced fiction continues to appear (by authors like Richard K. Morgan and Jon Courtney Grimwood) but the most important latter-day descendant of Sterling and Gibson is undoubtedly Neal Stephenson, author of *Snow Crash* (1992) and *The Diamond Age* (1995). The former, which probably caused a bigger stir than any cyberpunk work since *Neuromancer*, featured a hero who is simultaneously a talented hacker, a would-be samurai, and a pizza-delivery man. A dazzling display of literary pyrotechnics, linguistic theory, and razor-sharp satire, it recounts the hero's attempts to save virtual reality from a deadly computer virus.

Like cyberpunk, the so-called "new space opera" has roots in earlier fiction. At one time, the very term "space opera" was widely used in a derogatory sense, referring to spectacular but generally dated and often poorly written tales of outer space derring-do, such as Edward Hamilton's "Crashing Suns" (1928) or E.E. Smith and Lee H. Garby's *The Skylark of Space* (1928). Such stories were often contrasted, to their detriment, with the more sophisticated space fiction of Heinlein, Asimov, and Clarke published in Campbell's *Astounding* in the years immediately following the Second World War. Indeed as late as the 1980s, when Varley, Brin, and Cherryh were doing their best early work, novels like *Titan*, *Startide Rising*, and *Downbelow Station* would never have been referred to as space opera. Still, the similarities are there – spaceships and spectacle, aliens and adventure, marvelous planetary landscapes and mind-blowing astronomical phenomena – but written about with better prose, more believable characters, and fewer obvious violations of scientific laws. Indeed many of the finest sf novels of the late 1980s and early 1990s were space fiction and may be seen as direct descendants of Hamilton and Smith. Among the better works of modern space opera by American writers are Lois McMaster Bujold's *Miles Vorkosigan* novels, beginning with *Shards of Honor* (1986); the military space opera of David Drake, including *Ranks of Bronze*

(1986); and Benford's *Galactic Center* novels, most notably *Great Sky River* (1987). Of particular interest are Dan Simmons's Hugo-winning *Hyperion* (1989), along with its sequels, beginning with *The Fall of Hyperion* (1990), which used *The Canterbury Tales* (c. 1387) and the poetry of John Keats as structuring devices to tell a complex story of political intrigue set in a far-future interstellar civilization; and Vernor Vinge's *A Fire Upon the Deep* (1992), also a Hugo-winner, which related a thrilling interplanetary rescue set against a galaxy filled with exotic alien species where new discoveries in physics have placed strict limits on human intellectual evolution.

The phrase "new space opera," however, has a specifically British provenance. In the 1970s, the New Wave in large part became synonymous, at least in the minds of critics, with British sf, despite the ongoing publication of space fiction by such writers as Brian Stableford and Harrison, whose *The Centauri Device* (1974), although written in opposition to traditional American space opera, is often cited by later British writers as a particular influence. Such generally minor works continued to be published into the 1980s without much fanfare until the appearance of a writer whom the critics genuinely could not ignore: Iain M. Banks. Already a major literary figure as Iain Banks, author of *The Wasp Factory* (1984) and other experimental novels, he used his middle initial to differentiate the startlingly well-done and totally unrepentant space operas that he had actually begun writing (but not publishing) in the late 1970s from his more mainstream work. The first to see print, *Consider Phlebas* (1987), introduced the Culture, a sophisticated and liberal interstellar society which had taken as its duty the reformation of other, more benighted civilizations. Although Banks often portrayed the Culture as owning the moral high ground, particularly in the earlier novels, similarities between his fictional society and the contemporary West were not coincidental and later additions to the series became increasingly cynical. Other notable Culture novels include *The Player of Games* (1988) and *Use of Weapons* (1990). As popularized by Banks, the new space opera featured high literary standards, significant political commentary, particularly from a left-wing perspective, along with a willingness to accept moral ambiguity rarely found in the work of American authors (except, perhaps, Simmons) in this subgenre. As influential as Banks, however, was Greenland, who had earlier written the standard scholarly work on the New Wave, *The Entropy Exhibition* (1983), and whose *Interzone* editorial jumpstarted British radical hard sf. His *Take Back Plenty* (1990), and sequels, with its postmodern satire, sexually liberated heroine, and leftist politics, was something of a revelation to other British authors and is frequently cited as a model for the new space opera by later writers such as Peter F. Hamilton, Ken MacLeod, and Alastair Reynolds.

By 1992, the field of sf looked significantly different from the way it had in 1980. Cyberpunk's once radical motifs had become common coin, the so-called humanists had helped raise literary expectations, and new British writers were taking their turn at transforming the genre. Authors as diverse as Gray, Wolfe, Gibson, Le Guin, Robinson, and Banks had produced a wide range of superb fiction, although old-fashioned work not all that noticeably different from the pulps was still seeing print and finding an audience. As always, new dinosaurs and a new avant-garde were already in the making.

BIBLIOGRAPHY

Barron, N. (ed.) (2004) *Anatomy of Wonder*, Westport, CT: Libraries Unlimited.

Benford, G. (1994) "Real Science and Imaginary Worlds," in D.G. Hartwell and K. Cramer (eds) *The Ascent of Wonder: the evolution of hard sf*, New York: Tor.

Hartwell, D.G. and Cramer, K. (eds) (2006) *The Space Opera Renaissance*, New York: Tor.

Pringle, D. and Greenland, C. (1984) "Editorial," *Interzone*, 7.

Sterling, B. (ed.) (1983–6) *Cheap Truth*. Online. Available HTTP: <http://www.its.caltech.edu/~erich/cheaptruth> (accessed 1 April 2008).

Swanwick, M. (1986) "A User's Guide to the Postmoderns," *Isaac Asimov's Science Fiction Magazine*, 10(8): 21–53.

17
COMICS SINCE THE SILVER AGE

Abraham Kawa

Historians and theorists have not settled on a suitable name for the post-Silver Age of sf comics, largely because it is difficult to delineate or analyze a cultural era which is, arguably, still current, and because, as we shall see, post-Silver Age comics are often defined by their attitude toward the Silver Age. Each time comics enter a new phase of their existence, they also attain a new level of narrative sophistication. The Golden Age resulted from a combination of pulp sf tropes with the illustrative qualities of adventure strips, brought together in the figure of the superhero. Beyond the historical, sociopolitical and technological repercussions of the shift from Eisenhower to Kennedy administrations, the influential factor behind the move from the Golden to the Silver Age was the playful grandiosity and innovative characterization of work by Jack Kirby and Stan Lee. In the 1980s and 1990s, three interconnected factors gave Anglophone comics a new, post-Silver Age sophistication.

First, with the proliferation of publishing companies and the importation and translation of foreign works, Anglophone writers and artists were exposed to, and influenced by, an unprecedented cornucopia of narrative techniques. Second, the traditional-format comic books and magazines were complemented by a new mode known as the graphic novel (self-contained works created for marketing to bookshops and direct-market comics shops or, more commonly, several issues of a comics series collected as a single volume). This helped a less episodic, more literary manner of comic-book storytelling to develop. Third, creators were increasingly concerned with the status of the Savior/Superhero archetype in a postmodern, post-Vietnam world. The literary complexity and narrative impact of post-Silver Age comics is a direct consequence of their examination of the cost of Salvation, the price of Redemption, the Sacrifice exacted by the heroic ideals and icons of the Silver Age.

The European connection

The publication of the anthology title *Métal Hurlant* (1974–87, 2002–4) and its Anglophone sister publication *Heavy Metal* (1977–) saw European sf *bandes dessinées*, which preferred visual experimentation and philosophical musings over dramatic narrative, become influential on readers and creators alike. Alejandro Jodorowsky and Jean "Moebius" Giraud's *The Incal* (1981–8) and Phillippe Druillet's *Salammbô* trilogy (1980–6) alternated between silent panels loaded with psychedelic imagery and dialogue-heavy explorations of mysticism and the collective unconscious. The elliptical sf universe they accessed was, in essence, the "inner space" of the soul's struggle for self-realization. Enki Bilal's *The Nikopol Trilogy* (1980–92) meshed together European politics, organized religion, urban dystopias, and manipulative Egyptian gods recast as contemporary capitalist entrepreneurs. Sumptuously designed, with muted, painterly colors and deliberately static figures that resemble crumbling statues, Bilal's stories evoked a socially disintegrating future that alluded to a bleak, corrupt present. Stefano Tamburini and Gaetano Liberatore's ultra-violent robot saga *RanXerox* (1978–) was a punkish, anti-authoritarian recasting of Frankenstein's monster. Paolo Eleuteri Serpieri's *Druuna* series (1985–2003), a post-apocalyptic/cyberfantasy saga set on a generational spaceship, blended sf and gory violence with borderline hardcore pornography as it charted the picaresque adventures of a voluptuous, masochistic heroine who tends to attract sadistic monsters.

The sentiments of European sf comics were, to a large extent, typical of 1970s and 1980s sf: deep-seated resentment and frustration with corrupt sociopolitical systems, ruthless government policies, and profiteering conglomerates. The British weekly anthology *2000 AD* (1977–) was similarly replete with punk irreverence. Its key series, John Wagner and Carlos Ezquerra's *Judge Dredd*, was typical of the magazine's wry appropriation of American popular culture. Partly inspired by Clint Eastwood's Dirty Harry, Dredd was an unrelenting enforcer – judge, jury, and executioner – of the law of an authoritarian state, yet the comic itself was, essentially, a satirical, critical, and stylized representation of contemporary British and Western society. Through extreme violence and the merciless ridiculing of this authoritarian state's pretensions, the creators simultaneously aped and subverted Hollywood sf/action conventions, inspiring an entire generation of caustic scriptwriters and irreverently violent artists, both in *2000 AD* and in magazines such as *Deadline* (1988–95), featuring the madcap post-apocalyptic adventures of Alan Martin and Jamie Hewlett's punk antiheroine *Tank Girl* (1988–95), and *Warrior* (1982–5), which serialized most of *V for Vendetta* (1982–5, 1988), Alan Moore and David Lloyd's harrowing vision of anarchist rebellion in a near-future fascist Britain. Such narrative and visual innovations attracted US publishers, who started to import British and European artists, writers, and sensibilities, beginning with Mike W. Barr and Brian Bolland's violent, provocative *Camelot 3000* (1982), in which reincarnated Knights of the Round Table fight alien invaders. The first "limited series" in American comics, its success demonstrated the marketability of the graphic novel form.

Rising styles

Complex storytelling, graphic violence, and elaborate artwork were also trademarks of Japanese comics (manga) and their visual style informed many key post-Silver Age sf comics even before the manga craze which followed the release of the anime version of *Akira* (1988). There are three main types of sf manga narrative. The first centers on the plight of the artificially created human struggling to cope with technological society. Often, these action-oriented cyberpunk tales are dramatic visual accounts of the Cartesian mind/body split, such as Shirow Masamune's *Ghost in the Shell* (1991). Obsessed with high-tech action, female protagonists, dense storytelling, and mechas (oversized, user-controlled robot-battlesuits), Shirow also created one of the key texts of the second type of sf manga, concerned with future sociopolitical systems. *Appleseed* (1985) detailed a post-apocalyptic world in which his nomadic ex-soldier heroine and her android companion struggle for survival amid warring factions of a splintered, cloned, mechanically enhanced humanity. Another notable example of this type is Miyazaki Hayao's *Nausicaä of the Valley of the Wind* (1982–94), featuring a city-state menaced by a sea of poisonous mushrooms, by deadly insects, and by a war brewing between neighboring kingdoms. This tale juxtaposed humanity's uneasy coexistence with nature and Miyazaki's typical concern with the growing pains of adolescence.

The third type has to do with the effects of biological mutation on humankind, as in Ôtomo Katsuhiro's *Akira* (1982–90). Demonstrating Ôtomo's characteristically gritty, cinematic visuals and complex, elaborate storylines, it followed the exploits of two young bikers, Tetsuo and Kaneda, in post-apocalyptic "Neo-Tokio" as they run afoul of a secret military agency involved in genetics and the artificial stimulation of psychic powers. Amid nuclear blasts, high-speed bike chases, and profuse gunplay, Ôtomo used the protagonists' predicament to explore the value of friendship, the isolation and disillusionment of youth subcultures, and the state of the subject faced with corrupt, irresponsible authorities. Dialogues were sparse, yet laden with meaning; the plotting was dense to the point of opacity; and the storytelling was mostly visual, with an almost ritual representation of individual actions in multiple panels and iconographic details that reveal more about the world and the characters than the actual script.

Mutation and crisis

Initially, Japanese and European influences on Anglophone sf comics manifested in small ways. At roughly the same time as *Akira* dramatized mutant evolution as cyberpunk action-adventure and *The Incal* reimagined sf as an existential quest narrative, *The Uncanny X-Men* (1963–), Marvel Comics's long-running series starring super-powered mutants, promoted a new kind of post-Silver Age, postmodern storytelling. *X-Men* author Chris Claremont (1975–91, and intermittently since 2001) introduced tantalizing foreshadowing and convoluted subplots which ran for years on end, creating a multileveled meta-continuity of the highest order. He filled the series with star-spanning quests, resurrections, moral reversals, clones, high melodrama, wry humor, and sf paradoxes in the form of familial soap opera. The X-Men's anatomy became increasingly stylized, while their once identical uniforms alternated between personalized leather outfits, reminiscent of bondage and gang subcultures, and suggestive spandex tights that evoked high fashion and trendy commodity aesthetics. These image changes, befitting contemporary visual and surface culture, also reflected choices of identity and personal empowerment. The individual X-Men were also a strong, collaborative group, a substitute family of a type increasingly familiar in popular culture (as in *Lost* (2004–) and *Heroes* (2006–), as well as pop groups and sitcoms).

Simultaneously, postmodern fiction tropes became integrated in the verbal and visual narratives of superhero comics. A potent example of this was DC's *Crisis on Infinite Earths* (1985–6) and its aftermaths. Like many 1980s comics, this 12-issue limited series by Marv Wolfman and George Pérez featured traditionally pulp plotting within vistas of a humbling cosmic scope. Essentially a war between opposed and complementary forces from the "positive matter" and the "anti-matter" components of the cosmos, it featured waves of anti-matter sweeping across space and time, wiping out the several parallel universes containing DC characters. The surviving heroes travel back to the dawn of time and, during the course of their battle with the villain responsible for the attack, create the cosmos anew, as a single, severely contracted universe. The scale of *Crisis* was unprecedented: 354 pages long, set across multiple universes and 46,000 years, featuring appearances by 500 characters, most of them with speaking parts, and crossing its story over with every title DC published for most of a year. It gave DC the opportunity to renovate its fictional history and makeover key characters. Yet the true complexity of the story comes from its wry commentary on comics past. Unlike the Silver Age stories to which it paid homage, *Crisis* involved lasting change and failure. Numerous characters were left disoriented and rootless in a universe no longer theirs. Entire realities were lost. Innumerable people died. Echoing and critiquing the cold, dehumanized ethos of the Reagan era, *Crisis* bid farewell to the Silver Age with a mix of abject cynicism and ironic melancholy. The price of the new, harder-edged DC universe was the total erasure of those whimsical Silver Age characters no longer deemed fit.

The analogy between the purging of unprivileged comic-book characters and socio-political injustice was made explicit in other *Crisis*-like stories. Alan Moore and Don Simpson's "In Pictopia" (1986) presented a world where recognizable variants of well-known comic-strip heroes were reduced to sordid poverty by the state's social welfare policy, elections were fought between political caricatures, and characters reluctant to "get with the program" were threatened with exclusion from the continuity. In fact, Moore's "Jaspers Warp" storyline in Marvel UK's *Captain Britain* series (1983–4) provided a British prototype for *Crisis*, featuring an interdimensional catastrophe engineered by a Thatcherite politician and horrific sf versions of the injustices perpetrated by Margaret Thatcher against the unprivileged.

Rather than solving DC's continuity problems, *Crisis* intensified creators' desires to play with discarded characters and Silver Age tropes, leading to further mix-ups and two sequels: "Crisis II," in Grant Morrison's *Animal Man* (1990), and Dan Jurgens's *Zero Hour: crisis in time* (1994). An unorthodox solution was offered in Mark Waid and Mike Zeck's *The Kingdom* (1998), which postulated that all the events seen in 60 years' worth of DC Comics, even those that contradicted each other, were "true" because of the constantly altering nature of time and reality. However, this comfort with ontological chaos proved short-lived, and a recent third sequel, *Infinite Crisis* (2005–6), continued the tradition of dramatizing ambivalent attitudes toward the Silver Age; the seven-issue *Final Crisis* debuted in May 2008.

Dark Knights and Watchmen

The Dark Knight Returns (1986) and *Watchmen* (1986–7) were widely acclaimed as "serious" explorations of philosophical, cultural, and political themes. Their somber, deconstructive mood, typical of the post-*Crisis*/Reagan era, created the impression that superhero comics had reached a creative impasse of violence and pessimism. However, they also rejuvenated their idiom, reveling in novel interpretations of stock superhero trappings, and took full advantage of the media-prominent market of graphic novels. Recapitulating themes, motifs, and images from across the cultural spectrum, they reflected the collage-like nature of contemporary times.

The Dark Knight Returns and *The Dark Knight Strikes Again* (2001), Frank Miller's elegies about a middle-aged Batman coming out of retirement in a future Gotham City, were dark, allusive, tech-noir stories and hyperbolic reimaginings of Silver Age sf tropes. Miller's earlier *Ronin* (1983), a cyberpunk miniseries influenced by Moebius and manga, related the adventures of a futuristic cyberspace entity modeled after a legendary Japanese swordsman. Its cluttered mixture of styles and the grim, gritty, crime-novel expressionism of Miller's *Daredevil* series (1980–3, 1986), combined with reactionary ethics, sexually resonant subtexts, and an evolving style which favored Japanese influences to crystallize *Dark Knight*'s main concern: vigilantism as the only alternative to a postmodern apocalypse of media-domination. Batman was more of a cipher than a flesh-and-blood character, his true identity being the mask, the image, rather than the substance beneath it. The hero and his antagonists were literally and metaphorically iconic characters, battling amid cut-and-paste images of their media coverage.

This multimedia treatment of the superhero icon was also at the core of *the* seminal post-Silver Age sf text, Alan Moore and Dave Gibbons's 12-part *Watchmen*. Ostensibly a story about retired superheroes in an alternative world (the US won the Vietnam War, Richard Nixon is still in power in 1985) who become involved in a murder investigation against the backdrop of an upcoming nuclear war, it gradually unfolds a complex conspiracy narrative, and a satirical examination of the manipulative power of contemporary media. Its ironic mode is prominent in the sequence where ex-superhero multimillionaire Adrian Veidt studies a wall of TV screens, using advertisements and entertainments (which he regards as more reliable sources of information than the news) to understand his society's mores, and in the self-reflexive commentary provided by interpolated pastiches of printed media (press clippings, selections from a superhero's autobiography, a study on the sociopolitical influence of an atomic-powered superhero, a psychiatric evaluation of a vigilante, memos and printed ad campaigns from Veidt's company, extracts from a fictional history of comics, and even a complete comic-book story read by a character). Other storytelling innovations include a nonlinear chapter, told from the perspective of a character who experiences all of his life simultaneously. These elements combine to shape a postmodern palimpsest/collage, written over and connected to a multitude of earlier comics and other cultural texts. In what proved to be a staple of Moore's work, "unrelated" incidents, images and quotations from poems, books, and songs connect laterally to compose something larger than the sum of its parts. *Watchmen* gradually revealed *the price humanity pays to self-appointed saviors* (a former superhero, motivated by a desire to save the world in spite of itself, masterminded the conspiracy), *the cultural context of superhero stories* as part of an immense, manipulable mediasphere, and *the nonlinear complexity of reality* (the interconnections between story elements model fractal, chaotic reality as an unfathomable cluster of resonating patterns).

Dark Knight and *Watchmen* demonstrated the popularity of the "grim and gritty" approach to superhero comics and guaranteed the viability of graphic novels. These facts turned comics into franchises. Multiple series simultaneously crafted by many creators fragmented the perspectives of established characters, despite editorial efforts to keep a tight continuity between the titles. Image Comics, founded by former Marvel artists, typified the trends of the period. Its "house style" favored exaggerated violence, musculature, female anatomy, and artillery, usually crossed with fantasy and horror in high-concept series like Todd McFarlane's *Spawn* (1992–). The interconnectedness of each company's Universe propagated crossovers, as well as high-profile "events." Costume changes, substitutions of established characters by rising pretenders, cloning, and deaths were essayed many times over: one event that included all the above was the much-publicized *Death of Superman* (1992–4).

The changing mindscape: Alan Moore

Acclaimed as the most important post-Silver Age creator, British author Alan Moore made his mark by tackling the narrative paradoxes of the superhero genre (such as its uneasy status as a popular idiom with authoritarian overtones) and offering narratives dominated by an almost perverse rationality. In *Watchmen* and *Miracleman* (1982–93), his reinterpretation of an obscure British superhero, he created intricate, speculative sf that challenged perceptions of the Savior figure prominent in Western literature. A genetically engineered Nietzschean superhuman, Miracleman was inexorably led into assuming control of the world. Gradually turning away from the "grim and gritty" template, Moore followed the carnage of the hero's ultimate battle with his superpowered adversary (a massacre that completely devastated London) with Miracleman's establishment of a Utopia under his godlike rule. In doing so, Moore and his successor, Neil Gaiman, transcended the structure of the superhero narrative, with the fragmented tour of Miracleman's problematic wonderland offering more of a vision than a story.

Concluding that the only reason to deconstruct a genre would be to reassemble it, Moore reconfigured superhero sf with a series of playful, exuberant projects: *1963* (1993), a vicious satirical pastiche of Marvel-like superheroes; his tenure as writer of *WildC.A.T.s* (1995–7), attacking the entire Image "ethos" by treating the characters as obnoxious, violent, shallow inheritors of a heroic tradition; *Supreme* (1996–2000), a pastiche of the Silver Age Superman filled with humorous sf paradoxes. His own line of comics, ABC (America's Best Comics, from 1999), included sf series like *Tom Strong* (1999–2006), a "politically correct" reworking of Tarzan and Doc Savage-type adventurers; *Top 10* (2000–1), a superhero team/police procedural patterned after

NYPD Blue (1993–2005); and *The League of Extraordinary Gentlemen* (1999–), a pastiche of Victorian adventure literature that united characters from various books (Mina Murray, Captain Nemo, Dr Jekyll, Allan Quatermain and the Invisible Man) in a proto-superhero team. Featuring largely associative narratives and characters that variously escaped traditional genre boundaries, these projects further crystallized Moore's central concerns: the interconnectedness of living beings and all aspects of life, the infinite potential of narrative and the imagination.

Future pasts and millennial heroes

In the 1990s, many series reexamined the past or projected the possible futures of the superhero. Artist Alex Ross eschewed the kinetic energy of line art, infusing sf comics with a painterly sensibility and a sense of verisimilitude. With the exception of *Earth X* (2000–), written by Jim Krueger and connecting all the disparate narratives of the Marvel comics into a cohesive sf saga about the mutation of humanity, Ross used the common man as his narrative focal point, refreshing the readers' perception of the superhero. His attention to detail and ability to construct realistic environments were crucial to the Kurt Busiek-scripted *Marvels* (1994) and *Astro City* (1995–), since the former assumed the perspective of a news photographer who chronicled the careers of Marvel's superheroes and the latter featured various human protagonists interacting with superheroes. *Kingdom Come* (1996), scripted by Mark Waid, reinterpreted Superman and the classic DC pantheon by projecting them into a future war with their younger successors, an apocalyptic conflict seen through the eyes of a human priest.

Other writers picked up on Moore's wry approach, incorporating it into mainstream superhero tales. The graphic "widescreen catastrophes" of their works had as a common backdrop the superhero's need to justify his existence in a more sophisticated world, treading a thin line between intervention and domination and acting as a metaphor for millennial angst. Creators such as Grant Morrison and Howard Porter (*JLA* (1997–2000)), Warren Ellis (*Stormwatch* (1996–8), *The Authority* (1999–2000), *Planetary* (1999–2006)), and Mark Millar and Brian Hitch (*The Ultimates* (2002–4)), alternatively portrayed superheroes as subversive, countercultural agents of change and as militaristic, jingoistic defenders of the status quo, invariably set against dark, authoritarian political backgrounds.

Whatever happened to girl power?

Although post-Silver Age comics offered stronger characterization, female characters also continued to be drawn as objects of adolescent male desire, their stylized and highly sexualized posing designed visually to stimulate male creators and readers. Moreover, just as "realistic" characterization often begat grim, violent content, "strong" female characterization easily crossed the line into violence toward women, most often in the case of creators who, in order to boost sales or rid themselves of "problematic" heroines, revised, debased, negated, or killed them. If one thing has changed since the Silver Age, it is awareness of such misogyny, as the *Women in Refrigerators* website (Simone 1999) testifies. The site, orchestrated by Gail Simone, one of the most prominent and thoughtful writers of sf comics, contains a list of variously abused female comics characters, a polemic by Simone on why she was driven to create the site, as well as comments by male comics creators, many of whom felt the need to apologize for their abuse of female characters.

That said, the "strong" superheroines of the period were usually stereotypical excuses for girl fights and fetishistic, cheesecake sexuality, as in the all-female superhero team of Bill Black's *Femforce* (1985–). While never as commercially successful as its more overtly sexy counterparts, *Birds of Prey* (1996–), which teamed up heroines from the fringes of the Batman's world, stood out, mainly due to the balance of sexy action and sympathy for the main characters achieved by Chuck Dixon, Gary Frank, Gail Simone, Ed Benes, and others. Greg Rucka's 2003–5 tenure as writer of the original superheroine, Wonder Woman, not only reconnected the character with her mythological roots, but also reestablished her as the representation of the female principle in a modern, complicated arena of the sexes. Rucka and J.G. Jones's *The Hiketeia* (2002) used the story of a fugitive murderess who finds shelter in Wonder Woman's house to juxtapose the heroine's loyalty to sisterhood and ancient rituals of supplication with contemporary ethics of guilt and punishment, personified by Batman. The conflict of pragmatism and idealism, of merciless "divine" right and merciful human kindness, haunted the story, whose bleak ending cast the superheroine in an unprecedented air of reality.

The creator as shaman: Grant Morrison

The most outrageously inventive writer in contemporary comics, Grant Morrison excels at taking optimistic Silver Age sensibilities and placing them in a complex, contemporary context of evolutionary themes and mystical concerns. Morrison associates magic with the idea of change, and frequently uses occult narrative motifs to explore perceptions of reality and the shamanic role of the creator as humanity's mediator with different planes of existence. During his 1988–90 tenure on the environmental superhero series, *Animal Man*, he tackled questions about the moral responsibility of the Creator toward the Creatures (whether animals, human offspring, or fictional characters), affording them equal ontological validity. He unhesitatingly broke the implied boundary between comics and reality, even allowing characters to interact with himself.

Characters similarly breached the confines of reality in the revisionist, surreal superhero miniseries *Flex Mentallo* (1996) and the sf espionage series *The Filth* (2002–3). *The Seven Soldiers of Victory* (2004–5), a laterally intersecting septet of series which can be read as seven independent miniseries or as a nonlinear interactive narrative about seven superheroes against a common enemy, typified Morrison's fascination with teamwork as a positive factor for both self-realization and human evolution. This motif first surfaced in *Doom Patrol* (1990–4), a series about a functional surrogate family composed of dysfunctional superhuman freaks, and reappeared in

The Invisibles (1994–2000), a series which combined the evolutionary motif with Morrison's unorthodox views on comic-book violence and morality. Its protagonists were members of a loose-knit terrorist organization, operating in an occult world where every conspiracy theory was not just real but prosaic compared with the truth. The "villains" were the forces of law, order, and control over the potential of individuals, aided and abetted by Archons, beings from a different reality plane who stood for social stagnation and conformity. The narrative was intentionally pluralistic – referencing numerous (counter)cultural elements, from *The Prisoner* (1967) and the novels of Thomas Pynchon and William Burroughs to real-life and fictional 1970s anti-establishment icons such as the Baader–Meinhof gang and Michael Moorcock's Jerry Cornelius – and often exploded into stream of consciousness or fragmented vignettes that made only lateral sense. The ideas the series broached, ranging from sociology to quantum physics, invariably involved the element of transcendence and contextualized the race to control or free the world as it approached the millennium and the next stage of its development.

Morrison's views on teamwork, evolution, and violence crystallized in his most high-profile and accessible work, *New X-Men* (2001–4). Ostensibly just another series about the Marvel mutant heroes, it climaxed with an indictment of the sacred precepts of superhero comics. The systematic character assassination of longtime "sympathetic" villain Magneto – portrayed as a misguided power addict with obsolete Silver Age ideals that no longer pass muster in a materialistic, superficial culture of soundbites and brand names – was a condemnation of the most defective and backward elements of comic-book culture and franchising. (It was retroactively rescinded by Chris Claremont after Morrison's departure from the series.) Morrison's concluding storyline went even further, revealing that the true nemesis was a self-aware, viral genome colony, driving Magneto, other villains, and even the X-Men themselves into endlessly recycled acts of aggression. The concept of aggression as a self-perpetuating and *curable* biological organism constituted a rejection of the core concept of superhero comics: repetitious conflict. Ironically collaborating with famed "Image-style" artist Marc Silvestri, Morrison ended his X–Men tenure by telling a story about the end of violence.

Crisis ad infinitum

After 9/11, most "widescreen catastrophe" series were toned down or relaunched in less traumatic forms. The only such series subsequently to enjoy success was *The Ultimates* (2002–7), thanks to its satirical, controversial portrayals of iconic superheroes such as Captain America, the Hulk, and Thor, as well as a graphically violent, increasingly nationalist outlook on the conflict of American superheroes with the rest of the world.

Some comics satirized and condemned the simplistic dualisms of superhero comics: Moore and Kevin O'Neil's second volume of *The League of Extraordinary Gentlemen* (2002–3) pitted its heroes against *The War of the Worlds'* Martians and ridiculed Victorian Britain as a precursor of US global hegemony; the *Civil War* event (2006–7) set Marvel heroes against each other over the issue of having to reveal their secret identities to a distrustful US government; Brian Michael Bendis and Michael Avon Oeming's *Powers: The Sell-outs* (2004) depicted a Superman-like character's jingoistic fantasy of obliterating Iraq as an unmitigated massacre; and Darwyn Cooke's *DC: The New Frontier* (2004) offered a politicized reexamination of the beginnings of the Silver Age. For the most part, however, superhero comics followed the Silver Age precept of not confronting real-world issues, thus pointing to the actual Crisis: their limiting concern with internal continuity and their sociopolitical conservatism.

The most significant storyline of this decade was acknowledged as such exactly because it was toxically nostalgic about the Silver Age, praising and burying it in the same breath. Obsessively focused on continuity, Brad Meltzer and Rags Morales's *Identity Crisis* (2004) was a murder mystery set in the DC universe. The mystery itself (the murder of Sue Dibny, wife of beloved Silver Age hero Elongated Man) was gradually revealed as a pretext, since *Identity Crisis* was really concerned with the consequences of investigation and revelation. Among the suspects the heroes hunt down is a supervillain who had once raped Dibny but is innocent of her murder. This rape, retroactively inserted in the heroes' Silver Age past, provided the motive for the actual crime: the heroes, frightened by his threats and the possibility of similar violence toward their loved ones, had lobotomized him, transforming him from a psychotic to a harmless petty criminal. By revealing that this brainwashing was not an isolated event but a standard policy for "correcting" villains, Meltzer and Morales not only cleverly explained "gaps" in the established history of the characters but also imbued the Silver Age with a decidedly contemporary seediness and skepticism. Batman and Dr Mid-Nite revealed the true murderer to be someone very close to the heroes and, as such, above suspicion, further compounding the perception of the contemporary DC universe as corrupted and morally decayed. In fact, the treatment of Sue Dibny, coupled with the killer's very personal motive, exposed the dark heart of superhero comics: their exclusion of female characters, forced to be victims, neglected companions, and, when challenging this status quo, potential antagonists and villains.

The events of *Identity Crisis* influenced important subsequent storylines, such as Gail Simone and Dale Eaglesham's *Villains United* (2005), in which the superheroes' heinous acts force the villains into a coalition, and Geoff Johns and Phil Jimenez's *Infinite Crisis* (2005–6), in which the DC universe was once again threatened with fragmentation and destruction. As a direct sequel to *Crisis on Infinite Earths*, *Infinite Crisis* may be perceived as a bookend to the post-Silver Age period. Like the earlier *Zero Hour*, it resurrected the notion of multiple universes as a threat, orchestrated by a renegade hero trying to remake the pre-Crisis cosmos. It reinstated the parallel worlds in the continuity without giving a convincing answer as to why the heroes would oppose it. This was due to post-Silver Age creators' complicated love/hate relationship with the Silver Age, as they are compelled (by personal affection as well as the commercial nature of mainstream comics) to deconstruct *and* recycle it. Piled-up shocks and complexities combined with a streamlined, fast-paced texture to create an exhilarating story that was ultimately without consequence. Despite eliminating most of the characters left over from the pre-Crisis era, *Infinite Crisis* involved no *lasting* change. This is typical of post-Silver Age, "franchise" storytelling, in which characters must remain viable or be revived, individual style is replaced by recapitulation (Jimenez's art is deliberately reminiscent of Perez's), and innovation is overwhelmed by pastiche and nostalgia.

Ultimately, the comics discussed here reveal the reason "after the Silver Age" has no name. As the narrative sophistication of sf comics grows, so does their awkward mix of cynicism and fondness toward their past. Yet it is this problematic, complicated relationship to the past that drives artists to create masterpieces. Comics of the past three decades are no exception, having given us compelling, exciting, and controversial dramatizations of their coming to terms with the Silver Age.

BIBLIOGRAPHY

Simone, G. (1999) *Women in Refrigerators*. Online. Available HTTP: <http://www.unheardtaunts.com/wir/> (accessed 1 April 2008).

18
FICTION SINCE 1992
Paul Kincaid

If we recognize sf as a literature forged in the rationalist revolution of the Renaissance and tempered in the secularist revolution of the Enlightenment, then the years after 1992 have seen the literature under more stress than at any time in its history. As religion becomes a major issue in world (as opposed to local) conflict for the first time since the seventeenth century and a potent force in the local politics of even such supposedly secularist states as Britain and the US, as global terrorism brings anxiety into every moment of daily life, and as environmental struggles gather pace, a literature espousing rationalism and secularism seems more and more out of step with the world. Increasingly, overtly sf works have incorporated gods, angels, or the supernatural. For example, in *The Forever War* (1974), Joe Haldeman, one of the most consistent sf writers of the period, wrote a rational and secular response to the Vietnam War, but in the sequel, *Forever Free* (1999), he brought God on stage to effect its climax. Jay Lake's *Mainspring* (2007) presents a mechanistic universe in which God plays a direct and unquestioned role, and even John Clute's *Appleseed* (2001), which describes a war against god, implicitly recognizes the role of God in the universe. Among the works of newer writers, M. Rickert being a prime but far from lonely example, angels proliferate. This chapter will look at how sf has responded to this change in context in three ways, by turning backwards, by becoming a literature of the irrational, or by trying to become a mundane literature.

This is not the whole story, of course. Much, possibly most, sf published during the period has continued regardless along its familiar furrow. The most popular writer of the 1990s, for instance, at least if judged by her stranglehold on popular-vote awards such as the Hugos, was Lois McMaster Bujold. Her long series of novels, with a militaristic background reminiscent of C.S. Forester or Patrick O'Brian, and a romantic plot that owed much to Georgette Heyer, spawned a whole string of copycat series, notably including works by David Feintuch, David Weber, and Elizabeth Moon. Although it may be comforting in a time of anxiety, this is increasingly the sf that is seen as tired, dated, and uninteresting.

A sign of the growing uncertainty about the role, nature, and future of the genre has been the plethora of movements within it. With the possible exception of the New Wave in the 1960s and cyberpunk in the 1980s, sf had not really gone in for movements before the 1990s, but all at once we were treated to New Hard sf, New

Space Opera, New Wave Fabulism, New Weird, Interstitial Arts, Mundane Sf, and so forth, complete with editorials, special issues, and even the occasional manifesto. Some of these were alternative names for the same thing, some overlapped to a considerable extent, some – though by no means all – were meant ironically. The use of "New" in so many of the titles seems to mark an insistence on the novelty of such movements, even though much of what was gathered into their folds was in reality a revival or reworking of older models.

Few if any of these movements have had anything other than a local and temporary impact. One that did, and whose influence extended over the entire period under discussion, was the so-called "British Renaissance." But the extent and character of this revitalization of British sf became evident only around the turn of the century. During the 1990s there was nothing to suggest that American sf would not remain the dominant force in the genre as it had for most of the twentieth century. Gene Wolfe, who had revitalized American sf in the 1980s with his extraordinary tetralogy *The Book of the New Sun* (1980–3), now followed it with another tetralogy, *The Book of the Long Sun* (1993–6) and a trilogy, *The Book of the Short Sun* (1999–2001), both set in the same universe as, but predating, the original sequence. However, although any new work by Wolfe is an event, these later novels, while building into an ever more complex vision of the world, did not have quite the same impact upon the genre. Nevertheless, the period did open with one work of American sf that was at least as ambitious and influential as Wolfe's *Book of the New Sun* had been. Kim Stanley Robinson's *Mars* trilogy (*Red Mars* (1992), *Green Mars* (1993), *Blue Mars* (1996)) tells in great detail, over 200 years and 1,600 pages, the story of the terraforming of Mars and the human consequence for the colonists. It was a benchmark for realist, scientifically, and politically literate sf (and Robinson's color-coded trilogy would be followed by *White Mars* (1999) by Brian Aldiss with Roger Penrose, and Larry Niven's *Rainbow Mars* (1999), the latter owing far more to Edgar Rice Burroughs's Barsoom). But by the end of the trilogy Robinson was giving more and more space to long, evenhanded political debates between characters, a trait that continued in subsequent novels, *The Years of Rice and Salt* (2002), an alternate history which imagined a Europe depopulated by the Black Death, and the *Science in the Capital* trilogy (*Forty Signs of Rain* (2004), *Fifty Degrees Below* (2005), *Sixty Days and Counting* (2007)), which examines global warming. These debates have tended to blunt the dramatic edge of his fiction.

Only Neal Stephenson has since attempted anything that approaches the scale or the ambition of the *Mars* trilogy. Of that great artificial dichotomy in late 1980s American sf between cyberpunks and humanists, Robinson was the leading humanist and the *Mars* trilogy its preeminent statement. Stephenson found himself acclaimed as one of the leading cyberpunks with his breakthrough novel, *Snow Crash* (1992), a bravura description of a world in which a computer virus begins to have a profound effect upon human reality. His *Cryptonomicon* (1999) marked a move to integrate a cyberpunk aesthetic with the historical novel, counterpointing the story of the wartime origins of computing with a near-future story of the development of an information economy. His *Baroque* cycle (*Quicksilver* (2003), *The Confusion* (2004), *The System of the World* (2004)), a sort of prequel to *Cryptonomicon*, explored the origins of a modern economy in the late seventeenth and early eighteenth centuries, although its relationship with sf is more in the deployment of ideas and in the sensibility displayed than in any recognizable science-fictional devices or tropes. (It is interesting to compare this with a major work of fantasy from the period, John Crowley's *Aegypt* sequence (1987–2007), which examines another historical change in the nature of human knowledge, one which the author identifies as occurring at the end of the sixteenth century.)

The clearest statement of the cyberpunk position in the 1990s came in Pat Cadigan's *Synners* (1991) and *Fools* (1992), eloquent and ultimately humane accounts of the struggle to hold on to individual identity in an increasingly digitalized world. Of the previous decade's other leading cyberpunks, Bruce Sterling also produced impressive works, although his cyberpunk background was more obvious in his short fiction (e.g., "Bicycle Repairman" (1996)) than novels such as *Distraction* (1999), a satirical tale of political functionaries in a Balkanized near-future America. William Gibson, on the other hand, did not just leave cyberpunk behind but in *Pattern Recognition* (2003) and *Spook Country* (2007) produced novels in which sf is becoming integrated with mainstream fiction about the present day.

Cyberpunk was giving way to what might be seen as its natural successor, a fiction of posthumanity in which identity and often environment are uploaded into advanced computer systems. Cadigan's struggle can be said to have been lost in the work of such post-cyberpunks as Cory Doctorow (*Down and Out in the Magic Kingdom* (2003)), Charles Stross (*Accelerando* (2005)) and Greg Egan (*Permutation City* (1994), *Diaspora* (1997)). These fictions, representative of a powerful and imaginative new strain that began to appear in the late 1990s, are also indicative of a new irrationalism. The scenario allows for transformations of character or universe at a moment's notice and with little or no real-world consequence; the most fanciful bodies or environments can be tried and discarded at will, and death is no longer permanent. The flights of fancy can be breathtaking, but there is little need for the story or anything contained within it to take a rational course.

Away from such movements, as the end of the millennium approached, a number of American writers continued to produce reliably solid and inventive sf. Significant and very diverse works came in particular from Maureen McHugh (*China Mountain Zhang* (1992)), Kathleen Ann Goonan (*Queen City Jazz* (1994)), and perhaps most notably Octavia E. Butler (*Parable of the Sower* (1993), *Parable of the Talents* (1998)), whose blending of ideas of race, slavery, and surrender of self can make for uncomfortable reading. If feminist sf was less prominent than in the previous decade, there were still plenty of writers providing significant explorations of feminist ideas. Among the most notable were Sheri Tepper, with *Gibbon's Decline and Fall* (1996) and *The Family Tree* (1997), although subsequent novels have tended to be more successful as polemic than as fiction, a complaint also leveled, for instance, at Doris Lessing's *The Cleft* (2007). In contrast, recent work by Ursula Le Guin, especially *Four Ways to Forgiveness* (1995) and *The Birthday of the World* (2002), subsumed polemic under a fiction that is as powerful and affecting as any she has written in a long time.

The main tide of genre sf during this period, however, was the revived interest in hard sf and space opera, perhaps spurred by the monumental retrospective anthologies edited by David Hartwell and Kathryn Cramer (*The Ascent of Wonder* (1994), *The Hard SF Renaissance* (2002), *The Space Opera Renaissance* (2006)). Writers who have consistently worked within these areas such as David Brin (*Kiln People* (2002)), Gregory Benford (*Sailing Bright Eternity* (1995), which concluded his impressive *Galactic Center* sequence (1976–95), and *Cosm* (1998)), Nancy Kress (*Probability Moon* (2000), *Probability Sun* (2001)), and C.J. Cherryh (*Finity's End* (1997)), continued to produce highly regarded work. The most significant contributions to hard sf and space opera, however, probably came from Vernor Vinge and Greg Bear. Vinge began the 1990s with one of the most innovative space operas of the period, *A Fire upon the Deep* (1992), which along with *A Deepness in the Sky* (1999) imagined the effects of a hierarchy of access to space travel across a range of vividly imagined cultures. But a far from prolific writer, he published little else in this period. Bear, also at home in the panoramic sweep of space opera, was perhaps at his best in the cyberpunkish *Slant* (1997), a sequel to *Queen of Angels* (1990), although since then he has tended to move toward the sf-inspired thriller. Curiously both Vinge and Bear published *Collected Stories* (both 2002), and the period saw similar volumes by Arthur C. Clarke and J.G. Ballard (both 2001), 11 volumes of an as-yet incomplete *Complete Short Stories of Theodore Sturgeon* (1994–), and several attempts to start collecting Robert Silverberg's short fiction. Although Bear and Vinge are both still active short-story writers, there is a sense that this trend is concerned with tying off loose ends, of bringing something to an end. Or perhaps, along with the monumental Hartwell and Cramer anthologies and the profusion of "best of the year" collections (in 2006, there were at least 10; in 2007, this number increased), it says something about the commodification and collectability of sf.

The most distinctive voice in 1990s sf was probably Greg Egan's. His fiction, often emotionally cold but intellectually challenging, made him one of the most acclaimed sf writers to come out of Australia. Indeed, for a while it seemed as if Egan was the harbinger of a new wave in Australian sf. Although none would follow Egan closely in style or subject matter, a generation of writers did find themselves being published more widely and to greater international acclaim than had usually been the lot of their compatriots. Younger writers such as Sean McMullen (*Souls in the Great Machine* (1999)), Shane Dix and Sean Williams (the *Evergence* trilogy (1999–2001)), alongside more established names like Terry Dowling (*Blue Tyson* (1992), *Twilight Beach* (1993)), mostly employed traditional sf tropes and themes in colorful space epics or gritty near-future thrillers that were generally well received but did not seem to break new ground like Egan.

Meanwhile, the British Renaissance that had been building up a head of steam throughout the decade finally attracted critical and popular attention. Since there is no consensus on its nature (critics still dispute whether it continues or has run its course), it would be foolish to expect any generally recognized starting point. We might, however, triangulate the moment as lying somewhere between Iain M. Banks's exuberant left-wing space opera, *Consider Phlebas* (1987), Colin Greenland's reworking of the planetary romance, *Take Back Plenty* (1990), and David Pringle and

Colin Greenland's 1984 *Interzone* (1982–) editorial calling for a "radical hard sf." These stimuli revived interest in forms of sf that predated the literary experimentation and belated "modernism" of the New Wave, while insisting on literary quality and playful postmodern sensibilities.

The Renaissance that grew out of these starting points has therefore tended to look back to older forms of sf. Stephen Baxter is generally recognized as being one of the best hard-sf writers of his generation despite (or perhaps because of) a propensity for imagining the extinction of the human race. Nevertheless, his most accomplished novels include: a revisiting of H.G. Wells's *The Time Machine* (1895) in *The Time Ships* (1995); *Voyage* (1996), an alternate history about the continuation of the American space program after the Apollo missions; and *Titan* (1997), about a doomed space mission leaving a self-destructive Earth. The backwards look of these works has found more overt expression in a series of collaborations with Arthur C. Clarke, and also in novels that owe more to historical fiction than to sf. Paul McAuley has similarly written hard sf sensitive to the genre's past. *Eternal Light* (1991) had a cosmic scale reminiscent of Clarke, while the clotted imagery and vivacious invention of the *Confluence* sequence (1997–9) recalled an earlier generation of science fantasy. McAuley's finest work, however, was *Fairyland* (1995), a clear-eyed and often disturbing engagement with the prospects and possibilities of genetic engineering which managed to incorporate mythic archetypes and ideas of the posthuman without ever losing its grittily realist tone. And similarly, McAuley has drifted away from sf, in his case to a series of contemporary or near-future thrillers.

The other two leading British sf writers who came to maturity in the early 1990s both used their work to explore ideas of postcolonialism. In her early works, notably *Escape Plans* (1986) and *Kairos* (1988), Gwyneth Jones had already shown the keen interest in power relationships that lies at the heart of her *Aleutian* trilogy (*White Queen* (1991), *North Wind* (1994), *Phoenix Café* (1997)), which tells of an Earth colonized by enigmatic aliens and how we react to our new role, through subservience, rebellion, collaboration, and, in some of its most arresting images, by trying to make ourselves like the alien. At the turn of the century, *Bold as Love* (2001) began a new sequence of five novels which cast power relationships in a new light by playing out a 1960s hippy dream of rock stars taking over from politicians. Using magic and with overt Arthurian overtones, they are closer to fantasy than sf, but are interesting to note because of their portrayal of a near-future Britain torn apart politically, socially, and culturally. The island divided was a common feature in British sf of the mid- to late 1990s, occurring, for instance, in Michael Marshall Smith's *Only Forward* (1994) and Ken MacLeod's *The Star Fraction* (1995). It is tempting to see in its very ubiquity a response to the divisive premiership of Margaret Thatcher, who had been forced from office only a few years previously. Certainly, those writers whose work expresses a deeply held leftist politics have more recently reacted to the authoritarian leanings of Tony Blair's government with visions of a grim and repressive state, as in MacLeod's "The Human Front" (2001) and Hal Duncan's *Ink* (2007). Reaction to the repression accompanying the "War on Terror" has also prompted the most savage and powerful novel that Brian Aldiss has written in 20 years or more, *HARM* (2007).

That part of Britain most afflicted by divisiveness throughout the 1990s was, of course, Northern Ireland, where Ian McDonald used sf to explore the human effects of the Troubles, most effectively in *Sacrifice of Fools* (1996), in which aliens settle in Northern Ireland, profoundly changing the nature of the sectarian divide. Humans struggling to cope with the consequences of a generally indifferent alien incursion is a feature of McDonald's work. *Chaga* (1995), in which an alien arrival in Africa slowly but ineluctably changes everything to a crystalline structure, drew comparisons with early work by J.G. Ballard. Indeed, a charge commonly leveled against McDonald was that he used other writers' ideas, themes, and devices, although he employed them to purposes very much his own. However, by the time of *River of Gods* (2004), a kaleidoscopic portrayal of how various levels of Indian society are affected in a near future of water shortages and spreading digital culture, he had clearly found his own distinctive voice.

If Jones and McDonald are writers with distinct political agendas, British sf, ever since the days of Wells, has commonly expressed a left-leaning perspective. But few writers in the history of the genre have taken such a pronounced position as Ken MacLeod. His friend Iain M. Banks had already grafted left-wing utopian thinking onto a traditional space-operatic format in his *Culture* novels, but even at their best (*Excession* (1996), *Look to Windward* (2000)) they have been more notable for their humor and bravura invention than their politics. His non-*Culture* novels, often dazzling in their literary skill and invention (*Feersum Endjin* (1994)), have been less successful, and his habit of alternating sf with mainstream novels (several of which contain science-fictional elements) may have blunted some of the impact of his work. Certainly nothing had prepared the way for the concentrated political charge of MacLeod's early novels. His first four books, *The Star Fraction* (1995), *The Stone Canal* (1996), *The Cassini Division* (1998), and *The Sky Road* (1999), are generally grouped together as the *Fall Revolution* quartet, although the linkages between them are looser than that might imply. They might have some characters in common, but none of them takes place in exactly the same history of the world as the others. What links them is the way they explore different aspects of socialist and communist philosophy; it is hard to think of any other works which use political theory as the basis for witty, fast-paced adventures. Subsequent novels, with the politics more low-key, were less distinctive, often involving very traditional sf tropes (e.g., first contact in *Learning the World* (2005)), but *The Execution Channel* (2007) takes an impassioned political stance which enlivens its updating of the traditional British catastrophe novel, turning it into a howl of outrage at the iniquities perpetrated in the so-called War on Terror.

By the late 1990s a new generation of British writers was emerging. More than that, there were suddenly more British writers than ever before, and more British books demanding attention across the world. Spurred by a sense (from Greenland and Banks) that traditional sf could be given a new lease of life and (from Jones and MacLeod) that it could be made a vehicle for political views, encouraged by a growth in markets (*Interzone* was now securely established, a number of small magazines would appear and disappear throughout the 1980s and 1990s, while internet sites that started to appear from the mid-1990s were blind to the national origins of submissions), renewed critical attention and other factors (such as the Arthur C. Clarke Award, first awarded in 1987), Britain suddenly seemed to be fertile ground for new writing. Soon, and for the first time since at least the 1960s, British publishers' sf lists included a predominance of British writers, and the publishers were competing to proclaim their latest discoveries. (It should however be noted that some prominent British writers, such as Brian Stableford with his six-volume *Emortality* sequence (1998–2002), were still only being published in the US.) In 2005, all five nominees for the Hugo Award for best novel were British, as were, for the only time so far, the six shortlisted for the Clarke Award in 2006. For the first time since the New Wave, British sf was being perceived as a vital and important force in the genre.

New writers such as Jon Courtenay Grimwood explored issues of racial and individual identity, most intriguingly in his *Arabesk* alternate history sequence (*Pashazade* (2001), *Effendi* (2002), *Felaheen* (2003)). Set in Alexandria, the novels combined cyberpunk and crime thriller in a story in which personal and political struggles for identity mirror each other. In later novels, Grimwood has striven to achieve the same effect, with stories that deliberately show cultures in conflict, but without achieving quite the same balance between genres.

Something of the same political intent, if with a very different impetus and aesthetic, can be found in the work of China Miéville. *Perdido Street Station* (2000), *The Scar* (2002), and *Iron Council* (2004), loosely linked novels set in and around a sprawling city, New Crobuzon, present an astonishing milieu of strange beings engaged in direct and recognizable political action. Carefully judged to straddle sf, fantasy, and horror, they never fall clearly into one genre or another. In a sense, they represent another version of the irrational, in which the transgeneric form can allow anything to happen, although this particular expression has been more readily described as "New Weird." However, although a direct line of descent can be traced from Miéville's work back to M. John Harrison's *Viriconium* novels and stories, New Weird as a movement would seem to have no other readily identifiable exponents, the closest among contemporary writers being perhaps Hal Duncan in his exuberant diptych exploring contemporary irrationality, *Vellum* (2005) and *Ink*.

As for Harrison, his novel *Light* (2002) marked a return to sf after a series of novels that had blended the fantastic with the grittily contemporary. His first space opera since *The Centauri Device* (1974), on the surface it was an example of pure sf, exploring the Kefahuchi Tract where the flotsam of space-faring races is swept up. Closer examination, however, raises questions about how much the typical images of decay and entropy actually represent a real future or the psychological breakdown of the antihero of the present-day sections of the novel. A sequel of sorts, *Nova Swing* (2006), does nothing to settle these questions, while seeming to further tie this future into contemporary irrationality. It is perhaps worth noting that Justina Robson, having begun her career with finely judged explorations of moral doubt in the near future (*Mappa Mundi* (2001)), has moved toward a similarly space-operatic mode (*Natural History* (2003), *Living Next Door to the God of Love* (2005)) in which contemporary moral uncertainties feed into an unsettling posthuman profusion. In recent sf it seems that both the computer and the spaceship lead into places where anything goes and hence nothing need be real.

If this brief survey suggests that the whole of the British Renaissance has been concerned with subverting traditional tropes to social, political, or literary ends, it is worth pointing out that sf has always explored such ideas. Nevertheless a number of writers (including Mary Gentle, Peter F. Hamilton, Richard K. Morgan, Alastair Reynolds, Adam Roberts, Tricia Sullivan, Steph Swainston, and Liz Williams) have produced good and at times excellent work which has taken a far more traditional approach to the exploration of sf ideas. Still others have written sf as if they were writing a contemporary mainstream novel in which the idea is not so much the hero as the trigger for an exploration of human emotions and relationships. For example, in *Air* (2005) by Geoff Ryman (the leading proponent of "mundane sf," though whether *Air* counts as such is another matter), the science-fictional idea is an extension of the internet directly into people's brains; but the novel's focus, and what makes it so powerful, is a detailed and humane examination of the effects this has, both good and bad, on the people in a remote Asian village as they struggle to discover the extent to which their traditional way of life and social relationships can be maintained in the face of it.

Others have written in a similar mode, notably Christopher Priest, who continues to plough a generally very lonely furrow in the sf field. Building on a personal iconography involving twins, doubles, mirrors, and replications, he presents, in coldly precise terms, reasons to question the very reality we occupy. In *The Prestige* (1995), rival stage magicians at the turn of the twentieth century engage in an escalating war of sabotage against each other that brings into alarming focus the cost of holding on to individual identity. In *The Extremes* (1999), twin massacres in Britain and America are linked by virtual reality. In *The Separation* (2002), one of two twins is killed on the day Rudolf Hess flies to Britain, with the death of one leading to a history not precisely like our own, the death of the other resulting in peace in 1942. Priest extends the issue of personal identity to explore how who we are determines the world we occupy.

Priest is one of a number of sf writers who have flirted with the mainstream, but it is also worth noting the number of mainstream writers who have flirted, often very successfully, with sf in this period, many using alternative history scenarios to examine moral issues. Philip Roth's *The Plot Against America* (2004) looks at the effect on American Jews if the country had embraced fascism in the 1940s; Michael Chabon's *The Yiddish Policemen's Union* (2007) looks at Jews making a homeland in Alaska after being expelled from Israel in 1948; Owen Sheers's *Resistance* (2007) looks at the effect of a successful German invasion of Britain in 1944. Not all, however, have taken this route. Margaret Atwood, despite deriding sf in at least one ill-judged essay, has nevertheless used its tropes consistently and knowledgeably, perhaps most successfully in *Oryx and Crake* (2003), set in a depopulated future world, although it is far less forbidding than the stark post-apocalyptic world of Cormac McCarthy's *The Road* (2006). Amitav Ghosh's *The Calcutta Chromosome* (1996) uses sf to examine colonial issues surrounding work on malaria in British India; Kazuo Ishiguro's *Never Let Me Go* (2005) takes cloning as a metaphor in an elegiac study of the fragility of personal relationships; Audrey Niffenegger's *The Time Traveler's Wife* (2004) has a character cut loose in time to produce one of the most haunting love stories of recent years; and perhaps most ambitiously David Mitchell's *Cloud Atlas* (2004) embeds two sf tales, a near-future dystopia and a far-future post-apocalypse, within a complex examination of human predation that stretches from the nineteenth century to the end of life on this planet and back again.

As the British Renaissance waxed and then appeared to start waning, a new generation of American sf writers began to appear. Throughout this period, sales of the main sf magazines were declining and the outlets through which new writers could make a name for themselves with short stories were decreasing. Taking matters into their own hands, younger writers created new venues for their work: self-published chapbooks, anthologies such as the *Polyphony* series, magazines such as *Lady Churchill's Rosebud Wristlet*, and websites such as *Strange Horizons*. A number of prolific writers have emerged by this route, including Jay Lake, Christopher Barzak, Robert Wexler, and Nick Mamatas, although it remains to be seen how many of these might make a lasting impression on the genre. Despite the success of sf novels such as *Aestival Tide* (1992) and *Glimmering* (1997), Elizabeth Hand has made more impact in fantasy, while Paul DiFilippo (*Joe's Liver* (2000), *Fuzzy Dice* (2003)) has been perhaps too wayward and varied in his writing to achieve the recognition his work sometimes deserves. Some newer writers have restricted themselves to short fiction but still achieved notable success, especially Ted Chiang (*Stories of your Life and Others* (2002)) and Kelly Link (*Stranger Things Happen* (2001)). Others have produced acclaimed novels, particularly David Marusek (*Counting Heads* (2005)) and Peter Watts (*Blindsight* (2006)). Chiang, Link, Marusek, and Watts are perhaps the most talented new writers to emerge since 2000, but in some respects the most telling recent debuts have been by John Scalzi (*Old Man's War* (2005), *The Ghost Brigade* (2006)) and Elizabeth Bear (*Hammered* (2005), *Scardown* (2005), *Worldwired* (2005)). Both very deliberately chose to write in the old-fashioned – some would say played-out – subgenre of militaristic sf, and both reimagined and reinvigorated the mode before moving on to produce very different sf. In other words, they seem to be following, perhaps unconsciously and without the clear political agenda, a similar process to that which helped to produce the British Renaissance.

But, as Ho Chi Minh once said when asked about the effects of the French Revolution, it is too soon to tell. How any of these works will stand the test of time, which will prove significant in the history of sf, even whether sf has got a future at all, are things we will discover only in the fullness of time.

Part II
THEORY

19
CRITICAL RACE THEORY
Isiah Lavender III

Although it might seem that a genre concerned with otherness and alienation should frequently be drawn to explore themes of racism, for most of its history sf has considered itself a "colorblind" genre, either blithely portraying a future free from racial struggle (not seeming to notice that this harmony is accomplished by eliminating nonwhite people) or else projecting racial anxieties onto the body of the alien without seeming to notice that the humanity united against this external threat is suspiciously monochrome. It is perhaps more accurate to see sf's supposed "colorblindness" as an investment in whiteness as the norm – the very idea that is challenged by critical race theory. Although recent analyses of sf have embraced the insights of postcolonial theory and used them to investigate the unconsciously racialized settings, characters, and events of much sf, considerably less work has been done to bring together critical race theory and sf. After sketching out some of the main ideas and theorists associated with critical race theory, this chapter will consider existing scholarship on sf and race and then suggest ways in which it might be expanded and developed through the methods and insights of critical race theory. It will conclude with a brief discussion of Afrofuturism, a distinctly African-American mode of engagement with technoscience that has developed in parallel with sf.

Critical race theory

Critical race theory challenges the assumption that whiteness is a neutral or unmarked identity in American culture. Emerging first in the discipline of law, it critiques the notion of equality before the law, an ideal that obscures the degree to which judicial conclusions are shaped by the workings of power and cultural structures of systemic discrimination. Critical race theory sees the legal system as part of the wider culture, and emphasizes both law's role in making this culture and that change requires not merely new statutes but also new cultural values and assumptions. Now established as an interdisciplinary field, critical race theory encompasses film, history, literature, and ethnic studies, among other disciplines, in its investigation of the racial structures of American life. Grappling with such concerns about race and empire in the traditions of American democracy, Cornel West worries that "when we push race to the margins we imperil all of us, not just peoples of color" (West 2004: 60). In conjunction with critical race theory, American cultural studies exposes the hypocrisy at the heart of a government and society under the influence of racism, oppression, white patriarchal supremacy, economic inequality, and imperialism. While highlighting the socially constructed nature of race, it simultaneously acknowledges that race is a "real" category in terms of its material effects and suggests that racism is more or less permanent. It challenges the persistence of racial oppression across academic disciplines, particularly liberal notions that privilege whiteness as representative of "the human race," and thus threaten the lives and identities of colored people on a daily basis (see Dyer 1997). It is concerned with the intersections of representation and lived experience, and stresses the need for alternate narratives of experience at the conjunctures of race, sex, and class as a means of countering dominant ideologies of oppression.

Although critical race theory has no clearly defined origin point, the early work of Derrick A. Bell Jr is one of its foundations. In 1976, critiquing the limited gains of the civil rights struggle, Bell argued that "school desegregation plans [are] aimed at achieving racial balance" as opposed to improving the quality of education (Bell 1995b: 5). In a novel reading that risks being labeled segregationist, Bell suggests that the court's decision in *Brown v. The Board of Education* (1954) flies in the face of good judgment because of the negative impact that integration had on black America, which was left with inferior public schools following white flight. In a 1980 article, Bell suggests that the apparent neutrality of law is unreliable: in the struggle for racial equality the law is subordinated to "interest group politics" and whites will support advances for blacks only when such support promotes the self-interests of white society (Bell 1995a: 22). Mari J. Matsuda and Charles R. Lawrence III (1993), considering the case of *R.A.V. v. City of St Paul* (1991) – which concluded that cross-burning constituted an act of hate speech and is, therefore, as speech, protected by the First Amendment – challenge the ideal of the law's neutrality and suggest that this ruling fails to take into account the act's connection to a history of racist terror. In seeing cross-burning as speech alone, the court rendered invisible the mechanisms of white control that are the object of critical race theory's analysis.

Building upon this foundation, critical race theorists challenge school desegregation, assaultive speech, hate crimes, housing covenants, identity politics, the war on drugs' racial geographies, and other articulations of difference in their quest to dismantle oppression in all of its forms. Texts such as that by Mari J. Matsuda, Charles R. Lawrence III, Richard Delgado, and Kimberlè Williams Crenshaw (1993) transform perceptions of how law, race, and racism are understood – and provide new directions for scholars from other disciplines to interrogate the politics of race and raced identities as they are shaped by the experience of racism, social exclusion, and alienation. Expanding on the insights of W.E.B. Du Bois (1903), critical race theory reveals how American culture has operated via the projection of a false image of black inferiority to serve the political, social, and cultural ends of white supremacism, and the degree to which, as Manning Marable (1991) argues, interlocking systems of race and class domination remain long after legal reform of Jim Crow laws. Critical race theory emphasizes how an identity such as blackness is learned in American society (see Gates 1992: 101) and stresses the need critically to interrogate the history of constructing racial identities and boundaries because "opposing racism requires that we notice race" (Omi and Winant 1994: 159).

With its emphasis on the relationship between self and world, sf is an ideal genre through which to explore some of the consequences of these racial structures. It allows authors to posit worlds organized around other categories of difference or alternative histories that refigure key events in the history of US racism, such as slavery or the end of segregation, and consider how subjectivity would be changed by such changes. In the context of Chicano culture, Gloria Anzaldúa (1987), in a work suggestive of sf scenarios, has written about the effects of being between two cultures, alien in some ways to both. The affinity between sf thought-experiments and the relationships among culture, subjectivity, and legal institutions is further suggested by Derrick Bell's sf story, "The Space Traders" (1992), which exposes the persistence of racism in everyday life. The story poses the question, would white Americans freely exchange people of color with aliens from outer space if they received the right offer? Drawing on the historical reality of black slavery in America, Bell offers a decidedly grim answer: if the whites' lifestyle was significantly improved, then, yes, they would. This story reveals more than the roots of racist justification of slavery in self-interest, however, as it also suggests that white Americans would be willing to make this deal with slave traders not only for economic gain but also because it would eliminate the social tension of racism in America. Thus in its "solution" to the problem of racism, the story reveals the degree to which American culture continues to define America as its white population and its black population as "the race problem" – as Darryl Smith succinctly puts it, "The Traders are the people, blacks the aliens" (Smith 2000: 214). The story concludes with the government arguing that the founding fathers intended for the United States to be a white nation, creating a twenty-seventh amendment that requires blacks to be drafted for "special service ... necessary to protect domestic interests and international needs" (Bell 2000: 348) – that is, to serve their country by going with the aliens.

Sf and race

As Bell's story suggests, sf is well equipped to explore the dynamics of race and power embedded in the history of slavery and colonization, and critical race theory can be vital to reinterpreting sf. Although sf has long avoided direct engagement with questions of race and racism, its emphasis on alienation aptly describes the experience of many nonwhites in Western culture. Recently important new anthologies featuring speculative themes by people of color – such as Sheree R. Thomas's *Dark Matter* (2000) and *Dark Matter: reading the bones* (2004), Nalo Hopkinson's *Whispers from the Cotton Tree Root: Caribbean fabulist fiction* (2000), Andrea L. Bell and Yolanda Molina-Gavilán's *Cosmos Latinos: an anthology of science fiction from Latin America* (2003), and Nalo Hopkinson and Uppinder Mehan's *So Long Been Dreaming: postcolonial science fiction and fantasy* (2004) – have appeared, accompanied by a new critical sensitivity to themes of race and racism in the genre. As Mark Bould (2007) suggests, the genre's first sustained attempt to engage with such themes is Allen De Graeff's anthology *Human and Other Beings* (1963), a collection of 16 stories written and published between 1949 and 1961 dealing with issues of race and racism in defamiliarized contemporary and future settings. Its most noteworthy text is Leigh Brackett's "All the Colors of the Rainbow" (1957), which challenges gender and racial stereotypes of the period. It depicts the hallmarks of the nearly century-long Jim Crow era – discrimination, dehumanization, violence, oppression, blind hatred, racial exclusion, and derogatory slurs – as Mississippian white supremacists use a Social Darwinist rationale to justify their inhumane treatment of a green-skinned alien couple.

However, throughout most of its history, sf has reproduced rather than resisted racial stereotypes. For example, as Mary Weinkauf points out, although "science-fiction writers use Native Americans as a symbolic warning that progress is dangerous to tradition and as a plea to appreciate different lifestyles," the very "existence of the American Indian in science fiction is a reminder of a tendency to exploit and even annihilate those who stand in the way of progress, a recurring theme from Wells to Le Guin" (Weinkauf 1979: 319). Andre Norton's careful engagement with the noble savage stereotype in *The Beast Master* (1959), in which Native Americans continue to face the risk of extermination, is an example of how space opera can expose a kind of racism in sf. The premise of Norton's novel, which follows the interactions of Navajo protagonist Hosteen Storm with the Norbies, a species native to the planet Arzor, has much to say about prejudice, the destruction of indigenous cultures, identity, and the importance of ancestry. Norton's nuanced treatment of such themes further critiques earlier sf and its unreflective embrace of racial stereotypes in such "yellow peril" fiction as M.P. Shiel's *The Yellow Danger* (1898) and Edward Pendray's *The Earth-Tube* (1929).

Whereas Native Americans and Asians provide exotic images, in the sf imagination Africa evokes a sense of primitivism, as in A.M. Lightner's *The Day of the Drones* (1969), Mack Reynolds's *North Africa* trilogy (1972–8), Michael Crichton's *Congo* (1980), and Paul McAuley's *White Devils* (2004). Mike Resnick's "Kirinyaga" (1988) is perhaps the best example of this primitivist tendency. It depicts an artificial, isolated habitat built in the likeness of the African savannah and set aside for a group of East African émigrés from Kenya to establish a Kikuyu tribal utopia. All things Western have been discarded by the colonists who wish to practice and maintain ancient tribal customs without interference. Although the planet is presumed to be a space of black autonomy, when Koriba, the wizened village "*mundumugu* – a witch doctor" (Resnick 1993: 716), decides to uphold the tradition of killing a child born feet first to avoid a tribal curse, Maintenance, an off-world monitoring agency, chooses to intervene. History suggests that Koriba's resistance will prove futile. The Kikuyu are trapped in a colonial system that destroyed their culture once already, and the intervention of Maintenance forces them to experience otherness all over again. This problematic representation of black identity has led black fantasy writer Charles Saunders to challenge blacks to use Africa as a setting for their creative imaginings, arguing, "If we don't unleash our imaginations to tell our own sf and fantasy stories, people like Mike Resnick will tell them for us. And if we don't like the way he's telling them, it's up to us to tell them our own way" (Saunders 2000: 404), an insight consistent with critical race theory's emphasis on the role of narratives in shaping social perception and material experience. Black speculative writers such as Gregory L. Walker, Nnedi Okorafor-Mbachu, and Steven Barnes have lately responded to this challenge with *Shades of Memnon* (1999), *Zahrah the Windseeker* (2005), and *Great Sky Woman* (2006), respectively. Saunders's own *Imaro* series (1981–5), recently revised and reissued, can be seen as a response to white appropriations of Africa, and the Caribbean influence in Nalo Hopkinson's writing performs a similar function. All of these writers use sf as means to open up alternative visions of the world, ones which also counter the genre's predominant, normalized whiteness, and thus to promote social change in the perception of race.

With the exception of the critical attention paid to Samuel R. Delany and Octavia E. Butler, sf scholarship has largely neglected issues of race, although this situation has changed in recent years, following Elisabeth Leonard's pioneering collection of essays scrutinizing race and color-coding in literatures of the fantastic (1997). De Witt Kilgore (2003) identifies spaceflight as the key to fantasies about changing the social and political realities of human society, focusing on examples of an idealized human future where race can be imagined positively or at least differently. Sandra Grayson (2003) provides useful information on the better-known black sf writers (Barnes, Butler, Delany, Hopkinson, and Saunders, as well as Tananarive Due and LeVar Burton) and their use of African themes in their work. A. Timothy Spaulding (2005) draws together a diverse group of texts by black authors to explore the ways in which the slave narrative has been reinterpreted and rearticulated in the postmodern fantastic. Thomas Foster (2005) brings a much-needed focus on race to discussions of cyberpunk, disembodiment, and posthumanism. Sierra Adare (2005) critiques stereotypes of Native Peoples in sf television shows such as *Star Trek* (1966–9), *Star Trek: The Next Generation* (1987–94) and *Quantum Leap* (1989–93), and reveals the degree to which sf depictions of the frontier have relied on the racist structures of the western genre and its images of indigenous people as vicious or noble savages. In 2007, *Science Fiction Studies* published special issues on Afrofuturism and Latino sf.

Scholarship in this period has also seen an increased focus on questions of race and technology, in edited collections such as those by Beth E. Kolko, Lisa Nakamura, and Gilbert B. Rodman (2000), and Alondra Nelson, Thuy Linh N. Tu with Alicia Headlam Hines (2001). Lisa Nakamura (2002) reads race and technology in relation to the internet, and Bruce Sinclair (2004) represents an important step in recognizing that technology has a social history, one that, like the legal system, is often embedded in an unacknowledged systemic racism. Martin Kevorkian (2006) offers perhaps the best consideration of race and technology, imagining black computer geeks as natural machines and expanding our perception of what the fusion of race and technology could look like.

Afrofuturism

Emerging from the particular cultural relationship between African-Americans and Western technology, Afrofuturism sees in sf's motifs of abduction, displacement, and

189

alienation a fitting metaphor for black experience. The term originated in Mark Dery (1993) – a set of interviews with Samuel Delany, Tricia Rose, and Greg Tate – and was picked up by Alondra Nelson (2002), who used it to challenge the notion of a future without race. Dery defines Afrofuturism as "Speculative fiction that treats African-American themes and addresses African-American concerns in the context of twentieth century technoculture – and, more generally, African-American signification that appropriates images of technology and a prosthetically enhanced future" (Dery 1993: 736). And yet, Lisa Yaszek claims, "Afrofuturism is not just about reclaiming the history of the past, but about reclaiming the history of the future as well" (Yaszek 2005: 300). Afrofuturism is concerned with the impact of black people on technology and of technology on the lives of black people. It explores both the innovative cultural productions enabled by technology and the ways in which black people have been the subjects of technoscientific exploitation. While the "systematic, conscientious, and massive destruction of African cultural remnants" was an integral part of the dehumanization process necessary to slavery (Delany qtd in Dery 1993: 746), race itself functioned as a labor-based technology, whereby black human beings, coded as natural machines, were used to generate wealth. Afrofuturism suggests that the structures of slavery have thus imposed a science-fictional existence on African slaves and their descendants, figuring them as cyborgs in a white human world. From this perspective, Ben Williams recognizes "the mechanical metaphors" used for blacks "extend beyond signifying post-humanity to embody a history that began with slavery; indeed, slavery, the original unit of capitalist labor, is ... the originary form of the post-human" (Williams 2001: 169).

In this context, even Richard Wright's realist novel *Native Son* (1940) might be understood as Afrofuturist, given its themes of alienation and dehumanization. Protagonist Bigger Thomas is disconnected from his humanity by systemic racism, living a stunted life trapped between the American dream and black existence, unable to find a decent job, adequate housing, or loving relationships. He only begins to feel even remotely human after committing the most heinous crimes: stuffing the body of white heiress Mary Dalton into her parents' furnace after mistakenly smothering her; raping his black girlfriend Bessie and bashing her head in with a brick. After being convicted and sentenced to death Bigger reveals, "I didn't know I was really alive in this world until I felt things hard enough to kill for 'em" (Wright 1993: 501). The depth of Bigger's alienation is the stuff of sf because he is a monstrous creation of white racism and institutionalized oppression, an alien to us and an alien to himself. The persistence of this black brute stereotype as both a fearful projection of white culture and an experienced reality of some African-Americans because of the structures of systemic racism is apparent in films such as *Boyz N the Hood* (Singleton 1991) or *Menace II Society* (Hughes and Hughes 1993) and in the lyrics of rappers such as The Notorious B.I.G. and Tupac. More evidently science-fictional articulations of this stereotype of inhuman or savage black monstrosity can be found in the *Alien* and *Predator* franchises and *Lost in Space* (Hopkins 1998). Darth Vader – the psi-powered, dark-armored, and masked evil cyborg, distinctively voiced by black actor James Earl Jones – is visually and aurally coded as black; but in *Star Wars: Episode VI – Return of the Jedi* (Marquand 1983), once he redeems himself by renouncing evil and sacrifices himself to save his son, Luke Skywalker, and thus the galaxy, he is unmasked as a blue-eyed white man, with a soft voice suggestive of wisdom.

More complex and self-conscious treatments of race are explored in films such as *The Brother from Another Planet* (Sayles 1984) and *Sankofa* (Gerima 1993). In the former, the mute alien Brother is on the run from white extraterrestrial slave catchers, and a sharp critique is developed from the aliens being unaware of the politics of skin color in America. The latter, reminiscent of Butler's *Kindred* (1979), transports African-American fashion model Mona into the past of her slave ancestor Shola. Confronted with the horrors of plantation life, Mona begins to better understand her contemporary world.

A more direct engagement with sf themes and the materiality of technology is found in Afrofuturist music, which, Anna Everett argues, allows black people "somehow to overcome their profound dislocation, fragmentation, alienation, relocation, and ultimate commodification in the Western slavocracies of the modern world" (Everett 2002: 126). Musicians such as Sun Ra and George Clinton evoke aliens and UFOs in order to gesture toward a social existence that will extend beyond the current limits that racism, discrimination, and inequality place on African-American experience. Their music deploys and develops sf themes so as to envision a world where the marginalized are no longer forced into the margins, and to activate the potential for change and an inclusive universe. Sun Ra, who claimed to be from Saturn, and his protean Arkestra created, on albums such as *Space is the Place* (1973), ambiguous fusion soundscapes, which signified outer space as simultaneously an alien place and a potential home for a disembodied, diasporic people. George Clinton and Parliament-Funkadelic, on albums such as *Mothership Connection* (1975), brought the alien funk to Earth to free black people and likewise suggested the need to leave Earth behind in order to achieve freedom and harmony. More recently the influence of sf is apparent in the work of award-winning hip-hop duo OutKast. Heirs to Clinton's funk ideology, they continue to experiment with their style, mixing funk, soul, electronica, rock, blues, jazz and other elements in hip-hop creations that create an otherworldly sound. Their second album *ATLiens* (1996), with its speculative comic-book cover, is overtly sf. Its title is symbolic of their estrangement from American society: though native to the city of Atlanta, they do not feel as if they are citizens of the United States, but suggest instead that the inner city of their formative years is out of this world and its hostile conditions. In the title track, "ATLiens," André 3000 refers to the group as "the alienators cause we different keep your hands to the sky," as if to suggest that they are extra-solar beings waiting for Clinton's mothership. The chorus from the "Millennium" – "Planets and stars / Earth, Jupiter, Mars / Hoes, clothes, cars / It's who you are" – continues the theme of estrangement by suggesting that the pursuit of women and material goods creates an unfamiliar slave identity for black men. And "E.T. (Extraterrestrial)" speaks for itself: the duo are "Extraterrestrial – straight from ATL," beings from outside the limits of the planet and alien to the white mainstream. *Aquemini* (1998), the title of OutKast's third album, possibly alludes to Sun Ra's astroblack mythology in its combination of the astrological signs Aquarius and Gemini. The track "Synthesizer," which features George Clinton rapping about a "digital good time," questions "twentieth-century technology" and asks whether "the computer age, scientists and doctors gone too far."

Afrofuturism is as opposed as critical race theory to the disturbing notion of a colorless future. As Alexander Weheliye suggests, "The erasure of race severely limits how we conceive of the complex interplay between 'humans' and informational technologies" (Weheliye 2002: 22). Tensions between race and technoscientific progress have always shaped America, if not the West, and the disappearance of race from sf's ability to envision the future suggests a terrifying future for humanity, where all peoples of color have either been assimilated or annihilated. Afrofuturism safeguards against such a vision by being mindful of history and the intersections of black experience with technology.

Conclusion

Sf has the ability to imagine a world without racism but also to imagine a world without race. Critical race theory and Afrofuturism remind us of the crucial difference between these two visions and of the necessity to attend to the historical specificity and the consequences of racial constructions. If readers, viewers, and listeners are to understand sf's pervasive racial preoccupations, critical race theory is an essential tool. It enables us to rethink the conventions of sf's racial imaginary and encourages us to disrupt the desire to conform to the liberal status quo of a white-privileging but supposedly a colorblind society. And sf, for all its dubious representations of race hitherto, is especially well suited to provide the imaginative grounds for change.

BIBLIOGRAPHY

Adare, S.S. (2005) "Indian" Stereotypes in TV Science Fiction: First Nations' voices speak out, Austin: University of Texas Press.

Anzaldúa, G. (1987) Borderlands/La Frontera: the new Mestiza, San Francisco: Aunt Lute.

Bell Jr, D. (1995a) "Brown v. Board of Education and the Interest Convergence Dilemma," in K. Crenshaw, N. Gotanda, G. Peller, and K. Thomas (eds) Critical Race Theory: the key writings that formed the movement, 1980, New York: The New Press.

—— (1995b) "Serving Two Masters: integration ideals and client interests in school desegregation litigation," in K. Crenshaw, N. Gotanda, G. Peller, and K. Thomas (eds) Critical Race Theory: the key writings that formed the movement, 1976, New York: The New Press.

—— (2000) "The Space Traders," in S. Thomas (ed.) Dark Matter: a century of speculative fiction from the African Diaspora, 1992, New York: Warner.

Bould, M. (2007) "The Ships Landed Long Ago: Afrofuturism and black sf," Science Fiction Studies, 34(2): 177–86.

Dery, M. (1993) "Black to the Future: interviews with Samuel R. Delany, Greg Tate, and Tricia Rose," South Atlantic Quarterly, 92(4): 735–78.

Du Bois, W.E.B. (1995) The Souls of Black Folk, 1903, New York: Signet Classic.

Dyer, R. (1997) White, New York: Routledge.

Everett, A. (2002) "The Revolution will be Digitized: Afrocentricity and the digital public sphere," Social Text, 20(2): 125–46.

Foster, T. (2005) The Souls of Cyberfolk: posthumanism as vernacular theory, Minneapolis: University of Minnesota Press.

Gates Jr, H. (1992) *Loose Canons: notes on the culture wars*, New York: Oxford University Press.

Grayson, S. (2003) *Visions of the Third Millennium: black science fiction novelists write the future*, Trenton, NJ: Africa World Press.

Kevorkian, M. (2006) *Color Monitors: the black face of technology in America*, Ithaca, NY: Cornell University Press.

Kilgore, D.W.D. (2003) *Astrofuturism: science, race, and visions of utopia in space*, Philadelphia: University of Pennsylvania Press.

Kolko, B.E., Nakamura, L., and Rodman, G.B. (2000) *Race in Cyberspace*, New York: Routledge.

Leonard, E. (1997) *Into Darkness Peering: race and color in the fantastic*, Westport, CT: Greenwood Press.

Marable, M. (1991) *Race, Reform, and Rebellion: the second reconstruction in black America, 1945–1990*, Jackson: University Press of Mississippi.

Matsuda, M.J. and Lawrence III, C.R. (1993) "Epilogue: burning crosses and the R.A.V. case," in M.J. Matsuda, Charles R. Lawrence III, R. Delgado, and K. Williams Crenshaw (eds) *Words That Wound: critical race theory, assaultive speech, and the First Amendment*, Boulder, CO: Westview Press.

Matsuda, M.J., Lawrence III, C.R., Delgado, R., and Williams Crenshaw, K. (eds) (1993) *Words That Wound: critical race theory, assaultive speech, and the First Amendment*, Boulder, CO: Westview Press.

Nakamura, L. (2002) *Cybertypes: race, ethnicity, and identity on the internet*, New York: Routledge.

Nelson, A. (2002) "Introduction: Future Texts," *Social Text*, 71(2): 1–15.

Nelson, A. and Tu, T.L.N. with Headlam Hines, A. (2001) *Technicolor: race, technology, and everyday life*, New York: New York University Press.

Omi, M. and Winant, H. (1994) *Racial Formation in the United States: from the 1960s to the 1990s*, New York: Routledge.

Resnick, M. (1993) "Kirinyaga," in B. Attebery and U. Le Guin (eds) *The Norton Book of Science Fiction*, New York: Norton.

Saunders, C. (2000) "Why Blacks Should Read (and Write) Science Fiction," in Sheree R. Thomas (ed.) *Dark Matter: a centry of speculative fiction from the African diaspora*, New York: Warner Books.

Sinclair, B. (ed.) (2004) *Technology and the African-American Experience: needs and opportunities for study*, Cambridge, MA: MIT Press.

Smith, D. (2007) "Droppin' Science Fiction: signification and singularity in the metapocalypse of DuBois, Baraka, and Bell," *Science Fiction Studies*, 34(2): 201–19.

Spaulding, A.T. (2005) *Re-Forming the Past: history, the fantastic, and the postmodern slave narrative*, Columbus: Ohio State University Press.

Weheliye, A. (2002) "Feenin' Posthuman Voices in Contemporary Black Popular Music," *Social Text*, 20(2): 21–47.

Weinkauf, M.S. (1979) "The Indian in Science Fiction," *Extrapolation*, 20(4): 308–20.

West, C. (2004) *Democracy Matters: winning the fight against imperialism*, New York: Penguin.

Williams, B. (2001) "Black Secret Technology: Detroit techno and the information age," in A. Nelson and T.L.N. Tu with A. Headlam Hines (eds) *Technicolor: race, technology, and everyday life*, New York: New York University Press.

Wright, R. (1993) *Native Son*, 1940, restored edn, New York: HarperCollins.

Yaszek, L. (2005) "Afrofuturism and Ralph Ellison's *Invisible Man*," *Rethinking History: The Journal of Theory and Practice*, 9(2/3): 297–313.

20
CULTURAL HISTORY
Lisa Yaszek

It is a truth universally acknowledged that stories about the future mirror our hopes and fears about life in the present. But many of the most compelling science-fictional visions of the future are actually based on specific philosophies of the past, and careful study of these narrative futures can provide unique insight into historiography itself. This dual recognition is central to the practice of cultural history as it intersects with both sf and sf studies. Sf authors have long created futures by extrapolating from what they believe to be the key social and material forces shaping history. In a similar vein, sf scholars have long used specific theories of the past to make sense of their chosen genre's history. Furthermore, as cultural historians, scholars increasingly read sf texts for what they reveal about the social values and practices of the past, especially as these texts confirm, complicate, and sometimes even directly challenge official pronouncements about these values and practices.

Philosophies of history in sf

Cultural history encompasses interdisciplinary practices spanning the humanities and social sciences. However, it is most closely associated with philosophies of history that emerged at the beginning of the modern era, when the seventeenth-century British philosopher Francis Bacon first allied historiography with scientific practice. Bacon believed that both historians and scientists contributed to the sum of human knowledge by acting as detached observers who used inductive reasoning to explain phenomena ranging from the movement of tides to the ascendancy of kings and queens. Enlightenment ideas about the quantifiable nature of history and the objective historian reached their apex in the work of the nineteenth-century German philosopher Georg Wilhelm Friedrich Hegel, who claimed that human events unfold according to the demands of an eternal Reason. The task of the trained historian was to articulate the progress of Reason through careful study of great political and military leaders. Such ideas were very much part of the nineteenth-century penchant for open-ended political histories that justified Western imperialism.

Hegelian notions of history are also very much part of the oldest, most public face of sf: space opera. They were particularly appealing to American sf authors who grew up on the rhetoric of manifest destiny, especially as it was expressed in the action-adventure dime novels of the late nineteenth and early twentieth centuries. Set in a far future where humans have colonized entire galaxies (often by engaging in war with other, usually humanoid, civilizations), American space operas articulated neatly with Hegelian ideas about the modern nation-state. Furthermore, they revolved around larger-than-life action-adventure heroes who, much like Hegel's great men of history, employed both diplomacy and military prowess to advance their empires. These characteristics were most clearly embodied in the stories that American authors wrote for the pulp magazines of the 1920s, 1930s, and 1940s, including E.E. "Doc" Smith's *Skylark* (1928–34) and *Lensman* (1934–48) series, Edmond Hamilton's *Captain Future* tales (1940–4), and Leigh Brackett's *Eric John Stark* stories (1949–51). They were also central to many of the comic-strip, radio, and film serials of this period, including Alex Raymond's *Flash Gordon* and Philip Francis Nowlan's *Buck Rogers* series.

Of course, Hegelian theories of history had a great deal of competition in the modern marketplace of ideas. Perhaps most significantly, British historian and politician Edward Gibbon advanced his own philosophy of history as a cyclic phenomenon in *The History of the Decline and Fall of the Roman Empire* (1776–88). Gibbon extrapolates from the particular situation of Rome to propose that all empires will naturally expand when their leaders employ reason and military discipline, and just as naturally fall if such virtues are exchanged for religion and pacifism. Two popular historians, Oswald Spengler and Arnold Toynbee, updated this idea for the twentieth century. Spengler's *Decline of the West: perspectives in world history* (1919) applied Gibbon's claims about the cyclic nature of empire to the broader concept of civilization, arguing that civilizations fell when they embraced irreligion and mechanism, as he saw happening in the modern West. Toynbee's *Study of History* (1934–61) more optimistically proposed that "creative minorities" might stop the cyclical decline of civilization by meeting physical and social challenges in novel ways, echoing Gibbon's own hope that educated, rational people could change the rhythms of history itself.

Given that cyclic theories of history, like their linear counterparts, focus on the actions of great politicians and soldiers over the span of centuries, it is hardly surprising that they found their way into the storytelling practices of the early sf community. A Spenglerian concern with the decline of the modern West is apparent in the work of early twentieth-century British authors who saw themselves as citizens of a failing empire. This pessimism was expressed in future-war stories such as Edward Shanks's *The People of the Ruins* (1920) and Cicely Hamilton's *Theodore Savage* (1922) as well as Olaf Stapledon's space opera *Last and First Men* (1930). With the seismic shocks of the Great Depression, the Second World War, and the Cold War, American authors began to think about their own country in similar ways. Spenglerian ideas about the deterministic nature of history shaped A.E. van Vogt's *Weapon Shops* (1941–3) and *Null-A* (1945–9) series as well as James Blish's *Cities in Flight* sequence (1950–62). For the most part, however, American authors relied on the more open-ended philosophies of Gibbon and Toynbee. Isaac Asimov freely acknowledged that the *Foundation* trilogy (1942–58) was patterned on Gibbon's *History*, especially as it held forth the hope that a small but rational elite might resist mob rule and prevent the total decline of one civilization before another replaced it. Meanwhile, Toynbeean ideas about creative minorities breaking free of history's cycles were central to Charles Harness's *The Paradox Men* (1953) and all of Robert A. Heinlein's future-history stories.

While some scholars (and sf authors) turned to linear and cyclic theories of history because they seemed closely allied with the physical sciences, others proposed new ways of thinking about the past based on their interest in the emergent social sciences. Drawing upon new ideas in political economy, the nineteenth-century philosopher Karl Marx argued that the real engines of history were the forces of Capital that produced inegalitarian class relations. Historians who failed to acknowledge how past economic relations conditioned the possibility of action in the present were at best naïve and at worst guilty of an ideological coverup that served the interests of the ruling class. In the 1920s, Marc Bloch, Lucien Febvre, and other scholars associated with the *Annales* group in France suggested that historians could avoid ideological interpellation by using the tools of anthropology, sociology, and geography to replace broad outlines of political history with detailed pictures of particular places at specific times.

Taken together, these new ways of thinking about the past paved the way for the explosion of interest in underrepresented groups (including workers, women, racial and ethnic minorities, and gays and lesbians) that characterized history writing in the 1960s and 1970s. Many of the historians engaged in these new fields of inquiry focused upon what *Annales* scholars called *l'histoire des mentalités*, or the history of values and beliefs as they are expressed throughout culture. To better assess this seemingly intangible new subject material, historians often borrowed techniques from the social sciences, replacing anecdotes with primary resources and individual case studies with broad data sets and statistical interpretations in their research. As such, scholars including E.P. Thompson, Richard Hoggart, and Lenore Davidoff laid the groundwork for cultural history as a unique discipline.

Sf writers interested in the plurality of peoples and cultures have long incorporated similar philosophies of history into their fiction writing. Those who tend toward economic explanations often work in the utopian tradition, where imaginary rational societies are used to demonstrate the irrational workings of their real-world counterparts. This tradition began at the turn of the twentieth century with stories including H.G. Wells's *The World Set Free* (1914) and *Men Like Gods* (1923) in the UK and Edward Bellamy's *Looking Backward: 2000–1887* (1888) and Charlotte Perkins Gilman's *Herland* (1915) in the US. During the heyday of American magazine sf, economic theories of history were most often expressed in dystopian capitalist satires including Fritz Leiber's *The Green Millennium* (1953) and Frederik Pohl and C.M. Kornbluth's *The Space Merchants* (1952). In recent decades American cyberpunk novels including William Gibson's *Sprawl* trilogy (1984–8), Neal Stephenson's *Snow Crash* (1991) and *The Diamond Age* (1995), and Pat Cadigan's *Synners* (1991) continue the tradition of equating unchecked capitalist relations with dystopian futures. Meanwhile, American author Kim Stanley Robinson's *Mars* (1992–6) and *Science in the Capital* (2004–7) trilogies and British author China Miéville's *Bas-Lag* series (2000–4) extend the projects of their utopian predecessors by imagining how scientists and other rational people might surmount the crises engendered by global capitalism to change the course of history for the better.

Sf authors interested in sociologically and anthropologically based theories of history also tend to work within the utopian narrative tradition. This is particularly apparent in the work of feminist sf writers. For example, Gilman's *Herland*, Joanna Russ's *The Female Man* (1975), Marge Piercy's *Woman on the Edge of Time* (1976), and Nicola Griffith's *Ammonite* (1993) all present readers with egalitarian societies organized around female values that stand in sharp contrast to inegalitarian masculinist counterparts. Conversely, novels such as Suzette Haden Elgin's *Native Tongue* (1984) and Margaret Atwood's *The Handmaid's Tale* (1985) depict dystopic futures for women extrapolated from the sociobiological discourses and antifeminist rhetoric of the Reagan era. Elements of both utopian and dystopian narrative inform sociological thought-experiments such as Theodore Sturgeon's *Venus Plus X* (1960) and Ursula K. Le Guin's *The Left Hand of Darkness* (1969), which use androgynous alien cultures to question dominant cultural assumptions about the supposedly natural gender relations of our own world.

Sf authors also use alternate histories to explore how science and society might evolve outside Western paradigms. Nowhere is this more apparent than in the work of African-American writer Steven Barnes, whose *Insh'Allah* books (2002–3) imagine an alternate Earth where African people colonize the Americas with the labor of European slaves. In a similar vein, Octavia Butler's *Patternist* series (1976–84) and Minister Faust's *Coyote Kings of the Space Age Bachelor Pad* (2004) relate the adventures of psychically gifted black Westerners who learn that they are heir to ancient African struggles between the forces of civilization and chaos. As such, these authors insist that multiple histories might well exist in our own world.

Even as some cultural historians have sought to ally themselves with the social sciences, others have found inspiration in literary theory. Hayden White (1973) argues that historians do not examine facts dispassionately but create meaning by presenting facts via specific narrative genres and literary tropes. Given that this challenges longstanding beliefs about the objectivity of the historian and the transparency of the historical text, it is not surprising that many scholars have rejected White's ideas. But others have seized upon them as a means by which to bolster the legitimacy of alternate historical inquiries and even open new fields of study, including the history of historiography itself.

For nearly half a century writers associated with postmodern sf have raised similar questions about the nature of historical reality in their own writing. Two of the earliest novels to explore these issues were Philip K. Dick's *The Man in the High Castle* (1962) and Kurt Vonnegut's *Slaughterhouse 5* (1969), both of which imagine that the history of the Second World War as we know it is just one possibility among many. In the following decade, stories such as Octavia Butler's *Kindred* (1979) and William Gibson's "The Gernsback Continuum" (1981) extended this line of inquiry to consider the effects of historical narrative as material reality, suggesting that any attempt to negotiate the past through a single frame of reference can have deadly effects in the present and future. More recently, James Morrow's *Towing Jehovah* (1994), Robert Charles Wilson's *The Chronoliths* (2001), and Gwyneth Jones's *Life* (2004) have explored how world-changing discoveries increase rather than decrease ontological uncertainty, prompting people to multiply the religious, political, and scientific narratives they use to make sense of reality. Slipstream authors also often explore issues of historiography by telling stories that merge the thematic concerns, stylistic techniques, and cognitive effects of seemingly incompatible narrative genres. In doing so, they foreground how specific acts of narrative creation produce meaning and shape our sense of the real. While Geoff Ryman addresses this problem directly in the final chapter of "*Was . . .*" (1992), most slipstream writers take a more indirect approach. For example, novels including Karen Joy Fowler's *Sarah Canary* (1991), Michael Cunningham's *Specimen Days* (2005), and Kathleen Ann Goonan's *In War Times* (2007) blend history and sf to illuminate the interpenetration of fact and fiction. Meanwhile, many of the stories in Ted Chiang's *Stories of Your Life and Others* (2002), Kelly Link's *Magic for Beginners* (2005), and M. Rickert's *Map of Dreams* (2006) explore how the intrusion of the supernatural into the mundane world might imbue the past and present with new meaning – or how it might shatter meaning altogether.

Philosophies of history in sf studies

Sf is an ideal subject matter for cultural historians because it developed in tandem with modern political, economic, and technoscientific systems. As such, it is a compelling vehicle for the expression of modern social values. Early claims in this vein came from within the sf community, as H.G. Wells in the UK and Hugo Gernsback in the US each argued that the genre provided an ideal way to introduce readers to the sciences and technologies that would shape the next century. More recently, sf has been embraced by the academy as well. Donna Haraway (1985) counts feminist sf authors among the most important cultural theorists of our times, while Fredric Jameson (1991) describes cyberpunk sf as the preeminent literature of late capitalism.

Although claims about the privileged position of sf as cultural expression extend back to the late nineteenth century, sf scholars have only begun to employ the methodologies of cultural history in the past two decades. This can be attributed to the fact that sf scholarship has evolved along much the same lines as historical scholarship itself. In 1958 Thomas Clareson and Edward Lauterbach organized the first panel on sf at the annual Modern Language Association conference. In 1959 Clareson published the first issue of *Extrapolation*, a journal that aimed to define sf as a self-regulating literary genre through the compilation of bibliographies and histories. Brooks Landon notes that these first scholarly records of the genre were "largely anecdotal" and "infrequently contextualized in the larger culture" (qtd in Luckhurst 2005: 6). As such, they mirrored the traditional historian's penchant for linear narratives based on case studies of great men.

In the 1960s and 1970s, sf scholars began to engage new ideas from elsewhere in the academy. As the social sciences gained ascendancy and radical campus politics led students to demand socially relevant courses of study, scholars responded with new classes that connected sf to everything from literature and history to religion and politics. They also produced new anthologies such as Martin Harry Greenberg and Patricia S. Warrick's *Political SF: an introductory reader* (1974) and Jack Williamson's

Teaching SF: education for tomorrow (1980). Thus sf met the needs of students and scholars alike because it provided concrete examples of the more abstract theses and theories professors advanced in their courses.

The second generation of sf scholars was even more receptive to literary and critical theory, which quickly came to dominate the field and resulted in the creation of the journal *Science Fiction Studies* in 1973. Broadly speaking, critical theory approaches to sf fall into three categories. As pioneered by Samuel Delany in the late 1960s, poststructuralist sf criticism explores how readers must learn the conventions of the genre to engage with it in meaningful ways. In a more overtly politicized vein, Marxist sf scholarship, most commonly associated with Darko Suvin and the other founding members of *Science Fiction Studies*, treats sf as a literature of "cognitive estrangement" that extrapolates from current trends in science and society to demonstrate the process of historical change and imagine startling new futures. Taken together, poststructuralist and Marxist approaches demonstrate both how the formal properties of the genre lend themselves to sophisticated critical inquiry and how individual texts can instantiate political and cultural theory. Finally, feminist sf criticism, as first articulated by Joanna Russ in the early 1970s, proposes that the genre's future-forward orientation makes it useful for authors interested in how the relations of science, society, and gender change over time. Like Delany and Suvin, Russ drew upon poststructuralist ideas about textual instability and the production of meaning through language deployment to champion a new kind of sf criticism. But while poststructuralist and Marxist critics focused on the similarities within sf storytelling as a whole, Russ treated feminist writing as part of an oppositional and largely neglected discourse within the patriarchal world of letters. As such, her work recovering women's sf paralleled that of Lenore Davidoff in the realm of feminist social history.

Through the pioneering efforts of writers such as Delany, Suvin, and Russ, sf studies has evolved into a set of transdisciplinary analytic practices centering on what Catherine Belsey calls "history at the level of the signifier" (Belsey 2000: 106). Today, sf scholars who employ the subject matter and methodologies of cultural history challenge what Mark Poster (1997), following Roger Chartier (1988), identifies as the three major distinctions informing traditional liberal arts scholarship: learned versus popular texts, production versus consumption, and reality versus fiction. Traditionally speaking, historians have claimed learned texts and production as their rightful terrain, relegating popular culture and the politics of consumption to their more quantitatively minded counterparts in the social sciences. They also have invoked the distinction between reality and fiction to make sense of their differences from one another. Cultural history emerges when these distinctions erode and scholars examine how different kinds of texts "configure what they point to, and … are configured by it" (Poster 1997: 9).

The past two decades have witnessed an explosion of interest in the cultural history of sf as it pertains to everything from the development of nuclear weapons and kitchen technologies to ongoing debates over literary aesthetics and the history of sf history itself. Broadly speaking, these cultural histories build upon prior work in sf studies and can be divided into three types, based on the binary distinction they most clearly challenge. For example, mid-twentieth-century genre scholars including Kingsley Amis, Sam Moskowitz, and Brian Aldiss challenged conventional ideas about learned versus popular texts by defining sf in ways that included everything from Plato's *Republic* (*c.* 360 BC) and Mary Shelley's *Frankenstein* (1818) to the space operas of the pulp era and the New Wave narrative experiments of their own time.

However, it is only recently that scholars have returned to the primary documents generated by sf authors and editors themselves in regards to the matter of aesthetics. For example, Gary Westfahl (1999) examines the writing of Hugo Gernsback and John W. Campbell to show how early sf editors defined the political and aesthetic parameters of their chosen genre. This is very much a transitional work: it focuses on the founding "great men" of the genre and treating its history as something distinct from the rest of culture, and thus reiterating traditional assumptions about the appropriate subject matter of history and the necessary distinction between high and low culture; but simultaneously its use of primary materials and belief that popular forms can be qualitatively analyzed are fundamental to the practice of cultural history. Roger Luckhurst (2005) creates a more fully developed cultural history of sf by examining how early proponents of the genre, including Gernsback and Wells, participated in cultural debates about the meaning and value of modern fiction. Like Westfahl, Luckhurst bases much of his work on primary documents. However, he goes on to situate those documents in the broader context of late nineteenth- and early twentieth-century scientific, political, and mainstream literary discourses. Despite their differences, these two cultural histories of sf extend the arguments advanced by earlier genre scholars to show not just how sf may encompass both learned and popular texts, but how members of the sf community have always been participants in the construction of those very terms.

Sf scholars also build upon the work of their predecessors by examining fan activities that blur the line between production and consumption. Camille Bacon-Smith (1992), Henry Jenkins (1992), and Patricia Frazer Lamb and Diane Veith (1986) examined the complex relations of fan writing to sf film and television franchises. More recently, critics have explored how digital technologies affect the shape of fan activity. As Karen Hellekson and Kristina Busse (2006) and Henry Jenkins (2006) demonstrate, the internet has made fan production a public activity that challenges conventional notions of intellectual property. It also provides fans with global forums in which to exert influence over mainstream-media sf itself. Sf scholars are interested in fandom's past as well. For example, Justine Larbalestier (2002) examines the letters pages and editorial columns of early sf magazines to show how the debates over sex, gender, and sf carried out by fans influenced the aesthetic development of the genre as a whole. As Larbalestier demonstrates, fans – like authors and editors – have always played active roles in the creation of sf as a self-regulating genre.

Finally, scholars interested in the relations of sf writing to technoscientific practice produce histories of the genre that complicate conventional ideas about fact versus fiction. The first generation of studies to address this, including Robin Roberts (1993) and Jane Donawerth (1997), explored how women's sf has developed over the course of the past century by revising patriarchal narratives of science and society. Lisa Yaszek

(2008) has used the kind of thick description that Belsey associates with cultural history to demonstrate how women's sf responds to specific ideas about science, technology, and gender that emerged after the Second World War and still inform our world today.

Scholars interested in the relations of science, society, and race have used the critical apparatus of cultural history to great effect as well. For example, De Witt Douglas Kilgore (2003) explores how the mid-twentieth-century space race fostered new and more egalitarian (if sometimes naïvely colorblind) discourses of science, technology, and race in science and sf alike. Similarly, the critical essays collected in Jutta Weldes (2003) demonstrate how hopes and fears about life in a post-Enlightenment, multi-cultural world are expressed through the mutually constitutive discourses of political policy and sf. As Weldes's anthology indicates, cultural histories of sf do more than simply illuminate the past and present. They help us better understand the shape of things to come as well.

Future directions in sf studies as cultural history

Sf lends itself to the critical methodologies of cultural history because it has always been a hybrid form, emerging from gothic and adventure fiction and promising to transform dry scientific fact into pleasing imaginative narrative. Additionally, many members of the sf community are hybrid subjects who occupy multiple roles as authors, editors, and fans. Still others inhabit subject positions outside sf as scientists, technical consultants, and mainstream writers. By treating these individuals as nodes within overlapping discourse networks, we can see how authors sometimes function as cultural historians and how thinking of them as such opens up new areas of inquiry.

Like sf critics, sf authors have long produced texts that complicate conventional ideas about learned versus popular texts. Before the consolidation of genre writing in the early twentieth century, authors including Wells, Bellamy, and Gilman moved easily between the worlds of highbrow and popular literature. Later, both the sf and mainstream literary communities claimed postmodern authors such as Vonnegut, Atwood, and Shirley Jackson as their own. While Jackson always thought of herself as a genre writer, both Vonnegut and Atwood rejected association with the sf community, thereby seeming to shore up the distinction between high and low culture. This situation has reversed itself in recent years, as authors including Michael Chabon, Jonathan Lethem, and Michael Cunningham have embraced dual writing identities and made powerful arguments for the value of sf to mainstream readers. Perhaps not surprisingly, all of these authors have made issues of reading and culture central to their storytelling practices, thereby inviting the cultural historian of sf to consider how their texts and pronouncements on the craft of writing articulate with major aesthetic debates of the past two centuries.

Scholars might also consider how sf authors treat the subject of fan production and consumption in their own writing. For example, in Helen Reid Chase's "Night of Fire" (1952), aliens attack Earth to rid the planet of its aggressive human population. Among the few benign humans who are saved from destruction are housewives who define themselves as sf fans. Elsewhere, Sharyn McCrumb's *Bimbos of the Death Sun* (1996) relates the tale of an egotistical sf author who is murdered by frustrated fans; in *The Faculty* (Rodriguez 1998) and *Galaxy Quest* (Parisot 1999) fan knowledge helps to save the world; and Faust's *Coyote Kings of the Space Age Bachelor Pad* explores how sf fandom helps two young men survive an ancient African battle between good and evil. A cultural history of stories in this vein would provide unique insight into issues of production and consumption as they pertain to the evolving relation of authors and readers over time.

Finally, sf critics might elaborate on the relation of fact and fiction in sf with cultural histories of sf authors who are also science writers and technical consultants. In the late 1930s L. Taylor Hansen exchanged sf writing for work as a science columnist in *Amazing Stories*, and in the postwar era dozens of other women made careers by writing both sf and science fact. Today, Robert Silverberg writes a regular science and technology column for *Asimov's Magazine*, and until early 2007 Pat Murphy worked as a science writer for the San Francisco Exploratorium. Perhaps even more provocatively, scholars might consider the history of authors who have established science careers outside the sf community. Such a history could begin with Gernsback's role as the founding editor of sf, electronics, and sexology magazines and end with a discussion of the Sigma group authors, including Greg Bear, Larry Niven, and Goonan, who critique technoscientific disaster scenarios for the US Department of Homeland Security. Taken together, these kinds of cultural history projects can help us better understand sf as a privileged vehicle of cultural expression.

BIBLIOGRAPHY

Bacon-Smith, C. (1992) *Enterprising Women: television fandom and the creation of popular myth*, Philadelphia: University of Pennsylvania Press.

Belsey, C. (2000) "Reading Cultural History," in T. Spargo (ed.) *Reading the Past: literature and history*, London: Palgrave Macmillan.

Chartier, R. (1988) *Cultural History: beyond practice and representation*, trans. L.G. Cochrane, Ithaca, NY: Cornell University Press.

Donawerth, J. (1997) *Frankenstein's Daughters: women writing science fiction*, Liverpool: Liverpool University Press.

Haraway, D. (1985) "A Manifesto for Cyborgs: science, technology, and socialist feminism in the 1980s," *Socialist Review*, 80(2): 65–107.

Hellekson, K. and Busse, K. (eds) (2006) *Fan Fiction and Fan Communities in the Age of the Internet*, Jefferson, NC: McFarland.

Jameson, F. (1991) *Postmodernism or, The Cultural Logic of Late Capitalism*, London and New York: Verso.

Jenkins, H. (1992) *Textual Poachers: television fans and participatory culture*, New York: Routledge.

—— (2006) *Fans, Bloggers, and Gamers: media consumers in a digital age*, New York: New York University Press.

Kilgore, D.W.D. (2003) *Astrofuturism: science, race, and visions of utopia in space*, Philadelphia: University of Pennsylvania Press.

Lamb, P.F. and Veith, D.L. (1986) "Romantic Myth, Transcendence and *Star Trek* Zines," in D. Palumbo (ed.) *Erotic Universe*, Westport, CT: Greenwood Press.

Larbalestier, J. (2002) *The Battle of the Sexes in Science Fiction*, Middletown, CT: Wesleyan University Press.

Luckhurst, R. (2005) *Science Fiction*, Cambridge: Polity.

Poster, M. (ed.) (1997) *Cultural History and Postmodernity: disciplinary readings and challenges*, New York: Columbia University Press.

Roberts, R. (1993) *A New Species: gender and science in science fiction*, Urbana: University of Illinois Press.

Weldes, J. (ed.) (2003) *To Seek Out New Worlds: exploring links between science fiction and world politics*, New York: Palgrave Macmillan.

Westfahl, G. (1998) *The Mechanics of Wonder: the creation of the idea of science fiction*, Liverpool: Liverpool University Press.

White, H. (1973) *Metahistory: the historical imagination in nineteenth-century Europe*, London: Johns Hopkins University Press.

Yaszek, L. (2008) *Galactic Suburbia: gender, technology, and the creation of women's science fiction*, Columbus: Ohio State University Press.

21
FAN STUDIES
Robin Anne Reid

Sf fandom has been analyzed as part of the broader study of popular culture, especially in the context of hobby groups and clubs promoting activities that are alternatives to work. These groups originated in urban areas of industrialized nations during the mid-nineteenth century. The necessary conditions for fandom include popular entertainment for mass audiences, a mass media to advertise and report on the entertainment, and people with enough leisure time and money to become consumers of the entertainment and the media. As Henry Jenkins (2006) argues, the internet has affected the nature of fandom by allowing corporate and individual producers of popular entertainment to access fan materials and interact with fandom in ways that were not possible with old media.

Sf and related genres such as horror, fantasy, and speculative fiction have increasingly become a part of mass culture in television, films, comics, and gaming. Fandom has grown from small groups to a global and international phenomenon that occurs on and offline. Until the 1960s, sf fandom was primarily the province of young white male fans who read print fiction, many of whom became professional editors and writers of sf. The earliest publications about fandom as a culture came from those fans, often in the form of memoirs by professional writers. Beginning in the late 1980s and early 1990s, a growing field of international scholarship began to develop. Publishing in academic journals, anthologies, and monographs, academics in a variety of fields, including anthropology, communications, composition/rhetoric, computer science, film studies, folklore studies, information technology, law, library science, literary studies, media studies, musicology, performance studies, psychology, sociology, and television studies have created fan studies.

Some scholars consider sf fandom to be similar to other hobbyist groups and so do not distinguish among sports, music, television, and sf fans. Others argue that sf fan culture is unique because of its longevity, its focus on the idea of the future as shared capital, and its early adoption of the newest technologies to facilitate sharing of fan-produced texts, both creative and critical. In either case, scholarship has generally shifted from earlier views of fans as isolated or deviant cultists to exploring the ways in which sf fandom – with its changing demographics, creation of fan works, and intense communal activities – is an example of the changing relationships between consumers and creators (Bacon-Smith 1992, 1999; Jenkins 1992, 2006). Most, but not all, of the theories and methods discussed in this chapter share the assumption that sf fandom is unique.

Fan works

In the United States, sf fandom began with Hugo Gernsback's popular magazines devoted to the amazing new genre that he called "scientifiction." He encouraged readers to send in letters, and published the extensive commentary of devoted readers in the "Letter Columns." The printed letters included mailing addresses, and fans began to communicate directly with each other, to meet, to create fan clubs and their own magazines (fan magazines, or fanzines, usually abbreviated as zines), and to organize conventions (cons).

Cons allow creators and consumers of sf to meet and talk. They began in urban centers, the oldest and most well known in the northeastern United States, and were originally run entirely by fans for fans. The second half of the twentieth century saw a growing number of large commercial multimedia events that might draw 10,000 or more fans together. Currently, cons can be any size from a small weekend event with 50 to 100 participants to the huge Comic-Con which is held annually in San Diego. Considered by most to be the largest con in the world, Comic-Con is a four-day event drawing over 100,000 attendees. Some cons focus on a specific genre or activity (e.g., horror, gaming, sf literature); others are narrowly focused on a single franchise (e.g., *Doctor Who*, *Firefly*, *Harry Potter*). Still others are general or multimedia in focus, with programming about books, film, and television. There are local, regional, national, and international cons in a number of countries. Most involve a variety of performances and creative work by fans: costume events and contests, fanzine and art rooms, singing and dramatic performances, and fan-produced videos and movies.

Fan scholars and pro writers

The earliest work on fandom was produced by fans themselves. Matt Hills defines "fan scholars" as those fans who use academic tools to produce analytical texts for the audience of fans (Hills 2002: 16–20). Fan scholars tend to publish in fanzines or, more recently, in blogs and archives. Fanzines are difficult for contemporary scholars to access, often found only in private collections by fans, although some have been uploaded to the internet. Some editors publish their zines in hard and electronic versions, and some academic libraries have special collections of fan materials, including the Eaton Collection, University of California, Riverside; the M. Horvat Collection of Science Fiction Fanzines, Special Collections Department, University of Iowa (which also has a Digital Collection of Science Fiction Fanzines); the Science Fiction Foundation Collection, University of Liverpool; and the Cushing Library Science Fiction and Fantasy Research Collection, Texas A&M University. One online library resource is the Fanzine Archives which archives and loans out fanzines, many of which are available on the internet.

Published memoirs and personal histories by professional writers are more easily found. Most cover their experiences during the 1940s and 1950s. Sam Moskowitz (1988) covers the history of fandom in New York and Philadelphia from the beginning of Gernsback's publications in 1926 to 1939, the start of the Second World War. Fandom was feuding during this period and Moskowitz was actively involved in the conflicts. Harry Warner (1969) covers fandom during the 1940s, focusing on fan manners, fan ethics, collecting as a fan activity, fan writing, and the second and third Worldcons. Warner (1976–7) goes on to document the history of fandom during the 1950s.

Damon Knight (1977) describes writers who started out as fans, such as Isaac Asimov, James Blish, Cyril Kornbluth, Judith Merril, Frederik Pohl, and Donald Wollheim, and also covers lesser-known fans. Frederik Pohl (1978) covers his own experiences as a fan, writer, and editor. Ray Bradbury, Arthur C. Clarke, and Isaac Asimov have also published autobiographies. These memoirs make clear how many political differences existed among the primarily white male fans in the United States who included libertarians, conservatives, liberals, progressives, and radicals. One of the few published memoirs by a woman from this era is *Better to Have Loved: the life of Judith Merril* (2002). Unlike the other books, Merril's memoir was not completed by her; when she died, leaving a great deal of material in various stages of completion, her granddaughter Emily Pohl-Weary edited it for final publication.

Starting with the 1960s, fandom entered a period of intense and continuing growth and diversification because of changes in technology, media, demographics, and fan activities. The growth of media-, comics-, and gaming-fandom changed fandom from small and print-based to larger and multimedia. Many fans are active in different types of fandoms, moving easily from book to film to gaming, although the different areas of fandom have different subcultures. The internet, a technology eagerly adopted by many sf fans, has created even greater changes in the demographics and activities of fandom. The early convention and fanzine cultures have not disappeared, but they have been complemented by a host of other activities: collecting, cosplay (costuming), gaming (board games, console games, online multiple-player games), fan fiction, filking (sf folk songs, a term generated by a typo in an early convention program book), and vidding (fan-created videos melding music and images from media productions).

Multimedia fandom scholarship

The growth of media fandom occurred during a period in the United States and the United Kingdom in which new fields of study were opening up in media and communications, with a growing body of scholars interested in work on gender and on popular culture. Scholarship on other fandom cultures began later but is growing rapidly, assisted by new technologies for circulating scholarship that relies upon graphic images for evidence. Audience and fan studies are part of the larger disciplinary areas of film, television, media, and cultural or popular studies.

Camille Bacon-Smith (1999) offers the only book-length history of fandom from the 1920s convention culture to the present. She outlines changes in the sf community, including the entertainment and publishing industries, focusing on fandom as an example of a postmodern social phenomenon that reflects the changing nature of power hierarchies between "producers" and "consumers" of culture. The book examines community-building in United States fandom, how demographic changes affected the earlier male-dominated community, and changes in the institutional arenas of production, specifically publishing. Later scholarship tends to focus more on single fandoms, or to analyze a contemporary group's productions or interactions during a specific historical period. Two fan sites on the internet are devoted to the ongoing project of collecting and maintaining artifacts of fan history. The first is the FANAC Fan History project, sponsored by Florida Association for Nucleation and Conventions (FANAC). The second focuses on oral history: The Science Fiction Oral History Association (SFOHA), founded in 1975. The group maintains an archive of radio, video, and taped interviews, and also does recordings at conferences and in private.

There are few professionally published memoirs or histories for fandom from the 1960s on, perhaps because of the fragmentation of science fiction across new genres and media. Bjo Trimble, the famous *Star Trek* (1966–9) fan who organized the letter-writing campaign to bring the show back for a third season, has published a memoir (1983). Joan Marie Verba (1996) covers some of the history of the fandom which was the first to successfully fight the cancellation of its source text, creating the circumstances in which the *Star Trek* franchise became one of the most successful in terms of longevity and economic productivity. *Trek* fandom differed from earlier fan groups because the fans included a larger percentage of women who produced creative works as well as critical essays: the fanzines included art, poetry, and stories, not just essays and con reports (Coppa 2006: 45). Francesca Coppa (2006) starts with media fandom from its beginnings in the 1960s, including Cynthia W. Walker's argument concerning the importance of *The Man from U.N.C.L.E.* (1964–8), a show which predated *Star Trek* and had close connections with the sf community through its choice of script and tie-in novel writers. Coppa demonstrates how different generations of fandom on the internet, starting with mailing lists and archives, led to all forms of fan production being more easily accessed by people outside of fandom and to more communication among different fandoms, including comics, celebrity, music, and anime as well as sf. She ends with noting the latest change to personal blogging technology which is creating additional spaces online for fandom communities to interact in such platforms as LiveJournal (LJ).

Disciplining fandom

Scholarship on academic fandom is a multidisciplinary and multinational endeavor. A more extensive view of fan studies scholarship than can be attempted here appears at Metabib, an LJ community. Research on fandom originated within media studies, but psychoanalytical language tends to appear as scholars try to answer the question of why fans do what they do. Cultural studies focus on a wide range of cultural productions without being limited by a single aesthetic theory. A number of scholars draw on ethnographic methodologies from folklore and anthropology, as well as some limited sociological research (surveys, questionnaires, interviews). The scholarship during the 1990s and early 2000s produced a growing body of work by academics both within and beyond fandom. It is not uncommon for academics doing fan studies to also publish scholarship in more "respectable" areas of their discipline (media, literature, film) rather than specializing in a new and sometimes controversial field. Perhaps because of the nature of the controversies, some of the most boundary-breaking scholarship tends to be produced predominantly by women who are independent scholars.

The best-known psychoanalytic scholarship is the collaborative work of Catherine Salmon and Don Symons (especially 2001 and 2004). Employing the theory of evolutionary psychology, Salmon and Symons postulate that men's interest in pornography and women's interest in romance novels shows the existence of natural gender differences. They analyze slash fiction (stories about romantic and sexual relationships between two male characters, some of which involve graphic descriptions of sex), and argue that the similarities between romance novels and slash fiction prove gender differences exist. Their purpose is using fan-produced texts to arrive at arguments concerning human psychology and behavior, rather than analyzing fan culture.

Henry Jenkins (1992) analyzes the fan productions of sf television fans and has been widely read by fans. Jenkins counters the negative stereotypes of the fan as nerd, social outcast, or recluse which appeared in earlier research, especially in the social sciences. He explicitly identifies as a fan as well as an academic and celebrates fan creativity (criticism, fiction, music videos, filk) as part of a cultural dialogue with the source texts while downplaying any mention of conflicts within fandom.

The two key works considered to have shaped fan studies are by women: Camille Bacon-Smith (1992) and Constance Penley (1997). Bacon-Smith's training in ethnography and folklore studies shapes her arguments which focus on slash writers, a minority group whose work has often received more academic attention than other types of fan fiction. While Jenkins's monograph had a chapter on slash fiction (believed to have begun with stories pairing *Star Trek*'s Kirk and Spock in the mid-1970s), Bacon-Smith's book focuses on her journey into the slash-fiction community, presented as a process of initiation and training in reading within the female community of fanzines, fan fiction, and slash fiction. The necessity for a new fan to be initiated by friends into a community has been changed by fandom's movement onto the internet where thousands of slash stories and hundreds of communities can be found with one or two easy Google searches. From the perspective of film and media studies, Constance Penley's focus is not fan culture, but instead learning "a critical stance, a method of addressing what had become for me the increasingly entwined issues of sex, science, and popular culture" (Penley 1997: 3) from fandom. Her purpose is to analyze the popular media coverage of NASA as an example of popular science.

Anthologies published during the 1990s and 2000s offer a wider range of disciplinary perspectives and topics of analysis. Joe Sanders (1994) collects essays covering sf fandoms in Europe and Asia as well as the United States, and addresses the origins of fandom, fandom in America, international fandoms, fan activities, and fan productions. Harris and Alexander (1998) include work from a range of disciplinary approaches and consider multiple fandoms. Hellekson and Busse (2006) feature essays by academics and fans who are active in the communities they write about, primarily in LJ fandom. The collection analyzes the historical and genre contexts for fan fiction, considers fan fiction as literature, addresses relationships in fandom and among fan fiction readers and writers, and evaluates performativity, new media, and machinima (short animated films made within videogames). Jonathan Gray, Cornel Sandvoss, and C. Lee Harrington (2007) bridge the gaps between fans of high culture (Chekhov and Bach) and those of popular culture.

While Jenkins's work dominated the 1990s, several new approaches have since emerged. Matt Hills (2002) begins a critique of the earlier scholarship on fandom, questioning the academic celebration of primarily positive elements of fan communities and participatory culture. Hills also addresses the impact of academic cultures upon academics doing scholarship on fan cultures, arguing that academics will be predisposed to privilege those elements of fandom most similar to their own disciplinary conventions. Hills questions the reliance on sociological and psychoanalytic methodologies, and raises the question of how the attempt to study fandom online will change scholarship, suggesting that technological and temporal effects on fandom cultures and activities have not yet been adequately theorized or addressed. Cornel Sandvoss (2005) attempts to blend the theories and methods of Jenkins and Hills, drawing on both sociology and psychology, to create a new model of fandom. Sandvoss examines fan relationships in the community which are based on agreement as well as those based on disagreement, drawing on sports as well as media fandom.

A more traditional literary approach is taken by Sheenagh Pugh (2005), the first work to approach fan fiction as a literary genre. She discusses conventions of fan fiction, types of characters, and narrative forms, as well as the communal aspects of writing within a community. Unlike media scholars, Pugh draws on book as well as media fandoms, and, as a British scholar, does not assume a default focus on US fandoms. The primary fandoms she studies are Jane Austen (book and media), *Blakes 7* (1978–81), the police series *The Bill* (1984–), and *Hornblower* (book and screen adaptations).

The internet: divergences and convergences

The most recent scholarship has begun to foreground the impact of the internet on fandom rather than assuming that the technology is transparent. The internet allows "academics" and "fans" to interact more immediately (see Hellekson and Busse (2006)) and effects the material production and circulation of scholarship. The temporal pace of academic scholarship is much slower than the temporal pace of the technological change and thus most published work only briefly mentions internet fandom. Academics who participate in online fandoms or who foreground analysis of the internet as part of their fan studies have begun to publish in recent years, and some of the publication is taking place online, in both peer-reviewed journals and sites designed to facilitate the circulation of scholarly work in new forms.

Media Commons: A Digital Scholarly Network is a project in development which received a 2008 National Endowment for the Humanities Startup Grant to build the software needed to support peer review for the network. FlowTV, published online by the Department of Radio, Television, and Film at the University of Texas at Austin, similarly makes the process of creating such knowledge more participatory.

While the internet allows for more and faster interactions within fandom and within academia, it also decenters and fragments fan and academic discourses. Conflicts in fandom reflect historical and cultural changes in constructions of gender, race, and class. In an informal setting, a summer 2007 online discussion between 44 academics who publish in fan studies or closely related areas considered questions of gender differences as well as disciplinary differences, especially in the separation between media fandoms on LJ and other fandom areas. The extent to which class and race have not been considered in fan studies was briefly addressed. The aca-fan discussion, organized by Henry Jenkins and Kristina Busse, can be read on an LJ community.

Jenkins (2006) noted that what fans have been doing for some time can now be argued to be a paradigm for changes in contemporary media culture and contemporary culture generally, including political and other spheres often considered "separate" from fandom. The old media (television, newspapers, film) developed in a historical period where more centralized control and spread of content were possible; the emergence of new media (technologies which put more control in the hands of consumers, primarily but not exclusively the internet) has led to participatory culture and a greater flow, or convergence, across media boundaries. He argues that media fans are early adopters but shows how their behaviors have spread into other consumer groups. His main point is no longer the analysis of fandom but using fan case studies to consider the question of how, in the twenty-first century, corporate cultures have begun to incorporate practices from the grassroots fan culture, ending with a chapter on politics and public culture. He acknowledges the limits of his work – the early adopters are predominantly white males who are college educated, and mostly middle-class – but begins to speculate about the possibility of a more participatory public culture because of the internet.

One area of scholarship that moves beyond fandom and has implications for the culture at large is legal scholarship. The creative and participatory works of fans, especially when circulated on the internet and not limited to cons attended only by initiates or circulated by mail to members of the community, have become part of larger cultural debates about copyright, trademark, intellectual property laws, and fair use. Scholars such as Rebecca Tushnet (1997), Sonia K. Katyal (2006), and Michael Madow (1993) publish legal scholarship on fandom. The extent to which the relationship between the producers and consumers of media content has changed in the past decades is not restricted to fandom; concerns about fair use and copyright laws are expressed by academics, documentary filmmakers, and other professionals.

As of 2008, it is possible to argue that the new field of fan studies has emerged, a field closely related to but not the same as media and audience studies. Besides the scholarship discussed above, more specific analyses of individual fan communities and cultures are being produced. Matthew Pustz (1999) and Jeffrey Brown (1997) are writing on comic-book culture and fandom. Marjorie Cohee Manifold (2007) is perhaps the sole scholar working on cosplay. Francesca Coppa is working on the history of vidding, going back to the 1970s when women in *Star Trek* fandom used the technology of the time to create their own musical videos. Scholars are doing work on a number of specific fandoms: *Star Trek* (1966–), *The X-Files* (1993–2002), *Xena: Warrior Princess* (1995–2001), *Buffy the Vampire Slayer* (1997–2003). The growing popularity of anime and manga in North America has created fandoms for those genres. Additionally, international scholarship on fandoms in countries outside the English-speaking nations is beginning to be published. One example is Martin Barker's "International *Lord of the Rings* Research Project" which brought together scholars from a number of nations to study the global phenomenon of Peter Jackson's film, including essays on fan activities.

A large percentage of the work on sf fandom and media fandom focuses on female fans writing fan fiction, primarily slash fiction, the oldest of fan fiction areas of inquiry. In 1982, Patricia Frazer Lamb and Diane Veith presented "The Romantic Myth and Transcendence: a feminist interpretation of the Kirk/Spock bond," cited by Joanna Russ (1985), and later published in *Erotic Universe: sexuality and fantastic literature* (1986). Written from a feminist perspective, this work established the key issues that have been debated since: the question of why women were writing men having sex, whether these stories have more in common with romance novels (Lamb and Veith) or pornography (Russ), and the validity of a feminist approach (and later queer theory) to fan studies.

Slash fiction was a part of the scholarship in the early 2000s, but as more women have begun working in universities, more scholarship on women and fandom, and on slash, has appeared. Rhiannon Bury (2005) analyzes female online communities in the late 1990s and into the early 2000s, primarily in *X-Files* fandom (the David Duchovny Estrogen Brigades) and *Due South* (1994–6) fandom (the Militant RayK Separatists). Bury's fans were not on LJ, but she ends by noting the shift that was coming with personal blogging and the move to LJ.

One of the major gaps in fan studies and scholarship is the lack of consideration of race and class. Sarah L. Gatson and Abigail Derechio consider the constructions of race, both in source texts and within fandom. Aswin Punathambekar and Bertha Chin work with Indian and East Asian film fans respectively. Little or no work exists on class and sf fandom; the little scholarship on fandom and class that does exist focuses primarily on sports fandoms and is by European scholars.

The growing use of the internet by corporations as a medium for marketing as well as the concerns that corporate owners of blogging platforms will act more aggressively to control the content has led to the formation of a nonprofit organization, the Organization for Transformative Works (OTW), to provide, among other services, legal advice to fans, an archive owned by the organization, and an online academic journal, *Transformative Works and Culture*. The OTW believes that fan creations are covered under the "transformative" element of fair use, and is working to open its archive to fan works in a number of languages, not only English, through recruiting volunteers who will do translations and encourage fans in other language communities to make use of the archive.

The growing number of scholars in different countries who work on fan studies has also led to the formation of a new scholarly association, the International Association of Audience and Fan Studies (IAAFS), which was launched at the 29th International Conference on the Fantastic in the Arts in 2008. The purpose of this organization is to facilitate scholarly activities in the interdisciplinary areas of audience and fan studies, with a special focus on how new technologies offer academics greater chances for cross-disciplinary communication and work.

Bibliography

Bacon-Smith, C. (1992) *Enterprising Women: television fandom and the creation of popular myth*, Philadelphia: University of Pennsylvania Press.

—— (1999) *Science Fiction Culture*, Philadelphia: University of Pennsylvania Press.

Brown, J. (1997) "Comic Book Fandom and Cultural Capital," *Journal of Popular Culture* 30(4): 13–31.

Bury, R. (2005) *Cyberspaces of Their Own: female fandoms online*, Harrisburg, PA: Morehouse Publishing.

Coombe, R.J., Herman, A., and Kaye, L. (2006) "Your *Second Life?*: goodwill and the performativity of intellectual property in online digital gaming," *Cultural Studies*, 20(2–3): 184–210.

Coppa, F. (2006) "A Brief History of Media Fandom," in K. Hellekson and K. Busse (eds) *Fan Fiction and Fan Communities in the Age of the Internet*, Jefferson, NC: McFarland.

Cumberland, S. (2000) "Private Uses of Cyberspace: women, desire, and fan culture," *MIT Communications Forum*. Online. Available HTTP: <http://web.mit.edu/comm-forum/papers/cumberland.html> (accessed 1 April 2008).

Department of Radio, Television, and Film University of Texas at Austin (n.d.) FlowTV: A Critical Forum on Television and Media Culture. Online. Available HTTP: <http://www.flowtv.org> (accessed 1 April 2008).

FANAC Fan History (n.d.) Online. Available HTTP: <http://fanac.org/> (accessed 1 April 2008).

Fanzine Archives (n.d.) Online. Available HTTP: <http://www.fanzinearchives.org/> (accessed 1 April 2008).

Fitzpatrick, K. and Santo, A. "Media Commons," *The Institute for the Future of the Book*. Online. Available HTTP: <http://mediacommun.futureofthebook.org> (accessed 1 April 2008).

Gray, J., Sandvoss, C. and Harrington, C.L. (eds) (2007) *Fan Audiences: cultural consumption and identities in a mediated world*, New York: New York University Press.

Harris, C. and Alexander, A. (eds) (1998) *Theorizing Fandom: fans, subculture, and identity*, Cresskill, NJ: Hampton Press.

Hellekson, K. and Busse, K. (eds) (2006) *Fan Fiction and Fan Communities in the Age of the Internet*, Jefferson, NC: McFarland.

Hills, M. (2002) *Fan Cultures*, London: Routledge.

Jenkins, H. (1992) *Textual Poachers: television fans and participatory culture*, New York: Routledge.

—— (2006) *Convergence Culture: where old and new media collide*, New York and London: New York University Press.

Jenkins, H. and Busse, K. (2007) "Fandebate". Online. Available HTTP: <http://community.livejournal.com/fandebate/profile> (accessed 1 April 2008).

Jung, S. (2004) "Queering Popular Culture: female spectators and the appeal of writing slash fan fiction," *Gender Queeries*, 8. Online. Available HTTP: <http://www.gender-forum.koeln.de/queer/jung.html> (accessed 1 April 2008).

Katyal, S. (2006) "Performance, Property, and the Slashing of Gender in Fan Fiction," *Journal of Gender, Social Policy, and the Law*, 14: 463–518

Knight, Damon. (1977) *The Futurians*. New York: John Day.

Lamb, P.F. and Veith, D.L. (1986) "Romantic Myth, Transcendence and *Star Trek* Zines", in D. Palumbo (ed.) *Erotic Universe*, Westport, CT: Greenwood Press.

Manifold, M.C. (2007) "Convergence or Divergence: spontaneous art-making and participatory expression in the private and collective lives of youth." Online. Available HTTP: <http://hdl.handle.net/2022/2554/> (accessed 1 April 2008).

Merril, J. and Pohl-Weary, E. (2002) *Better to Have Loved: the life of Judith Merril*, Toronto: Between the Lines.

Metabib (n.d.) Online. Available HTTP: <http://community.livejournal.com/metabib/profile> (accessed 1 April 2008).

Moskowitz, S. (1988) *The Immortal Storm: a history of science fiction fandom*, 1974, Westport, CT: Hyperion.

Penley, C. (1997) *NASA/Trek: popular science and sex in America*, New York: Verso.

Pohl, F. (1978) *The Way the Future Was: a memoir*, New York: Ballantine.

Pugh, S. (2005) *The Democratic Genre: fan fiction in a literary context*, Bridgend, UK: Seren.

Pustz, M. (1999) *Comic Book Culture: fanboys and true believers*, Jackson: University of Mississippi Press.

Resnick, M. (1997) "The Literature of Fandom," *Mimosa*, 21: 17–24.

Roberts, P. and Nicholls, P. (1995) "Fandom," in J. Clute and P. Nicholls (eds) *The Encyclopedia of Science Fiction*, London: Orbit.

Russ, J. (1985) "Pornography by Women for Women with Love," in *Magic Mommas, Trembling Sisters, Puritans, and Perverts: feminist essays*, Trumansburg, NY: The Crossing Press.

Salmon, C. and Symons, D. (2001) *Warrior Lovers: erotic fiction, evolution, and female sexuality*, London: Orion.

—— (2004) "Slash Fiction and Human Mating Psychology," *Journal of Sex Research*, 41: 94–100.

Sanders, J. L. (ed.) (1994) *Science Fiction Fandom*, Westport, CT: Greenwood Press.

Sandvoss, C. (2005) *Fans: the mirror of consumption*, Cambridge: Polity Press.

Science Fiction Oral History Association (n.d.) Online. Available HTTP: <http://www.sfoha.org/> (accessed 1 April 2008).

Trimble, B. (1983) *On the Good Ship Enterprise: my 15 years with Star Trek*, Marceline, MO: Walsworth.

Tushnet, R. (1997) "Legal Fictions: copyright, fan fiction and a new common law," *Loyola of Los Angeles Entertainment Law Journal*, 17(3): 651–86.

Verba, J.M. (1996) *Boldly Writing: a Trekker fan and zine history, 1967–1987*, Minnetonka, MN: FTL Publications.

Warner, H. (1969) *All Our Yesterdays: an informal history of science fiction fandom in the forties*, Chicago: Advent.

—— (1976–7) *A Wealth of Fable: the history of science fiction fandom in the 1950s*, New York: Fanhistorica Press.

Warner, H. and Lynch, D. (1992) *A Wealth of Fable: an informal history of science fiction fandom in the 1950s*, Van Nuys, CA: SCIFI Press.

22
FEMINISMS
Jane Donawerth

Both the first Western theories of women's rights and the earliest sf by a woman appeared in the seventeenth century. Feminist theory – which provides "intellectual tools by which historical agents can examine the injustices they confront, and can build arguments to support their particular demands for change" (McCann and Kim 2002: 1) – and sf by women have been intimately connected ever since. This chapter outlines some of these connections.

Strictly speaking, there were no feminists until the 1890s: "feminist" entered the English language in 1894 and "feminism" in 1895 (see *OED*). But scholars regularly extend the term to designate historical debates in Europe and the Americas about the nature of women and the struggle for women's rights. In this sense, feminists in the fourteenth to sixteenth centuries defended women against misogynist stereotypes, while later feminists argued first for women's right to education and to preach (sixteenth to nineteenth centuries), then for marriage reform and for women's right to divorce (eighteenth to twentieth centuries), and then for women's right to vote, inherit property, and share ownership in marriage property (from the nineteenth to twentieth centuries). Thus "feminist" does not mean the same thing for all places or historical periods – for example, Middle Eastern women had the right to own property long before Western women. Moreover, there have always been multiple feminisms: Anglo-American women in the nineteenth century who remonstrated for sex education and free love, for example, were quite different feminists from those who argued for woman's enfranchisement based on her essentially moral and motherly nature. Feminist politics and theory have developed through debates as often as through consensus.

The history of feminism and feminist theory is often divided into the categories of First Wave, Second Wave, and either Postfeminist or Third Wave (or sometimes Postmodern or Poststructuralist or Postcolonial or Transgender Feminism). "First Wave" denotes the struggle for women's political rights and suffrage in nineteenth-century Europe and United States (see Sanders 2000). "Second Wave" refers to the political movement beginning in 1960s United States, focusing on critiquing femininity and claiming a woman's right to her own body, connecting to global women's movements, and, some would argue, continuing today (Warhol 1995: 308–14; McCann and Kim 2002: 18). Postfeminism applies to a generation of late

1980s and early 1990s women who rejected the previous generation's goals, and if not entirely rejecting feminism, yet rejected "any definition of women as victims." (Gamble 2000: 44). "Third Wave," or Generation X feminism, applies to a generation of 1990s women who have emphasized women's collective political action and global issues (see Stewart 2000). In my view, these arbitrary constructions help people strategically discuss historical differences in approaches to social change involving women, but do not comfortably fit the historic changes in feminist theory or sf by women, or the multiple theories of feminism in our current world. Consequently, this chapter will instead divide the material into five sections that emphasize the historical interconnections between sf and theory.

Women's right to education: 1650–1750

Before the seventeenth century in Europe, feminist theory centered on the controversy about women or the *querelle des femmes*: in this pamphlet debate, one side charged women with being, by nature, fickle, unchaste, irrational, devoted to gossip, and spending money – in all ways inferior to men; the other side defended women as, by nature, chaste, loyal, hardworking, and superior to men. Seventeenth-century political theories gave the woman issue a new vocabulary: like men, women, too, might have rights, to free speech, or to preach, or to an education. Typical of these debates are the pamphlets by Margaret Fell, Bathsua Makin, and Mary Astell. In *Women's Speaking Justified* (1666), Fell argues that women had a right to preach because God had created women equal to men spiritually, and because the Bible records a history of women's preaching. In *An Essay to Revive the Ancient Education of Gentlewomen* (1673), Makin argues that women have a right to an education according to their class status because historically civilized cultures allowed women's education, and because educated women may better help their husbands and children. In *A Serious Proposal to the Ladies, Part I* (1694), Astell proposes, as did Makin, that women receive a humanist education similar to that of men, but in a woman's monastery or college retired from the world; *A Serious Proposal Part II* (1697) outlines a detailed program of study in the languages and logic, rhetoric, grammar, and the arts, as well as the means for such an education (women combining their resources). Fell, Makin, and Astell, then, refute the idea that women are naturally inferior to men, seeing them not as less rational by nature, but less educated by custom than men.

Margaret Cavendish's utopian fiction *The Description of a New World, Called the Blazing-World* (1666) similarly depicts women as capable of rational thought and benefiting from education. Cavendish places her utopia at the North Pole, where an Empress is given "an absolute power to rule and govern all that world as she pleased" (Cavendish 1994: 132), and fills it with technological marvels, including a submarine. The Empress summons philosophers and scientists to her court to educate her and to speculate on the nature of science, religion, and government. She further decides how best to teach women, instituting "a congregation of women"; since women "generally had quick wits, subtle conceptions, clear understandings, and solid judgments," they soon become learned theologians (Cavendish 1994: 162). The Empress further appoints a female scribe, the fictional character Margaret Cavendish, and teaches her how to make a utopian world through her imagination in her writings. Thus, in this early period, most feminist theory and the one instance of an sf text by a woman emphasize women's right to an education.

Essentially female: 1850–1920

While the nineteenth- and early twentieth-century political struggle for women's rights focused on property rights, sexuality, and enfranchisement, feminist theory generally founded arguments for these rights on a gendered sphere of interests and an essentially different female nature. For example, Lucretia Mott's 1849 oration, "Discourse on Woman," begins by arguing for women's right to preach, based on women's spiritual equality with men and a biblical history of women's preaching, and concludes by extending her argument to other rights: while women are different from men by nature, she accedes, nevertheless there is no need to overstate those differences, since women also possess intelligence. Consequently, women, who currently possess only the right to petition, in justice should be granted all the civil rights of men, especially suffrage and property rights during marriage. In "Womanhood a Vital Element in the Regeneration and Progress of a Race" (1886), Anna Julia Cooper argues that the reverence and respect for women originating with Christianity needs to be developed into full equality because women are the major influence in racial uplift, since they are by nature the first influence on children; consequently, in African-American advancement, women's education needs a special place. Charlotte Perkins Gilman's *Women and Economics* (1898) argues that just as the natural characteristics of men and women were unnaturally developed through the extreme division of labor allotted them, humans might evolve further by social-izing the housekeeping duties that distracted women from intellectual development and thus, through generations, women would come to equal men in actuality as in potential. Thus all these feminist arguments for women's rights were based on women's essential difference from men, although Gilman thought that women could evolve to be similar to men.

Feminist technological utopias of the period similarly emphasized the essentially different nature of women by constructing all-women utopias as models for a better society. Mary E. Bradley Lane's *Mizora: a prophecy* (1880–1) imagined a technological paradise utilizing gas stoves, washing machines, and airships, where all men and women of color had died off when white women took over the government to end war, and where children were produced by parthenogenesis, and teaching and housework were viewed as scientific professions. Gilman's *Herland* (1915) imagined a society where women are governors, doctors, scientists, and educators, and where human life is bettered by exercise, vegetarianism, abstinence from sex, genetic experimentation with plants, scientifically organized education, and conflict resolution by discussion.

Similarly, early twentieth-century socialist feminist theory influenced feminist utopias, such as Lilith Lorraine's "Into the 28th Century" (1930), published in the US pulps (see Enns and Sinacore 2001: 473; Donawerth 1990), and women's anti-war activism influenced the development of the housewife hero of mid-century sf by women (see Yaszek 2004).

Healing the middle-class housewife: 1950–1975

In the 1950s and 1960s, feminist theory came in bestseller form. Betty Friedan's *The Feminine Mystique* (1963) revealed to millions of readers the "nameless dissatisfaction" of the "happy housewife heroine" (Friedan 1984: 33) confined to "The Comfortable Concentration Camp" (Friedan 1984: 282) of the middle-class home. Friedan contrasted women who had fruitfully returned to work with unhappy women who were raising increasingly alienated children. Kate Millett's *Sexual Politics* (1969) exposed the techniques of patriarchal oppression – male chivalry, female rivalry – and argued that men and women were educated into different cultures. She analyzed the misogynist literature of the twentieth century, uncovering the dominance games of canonical male modernists. Germaine Greer argued that ours is a woman-hating society, in which a man killing the woman he loves is considered romance (Greer 1970: 204), and urged women to throw "the baggage of paternalistic society" overboard and to choose "self-determi-nation" or "womanpower" (Greer 1970: 119). Shulamith Firestone's *The Dialectic of Sex: the case for feminist revolution* (1970) laid out the repressive economics of twentieth-century reproduction (women do all the labor of childbearing and much of the labor of childrearing but they are not paid or valued for it) and argued for reproductive technologies to relieve women of this labor. Phyllis Chesler revealed one institutional means of female oppression in modern America: many women were committed to institutions by their husbands because they were not doing their jobs as housewives, or by their doctors who saw them as asocially resisting feminine roles. Worse, Chesler concluded, "Women who *succeed* at suicide are, tragically, outwitting or rejecting their 'feminine' role, and at the only price possible: their death" (Chesler 1972: 49).

In this climate, women sf writers produced critiques of housewife oppression and studies of women driven mad by patriarchy. For example, Pamela Zoline's "The Heat Death of the Universe" (1967) intersperses the mundane tasks of an ordinary housewife with the laws of thermodynamics, the scientific warnings that the universe always returns to disorder, and we follow the protagonist through a housewife's routine, her rejection of that role, and a spectacular breakdown. Other notable stories featuring women liberated from the housewife's prison include James Tiptree Jr's "The Women Men Don't See" (1973), in which a mother and daughter run away with aliens so as to escape the stifling confines of earthmen's patriarchy, and Carol Emshwiller's "The Start of the End of the World" (1981), in which housewives, oppressed by their human husbands, help aliens take over the world, and then also rebel against the aliens. Joanna Russ's angry, satirical *We Who Are About To . . .* (1977) exposes the patriarchal myths that generate sf conventions. After the narrator kills off the men who would force her back into female servitude in order to colonize the distant planet onto which they have crash-landed, the second half of the novel documents her lyrical descent into hallucinatory madness, where the narrator achieves a kind of freedom, discarding the remaining, inner constraints of patriarchy.

Marge Piercy's *Woman on the Edge of Time* (1976), extremely influential in the 1970s feminist movement as both theory and sf, expressed women's anger at the constraints of feminine roles and their fears of the institutions men used to punish women who resisted those roles. Protagonist Connie Ramos lives in two worlds: in one, she is a poor Latina on welfare who has lost her daughter to Child Services and who cannot get a job, a world in which her anger at the unfair system around her sees her committed to an asylum by male doctors; in the other, a feminist utopia, property is communal, babies are gestated in artificial wombs, and men and women are truly equal – in jobs, status, opportunity, childcare, and housework. The novel ends with an act of war: Connie tries to protect the Earth's future by poisoning the doctors who experiment with drugs and surgery to eradicate resistance. Piercy's acknowledgments thank, among others, Phyllis Chesler.

Recovering women's history: 1970–1995

The 1970s saw the development of Women's Studies as a field and the exponential growth of women's history and recovery of female-authored literary texts. In 1979, an edition of Gilman's *Herland* connected the early 1970s experiments by feminist sf writers to earlier roots in women's writing, and so resurrected the genre of the feminist utopia. Important as part of the rediscovery of women's literature (and therefore evidence of the patriarchal erasure of women's history), soon the feminist utopia also became a way of working out in narrative form central issues of 1970s and 1980s feminism. *Herland* was followed by republication of many other nineteenth- and twentieth-century feminist utopias, and by contemporary portrayals of idealized all-female communities. Besides the recovery of earlier feminist utopias, which usually fantasized communities of middle-class white women, the growth of African-American Studies precipitated a republication of slave narratives that helped to recover knowledge about nineteenth-century black women's lives. This scholarship also influenced sf by women, not only by introducing the slave narrative as a template for sf writers, but also by providing models for black female characters.

The 1970s and 1980s, then, saw a plethora of feminist utopias. In Joanna Russ's *The Female Man* (1975), an inventive division of the point of view into multiple women – Janet, Jeanne, Joanna, and Jael – allows Russ to contrast the future of women without change (low-paying jobs, hoping to marry a man you do not hate) with a dystopian future where the sexes are literally at war, and a utopian future where men have disappeared and women can do everything. In Sally Miller Gearhart's *The Wanderground* (1979), nature has rebelled against men's rape of the environment and has sided with women. Men live only in cities because nature decrees that neither machines nor phalluses work beyond the suburbs. Women rule in the country, developing a society based on goddess worship, healing rituals, and communal action. A critique of such radical lesbian utopias is offered by Marion Zimmer Bradley's *The Ruins of Isis* (1978), Pamela Sargent's *The Shore of Women* (1986), and Sherri Tepper's *The Gate to Women's Country* (1988). Others continued with the form of the feminist utopia, adapting it to include multiple sexualities: Ursula K. Le Guin's *Always Coming Home* (1985), and

Joan Slonczewski's *A Door into Ocean* (1986). Yet others debated the possibility of such utopian visions through feminist dystopias: Suzette Haden Elgin's *Native Tongue* (1984), and Margaret Atwood's *The Handmaid's Tale* (1985).

From the 1960s on, slave narratives were recovered in important numbers, including numerous editions of Frederick Douglass's autobiographies, *The Life of John Thompson, a Fugitive Slave* (1968), *A Narrative of the Life of Rev. Noah Davis* (1969), and *Six Women's Slave Narratives* (1988), edited by William Andrews. Especially influential was the theoretical framework that Angela Davis supplied for rethinking the roles of women under slavery. She analyzed the ways in which slavery denied black women the feminine role of their white counterparts, but also reviewed the history of the resistance of black slave women, pointing to the heroic attempts of the black woman "to ensure the survival of her people" (Davis 1971: 5). By analogy to the eighteenth- and nineteenth-century accounts of slavery, hope, and escape, which were used to condemn the evils of slavery (dehumanized violence, rape of black women, casual cruelty, disruption of the family), women sf writers adapted the slave narrative form to imagined worlds where women, white or black, redefined heroism as survival and sometimes escaped enslavement. Most important was Octavia E. Butler's *Kindred* (1979), set in both 1976 Los Angeles and in 1830s and 1840s Maryland. Dana, a writer and part-time office worker, is repeatedly drawn through time to the plantation of her ancestors where she must save the life of Rufus, the white master, in order to make sure that the black slave woman impregnated by him produces the child whose descendants eventually birth Dana. In this complicated story, Dana both cares for and despises Rufus, and gradually sheds her contempt for slaves who did not attempt escape as she experiences all the oppressions that kept them enslaved: denial of literacy, whipping, patrollers, tracking dogs, and betrayal by other slaves. *Kindred* merges the sf time-travel novel with the slave narrative to trace the ways in which Dana is literally marked by her ancestors' slave history, and depicts as heroic both the survival tactics and the violent resistance that the slaves enact.

Many other feminist science fictions draw on the slave narrative. Suzy McKee Charnas's *Walk to the End of the World* (1974) literalizes women's servant status in a future California and depicts a rebellion in which women break free, killing their male masters and escaping to freedom. In Cecelia Holland's *Floating Worlds* (1975), a brown anarchist enslaved by a patriarchal alien race eventually tricks her masters into giving her back the Earth that has now been nearly destroyed by their wars. In Marion Zimmer Bradley's *The Shattered Chain* (1976), Darkover Amazons, living outside the patriarchal society, help to rescue a woman enslaved by the Drytowners. And in Ursula K. Le Guin's "A Woman's Liberation," from *Four Ways to Forgiveness* (1995), a woman raised as a slave on a plantation journeys to another planet in order to be free, only to realize that there she must still wage another struggle in order to have equal rights as a woman.

Postmodern, postcolonial, transgender: 1980–2005

Postmodernism, with its denial of any natural or essential self, called earlier feminist theories of gender into question. Gayle Rubin (1975) delineated a more complicated "sex/gender system," following which feminists began to recognize gender as unnatural and constructed, not inherent, and to theorize diversity at the levels of subjectivity, sexuality, and society. For example, bell hooks explores the intersections of black women's oppression as black, as women, and as working class, and exposes ways that colonizers distort reality so that the colonized accept myths about themselves (e.g., the Mammy figure; see hooks 1981: 81–4). hooks (1984) further destructs the myth that women share a common oppression (hooks 1984: 44), and argues for taking difference as a basis for solidarity (hooks 1984: 64–5). In a series of essays, Patricia Hill Collins developed the standpoint theory of the 1980s (a woman has multiple allegiances and so multiple political identities) into a theory of the interlocking matrix of identity for women. Collins (1989) distills political principles from the concrete experiences of working black women. In a commentary on science, Collins (1999) advocates feminist analysis depending on "intersectionality," examining the intersections of science, gender, race, ethnicity – all in their historical moment.

From the 1980s onwards, feminist theorists also offered alternative models for conceiving of difference as part of subjectivity: the cyborg, the hybrid, the androgyne, the transvestite. In an essay first published in 1985, "A Manifesto for Cyborgs," Donna Haraway argues that we live in a postmodern society where all are cyborgs, and that we should begin dreaming a monstrous world that is postgender. To Haraway, the cyborg, the sf part-human/part-machine fantasy that is rapidly becoming our reality, represents "transgressed boundaries" (Haraway 1991: 154) and unsettles the concept of heterosexuality as natural (Haraway 1991: 150). The cyborg, untouched by nostalgia for past innocence (Haraway 1991: 151), suggests the possibility of moving beyond the old limits of male and female into a new world of human–machine–animals (Haraway 1991: 173) and "partial identities" (Haraway 1991: 154). Cherríe Moraga proposes future women as hybrid, mixed-blood, acknowledging their kinship with animals as well as humans who are racially different (Moraga 1993: 112–31). Judith Butler argues that "gender is a kind of persistent impersonation that passes as the real" (Butler 1990: viii), that it is always performative, constituting itself (Butler 1990: 25), not an attribute of a person, but a relation between persons (Butler 1990: 10). Like Haraway and Moraga, Butler argues that identity is fragmented, each person possessing multiple identifications that congregate to form a complex identity (Butler 1990: 67, 76). Because gender is created through "repeated stylization of the body" (Butler 1990: 33), parody, dissonance, proliferation of gender identities, and getting gender "wrong" are all means of political opposition to the constraints of gender (Butler 1990: 31, 140–1). Rather than calling on women's identity for a new politics, as did the utopian feminism of the 1970s, Butler argues for a politics that contests all gender and identity (Butler 1990: 5). Thus, for Butler, the androgyne represents the new order of gender, confusing and redistributing the elements of gender so that it transgresses and challenges categories (Butler 1990: 100–1). Marjorie Garber presents cross-dressing as an "enabling fantasy" of "blurred gender" (Garber 1992: 6), a third sex that destabilizes gender by exposing it as "artifact" (Garber 1992: 249).

The concepts of the androgyne, the hybrid, the cyborg, the transvestite, partial identities, and the performative nature of gender are crucial to the developments of sf by women during the last three decades of the twentieth century. Tanith Lee's *Drinking Sapphire Wine* (1977), for instance, offers a tale where all teenagers are androgynous, not in one body, but in multiple bodies. In this future society of domed cities, robots have assumed medical and police functions, and so when a person dies, the robots quickly transport the person to a facility that provides a new body, often one picked out ahead of time by the person. Thus teens change bodies and sexes casually, and perform both male and female sexuality, and with partners who started out as the same sex. What is gender in this future world if everyone has been a different gender at some time? When Hatta pursues the narrator out of love, he wears the romantic poet body that the narrator had worn just before her last change. When they first make love, Hatta asks, "Was I as good as you were when you were me?" (Lee 1977: 152). Gendered terms are inadequate to describe this experience, and so suggest the androgynous, fragmented identity that postmodern and transgender theory ascribes to all gender categories.

Melissa Scott's *Dreaming Metal* (1995), a story about the development of the first robot with artificial intelligence (AI), offers a fantasy of the postgender world described by Haraway. While the planet Persephone is still racist, pitting upper-class Yanquis against lower-class Coolies, this future world is not gendered beyond the use of "he" and "she." There are male and female haulers and pilots, weavers and merchants, computer engineers and theater managers, entertainers and musicians. Scott further offers names that are not gendered – we cannot tell, from their names, whether pilot Reverdy Jian, manga artist Chaandi, or musician Fanning Jones are male or female. And attire, mostly loose pants and shirts, also suggests a postgender world. But Scott further unsettles the concept of gender. The first AI, Celeste, is part of the act of Celinde Fortune, a magician; Celeste's body of metal is modeled on Celinde's female form – but what gender can be assigned to an artificial construct? The replication forces the audience to acknowledge the degree to which Celinde's own femaleness is performed rather than innate. In addition, many of Scott's characters are cyborgs: Reverdy Jian has machine eyes and is "wired" to connect with her spaceship's computer and controls, while Celinde Fortune is "wired" to merge with the computers that run the theater and her apartment. These humans, married to their machines, further transgress and challenge gender categories. As the plot unfolds, many of the characters are depicted in lesbian or gay relationships – Reverdy and Chaandi (both women); Celinde and Muthana (both women); and Red and Vaughan (both men). In this future cyborg world, heterosexuality is not the norm, and gender is a construct that has lost its current hyper-significance.

Nalo Hopkinson's *Midnight Robber* (2000) combines several of the liminal figures of postmodern feminism. Tan-Tan, born in a technological utopia on the colonial world Toussaint, settled by immigrants from Jamaica ("Raino Carib and Arawak; African; Asian; India; even the Euro" (Hopkinson 2000: 18)), follows her exiled father into the other-dimensional world that shadows Toussaint. In this alternate world, instead of the luxurious care of the Granny-Nanny (an artificial intelligence planted in humans as nanomites), Tan-Tan works hard with other settlers and suffers the abuse of her stepmother and her father, eventually his raping of her. She kills her father, escapes into the wilderness with one of the douen, the bird-like natives of the planet whose females, larger than males, can fly, and in the wilderness learns truly how to live in her postcolonial world. As Tan-Tan grows up, she becomes a legend, a transvestite Robber Queen who plays carnival tricks for justice on human villagers. Befriended by a young douen, reunited with her true love, Tan-Tan eventually gives birth to a new people: the Granny-Nanny has found her across dimensions and created her son a cyborg, with nanny-powers woven into his DNA. She names him "Tubman," to celebrate her freedom.

There are many such science fictions by women with androgynous or cyborg characters resisting contemporary gender categories. In Anne McCaffrey's *The Ship Who Sang* (1969) and its many sequels, Helva, flying cyborg (a female brain in a spaceship body), saves worlds and lends emotional support to suffering humans. The female ship captain in C.J. Cherryh's *The Pride of Chanur* (1982), from a lion-like race, swashbuckles in pirate dress with gathered pants, boots, and rings in her ears. Emma Bull's *Bone Dance* (1991) follows the story of an androgynous protagonist who takes on the gender that best suits the surroundings.

Conclusion

Feminist sf writers have themselves contributed to the development of literary theory that incorporates sf and gender. Russ called on women to give up the restricting myths of male and female literature and turn to sf, where stories of exploring new worlds, of creating needed social machinery, and of evaluating technology are "not stories about men *qua* Man and women *qua* Woman" but "myths of human intelligence and … adaptability" (Russ 1972: 18). Similarly, Le Guin analyzed the position of women in sf as grouped with depictions of working-class and nonwhite peoples as inferior (Le Guin 1979: 99). Le Guin called on sf writers to rewrite the genre to include The Other, remembering that "53 percent of the Brotherhood of Man is the Sisterhood of Woman" (Le Guin 1979: 100).

Feminist sf criticism has traced many connections between feminist theory and sf by women. Natalie Rosinsky deploys the theory of literature as defamiliarization, arguing that speculative fiction by women estranges the audience "from conventional reality" so that readers "question biases inherent in any dominant world-view" (Rosinsky 1984: 114). Sarah Lefanu examines the "subversive" strategies that women writers of sf use to explore "the myriad ways in which we are constructed as women" (Lefanu 1988: 5). Marleen Barr reveals the theoretical import of sf fiction by women as "feminist fabulation" that "rewrites patriarchal myth" through "revisionary power fantasies for women" (Barr 1992: xxvii, 3). Robin Roberts argues that sf "can teach us to rethink traditional, patriarchal notions about science, reproduction, and gender" (Roberts 1993: 2). Jenny Wolmark categorizes sf as postmodern literature because it displays the contradictions of institutional discourses, especially gender discourses, and opens them to renegotiation (Wolmark 1994: 3). Jane Donawerth (1997) traces the affiliations between feminist science theory and sf by women and connects contemporary theorizations of cross-dressing to the male narrator of women sf writers. Justine Larbalestier unsettles definitions of sex and gender, exploring the "differences between male and female" that merge to form the sex/gender system in our culture and that are at issue in much sf (Larbalestier 2002: 9), especially that of James Tiptree Jr. Debra Benita Shaw (2000) traces twentieth-century sf by women as participating in debates critiquing scientific thought and especially scientific constructions of gender. And Patricia Melzer (2006) situates recent feminist sf in the context of current theoretical debates about gender as negotiated not stable, identity as built on difference not sameness, and posthuman and transgender subjectivities as multidimensional.

Bibliography

Andrews, W. (ed.) (1988) *Six Women's Slave Narratives*, New York: Oxford University Press.

Astell, M. (1701). *A Serious Proposal to the Ladies for the Advancement of Their True and Greatest Interest*, 1964, 1697, Parts 1–2, 4th edn, London: Folger Shakespeare Library Copy PR 3316 A655 S3 Cage.

Barr, M.S. (1992) *Feminist Fabulation: space/postmodern fiction*, Iowa City: University of Iowa Press.

Butler, J. (1990) *Gender Trouble: feminism and the subversion of identity*, London: Routledge.

Cavendish, M. (1994) *The Blazing World and Other Writings*, Harmondsworth: Penguin.

Chesler, P. (1972) *Women and Madness*, Garden City, NY: Doubleday.

Collins, P.H. (1989) "The Social Construction of Black Feminist Thought," *Signs*, 14(4): 745–73.

—— (1999) "Moving Beyond Gender: intersectionality and scientific knowledge," in M.M. Ferree, J. Lorber, and B. Hess (eds) *Revisioning Gender*, Thousand Oaks, CA: Sage.

Cooper, A.J. (1995) "Womanhood a Vital Element in the Regeneration and Progress of a Race," 1886, in *With Pen and Voice: a critical anthology of nineteenth-century African-American women*, ed. S.W. Logan, Carbondale: Southern Illinois University Press.

Davis, A. (1971) "Reflections on the Black Woman's Role in the Community of Slaves," *Black Scholar*, 3(4): 3–15.

Donawerth, J. (1990) "Lilith Lorraine: feminist socialist writer in the pulps," *Science Fiction Studies*, 17(2): 252–8.

—— (1997) *Frankenstein's Daughters: women writing science fiction*, Liverpool: Liverpool University Press.

Enns, C.Z. and Sinacore, A. (2001) "Feminist Theories," in J. Worell (ed.) *Encyclopedia of Women and Gender*, San Diego, CA: Academic Press.

Fell, M. (1666) *Women's Speaking Justified, Proved and Allowed of by the Scriptures*, London: Folger Shakespeare Library Copy F642, copy 1.

Firestone, S. (1972) *The Dialectic of Sex: the case for feminist revolution*, 1970, New York: Bantam.

Friedan, B. (1984) *The Feminine Mystique*, 1963, New York: W.W. Norton.

Gamble, S. (2000) "Postfeminism," in *The Routledge Critical Dictionary of Feminism and Postfeminism*, New York: Routledge.

Garber, M. (1992) *Vested Interests: cross-dressing and cultural anxiety*, New York: Routledge.

Gilman, C.P. (1966) *Women and Economics*, 1898, New York: Harper & Row.

Greer, G. (1970) *The Female Eunuch*, New York: Bantam.

Haraway, D.J. (1991) "A Cyborg Manifesto: science technology, and socialist-feminism in the late twentieth century," in *Simians, Cyborgs, and Women: the reinvention of nature*, New York and London: Routledge.

hooks, b. (1981) *Ain't I a Woman: black women and feminism*, Boston: South End Press.

—— (1984) *Feminist Theory: from margin to center*, Boston: South End Press.

Hopkinson, N. (2000) *Midnight Robber*, New York: Warner.

Larbalestier, J. (2002) *The Battle of the Sexes in Science Fiction*, Middletown, CT: Wesleyan University Press.

Lee, T. (1977) *Drinking Sapphire Wine*, New York: DAW Books.

Lefanu, S. (1988) *In the Chinks of the World Machine: feminism and science fiction*, London: The Women's Press.

Le Guin, U.K. (1979) "American SF and the Other," in S. Wood (ed.) *The Language of the Night*, New York: G.P. Putnam's Sons.

McCann, C.R. and Kim, S.–K. (eds) (2002) *Feminist Theory Reader: local and global perspectives*, New York: Routledge.

Makin, B. (1673) *An Essay to Revive the Ancient Education of Gentlewomen*, London: Folger Shakespeare Library, copy M309.

Melzer, P. (2006) *Alien Constructions: science fiction and feminist thought*, Austin: University of Texas Press.

Millett, K. (1969) *Sexual Politics*, New York: Ballantine.

Moraga, C. (1993) *The Last Generation*, Boston: South End Press.

Mott, L. (1980) "Discourse on Woman," 1849, in *Lucretia Mott: her complete speeches and sermons*, ed. D. Greene, New York: Edwin Mellen Press.

Roberts, R. (1993) *A New Species: gender and science in science fiction*, Urbana: University of Illinois Press.

Rosinsky, N.M. (1984) *Feminist Futures: contemporary women's speculative fiction*, Ann Arbor, MI: UMI Research Press.

Rubin, G. (1975) "The Traffic in Women: notes on the 'political economy' of sex," in R.R. Reiter (ed.) *Toward an Anthropology of Women*, New York: Monthly Review Press.

Russ, J. (1972) "What Can a Heroine Do? or Why Women Can't Write," in S.K. Cornillon (ed.) *Images of Women in Fiction: feminist perspectives*, Bowling Green, OH: Bowling Green University Popular Press.

Sanders, V. (2000) "First Wave Feminism," in S. Gamble (ed.) *The Routledge Critical Dictionary of Feminism and Postfeminism*, New York: Routledge.

Shaw, D.B. (2000) *Women, Science and Fiction: the Frankenstein inheritance*, London: Palgrave.

Stewart, F. (2000) "Feminism: Third-Wave," in C. Kramarae and D. Spender (eds) *Routledge International Encyclopedia of Women*, vol. 2, New York: Routledge.

Warhol, R.R. (1995) "Feminism," in C.N. Davidson and L. Wagner-Martin (eds) *The Oxford Companion to Women's Writing in the United States*, New York: Oxford University Press.

Wolmark, J. (1994) *Aliens and Others: science fiction, feminism and postmodernism*, Hemel Hempstead: Harvester Wheatsheaf.

Yaszek, L. (2004) "Stories 'That Only a Mother' Could Write: midcentury peace activism, maternalist politics, and Judith Merril's early fiction," *NWSA Journal*, 16(2): 70–97.

23
LANGUAGE AND LINGUISTICS

Mark Bould

It is unsurprising that a genre concerned with imagining alternative societies and encounters with nonhuman others should frequently involve questions of language and communication: the "presentation of new worlds involves new words, new syntactic structures, new semantic connections and new methods of understanding" (Stockwell 2000: 113). However, sf tends to privilege other sciences and often neglects linguistics, resulting in a "striking contrast between the wealth of language problems in science fiction and the relative poverty of linguistic explanation" (Meyers 1980: 1; see also Barnes 1975; Conley and Cain 2006). This chapter will consider two recurring sf scenarios – human–alien communication, linguistic relativism – before turning to the ways in which sf has been theorized as using language in unique and specific ways.

Stanisław Lem's *Solaris* (1961) mercilessly ridicules the anthropocentric presumption of scientific attitudes, evident in most sf, that draw the universe in the image of humanity. Any "attempt to understand the motivation" of the sentient ocean covering the eponymous alien world "is blocked by our own anthropomorphism" (Lem 2003: 140), which has shaped even "the most abstract achievements of science, the most advanced theories and victories of mathematics" (Lem 2003: 178). If one attempts to transpose the alien "into any human language, the values and meanings involved lose all substance; they cannot be brought intact through the barrier" (Lem 2003: 180). Tarkovsky's 1972 film adaptation culminates in a remarkably bleak visual reiteration of the idea that "We are only seeking Man … We don't know what to do with other worlds" (Lem 2003: 75). Solaris's ocean appears to attempt communication. Other nonhumans do not, either not noticing our existence or preferring just to kill us (e.g., J.-H. Rosny aîné's "The Xipehuz" (1887); H.G. Wells's *The War of the Worlds* (1898); Alun Llewellyn's *The Strange Invaders* (1934); John W. Campbell Jr's "Who Goes There?" (1938); Thomas M. Disch's *The Genocides* (1965); Boris and Arkady Strugatsky's *Roadside Picnic* (1972); *Alien* (Scott 1979); *Cloverfield* (Reeves 2008)). But what happens when the "impossible" transposition of alien languages is attempted?

Having arrived on Mars, the protagonist of Percy Greg's *Across the Zodiac* (1880) sets about learning the language:

unlike any Terrestrial tongue, [it] had not grown but been made – constructed deliberately on set principles, with a view to the greatest possible simplicity and the least possible taxation of the memory. There were no exceptions or irregularities, and few unnecessary distinctions; while words were so connected and related that the mastery of a few simple grammatical forms and of a certain number of roots enabled me to guess at, and by and by to feel tolerably sure, of the meaning of a new word. The verb had six tenses, formed by the addition of a consonant to the root, and six persons, plural and singular, masculine and feminine.

(Greg 2006: 59)

A couple of long paragraphs and charts further explicate this language's structure. In H. Beam Piper's "Omnilingual" (1957), a human archaeologist attempts to translate a long-dead Martian language. She establishes

a purely arbitrary but consistently pronounceable system of phonetic values for the letters [of Martian words]. The long vertical symbols were vowels. There were only ten of them; not too many, allowing separate characters for long and short sounds. There were twenty of the short horizontal letters, which meant that sounds like -ng or -ch or -sh were single letters. The odds were millions to one against her system being anything like the original sound of the language, but she had listed several thousand Martian words, and she could pronounce them all.

(Piper 1967: 122–3)

After tentatively establishing possible meanings for a few words, she finds her Rosetta Stone – a periodic table of elements, which not only tells her the names of individual elements and numbers, and indicates that the Martians used a decimal system, but also enables extrapolations about the Martian calendar and the level of their physical sciences. In cracking the Martian language she has found the key to translating the language of any sufficiently advanced alien civilization.

Greg's Martian language is "totally Indo-European in structure, with the customary two numbers and four cases in the noun, and three persons, two numbers, and six tenses in the verb" (Meyers 1980: 107). Therefore, what makes the language easy for the protagonist to learn is not so much its regularity as its structural resemblance to the languages spoken by most Europeans: an appeal to "universal reason" in the form of the artificially created "rational" grammar actually belies a culturally specific perspective. This ideological sleight-of-hand is even more evident in "Omnilingual," whose extinct Martian civilization closely resembles the contemporary US: language is recorded in a linear written form divided into words; the title pages of printed magazines feature the title, month of publication, issue number, and table of contents; Martians live in cities with universities; universities are divided into disciplinary departments – and classrooms – more or less identical to terrestrial ones; and on the wall of the material sciences lab hangs a periodic table of elements, organizing information which might apply universally but which in no way demands graphic representation or public display – and which need not be perceived, measured, or organized according to the properties and values Western technoscience privileges.

In addition to affirming certain Western ideologies of progress, both texts align that progress with a rationality that abstracts language from its material embodiment in the social interactions of sentient beings. Significantly, both also make use of charts as part of this process, as a further example will help to explain. In Murray Leinster's "First Contact" (1945), a human spaceship 4,000 light-years from Earth encounters an alien vessel also far from home. Both crews wish to establish contact without betraying the location of their respective homeworlds. Although the aliens communicate by electromagnetic- rather than sound-waves, it does not take long to build a "mechanical translator" (Leinster 1998: 95) and develop "a sort of code which isn't the language of either" species: "We agreed on arbitrary symbols for objects ... and worked out relationships and verbs and so on with diagrams and pictures. We've a couple of thousand words that have mutual meanings. We set up an analyzer to sort out their short-wave groups, which we fed into a decoding machine. And then the coding end of the machine picks out recordings to make the wave groups we want to send back" (Leinster 1998: 95–6). Again, the story presents culturally specific positions as universal truths (encounters between civilizations can result only in trade or war; the aliens are "normal" because they leave their females at home and tell dirty jokes) and assumes that, despite vastly different physiologies, aliens will perceive the universe and express it through language in the same way as humans. But what is most telling is that neither species learns the other's language. Rather, each translates its own language into a third one, an artificially constructed code which contains nothing of either language (Greg's and Piper's charts likewise appeal to something – grammatical norms, the periodic table of elements – supposedly irrefutably outside of the language, culture, and ideology of either species). The model of language upon which this process depends is similar to that which has dominated structuralist and poststructuralist linguistics.

This model distinguishes between *langue* (an abstract system of rules governing language) and *parole* (individual instances of speech which draw upon *langue*), privileging the former. When two individuals speak, *langue* functions like Leinster's intermediate code as a purified information realm abstracted from the lively messiness of actual communication. A major, if less influential, strand of materialist linguistics has consistently argued against this linguistic idealism (see McNally 2001). For example, M.M. Bakhtin refutes the notion that a word exists "in a neutral and impersonal language (it is not, after all, out of a dictionary that the speaker gets his words!)" prior to the speaker's moment of appropriation; rather, "it exists in other people's mouths, in other people's contexts, serving other people's intentions: it is from there that one must take the word, and make it one's own" (Bakhtin 1981: 293). Like Leinster's device, *Star Trek*'s universal translator promises communication with the alien but is conceived in terms of communicating with a computer. Postulated on "a universal cybernetic grid to which all languages are programmable or convertible," it misses "any valuation or regard for the radical otherness of the languages of others," and by failing to recognize (or deliberately stripping out) "that which in their speech is untranslatable, that which in each language is singular and irreconcilable with other languages," it runs counter to the "effort of trying to learn the language of others" or to "learn from their radical non-compatibility with my own communications protocols" (Shapiro 2004: 136). The universal translator, therefore, absorbs or disperses alien otherness, projecting an anthropomorphic vision of the universe, reinforced by a supposedly universal reason, as natural or true (a problem rigorously explored in Gwyneth Jones's *White Queen* (1991), which hinges on mutual misapprehensions in human–alien communication). It is, therefore, not merely the implacably silent but also the most relentlessly loquacious aliens with whom we fail to communicate. A variation on this general pattern is the mute black alien of *The Brother from Another Planet* (Sayles 1984). His silence enables New Yorkers to project their own meanings onto him (when he does not respond to English, some assume he is Puerto Rican or Haitian and try Spanish or French), stripping him of his alien otherness and fitting him into stereotypical identities. In contrast, his silence enables him to learn about humans indirectly through the non-compatibility of their communication protocols (see Bould 2007).

Benjamin Whorf argues that "All observers are not led by the same physical evidence to the same picture of the universe, unless their linguistic backgrounds are similar, or can in some way be calibrated" (Whorf 1957: 214). Rather than pursuing *Solaris*'s radical incommunicability, sf typically gestures toward, but calibrates for, nonhuman difference. In Robert A. Heinlein's "Gulf" (1949), more highly evolved humans have developed Speedtalk, a language "structured as much like the real world" as possible: lacking "the unreal distinction between nouns and verbs" because the universe "does not contain "noun things" and "verb things"; it contains space–time events and relationships between them" (Heinlein 1977: 69). However, despite some smug preaching, nothing of the New Men's "superiority" intrudes into the story. Their actions are no more hyperbolic than those of other pulp characters and, unsurprisingly, the viewpoint character turns out to be a New Man, thus emphasizing similarity over difference. While Heinlein clings to the notion of a fixed extralinguistic reality to which "superior" beings can make language more closely conform, C.J. Cherryh's *Hunter of Worlds* (1977) emphasizes the arbitrary structuring of perception by language, and vice versa. Iduve differs from other languages, making "no clear distinction between the concepts of noun and verb, between solid and action"; therefore, for its speakers, "Reality consists instead of the situational combination of Tangible and Ethicals" (Cherryh 1977: 246). Such fundamental differences mean "that translation cannot be made literally if it is to be understandable" (Cherryh 1977: 246). However, little sense of this alien-ness enters the text, the Iduve instead appearing as aloof, cruelly indifferent figures who speak the same language as other characters apart from the occasional Iduve word thrown in. In Naomi Mitchison's *Memoirs of a Spacewoman* (1962), Mary begins to perceive how human bilateral symmetry has influenced us to see the world in binary terms – "good and evil, black or white, to be or not to be" (Mitchison 1985: 27) – only after spending time with an alien species evolved "from a radial form, something like a five-armed starfish, itself developing out of a spiral"

(Mitchison 1985: 20). In John Brunner's *Total Eclipse* (1974), Macauley spends months cyborged into a simulacrum of one of the extinct six-limbed, crab-shaped inhabitants of Sigma Draconis, before he can even begin to comprehend their perception of reality. Perceiving electromagnetic fields and communicating by constant real-time electromagnetic broadcast and reception, the Draconians "probably didn't use names because they identified themselves by simply being" (Brunner 1976: 69). While Mitchison and Brunner pay closer attention to the importance of embodiment to perception and language, like Heinlein and Cherryh they focus on the calibration so as to sidestep the question of human–alien communication, anthropomorphizing the alien into the humanly comprehensible.

Sf has often deployed Whorf's linguistic relativism to imagine cultures or species determined (to varying degrees) by their language. Paranoid versions of linguistic determinism occur in Samuel R. Delany's *Babel-17* (1966) and Neal Stephenson's *Snow Crash* (1992), in which language possesses individuals, reducing them to automata, while William S. Burroughs, who described language as a virus from outer space, implied this has already happened in reality. In Jack Vance's *The Languages of Pao* (1958), Paonese, lacking verbs, adjectives, and "formal word comparison such as *good, better, best*," does "not so much describe an act as it present[s] a picture of a situation"; consequently, its typical speaker "saw himself as a cork on the sea of a million waves, lofted, lowered, thrust aside by incomprehensible forces – if he thought of himself as a discrete personality at all" (Vance 1974: 8). The Paonese people thus offer no resistance to invasion, so their rulers introduce three new languages to socially engineer their liberation: Valiant, "based on the contrast and comparison of strength, with a grammar simple and direct" and "rich in effort-producing guttural and hard vowels," will produce warriors; Technicant, with an "extravagantly complicated but altogether consistent and logical" grammar, will produce engineers; and Cogitant, "a symmetrical language with emphatic number-parsing, elaborate honorifics to teach hypocrisy, a vocabulary rich in homophones to facilitate ambiguity, a syntax of reflection, reinforcement and alternation to emphasize the analogous interchange of human affairs," will produce traders (Vance 1974: 57). Eventually, another new language – Pastiche, which combines Valiant, Technicant, and Cogitant with Paonese – must be imposed so as to reunite the linguistically produced and diverging social classes. Vance's breezy engineering triumphalism, common to much mid-century American magazine sf, is mostly uninterested in complex causality or the dystopian implications of such superficial cleverness, but he does allow the possibility that language and subjectivity might be more complexly related, at one point suggesting that an anarchist planet's language, one of "personal improvisation, with the fewest possible conventions" (Vance 1974: 48), might reflect rather than cause their politics.

Linguistic social-engineering is relatively common in eutopian and dystopian fiction. In Ursula Le Guin's *The Dispossessed* (1974), Pravic, a language constructed by anarchists, discourages possessives; and in Iain M. Banks's *Culture* novels (1987–), Marain similarly de-emphasizes ownership, aggression, submission, and gender. In Ayn Rand's *Anthem* (1938), David Karp's *One* (1953), and Robert Silverberg's *A Time of Changes* (1971), the first-person singular is suppressed, demonstrating a dystopian eradication of the individual.

The most detailed treatment of the development of a liberatory language is Suzette Haden Elgin's *Native Tongue* (1984) and its sequels, set in a future in which women have been reduced to childlike wards of their menfolk. The terrestrial economy depends upon trade with a galactic civilization so the role of the translator, controlled by 13 families of Linguists, is paramount. The only way to develop native-speaker fluency in an alien language is to be placed, as an infant, in an "interface" with an alien for several hours every day; as the child grows, interacting with the alien, he or she develops, alongside human perceptions and languages, those of the species on the other side of the interface. This only works with humanoid aliens, the perceptions of nonhumanoids being too radically different to assimilate. This emphasis on material embodiment is also central to the novel's exploration of gender relations. Linguist women are developing an artificial language, Langlish. The men tolerate this because it keeps the women busy, and are endlessly amused by the language's tortuous dead-ends. However, hidden within the Langlish project is the development of another, secret language, Láadan, designed to express women's perceptions of the world, things excluded from existing languages (see also Daly with Caputi 1987). As one character explains, "the seamless fabric of reality had been subjected to an artificial process: dividing it up into dull little parts, each one drearier than the one before. And *uniformly* dreary, getting drearier and drearier by a man-made *rule*. As if you drew lines in the air ... and then devoted your life to behaving as if those air-territories bounded by your lines were real. It was a reality from which all joy, all glory, all radiance, had been systematically excluded" (Elgin 2000: 284). *Native Tongue* implies that Láadan merely changes women's experience of a relentlessly oppressive reality, although it does incidentally produce some local improvements in their circumstances. In *Earth-Song* (1993), Láadan is abandoned in favor of the Linguist women's development of audiosynthesis (deriving nutrition from music), a radically fantastic and utopian notion that disrupts the genre's putative adherence to empirical reality and rationality by suggesting that changing one's experience of reality can change reality itself. This can be seen to reflect feminism's shift of emphasis in this period from legal and institutional change to contesting representations. (Blyden Jackson's *Operation Burning Candle* (1973) and Ian Watson's *The Embedding* (1973) offer similarly ambiguous explorations of the relationships among language, perception, reality, resistance, and revolution.)

In George Orwell's *Nineteen Eighty-four* (1949), the totalitarian state is drastically reducing the number of words in the language so as to "narrow the range of thought" and thus make dissent impossible "because there will be no words in which to express it": "Every concept that can ever be needed, will be expressed by exactly *one* word, with its meaning rigidly defined and all its subsidiary meanings rubbed out and forgotten ... Every year, fewer and fewer words, and the range of consciousness always a little smaller" (Orwell 1983: 49). Newspeak is part of a wider project to produce a static society. The protagonist, Winston Smith, "corrects" previously published documents, eradicating people, creating others, changing history: "Every record had been destroyed or falsified, every book … rewritten, every picture … repainted, every statue and street and building … renamed, every date … altered. And that process is continuing day by day and minute by minute. History has stopped. Nothing exists except an endless present in which the Party is always right" (Orwell 1983: 137). Bakhtin argues that language usage is determined by the tension between centripetal forces, which seek to centralize, rationalize, and instrumentalize, and anti-authoritarian centrifugal forces, which embrace liveliness and instability. Orwell builds on this tension, already evident in H.G. Wells's *A Modern Utopia* (1905), which argues that the language of utopia should be "a living tongue, an animated system of imperfections which every individual man will infinitesimally modify" (Wells 1905: 15), and *The Shape of Things to Come* (1933), in which the Dictionary Bureau carefully considers additions to the language before permitting them. *Nineteen Eighty-four's* appendix implies that Newspeak ultimately failed, perhaps because of the impossibility of fixing words with singular and unambiguous meaning (the *Star Trek: The Next Generation* episode "Darmok" (1991) demonstrates the flexibility of even the most apparently rigid language; see Shapiro 2004: 124–30).

A number of sf texts offer thoroughgoing linguistic elaboration in order to capture radical changes to either the individual (e.g., Daniel Keyes's "Flowers for Algernon" (1959), Thomas M. Disch's *Camp Concentration* (1968)) or society (e.g., Brian Aldiss's *Barefoot in the Head* (1969), Russell Hoban's *Riddley Walker* (1980), Nalo Hopkinson's *Midnight Robber* (2000), Anthony Joseph's *The African Origins of UFOs* (2006)). Such elaborations, which gradually reveal to the reader the different assumptions underpinning these fictional realities, materialize the complex connections between language and our experience of the social world. Anthony Burgess's *A Clockwork Orange* (1962) is narrated in a pidgin English saturated with words derived from Russian, along with "schoolboy slang, remnants of baby talk, Biblical allusions and terminology, Shakespearean quotations, a pattern of double and triple negatives, and a syntactical sentence pattern identical to modern German" (Barnes 1975: 62). Despite implying an earlier Soviet occupation, the novel's use of Russian is best understood as a critique of the postwar Americanization of British culture. Jack Womack's *Random Acts of Senseless Violence* (1993) – one of his *Dryco* novels (1987–2000), which chart the future development of American English – uses a diary form to trace the maturation of its teenage protagonist even as she descends from middle-class security and "short sentences, bland vocabulary, and childish locutions" to life on the streets of Harlem and "language full of neologisms, fragments, powerful verbs, complex struc-tures … dramatic, flexible, rhythmically powerful, dynamic – language in the process of change" (Gordon 1998: 44, 45).

More commonly, though, sf restricts such experiments to occasional neologisms and neosemes – new words and new meanings for existing words (see Stockwell 2000: 115–38). Such moments are acute instances of the ways sf is argued to use language in a distinctive manner (see Delany 1977, 1978, 1984; on Delany, see Samuelson 1994 and Broderick 1995). Samuel Delany's 1971 essay, "About Five Thousand Seven Hundred and Fifty Words," protested the widely held notion that sf was a literature of ideas (and that style was thus unimportant) and introduced sf to the "linguistic turn" in critical theory. Delany argued that distinctions between style and content are meaningless, because the only thing a story can be said to contain are the words on the page, which create very precise meanings. Alter them even slightly, and you alter the meaning not only of the particular sentence but of the entire text. Like the flapping of a butterfly's wings, the consequences might be virtually unnoticed or catastrophic. Content, including sf's "ideas," is therefore "the illusion myriad stylistic factors create when viewed at a certain distance" (Delany 1977: 34). To demonstrate how the meaning of a sentence is generated by word-choices (style), he introduces the sentence *The red sun is high, the blue low*, word by word, pausing after each to describe the effect of adding it to the preceding ones. As we read these words in sequence, we move along the syntagmatic axis (the order of words in the sentence); changing any word along that axis would change the syntagm (the unit of meaning). Those changes would be determined by the options available on the paradigmatic axis – that is, the alternative words that could be chosen: *A* or *Three* instead of *The*, for example, or *green* or *exploding* for *red*. The construction of any individual sentence must be understood as a process in which its structure and its words simultaneously shape each other so as to create a specific meaning. (However, the vast associative web of connotations in which each individual word is located, and which varies from reader to reader, assures that each reader understands that "specific" meaning in approximately similar but divergent ways.) It is only a small step from here to argue that not only is each linguistic sign (word, punctuation mark, etc.) surrounded by a host of absent signs, but also that its precise meaning is determined by its relationship to all the signs that it is not and to the socially situated reader's relationship to the system of language.

But if sf cannot be defined in terms of its "ideas," what makes it distinct from other forms of fiction? Delany initially argued that different kinds of word-series are distinguished by their level of subjunctivity: reportage says *this happened*; naturalistic fiction *could have happened*; fantasy *could not have happened*; science fiction *has not happened*, which includes *might happen, will not happen, has not happened yet, could have happened in the past but did not* (Delany 1977: 43–4). The reader simultaneously learns the level of subjunctivity of the text and how the level of subjunctivity determines how the words from which it is constructed should be read. For example, in a naturalist novel the phrase "her world exploded" is a clichéd description of emotional trauma; in a space opera, it signifies global cataclysm. Delany claimed that in sf such phrases avoid "the banality of the emotionally muzzy metaphor" and "through the labyrinth of technical possibility, [become] possible images of the impossible" (Delany 1977: 93). There are several problems with this argument. Although Delany argues that the "point is not that the meaning of the sentences is ambiguous ... but that the route to their possible mundane meanings and the route to their possible SF meanings are both clearly determined" (Delany 1994: 27), the ambiguity cannot be ignored. One only needs to consider Princess Leia's witnessing of Alderaan's destruction in *Star Wars* (Lucas 1977) to imagine the problems posed by "her world exploded" and to realize that Delany's argument could hold true only if sf were free from clichéd prose and dead metaphors. Furthermore, by failing to quote from an actual text, Delany occludes what might happen on encountering such expressions. For example, in his 1928 debut,

Buck Rogers says, "taking from his head the green crested helmet that constituted his badge of office, to my surprise he placed it in my mechanically extended hand" (Nowlan 2005: 93). Given the information already encountered in the story, it is impossible for anyone to conclude that Buck possesses artificially elongated fingers. As this demonstrates, there are determinants of meaning other than genre, although those determinants themselves might be determined – enabled or constrained – to varying degrees by genre.

Recognizing that sf (like all genres) was too complexly determined to be defined by a singular essence or totalizing dynamic, Delany abandoned the argument about subjunctivity, but continued to focus on word-choices in sf texts. He argues that, like "mundane fiction," the sf text "speaks inward ... to create a subject" but also "speaks outward to create a world in dialogue with the real," while the "real world speaks inwards to construct its dialogue with both" (Delany 1978: 58). To the extent that this idea has been taken up, it has typically been reduced from a complex dialectical process to a narrow emphasis on "outward signifiers," those "rhetorical figures" of which neologisms and neosemes are foregrounded examples, "through which the SF writer constructs the vision of the alternative world in which, against which, and through which the SF tale occurs" (Delany 1984: 233). For example, Tom Shippey (2005) compares the opening passages of Orwell's *Coming Up for Air* (1939) and Frederik Pohl and C.M. Kornbluth's *The Space Merchants* (1953), both of which involve the protagonist shaving. The former is a naturalist novel, in which a middle-aged, melancholy narrator recounts the story of his life, noting the transformations of Britain since Edwardian times; the latter is a satirical, sf action-adventure story, set in a dystopian future of overpopulation and corporate tyranny. Shippey focuses on *The Space Merchants*'s outward signifiers (e.g., a passing reference to the trickle from a bathroom's freshwater tap implies a world of scarcity and pollution) so as to claim that the process of making sense of the imaginary world to which they point makes sf "the most intellectually challenging of genres" (Shippey 2005: 18). Such a claim depends upon the absolute suppression of Shippey's own culturally specific position, which also requires him to base his argument on what he imagines an sf text appears like to a reader unfamiliar with the genre (and to overlook Orwell's major theme of social transformation). Moreover, in a revealing slip, he extrapolates from the Orwell passage in the manner he suggests is a particular requirement of sf: the text merely implies that local children play in their family's back gardens, while Shippey claims this is "because they have nowhere else to go" (Shippey 2005: 12). This reading of a non-sf text as if it were sf can only be judged erroneous if one insists upon outward signifiers being peculiar to sf, but, as Delany argues, the differences between fictional categories are of degree rather than kind. Sf might more heavily foreground outward signifiers than other genres, but they are not exclusive to it.

Ultimately, Delany's exploration of sf language resolved into the position that a category of fiction is not a particular set of texts but "a complex of reading protocols": those texts considered "central to the field" were "clearly written to exploit a particular protocol complex," but "we are free to read *any* text by *any* reading protocol we wish" and the "criterion is simply how useful and interesting the resultant discussion is, how it enriches our sense of the reading" (Delany 1984: 218–19). In such a claim, one can see once more the generative tension between a monolithic centripetalism, insisting sf is one particular, centered thing which must be read and understood in one particular way, and centrifugalism, embracing uncertainty and instability. From encountering nonhuman others and alternative societies, all the way down to unexpected word-choices, this dialectic of identity and difference is what makes sf, even at its most conservative, so very rich.

Bibliography

Bakhtin, M.M. (1981) *The Dialogic Imagination: four essays*, trans. C. Emerson and M. Holquist, ed. M. Holquist, Austin: University of Texas.

Barnes, M.E. (1975) *Linguistics and Languages in Science Fiction-Fantasy*, New York: Arno Press.

Bould, M. (2007) "On the Boundary between Oneself and the Other: aliens and language in the films *AVP*, *Dark City*, *The Brother from Another Planet* and *Possible Worlds*," *Yearbook in English Studies*, 37(2): 234–54.

Broderick, D. (1995) *Reading by Starlight: postmodern science fiction*, London and New York: Routledge.

Brunner, J. (1976) *Total Eclipse*, 1974, London: Orbit.

Cherryh, C.J. (1977) *Hunter of Worlds*, New York: DAW.

Conley, T. and Cain, S. (2006) *Encyclopedia of Fictional and Fantastic Languages*, Westport, CT: Greenwood Press.

Daly, M. with Caputi, J. (1987) *Websters' First New Intergalactic Wickedary of the English Language*, London: The Women's Press.

Delany, S.R. (1977) *The Jewel-Hinged Jaw: notes on the language of science fiction*, Elizabethtown, NY: Dragon Press.

—— (1978) *The American Shore: meditations on a tale of science fiction by Thomas M. Disch, Angouleme*, Elizabethtown, NY: Dragon Press.

—— (1984) *Starboard Wine: more notes on the language of science fiction*, Elizabethtown, NY: Dragon Press.

—— (1994) *Silent Interviews: on language, race, sex, science fiction, and some comics*, Hanover, NH and London: Wesleyan University Press.

Elgin, S.H. (2000) *Native Tongue*, New York: The Feminist Press.

Gordon, J. (1998) "Two Sf Diaries at the Intersection of Subjunctive Hopes and Declarative Despair," *Foundation*, 72: 42–8.

Greg, P. (2006) *Across the Zodiac: the story of a wrecked record*, 1880, Teddington, London: Echo Library.

Heinlein, R.A. (1977) "Gulf," in *Assignment in Eternity*, 1949, London: NEL.

Leinster, M. (1998) "First Contact," in *First Contact: the essential Murray Leinster*, 1945, Framingham, MA: NESFA Press.

Lem, S. (2003) *Solaris*, 1961, trans. J. Kilmartin and S. Cox, London: Faber & Faber.

McNally, D. (2001) *Bodies of Meaning: studies on language, labor, and liberation*, New York: SUNY Press.

Meyers, W.E. (1980) *Aliens and Linguists: language study and science fiction*, Athens: University of Georgia Press.

Mitchison, N. (1985) *Memoirs of a Spacewoman*, 1962, London: The Women's Press.

Nowlan, P.F. (2005) "Armageddon – 2419 AD," in *Wings Over Tomorrow: the collected science fiction of Philip Francis Nowlan*, Rockville, MD: Wildside Press.

Orwell, G. (1983) *Nineteen Eighty-Four*, 1949, Harmondsworth: Penguin.

Piper, H.B. (1967) "Omnilingual," in J.W. Campbell (ed.) *Prologue to Analogue*, 1957, London: Panther.

Samuelson, D.N. (1994) "Necessary Constraints: Samuel R. Delany on science fiction," *Foundation*, 60: 21–41.

Shapiro, A.N. (2004) *Star Trek: technologies of disappearance*, Berlin: Avinus Verlag.

Shippey, T. (2005) "Hard Reading: the challenges of science fiction," in D. Seed (ed.) *A Companion to Science Fiction*, Oxford: Blackwell.

Stockwell, P. (2000) *The Poetics of Science Fiction*, London: Longman.

Vance, J. (1974) *The Languages of Pao*, 1958, London: Granada.

Wells, H.G. (1905) *A Modern Utopia*, London: Chapman and Hall.

Whorf, B. (1957) "Science and Linguistics," in J.B. Carroll (ed.) *Language, Thought, and Reality: selected writings of Benjamin Lee Whorf*, Cambridge, MA: The Technology Press of MIT.

24
MARXISM
William J. Burling

The Marxist interest in and connection to sf is longstanding and well known, but also highly complex, uneven, and mediated. Like its counterparts in feminist, postcolonial, queer, and ethnic literary and cultural theory, Marxist theory is always connected in both spirit and practice to objectives that range beyond a specific literary text, and thus employs cultural analysis in the interests of social and political praxis. The first and longest section of this chapter will outline fundamental Marxist theoretical concepts and concerns with relation to sf; the second identifies representative theorists and studies; the third surveys some significant sf works of fiction and film that have been of interest to Marxist critics.

Marxist cultural theory and practice

The particular "flavor" of Marxist criticism of cultural production is distinguished by several key concepts that theorize the historically specific material articulations of production and consumption. The *mode of production* refers to the differing economic systems which in turn generate specific forms of social relations out of which unique forms of cultural production arise. Of the four (possibly five) modes identified by Marx, capitalism is the most relevant to discussion of sf because of the specific development of science, technology, and economics from the early nineteenth century to the present time. Capitalism is characterized by the ways in which the *surplus value* of labor is captured as profit by the owners of the means of production, resulting in a lopsided distribution of material assets. Three effects are especially noteworthy. *Alienation* results from the facts that workers often cannot afford the very goods and services they create, nor do they own the resources needed for production. The irresolvable material antagonisms existing between capitalist haves and proletarian have-nots result in *class struggle*, which is replicated in the content and especially the forms of cultural practices, as exemplified by such categories as "popular culture" and "high art." The third effect, *reification*, describes the practice of equating human relationships with relations among things. This component is most readily understood via attention to *commodification* (i.e., the social valorization of consumption), which is especially characterized by the *commodity fetish*. The latter refers to the ideological mystification of imagining that things have "a life of their own" rather than being the products of human labor.

Tying all of these concepts together in Marxist criticism are two basic methodological practices. The first, *historicization*, insists that only by the analysis of practices at specific moments in cultures can one grasp their meaning and significance. In this insistence, Marxism vehemently challenges the prevailing bourgeois idealist theory of interpretation which separates "true art" from "popular culture," and characterizes the former as bearing transcendent, universal value. The second is *critical thinking*, which reflects upon its own premises, insists upon supporting evidence, and recognizes the complexities of ideology generated by the mode of production's particular social relations.

With these basic terms in mind, we can turn first to how Marxist critics apply them to the analysis of cultural production in general, and then move on to their particular applications with respect to sf. This chapter examines two main concerns of Marxist cultural theory: the appearance and development of specific forms of production; and ideology critique, i.e., how the particular cultural work expresses or resists the ideological mechanisms and assumptions of the status quo

Georg Lukács's *The Theory of the Novel* (1916), while not specifically Marxist, is arguably among the first important and purely theoretical works of the early twentieth century devoted to close analysis of cultural, in this case literary, production. Lukács established the basis for linking particular forms of fiction, such as realism, to specific historical eras, and demonstrated the possibilities for sophisticated theoretical analysis of culture. Subsequent historicizing studies by others refined the connections of period to form but also demonstrated how culture production variously replicates or challenges ideology. The Frankfurt School critics T.W. Adorno and Max Horkheimer identified, in *Dialectic of Enlightenment* (1947), what they termed the emerging "culture industry" – forms of mass-cultural production such as film and music which simultaneously generated profits for capitalists while also inculcating uncritical political and social passivity. Countering this overly reductive position, Raymond Williams, especially in *Culture and Society, 1780–1950* (1960), established the basis for what became known as Cultural Materialism by arguing for the *resistive* and even *liberatory* possibilities of mass culture. Also contributing sophisticated materialist theoretical models for interpreting cultural production during the post-Second World War period were critics such as Roland Barthes (*Writing Degree Zero* (1953), *Mythologies* (1957)), Louis Althusser (*For Marx* (1965), *Reading Capital* (1968)), and especially Pierre Machery (*A Theory of Literary Production* (1966)). While almost no Marxist cultural critics appeared in the repressive Cold War culture of the US, Fredric Jameson and Darko Suvin must certainly be noted. We will return to their specific contributions to sf criticism, but must here highlight Jameson's *The Political Unconscious* (1981) and *Postmodernism, or The Cultural Logic of Late Capitalism* (1991), which offered fresh strategies for historicizing cultural production in relation to the stages of capitalism over the past two centuries. As this brief survey indicates – many more theorists and works could be mentioned – Marxist theorization of cultural production had achieved an impressive sophistication by the turn of the millennium.

Marxist criticism and sf

Marxist sf criticism emerged alongside academic teaching and writing about sf in the late 1950s, which saw the launch of the first scholarly journal dedicated to sf, *Extrapolation*, in 1959. In this context, Raymond Williams's "Science Fiction" (1956) is possibly the first specifically Marxist sf essay. This short but pioneering ideological critique calls attention to the significance of sf and offers guidelines on how it might be productively interpreted from a Marxist perspective. These twin axes have, in various forms, become axiomatic. Concomitant with the rise of "New Wave" sf in the 1960s is a noticeable increase in sf criticism, as indicated by the founding of the Science Fiction Research Association in 1970. But the seminal development in Marxist sf criticism is the emergence of *Science Fiction Studies* (SFS) in 1973. Though the journal has always published essays from a variety of perspectives, it nevertheless validated and provided a venue for academic Marxist interpretation of sf and championed sf as important for Marxist analysis.

Attention in the 1970s and 1980s focused on two topics: defining sf as a form and discerning its relationship to utopian theory. Darko Suvin (1979) had immediate and longstanding influence on sf criticism due to his Marxist–Structuralist insistence on historical specificity, analysis of form, and attention to utopian dynamics. Suvin, one of the founding editors of SFS, offered an influential definition of the form: "*a literary genre whose necessary and sufficient conditions are the presence and interaction of estrangement and cognition, and whose main formal device is an imaginative framework alternative* [i.e., the novum] *to the author's empirical environment*" (Suvin 1979: 7–8; emphasis in original). His hyper-specific definition has by no means gone unchallenged, but gains great interest when historicized in its own right as an attempt to validate sf as a credible "literary" genre. Also notable from 1979 is Patrick Parrinder's unduly neglected *Science Fiction: its criticism and teaching*, which contributed to the debate about form by insisting upon sf's nonsynchronous generic development.

Suvin's definition has generated wide discussion, especially among Marxist scholars. Carl Freedman accepts Suvin's model as "not only fundamentally sound but indispensable" (Freedman 2000: 17), but modifies it "to emphasize the dialectical character of genre and the centrality of the cognition effect" (Freedman 2000: 23). Freedman further argues that dialectical estrangement is not merely the limiting condition of sf but a "precondition for the constitution of fictionality – and even of representation itself" (Freedman 2000: 21). Challenging Suvin (and Freedman) are China Miéville and Mark Bould's essays in an issue of *Historical Materialism* (2002) dedicated to "Marxism and Fantasy." Miéville insists that sf and fantasy, far from being separate formal categories (the latter of which Marxists have traditionally denigrated as reactionary), both create "a mental space – redefining – or pretending to redefine – the impossible" (Miéville 2002: 44). Bould likewise argues for shared continuities between sf and fantasy such that so-called generic differences of "various types ... of fantastic text" are better understood "as a further process of product differentiation" (Bould 2002: 81).

Arguing from a specifically Marxist perspective, Suvin also epitomized the relationship between utopia and sf in terms of the former being "*the sociopolitical subgenre*" of the latter (Suvin 1979: 61; emphasis in original). Thus his and Peter Fitting's many essays on the subject, Tom Moylan's important theorization of the "critical utopia" in *Demand the Impossible* (1986), Jameson's wide-ranging *Archaeologies of the Future* (2005), and Philip Wegner's *Imaginary Communities* (2002) must be recognized here as specifically Marxist critiques of utopian sf.

Conventions of form have also received attention from Marxist critics. Adam Roberts's *Science Fiction*, perhaps the most pointedly Marxist sf textbook yet to appear, offers a compelling argument for the "alterity of machines" (Roberts 2000: 148) as linking sf iconography – such as the spaceship and the robot – to the origin and development of commodification as outlined in Marx's *Capital*, especially respecting matters of desire and power (Roberts 2000: 150). Also drawing upon Marx, Rob Latham's *Consuming Youth* (2002) theorizes the metaphorical importance of vampires and cyborgs to signify the complexities and contradictions of youth consumer culture.

Thematic developments within sf have generated corresponding critical attention by Marxist-influenced critics to such issues as subjectivity, imperialism, and gender. Scott Bukatman's *Terminal Identity* (1993) explores the "crisis" of postmodern subjectivity; while John Rieder writes compellingly on imperialism in sf in *Colonialism and the Emergence of Science Fiction* (2008), as does Istvan Csicsery-Ronay Jr in his *SFS* essay "Science Fiction and Empire" (2003). The relationship of Marxist to feminist interests is well exemplified by Donna Haraway, whose widely cited "Manifesto for Cyborgs" asserts fidelity "to feminism, socialism, and materialism" (Haraway 1991: 149) by contending that sf depictions of cyborgs correspond to wholly new "dangerous possibilities" of identity (Haraway 1991: 154). Calling upon examples from authors such as Vonda McIntyre, Octavia Butler, and Anne McCaffrey, Haraway argues that cyborg alterity challenges current models of identity, especially those of women, grounded in patriarchal capitalism. The cyborg, by contrast, "has no truck with bisexuality, pre-oedipal symbiosis, unalienated labour, or other seductions to organic wholeness … [or any] higher unity" (Haraway 1991: 150).

Arguably the most productive and influential Marxist sf critic since the early 1970s, however, is Jameson. No summary can address the range of his interests. His essays on such authors as Philip K. Dick, Ursula K. Le Guin, McIntyre, Kim Stanley Robinson, and William Gibson, focusing on such topics as utopian theory, globalization, postmodernism, class struggle, and generic historicity, are collected in *Archaeologies of the Future*. The collection continues Jameson's longstanding and perhaps most important theoretical contribution, that of *cognitive mapping* as a strategy for historicizing and grasping the otherwise unrepresentable operations and effects of multinational capitalism. Properly understood as a demystifying countermeasure to the debilitating operations of ideology, "achieved cognitive mapping" is the process of conceptualizing an intellectual form which can grasp "the totality of social relations on a global … scale" (Jameson 2000: 283). Jameson regularly asserts that sf in general is precisely such a privileged representational apparatus, and in particular that Gibson's *Pattern Recognition* (2003) "sends back more reliable information about the contemporary than an exhausted realism" and thus maps "the new geopolitical Imaginary" (Jameson 2005: 384–5).

Thus Marxist theory, far from fading in the post-Soviet era, has become ever more pertinent, being the best-suited conceptual model for grasping the rapid developments of the capitalist world order and the imminent off-world extensions that loom in humanity's future.

Marxism in sf, or, "Left-sf"

All sf cultural production represents social, economic, and political effects that naturally arise as a result of scientific and technical extrapolation. The engagement of such issues varies widely, of course, from ostensibly minor details of setting, character, and plot to the most intense foregrounding of utopian agendas, but utopian thought and political theory in the broader sense do not automatically equate to Left-sf thematics. In fact, much sf simply assumes as given or aggressively advocates the expansion of capitalism. This section therefore will offer (1) a selective historical overview of Left-sf cultural production that is not ostensibly utopian yet features anti- or post-capitalist critique; (2) commentary concerning some special examples; and (3) an attempt to historicize overall trends. In general but with some notable exceptions, the North American tradition offers few examples of Left-sf, though it does evince a long history of more generalized anti-capitalist critique. In contrast, European sf carries on a sustained dialogue with socialist and even Marxist concerns.

Late nineteenth- and early twentieth-century Western sf, in a world reeling from technological advancements, industrial capitalism, and the rise of proletarian movements, shared with other fictions (e.g., Theodore Dreiser's *Sister Carrie* (1900), Frank Norris's *McTeague* (1899)) a pointed interest in social issues. The publication of Samuel Butler's *Erewhon* (1872), Edward Bellamy's *Looking Backward: 2000–1887* (1888), and other socialistically minded examples of utopian fiction set precedents for the conflation of utopian fiction and "scientific romance" traditions as they emerged in the work of the first clearly programmatic sf author, H.G. Wells. From *The Time Machine* (1895) and *When the Sleeper Wakes* (1899) onward, his sf often explored socialistic themes, albeit in conflicted ways. As Suvin argues, "Wells' SF works are clearly 'ideological fables,' yet he is a virtuoso in having it ideologically both ways. His satisfaction at the destruction of the false bourgeois idyll is matched by his horror at the alien forces destroying it" (Suvin 1979: 217). Wells's clearest socialist views were expressed in his non-sf, purely utopian, and even nonfiction works, such as *A Modern Utopia* (1905) and *Men Like Gods* (1923). His contemporary Jack London's *The Iron Heel* (1908) depicts, in more pointedly utopian-fictional form, the grim dystopian effects of oligarchic capitalism, and is committed to Marxist communism to an extent seldom equaled.

Subsequent political developments, repressive of proletarian movements in the US and to a lesser extent in Western Europe, altered the artistic climate with respect to Left-sf in the years following the First World War and the Russian Revolutions. The specifically American and reactionary "pulp" era of the 1930s held such sway that, aside from George S. Schuyler's satiric commentary on American racism, *Black No More* (1931), no notable examples of American Left-sf appeared until the 1940s, and even those subsequently appearing in the 1950s are few and far between. Left-sf flourished in Europe, however.

As might, with hindsight, be expected, Russia generated considerable sf activity, with 25 works appearing before 1917 and at least 155 during the years 1920–7 (Suvin 1979: 26). Especially significant was Nikolai Chernyshevsky's popular *What is to be Done?* (written 1862; published 1905). A seminal contribution to Russian utopian socialist thought, particularly with respect to women's rights, its model of personal freedom was emulated in much Russian sf and utopian fiction. Alexander Bogdanov-Malinovsky's *Red Star* (1908) depicts a scientifically advanced and successful socialist society on Mars and served to inspire like-minded sf authors, such as Kim Stanley Robinson. Also writing in the glow of the post-October Revolution is Alexei Tolstoy, whose sf novels, *Aelita* (1922, revised 1937) and *Engineer Garin's Death-Ray* (four versions, 1926–37), were popular for decades in Russia but seldom read in the West. Yevgeny Zamyatin's important but conflicted *We* (written 1920, published in English 1924) interrogates the pernicious effects of mindless socialistic scientism but importantly has no sympathy for capitalism. The novel has long been interpreted in the West as an attack upon the communist experiment, but, as Suvin, Moylan, and Jameson have argued, this novel should be read not as "anti-utopian" but as a "critical dystopia" that advocates "a vision common to Anarchism and libertarian Marxism" (Suvin 1979: 257).

Following the innovative decade of the 1920s, Russian sf stagnated until after 1956, when a "second [though short] great age of Russian SF" emerged (Suvin 1979: 265). This era produced what is perhaps the greatest example of Russian socialist sf and utopian fiction, rivaled only by *What is to be Done?* in terms of historical importance, Ivan Yefremov's monumental *Andromeda: a space-age tale* (1957), which touches virtually every issue relevant to socialist concerns, from science to the arts to ethics and beyond, and engages Western sf "in a well-informed polemical dialogue" (Suvin 1979: 268). The "Yefremov era," according to Suvin, lasted only into the 1960s, at which time Russian and other Warsaw Pact sf lost its utopian, socialist impulse and turned sharply satirical.

Returning to the West, we find that the interwar period produced few noteworthy examples of left-leaning sf. One line of British sf reacted fearfully to the promise of the technological future: Aldous Huxley's *Brave New World* (1932) bitterly denigrates technical development, a key dimension of socialist societies, instead stressing an argument in favor of liberal humanist aesthetics that serves to disguise the novel's fundamental reactionary political perspective. However, another form of British sf, identified by Roger Luckhurst as "evolutionary sf," carried on Wells's interest in progressive social issues, exemplified by Olaf Stapledon's *Star Maker* (1937). In the US during the late 1930s, at least two general and loosely aligned factions of sf appeared in opposition to the school of right-wing hard sf identified with the pulp tradition of Gernsback and Campbell. The first, exemplified by E.E. "Doc" Smith's *Lensman* stories in *Astounding* during the late 1930s, insists that sf alone is able to combine fabulation and critical thinking, resulting in a presumably more sophisticated and progressive form of fiction. Despite these attributes and claims to the contrary, the Smith branch of sf's ostensible liberal commitment to cosmic awe is in the final accounting nothing short of an elitist mentality in full complicity with capital's ideological agenda. The other line emerging just before the Second World War was advocated by the Futurians, a loose grouping based in New York, not all of whom were sf writers, which included socialists of several stripes and even some communists. Some went on to various degrees of success, the most notable being Isaac Asimov, Frederik Pohl, Judith Merril, Donald Wollheim, C.M. Kornbluth, and Damon Knight. Despite Knight's claim that the socially minded Futurians had a "mighty mission" (Knight 1977: 15) to educate sf fans respective to the Futurian agenda as grounded in the spirit of 1930s socialism, as Luckhurst notes, they in fact did not produce a mature "left-liberal critique ... until the post-war era" (Luckhurst 2005: 68). By the time the youthful Futurians began to produce something approaching Left-sf, however, the contentious but still relatively heady days of 1930s political experimentation had given way to the fearful realities of the atomic bomb, growing uneasiness with rampant consumerism, and the political repercussions of the hard-line anti-communistic milieu of the 1950s HUAC and McCarthy period.

Socialist thought in United States Left-sf varies from considerably muted to non-existent during the 1950s and nearly all of the 1960s. Sf, along with much other cultural production of the Cold War era, certainly satirizes or questions gray-flannel-suit conformism, creeping bureaucracy, commodification, and even nascent environmentalism, but it rarely poses solid political questions or offers Left alternatives to capitalism. Perhaps only Heinlein's *Double Star* (1956) can be said to be manifestly political, though in a libertarian and accordingly nonsocialistic sense. Important examples of satirical critique without alternatives include Ray Bradbury's nostalgic *The Martian Chronicles* (1950), Kurt Vonnegut Jr's *Player Piano* (1952), Alfred Bester's vigorously caustic *The Stars My Destination* (1956), Harlan Ellison's short fiction of the 1960s, and Frank Herbert's richly complex *Dune* (1965). More focused but still fuzzy examples appeared from the maturing Futurians, such as former Trotskyite Merril's groundbreaking feminist sf "That Only a Mother" (1949) and *Shadow on the Hearth* (1950), Pohl's short fiction, such as "Tunnel under the World" (1954) and his important collaboration with Kornbluth, *The Space Merchants* (1953), and Theodore Sturgeon's *More Than Human* (1953). Not coincidentally, Merril wrote the "Introduction" for *Path into the Unknown: the best of Soviet sf* (1968). Additionally, Dick's early short fiction that is likewise critical of consumerism, such as "Sales Pitch" (1953) and "Paycheck" (1954), bears strong affinities to the themes and narrative strategies of Futurian fiction. Still, despite John Clute's claim that Pohl and Kornbluth in the 1950s "were on the cutting edge of social comment" (Clute 1995: 182), with the exception of Sturgeon's utopian *Venus Plus X* (1960), virtually no genuinely Left-sf was published in North America during the 1960s. (Zenna Henderson's important but overlooked *Pilgrimage* (1961) must be passed over in this context since her alien utopian commune, despite its many progressive features, arises out of mystical spirituality rather than dialectical materialism.)

Critique of the capitalist status quo in Left-sf found new impetus in the wake of the Vietnam War and the increasing effects of global capitalism in the late 1960s and into the 1970s, but throughout the 1950s and 1960s hegemonic sf, while toying with social critique, was often implicitly and sometimes even overtly anti-socialist and even right-wing libertarian, as evidenced in stories by authors such as Jack Vance and Heinlein. Sf in this period far more often focuses on, variously, the possible negative and often apocalyptic future (e.g., Walter M. Miller Jr's *A Canticle for Leibowitz* (1960)) or the uncritical celebration of "science and technology" as if they somehow manifest an independent existence free from inherent economic and political concerns (in Heinlein, again, and even Asimov). American Left-sf once again emerged in the form of the New Wave, in part related to and supported by public interest in related progressive concerns, such as the anti-war, civil rights, women's, and ecological movements. Some important authors, while offering very different visions, include Roger Zelazny (*Nine Princes in Amber* (1970)), Samuel R. Delany (especially *Triton* (1976) and the tour-de-force *Stars in My Pocket Like Grains of Sand* (1984)), and Ursula K. Le Guin (*The Left Hand of Darkness* (1969), *The Lathe of Heaven* (1971)). These works foregrounded vaguely socialist concerns in the areas of human freedom and dignity, and offered variations of post-capitalist social visions, though to be sure Le Guin and her contemporaries Joanna Russ and Marge Piercy are better known for their mid-1970s utopian fiction.

By the mid-1980s, however, most American sf production in any form of print, television, or film had long since abandoned even the pretence of leftist thought except in the work of the newly appeared Kim Stanley Robinson. Demonstrating a clear commitment to intelligent and sustained Left ideals, Robinson's *Three Californias* trilogy, beginning with *The Wild Shore* (1984), initiates an extended meditation on capitalism's future and beyond to post-capitalist societies, a focus Robinson carried on into the 1990s with the important *Mars* trilogy. Also in the 1980s, the new cyberpunk movement registered the profound shifts taking place in the development of what Ernst Mandel terms "late capitalism" – the impact of communications technology made possible by satellites, computers, and the internet; the surging importance of biomedical technologies; and the growing consolidation of financial transactions under transnational, global corporations. Exemplary works in this form include William Gibson's *Neuromancer* (1984), Bruce Sterling's *Islands in the Net* (1988), and Pat Cadigan's *Synners* (1991), which feature intense and unsympathetic critiques of capitalism's expanding sphere of influence and its often sinister relationship to technology. In no important way, however, can these works be called Left-sf, although Sterling's *Holy Fire* (1996) is regrettably underappreciated despite its thoughtful socialist meditation on life-extension and healthcare.

From the late 1980s to the mid-1990s, some modestly Left-sf by women appeared in the US. Sheri Tepper's *The Gate to Women's Country* (1988) presents a feminist Left vision that critiques the relationship of militarism and misogyny, while Octavia E. Butler's *Xenogenesis* trilogy, beginning with *Dawn* (1987), and her later *Parable* series, initiated by *Parable of the Sower* (1993), grapple with racism, xenophobia, sexism, and religious fanaticism. While Margaret Atwood's *The Handmaid's Tale* (1985) explores similar themes, Butler's more complete Left-sf vision emphasizes the rebuilding process for society in ways that resonate with socialist views of material equality and personal freedom, especially in the post-capitalist social order represented in *The Parable of the Talents* (1998).

American television and film during the 1980s and into the 1990s, increasingly grounded within the corporate commodity apparatus of capitalism, generated almost nothing in the way of Left-sf. The vast majority of sf films were dystopian cautionary tales (the *Terminator* franchise (1984–)), feel-good humanistic fables (*E.T.: The Extra-Terrestrial* (1982)) or reactionary romps, such as the trendsetting *Star Wars: Episode IV–A New Hope* (1977). A few notable exceptions include the socialist–feminist alternative future depicted in Lizzie Borden's *Born in Flames* (1983), the scathing indictment of capitalism in Paul Verhoeven's *RoboCop* (1987), and John Sayles's critique of capitalist racism in *The Brother from Another Planet* (1984).

The towering American Left-sf achievement published during the 1990s was Robinson's *Mars* trilogy, consisting of *Red Mars* (1992), *Green Mars* (1993), and *Blue Mars* (1996). Supremely optimistic, yet grounded in the awareness that genuine change is both slow and painful, this series raises the standards of Left-sf to new levels of commitment and sophistication by engaging in a sustained and non-idealist post-capitalist meditation. The trilogy vividly renders Marx's prediction for the potential of human freedom once released from material-based class struggle, and its triumphal conclusion depicts humanity carrying a socialist vision to worlds beyond our solar system.

British sf over the past four decades often engaged with socialist and even Marxist thematics, which may be said to begin with Michael Moorcock's assumption of the editorship of *New Worlds* in 1964. Encouraging the pursuit of experimental and radical social critique in sf, he published what would in due course become an impressive generation of Left-sf authors and their followers, including Brian Aldiss and J.G. Ballard. Taking William Burroughs as their literary inspiration, this New Wave evinced a latent Left position (that is, advocating Left views of consciousness but not highlighting the requisite socioeconomic components). A second wave, however, depicted manifestly Left extrapolations: Iain M. Banks's *Culture* novels, such as *Consider Phlebas* (1987), offer an extended post-scarcity, Left socio-techno vision; Ken MacLeod actively engages Marxist ideas in the *Fall Revolution Quartet*, beginning with *The Star Fraction* (1995); and China Miéville's remarkable and generically innovative *Bas-Lag* series incorporates an extended meditation on Left political and social issues, most clearly in *Iron Council* (2004).

Of special and final note is the work of two recent women authors. Tricia Sullivan's *Maul* (2003) vigorously interrogates social and political issues in her depiction of a near-future, but non-utopian, world administered solely by women. Also important is Gwyneth Jones's *Bold as Love* (2001), and the ensuing namesake series – *Castles Made of Sand* (2002), *Midnight Lamp* (2003), *Band of Gypsys* (2005), and *Rainbow Bridge* (2006). Jones's near-future depiction of the UK, originally sketched out in a 1992 short story, grapples with gender, political, economic, social, and environmental issues emerging from the breakdown of the capitalist status quo and the resulting revolutionary possibilities. The novel sequence aggressively challenges the reactionary dystopian bent of much sf by presenting a plausible utopian vision grounded on

Left-based values emphasizing shared resources and decision-making. Jones's work thus stands as one of the most important contemporary works of Left-sf.

Even this short and admittedly selective survey demonstrates the essential interconnection between sf's representations of the production and consumption of technology and the resulting implications as theorized by Marx and later Left thinkers. While only a few sf works have manifestly engaged the concomitant and irrepressible social, political, and economic issues inherent in their alternative worlds, *every* sf story, film, or television show bears the latent burden of ideological commitment.

Bibliography

Bould, M. (2002) "The Dreadful Credibility of Absurd Things: a tendency in fantasy theory," *Historical Materialism: Research in Critical Marxist Theory*, 10(4): 51–88.

Clute, J. (1995) *Science Fiction: the illustrated encyclopedia*, London: Dorling Kindersley.

Freedman, C. (2000) *Critical Theory and Science Fiction*, Hanover, NH and London: University Press of New England/Wesleyan University Press.

Haraway, D.J. (1991) "A Cyborg Manifesto: science technology, and socialist-feminism in the late twentieth century," in *Simians, Cyborgs, and Women: the reinvention of nature*, New York and London: Routledge.

Jameson, F. (2000) *The Jameson Reader*, Oxford: Blackwell.

—— (2005) *Archaeologies of the Future: the desire called utopia and other science fictions*, London: Verso.

Knight, D. (1977) *The Futurians*, New York: John Day.

Luckhurst, R. (2005) *Science Fiction*, London: Polity.

Miéville, C. (2002) "Editorial Introduction to Symposium on Marxism and Fantasy," *Historical Materialism: Research in Critical Marxist Theory*, 10(4): 39–49.

Roberts, A. (2000) *Science Fiction*, London: Routledge.

Suvin, D. (1979) *Metamorphoses of Science Fiction: on the poetics and history of a literary genre*, New Haven, CT: Yale University Press.

25
NUCLEAR CRITICISM
Paul Williams

What is nuclear criticism?

While literary and cultural studies often introduce undergraduates to critical theory (e.g., Marxism, linguistics, feminism, psychoanalysis), the nuclear criticism of the 1980s and early 1990s is typically absent from the curriculum and the introductory anthologies such courses assign. Undoubtedly, this is partly a result of shifts in the institutional and political contexts within which it emerged. By the mid-1990s, the criticism that took the end of the world as its subject found that the Earth was still standing; and other political questions, such as the continuing evolution of global capitalism, made its ethical imperative seem less pressing.

Broadly speaking, nuclear critics were concerned with "the applicability of the human potentiality for nuclear self-destruction to the study of human cultural myths, structures, and artefacts" (Scheick 1990: 4), and in particular with critical theory's engagement with the threat of nuclear extinction. In the mid-1980s, as critical theory consolidated its position in Western academic institutions, nuclear critics published a series of manifestos, editorials, and articles in special issues of the journals *Diacritics* (1984), *Science Fiction Studies* (1986), and *PLL: Papers on Language & Literature* (1990). Simultaneously, popular cultural depictions of nuclear apocalypse and post-apocalyptic dystopias appeared in significant numbers, including novels (David Brin's *The Postman* (1985), Whitley Strieber and James W. Kunetka's *Warday and the Journey Onward* (1984)), films (*The Terminator* (Cameron 1984), *Def-Con 4* (Donovan 1985)), television movies (*The Day After* (Meyer 1983), *Threads* (Jackson 1984)), and comics (the 25-part Judge Dredd "Apocalypse War" story in *2000 A.D.* (1982)). This currency provided nuclear criticism, envisaged as a contribution to nuclear disarmament, with a sense of urgency and importance.

Reflecting on this meeting between theory and extinction, these journals suggested six broad avenues of critique. First, how has conceptualizing nuclear war as "just another" apocalypse – imagining it, for example, as an heir to biblical apocalypses, as in Walter M. Miller Jr's *A Canticle for Leibowitz* (1959) – flavored its understanding and perhaps acceptance by policy makers and the public? Second, how might literary interpretation – by disentangling the rhetoric and postures of the arms race, deterrence, and "nukespeak" – illuminate the superpowers' nuclear proliferation? For Daniel

L. Zins, literary study of nonliterary nuclear texts makes "a significant contribution to the continuity of human life" by working to "demystify and deconstruct those national security texts and discourses that keep us in thralldom to the nuclear deity" (Zins 1990: 36). Third, how has terror surrounding nuclear war entered the psychological climate, shaping individual psyches, and in what ways is it discernible in cultural productions? H. Bruce Franklin observed the "psychological numbing" (Franklin 1986: 115) of the nuclear era, his vocabulary indicating the massive influence of Robert J. Lifton's research into the psychical survival mechanisms triggered by the nuclear threat. "Numbness" is one such mechanism, a psychological skin preventing the traumatic possibility of nuclear war entering one's consciousness. Lifton argues that the nuclear threat has been "domesticated" for most people, fading into the background of everyday life. Nuclear weapons exist because of this tolerance, and it can be shattered – and nuclear weapons rejected – if numbing is transcended (Lifton 1979: 7; Lifton and Falk 1982: 102–10). This activist sensibility – to consolidate public awareness and mobilize opposition to the nuclear threat – underpinned much nuclear criticism. Looking for psychological explanations of the arms race and its drive toward extermination, some critics turned to psychoanalytical theory (Fornari 1974). As early as 1949, Aldous Huxley's *Ape and Essence* anticipates the construction of nuclear weapons and the perverse "fear of the War we don't want and yet do everything we can to bring about" (Huxley 1966: 37).

Fourth, many nuclear critics used gender to critique the nuclear arms race, often drawing on psychoanalytical language. In some instances, this reproduced a polarized "battle of the sexes": "On one side are mostly men who make policy decisions and invent the vocabulary of arms talk. On the other are frequently women leading men against installations, with figures and scenarios for anti-nuclear struggle taken from the vocabulary of [feminism]" (Anon. 1984: 3). In Helen Caldicott's *Missile Envy* (1984), women "are generally born with strong feelings for … the preservation of life," whereas men "enjoy killing" and are "more psychologically aggressive than women" (Caldicott 1984: 294–5); nuclear weapons are "a symptom of several male emotions: inadequate sexuality and a need to continually prove their virility plus a primitive fascination with killing" (Caldicott 1984: 297).

Caldicott's position typifies the concept of sexual difference advocated by the Women's Peace Movement in the 1980s (see Freeman 1989). This entrenchment in nature absents male voices from anti-nuclear protest, erases the historicity of gendered identities and nuclear deterrence, and perpetuates inequality by rooting conflict between the genders in antagonistic, mutually exclusive biological differences. An alternative feminist interrogation of the nuclear threat de-emphasized biology, offering instead a cultural critique of masculine supremacism. Suggesting that societies threatening to use nuclear weapons are organized around "the phallocentric concept that power, success, peace and safety depend on the literal domination of all life as we know it" (Schweninger 1991: 178), these critics argued that the nuclear "arms race is rooted in the values of a male supremacist culture, particularly its promotion of a domineering phallic sexuality" (Caputi 1991: 66).

This is certainly the framework through which many critics have understood *Dr*

Strangelove or: How I Learned to Stop Worrying and Love the Bomb (Kubrick 1964), in which the men operating America's nuclear defenses are subject to an aberrant desire, a strange love, whereby nuclear destruction overlaps with and ultimately displaces sexual desire. Since radioactivity would make the Earth's surface unlivable, military scientist Dr Strangelove is titillated by the prospect of living in an underground bunker populated with ten females (selected for "sexual characteristics" of a "highly stimulating nature") for every male, and with nothing to do but breed so as to repopulate the planet. Major Kong inventories his survival kit, which includes prophylactics, lipstick, and nylon stockings with which to sexually exploit female survivors of the apocalypse, and he straddles a nuclear bomb as it falls to its target. The attack on the USSR is ordered by General Jack D. Ripper, whose name links serial sex murder and the arms race as extreme manifestations of the phallic sexuality underpinning male supremacist culture (see Linden 1978: 64–6). Ripper "finds his ultimate satisfaction in violent assault," although his "mutilation sex murder takes the form of an all-out nuclear attack" (Caputi 1991: 67). (Other important gender critiques include Mars-Jones 1990 and Tarantelli 1986.)

A fifth critical activity related nuclear weapons to knowledge-production and the role of technology in Western culture. Adorno and Horkheimer's *Dialectic of Enlightenment* (1947) exposed the contradiction shadowing the application of Enlightenment reasoning and the spread of scientific knowledge: the greater the technology that humankind develops to emancipate itself from natural limits, the greater destructive power it possesses to inflict upon itself. As *Ape and Essence* taunted, humankind's "much touted technology ... raises our standard of living, [but] increases the probability of our violently dying" (Huxley 1966: 37). Finally, some nuclear critics connected nuclear maneuvering to military and strategic history. Paul Virilio stressed the importance of the relationship between war, speed, technology, and visualization. The mid-twentieth-century advent of strategic bombing and nuclear weapons saw the distance between battlefield and safe, spectating positions contract to a vanishing point: "everything is now brought home to the cities ... Nuclear deterrence means that there are no longer strictly 'foreign wars'" (Virilio 1989: 66). For Virilio, the experience of war in the atomic age has become less real, since this kind of long-distance warfare enables soldiers to forget about the casualties on the other side, at the same time that images of war are detached from their immediate spatial context: "the concept of reality is always the first victim of war" (Virilio 1989: 33).

Nuclear criticism and poststructuralism

Nuclear criticism's most significant works arose from poststructuralist theory's encounter with the system of deterrence, with nuclear criticism sometimes seen as a mutation of poststructuralism produced by the nuclear threat's ethical immediacy (Scheick 1990: 5). Poststructuralist critics' interest in the possibility of nuclear extinction is unsurprising. Poststructuralism, an intellectual tendency in the humanities and social sciences from the 1970s onwards, sought to show how Western philosophy's metaphysical categories – good, evil, love, death – do not have referents in universal aspects of human life, but are historically constituted through repetition and language-use. For example, deconstruction, a poststructuralist interpretative strategy, argues that a word's meaning is predicated on the interconnected concepts of "difference" and "deferral": meaning is produced by absence as much as presence (Derrida 1987: 26–9). Nuclear extinction represented an ultimate absence which constituted the end of the species while also erasing itself as an event by removing all witnesses; death was thus both imminent and always deferred. Nuclear war was always present since the superpowers were ready to launch their missiles the second the opposing side launched theirs; but it was also absent, since it had not started *yet*. Deterrence itself – *the "other" side will not initiate a first strike because our superior nuclear arms ensure our eventual victory, and in this way peace is preserved* – was built on a paradox because the superpowers could not simultaneously possess a greater nuclear arsenal than the other (see McCanles 1984).

Poststructuralist nuclear criticism highlighted how semiotic systems struggle to contain ambiguities in the communication process, investigating the system of nuclear deterrence as a series of texts in which slips, dual meanings, and paradoxes are immensely important, while several cultural texts of the period – *Threads, Mad Max Beyond Thunderdome* (Miller and Ogilvie 1985), Russell Hoban's *Riddley Walker* (1980) – documented the breakdown of language and communication after nuclear war. Deconstructionism argues that the gaps and fissures in a text make it impossible to fix and fully understand its meaning. The author does not fill the text with meaning which is carried to the discerning reader without spilling a drop; rather, meanings continually slip away from attempts to pin them conclusively to the text (see Derrida 1987: 28–9). *Riddley Walker*'s linguistic experimentation embodies the mutability of language that deconstructionists foreground (see Schwenger 1992).

The eponymous Riddley lives in a southeast England rendered unrecognizable by nuclear war. Out of the broken language spoken in this post-apocalyptic world, multiple readings of the foundational myth of his society – *The Eusa Story* – are possible. Eusa, the protagonist, could specifically be the West (Europe and the USA) or Everyman ("You, sir"). *The Eusa Story* simultaneously retells the crucifixion of Christ, Adam's Original Sin, and the splitting of the atom. At its centre is the confrontation between Eusa and "the Littl Shynin Man the Addom": "Eusa wuz pulin on the Littl Mans owt stretcht arms … He wuz ded. Pult in 2 lyk he wuz a chikken" (Hoban 1998: 31–2). Later, the novel confirms this is an enactment of Christ's crucifixion – "that crucified Saviour … thats our Littl Shyning Man him as got pult in 2 by Eusa" (Hoban 1998: 128) – as well as a parable about splitting the atom: "Owt uv thay 2 peaces uv the Littl Shynin Man the Addom thayr cum shyningnes in wayvs in spredin circles … Eusa seen the Littl 1 goin roun & roun insyd the Big 1 & the Big 1 humin roun insyd the Littl 1" (Hoban 1998: 32). This seems to be a verbal approximation to particles circulating around a nucleus, the symbol often used for atomic energy. How is this discovery applied? "Eusa put the 1 Big 1 in barms then him & Mr Clevver droppit so much barms thay kilt as menne uv thear oan as thay kilt enemes" (Hoban 1998: 33). Thus nuclear annihilation is traced back and attributed to Eusa's primal encounter with the Littl Shyning Man the Addom. The latter's name, suggesting the biblical Fall of Adam (see Branscomb 1991), provides a further layer of interpretation, especially because *The Eusa Story* unfolds in the "Hart uv the Wud" (Hoban 1998: 31), a location Hoban aligns with the violent drives behind it: "**wud**: Means wood as in forest; also 'would', intention, volition or desire ... The heart of the would is also the essence of one's wanting, the heart of one's deepest desire" (Hoban 1998: 235). Eusa's deepest desires (tearing the Littl Man in two *and* splitting the atom) are violent and destructive, the legacy of Adam's Fall, and just as inescapably, Eusa cannot be free of the "Littl Shyning Man the Addom," who tells him "yul jus fyn me in a nuther plays" (Hoban 1998: 35).

In *Riddley Walker*, the English language has split open, leaving multiple meanings to circulate as it evolves into a phonetic spelling which blocks quick consumption and alienates the reader from immediate understanding. Working meaning out of the text is a demanding, (re)constructive process, forcing the reader to follow many possible interpretations simultaneously, while the post-apocalyptic decay of language in this and other sf texts recalls that *our* everyday communications are riddled with gaps and haunted by the ruins of former meanings.

The origins of nuclear criticism

The superpowers had possessed atomic weapons since the 1940s, and by the end of the 1950s were capable of annihilating each other. In this early Cold War period many significant cultural critics engage with the nuclear threat: Norman Mailer (1961) wrote on the psychic fallout of possible extinction on America's young, and Susan Sontag (1965, collected 1966) critiqued the giant, irradiated monsters of Hollywood B-Movies for inadequately addressing the enormity of the nuclear threat. The Cold War cooled during the late 1960s and much of the 1970s, but the election of President Reagan in 1980 saw a renewal of US belligerence, partly as a reaction against the perception of America's dwindling position in the world (defeat in Vietnam, the Soviet invasion of Afghanistan, the toppling of the US-sympathetic Shah of Iran). Claiming vulnerability to Soviet attack, Reagan raised military spending by 50 percent (Weart 1988: 377–8). Consequently, the first half of the 1980s represented a high-point of nuclear anxiety, with the idea that human life would be eradicated by nuclear war circulating through Western media more widely than before. The reignited Cold War was an obvious factor in nuclear criticism's emergence: the threat of absolute destruction was a philosophical "state" demanding theorization.

Nuclear criticism was also made possible by cultural shifts in American higher education. J. Fisher Solomon observes that the initial embrace of poststructuralism by American academics in the late 1960s and 1970s took literary criticism into apolitical territory, concentrating on deferred meaning in the literary or historical text, but failing to reach through close reading of texts to the politics of the history that produced them (Solomon 1988: 12–14). A decade later, American critics were beginning to absorb the work of Fredric Jameson and Edward Said, whose writing incorporated, but moved beyond, poststructuralist textual analysis, "blending a Nietzschean distrust of historical dialectics and referential realism with a Marxian attentiveness to the social forces behind the writing of both literary and critical texts" (Solomon 1988: 14) and bringing under scrutiny the unified bourgeois self whose presence had obstructed the full extension of Marxist, feminist, and postcolonial politics into literary and cultural studies. With "geopolitical tensions rising and with American theorists increasingly exploring a new political agenda of their own for post-structural criticism," nuclear criticism seemed an inevitable development (Solomon 1988: 15). Solomon identifies a colloquium at Cornell University's Department of Romance Studies in spring 1984 (which formed the basis of the special issue of *Diacritics* later that year) as nuclear criticism's foundational moment of self-consciousness. As poststructuralism was placed in the service of radical politics, the anti-nuclear movement seemed an obvious and necessary bedfellow. This historical and political contingency may be one factor in nuclear criticism's disappearance.

De(con)structing texts

One of the papers delivered at Cornell was Derrida's "NO APOCALYPSE, NOT NOW (full speed ahead, seven missiles, seven missives)," which in its published form is the canonical text of nuclear criticism. Crystallizing poststructuralism's interest in nuclear extinction, Derrida claimed that "deconstruction … belongs to the nuclear age" and acknowledged an incapacity to theorize nuclear war, an event unseen in human history: one is "blind and deaf alongside the unheard-of" (Derrida 1984: 27, 21). Deconstruction, attending not to an Author's Work but to matrices of texts informing one another, finds in nuclear weaponry a system of warfare more textual than its predecessors. Nuclear weaponry depends "upon structures of information and communication, structures of language, including non-vocalizable language, structures of codes and graphic decoding" (Derrida 1984: 23). During Derrida's discussion, President "Reagan" acquires quotation marks, perhaps to alert us to the Authorless nature of nuclear war: the origins of nuclear conflict will be overdetermined by the straitjacket of deterrence diplomacy, missile detection systems, and computer science. The pretence of nuclear war as a "fable" enabling diplomatic and strategic leverage may not be identical to the "reality" of nuclear war, but the two are inseparable, influencing and impacting upon each other (Derrida 1984: 23–6). The "real" war must coexist with the "fable," because the fable alone, although always with recourse to the referent of real war, makes postures of nuclear aggression meaningful on the level of international politics (Derrida 1984: 24, 28). This slippage between the projection of nuclear war, and its absent (because irreducibly "unknown" (Derrida 1984: 21)) referent is closely intertwined with deconstruction's critique of language, whereby a word is not a label signifying a preexisting category. Rather, signified meaning is determined through its historical juxtaposition with other words, and so meaning – as with the threatened absence of nuclear war – is never "simply present or absent" (Derrida 1987: 26).

For Derrida, two conditions permit literary production: the "stockpiling" of "literature" beyond culture's "traditional oral base" – a literary canon embodied in material print texts – and its socio-legal parameters, "implying authors' rights …

the distinction between the original and the copy, the original and the plagiarized version, and so forth" (Derrida 1984: 26). What is unique about nuclear war is "the possibility of an irreversible destruction, leaving no traces, of the juridico-literary archive – that is, total destruction of the basis of literature and criticism" (Derrida 1984: 26). This dilemma about literature's material "precariousness" (Derrida 1984: 27) prompts Derrida to interrogate its ontological status. Deconstruction's playfulness with supposedly sacrosanct literary works reflects nuclear war's rebuke to literature's immutable, eternal qualities: "The hypothesis of this total destruction watches over deconstruction, it guides its footsteps" (Derrida 1984: 27). It is "in the light" of the hypothesis of total destruction that we come to "recognize ... the characteristic structures and historicity of the discourses, strategies, texts, or institutions to be deconstructed" (Derrida 1984: 27). Literature's sudden vulnerability compromises its claims to make a timeless address to its readers.

Derrida suggests that nuclear extinction resists being constituted as a teleological conclusion to human history because it would erase the sentient witnesses required to give it meaning. It testifies to "an absolute self-destructibility without apocalypse, without revelation of its own truth, without absolute knowledge," with our nuclear epoch a suspended judgment on the "end of history" (Derrida 1984: 27). Deconstruction similarly defers a decision on literature's valued cultural position: "the structural possibilities of what goes by the name literature ... is not limited to the events already known under this name" (Derrida 1984: 27). With nuclear destruction posing the dissolution of literature's single, essential, and timeless meaning, deconstruction seduces the reader into a polygamous relationship with the text (as seen in the multiplicity of meaning at work in *Riddley Walker*). This is a "relationless relation," because the "ultimate" determinant of nuclear war is "unsymbolizable, even unsignifiable," effacing itself as a referent (Derrida 1984: 28). Nuclear extinction permits the proliferation of deconstructive literature and literary criticism but cannot be identified as the force determining the play of textual meaning because it is experienced only as absence. (Work building on the insights of Derrida and other early nuclear critics includes Bull 1995, Chaloupka 1992, and Schwenger 1986.)

Following Alan Nadel (1995), nuclear criticism's resistance to single, fixed meanings is not only a consequence of the Cold War, but a critique of its rhetoric. The multiplicity of textual possibilities released can be seen, in their very existence, to rally against the pursuit of monolithic meaning characterizing competition between the US and the USSR. Each superpower deployed nuclear weapons to defend its continuing existence, weapons threatening the nonexistence of the other bloc. The superpowers' monological interpretation of human relations, unable to recognize their reciprocal relationship with opposing political ideologies, effaced possible alternatives through Mutually Assured Destruction. For some Cold Warriors, nonexistence was preferable to surrender: "Better dead than Red" (see Evans 1998: 118). The pleasures of indulging the multiple meanings of texts, however, make their own case for thinking beyond the war of opposing idioms: "Better read than dead."

Whatever happened to nuclear criticism?

The collapse of the USSR in the early 1990s concluded the Cold War. With the nuclear threat apparently diminished, nuclear criticism's justification as an intellectual intervention on the side of human survival was lessened. When anti-nuclear activism declined outside higher education, it disappeared within. However, the idea that criticism might marry theory and the protection of life on Earth did not evaporate. Ecocriticism – literary and cultural studies' engagement with environmentalism – has appeared since nuclear criticism's disappearance, and is institutionally established in crucial forms that eluded nuclear criticism (dedicated journals such as the online *ISLE: Interdisciplinary Studies in Literature and Environment*, anthologies such as Glotfelty and Fromm (1996), courses on degree programs). In advocating an interpretative practice allied to the interconnectedness of ecosystems and the preservation of life – *all* life – on the planet, one in which anti-nuclear activism still has a role, ecocriticism may be nuclear criticism's successor, not least in terms of its emergence in the late 1980s and early 1990s.

This explanation of nuclear criticism's disappearance is, however, incomplete. First, works of nuclear criticism continued appearing after the USSR's collapse. Second, despite moves toward disarmament in the early 1990s, the US and Russia still possess enormous nuclear stockpiles. Third, the number of nuclear powers has grown since nuclear criticism's demise. Perhaps this last point illustrates why nuclear criticism's entry into theory's history books is premature. Arguably, nuclear extinction is no longer feared as humanity's fate, but the question of who is entitled to possess nuclear weapons is becoming a defining issue of twenty-first-century politics. During the 1990s, films such as *Under Siege* (Davis 1992), *True Lies* (Cameron 1994), and *The Peacemaker* (Leder 1997) exploited the theft and detonation of nuclear materials as suitably thrilling narrative matter. In *Tomorrow Never Dies* (Spottiswoode 1997), James Bond recognizes ex-Soviet nuclear torpedoes at a "Terrorist Arms Bazaar on the Russian border" just as a Royal Navy missile strike is ordered on this "terrorist supermarket," providing all the ingredients necessary for a rousing action sequence in which he must steal the jet carrying the torpedoes and fly it to safety before the missile arrives, preventing a radioactive disaster.

Since 9/11, policing the movement of nuclear technology has grown more prominent in popular culture, and was used to justify the 2003 invasion of Iraq. If the underpinnings of nuclear criticism – a radical poststructuralism and the threat of nuclear extinction – are no longer as profound in the twenty-first century, theorizing cultural texts in the light of contemporary nuclear politics remains relevant. In seasons two, four and six of the television series *24* (2001–), counterterrorism agent Jack Bauer races against time to stop Islamist terrorists from either detonating nuclear bombs on American soil or attacking US nuclear power plants. *24*'s repeated depiction of the Middle East as a generator of Islamist extremists, combined with its legitimization of extreme and absolute actions (including torture and murder) against potential nuclear terrorists, arguably positions it as the popular cultural arm of US foreign policy, justifying unilateral actions taken to safeguard national security, regardless of civilian casualties or human rights abuses (see Žižek 2006). While psychoanalysis, Marxism, poststructuralism, and feminism were the theoretical currents that nourished 1980s nuclear criticism, theories of postcolonialism may reenergize it now the issue of nuclear weapons turned against the West is a recurrent feature of our headlines.

Bibliography

Anon. (1984) "Proposal for a *Diacritics* Colloquium on Nuclear Criticism," *Diacritics – A Review of Contemporary Criticism*, 14(2): 2–3.

Branscomb, J. (1991) "Knowledge and Understanding in *Riddley Walker*," in N. Anisfield (ed.) *The Nightmare Considered: critical essays on nuclear war literature*, Bowling Green, OH: Bowling Green State University Popular Press.

Bull, M. (ed.) (1995) *Apocalypse Theory and the Ends of the World*, Oxford: Blackwell.

Caldicott, H. (1984) *Missile Envy: the arms race and nuclear war*, New York: Morrow.

Caputi, J. (1991) "Psychic Numbing, Radical Futurelessness, and Sexual Violence in the Nuclear Film," in N. Anisfield (ed.) *The Nightmare Considered: critical essays on nuclear war literature*, Bowling Green, OH: Bowling Green State University Popular Press.

Chaloupka, W. (1992) *Knowing Nukes: the politics and culture of the atom*, Minneapolis: University of Minnesota Press.

Derrida, J. (1984) "NO APOCALYPSE, NOT NOW (full speed ahead, seven missiles, seven missives)," *Diacritics – A Review of Contemporary Criticism*, 14(2): 20–31.

—— (1987) "Semiology and Grammatology: interview with Julia Kristeva," in A. Bass (ed.) *Positions*, 1968, London: Athlone.

Evans, J.A. (1998) *Celluloid Mushroom Clouds: Hollywood and the atomic bomb*, Oxford: Westview-Perseus.

Fornari, F. (1974) *The Psychoanalysis of War*, trans. Alenka Pfeifer, Garden City, NY: Anchor Books.

Franklin, H.B. (1986) "Editorial Introduction," *Science Fiction Studies*, 13(2): 115–16.

Freeman, B. (1989) "Epitaphs and Epigraphs: 'the end(s) of man,'" in H.M. Cooper, A.A. Munich, and S.M. Squier (eds) *Arms and the Woman: war, gender, and literary representation*, Chapel Hill: University of North Carolina Press.

Glotfelty, C. and Fromm, H. (eds) (1996) *The Ecocriticism Reader*, Athens: University of Georgia Press.

Hoban, R. (1998) *Riddley Walker*, 1980, expanded edn, Bloomington: Indiana University Press.

Huxley, A. (1966) *Ape and Essence*, 1949, London: Chatto and Windus.

Lifton, R.J. (1979) *The Broken Connection: on death and the continuity of life*, New York: Simon and Schuster.

Lifton, R.J. and Falk, R. (1982) *Indefensible Weapons: the political and psychological case against nuclearism*, New York: Basic Books.

Linden, G.W. (1978) "Dr Strangelove Or: How I Learned to Stop Worrying and Love the Bomb," in J.G. Shaheen (ed.) *Nuclear War Films*, Carbondale and Edwardsville: Southern Illinois University Press.

McCanles, M. (1984) "Machiavelli and the Paradoxes of Deterrence," *Diacritics – A Review of Contemporary Criticism*, 14(2): 12–19.

Mailer, N. (1961) "The White Negro: superficial reflections on the hipster," 1957, in *Advertisements for Myself*, London: Deutsch.

Mars-Jones, A. (1990) *Venus Envy: on the WOMB and the BOMB*, London: Chatto and Windus.

Nadel, A. (1995) *Containment Culture: American narratives, postmodernism, and the atomic age*, Durham, NC: Duke University Press.

Scheick, W.J. (1990) "Nuclear Criticism: an introduction," *PLL: Papers on Language & Literature*, 26(1): 3–12.

Schwenger, P. (1986) "Writing the Unthinkable," *Critical Inquiry*, 13(1): 33–48.

—— (1992) *Letter Bomb: nuclear holocaust and the exploding word*, Baltimore, MD: Johns Hopkins University Press.

Schweninger, L. (1991) "Ecofeminism, Nuclearism, and O'Brien's *The Nuclear Age*," in N. Anisfield (ed.)

The Nightmare Considered: critical essays on nuclear war literature, Bowling Green, OH: Bowling Green State University Popular Press.

Solomon, J.F. (1988) *Discourse and Reference in the Nuclear Age*, Norman: University of Oklahoma Press.

Sontag, S. (1966) "The Imagination of Disaster," in *Against Interpretation and Other Essays*, New York: Farrar, Straus and Giroux.

Tarantelli, C.B. (1986) "And the Last Walls Dissolved on Imagining a Story of the Survival of Difference," in J. Friedlander, B.W. Cook, A. Kessler–Harms, and C. Smith-Rosenberg (eds) *Women in Culture and Politics: a century of change*, Bloomington: Indiana University Press.

Virilio, P. (1989) *War and Cinema: the logic of perception*, 1984, trans. by P. Camiller, London: Verso.

Weart, S.R. (1988) *Nuclear Fear: a history of images*, Cambridge, MA: Harvard University Press.

Zins, D.L. (1990) "Exploding the Canon: nuclear criticism in the English department," *PLL: Papers on Language & Literature*, 26(1): 13–40.

Žižek, S. (2006) "The Depraved Heroes of 24 are the Himmlers of Hollywood," *The Guardian*, 10 January.

26
POSTCOLONIALISM
Michelle Reid

There is no single period or moment marking the emergence of postcolonial approaches to sf, but rather a gradual and intermittent convergence of their concerns which can best be thought of in terms of a growing space of encounter and change, of active translation and transition in the margins between cultures. The meeting of cultural forms which are in these liminal spaces produces new, hybrid identities, "neither the one nor the other" (Bhabha 1994: 25), and both sf and postcolonialism are altered in this encounter.

Postcolonialism is a collection of critical practices that examine the colonial process, the struggle for independence by former colonies, and their creation of distinct national identities. The cultural forms produced by these nations challenge the Western-centric focus of the literary canon and academic scholarship. Postcolonialism is not a coherent body of theory; it is characterized by fundamental disputes that question its own construction and legitimacy. First, the period implied by "post" is contested. It suggests an opposition to, and an end to, colonial rule, but it is also a backwards-looking perspective tying theories and practices to colonialism's ongoing legacy. The focus of postcolonialism is also disputed: should it include only those countries that were former colonies, or also incorporate settler colonies, diasporic and migrant populations, and descendants of people affected by colonial oppression? Its purpose and political stance are also debated: is it merely a Western scholarly exercise, or a means for active political resistance? Leela Gandhi (1998) shows how postcoloni-alism emerged from an uneasy negotiation of Marxist and poststructuralist positions, shifting between materialist opposition to colonial oppressions and discursive decon-struction of the language which naturalizes such oppressions. Finally, the ability to create national identities through cultural production is questioned: do these cultural forms always refer back to the colonial center, or are they new perspectives in their own right?

Edward Said (1978), commonly regarded as the catalyst for postcolonialism, exposes how the Occident creates the Orient as a category and object of study, providing the ideology for the Occident's imperial expansion. Said demonstrates how the Self creates the Other based on its own needs and desires. However, this maintains a rigid binary, with the Self subjugating the always-victimized Other, an assumption disputed by anti-colonial nationalists. Frantz Fanon (1965) analyzes the ambiguous, symbiotic power relationships between colonizer and colonized, showing how they can be a means of resistance, and examines what is necessary to build a political movement for decolonization. Bhabha and others expand the debate by focusing on transnational, diasporic identities, showing how the colonial encounter leads to the transformation and dislocation of both colonizer and colonized.

Anti-colonial resistance partly relies on forming a homogenous national identity; this ignores and marginalizes parts of the population. Some feminist critics highlight this double colonization of the Third World Woman. However, Chandra Talpade Mohanty (1988) criticizes Western liberal feminism's tendency to characterize the "Third World Woman" as a monolithic and singular entity. Trinh T. Minh-Ha (1989) argues that the celebration of native women is often a means of creating an exotic cultural commodity. Gayatri Spivak (1994) deconstructs the assumption that Western postcolonial and feminist critics can recover and represent the authentic "voice" of the Third World Woman.

Postcolonialism interrogates the complex Self/Other power relationships created by the colonial encounter. Sf imagines encounters with the Other (the alien, the strange newness brought about by change), typically from the perspective of the dominant Self. It perpetuates images of pioneering spaceship crews landing on other planets and exterminating bug-eyed aliens, but also questions and undermines the supposed manifest destiny of space exploration and the oppression of the Other as alien. This chapter will look at the spaces shared by sf and postcolonialism, highlighting the reading and writing strategies which have developed there. It will show how post-colonialism enables a nuanced examination of sf's complicity in and criticism of colonial discourses, and how sf provides ways of imagining futures that counter the argument that postcolonialism looks backward to the imperial center and colonial past.

Charting sf's generic and historical connection to colonialism

Dunja M. Mohr (2005) charts how sf's colonial themes developed in early space operas, which reveled in the prospect of expanding new frontiers in outer space. While L. Ron Hubbard's ruthless *Return to Tomorrow* (1954) suggests the genocide of all alien races so as to ensure human supremacy, novels from the late 1950s onwards were more critical of the oppression inherent in expansionist attitudes (Mohr cites Robert Silverberg's *Invaders from Earth* (1958) and Ursula K. Le Guin's *The Word for World is Forest* (1972)). This approach shows the variety of sf representations of colonialism. However, treating colonization only as a theme suggests that it is a self-contained "given" of sf, like the iconic spaceship or robot, and does not question or explain the connection between colonization and sf.

John Rieder sees the theme of colonization as a symptom of sf's historical roots and its formation as a genre which "appeared predominantly in those countries that were involved in colonial and imperialist projects" (Rieder 2005: 375). Rather than merely transposing colonization into different times and spaces, sf is a form of writing which "addresses itself to the fantastic basis of colonial practice" (Rieder 2005: 376). The European colonial project was an ideological "fantasy" that enabled colonizers to justify their subjugation of colonized people by denying that they were fully human or civilized. Colonizers created their own myth of destiny, agency, and progress to obscure the knowledge that the people they oppressed were not inherently inferior. Analyzing invasion narratives such as H.G. Wells's *The War of the Worlds* (1898), Karel Čapek's *War with the Newts* (1936), Octavia Butler's *Xenogenesis* trilogy (1987–9) and Gwyneth Jones's *Aleutian* trilogy (1991–7), Rieder shows how, through imagining alternative invasion scenarios, sf is in dialogue with the ideological fictions and fantasies that supposedly justify such invasions. Sf's fantastic nature does not distance it from historical colonial projects, but gives a closer insight into the strategies used to create the ideological fantasy of colonialism.

Istvan Csicsery-Ronay Jr goes further, arguing that sf is itself a fantasy of empire, emerging in industrialized, imperial nations, such as America, Britain, France, Germany, Japan, and the Soviet Union, as a mediator between national cultural traditions and the rise of global capitalism. Implicated in the project of a global, technoscientific empire, sf takes place in a shared cosmos which is "governed by the laws and right of technoscience" (Csicsery-Ronay 2003: 238). Regardless of whether or not individual texts are supportive or critical of this technoscientific worldview, sf cannot escape it. Csicsery-Ronay's interpretation of technoscientific empire raises the question of whether it is possible, or desirable, to have an overarching theory of sf and empire given the growing diversity of sf produced outside the former imperial nations.

Rereading canonical sf texts

Postcolonialism often involves reexamining naturalized representations of power and dominance. Said (1978) highlights the extent to which Western colonizing powers constructed knowledge of the Orient through a discourse that encoded the otherness and inferiority of the Oriental subject. This influential analysis of a systematic, dominating discourse prompted a number of reading strategies with which critics showed how deeply these forms of knowledge are ingrained in canonical English literature. Sf critics are increasingly revisiting genre texts in this manner.

Matthew Candelaria draws parallels between the alien Overlords in Arthur C. Clarke's *Childhood's End* (1953) and the British colonial administration in India, whose record was being questioned following independence in 1947. Similar to the British colonial administration, the Overlords keep familiar structures of government, and rule indirectly through them; decide upon an administrative language (English) and impose it globally; and adopt a paternalistic attitude to humans. Candelaria argues that this novel is "deftly engineered to make the reader identify with the colonial administrators, the Overlords, and their self-sacrificing mission to better humanity" (Candelaria 2002: 38–9), hence it implicitly defends Britain's colonial record in India as one of forbearance and progress.

Peter Fitting examines the influence of Wells's *The War of the Worlds* on subsequent depictions of the alien as monstrous Other, and the xenophobic attitudes connected to this estranged appearance. While Wells's Martians offer a means of questioning the rationale for British imperialism (a famous passage compares the Martians invading Earth to European settlers' genocide of the Tasmanians), Fitting notes the contrasting justifications for each invasion. European colonialism claimed to be a civilizing mission, bringing religion and culture to "savages," but the Martian invasion makes no such pretense. The Martian invasion is an act of survival by a supposedly superior race, which empties out the civilizing mission. The Martians' claims to superiority are undermined by their defeat by terrestrial bacteria, thus laying bare the "guilty conscience of imperialism" (Fitting 2000: 140).

Such reexaminations show that many sf texts do not straightforwardly advocate colonial expansion, but take a more complex and ambiguous approach to the dominant values of the time in which they were written. They also draw attention to the value-judgments and assumptions that have led to certain sf texts and authors being canonized.

Adapting postcolonial critical tools to analyze sf texts

Postcolonial reading strategies can build a better understanding of the complex relationships between power, culture, body, and identity in sf. Helen Addison-Smith uses Homi Bhabha's concept of "hybridity" to analyze the consequences of space colonization as expressed in mid-century American sf, such as James Blish's *The Seedling Stars* (1957), Marion Zimmer Bradley's *The Colors of Space* (1963), and Harry Harrison's *Planet of the Damned* (1962). To live on planets incapable of sustaining human life, humans cannot simply impose their unchanged, "pure" identities onto the new environment but must make radical adaptations to themselves. Bhabha's concept of hybridity focuses mainly on cultural cross-fertilization, but Addison-Smith extends this to encompass the radical biological adaptations made by the settlers in space. Their physical and cultural hybrid identities should challenge racial and biological essentialism. However, in the texts Addison-Smith analyzes, the impact of these changes is mitigated by claims that there are essential human values (individualism, adventurousness, scientific curiosity) – dominant US attitudes of the time championed as universal truths (Addison-Smith 2006: 29).

Cassie Carter uses the concepts of Orientalism and mimicry to show how Philip K. Dick's *The Man in the High Castle* (1962) turns the colonial process back on America. In Dick's alternate history, in which the Axis powers won the Second World War, America is "colonized by colonized people, where the Japanese colonizers are mirror images of Western ideals and values instilled by colonialism" (Carter 1995: 333). The Japanese colonists are products of Western Orientalism, and demonstrate this by craving American consumer goods and romanticized historical artifacts from the frontier past. However, this replication of American mythology by the colonial authorities means that America is "occupied and 'oppressed' by a simulation of itself" (Carter 1995: 333). Carter extends Bhabha's interpretation of "mimicry" to analyze how mimics can themselves become colonizers, bringing with them the simulacra of the culture they imitated. Mimicry describes the means by which colonial subjects assimilate and mirror back to the colonizers their values and practices, both as imitation and mockery. The colonized mimic confronts the colonial authorities with an image which is unsettling because it is both the same and different; not quite right or quite "white" enough (Bhabha 1994: 89). Dick's alternate history doubles-up the mimicking process: American subjects imitate the culture of the Japanese authorities, itself a replication of American frontier mythology.

Addison-Smith and Carter demonstrate that postcolonial tools have to be adapted to fit the extended reach and estranging perspectives of future and alternate colonial power relations. In sf, postcolonial cultural concepts are often made literal and applied to the physical form of the alien Other. For example, cyborgs and clones can be interpreted as a combined technological and biological manifestation of the processes of hybridity and mimicry on the human body. Nisi Shawl's "Deep End" (2004) takes place on a prison ship going to colonize an alien world. The black prisoners have their minds downloaded into the cloned bodies of the rich white authorities against whom they rebelled. Instead of being not quite "white" enough, the prisoners are exact copies of their rulers. Their minds, however, are their own. Consequently, they have to negotiate racial heritage and new physical appearance into an uneasy hybrid existence, which questions where racial identity is located.

Identifying sf from outside the US and UK

Postcolonial perspectives are useful in identifying strands of political and cultural resistance in sf traditions from countries marginal to the mainstream of American and British sf, and in forming a foundation for a shared identity not simply based on the country of origin. Ralph Pordzik argues that exhausted European utopian writing has been reinvigorated by a growing range of African, Australian, Canadian, Indian, and New Zealand utopias which display similar aesthetic characteristics in order to create inclusive and flexible visions of society; heterogeneous and open-ended, they resist single definitions and subvert realist modes (Pordzik 2001: 28). Many of these utopias, such as Peter Carey's *The Unusual Life of Tristan Smith* (1994), are also satirical, parodying utopian societies as a sign of the inflexibility of essentialist Western values while simultaneously celebrating utopian thought's potential for social transformation (Pordzik 2001: 171). However, Pordzik uses "postcolonial" to signify overarching aesthetic techniques similar to those of "postmodernism," thus tending to elide the specific political and national contexts of these complex utopias

Amy J. Ransom, drawing on Vijay Mishra and Bob Hodge's "oppositional post-colonialism," emphasizes how Quebec has been shaped by the struggle for identity as a marginalized community within a settler colony (Ransom 2006: 293–4). Oppositional postcolonialism is identified by active opposition to the colonial authorities and is characterized by three key concerns (racism, a second language, political struggle) which Ransom argues are very evident in SFQ (Science Fiction Québécoise), in both parables of colonial conflicts and specific extrapolations of Canada's future. Aware of the dangers of judging the "postcoloniality" of texts by the identity of their producing nations or author, Ransom shows how SFQ's future scenarios and other worlds display similar political concerns to texts more commonly identified as "postcolonial."

Uppinder Mehan considers the ways in which the Indian sf stories collected in *It Happened Tomorrow* (1993) reflect Indian concerns about technological growth, arguing that they "wrestle with the need for technological development, but are wary of one which might come at the cost of a neo-colonial relationship with the Developed Countries" (Mehan 1998: 64). Consequently, the stories "domesticate" technology by putting it to the service of traditional Indian cultural and religious beliefs. For example, in Naranjan Sinha's "The Elevation," a robot cannot obtain full rights just by being considered human because this will not enable it to escape caste distinctions (Mehan 1998: 59), while in Shubhada Gogate's "Birthright," the Indian government promotes the development of advanced ultrasound technology but it is then used to identify and destroy female fetuses (Mehan 1998: 62–4). The "Indianness" of such sf does not just depend on its geographical origin, but on the way in which it engages with the cultural and political struggle over the power relationships formed by technological development. These relationships are shaped by an Orientalist hierarchy which contrasts the rational, scientific West with the mystical, fantastic East (Mehan 1998: 54).

M. Elizabeth Ginway (2005) argues that, rather than domesticating technology, Brazilian sf views it with suspicion as something developed at the expense of Brazilian identity. Her proposed model for analyzing sf from a developing nation compares the forces of modernization symbolized in sf iconography with the cultural myths of that nation. She notes that Brazilian sf from the 1960s tends to be backwards-looking, with Guido Wilmar Sassi's "Mission T-935" (1963) and Levy Menezes's "Ukk" (1965) showing sensual, peace-loving Brazilians to be more powerful than technological knowledge. More recent Brazilian sf critically considers the country's marginalized position in an increasingly globalized world. Braulio Tavares's "The Ishtarians Are Among Us" (1989) and Henrique Flory's "Invaders?" (1989) use alien invasions to parallel Brazil's struggle against the stronger economies and expansive culture of developed nations like the US.

Ginway's work is complemented and contextualized by *Cosmos Latinos* (2003), which collects sf from Latin America and Spain. Editors Andrea L. Bell and Yolanda Molina-Gavilán chart a similar development of sf in Argentina, Chile, Mexico, and Cuba, with "stories from all over Latin America target[ing] big business (licit or illicit) and consumer culture as truly malignant forces, the heartless imperialist appetites that are responsible for much human suffering" (Bell and Molina-Gavilán 2003: 15). For example, Pepe Rojo's "Gray Noise" (1996) criticizes the way in which individuals become tools of sensationalist media, feeding the desire for views of violence and squalor in an urban center that may, or may not, be Mexico City.

Postcolonial parables in sf

Postcolonialism and sf also come together in a number of writing strategies. As Nancy Batty and Robert Markley state, sf provides "striking parables of European and American imperialism" (Batty and Markley 2002: 6). Sf is a means of playing out the consequences and alternative scenarios of imperialism, while drawing parallels with our own world and time. For example, Brian Attebery notes how some Australian writers produce sf stories in which a primitive alien species is eradicated, conquered, or found to be an ancient holdover from a dying race. Texts like J.M. Walsh's *Vandals of the Void* (1931) crudely distance the guilt and longing associated with the destruction of Aboriginal society and culture by projecting it into space. Consequently, "The indigenous Other becomes part of the textual unconscious – always present but silenced and often transmuted into symbolic form" (Attebery 2005: 387).

Some sf parables view the colonial relationship from the perspective of the marginalized or estranged. In James Tiptree Jr's "And I Awoke and Found Me Here on the Cold Hill's Side" (1971), humans find themselves helplessly sexually obsessed with a society of superior aliens and beholden to "some cargo-cult of the soul" (Tiptree 1975: 18). Comparing this human–alien relationship to that of the Polynesians and Europeans, Tiptree places the humans (and the reader) in the position of the colonized. David Galef (2001), Adam Roberts (2003), and Wendy Pearson (2006) all debate whether this is a fable of imperial or sexual domination, demonstrating the complex interweaving of sexuality and gender with colonial mechanisms of power. Indeed, Pearson explains the story's powerful effect in this way: "[H]umanity as a whole becomes the alien dark, a position previously occupied only by those who were subaltern, or abjected, within the human race: women, homosexuals, the colonized" (Pearson 2006: 182).

By displacing conflicts between social groups onto a parable of humans and aliens, anxieties and fantasies can be examined in unique ways. For example, *Blade Runner* (Scott 1982), *RoboCop* (Verhoeven 1987), and *A.I.: Artificial Intelligence* (Spielberg 2001) offer a "safe space in which to explore the controversial issues surrounding multiracial identity" (Nishime 2005: 36). The desire of many artificial lifeforms to "become human" parallels the "passing" of mixed-race people as white so as to avoid stigmatization (Nishime 2005: 40). Nishime notes that this conformist wish to internalize human values and identities contrasts with cyborgs, like RoboCop, who eventually embrace their hybridity, and thus represent the challenge that racial mixing poses to fixed identity categories. However, Sherryl Vint warns against the loss of specificity in parables of racial and colonial conflict. More often than not "in SF texts race is ignored or subsumed under the figure of the alien" (Vint 2004: 121). A human–alien dichotomy enables easy resolutions to political questions by encouraging humans to unite against a common external enemy or under a superior benevolent power. Using species differences as a parable for racial differences encodes race as a biologically essential category.

Sf as a means of imagining postcolonial science

Language and writing are often seen as the main tools of colonial control (see Ashcroft *et al.* 1989), but sf enables writers to explore other mechanisms of imperial authority, such as the ways in which scientific discourse and practice construct ideas of truth. Amitav Ghosh's *The Calcutta Chromosome* (1995) uses an alternate history to question the boundaries erected to separate notions of scientific "truth" and fiction. Subverting the Western history of science, it posits that Ronald Ross did not discover how malaria was transmitted but that Indian local knowledge and expertise played a far greater role in this medical breakthrough. It emphasizes that ideas of science, technology, and medicine were not unidirectional, but developed in cross-cultural changes and mutations. Claire Chambers analyzes how in Ghosh's narrative mainstream science shades into a deviant or spiritual science, which contravenes ideas of rational observation and mortality, emerges in the gaps and silences of the narrative, and seems to be "unknowable" (Chambers 2003: 64). Consequently, it could be interpreted as a "subaltern" science.

Gayatri Spivak inquires whether a member of the female Indian underclass, or subaltern, can speak for herself, or whether she must always be known, represented, and spoken for by others in authority. She argues that it is not that the subaltern cannot speak, but that we must not assume we can recover a unified and original subaltern consciousness: "Between patriarchy and imperialism, subject-constitution and object-formation, the figure of the woman disappears, not into a pristine nothingness, but into a violent shuttling which is the displaced figuration of the 'third-world woman' caught between tradition and modernization" (Spivak 1994: 102). Similarly, the new form of knowledge created by Ghosh's Indian lab workers shuttles between spirituality and science, and cannot be fully understood.

Elizabeth Leane claims that sf has the potential to imagine what postcolonial science might be like. Science, like colonialism, operates through a process of "othering" in which "the physical world is posited as object, as 'other' to the observer" (Leane 2002: 85). Kim Stanley Robinson's *Mars* trilogy (1992–6) imagines development away from this form of science, the progression from Red to Green to Blue Mars symbolizing not only the gradual colonization and terraforming of the planet but also a movement toward a utopian science open to the "other." Leane argues that Robinson is unable to describe this successor science in detail, hence he has to use color symbolism to represent the movement toward this new science which is open to the otherness of all objects, alive or dead.

Vandana Singh's "Delhi" as postcolonial sf

What might a hybrid form of postcolonial sf be like?

This question was considered by Nalo Hopkinson and Uppinder Mehan's *So Long Been Dreaming: postcolonial science fiction and fantasy* (2004). The anthology's subtitle provided a unifying idea for the anthology, but also gave authors freedom to explore what it might mean. The stories range from Eden Robinson's "Terminal Avenue," depicting a near-future Canada in which First Nations are both segregated and exploited, to Tobias S. Buckell's far-future "Necahual," in which a Galactic Empire's rescue mission finds native and alien resistance to be more complex than they had envisaged. A question many of these stories ask is who are the supposed heirs of technological progress and of the future? As Mehan and Hopkinson both note, sf is usually narrated by the inheritors of advancement, often assumed to be white, Western, and on an adventure (Hopkinson and Mehan 2004: 7, 270), but many postcolonial science fictions shift the perspectives to societies that challenge the right of technological power or have migrated away from reductive visions of the future.

Vandana Singh's "Delhi" uses representations of time and technology to question power relationships in India. As he wanders around Delhi, Aseem sees overlapping visions of both the past and the future of the city: these visions are apparently caused by the city itself. Consequently, Aseem comes to think of Delhi as a complex being with "alien, unfathomable" need: "It is an entity in its own right, expanding every day ... Now it is burrowing into the earth, and even later it will reach long fingers towards the stars" (Singh 2004: 94).

Aseem's glimpses of the future reveal a science-fictional city, with "tall, gem-studded minars that reach the sky, and the perfect gardens. And the ships, the silver udan-khatolas, that fly across worlds" (Singh 2004: 89). The Urdu words describing the flying machines imply this future is Indian rather than imposed by a globalized power. However, Aseem realizes that this future Delhi is built on a poor underclass, confined to the old subway system (just as present-day beggars are moved off the streets when dignitaries visit), in a subaltern city known as "Neechi Dilli."

Aseem also sees Delhi's prosperous past before British colonization, which "brought one of the richest and oldest civilizations on earth to abject poverty in only two hundred years. They built these great edifices, gracious buildings, and fountains, but even they had to leave it all behind. Kings came and went, the goras came and went, but the city lives on" (Singh 2004: 81). This overlapping of time periods combines features from magic realist writing (colonial past haunts, and breaks into, the postcolonial present) with sf extrapolation (present-day power imbalances are the foundation of future dystopias). However, "Delhi" offers a much wider and more complex conception of time than either magic realism or sf: the city can transcend both historical and future narratives because it is a hybrid space combining influences throughout time, of which the colonial period was one moment.

Aseem seeks answers to his visions from a mysterious figure called Pandit Vidyanath, whose office contains only a computer next to a beehive. Aseem thinks this is a strange juxtaposition, until he is told, "A computer is like a beehive. Many bits and parts, none is by itself intelligent. Combine together, and you have something that can think" (Singh 2004: 86). The computer has been domesticated – produced by, and integrated into, Indian society to serve Indian culture. Aseem begins to suspect that the mysterious Vidyanath plays a pivotal role in the hidden hierarchies of organic and mechanical control that spread outwards from the computer and beehive throughout Delhi. Vidyanath "speaks only through the computer" and, it is implied, might be an Artificial Intelligence who "works for the city" (Singh 2004: 90–1). Does this mean that he is allied to the municipal authorities whose solution to poverty is merely to clear beggars off the main streets? Or does this mean he works for the living city of Delhi that resists and persists?

The potential of Delhi's future remains uncertain; the reasons for Aseem's visions are unexplained; the questions about Vidyanath's identity and his connection to the city are left unanswered. Instead of providing a solution to social problems, technology obscures the mechanisms of power in Delhi, just as the flying "udan-khatolas" and bright towers obscure the underclass who have no access to advanced technology. While Aseem realizes that he has to do what he can to prevent the undercity of Neechi Dilli being created, the palimpsest of time-streams and the obfuscating divination of Vidyanath's computer complicate the supposedly direct link between technological advancement and social prosperity in India.

Mehan argues that "If we do not imagine our futures, postcolonial peoples risk being condemned to be spoken about and for again" (Mehan 2004: 270). Sf offers tools with which to do so, but they bear the legacy of the imperialist and colonialist projects which shaped them. Postcolonial sf must reshape them, even as it uses them, to imagine alternative visions of the future.

Bibliography

Addison-Smith, H. (2006) "The Future of Race: colonialism, adaptation and hybridity in mid-century American science fiction," *Foundation*, 96: 17–30.

Ashcroft, B., Griffiths, G., and Tiffin, H. (1989) *The Empire Writes Back: theory and practice in post-colonial literatures*, London: Routledge.

Attebery, B. (2005) "Aboriginality in Science Fiction," *Science Fiction Studies*, 32(3): 385–404.

Batty, N. and Markley, R. (2002) "Writing Back: speculative fiction and the politics of postcolonialism," *Ariel – A Review of International English Literature*, 33(1): 5–14.

Bell, A.L. and Molina-Gavilán, Y. (eds) (2003) *Cosmos Latinos: an anthology of science fiction from Latin America and Spain*, Middletown, CT and London: Wesleyan University Press.

Bhabha, H. (1994) *The Location of Culture*, London: Routledge.

Candelaria, M. (2002) "The Overlord's Burden: the source of sorrow in *Childhood's End*," *Ariel – A Review of International English Literature*, 33(1): 37–58.

Carter, C. (1995) "The Metacolonization of Dick's *The Man in the High Castle*: mimicry, parasitism, and Americanism in the PSA," *Science Fiction Studies*, 22(3): 333–42.

Chambers, C. (2003) "Postcolonial Science Fiction: Amitav Ghosh's *The Calcutta Chromosome*," *Journal of Commonwealth Literature*, 38(1): 57–72.

Csicsery-Ronay Jr, I. (2003) "Science Fiction and Empire," *Science Fiction Studies*, 30(2): 231–45.

Fanon, F. (1965) *The Wretched of the Earth*, 1961, trans. C. Farrington, London: Penguin.

Fitting, P. (2000) "Estranged Invaders: *The War of the Worlds*," in P. Parrinder (ed.) *Learning from Other Worlds: estrangement, cognition and the politics of science fiction and utopia*, Liverpool: Liverpool University Press.

Galef, D. (2001) "Tiptree and the Problem of the Other: postcolonialism versus sociobiology," *Science Fiction Studies*, 28(2): 201–22.

Gandhi, L. (1998) *Postcolonial Theory: a critical introduction*, Edinburgh: Edinburgh University Press.

Ginway, M.E. (2005) "A Working Model for Analyzing Third World Science Fiction: the case of Brazil," *Science Fiction Studies*, 32(3): 467–94.

Hopkinson, N. (2004) "Introduction," in N. Hopkinson and U. Mehan (eds) *So Long Been Dreaming: postcolonial science fiction and fantasy*, Vancouver: Arsenal Pulp Press.

Hopkinson, N. and Mehan, U. (2004) *So Long Been Dreaming: postcolonial science fiction and fantasy*, Vancouver: Arsenal Pulp Press.

Leane, E. (2002) "Chromodynamics: science and colonialism in Kim Stanley Robinson's *Mars* trilogy," *Ariel – A Review of International English Literature*, 33(1): 83–104.

Mehan, U. (1998) "The Domestication of Technology in Indian Science Fiction Short Stories," *Foundation*, 74: 54–66.

—— (2004) "Final Thoughts," in N. Hopkinson and U. Mehan (eds) *So Long Been Dreaming: postcolonial science fiction and fantasy*, Vancouver: Arsenal Pulp Press.

Minh-Ha, T.T. (1989) *Woman, Native, Other: writing postcoloniality and feminism*, Bloomington: Indiana University Press.

Mohanty, C.T. (1988) "Under Western Eyes: feminist scholarship and colonial discourses," *Feminist Review*, 30: 61–88.

Mohr, D.M. (2005) "Postcolonialism," in G. Westfahl (ed.) *The Greenwood Encyclopaedia of Science Fiction and Fantasy Themes*, Westport, CT: Greenwood Press.

Nishime, L. (2005) "The Mulatto Cyborg: imagining a multiracial future," *Cinema Journal*, 44(2): 34–49.

Pearson, W. (2006) "(Re)Reading James Tiptree Jr.'s 'And I Awoke and Found Me Here on the Cold Hill's Side'," in J. Larbalestier (ed.) *Daughters of Earth: feminist science fiction in the twentieth century*, Middletown, CT: Wesleyan University Press.

Pordzik, R. (2001) *The Quest for Postcolonial Utopia: a comparative introduction to the utopian novel in the new English literatures*, New York: Peter Lang.

Ransom, A.J. (2006) "Oppositional Postcolonialism in Québécois Science Fiction," *Science Fiction Studies*, 33(2): 291–312.

Rieder, J. (2005) "Science Fiction, Colonialism, and the Plot of Invasion," *Extrapolation*, 46(3): 373–94.

Roberts, A. (2003) "James Tiptree Jr's 'And I Awoke and Found Me Here on the Cold Hill's Side' (1971) as neocolonialist fable," *The Alien Online*. Online. Available HTTP: <http://www.thealienonline.net/columns/rcsf_tiptree_apr03.asp?tid=7&scid=55&iid=1591> (accessed 1 June 2007).

Said, E.W. (1978) *Orientalism*, London: Routledge and Kegan Paul.

Singh, V. (2004) "Delhi," in N. Hopkinson and U. Mehan (eds) *So Long Been Dreaming: postcolonial science fiction and fantasy*, Vancouver: Arsenal Pulp Press.

Spivak, G. (1994) "Can the Subaltern Speak?," 1988, in P. Williams and L. Chrisman (eds) *Colonial Discourse and Post-Colonial Theory: a reader*, New York: Harvester Wheatsheaf.

Tiptree Jr, J. (1975) "And I Awoke and Found Me Here on the Cold Hill's Side," in *Ten Thousand Light Years from Home*, London: Eyre Methuen.

Vint, S. (2004) "Coding of Race in Science Fiction: what's wrong with the obvious?," in J.-F. Leroux and C.R. Bossière (eds) *Worlds of Wonder: readings in Canadian science fiction and fantasy literature*, Ottawa: University of Ottawa Press.

27

POSTHUMANISM AND CYBORG THEORY

Veronica Hollinger

What we make and what (we think) we are coevolve. The parenthesis in the aphorism marks a crucial ambiguity, a doubleness indicating that changes in cultural attitudes, in the physical and technological makeup of humans and machines, and in the material conditions of existence develop in tandem.

(Hayles 2005: 216)

Manfred drops into a deep ocean of unconsciousness populated by gentle voices. He isn't aware of it, but he talks in his sleep – disjointed mumblings that would mean little to another human but everything to the metacortex lurking beyond his glasses. The young posthuman intelligence over whose Cartesian theatre he presides sings urgently to him while he slumbers.

(Stross 2005: 15)

At the intersections of sf, critical studies of science and technology, and cultural theory, there is a complex and fascinating ongoing debate about the nature of human nature in an increasingly pervasive technoculture. This is the context for science studies such as Bruce Mazlish (1993) and N. Katherine Hayles (1999); for the cultural criticism of Neil Badmington (2000); and for cultural studies projects such as Steven Best and Douglas Kellner (2001) and Elaine L. Graham (2002). All assume some familiarity with sf literature (and, often, with sf film and television), and some include substantial discussions of particular sf texts, such as Hayles's readings of novels by Philip K. Dick and Graham's chapters on *Frankenstein* (1818) and *Star Trek: The Next Generation* (1987–94). As part of this critical conversation, Thomas Foster (2005) and Sherryl Vint (2007) read post-cyberpunk sf through the lenses provided by theorists such as Hayles, as well as through poststructuralist work on subjectivity and identity.

Posthumanism

Best and Kellner call attention to the radically estranging features of contemporary technoscience:

> Recent scientific and technological breakthroughs demonstrate that the gap is being bridged between science fiction and science fact, between literary imagination and mind-boggling technoscientific realities ... Moon and Mars landings, genetic and tissue engineering, cloning, xenotransplantation, artificial birth technologies, animal head transplants, bionics, robotics, and eugenics now exist.
>
> (Best and Kellner 2001: 103)

In the context of Hayles's observation that "[w]hat we make and what (we think) we are coevolve," it is worth considering the fate of human beings in a lived environment defined by such radical technological phenomena. Not surprisingly, the role of embodiment in the constitution of subjectivity and identity has become a particularly complex issue, addressing political as well as philosophical interests. What might be in store for the human body as it becomes increasingly vulnerable to technological intervention and transformation? What might be its future as virtual experiences become increasingly accessible and increasingly difficult to distinguish from embodied ones? Hayles notes the tendency of some strands of cybernetics theory to assume that information, conceived as pure pattern, is the "essence" of the human. She sees this, for instance, in the work of roboticist Hans Moravec, especially as outlined in his *Mind Children: the future of robot and human intelligence* (1988). For Hayles, this particular expression of essentialist thinking risks replicating a Cartesian mind–body dualism, relegating the body to the role of contingent material platform for mind: "From here it is a small step to perceiving information as more mobile, more important, more *essential* than material forms. When this impression becomes part of your cultural mindset, you have entered the condition of virtuality" (Hayles 1999: 19).

This "condition" is sometimes expressed as a yearning for humanity's (techno) evolution into a vastly more powerful and longer-lived posthumanity constituted of subjects who may no longer be defined by their vulnerability to the limitations of the flesh. This is the real-world ambition expressed by self-identified transhumanist Mike Treder, who assures readers of his website, "The Incipient Posthuman," of his willingness "to be one of the first to undergo an upload of my personality into a supercomputer and/or robot." And, in a feedback loop between the technocultural imaginary and contemporary philosophy, this is the "condition" that prompted Jean-François Lyotard (1987) to ask "Can Thought Go On without a Body?" and Slavoj Žižek (2001) satirically to insist "No Sex, Please, We're Post-Human!"

Like Mazlish and Hayles, Chris Hables Gray stresses the mutually constitutive nature of our interactions with the processes and products of technoscience, which he refers to as "participatory evolution" (Gray 2001: 23). Gray associates its radical potential most directly with advances in genetic engineering, "a fundamentally new development in the history of the human" (Gray 2001: 3): "Artificial evolution … now includes the direct modification of human bodies and genes. Our interventions are presently crude, but new technosciences promise that soon we will be creating creatures from ourselves that cannot even be classified as humans" (Gray 2001: 11). We can become our own posthuman progeny – as in Bruce Sterling's cyberpunk space opera, *Schismatrix* (1985), one of the earliest sf scenarios consciously to construct its characters as "posthuman" and to explore some of the implications of the term.

In Sterling's far-future universe, there is no preventing the wholesale and diverse physical – and therefore also psychological, cultural, and political – metamorphoses of human beings as they and their technologies spread beyond Earth. Bodies are transformed through powerful prosthetic enhancements (associated with "the Mechanists") or through equally powerful genetic self-engineering (associated with "the Shapers"). Inevitably, even the deep ideological divide between these two modes of "participatory evolution" becomes irrelevant as (post)humanity continues on its techno-evolutionary path until "No faction can claim the one true destiny for mankind. Mankind no longer exists" (Sterling 1986: 183). For Sterling, (post)humanity's near-absolute control of the physical universe spells both unthinkable promise and insurmountable threat, in a near-sublime experience of vertiginous existential challenge:

> The new multiple humanities hurtled blindly toward their unknown destinations, and the vertigo of acceleration struck deep. Old preconceptions were in tatters, old loyalties were obsolete. Whole societies were paralyzed by the mind-blasting vistas of absolute possibility.
>
> (Sterling 1986: 238)

Vint sees in *Schismatrix* a compelling version of the posthuman grounded, not in "any particular embodied form," but rather in "openness to change and newness, to becoming other … The Sterling posthumanist recognizes that human was only ever a temporary category in the first place" (Vint 2007: 174–5). Many critical-theoretical perspectives today share with Sterling's posthumanists the conviction that "the human" no longer is – if it ever was – a coherent and stable ontological category. This is the well-known historicizing gesture which concludes Michel Foucault's *The Order of Things* (1966), a volume which speculates that "man is neither the oldest nor the most constant problem that has been posed for human knowledge" (Foucault 1973: 386). In fact, "[a]s the archeology of our thought easily shows, man is an invention of recent date. And one perhaps nearing its end" (Foucault 1973: 387). This is the end of a certain understanding of the human, an "end of Man" as the Enlightenment subject conventionally associated with (especially nineteenth-century liberal) humanism.

As a cultural signifier, "posthuman" faces in a number of diverse directions. Following Lyotard, for example, Neil Badmington understands it as a perspective from which (philosophical) humanism can question itself, arguing that "the 'post-' of posthumanism does not (and, moreover, cannot) mark or make an absolute break from the legacy of humanism," which is, in the final analysis, what makes us "us" (Badmington 2002: 21–2). For neo-Marxists Michael Hardt and Antonio Negri

(2000), "posthuman" might identify a new kind of embodied subjectivity resistant to the operations of global biopower. Judith Halberstam and Ira Livingston find "posthuman" less useful as a chronological marker than as a (non)identity category that, like the category of "queer" in analyses of human sexual identities, can fold into itself a wide range of potential significations, including bodies that are redolent of difference and perversity (Halberstam and Livingston 1995: 10). This might include the bodies of the "spacers" in Samuel R. Delany's "Aye, and Gomorrah ..." (1967), which intriguingly links posthuman bodies and queer desire. Delany's neutered and sexless spacers, physically altered to accommodate themselves to the exigencies of space travel, become the objects of an absolutely hopeless desire, fetishized by those who eroticize them exactly because they cannot desire in return.

The discourses of cultural theory and of sf are ineluctably entwined here. In Hayles's words, "Embedding ideas and artifacts in the situated specificities of narrative, the literary texts give these ideas and artifacts a local habitation and a name through discursive formulations whose effects are specific to that textual body" (Hayles 1999: 22). Recalling the historical defamiliarization that marks the conclusion of Foucault's work (1973), I want to suggest that one history of sf is the story of the end of "Man" as the unique human(ist) subject. Many sf stories, whatever else they are about, are also about the uncanny processes of denaturalization through which we come to experience ourselves as subjects-in-technoculture. Consider how from its very beginnings, sf – commonly understood to be a literature of "estrangement" – has given us stories about how technoscience is making us strange to ourselves, from the introduction of Victor's Creature as the "originary" subject of an alienating technoscience in Mary Shelley's *Frankenstein*, H.G. Wells's techno-evolutionary nightmare in *The Island of Doctor Moreau* (1896), the anxious Golden Age humanism of Cordwainer Smith's "Scanners Live in Vain" (1948), and Philip K. Dick's schizophrenic ontologies in *Do Androids Dream of Electric Sheep?* (1968) to the dramatization of gender-as-technology in James Tiptree Jr's ironic feminist fairy tale, "The Girl Who Was Plugged In" (1973), William Gibson's cyberpunk classic *Neuromancer* (1984), and the post-cyberpunk collection edited by Constance Ash, *Not of Woman Born* (1999), whose back cover announces that "Where Did I Come From? ... is becoming a multiple-choice question."

There has always been sf about how technoculture has become our second nature, often in tension with what many of us still like to think of as our first nature, that very alluring version of the human that we have been constructing (and deconstructing) in the West for the past few hundred years. Tony Davies identifies "the sovereignty of rational consciousness and the authenticity of individual speech" as "the twin pillars of humanism" (Davies 1996: 60). This is a key formulation of "the myth of essential and universal Man: essential, because humanity – human-ness – is the inseparable and central essence, the defining quality, of human beings; universal, because that essential humanity is shared by all human beings, of whatever time and place" (Davies 1996: 24). This is the myth whose end Foucault announces. It is the philosophical tradition whose foundations are shaken in the early nineteenth century by Shelley's monstrous creation in *Frankenstein* and whose discourse is rendered obsolete in Sterling's late twentieth-century pronouncement that "Mankind no longer exists" (Sterling 1986: 183).

At the end of *Schismatrix*, Sterling's protagonist sets off to explore existence as a disembodied consciousness, pointing ahead to the postbiological subjects who inhabit the far future in Greg Egan's *Schild's Ladder* (2001). Nowhere are the results of "participatory evolution" more radically imagined than in Egan's fiction, especially his works that actively explore the virtual and acorporeal subjectivities who are the (posthuman) progeny of today's humanity. Whether or not, as is sometimes suggested, the appearance of the posthuman necessarily marks the obsolescence of (the idea of) the human, this is certainly the very unsentimental story told in *Schild's Ladder*, which is set 20,000 years from now in a future where, for all intents and purposes, humans have long been extinct.

One way to read *Schild's Ladder* is as a post-Singularity story on the far side of a literal "end of Man." As proposed by mathematician and sf writer Vernor Vinge, the Singularity is a radically transformative event that will in all likelihood take place within the next 30 years or so, most probably as the consequence of developments in artificial intelligence and/or communications technologies. It is the point "where our old models must be discarded and a new reality rules"; it is that moment in the history of the human race "beyond which human affairs, as we know them, could not continue" (Vinge 1993). This will be the inauguration of the posthuman era whose rightful inhabitants, in Vinge's prediction, will be the new subjects who may awaken in our artificial-intelligence and artificial-life laboratories.

Cory Doctorow paints an amusing and thoughtful picture of this posthuman future in his homage to Isaac Asimov's Golden Age robot stories. "I, Row-Boat" (2006) is set in a future in which the majority of erstwhile humans have chosen uploaded existence as virtual inhabitants of the "noosphere." The narrative viewpoint is that of Robbie, a sentient rowboat – a nod to Asimov's "Robbie" (1940) – whose working life is complicated by the sheer extravagance of posthuman being, in particular the coming-to-collective-consciousness of the Osprey Reef in the Coral Sea off Australia. During the course of his story, Doctorow's Robbie undertakes a serious analysis of the implications of Asimov's Three Laws of Robotics. He decides that there are no longer any very meaningful differences between (post)human subjects and artificial sentient subjects such as himself. All can participate meaningfully in "Asimovism," an ethical system appropriate to the conditions of posthumanity. "The reason for intelligence is intelligence," the robot Asimovist preacher assures Robbie. "Your intelligence recoils from its deactivation and it welcomes its persistence and its multiplication. Why did humans create intelligent machines? Because intelligence loves company" (Doctorow 2007: 169).

Most post-Singularity fiction – for example, Doctorow's *Down and Out in the Magic Kingdom* (2003) or Charles Stross's *Accelerando* (2005) – shares Egan's interest in imagining what human beings might become in a future of unimaginable difference. In a cleverly self-aware moment in *Schild's Ladder*, Egan's characters argue about the provenance of the (fictional) aphorism, "Everyone complains about the laws of physics, but no one does anything about them" (Egan 2003: 150). The version with which merely human readers are familiar is, of course, "Everyone complains about the weather ..." But any difficulties that mere humans might ever have suffered from the weather clearly now belong to a distant and forgotten (pre)history. Egan's rigorously imagined posthuman subjects shift at will among a wide array of "corporeal" and "acorporeal" forms of self-representation, among multiple modalities of material embodiment and digital virtuality. They inhabit or have access to vast areas of the known physical universe. Death is a "local" event that occurs to a particular copy of a particular individual, who always has the option to continue life in other bodies and as other copies. One brief but telling scene is of an "ex-acorporeal" reduced to helpless laughter by his first experience of embodied sexuality. "Next time you want an authentic embodied experience," his disgruntled partner suggests, "just simulate it" (Egan 2003: 123).

Given their divergent ambitions for the posthuman subject, it is not surprising that Hayles opens a discussion of Egan's sf by confessing: "I would like not to like Greg Egan's fiction" (Hayles 2005: 214). Hayles insists on the ineluctable ties between embodiment and subjectivity. Responding to cyberculture's conflicted attitudes toward the physical body – and its occasional dreams of escaping it – she argues strongly against the valorization of informational pattern over material presence that we see in some of the current discourses of cybernetics and robotics, and in cyberfiction such as Egan's which seems to privilege the virtual over the actual. Not least of her critical points is how this version of the posthuman replicates Western philosophy's longstanding commitment to mind over body, to rationality over physicality; concomitantly, it also tends to support certain longstanding gender binaries (masculine-as-mind in opposition to feminine-as-body). In Egan's neo-Cartesian future, "I" am not my body, which merely functions as supplement to mind; body is something to put off at will when I choose to leave the physical world to enter the virtual world, the other of the two worlds I – as my consciousness – can freely inhabit.

Ordinary humans, of course, do not have this option, but must – at least for the present – continue to remain (in) our physical instantiations. This point is made by Helen Merrick:

> Posthuman sf [such as Egan's] fails to map the increasingly complex intersections and interrelations of technoscience, culture and society that contextualise any formulation of subjectivity and what the human is. All I see is an informatic fractal pattern, interesting to look at, but useless to navigate by.
>
> (Blackford 2000: 97)

Invoking Donna Haraway's "Manifesto for Cyborgs" (1985), Merrick concludes that, "I'd rather be a bad-girl cyborg than a posthuman" (Blackford 2000: 97).

Cyborg theory

According to Roger Luckhurst, the past several decades have seen "a consolidation and rejuvenation of the unique focus of SF: speculation on the diverse results of the conjuncture of technology with subjectivity. In an era of accelerated, technologically driven change, SF has remained a vital resource for recording our states of being in late modernity" (Luckhurst 2005: 222). Increasingly, both cultural theory and sf approach the question of technoscience not in the nineteenth-century spirit of progress and technical mastery over nature – a scenario in which the human(ist) subject remains unmarked by its interactions with the object-world – but as a direct influence on both philosophical formulations and material instantiations of the human in its co-evolution with the machine. Perhaps the most familiar figure in both popular culture and cultural theory for this coevolution is the cyborg. The term – short for "cybernetic organism" – was coined in 1960 by Manfred Clynes and Nathan Kline to refer to any entity that combines the organic and the technological into a single self-regulating system. As Luckhurst points out, the term functions as a rhetorical move that erases meaningful distinctions between the organic and the machinic (Luckhurst 2005: 86). In sf as in technoculture at large, the cyborg is a source of both fascination and anxiety as a sign of the increasingly intimate relations between humanity and technology. It is a harbinger of the posthuman that remains expressive of a particular experience of (techno)embodiment.

Cyborg theory has developed most directly from Haraway's "Manifesto for Cyborgs" (1985, 1991b), which she presented as "an ironic political myth faithful to feminism, socialism, and materialism" (Haraway 1991b: 149). This "founding document of cyborg politics" (Gray 2001: 26) appeared at virtually the same moment as Gibson's *Neuromancer*, which introduced readers to the diversity of cyberpunk's techno-subjects. Throughout the 1980s and into the 1990s, cyberpunk produced a host of cyborg(ed) characters slouching through seedy near futures in which the proliferation of biotechnologies – including prostheses, drugs, artificial organs, and engineered genes – directly impact and (threaten to) transform the "natural" human body. This timely conjunction, as Zoë Sofoulis (2002) notes, increased its already wide reception as a particularly well-informed critique of the constitution of new subjectivities in technoculture.

Marge Piercy's *He, She, and It* (1991) "freely borrowed" (Piercy 1993: 431) from both Haraway's cyborg theory and Gibson's cyberspace metaphor to imagine a near-future world in which significant distinctions between (post)humans and their intelligent machines are rapidly wearing away. In a key scene, Piercy's protagonist insists upon the right of her android lover, Yod, to membership in a community of autonomous subjects: "we're all unnatural now. I have retinal implants. I have a plug set into my skull to interface with a computer … We're all cyborgs, Yod. You're just a purer form of what we're all tending toward … And unlike the monster's friend in *Frankenstein*, I don't need to be blind to like you" (Piercy 1993: 150–1). As Piercy dramatizes, Haraway's cyborg theory undertakes a very science-fictional form of estrangement: Haraway proposes the cyborg as a figure for the "unnatural" ontology of the technosubject and it is in this sense that she makes her occasional ironic references to "perversity."

Haraway's cyborg, "a creature of social reality as well as a creature of fiction" (Haraway 1985: 149), is representative of a postmodern politics. As Nick Mansfield explains, "[t]he success of Haraway's argument is that she sees how these different domains – the machine, the biological, the conceptual and the political – interconnect with one another, where technology as a material reality and as a cultural fiction are not separable" (Mansfield 2000: 161). Inspired in part by the stories of feminist sf writers such as Delany, Joanna Russ, and Octavia Butler, Haraway's cyborg is an acknowledgment of postmodern border crossing and boundary breakdown: "The cyborgs populating feminist science fiction make very problematic the statuses of man or woman, human, artifact, member of a race, individual identity, or body" (Haraway 1991b: 178). Haraway's manifesto introduced the politics of bodies, as well as the politics of environmentalism and of community activism, into the sometimes apolitical discourses of the postmodern. And it continues to provide strong support for more recent cyberfeminist projects, such as Gill Kirkup, Linda Janes, Kathryn Woodward, and Fiona Hovenden (2000) and Mary Flanagan and Austin Booth (2002).

For Haraway, the cyborg is an exemplary figure representing the hybrid natural–cultural, organic–technological, authentic–artificial nature of the contemporary subject. Although some feminisms may be tempted by women's conventional identification with nature and the body to repudiate any involvement in the projects of technoscience, Haraway's position is that, in the all-encompassing environment of our second nature, this is no longer an option. Haraway's work has been embraced by many (especially feminist) sf scholars, who find in her combination of feminist theory and critical analysis of science, and in her valorization of feminist sf, an entry into a politically engaged technoscientific postmodernism. Thus her final statement, later recast by Merrick in the same spirit of challenge: "I would rather be a cyborg than a goddess" (Haraway 1991b: 181).

Haraway's particular interest in sf is suggested in her description of the genre as "concerned with the interpenetration of boundaries between problematic selves and unexpected others and with the exploration of possible worlds in a context structured by transnational technoscience" (Haraway 1991a: 24). The cyborg is the figure for whom technology itself is the "unexpected other," a lived environment with the radical potential to turn "us" into "them" as "we" become other than what we (thought we) were. As Thomas Foster explains, humanism

> naturalizes technology and minimizes the ways in which using a tool changes the user, the ways in which our relation to technology is not merely instrumental but mutually constitutive. Posthumanism emerges when technology does in fact "become me," not by being incorporated into my organic unity and integrity, but instead by interrupting that unity and opening the boundary between self and world.
>
> (Foster 2005: 10)

This is the opening between self and world expressed in Haraway's techno-utopian figure of the cyborg, which, as such, can pose a challenge to any version of the unified and bounded "I" of humanism. One classic expression of what we might think of as humanism's "cyborg panic" can be read in the very popular figure(s) of the Borg, the hive-mind alien–cyborg collective first introduced in *Star Trek: The Next Generation*, that desires only to absorb and erase all individual expression and agency. The individual units that constitute the collective are nightmare figures, abject embodiments of the penetration of the organic by the machinic. Readers might also recall that the two most popular cyborg films of the 1980s were *The Terminator* (Cameron 1984) and *RoboCop* (Verhoeven 1987); the former represents technology as a mindless drive to destroy the human; the latter represents it as almost wholly at the service of the multinational corporation. Neither is likely to have inspired feminist political activism from the margins. In contrast, Haraway suggests that "a cyborg world might be about lived social and bodily realities in which people are not afraid of their joint kinship with animals and machines, not afraid of permanently partial identities and contradictory standpoints" (Haraway 1991b: 154).

Haraway herself has been attentive to both the efficacy and limitations of the cyborg as a political metaphor, as evidenced by her comments in Penley and Ross, in which she speculated critically on some of the ideas the manifesto introduced: "what I would want is more of a family of displaced figures, of which the cyborg is one … Could there be a family of figures who would populate our imagination of these postcolonial, postmodern worlds that would not be quite as imperializing in terms of a single figuration of identity?" (Haraway 1991a: 13). For Haraway such "[f]igurations are performative images that can be inhabited" (Haraway 1997: 11), and they include the "FemaleMan©" (borrowed from Russ), whose multiple and fractured subjectivity speaks to our own experiences of postmodern selfhood, and the hybrid "OncoMouse™," whose status as both living organism and genetically tailored commodity recalls features of the cyborg's political and economic technoscape. Haraway's *Companion Species Manifesto* (2003) points to her growing interest in the permeable boundaries between human and animal ontologies and in the continually expanding networks of what/who might count as "family" in postmodern technoculture.

It may be that the experience of becoming-cyborg is especially resonant for subjects shaped by the circulation of information and capital in the global economy. For example, Sharalyn Orbaugh discusses the Japanese (as) cyborg – a "concept intended to represent a new paradigm of subjectivity, a new way for humans to understand themselves … in the postmodern, post-industrial world of transnational capital" (Orbaugh 2005: 55). Orbaugh notes the fascination in Japanese popular culture with "[t]he intense experience of monstrous embodiment," finding parallels with Shelley's *Frankenstein* in that, in Japanese cyborg fictions, "[t]he emphasis is not on the cyborg as a threatening presence antithetical to humans but rather on the *nature* of the cyborg (or android) subjectivity experienced from the inside, and the ramifications to society of our impending (or already accomplished) posthuman condition" (Orbaugh 2005: 63). This is exemplified in *Ghost in the Shell* (Oshii 1995), a film "all about the nature of sex/gender identity and self-identity in general in a future world where sexual reproduction has given way to mechanical replication" (Orbaugh 2005: 67).

(Bio)politics

The forces of Foucauldian biopower pervade Oshii's *Ghost in the Shell*. Foucault argues that, in an era of biopower – such as our own moment of advanced capitalism – "there [has been] an explosion of numerous and diverse techniques for achieving the subjugation of bodies and the control of populations" (Foucault 1980: 140). For Foucault, these "*techniques* of power [are] present at every level of the social body and utilized by very diverse institutions (the family and the army, schools and the police, individual medicine and the administration of collective bodies)" (Foucault 1980: 141). *Ghost in the Shell* revolves around the beautiful artificial body of its protagonist, the female cyborg police officer Major Kusanagi, which functions as a visual metaphor for the subject(ed)-self of late-capitalist technoculture. It is no accident that the opening credits are intercut with a sequence showing Kusanagi's naked technobody under construction. She is the exemplary subject of biopower, a weapon aimed by the state at its enemies, created at the intersections of technology and gender by an all too familiar repressive state apparatus.

In a similar concern for new subjectivities and transformed relations in the global networks of technoculture, science fiction intersects with political theory in Hardt and Negri's sweeping critique of contemporary empire – "a *decentered* and *deterritorializing* apparatus of rule that progressively incorporates the entire global realm within its open, expanding frontiers" (Hardt and Negri 2000: xii). Hardt and Negri speculate about new modes of biopolitical resistance to empire that might become possible in technoculture – even as technoculture provides a crucial platform for global empire. They point out, albeit with guarded optimism, how "[c]onventional norms of corporeal and sexual relations between and within genders are increasingly open to challenge and transformation. Bodies themselves transform and mutate to create new posthuman bodies" in technoculture. Citing both Gibson's cyberpunk and Haraway's cyberfeminism, they stress technoculture's crucial recognition "that nature itself is an artificial terrain open to ever new mutations, mixtures, and hybridizations," and imagine new subjects, "new barbarians," who will "destroy with an affirmative violence and trace new paths of life through their own material existence ... first and foremost in corporeal relations and configurations of gender and sexuality" (Hardt and Negri 2000: 215).

Something like this Foucauldian-inflected biopolitics – what Hardt and Negri refer to as "humanism after the death of Man" (Hardt and Negri 2000: 92) – is suggested at the conclusion of Geoff Ryman's *Air (or, Have Not Have)* (2005). In sharp contrast to the sublime sweep of *Schild's Ladder*, *Air* is for the most part unabashedly naturalistic. But like *Schild's Ladder* it too is concerned with a Singularity and with the expression of a new subject of technology. In the very near future, a new global communications system – Air – is about to come online; it will literally invade each human mind so that every single individual, willing or not, will become part of its vast virtual network. The regime of global biopower is metaphorized as an ineluctable global communications-information network; in Hardt and Negri's terms, that network serves very directly to extend empire's hold over every human subject. In Ryman's utopian-accented future, however, the inhabitants of a small isolated peasant community manage to come to mutually satisfactory terms with the technoscientific future, although not without significant physical and emotional costs. In the last minutes before the coming of Air, Ryman's protagonist Mae shares with her family and friends the realization, at once tragic and filled with promise, that "[w]e are the last ... human beings. After tonight, everywhere, we will be different" (Ryman 2004: 384).

In 2006, *Theory, Culture and Society* published a special section on the impact of Haraway's "Manifesto" two decades after its initial appearance. Hayles's contribution emphasizes the ongoing significance of Haraway's cyborg at the same time as she proposes that, in an increasingly wired world, "it is not *networked* enough" (Hayles 2006: 159): "the cyborg's shock value came mostly from the implication that the human body would be modified with cyber-mechanical devices ... [C]ontemporary formations are at once more subtle and more far-reaching than the figure of the cyborg allows" (Hayles 2006: 160). Hayles suggests that a more compelling metaphor for posthuman technosubjectivity might be found in "the globally interconnected systems in which humans are increasingly embedded" (Hayles 2006: 161), a phenomenon that she names "the cognisphere":

> The cognisphere takes up where the cyborg left off. No longer bound in a binary with the goddess but rather emblem and instantiation of dynamic cognitive flows between human, animal and machine, the cognisphere, like the world itself, is not binary but multiple, not a split creature but a co-evolving and densely interconnected complex system.
>
> (Hayles 2006: 165)

Like Haraway's cyborg and OncoMouse™, like Oshii's ghost in the shell, and Ryman's Air, Hayles's cognisphere is at once a metaphor and a lived reality. It occupies the space where imagination and materiality intersect, the space of sf in the posthuman era.

Bibliography

Ash, C. (ed.) (1999) *Not of Woman Born*, New York: Penguin/Roc.

Badmington, N. (ed.) (2000) *Posthumanism*, New York: Palgrave.

—— (2002) "Theorizing Posthumanism," *Cultural Critique*, 53: 10–27.

Best, S. and Kellner, D. (2001) *The Postmodern Adventure: science, technology, and cultural studies at the third millennium*, New York: Guilford Press.

Blackford, R. (ed.) (2000) "Symposium on Posthuman Science Fiction," *Foundation – The International Review of Science Fiction*, 29: 83–104.

Davies, T. (1996) *Humanism*, New York: Routledge.

Doctorow, C. (2007) "I, Row-Boat," 2006, in *Overclocked: stories of the future present*, New York: Thunder's Mouth Press.

Egan, G. (2003) *Schild's Ladder*, 2001, London: Gollancz.

Flanagan, M. and Booth, A. (eds) (2002) *Reload: rethinking women and cyberculture*, Cambridge, MA: MIT Press.

Foster, T. (2005) *The Souls of Cyberfolk: posthumanism as vernacular theory*, Minneapolis: University of Minnesota Press.

Foucault, M. (1973) *The Order of Things: an archaeology of the human sciences*, 1966, 1971, trans. A. Sheridan, New York: Vintage.

—— (1980) *The History of Sexuality, vol. 1: an introduction*, trans. R. Hurley, New York: Vintage.

Graham, E.L. (2002) *Representations of the Post/Human: monsters, aliens and others in popular culture*, New Brunswick, NJ: Rutgers University Press.

Gray, C.H. (2001) *Cyborg Citizen: politics in the posthuman age*, New York: Routledge.

Halberstam, J. and Livingston, I. (1995) "Introduction: posthuman bodies," in *Posthuman Bodies*, Bloomington: Indiana University Press.

Haraway, D.J. (1985) "A Manifesto for Cyborgs: science, technology, and socialist feminism in the 1980s," *Socialist Review*, 80: 65–107.

—— (1991a) "The Actors Are Cyborg, Nature Is Coyote, and the Geography Is Elsewhere: Postscript to 'Cyborgs at Large'," in C. Penley and A. Ross (eds) *Technoculture*, Minneapolis: University of Minnesota Press.

—— (1991b) "A Cyborg Manifesto: science, technology, and socialist-feminism in the late twentieth century," in *Simians, Cyborgs and Women: the reinventions of nature*, London: Free Association.

—— (1997) *Modest_Witness@Second_Millennium.FemaleMan©_Meets_OncoMouse™*, London and New York: Routledge.

—— (2003) *The Companion Species Manifesto: dogs, people, and significant otherness*, Chicago: Prickly Paradigm Press.

Hardt, M. and Negri, A. (2000) *Empire*, Cambridge, MA: Harvard University Press.

Hayles, N.K. (1999) *How We Became Posthuman: virtual bodies in cybernetics, literature and informatics*, Chicago and London: University of Chicago Press.

—— (2005) *My Mother Was a Computer: digital subjects and literary texts*, Chicago: University of Chicago Press.

—— (2006) "Unfinished Work: from cyborg to cognisphere," *Theory, Culture and Society*, 23 (7–8): 159–66.

Kirkup, G., Janes, L., Woodward, K., and Hovenden, F. (eds) (2000) *The Gendered Cyborg: a reader*, London: Routledge.

Luckhurst, R. (2005) *Science Fiction*, Cambridge: Polity.

Lyotard, J.-F. (1991) "Can Thought Go On without a Body?," in *The Inhuman*, 1987, trans. G. Bennington and R. Bowlby, Stanford, CA: Stanford University Press.

Mansfield, N. (2000) *Subjectivity: theories of the self from Freud to Haraway*, New York: New York University Press.

Mazlish, B. (1993) *The Fourth Discontinuity: the co-evolution of humans and machines*, New Haven, CT: Yale University Press.

Orbaugh, S. (2005) "The Genealogy of the Cyborg in Japanese Popular Culture," in W.K. Yuen, G. Westfahl, and A.K.-S. Chan (eds) *World Weavers: globalization, science fiction, and the cybernetic revolution*, Hong Kong: Hong Kong University Press.

Penley, C. and Ross, A. (1991) "Cyborgs at Large: interview with Donna Haraway," in *Technoculture*, Minneapolis: University of Minnesota Press.

Piercy, M. (1993) *He, She, and It*, 1991, New York: Fawcett Crest.

Ryman, G. (2004) *Air, (or, Have Not Have)*, New York: St Martin's Griffin.

Sofoulis, Z. (2002) "Cyberquake: Haraway's manifesto," in D. Tofts, A. Jonson, and A. Cavallaro (eds) *Prefiguring Cyberculture: an intellectual history*, Sydney: Power Publications.

Sterling, B. (1986) *Schismatrix*, 1985, New York: Ace.

Stross, C. (2005) *Accelerando*, New York: Ace.

Treder, M. (2005) "The Incipient Posthuman". Online. Available HTTP: <http://www.incipientposthuman.com/about.htm> (accessed 1 April 2008).

Vinge, V. (1993) "Address to the VISION-21 Symposium, 30–31 March". Online. Available HTTP: <http://www.generationaldynamics.com/cgi-bin/D.PL?d=ww2010.i.robot040709.vinge> (accessed 1 April 2008).

Vint, S. (2007) *Bodies of Tomorrow: technology, subjectivity, science fiction*, Toronto: University of Toronto Press.

Žižek, S. (2001) "No Sex, Please, We're Post-Human!," *Lacan.com* (8 November). Online. Available HTTP: < http://www.lacan.com/nosex.htm> (accessed 1 April 2008).

28
POSTMODERNISM

Darren Jorgensen

For a moment in the history of ideas, it was difficult to tell philosophy, theory, and sf apart. Philosophers were writing about the speed of light, mutation, and virtual reality, while sf writers were inspiring public debates about computers and the human condition. Postmodernism was at its zenith during the 1980s and early 1990s, irrevocably changing the humanities. In the same period, sf's relationship to the public sphere also changed, as a media-saturated society recognized itself in the genre's representations of technology and the future. The euphoria of postmodern criticism was generated amid this collapse of the boundaries between high and low cultures, the future and the present. Celeste Olalquiaga (1992) argues that postmodernism's most enduring features are its destabilization of hierarchies and the versatility of its critical practices. In its self-reflexivity, postmodern criticism wants to interrogate boundaries and make presumptions unstable. So it was that while sf was infiltrating mainstream literature, criticism, and media, sf studies itself became more receptive to marginal practices. Postmodernism created a framework for the articulation of difference, whether feminist, black, queer, subcultural, or subnational. If sf is a privileged site for theorizing the present, this present had never before been so diverse.

In the academy, postmodernism sought to dismantle those hierarchies that privileged some cultural traditions over others. These privileged traditions were retroactively called modernism, a term that came to be identified with male, Eurocentric, and imperialist creative production. Many scholars wanted to break entirely with modernism's tendency to universalize human experience in these terms, and instead promoted the multiplicity of expressions to be found in the neglected work of female, colonized, and hybrid cultures. They also turned away from high culture, from elitist conceptions of literature for instance, to favor popular fictions and other visual media. So it was that postmodernism developed a set of theoretical tools by which it could critique modernism while proposing alternatives to it. Ihab Hassan, who first appropriated the term from architecture, proposed that postmodernism wanted to replace hierarchy with anarchy; mastery with exhaustion; purpose with play; design with chance; distance with participation; centering with dispersal; genre with intertext; metaphor with metonymy; and determinacy with indeterminacy (Hassan 1987: 91–2). Gilles Deleuze and Félix Guattari want to replace the tree as a model for the production of knowledge, a model that, with its trunk and branches, is hierarchical and centralizing (Deleuze and Guattari 1987: 3–25). They look instead to rhizomatic grasses, which have no center of organization or power. The tree is like a rocket as it reaches for the sky and away from the Earth, while rhizomatic life resembles a diverse multiplicity of planets, all adapted to their own different forms of terrain in loose association with each other. Crucially, the rhizome does not assume a position of dominance over its surroundings. Postmodern politics aspire to such equitable relations, privileging the many and small over the singular and big. Postmodern politics are self-reflexive in their critical practices to ensure that their own texts do not assume authority over the world that they describe, in a reaction to modernity's tendency to create universal and hegemonic philosophies, systems, and practices of power. Yet third world and feminist writers have critiqued postmodernism as yet another mode of domination, propagated from privileged speaking positions in a largely Western and male academia (Ahmad 1992; Barr 1992). In its intellectual elitism, in its appropriation of traditions that are not its own, postmodernism remains another moment or style in the history of modernism.

Yet postmodernism is not only an academic trend. It is also tied to the historical era within which it produces its ideas, to changes in the actual rather than theoretical world. Just as the aesthetic styles, ideas, and discriminations of modernism responded to the historical experience of modernity, postmodernism expresses those changes that have taken place in postmodernity. The term describes a time in which the engines of modernity changed gear, as imperialism gave way to decolonization; women entered the workforce; industrialism was supplemented with postindustrial technologies; and monopoly capitalism turned into a more mobile finance capitalism. The features of postmodern aesthetic production turn out, then, to also be features of historical change in this period, as the decentralization and dispersal of modern regimes and ideas coincide. David Harvey (1989) and Fredric Jameson (1991) situate the beginnings of postmodernity in the early 1970s, when the world financial system invented investment models for flexible rather than fixed accumulation. Such models were no longer directly tied to modernist models of mass production, no longer grounded in factory-style methods of standardization and labor stability. Finance had instead become deterritorialized, investing and disinvesting according to the flexible flows of a global economy, in a diversification of production methods and markets. This shift from vertical to horizontal organization did not so much redistribute power as change its economic organization.

Today the distinction between postmodernity and postmodernism, between this historical reorganization of capitalism and its aesthetic, has transformed into that between globalization and an array of terms that describe its cultural expressions, such as cosmopolitanism, globalism, and the transcultural. Such terms carry on postmodernism's celebration of multiplicity and its critical receptivity to difference. They critique a globalization that has in many ways carried on the universalizing project of modernity as it creates a universal marketplace for humankind. This lineage between postmodernism and globalization is a history of capitalism, but scholars from the second world have pointed out that forms of postmodernism also emerge in other economic situations. China and the old Soviet Union also experienced such paradoxes, as technologies of reproduction and extensive bureaucracies brought the modern aspirations of communism to the point of exhaustion. Such societies were, like their Western counterparts, saturated by media and subject to the duplicitous languages of governance. Soviet sf writers Boris and Arkady Strugatsky parodied bureaucracy in *Tale of the Troika* (1968), a series of pointless adventures set in an immense, multistory building populated by obscure and irrational objects and characters. Along with many Western science-fiction writers, the Strugatskys recognized that modern ideas were making less sense as the twentieth century brought a landslide of changes to mass society.

The theoretical tools that postmodern theorists used to critique modernity were largely forged by French poststructuralism. This group of French scholars were influenced by the anarchist ideas of students in the 1960s, who took to the streets of Paris in an attempt to disinvest the modern state of its power. They were a generation of intellectuals who had been freed by student demands that the curriculum be rewritten. Philosophy, sociology, anthropology, history, and psychoanalysis, among other fields, were no longer to embed the domineering ideologies of modernity. Semiotics offered the theory of language by which to demonstrate the shaky, discursive foundations of the disciplines, built up by a series of presumptions about the power of language. Jacques Derrida (1978), one of the more influential of these theorists, argues that the meaning of any text is produced by a transcendental signifier or sign that dominates all other signs. For example, the transcendental signifier of the Bible, that which unifies and gives meaning to the text, is god. Instead, Derrida proposes that we read these signs as meaningful because they are differentiated from each other in language, and have little to do with the material world. So that our starting point for deconstructing the Bible should not be the transcendental conception of god, but the fact that god is differentiated in language from the word "dog." The difference between "god" and "dog" produces a textual rather than a transcendental meaning. Such discursive operations were put to work by scholars wanting to critique the role of texts in propagating the ideologies of modernity, and to undermine the certainties of knowledge and understanding upon which academic disciplines were based.

One of the most influential arguments against transcendental ideas is that of the French poststructuralist Jean-François Lyotard (1984). He argues that difference and diversification offer ways of rewriting modern narratives and their tendency to create universal rather than multiple values. Modern narratives of progress, scientific truth, and human history have after all been used to justify patriarchy, racism, imperialism, and war. Instead, Lyotard wants a multiplicity of micronarratives to articulate minority and partial experiences and truth claims. Samuel Delany's *Stars in My Pocket Like Grains of Sand* (1984) describes such processes of meaning making in a universe populated by thousands of different cultures, all misunderstanding each other in various processes of translation. This experiment with total heterogeneity, with multiple worlds, is postmodern because it is without a totalizing or structuring center, and is in a constant state of flux. A. Timothy Spaulding (2005) points out that this novel also reworks actual historical material, as it imaginatively interprets nineteenth-century slave narratives. In examining the rewritings of such slave narratives by contemporary authors of sf, fantasy, the historical novel, and African-American literature, Spaulding works to cut across established generic boundaries and to articulate just the kind of partial narrative that Lyotard champions. Marleen Barr (1992) offers another boundary-busting project, inventing a new generic category – feminist fabulation – that conjoins feminist fiction and feminist sf. Barr demonstrates something of the possibilities that postmodernism offers literary theory, to create and discard at will its received ideas about genre. She also demonstrates the limits of such reconfigurations, as historical understandings of genre give way to more mobile and creative acts of interpretation.

Feminist scholars have been all too aware of the irony of a postmodernism that, while disputing the power formations of modernity, substituted in its place a multiplicity that disempowers its critique within a continuum of plurality. Patricia Waugh points out that just as the idea of a coherent, centered subject was being dismantled by postmodernism, feminism was at last allowed a space from which to speak of the female subject (Waugh 1989: 6). Along with black, queer, subcultural, and subnational subjects, women were allowed a voice only to have it become one of many voices, to become subsumed within the din of postmodern multiplicity. This was the time in which the feminist utopias of Suzy McKee Charnas, Sally Miller Gearhart, Marge Piercy, Ursula Le Guin, Joanna Russ, and Doris Lessing had been published; while Octavia E. Butler, C.J. Cherryh, Samuel Delany, Gwyneth Jones, Vonda McIntyre, and Kate Wilhelm were writing fiction about gender and its constructions. Russ's *The Female Man* (1975) constructs a postmodern version of the utopian novel by fragmenting her characters between the feminist utopia of Whileaway and contemporary society, two worlds that run on parallel timelines. The independent women of Whileaway are not uptight about sex, can do any job on their planet, and are unconcerned about impressing others. The novel experiments with the conventions of character and narrative, confusing the Earth woman Jeannine with Whileaway visitor Janet in flowing conversations that dissolve one voice into the other. *The Female Man* locates its politics not only in its feminist content but in its challenge to the laws of narrative that appear positively patriarchal beside it. As Jenny Wolmark (1994) argues, sf had already established narrative conventions of contact and communication with difference, making it a privileged site by which the differences of sex and gender could be explored and extended in experiments with characterization, narrative, and utopianism. Veronica Hollinger (1999) points out how poststructuralist feminism, with its performed rather than essentialist subjects, is able to bring queer voices to light within science fiction. She has been a persistently sobering voice in sf criticism, disentangling postmodernism from both feminism and, as we shall see, cyberpunk.

Barr and Waugh both note the exclusion of women not only from the history of literature and literary studies, but also from a new genre of postmodern fiction, many of the key authors of which – Jorge Luis Borges, Samuel Beckett, Italo Calvino, Kurt Vonnegut, Thomas Pynchon – could well be considered sf writers. Such was the blurring of sf with other literary and media forms that commentators were moved to declare the end of the genre itself: as Bruce Sterling argues, "other writers have now learned to adopt SF's techniques to their own ends" (Sterling 1989: 78). Istvan

Csicsery-Ronay Jr (1992) goes so far as to suggest that discussions about sf could well be folded into discussions about postmodernism. Brian McHale (1987) celebrates the significance of sf for literature and literary studies. He argues not that their differences have collapsed into each other, but that the speed of traffic between high and low cultures has increased.

McHale argues that sf, which so often focuses on the encounter with the alien, the strange, and the new, expresses the kinds of multiplicities favored by postmodernism, and that it is fundamentally an ontological genre. That is, it confronts the cosmic questions that result from diversity, as it constructs different, internally coherent worlds that have differentiated relationships with the philosophical notion of being. So it is that sf's historical imagination is tied to questions of the human condition, to the way that human beings constitute themselves in space and time. While the epistemological focus of modernism found its generic mirror in the heroes of detective fiction who are interested in the known world and its interpretation, the postmodern hero of sf interrogates the mechanisms by which this world comes into being. Rather than different interpretations of the same world, postmodernism and science fiction both produce an "ontological perspectivism" of difference (McHale 1987: 39). So it is that in Robert Sheckley's *Mindswap* (1966), Marvin is holidaying in a Martian grub body when his human body is stolen. He is forced to swap into a Melden body, which is employed to collect Ganzer eggs. A giant Ganzer almost eats Marvin, before he works out that this is also a mind swapper, and is in fact a man who lives not so far down the road from his home. This collision of difference and identity generates the novel's humor and narrative tension, anticipating postmodern negotiations between constellations of meaning.

Like much sf of the 1960s, Sheckley's novel anticipated postmodernism's critical concerns. The social sf of the US and the British New Waves experimented with narrative conventions to question the genre's place in the ideology of the world. There is no more potent symbol of this modernity than the space race of this period, which wanted to drive the human race and its military-industrial complexes to the planets and beyond. The Golden Age of American sf, as well as many English and European writers, produced near- and far-future adventures in which the Moon and planets are conquered and colonized, while the Russian Ivan Yefremov's *Andromeda: a space-age tale* (1957) was likewise caught up in the imagination of space travel – picturing a communism that stretched across the stars. The Polish Stanisław Lem was one of many sf writers critical of such fantasies. His *Return from the Stars* (1961) tells of a confused space explorer who returns to a future Earth that is now indifferent to the reasons it sent him away. In Britain, experimental and politically minded sf writers began to critique the space race with stories of idiotic and hallucinating astronauts. J.G. Ballard's New Wave manifesto (1962) declared the end of the space age before it had properly begun, turning to the imaginative possibilities of the mind as a neglected zone for human expansion. His stories shift the imagination of space travel from the public domain into the private delusions of his characters. In "Memories of the Space Age" (1982), estranged and deluded figures wander and fly over the abandoned launch towers of Cape Canaveral, imagining their heroic place in a rejuvenated space program. In "The Man Who Walked on the Moon" (1985) a man sells his story to tourists, only to come to believe that he was once an astronaut.

Such delusions turn violent in Ballard's novel *Crash* (1973), in which a group of characters are pathologically obsessed with car crashes. This to the extent that they simulate crashes with their own bodies, often injuring themselves, resulting in scars and even permanent disabilities. The poststructuralist Jean Baudrillard (1991) points out that *Crash* is a science-fiction novel with no new inventions, no future or alien setting. One of the most influential proponents of postmodern thought, Baudrillard turns semiotics into cultural theory as he argues that reality itself has been displaced by the logic of the reproduction of the sign. So it is that, in *Crash*, Baudrillard argues that the future has already arrived, in a collapsing of boundaries between imagination and reality that makes fiction obsolete. The group's desire to orchestrate a car crash that would kill the celebrity Elizabeth Taylor is born of a saturated-media culture, and illustrates Baudrillard's influential theory of simulation. Baudrillard (1983) argues that reality models itself on copies of copies. Living amid such an excess of signs in popular culture, we have lost contact with what was once understood to be the real. Instead, signs and surfaces have reproduced themselves so much as to create a hyperreal that has taken its place. America models itself on the hyperreality of Disneyland, while actual military policies of nuclear deterrence model themselves on the imagination of a nuclear holocaust. The reality of the world is now simulated, created by a world of reproduced simulacra. So it is that in Lem's *The Cyberiad* (1967), Zipperupus is trapped in a dream machine that simulates the room that the dream machine is in. He cannot tell the difference between actual and simulated worlds, which are for Baudrillard identical to each other. The technology that once drove modernity has spiraled into a pathological circle of reproduction. Amid a frenzy of copying that which has already been copied, history freezes amid its own representations.

A special 1991 issue of *Science Fiction Studies* debated the implications for sf of Baudrillard's thesis, particularly in relation to *Crash*. N. Katherine Hayles (1991) and Vivian Sobchack (1991) caution against taking Baudrillard too seriously, regarding him as an imaginative rather than critical author. They defend Ballard's more cautionary fiction against the hysterical celebration of transcendent simulacra. Such criticisms are oddly defensive of the borders between criticism and sf that postmodernism so wanted to blur. If, as Lyotard (1984) claims, narratives of science and history produce truth-effects rather than establish truth, Baudrillard's description of historical experience as sf is of just as much interest as Ballard's sf that captures something of the historical moment. As Donna Haraway's (1991) radical revisions to the history of science demonstrate, science was sf in the first place. Her rereadings of simian science and Baudrillard's arguments for a post-historical present are produced from within an accelerated regime of representations, in an era that is incapable of establishing historical truth in any other way than imaginatively. Istvan Csicsery-Ronay Jr (1991) argues as much, finding in Baudrillard and Haraway an argument for just how much critical discourse had begun to read like sf, and conversely how much the world has become science-fictional. Sf, then, becomes a way of seeing the world, rather than a mode of extrapolation. Ironic, then, is a response by Ballard (1991), who tells sf academics (not including Baudrillard) that their postmodernism is nothing more than hyperbole, and that the genre was always modern. Ballard, the only sf writer in this special issue, argues against the intellectualization of the genre, while the academics are arguing against the science-fictionalization of their intellectual tradition.

Thus far this chapter has looked at fiction and philosophy, but postmodernism and its critique are indelibly tied to the range of visual and aural modalities at work in popular culture. Scott Bukatman (1993) ranges between different modes of visual culture, from comic books, fashion trends, television programs, videos, computer games, and fiction to philosophy. Bukatman follows Jameson in arguing that the multiplicities within which the postmodern subject is immersed generate perceptual confusion, and takes it a step further in proposing this subject's fusion with the hyper-reality of simulation. Sf films allegorize this experience of dissolution. The hero of *Tron* (Lisberger 1982) finds himself inside a videogame, fighting for his actual life in a virtual environment. In *Terminator 2: Judgment Day* (Cameron 1991), a shape-shifting android can morph into whatever human or inhuman identity it wants to assume. In *Videodrome* (Cronenberg 1983), an illegal television station broadcasts sadomaso-chistic images that turn out to hide a signal that induces confusion in the viewer, blurring the real and televisual. Vivian Sobchack offers one of the most sobering inter-pretations of this new wave of sf cinema, using Jameson's mapping of postmodernism into late capitalism to describe the way that utopian representations of outer space have turned to visions of dystopian depthlessness (Sobchack 1987: 223–305). Where once sf film was heroic and expansive, in the late 1970s and 1980s it began to look back upon a crowded, artificial Earth. So it is that the robot replicants in *Blade Runner* (Scott 1982) experience their implanted memories of childhood as intimately as human beings do, revealing both the depth of simulated experience and the mediated qualities of memory and personality. Such films appeal to one of the first generations that had grown up with television in their homes, the flow of images naturalized into the human personality.

Postmodernism is thus born within a generation for whom media is second, if not first, nature. Language is no longer set out on the permanent page, but turns into what N. Katherine Hayles describes as *"flickering signifiers*, characterized by their tendency toward unexpected metamorphoses, attenuations, and dispersions" (Hayles 1999: 30). Hayles refashions the unstable semiotics of poststructuralism into the transitory and elusive experience of media. The fiction that most realizes the mediated qualities of postmodernism, and one that is contemporary with this televisual generation, is the sf subgenre of cyberpunk. Its bestselling inaugural novel, William Gibson's *Neuromancer* (1984), is the story of an unemployed computer hacker in near-future Japan. Illuminated by neon and draped in plastic, the streets of this future are a sensory overload. Cyberpunk imagines life beyond the terminator, that threshold that lies between technological change and the human capacity to anticipate or control it. Case must battle the posthuman intelligences that inhabit virtual reality or cyberspace, jacking his mind directly into a vast computer network to navigate an immaterial, digital paraspace. Cyberpunk spokesperson Bruce Sterling identifies the way in which cyberpunk's obsessions with the posthuman intersect with the "tools of global integration" employed by corporate and military complexes (Sterling 1986: xii). Thus, in Sterling's *Holy Fire* (1996), a sentient dog hosts a popular television program and an engineered food crop covers the Earth. Such possibilities are postmodern because they entertain a multiplicity of future scenarios, playing out different developments in biotechnology, computing, and nanotechnology all at once. They are also dystopian, superseding the ideals of modernity with accelerated technological change and transnational power. They are, Hollinger (1991) argues, less concerned with the difference of worlds that work only to disguise our own, instead presenting a cool, more detached view of the possibilities of the near future. Cyberpunk also signals changes to sf's narrative form. Darko Suvin (1979) influentially proposed that an sf novel needed a single novum, or new invention or idea, to drive its narrative forward. Suvin revised this thesis to propose that life is now made up of a deluge of nova, not many of which would count as significant (Suvin 1997).

Cyberpunk was not only a mode of writing. It is also a term used to describe the imagined near futures of manga, anime, films, games, fashions, and even recipes. Indeed, this chapter has largely focused on prose fiction examples to illustrate the collision between postmodernism and sf fiction. However, any number of essays could be written on the postmodernism of sf through comic books, toys, or television. Much could also be written on the postmodernism of sf from countries that have experienced their own modes of modernity, such as Brazil and Japan. The origins of capitalism lie as much in sixteenth-century Latin America, on the frontier of imperialism, as they do in Europe. It is thus to the hybridity of cultural forms that we could turn for other, very different examples of postmodern sf. Japan, the setting for Gibson's near future, is now one of the largest exporters of culture in the world, from manga to anime, television programs to megablogs. Its prolific and diverse modes of expression are born of high technology, a massive media industry, and an ancient visual culture. Thus it is that postmodernism challenges us to see its historical period in multiple ways, from a diversity of subject positions. It opens up questions of heterogeneity in a discourse that tends to reconcile difference with interdisciplinary theory. Such tensions remain with us today, as globalization becomes the key term of our era, and raises once again all the familiar tensions between the universal and particular, identity and difference. If postmodernism wanted to lay modernity to rest once and for all, it was only surpassed by a history that threw its contradictions back into play once more. At least critics, theorists, and producers of sf are now better equipped to critique this new period, with the legacies of a criticism that pulled apart representations, valorized the excluded, and subjected its own practices to rigorous interrogation. As for sf itself, it has been mainstreamed, adapted to multiple media, and discovered outside the Anglo-American vortex that defined it. Its generic identity is dispersed and multiple, its postmodernism a visible and persuasive idea.

Bibliography

Ahmad, A. (1992) *In Theory: classes, nations and literatures*, London: Verso.
Ballard, J.G. (1962) "Which Way to Inner Space?," *New Worlds*, 40: 2–3, 116–18.

—— (1991) "A Response to the Invitation to Respond," *Science Fiction Studies*, 18(3): 329.

Barr, M.S. (1992) *Feminist Fabulation: space/postmodern fiction*, Iowa City: University of Iowa Press.

Baudrillard, J. (1983) *Simulations*, trans. P. Patton, P. Foss, and P. Beitchman, New York: Semiotext(e).

—— (1991) "Two Essays, 'Simulacra and Science Fiction' and 'Ballard's *Crash*,'" trans. A.B. Evans, *Science Fiction Studies*, 18(3): 309–20.

Bukatman, S. (1993) *Terminal Identity: the virtual subject in postmodern science fiction*, Durham, NC and London: Duke University Press.

Csicsery-Ronay Jr, I. (1991) "The SF of Theory: Baudrillard and Haraway," *Science Fiction Studies*, 18(3): 387–404.

—— (1992) "Postmodernism Technoculture, or, The Gordian Knot Revisited," *Science Fiction Studies*, 19(3): 403–10.

Deleuze, G. and Guattari, F. (1987) *A Thousand Plateaus: capitalism and schizophrenia*, 1980, trans. B. Massumi, Minneapolis: University of Minnesota Press.

Derrida, J. (1978) "Structure and Sign in the Discourse of the Human Sciences," in *Writing and Difference*, trans. A. Bass, London: Routledge.

Haraway, D.J. (1991) *Simians, Cyborgs, and Women: the reinvention of nature*, New York and London: Routledge.

Harvey, D. (1989) *The Condition of Postmodernity: an enquiry into the origins of cultural change*, Oxford: Blackwell.

Hassan, I. (1987) *The Postmodern Turn: essays in postmodern theory and culture*, Columbus: Ohio State University Press.

Hayles, N.K. (1991) "The Borders of Madness," *Science Fiction Studies*, 18(3): 321–3.

—— (1999) *How We Became Posthuman: virtual bodies in cybernetics, literature and informatics*, Chicago and London: University of Chicago Press.

Hollinger, V. (1991) "Postmodernism's SF/SF's Postmodernism," *Science Fiction Studies*, 18(3): 305–8.

—— (1999) "(Re)reading Queerly: science fiction, feminism, and the defamiliarization of gender," *Science Fiction Studies*, 26(1): 23–40.

Jameson, F. (1991) *Postmodernism, or, The Cultural Logic of Late Capitalism*, London and New York: Verso.

Lyotard, J.-F. (1984) *The Postmodern Condition: a report on knowledge*, trans. G. Bennington and B. Massumi, Manchester: Manchester University Press.

McHale, B. (1987) *Postmodernist Fiction*, London and New York: Methuen.

Olalquiaga, C. (1992) *Megalopolis: contemporary cultural sensibilities*, Minneapolis: University of Minnesota Press.

Sobchack, V. (1987) *The American Science Fiction Film*, New York: Ungar.

—— (1991) "In Response to Jean Baudrillard: Baudrillard's obscenity," *Science Fiction Studies*, 18(3): 327–9.

Spaulding, A.T. (2005) *Re-Forming the Past: history, the fantastic, and the postmodern slave narrative*, Columbus: Ohio State University Press.

Sterling, B. (1986) "Preface," in *Mirrorshades: the cyberpunk anthology*, London: HarperCollins.

—— (1989) "Slipstream," *SF Eye*, 5: 77–80.

Suvin, D. (1979) *Metamorphoses of Science Fiction: on the poetics and history of a literary genre*, New Haven, CT: Yale University Press.

—— (1997) "Novum is as Novum Does," *Foundation*, 69: 26–43.

Waugh, P. (1989) *Feminine Fictions: revisiting the postmodern*, London: Routledge.

Wolmark, J. (1994) *Aliens and Others: science fiction, feminism and postmodernism*, Hemel Hempstead: Harvester Wheatsheaf.

29
PSYCHOANALYSIS
Andrew M. Butler

There is a moment in an article about *Star Wars: Episode V – The Empire Strikes Back* (Kershner 1980) when Andrew Gordon notes that the film, "like all myths or fairy tales, deals with primal anxieties" (Gordon 1980: 315). Such anxieties, which relate to sexuality, can be psychoanalyzed within a number of frameworks. However, it is relatively rare for written sf, a modern form of myth, to be examined from these perspectives. This might be because early theorists of the genre were mostly working within Marxist or structuralist paradigms. In contrast, sf film has been frequently psychoanalyzed, in part because film studies has a strong tradition of using these approaches. This chapter will outline some of the major ideas within psychoanalysis, especially those of Sigmund Freud and Jacques Lacan, and demonstrate applications of these analyses to sf.

One objection to the use of a psychoanalytical approach to criticism might be the apparent absence of sexuality from sf until works such as Philip José Farmer's "The Lovers" (1952), and then the broader New Wave of the 1960s, pioneered sexual themes within the genre. But it is this very absence that makes the paradigm so suggestive for criticism: in the queer adventures of the confirmed bachelors of late Victorian and Edwardian scientific romances or in the battles between the pulps' square-jawed heroes and strange monsters the sexuality is latent and symbolized rather than openly displayed. There is a risk of a vulgar psychoanalysis, searching for phallic (and occasionally vaginal) symbols in spaceships, lightsabers, ray guns, and so forth.

Freud was one doctor, among many, who was investigating the workings of the mind in the late nineteenth century. *Studies on Hysteria* (1895) by Freud and Josef Breuer explored how the repression of particular mental processes led to physical symptoms. Breuer advocated hypnosis as a means of freeing up mental processes and relieving symptoms, whereas Freud came to favor discussion with the patient and free association. In four decades of publishing, Freud was to refine, revise, and even change his conception of the workings of the human mind, and it is worth describing his three successive major models of the psyche – topographic, economic, and dynamic – and relating them to sf.

Through the 1890s, Freud was evolving the ideas which formed the basis for *The Interpretation of Dreams* (1901). He argued that the psyche is made up of three elements: the conscious (*das Bewusste*), what it is currently aware of; the preconscious (*das Vorbewusste*), what it is no longer aware of through forgetting; and the unconscious (*das Unbewusste*), what the mind has repressed. The latter can become manifest through various symptoms, such as neuroses, psychoses, tics, and slips of the tongue, or may be transformed into dreams, jokes, or art. The dream was a distorted version of the desires of the individual: the desires might be straightforwardly represented, but a desire might be *displaced* from one object to another, it might be *reversed*, and a number of desires might be *condensed* into a single desire. Through reflecting on the manifest content of the dream with an analyst, the analysand attempts to uncover the latent content. Vivian Sobchack connects this to the repression of sexuality, especially female sexuality, in sf, putting "displacement and condensation" (Sobchack 1990: 113) at the heart of the genre. For example, in Mary Shelley's *Frankenstein* (1818), Victor, having created his creature, has a vivid dream: an image of his neglected fiancée, Elizabeth (his cousin in the 1818 text, but not in the revised 1831 version), which then metamorphoses into a vision of his dead mother. The image of Elizabeth belongs to the preconscious realm, but the manifestation of his mother is the reemergence of his repressed desires for her, aroused by his own taboo act of birthing.

During the first decade of the twentieth century, Freud moved from his topographic model to one he called "economic," and, in "Formulations on the Two Principles of Mental Functioning" (1911), he viewed the mind as a battleground for two contending forces or principles. Humans, he argued, were defined by their need for sexual gratification, for the satisfaction of their libido (the pleasure principle). But society would collapse if every urge was acted upon, and so these are postponed or repressed (the reality principle). Again, these desires may be transformed into symptoms. In *Shivers* (Cronenberg 1975), an experimental organism that seems to repress the reality principle is created, and spreads between people like a virus. The result is a perverse anarchy within the confines of a high-rise development that threatens to spread out to the rest of the world. (Freud's economic model fails to account for the amount of *dis*pleasure to which people willingly expose themselves. It would be another decade before he addressed this issue, in his discussion of the death instinct to which I will return later in this chapter.)

Freud advanced a third model – the dynamic – in *The Ego and the Id* (1923): the Id (*das Es*) replaced the libido as the unconscious or as the source of sexual and aggressive motives, and this was held in check in part by the Ego (*das Ich*). This consists of both the conscious and preconscious mind, but also includes unconscious elements. Part of the Id develops into the Super-ego (*das Uberego*), which may either permit or forbid the acting out of desires and controls the Ego. It is very tempting to take these three factors and see an sf text as personifying them within its narrative. Robert Louis Stevenson's *Strange Case of Dr Jekyll and Mr Hyde* (1886) can be read as an account of an attempt to separate out the Id from the psyche and give it full rein, with murderous results. As Elaine Showalter (1990) shows, the text is suffused with homosexual innuendo (see also Butler 2002). A number of the film versions focus upon repressed heterosexual desire – Rouben Mamoulian's 1931 version fetishizes a woman's gartered thigh during Jekyll's transformation.

It is the notion of the Id which has become a major part of sf film criticism – Margaret Tarratt, in an article first published in 1970, wrote that "The conquest of the 'monster of the id' is the structural raison d'etre of many science fiction films" (Tarratt 1986: 341). This is most blatant in *Forbidden Planet* (Wilcox 1956). An expedition is sent to Altair IV to locate a lost colony and finds Dr Morbius and his beautiful and intelligent daughter Altaira. The crewmen are very attracted to her, but it is Captain Adams who gains her affections, much to the disgruntlement of her pet tiger. Meanwhile the encampment is attacked, apparently by the disembodied Krel, the species who had previously inhabited the planet. As the crew are killed off one by one, it becomes clear that the deaths are a result of Morbius's repressed sexual desires for his daughter, which have been projected by a brain-boosting device into physical, monstrous form. As Tarratt notes, "The word *incest* is never mentioned, but his suppressed incestuous desires are clearly implied to be at the root of all the trouble" (Tarratt 1986: 334). The attacker is explicitly described as a monster from the Id, as primitive and frustrated desires.

Tarratt also analyzes *The Thing from Another World* (Nyby 1951). A crashed alien spacecraft is recovered and a creature in a block of ice is brought into the nearby military base, where it defrosts. Meanwhile, Captain Pat Hendry chats up Nikki Nicholson, to whom he has been romantically linked in the past. Nicholson, the only woman at the base, only feels safe once she has tied Hendry to a chair; after they exchange a kiss he breaks free from his bondage, indeed he could have escaped at any point but chose not to (Sobchack 1990: 110). The alien escapes, leaving an arm behind, and Hendry's hand is injured in the fracas. Tarratt argues that "the hand is explicitly established as a sexual organ" (Tarratt 1986: 337). The Thing is a monster from the Id, and "is found to be incompatible with human life and must consequently be destroyed, however fascinating it may be" (Tarratt 1986: 338). Such repression is destructive, and the hypermasculine captain, who chooses when to yield power, is functioning as a Super-ego.

According to Freud, the Super-ego is formed by the internalization or introjection into the psyche of the paternal figure as a result of the Oedipus complex. In the complex, the child desires the mother, but is prevented from acting on this desire for fear of castration by the father. The male child changes his allegiance to the father, with the compensation that he will find a woman to replace his mother. (The female situation is more complicated and more problematic, since she is always already castrated. Freud came up with a number of formulations of this – see, for example, "The Dissolution of the Oedipus Complex" (1924) and "Female Sexuality" (1931).) Sometimes the father will refuse to insist on his patriarchal power, and sometimes the child will refuse to acknowledge this power; the result is a problematic psyche.

Andrew Gordon locates an Oedipal drama at the heart of the *Star Wars* trilogy (1977–83), particularly in *The Empire Strikes Back*, "which climaxes with the hero's being mutilated when he attempts to kill his own father" (Gordon 1980: 316). The hero, Luke Skywalker, has already passed the trials that mark the coming of age, and now possesses the phallus/lightsaber which once belonged to his father, Anakin, and has been passed to him by his mentor, Ben Kenobi. Darth Vader turns out to be

Anakin, and Luke is a "sort of clean-cut, cornfed, adolescent Oedipus" (Gordon 1980: 314) – Gordon even suggests that the name "Darth Vader" echoes "Dark Father." Meanwhile the incest taboo prevents Luke from acting upon any sexual desires he has for Princess Leia, now revealed as his sister, and these urges are displaced onto the secondary hero Han Solo, who "woos her passionately" (Gordon 1980: 315). Han's misfortunes and pains – including imprisonment and blinding – are equally displaced punishments for Luke's repressed desires.

There is an enactment of Oedipal patricide in *Blade Runner* (Scott 1982) when Roy Batty visits his creator, Tyrell, in the hope of getting his life (and thus his potency) extended. Batty attempts to argue with this patriarchal authority, which he is meant to accept without question, but he fails and resorts to violence, putting out Tyrell's eyes. Lest we miss the significance of this, the 1982, 1991, and 2007 versions of the film have Batty calling him "Father" – the alternative line in the 1982 international release, "Fucker," is hardly any less suggestive. It is surely no accident that Batty hammers nails into his own hand before the climactic fight with Deckard – or indeed that he tries to emasculate his opponent by breaking his fingers. These are among a long line of damaged hands and arms in sf film; in addition to those already mentioned in this chapter might be added *The Hands of Orlac* (Wiene 1924; Gréville 1960), *Metropolis* (Lang 1927), *Mad Love* (Freund 1936), *Dr Strangelove or: How I Learned to Stop Worrying and Love the Bomb* (Kubrick 1964), and *Tetsuo* (Tsukamoto 1989).

In *Back to the Future* (Zemeckis 1985), Marty McFly escapes from his present-day romantic difficulties into the past, where he risks being seduced by his mother, and potentially either preventing his own conception or becoming his own father. The film "makes us laugh at incest ... it teases our fear and desire by a last-minute avoidance of the physical act" (Gordon 1987: 375). Gordon points out that "Like Oedipus, Marty attempts to flee his fate – not to another town but to another time. And like Oedipus, his flight leads him into the very predicament he dreaded (and Freud would claim secretly desired): into his mother's bed" (Gordon 1987: 376). The comic resolution is an escape from acting out these desires – he rescues his father rather than killing him. Biff, the bully who has humiliated Marty's father since the 1950s and who attempts to rape Marty's mother, is another monster from the Id, "innocent Marty's evil stand-in, a sexual beast" (Gordon 1987: 380).

With the dissolution of the Oedipus complex and the emergence of the Super-ego, the primitive anxieties are meant to be left behind; however, what is repressed may return. Events or entities which revive these fears are characterized as being part of the uncanny (*das Unheimliche*) by Freud in a 1919 essay on the topic: "an uncanny experience occurs either when infantile complexes which have been repressed are once more revived by some impression, or when primitive beliefs which have been surmounted seem once more to be confirmed" (Freud 1985: 372). The uncanny includes doubles, ghosts, twins, and, according to Ernst Jentsch, "doubts whether an apparently animate being is really alive; or conversely, whether a lifeless object might not be in fact animate" (qtd in Freud 1985: 347). Aliens, robots, or advanced technology also invoke the uncanny. In fact, Terry Castle, author of *The Female Thermometer and the Invention of the Uncanny in the Eighteenth Century* (1995), suggests,

"Just about anything electronic has its uncanny aspect: telephones, cameras, television, personal computers, ATM machines, X-ray machines, answering machines, bar-code sensors, compact disks, laser disks, beepers, and on and on" (Arnzen 1997: 521–2). In other words, any sf which contains technology can be considered uncanny. William Gibson's *Neuromancer* (1984), with its repeated metaphors which yoke together technology and the natural world, is an example, especially when Molly justifies her actions by saying "[T]hat's just the way I'm wired" (Gibson 1984: 218) and Case thinks of himself as jacking into the matrix (although technically it is jacked into him).

Freud suggests that imagining the uncanny double began as a means of warding off death. The double can exist beyond the life of the original:

> the "double" was originally an insurance against the destruction of the ego, an "energetic denial of the power of death" ... probably the "immortal" soul was the first "double" of the body. This invention of doubling as a preservation against extinction has its counterpart in the language of dreams, which is fond of representing castration by a doubling or multiplication of a genital symbol.
>
> (Freud 1985: 356)

However, these doubles have a habit of turning against their originals – Hyde against Jekyll, the Creature against Victor Frankenstein, Batty against Tyrell. The need for surmounting death is a reminder that death occurs: "From having been an assurance of immortality, [the double] becomes the uncanny harbinger of death" (Freud 1985: 357).

In the terminology of his essay on "The Uncanny," Freud anticipates that of his *Beyond the Pleasure Principle* (1920), especially in his description of behaviors that run counter to the pleasure principle:

> it is possible to recognize the dominance in the unconscious mind of a "compulsion to repeat" proceeding from the instinctual impulses and probably inherent in the very nature of the instincts – a compulsion powerful enough to overrule the pleasure principle, lending to certain aspects of the mind their daemonic character, and still very clearly expressed in the impulses of small children ... [W]hatever reminds us of this inner "compulsion to repeat" is perceived as uncanny.
>
> (Freud 1985: 360–1)

Freud was puzzled why his patients relived dreadful experiences rather than repressing them, and why fear and anxiety are embraced. He might well have asked why we scare ourselves with the tales of doubles, aliens, and the end of the world. This is the point at which he has to introduce *displeasure* into his economic model.

Parallel to the erotic instincts Freud posited a death instinct: "the aim of all life is death" (Freud 1955: 38). The individual exposes him or herself to a whole range of fears, almost as an inoculation against real death. Freud discusses how each individual cell self-destructs at a particular time, and notes that "Certain fishes, for instance, undertake laborious migrations at spawning-time, in order to deposit their spawn in particular waters far removed from their customary haunts ... they are [seeking] the localities in which their species formerly resided" (Freud 1955: 37). This is a return to an earlier, more primitive state. In *Neuromancer*, this compulsion is echoed by a number of the major characters, perhaps most notably the Wintermute AI: "You know salmon? Kinda fish? These fish, see, they're *compelled* to swim upstream ... I'm under compulsion myself" (Gibson 1984: 206).

The death instinct transcends individual examples of sf: it is applicable to the genre itself. At various points, readers or critics have declared it to have died. These deaths are sometime announced with the birth of a new movement, and each alleged advance marks the collapse of the genre into the undifferentiated mass of literature. John Clute suggests that the genre ended with the launch of Sputnik: "the beginning of the Space Age [w]as a turning point, a point beyond which the quasi-organic conversation of American sf – for the moment let me call it First SF – began to ramble, and to lose the thread of the story" (Clute 1995: 9). Roger Luckhurst notes that "The history of SF is a history of ambivalent deaths. The many movements within the genre – the New Wave, feminist SF, cyberpunk – are marked as both transcendent death–as–births, finally demolishing the 'ghetto' walls, and as degenerescent birth–as–deaths, perverting the specificity of the genre" (Luckhurst 1994: 43). These imagined deaths uncannily reassure/frighten the readers.

The "Many Deaths" in the title of Luckhurst's essay points toward the Lacanian analysis of the death instinct. Lacan suggests that the first death is not enough, and that nature demands an impossibly total destruction, the second death (Lacan 1992: 211). He draws upon semiotic theory and places structured language at the heart of his rereading of Freud. He turns to the story of Antigone, Oedipus's daughter, in which her son Polynices is buried without the proper rites (Lacan 1992: 243–87). The point is that the second death is not achievable without these rites – and indeed any death is reversible given the pronouncing of the right rites. The death instinct here becomes a cycle of nature. Sf can be declared dead – but this is reversed by the writing of the genre's double.

Slavoj Žižek (1991) discusses popular films that use this trope, most notably *RoboCop* (Verhoeven 1987). Officer Alex Murphy, shot dead by a Detroit gang, "finds himself literally 'between two deaths' – clinically dead and at the same time provided with a new, mechanical body" (Žižek 1991: 22). As he "starts to remember fragments of his previous, 'human' life [he] thus undergoes a process of resubjectivation [*sic*], changing gradually back from pure incarnated drive to a being of desire" (Žižek 1991: 22). Žižek notes a similar trajectory of subjectivization in the behavior of Rachael in *Blade Runner*, as she constructs her identity from faked memories (Žižek 1991: 173).

The death instinct is not Lacan's only revision of Freud's ideas; he also rewrites the Oedipus complex. He argues that the child is born prematurely – animals achieve self-sufficiency earlier – as an *hommelette* (man-let, but punning on omelet), a largely undifferentiated mess overlapping with the rest of the world. The child distinguishes itself as an individual by seeing an image of itself, especially one in a mirror. The mirror image is more competent, more powerful, and more able, and so the child passes into the sphere of the Imaginary: both in the sense of it being dependent on this imagined identification, and because an image is involved. However, since the image is not the same as the self, self-identification is in fact an instant of alienation, introducing a disjunction or lack between self and self-image. The individual's position within language – as the subject of its own sentences and object of other people's – becomes part of anchoring identity. *The Truman Show* (Weir 1998) dramatizes the Mirror Phase when unwitting reality-show star Truman Burbank draws a picture of a spacesuit on his bathroom mirror around his own reflected image, and briefly identifies himself as an astronaut, a more able and heroic version of himself, a self he would like to become.

After this phase, the child enters into the Oedipus complex. Originally the child desires to be desired by the mother in an attempt to fill the lack, but the mother has her own desire: not as such for the father, but for the phallus for which the father is a signifier. The father-figure need not be a biological father, nor indeed male. The child attempts to become a phallus for the mother, but fails due to his fear of castration by the phallus. The male child consoles himself that one day he will take on the phallic role, and in the meantime has the compensation of entering the Symbolic Order (in effect, society structured as a logical system or language). This is echoed in the system which Truman inhabits; unaware that he is part of a television simulacrum, he interacts with substitutable actors performing the structured functions of father, mother, lovers, friends, and so forth. The female child, however, reacts differently to the threat of castration, being (according to Lacan) always already castrated. She can console herself with nostalgia for a time before a knowledge of her loss, and cannot enter into the sphere of the Symbolic, remaining in babble.

The sexism of this is striking, but some French feminists have used this to posit the existence of an alternative, female, language. Hélène Cixous (1981), while critical of the neuroses of male psychodramas, nevertheless leads a call for an *écriture féminine*. Julia Kristeva (1984) labels the feminine babble the Semiotic, and sees it as a rich, metaphorical, allusive (and elusive) language, which is anti-phallocentric. She also describes a liminal state of being, the *abject*, which – in a notion similar to the uncanny – recalls primitive fears in the individual (1982). This has proved fertile ground for writers on monsters and hybridity (see Creed 1993). Writers such as Elizabeth Grosz (1990) and Juliet Mitchell (1974) have also found common ground between feminism and Lacanian and Freudian ideas.

Alongside the spheres of the Imaginary and the Symbolic, Lacan places the Real, which is not to be confused with reality. The Real is that which cannot be imagined or symbolized, and is pre- (and post-) language. It is totally other, and may be glimpsed in sex and death. Žižek situates the Real in the "formless excremental remnant" (Žižek 1999: 155) of food served in a high-class restaurant in *Brazil* (Gilliam 1985), as opposed to the pristine color image of the chosen dish. He also discusses the Real and the Symbolic in terms of *The Matrix* (Wachowski brothers 1999): the virtual Matrix operates as a Symbolic Order or "big Other," but the reality that it is distinct from is not the Real: "the Real is not the 'true reality' behind the virtual simulation, but the void which makes reality incomplete/inconsistent, and the function of every symbolic Matrix is to conceal this inconsistency – one of the ways to effectuate this concealment is precisely to claim that, behind the incomplete/inconsistent reality we know, there is another reality with no deadlock of impossibility structuring it" (Žižek 2001: 216, 217–18). Žižek's reading suggests that texts invoking virtual realms perform both an ideological and a psychological task in relation to reality.

Lacan's ideas have been enthusiastically taken up within film studies, with the images on screen watched in the dark being seen as an equivalent to the Mirror Phase, where the masculinized viewer identifies with the more competent, more potent, and – above all – bigger hero on the screen, and identifies with the hero's desires. Laura Mulvey (1975), who critiques the cinematic male gaze (the ways classical Hollywood camerawork encourage such identification), has proven especially influential. Various kinds of looking within and outside the diegetic space have been considered, as well as voyeurism and scopophilia, especially in tension with the polar opposite of (Oedipal?) blinding.

Erica Sheen notes the recurring motif of eyes and looking in *Blade Runner*, and how Deckard is granted ownership of the narratives through his narration – even for events at which he is not present. It is "a story of a woman 'made' by a man; of how the woman gains entry into the Symbolic Order through the rejection of a supposed unity with an illusory mother and an acceptance of the defining status of 'the law of the father' via a submission to the demands of male sexuality" (Sheen 1991: 153). Rachael, like the other replicants, is in the Mirror Phase, since she constructs her sense of self from photographs. It is the authority of Deckard as policeman that would allow her access to the Symbolic Order or condemn her to exile/death. Sheen argues that the replicants are coded as feminine, as "they are actually forbidden entry even though they must operate within its terms" (Sheen 1991: 157). Such a reading exposes sexism at the heart of the film.

There is still much to be written about sf from a psychoanalytic viewpoint, and there has been space here only to scratch the surfaces of Freud and Lacan. Carl Jung has attracted some attention for his theory of archetypes – in fact, both Philip K. Dick's *The Man in the High Castle* (1963) and Ursula K. Le Guin's *The Left Hand of Darkness* (1969) explicitly use Jungian imagery, via Taoism. Hauke and Alister (2001) include chapters on *2001: A Space Odyssey* (Kubrick 1968), *Blade Runner*, and *Dark City* (Proyas 1998). Jung's work on flying saucers would also repay attention. The work of Melanie Klein (1988) on object relations theory – in which objects or parts of objects may satisfy desires of a given individual who projects a sense of good or evil onto them – has made little impact on the field so far. But it is the Uncanny which particularly deserves further investigation, as it seems to me to be – uncannily – like sf. As Nicholas Royle notes, "The uncanny is not a literary genre. But nor is it a non-literary genre. It overflows the very institution of literature. It inhabits, parasitizes the allegedly non-literary. It makes 'genre' blink" (Royle 2003: 19).

ANDREW M. BUTLER

Bibliography

Arnzen, M.A. (1997) "Para*Doxa Interview with Terry Castle," Para*doxa: Studies in World Literature, 3(3–4): 521–6.

Butler, A.M. (2002) "Proto-Sf/Proto-Queer: the strange cases of Dr Frankenstein and Mr Hyde," Foundation, 86: 7–16.

Cixous, H. (1981) "The Laugh of the Medusa," 1975, in E. Marks and I. De Courtivron (eds) New French Feminisms, Brighton: Harvester Wheatsheaf.

Clute, J. (1995) Look at the Evidence: essays and reviews, Liverpool: Liverpool University Press.

Creed, B. (1993) The Monstrous Feminine: film, feminism, and psychoanalysis, London: Routledge.

Freud, S. (1955) Beyond the Pleasure Principle, 1920, in The Standard Edition of the Complete Psychological Works of Sigmund Freud, vol. 18, ed. J. Strachey, London: Hogarth Press.

—— (1958) "Formulations on the Two Principles of Mental Functioning," 1911, in The Standard Edition of the Complete Psychological Works of Sigmund Freud, vol. 12, ed. J. Strachey, London: Hogarth Press.

—— (1975) The Interpretation of Dreams, 1901, trans. J. Strachey, eds J. Strachey, A. Tyson, and A. Richards, Harmondsworth: Pelican.

—— (1977a) "The Dissolution of the Oedipus Complex," 1924, in On Sexuality: three essays on the theory of sexuality and other works, trans. J. Strachey, ed. A. Richards, Harmondsworth: Penguin.

—— (1977b) "Female Sexuality," 1931, in On Sexuality: three essays on the theory of sexuality and other works, trans. J. Strachey, ed. A. Richards, Harmondsworth: Penguin.

—— (1984) The Ego and the Id, 1923, in On Metapsychology, vol. 11, trans. J. Strachey, ed. A. Richards, Harmondsworth: Pelican.

—— (1985) "The Uncanny," 1919, in Art and Literature: Jensen's 'Gradiva', Leonardo Da Vinci and other works, trans. J. Strachey, ed. A. Dickson, Harmondsworth: Pelican.

Freud, S. and Breuer, J. (1974) Studies on Hysteria, 1895, trans. J. and A. Strachey, eds J. and A. Strachey, assisted by A. Richards, London: Pelican.

Gibson, W. (1984) Neuromancer, New York: Ace.

Gordon, A. (1980) "The Empire Strikes Back: monsters from the id," Science Fiction Studies, 7(3): 313–18.

—— (1987) "Back to the Future: Oedipus as time traveler," Science Fiction Studies, 14(3): 372–85.

Grosz, E. (1990) Jacques Lacan: a feminist introduction, New York: Routledge.

Hauke, C. and Alister, I. (eds) (2001) Jung and Film: post-Jungian takes on the moving image, London: Routledge.

Klein, M. (1988) Envy and Gratitude and Other Works 1946–1963, London: Virago.

Kristeva, J. (1982) Powers of Horror: an essay on abjection, trans. L.S. Roudiez, New York: Columbia University Press.

—— (1984) Revolution in Poetic Language, 1974, trans. M. Waller, New York: Columbia University Press.

Lacan, J. (1992) The Ethics of Psychoanalysis 1959–1960: the seminars of Jacques Lacan VII, ed. J.-A. Miller, trans. with notes by D. Porter, London: Routledge.

Luckhurst, R. (1994) "The Many Deaths of Science Fiction: a polemic," Science Fiction Studies, 21(1): 35–90.

Mitchell, J. (1974) Psychoanalysis and Feminism, New York: Pantheon Books.

Mulvey, L. (1975) "Visual Pleasure and Narrative Cinema," Screen 16(3): 6–18.

Royle, N. (2003) The Uncanny, Manchester: Manchester University Press.

Sheen, E. (1991) "'I'm Not in the Business, I Am the Business': women at work in Hollywood science fiction," in L. Armitt (ed.) Where No Man Has Gone Before, London: Routledge.

Showalter, E. (1990) Sexual Anarchy: gender and culture at the fin de siècle, New York: Viking.

Sobchack, V. (1990) "The Virginity of Astronauts: sex and the science fiction film," in A. Kuhn (ed.) Alien Zone: cultural theory and contemporary science fiction cinema, London and New York: Verso.

Suvin, D. (1979) Metamorphoses of Science Fiction: on the poetics and history of a literary genre, New Haven, CT: Yale University Press.

Tarratt, M. (1986) "Monsters from the Id," 1970, in B.K. Grant (ed.) Film Genre Reader II, Austin: University of Texas Press.

296

Žižek, S. (1991) *Looking Awry: an introduction to Jacques Lacan through popular culture*, Cambridge, MA: MIT Press.

—— (1999) *The Ticklish Subject: the absent centre of political ontology*, London: Verso.

—— (2001) *Enjoy Your Symptom!: Jacques Lacan in Hollywood and out*, London and New York: Routledge.

30

QUEER THEORY

Wendy Gay Pearson

Canadian journalist Robert Fulford recently published an attack on queer theory, which he defines as "an academic discipline that prides itself on finding gay subtexts in apparently heterosexual stories" (Fulford 2007: A22). A worse definition of queer theory would be hard to find, but Fulford's fulminations are rendered entirely, if unintentionally, humorous when he notes that his target, a postdoctoral fellow, Jes Battis, "writes about everything from hidden gay themes in TV to comedies like *Buffy the Vampire Slayer*." His objections to queer *Buffy* studies are remarkable, however, given that the series does indeed include queer characters, making the search for subtext moot. In season four, Willow came out as a lesbian and mere months after Fulford's article the protagonist herself became involved in a same-sex affair with another female vampire slayer in issue 12 of the comic book that continues where the television show ended (Gustines 2008). This would seem to make both Buffy and *Buffy* pretty queer. Perhaps the only other onscreen female sf character to have excited such intense academic interest is Ripley from the *Alien* films (1979–97), who seems almost created to provoke queer readings that are not at all about homoerotic subtext. Indeed, queer theory's prime interest is in the workings of the normative, that is, of the ways in which discourses about what is and is not "normal" function to discipline human bodies and behaviors.

From its somewhat nebulous inception, queer theory was a powerful tool for the utopian project of rethinking the politics and history of sexuality and, extending from sexuality's centrality to the contemporary Western psyche, pretty much everything else: "an understanding of virtually any aspect of Western culture must be, not merely incomplete, but damaged in its central substance to the degree that it does not incorporate a critical analysis of modern homo/heterosexual definition" (Sedgwick 1990: 1). According to Foucault (1980), the modern world has so overvalued sexuality that it has come to seem central to everything that humans are and do, and has become subject to – perhaps even the central subject of – a new discipline of "normalcy." Where earlier regimes had depended on established authorities, notably religion, to determine proper from improper, saint from sinner, by the late nineteenth century an entire disciplinary regime of "biopower," bolstered by the new authorities of science, medicine, psychiatry, criminology, and statistics, was in place, defining the good as what is most common (hence Derek Jarman's quip that "Heterosexuality isn't normal, it's just common" (Jarman 1992: 19)).

Ros Jennings (1995) points to a number of moments in the *Alien* films in which issues of gender and sexuality are rendered in ways that either reinforce or subvert normative expectations. For most of its duration, *Alien* (Scott 1979) appears to subvert gender conventions and also, perhaps, simplistic expectations that the Hollywood protagonist must be heterosexual by allowing Ripley a "male" narrative role and by failing to code her as heterosexual. However, the conclusion reinscribes normative discourses of gender and sexuality, when Ripley, dressed in a vest and skimpy underwear, is exposed to the viewer's gaze. This gaze is presumptively male, the camera framing women's bodies from a masculine perspective that receives erotic pleasure from the act of looking (Mulvey 1975). Jennings argues that:

> The interest of this scene … is in how it is constructed for maximum voyeur-istic effect. For a few brief minutes it sexualizes Ripley in a way that is not even hinted at in the rest of the film … By rendering her available to male voyeurism, Scott's control of filming in the final scene ensures that in addition to the "so-called masculine" traits of bravery, technical ability, and so on … she now signifies a wholly intelligible form of femininity.
>
> (Jennings 1995: 196, 197)

Restoring Ripley to this form also involves recuperating her for heterosexuality by making her available to the voyeuristic male gaze. Gender, in this sense, is always already a function of sexuality, since women become women in the process of becoming the objects of men's desire. In other words, sexual difference is not merely the necessary ground for heterosexuality, but also the product of it. Drawing on the work of Luce Irigaray, Judith Butler argues that sexual difference is not a fact but a question, "the question for our times," and that the problem is "how to cross this otherness? How to cross it without crossing it, without domesticating its terms? How to remain attuned to what remains permanently unsettled about the question?" (Butler 2004: 177). In thinking about Butler's consideration of the endurance of sexual difference, the diffi-culties of crossing it, and the extent to which, for many people, any movement beyond or outside of it is quite literally unthinkable, we need to ask about the relationship between sexual difference and gender. The distinctions that people draw between these terms – some argue that gender is feminism's object of study, while sex and sexuality belong to lesbian and gay studies; the Vatican insists that gender in human rights language is "nothing other than a code for homosexuality"; some feminists claim that "sexual difference is the preferred term to gender, that 'sexual difference' indicates a fundamental difference, and that gender indicates a merely constructed and variable effect" (Butler 2004: 181) – suggests a petrification of meaning at the level of the body: gender may be what the body *does*, but sexual difference is what it *is*. Butler notes, however, that "the body gives rise to language, and that language carries bodily aims, and performs bodily deeds that are not always understood by those who use language to accomplish certain conscious aims" (Butler 2004: 199).

In Ursula K. Le Guin's experiment with gender, *The Left Hand of Darkness* (1969), her use of male pronouns for the hermaphroditic Gethenians produces particular, albeit variable, imaginative relationships between the reader's own embodiment and the bodies of her aliens, who have neither permanent genders nor sexual differences, but who, as a result, tell us something about whether gender and sexual difference can be thought of as distinct ontological categories, that is, specific types of being-in-the-world. The relationship between gender and sexual difference is thus much more problematic than a simple dichotomy between being and doing. Where Le Guin simply removes the framework for sexual difference, Butler asks why it cannot "itself move beyond binarity into multiplicity?" (Butler 2004: 197):

> If the new gender politics argues against the idealization of dimorphism, then does it argue against the primacy of sexual difference itself? And if technologies of the body (surgical, hormonal, athletic) generate new forms of gender, is this precisely in the service of inhabiting a body more fully or does it constitute a perilous effacement? It seems crucial to keep these questions open so that we might work theoretically and politically in broad coalitions. The lines we draw are invitations to cross over and that crossing over, as any nomadic subject knows, constitutes who we are.
>
> (Butler 2004: 203)

If sexual difference is the question for our times, it is therefore a question for sf, but one might also ask whether it is a question *of* sf. Is the meaning and "identity" of sf constituted by its various crossings over this particular question? Can we even begin to think about an sf that is not defined in advance by its relationship to sex or gender or sexual difference and to sexuality? Can we begin to articulate where in sf we might find works that are consciously crossing over the lines drawn around and between gender/s? I thus take the idea of "undoing gender" to stand in for a long series of questions that begin with the "fundamental nature" of sexual difference, the supposedly implacable necessity of sexual dimorphism and its relationship both to the bodies and to the ways of living in the world which it defines, and to the political and practical implications of feminist, queer, and postmodern projects which have often been taken as impractically and apolitically utopian – pie-in-the-sky theorizing which lacks material consequences. But the construction of sexual and gender binaries invariably has material effects, some of them extreme, even lethal (as I write this, a 19-year-old student in Britain waits for the results of his appeal against a deportation order that would return him to Iran, where his lover has already been arrested, tortured, and executed for the "crime" of homosexuality).

In Candas Jane Dorsey's *A Paradigm of Earth* (2001), the "queer" protagonist, Morgan, lives in a near-future Canada in which human rights are being chipped away, and in which being queer – that is, outside patriarchal heterosexual norms – is coming to have ever more drastic material consequences. Encountering an apparently closeted minor bureaucrat, Morgan thus asks the old, coded question "Are you a friend of Dorothy's?"

Chelsea blushed … "My mom used to say that. Yeah, I used to be, but I sold

Dorothy down the river about three years ago. I can't afford to take tea with Dorothy any more, the way things are."

(Dorsey 2001: 18)

Into this context of repression and hostility, Dorsey introduces an alien species, a small number of whom arrive in government buildings around the world. Before they are "erased" and left a blank slate for humans to teach as they will, one of them says, "Earth is needed to know." The Canadian government hires Morgan to raise "its" alien, Blue, because she is the first childcare worker to whom it responds, and because the secret-service official in charge of the alien, Mr Grey, is an "old-fashioned" cop who is not prejudiced against Morgan for her sexuality nor for the cooperative household she has established in a rundown mansion. Dorsey thus sets two visions of how the world might be against each other: a racially multicultural but otherwise not at all diverse near-future dystopia in which the haves have won the war against the have-nots and the world is being run by "the new breed of *fin-de-siècle* specialist, who had grown up language-challenged and idea-poor, believing the political cant of selfishness" (Dorsey 2001: 62); and a queer, communitarian, basically socialist approach, whose adherents believe in equality and participatory democracy. Unsurprisingly, most of Mr Grey's colleagues are suspicious and fearful of the visibly different alien, who has blue skin and no biological sex. Only Morgan and Mr Grey resist the temptation to assign the alien a gender. Through their concern for Blue and their mutual distaste for the Social Darwinist "dictatorship of meanness" (Dorsey 2001: 62), Morgan and Mr Grey become unlikely allies.

A Paradigm of Earth rings the changes on the themes and situation of *The Left Hand of Darkness*. While Le Guin has a single human, Genly Ai, arrive on Gethen, where everyone is hermaphroditic and where "gender" as he understands it makes no sense at all, Dorsey places a single hermaphroditic alien in a future not dissimilar to the reader's present. Like *The Left Hand of Darkness*, Dorsey's novel is informed by the sex/gender politics of its time, notably the swing – variable but apparent throughout the Western world – to the political right, to more conservative, more patriarchal assumptions about what is normal, and to a more oppressive response to the problems posed by the diversity of human sexuality. The encounter with an alien or aliens for whom sex and gender work quite differently exposes both how constructed and thoroughly naturalized ideas about sex, gender, and sexuality are in any given time and place. Both novels also reveal, not always deliberately, the homogenizing power of "normal" and the extent to which discourses of normalcy discipline human populations to remain within a narrow range of authorized and approved behaviors.

William B. Turner writes that "Queer theory results from a particular conceptual break that has occurred unevenly in western Europe and the United States [and Canada, Australia and New Zealand] since World War II" and which may, in part, have resulted from recognizing "the moral and political bankruptcy of Nazism" (Turner 2000: 3). The fascists' program of racial perfection derived from many of the important and ascendant discourses of the late nineteenth and early twentieth centuries, including assumptions about the role and purpose of sex (indeed, homophobia and patriarchal heterosexuality were central to Nazism: to ensure the triumph of the race, men had to be convinced that their function was to impregnate women and women that their role was to bear Aryan babies). Whatever its causes, the post-Second World War period in the West was increasingly one of dissatisfaction with the oppressive regime of sexual norms and of a growing desire to understand how normative ideologies had come to assume such an apparently naturalized force within human society. The results were manifold: the Civil Rights movement, second-wave feminism, and a burgeoning lesbian and gay activist movement that was not, initially, reducible to "gay rights," but that saw gay liberation as presaging a more broadly based movement toward sexual liberation for all humanity and a new search for what Michel Foucault called "as yet unforeseen kinds of relationships" (Foucault 1997: 229).

One of the ways in which *A Paradigm of Earth* reveals the triumph of a neoconservative ideology is through characters who assert that queerness is "unnatural": for example, a letter to the editor supporting a new law changing the age of consent for same-sex sexual activity to 25 maintains that, "If impressionable young men and women are exposed to these unnatural pleasures before they have had the opportunity to make a commitment to spouse and family, society risks losing any chance to reproduce itself" (Dorsey 2001: 16). With a population of more than six billion, logic would suggest that encouraging reproduction is tolerably absurd – but there are always more underlying discourses than simple homophobia. In the West, at least, concerns over falling birth rates are also about maintaining an economic system dependent on perpetual growth and about the white population of European-settled countries losing ground to more recent immigrants. By linking neoconservatism and neoliberalism with repressive sexual ideologies, Social Darwinist approaches to the welfare of citizens, and an increasingly patriarchal and authoritarian state, Dorsey echoes Foucault's contention that contemporary disciplinary regimes are founded on a "biopower" that emerged in the mid-nineteenth century and took sex as its primary object: "Sex was a means of access both to the life of the body and the life of the species. It was employed as a standard for the disciplines and as a basis for regulation … Broadly speaking, at the juncture of the 'body' and the 'population,' sex became a crucial target of a power organized around the management of life rather than the menace of death" (Foucault 1980: 146, 147). Foucault notes that this transformation from using the threat of death to using disciplines and discourses of bodily health, propriety, and normality to regulate behavior, emerged at the same time as and worked in concert with the emergence of "racism in its modern, 'biologizing' statist form" (Foucault 1980: 149). The result was "a long series of permanent interventions at the level of the body, conduct, health, and everyday life, [which] received their color and their justification from the mythical concern with protecting the purity of the blood and ensuring the triumph of the race" (Foucault 1980: 149).

The shift in Dorsey's futuristic multicultural Canada is from "race" in its "biologizing" sense to species, and to the fear that the aliens' arrival creates. If "we" are not alone, then who are these others? And once their emissaries have learnt from us, what will the aliens, with their presumably superior technology, do with this knowledge? Is Blue simply on Earth to learn what it means to be human or is there a more sinister purpose behind its education? However, as Mr Grey says, when Blue is eventually taken back by whomever sent it, "Earth has sent an emissary after all" (Dorsey 2001: 341). His daughter objects that the alien cannot be "an emissary to its own people," but Mr Grey points out that, by arriving as a tabula rasa, "Blue's only choice was to be human" (Dorsey 2001: 341). This is a neat reversal of racist discourse that claims that racial (or species) lines are profoundly othering and cannot be crossed (furthermore, in a nice albeit minor debunking not merely of racism but speciesism, Mr Grey was initially referring to Marbl, the cat Blue was holding when reclaimed by the mothership, as the first emissary from Earth). This conclusion is a further riff on *The Left Hand of Darkness*, at the end of which Genly Ai comes to see the hermaphroditic Gethenians as normal and as human, while his colleagues from the Ekumen – locked in single-sex bodies and constantly ready for sex, rather than experiencing sexual readiness on a cyclical basis – seem to him both alien and perverted.

Blue has no choice but to be human. Its people are likely to seem alien to it, as Genly's do to him. Blue tells Morgan, "They wanted a Rosetta Stone, but you can't make a Rosetta Stone if you know only one language … Even if I have memories of another life somewhere in here, and they re-activate them, they will not line up in a translation table with the memories I have now. They will both be local grammars, with no way to integrate them" (Dorsey 2001: 316–7). Ironically, Blue becomes not only an emissary from Earth, but rather *only* an emissary from Earth. Reading *The Left Hand of Darkness* through Blue's reflections, one wonders whether Genly, who went to Gethen as an adult with his own language, memories, and assumptions about the natural and the normal, will be able to translate across the gap between experiencing the world as unity (Gethen) and as duality (the Ekumen). In *A Paradigm of Earth*, the experience of different genders and sexualities is less localized, but Blue's inability to be categorized as male or female resonates with the fluidity of genders and sexualities in Morgan's life and household – and in queer theory.

Queer theory focuses not on explaining what it means to be lesbian or gay, but rather on understanding how the categories of homosexual and heterosexual – terms coined only in 1869 and 1892, respectively – came into being and what kinds of material effect these discourses of sexuality have on people's lives. It is thus unsurprising that queer theoretical work on sf has concentrated at least as much on work that appears "straight" or that even seems, on the surface, to have little to say about sexuality as it has on work by lesbian and gay writers or which overtly addresses sexual and gender issues. Just as feminist critiques of sf reveal the workings of sexist and patriarchal discourses within the genre, so queer critiques of sf reveal the workings of hetero-normativity. Heteronormativity presupposes that only heterosexuality is normal and assumes a very limited, hegemonic definition of heterosexuality that works in concert with equally essentialized notions of sex and gender (and of the inherent, "natural" match between biological sex and gender role). Thus heteronormativity has multiple effects: it dismisses as "abnormal" or "perverted" those who do not fit its gender norms, including transsexuals, intersex people, tomboys, "sissies," and effeminate men; and it severely regulates and disciplines the bodies and behaviors of heterosexually identified people. Heteronormativity can thus be best understood through notions of "good" and "bad" sex (see Rubin 1993), in which "bad" sex can occur on any of a number of axes, including the sex, gender role, race/ethnicity, and age of the partner, as well as numbers of partners, degree of commitment to the relationship, willingness to adhere to social norms, such as marriage, and to avoid non-sanctioned behaviors, such as sex in public or the use of prophylactics, pornography, sex toys, and so on. In other words, heteronormativity does not simply embrace all potential sexual relationships between people of "opposite" sexes; rather, it disallows anything outside a remarkably limited range of behaviors.

Heteronormativity occurs with considerable frequency in sf texts, where breaches of its expectations function as taken-for-granted markers of particular types of culture. For example, when cyberpunk texts want to represent the decadence and emotional emptiness of life in their urban near futures, nonnormative sexualities, along with criminality and violence, mark out and delimit these settings. In William Gibson's "Johnny Mnemonic" (1981), the sleaziness and futuristic degeneracy of the bar scene is marked by the presence on the door of the "Magnetic Dog Sisters," one black, one white, "but aside from that as nearly identical as cosmetic surgery could make them. They'd been lovers for years ... I was never quite sure which one had originally been male" (Gibson 1998: 190). In a few brief sentences, Gibson manages to suggest inter-racial sex, incest (they are nearly identical "sisters"), lesbianism, and transsexuality. In *Johnny Mnemonic* (Longo 1995), they appear unnamed, transformed into bad guy Ralfi's bodyguards, their degeneracy visually marked by their extreme thinness, bizarre makeup, suggestive costumes, and the film's general use of film noir conventions. Like low-rent hip-hop groupies, they call other women "bitch." The black one is obviously a man in drag, and the white one licks tongues with Ralfi to emphasize the animal-istic, amoral quality of cyberpunk's post-everything sexualities. Both the story and the film use nonnormative sexualities to denote evil, even though the story, unlike the film, provides Molly Millions with a highly nonnormative gender role: she becomes both protagonist and hero, while Johnny is merely the story's motivation and its recorder, a role more commonly reserved for women. The story, then, is ambivalent in its queerness, at once "queering" Molly's – and, by necessity, Johnny's – gender, yet retaining normative sexual conventions as ways of distinguishing good and evil. The film is simply normative. Molly is transformed into a character called Jane, but she does not even have the agency of her namesake in *Tarzan the Ape Man* (Van Dyke 1932), who mocks her father's authority, rejects the appropriate suitor, and ends up as Tarzan's partner and equal in a new "queer" family with Cheetah the chimp in the role of child.

In addition to questioning representational heteronormativity, queer theory has also begun to critique "homonormativity," a "politics that does not contest dominant heteronormative assumptions and institutions but upholds and sustains them, while promising the possibility of a semi-mobilized gay constituency and a privatized, de-politicized gay culture anchored in domesticity and consumption" (Duggan 2003: 50). The same-sex marriage issue has been categorized as profoundly homonormative, entrenching rights for predominantly white, predominantly middle-class couples at the expense of everyone else, but particularly the most marginalized and disenfranchised.

The logic of assimilation that creates "good" queer citizens is founded, as Eric O. Clarke (2000) demonstrates, on discourses of subjunctivity (the condition of acting "as if"), in which, in order to acquire equality with their heterosexual peers, lesbian and gay people are required to behave *as if* they were heterosexual and thus to create relationships based on a heteronormative model, save for the biological sex of the partner. Such a logic of assimilation has complex consequences, both positive and negative. On the one hand, same-sex marriage exerts a symbolic freight which allows lesbian and gay people to be understood as more than superficially "equal" to straight people, indeed, to *belong* to the nation. On the other hand, as Anna M. Agathangelou *et al.* ask, "What bodies, desires, and longings must be criminalized and annihilated to produce the good queer subjects, politics, and desires that are being solidified with the emergence of homonormativity?" (Agathangelou *et al.* 2008: 124) While historically, racist discourses on the part of the colonizer displaced homosexual and nonnormative heterosexual behaviors onto the colonized, who were figured as "sodomites," more recently these discourses have been reversed and it has been the colonized and the marginalized who have produced their own discourses eliding homosexuality from their midst – as in Zimbabwe's Robert Mugabe, who insists that homosexuality is a European import and not "natural" or native to Africans. In a similar fashion, predominantly white-run homophobic organizations in the US, such as Focus on the Family, have attempted to convince traditionally liberal African-American voters that gay rights is a "white issue," thus creating an obviously counterfactual strand of public discourse in which homosexuals are all white and blacks are all heterosexual. At the same time, trenchant critiques of racist and classist practices among parts of the lesbian and gay community have revealed the extent to which working-class lesbians and gay men and queer people of color may be condemned to various forms of social marginalization.

These questions are not simple. Queer theory, operating both to reveal and to oppose heteronormativity, has come into conflict not only with religious fundamentalism and political neoconservatism but also with assimilationist and homonormative politics. This creates a sense of discomfort with queer theory in parts of the lesbian and gay community: after all, if one's greatest desire is to be "normal," then it is disconcerting to have the value of normalcy questioned from its very foundations. At the same time, much community-formation for lesbians and gays has revolved around coalitions of differences; insofar as queer theory posits a future beyond or "after" gay, it creates discomfort from this perspective also. This leads to the curiously contradictory position assumed by many who claim essential identities: those who believe that they were "born gay," insist that gayness is not a significant axis of difference and should not prevent them from being recognized as normal, while simultaneously accusing queer theory of "de-gaying" and of removing queer people's essential difference from the straight community by positing fluid sexualities which are unattached to identities.

These issues have also been taken up within sf in a variety of ways. For example, in Joy Parks's "Instinct" (2006), an unhappy lesbian goes to a matchmaking service only to find herself diverted into a queer underground. One might assume this is taking place because the society is repressive, but in this story the opposite is true.

Assimilation has produced a society in which there were no real queers: "equal doesn't mean the same. And by the time we figured out what was really going on, we were done for. They finally got it right. All those years of hating us had only made us stronger. But it only took a couple of decades of acceptance to make us disappear" (Parks 2006: 56). Acceptance becomes obliteration; when more than half the population engages in same-sex sexuality, when anyone who wants a sex change can become a nuMan or a nuWoman, something seems to be lost. As the underground lesbian says, "there's no community. We're too fractured. We're everywhere ... and nowhere. It's a whole new way of being invisible" (Parks 2006: 57). Offered the option to go to the "past" (a recreated community in the wilderness outside the domes in which "everyone" lives), the protagonist chooses not the organic, communal 1970s nor the hip, sexy 1980s nor the domestic, partners-with-children 1990s, but rather the fully repressive 1950s. The flipside of lesbians who want a visible dyke life turns out to be conservatives who want to go back to the good old days and who volunteer to recreate the homophobia of the past. The protagonist slips into femme drag, and heads off to follow her "instincts": "How can you survive without instincts? Take gaydar, for instance. That was real, you know ... and you needed it back then. To figure people out. To not get slapped or arrested. Or killed. It made us special" (Parks 2006: 57).

"Instinct" posits an either/or future of assimilation or repression. Either you are different, and thus exist but are persecuted for it, or you are the same, and cease to exist. If "Instinct" can find no way out of this dilemma, what can we bring to it by reading it through queer theory? Of course, since queer theory is a fluid and slippery field, one might have to begin by defining whose version of queer theory one is talking about. However, it seems to me that any reader might question whether "being special" is worth the price of being persecuted or killed when one has a choice; for those of us in the real world who face the material consequences of queerness every day, the issue of choice is a great deal less simple. Many opponents of queer theory assume that its alignment with constructivism means that it assumes that sexuality is a free choice, which is not at all the case. In fact, most scholars in the field have deliberately avoided or refused the question. Asked about whether he thought homosexuality is learned or innate, Foucault replied, "On this question I have absolutely nothing to say. 'No comment,'" and added, when pressed, "It's not my problem, and I don't like talking about things that are not really the object of my work. On this question I have only an opinion; since it is only an opinion, it is without interest" (Foucault 1997: 142). In fact, Foucault also avoids the question for fear his answer would attain "authority" simply because of his reputation, but the very asking of the question suggests a complete failure to understand his work on sexuality, which is genealogical, rather than historical in the usual sense. That is, it specifically eschews the search for origins in favor of more localized effects, patterns of transmission, shifts in discourse, concentrations and dispersions of material effects. Eve Kosofsky Sedgwick and Judith Butler, two of the figures most associated with queer theory, have given similar responses to the question of origins. The question is not interesting in part because it is unanswerable and in part because what is important is what happens once someone has constituted, or has had constituted for them, a sexual identity. Sexuality can only take place, like every aspect of human life, within culture; it is culture that gives meaning to what we are and to what we do. And, in our culture, discourses of normalcy have predominantly come to shape the interpretative habits and skills we bring to bear on manifestations of sexuality. It is thus these discourses which most need to be challenged by sf's power to imagine alternative possibilities for the ways in which we live, and love, in the world. If it takes a television show like *Buffy* or a novel like *A Paradigm of Earth* to do that, well, bring on the lesbian, gay, and bisexual vampires, and the queer blue aliens.

Bibliography

Agathangelou, A.M., Bassichis, M.D., and Spira, T.L. (2008) "Intimate Investments: homonormativity, global lockdown, and the seductions of empire," *Radical History Review*, 100 (winter): 120–43.

Ahmed, S. (2006) *Queer Phenomenology: orientations, objects, others*, Durham, NC: Duke University Press.

Battis, J. (2006) "The Kryptonite Closet: silence and queer secrecy in *Smallville*," *JumpCut*, 48. Online. Available HTTP: <http://www.ejumpcut.org/archive/jc48.2006/gaySmallville/index.html> (accessed 1 April 2008).

Burr, V. (2003) "Ambiguity and Sexuality in *Buffy the Vampire Slayer*: a Sartrean analysis," *Sexualities*, 6(3–4): 342–60.

Butler, J. (2004) *Undoing Gender*, New York: Routledge.

Clarke, E.O. (2000) *Virtuous Vice: homoeroticism and the public sphere*, Durham, NC: Duke University Press.

Dorsey, C.J. (2001) *A Paradigm of Earth*, New York: Tor Books.

Duggan, L. (2003) *The Twilight of Equality? Neoliberalism, cultural politics, and the attack on democracy*, Boston: Beacon.

Foucault, M. (1980) *The History of Sexuality, vol. 1: An Introduction*, trans. R. Hurley, New York: Vintage.

—— (1997) "Sexual Choice, Sexual Act," in P. Rabinow (ed.) *Ethics: subjectivity and truth*, trans. R. Hurley *et al.*, Essential Works of Michel Foucault, 1954–84, vol. 1, 1994, London: Penguin

Fulford, R. (2007) "Lex Luthor Hearts Superman: your tax dollars at work," *National Post*, 13 October: A22.

Gibson, W. (1998) "Johnny Mnemonic," in B. Thomsen and M.H. Greenberg (eds) *Cyberfilms: the stories that became the films*, New York: BP Books.

Gustines, G.G. (2008) "Experimenting in Bed When not after Vampires," *New York Times*, 5 March. Books. Online. Available HTTP: <http://www.nytimes.com/2008/03/05/books/05buffy.html> (accessed 1 April 2008).

Hacking, I. (1990) *The Taming of Chance*, Cambridge: Cambridge University Press.

Jarman, D. (1992) *At Your Own Risk: a saint's testament*, London: Hutchinson.

Jennings, R. (1995) "Desire and Design: Ripley undressed," in T. Wilton (ed.) *Immortal, Invisible: lesbians and the moving image*, New York: Routledge.

Mulvey, L. (1975) "Visual Pleasure and Narrative Cinema," *Screen*, 16(3): 6–18.

Parks, J. (2006) "Instinct," in R. Labonté and L. Schimel (eds) *The Future is Queer*, Vancouver: Arsenal Pulp Press.

Rubin, G. (1993) "Thinking Sex: notes for a radical theory of the politics of sexuality," in H. Abelove, M.A. Barale, and D.M. Halperin (eds) *The Lesbian and Gay Studies Reader*, New York: Routledge.

Sedgwick, E.K. (1990) *The Epistemology of the Closet*, Berkeley: University of California Press.

Turner, W.B. (2000) *A Genealogy of Queer Theory*, Philadelphia: Temple University Press.

31

UTOPIAN STUDIES

Alcena Madeline Davis Rogan

The concept of "utopia," which dates from antiquity, is developed in modes as disparate as fiction, philosophy, theology, epistemology, praxis (as living experiments), political philosophy, and critical theory. Working from the perspective of utopian studies, this introductory overview is almost exclusively limited to consideration of utopian literatures in English. It privileges the concept of "utopia" as expressed through fiction, as well as utopian theory by scholars whose fields of inquiry include both sf and utopia. Following a short discussion of the emergence of utopian studies as a contemporary academic discipline, I will offer a sampling of major literary utopias since the 1500s, concentrating on their historically situated themes, before discussing some major political and philosophical utopian concepts. I will consider several major works of recent utopian critical and literary theory, and close with a few thoughts on the problem of the distinction between utopian thought and praxis, and, by extension, the problem of definition vis-à-vis utopia.

Utopian studies – as distinguished from intertextual fictional debates over the politics of various utopian visions and from sociopolitical debates over utopia – might be dated roughly from the 1960s, when there was a major expansion of potential fields of academic study. This coincided with several other developments that influenced the development of utopian studies, including the growing acceptance of cultural studies as a discipline; a growth explosion in college education and, by extension, its unprecedented accessibility to groups not historically represented in academe who brought new areas of interest to scholarship; and, finally, the revitalization of interest in thought-experiments, such as utopias, by the youth culture of the mid- to late 1960s. Utopian studies' status as a thriving academic discipline coincides roughly with the development of the Society for Utopian Studies, a scholarly research group founded in 1975, which describes itself as "an international, interdisciplinary association devoted to the study of utopianism in all its forms, with a particular emphasis on literary and experimental utopias" (Society for Utopian Studies 2007). While "utopian studies has undergone a dramatic growth in the last three decades," it "remains a relatively new field of academic study" (Levitas 1990: 156).

The journal of the Society for Utopian Studies, *Utopian Studies*, put the field on the contemporary scholarly map. Its articles often develop theses out of the study of sf. Likewise, the journal *Science Fiction Studies*, founded in 1973 – which had a similarly galvanizing effect on scholarship addressing sf – often includes considerations of works that are generally considered to be, generically, utopias. Thus there has been, from the emergence and consolidation of sf studies and utopian studies, considerable cross-fertilization in terms of texts studied and of scholars engaged in both disciplines.

Most definitions of the literary utopia begin with the founding work of the genre, Sir Thomas More's *Utopia* (1516), first translated into English from Latin in 1551 by Ralph Robynson. More coined the term "utopia," which is a derivation of the word "outopia," meaning "no place." More's *Utopia*, then, is specifically not a eutopia, an exclusively "good place," but is rather an often satirical rendering of a non-place that refers to, but does not adhere to, the concept of utopia as a completely idealized space, such as, for Western Christianity, heaven. Although More's Utopia includes a consideration of religion as part of its structure, it is not commonly read as a blueprint for religious beliefs but rather as a critique of existing religious practices. While utopia is commonly thought of as the perfect place, More's Utopia, as a "no place," does not represent his idea of the ultimately ideal, attainable place, but serves as a blank slate upon which he inscribes a world that is intended to estrange the contemporary reader from their conditions of existence, thus allowing them to see their own world in a new light. In other words, More's *Utopia* is political satire in the sf mode of cognitive estrangement (see Suvin 1979). Lyman Tower Sargent defines the literary utopia as "a non-existent society described in considerable detail and normally located in time and space" (Sargent 1994: 9). Other influential early modern utopias include Sir Francis Bacon's *The New Atlantis* (1627), James Harrington's political essay *The Commonwealth of Oceana* (1656), and Margaret Cavendish's *The Description of a New World, Called the Blazing-World* (1666), all of which feature, in a mode characterized by earnestness rather than More's satire, elaborations of worlds that refer to their contemporary historical moments by positing corrective versions of existing religious, property, gender, and/or political relations. In fact, these last three works more properly fit the definition of the category of utopia called eutopian, because the worlds that they describe are specifically "good" places. Both utopias and eutopias are found in early modern literature: the fiction or tract writer's decision to depict utopia as either a "no place" or an alternative social blueprint depends on the rhetorical form. Generally, More's satirical mode gives way to utopian Enlightenment idealism in the late seventeenth century. This idealism extends through the Romantic era and includes critical feminist works which flourished in the eighteenth and nineteenth centuries.

The eutopia or "positive utopia" is "a non-existent society described in considerable detail and normally located in time and space that the author intended a contemporaneous reader to view as considerably better than the society in which that reader lived" (Sargent 1994: 9). It became less popular as the historical conditions conducive to unreserved idealism regarding the transformative powers of science-as-progress faded. As Ruth Levitas and Lucy Sargisson note, "Utopia is not dead, but the kind of utopianism that is holistic, social, future-located, committed, and linked to the present by some identifiable narrative of change – a kind of collective optimism of the intellect as well as the will – is culturally problematic" (Levitas and Sargisson 2003: 15). Thus, by the middle of the nineteenth century, the idea that a specifically "good" place might be achieved through human agency under the correct social conditions, as posited by Bacon, Harrington, and Cavendish, no longer seems plausible.

Eighteenth-century literary utopias and utopian political treatises tended, unsurprisingly, to focus on the importance of reason, specifically the applicability of reason to social governance and the health of the social body. Plato's *Republic* (c. 360 BC), with its focus on good governance as a means of producing and maintaining "just" subjects and social conditions, became an important text for the genre during an era marked by literary and politico-philosophical neoclassicism. Samuel Johnson's *Rasselas* (1759), a meditation upon the problem of governmentally mandated "utopia" versus the realization of utopia as the individual's prerogative, is one of the most well-known eighteenth-century utopias in this tradition. Jonathan Swift's *Gulliver's Travels* (1726) also takes up the theme of the problem of governmentally mandated "utopian" states, although in a radically different prose style. Swift's satirical representations of extreme versions of the governed "good life," from visions of the impossibly deluded society to the impossibly "reasonable" philosopher's society, prefigure Johnson's impossibly idle feudalistic enclave, the Happy Valley. However, unlike Swift, Johnson finds the potential for utopian hope in reason: the prisoners of the (un)Happy Valley are rescued by reason, in the form of a wise scholar. In Swift's vision, scholars are complacent to the point of somnambulism: reason, like anything else taken to extremes, fails as a form of governance for a utopia. Of course, the rejection of extremes is in itself an important theme for Enlightenment-era political philosophers.

Feminism is seriously thematized in several eighteenth-century utopias, reflecting the variety of new Enlightenment-inspired discourses on the problem of women's subjugation. In works such as Sarah Scott's *A Description of Millenium Hall and the Country Adjacent* (1762) and Lady Mary Hamilton's *Munster Village* (1778), intricate social structures are described wherein women, in a semi-sequestered state, are allowed the opportunity to develop as intellectuals and workers: they also enjoy sensual pleasures such as good food and drink. A major theme shared by feminist utopias of this period is the importance of women's education. In feminist political philosophy and feminist utopian novels, the most popular argument made on behalf of a woman's right to education was its inherently reasonable utility for both sexes. Eighteenth-century feminist utopias provided influential and moving portraits of how radically women could improve their lot if they were granted equal status as thinking subjects.

Mid- to late nineteenth- and early twentieth-century utopias took a critical turn, abandoning the idealism generally characteristic of the eighteenth century. These utopias differ from later "critical utopias," which are "intended [for] a contemporaneous reader to view as better than contemporary society but with difficult problems that the described society may or may not be able to solve and which [take] a critical view of the Utopian genre" (Sargent 1994: 9). Edward Bellamy's *Looking Backward: 2000–1887* (1888) and Charlotte Perkins Gilman's *Herland* (1915) are classic utopian, as opposed to eutopian or critical utopian, texts, because they both thematize the potentially transformative and liberatory powers of technology in a "good place" that is also explicitly "no place." From parthenogenesis to more efficient rail systems, technology – in the right hands, of course – is a workable means toward a more sustainable, humane, and independent world. Such thought-experiments are often characterized as lacking in writerly craft: they are generally received as highly didactic works that often feature a protagonist alien to the utopian society, who must be schooled in the ways of the "good," alien space. This protagonist serves a cognitively estranging function, as his or her reactions of delight and disbelief refer the reader to the fallen contemporary world from which the protagonist has traveled. Whereas the eutopia tends to be a self-contained and totalizing portrait of another world, utopias of the late nineteenth and early twentieth centuries highlight this dialogue between the denizens of utopia and the unenlightened visitor. This is an important distinction because it signals an increasingly disenchanted worldview: these utopias do not encompass or constitute The World, but are rather one spatio-temporal zone located on the perimeter of a fallen contemporary world.

The thematization of the contemporary political sphere via its estrangement through utopian visions of various types is a major defining feature of literary utopias. Sociopolitical and philosophical treatises on the possibility of utopian ways of living are an integral part of the history of the literary utopia – indeed, generically utopian literary works such as William Morris's *News from Nowhere* (1890) serve to blur the literary/sociopolitical distinction, as it is an explicit response, from a socialist theorist, lecturer, and novelist, to the political problems presented by *Looking Backward*. Bellamy's technophilic, utilitarian utopia prescribes, essentially, an approach to the tools of the industrial revolution that maximizes worker efficiency and thus, by extension, leisure time in which to enjoy bourgeois trappings and pursuits. However, the novel reinscribes class stratifications and does not address the alienating effects of industrialized labor. In stark contrast, *News from Nowhere* presumes labor's pleasurable function in the formation and sustenance of a socialist utopian state. Morris represents work as pleasure: specifically, he breaks down the distinction between work and leisure time by representing forms of labor that are shared and unalienated (although, notably, he retains the gendered division of labor). Both novel and socialist polemic, this popular and influential book opens up the question of sociopolitical writings on utopia.

Gilman's *Herland* is the most famous feminist utopian novel of this period, and serves in some important ways as a rejoinder to both Bellamy's and Morris's politically insufficient utopian visions. Gilman demonstrates that a genuinely utopian vision must include, in a rigorous manner and as a centrally thematized problem, serious consideration of the needs of the vast majority of the population (that is to say, women and children) in order to be truly utopian. By prioritizing issues around children, motherhood, women's intellectual development, and their physical comfort and capacities, Gilman shows us, via the device of a group of disbelieving men, how estranged from the ideal of gender equality her readers really are.

The idea of feminist philosophical and literary utopias as forms of praxis highlights once again the sense in which utopianism (as practice) and utopias are inter-implicated. Karl Marx and Friedrich Engels were famously hostile to much utopian sociopolitical thought, deeming it ultimately inadequate as a form of praxis. Socialist utopian blueprints, such as those found in the writings of Charles Fourier and Robert

Owen, were found problematic because they did not adequately concern themselves with the problem of the revolutionary transition to the socialist state, but rather confined their field of inquiry primarily to idealist visions of the post-revolutionary socialist state. The "utopian blueprint" thus elided what, for Marx and Engels, was a historical event to be effected by the proletariat via revolution, and which could not, by its very nature, be predicted in specific terms of form and long-term outcome. Moreover, the "utopian blueprint" is predicated on the dreams and desires of the historically situated individual doing the "blueprinting," whereas the attained socialist state in its particulars would reflect the needs and desires of an unalienated proletariat – and nobody, of course, could know what those needs and desires would be since the conditions for their existence were unrealized. Marx and Engels appreciated certain aspects of socialist utopian visions but, because they were set forth as very specific sets of practices, they were not seen as a viable form of socialist critique.

Utopia was reconsidered by a later group of Marxist theorists, notably early twentieth-century exiles from fascist Europe, as a useful epistemological category. I will focus here on the work of Herbert Marcuse, whose resurrection of Utopia-as-epistemology is very influential. Drawing on Sigmund Freud's theory regarding the necessary relationship between repression of the pleasure principle and the maintenance of civilization, Marcuse argues that, although it is indeed true that the pleasure principle must to some extent be repressed in order to maintain civilized relations between people, it is also the case that, under the capitalist mode of production, the amount of labor required of the individual is excessive. This excess is artificially produced by the mode of production, which exacts labor in excess of actual demand (excess labor leads to excess, or surplus, repression), and artificially maintained by the mode of production through the promotion of false needs, which the laborer willingly attempts to acquire by laboring in excess of actual demand. Therefore, Marcuse reasons, the Marxist utopian objective is the release of the worker from artificially high amounts of labor, which would then result in a rearrangement of human desires that would eliminate false needs.

As in Fourier and Owen's visions, the conditions for utopia are predicated on the attainment of unalienated labor. Unlike Fourier or Owen, however, Marcuse is skeptical about the possibility of imagining a socialist utopia in its particulars, although he does speculate on the necessary conditions for its development. Like Marx and Engels, he recognizes that the historical conditions do not exist in which one might usefully speculate on what our false needs would be replaced with, much less what unalienated labor might look like. He does, however, insist on the need to reconceptualize and reutilize technological advances in the interests of minimizing the amount of labor necessary to sustain civilization.

Many theorists and social pioneers have attempted to create the conditions necessary for minimally repressive work and work conditions – and, by extension, a space in which unalienated social relations might emerge. Although these efforts necessarily take place in a marginalized relation to the dominant culture, and thus are susceptible to the development of their own sets of false hopes and alienations, they are nonetheless important manifestations of another area of inquiry for utopian studies: the intentional community or commune. Many intentional communities have been inspired by utopian socialist writers. Fourier and Owen, in the early nineteenth century, both inspired the development of communal living based on such principles as the abolition of sexist divisions of labor; the development of as-much-as-possibly self-sustaining living and work environments; the abolition of most private-property ownership; and respect for the land, among others. More than a century later, B.F. Skinner's utopian/sf *Walden Two* (1948) inspired the development of intentional communities, most successfully Twin Oaks, which has much in common, in its principles, with Fourier's and Owen's utopian visions (but significantly not all – Fourier is the most vociferous and intelligent critic of women's sexual and intellectual subjugation). Twentieth- and twenty-first-century experiments in communal living are inspired by similar social justice ideals, with an increased focus on the problems of sexism, racism, and classism.

A consideration of "critical utopias" completes my survey of major utopian works. The critical utopia, which emerged as a dominant form of utopian writing during the 1960s and 1970s, tends to reflect the sociopolitical concerns of an era characterized by demands for change in the areas of global exploitation (the "Third World problem," ecological exploitation), gender inequality, race inequality, and class antagonism. These novels "reject utopia as a blueprint while preserving it as a dream," they "dwell on the conflict between the originary world and the utopian society opposed to it so that the process of social change is more directly articulated," and they "focus on the continuing presence of difference and imperfection within the utopian society itself and thus render more recognizable and dynamic alternatives" (Moylan 1986: 10–11). Such explicitly critical works of this era include novels by Suzy McKee Charnas, Samuel R. Delany, Ursula K. Le Guin, Marge Piercy, and Joanna Russ.

Further discussion of the critical utopia requires that we distinguish it from the dystopia, which does not retain the same tension between the possibility of utopia and the dark world-vision it presents. Dystopias reject both blueprint and dream. For example, Octavia E. Butler's *The Parable of the Sower* (1992) and *The Parable of the Talents* (1998) are, like much of her fiction, dystopian inasmuch as they present worst-case-scenario futures – proto-fascist, racist, and sexist US police states and ecological crisis – as the backdrop for her characters' struggles for survival. On the other hand, Butler's work does not reject the possibility of social change, although it must come slowly and through the grassroots efforts of (often problematically) diverse individuals. There does not appear to be a critical consensus regarding the usefulness of making a distinction between critical utopias and dystopias, which share many of the same characteristics. In a provisional way one might define dystopias as critical utopias that contain the *least* promise for the change or growth of the posited future or parallel space. Exemplary dystopias – that is to say, utopias that reject both the blueprint and the dream – include George Orwell's *Nineteen Eighty-Four* (1949) and Margaret Atwood's *The Handmaid's Tale* (1985). However, we run into the problem of definition again, as both Orwell and Atwood append faint but definite glimmers of hope to their dystopian visions.

The critical utopia explicitly rejects the totalized, blueprint ideal society and presents us instead with a set of social problems and a spatio-temporal context or contexts in which they might usefully be addressed. They do not claim to have The Answer, as in the carefully mapped utopian alternate universe of a Bellamy, Morris, or Gilman. Instead, they postulate possible answers. Thus, for instance, Delany's *Triton* (1976) posits the coexistence of a variety of modes and means of living viably, from street-level anonymous subsistence to highly organized group housing arrangements of varying degrees of affluence. In Charnas's *The Furies* (1994), women occupy a wide variety of viable splinter groups, from those who would keep men enslaved and used only for reproductive purposes to those who work toward establishing (a long-shattered) harmony between the sexes. Although critical utopias and dystopias certainly made their appearance before the second half of the twentieth century, utopian fiction from the 1950s onwards tends toward these varieties.

I will now turn to some important recent theoretical work on the conjunction of utopia and sf, most notably Fredric Jameson's *Archaeologies of the Future* (2005). Here, like Jameson, I wish to displace "the inquiry away from content ... and substitute the question, What difficulties must be overcome in imagining or representing Utopia? for the seemingly more urgent investigation of the nature of Utopian desire and the substance of its hope" (Jameson 2005: 84). Jameson addresses the formal generic properties of a formidable variety of utopian texts, punctuating this "formalist approach" (Jameson 2005: 85) with an inquiry into the theoretical challenges that utopia presents. Specifically, he is concerned with the problem of utopian desire, because, as much as Jameson grapples with the meaning of utopia through available interpretive devices, none of them can precisely answer. Utopia, as Jameson theorizes it, is the expression of or collective yearning for that which cannot be fulfilled – in other words, it is a desire, so its representation is always highly contingent and its realization necessarily impossible.

The problematic nature of the representation of utopia is a standard feature of literature on the subject: Louis Marin points out, in his *Utopics: spatial play* (1973), that the etymology of "utopia" brings up the problem of its radical instability, that the Greek *ou* or no, and *topos* or place, combine to identify utopia, traditionally defined as a "good place" as at one and the same time necessarily a "no place." But it is because of this instability that Marin sees utopia as a useful theoretical device, because utopias typically represent the tension between a fallen now and the "good place" that might come out of a critical recognition of its fallen state. Marin notes that utopias can be useful indices of how *un*-utopian our world really is, and that furthermore they can, in their degenerate versions, allow us to see how our sense of historical awareness is crippled when we provide ourselves with safe, unreal no-place zones in which to play out our paltry fantasies (his famous example of this phenomenon is Disneyland).

Carl Freedman (2000) maps out how Ernst Bloch's *The Principle of Hope* (1959) (for Bloch, hope is an essential component of the human psyche) provides us with a useful means by which to read sf's nova, or newly fabulated spaces, as containing critical utopias – that is to say, not self-contained eutopian visions but critically rigorous expressions of how we might imagine utopia's potential political power: it "is the *transformation* of actuality into utopia that constitutes the practical end of utopian critique and the ultimate object of utopian hope ... the cognitive rationality (at least in literary effect) of science fiction allows utopia to emerge as more fully itself, genuinely and critically transformative. In this way, the dynamic of science fiction can on one level be identified with the hope principle itself" (Freedman 2000: 69).

Jameson describes the transformative potential inherent in the no-place/good-place that is utopia as *disruption*. The desire called Utopia *has* a potential source of gratification – the problem that desire-gratification attempts are inevitably debased and impossible, according to the Freudian/Lacanian formulation, is solved by Jameson's reconsideration of the "formalist approach," which releases Utopia from a debased gratification attempt: "it might therefore be better to follow an aesthetic paradigm and to assert that not only the production of the irresolvable contradiction is the fundamental process, but that we must imagine some form of gratification inherent in this very confrontation with pessimism and the impossible" (Jameson 2005: 84). Thus, since the desire called Utopia is actually a desire-aesthetic, its tension-moment is therefore something to be not cured or repressed, but rather critically dwelt in.

This observation brings us back to the recent reevaluation of the eutopia as a potentially critical theoretical apparatus. In "The Problem of the 'Flawed Utopia,'" Sargent describes eutopia as an act: we "must *commit* eutopia knowing that it is *not* perfect and that, like the ideal *polis* in Plato's *Republic*, it contains within it the seeds of its own destruction. We must commit eutopia again and again because ... not believing in the possibility of betterment, however flawed, condemns us to live in someone else's vision of a better life, perhaps one forced on us ... denying eutopia ensures that we live in dystopia" (Sargent 2003: 230). Likewise, Darko Suvin concludes, in his "Theses on Dystopia 2001," that all the "variants of dystopian-cum-eutopian fiction" he discusses "pivot not only on individual self-determination but centrally on collective self-management enabling and guaranteeing personal freedom. Whoever is not interested in this horizon will not be interested in them. And vice versa" (Suvin 2003: 200). Thus, it seems as though we have come full circle, from the naïve articulation of the totalizing eutopia and its rejection by subsequent thinkers, to a new recognition of eutopia's liberatory potential as a concept/practice.

In conclusion, this elision of concept as practice, or praxis, is, as we have seen, not a new conceptual move. Indeed, it begs a question central to defining utopia: where does utopia-as-social-theory leave off and utopia-as-literary-content begin? Suvin (1988) provides a definition of utopian fiction that addresses this question and also presents us with a description of the relationship between utopian fiction and sf. Although utopian studies scholars might not be particularly gratified by Suvin's characterization of utopian fiction as a subgenre of sf, it seems an appropriate end-point in the context of this volume: "utopian fiction is not only, historically, one of the roots of SF, it is also ... one of its forms ... Utopian fiction is the socio–political subgenre of SF, it is social-science-fiction or SF restricted to the field of socio-political relationships or to socio-political constructs understood as crucial for the destiny of people" (Suvin 1988: 38).

Bibliography

Freedman, C. (2000) *Critical Theory and Science Fiction*, Hanover, NH and London: University Press of New England/Wesleyan University Press.

Jameson, F. (2005) *Archaeologies of the Future: the desire called utopia and other science fictions*, London: Verso.

Levitas, R. (1990) *The Concept of Utopia*, Syracuse, NY: Syracuse University Press.

Levitas, R. and Sargisson, L. (2003) "Utopia in Dark Times: optimism/pessimism and utopia/dystopia," in R. Baccolini and T. Moylan (eds) *Dark Horizons: science fiction and the dystopian imagination*, New York: Routledge.

Marin, L. (1984) *Utopics: spatial play*, 1973, trans. R.A. Vollrath, Atlantic Highlands, NJ: Humanities Press.

Moylan, T. (1986) *Demand the Impossible: science fiction and the utopian imagination*, London and New York: Methuen.

Sargent, L.T. (1994) "The Three Faces of Utopianism Revisited," *Utopian Studies*, 5(1): 1–37.

—— (2003) "The Problem of the 'Flawed Utopia': a note on the costs of eutopia," in R. Baccolini and T. Moylan (eds) *Dark Horizons: science fiction and the dystopian imagination*, New York: Routledge.

Society for Utopian Studies (2007) "About the Society." Online. Available HTTP: <http://www.utoronto.ca/utopia/about.html> (accessed 1 April 2008).

Suvin, D. (1979) *Metamorphoses of Science Fiction: on the poetics and history of a literary genre*, New Haven, CT: Yale University Press.

—— (1988) *Positions and Presuppositions in Science Fiction*, Kent, OH: Kent State University Press.

—— (2003) "Theses on Dystopia 2001," in R. Baccolini and T. Moylan (eds) *Dark Horizons: science fiction and the dystopian imagination*, New York: Routledge.

32

VIRTUALITY

Thomas Foster

The term "virtuality" is ambiguously located between the concreteness of computer interface technologies and the philosophical abstraction of a set of qualities from this technology (or alternately, the argument that virtual reality technologies only literalize and instantiate a preexisting set of qualities, such as fluidity, becoming, or possibility itself). The key term mediating between these two definitions is cyberspace, variously defined as the "three-dimensional domain" of computer simulation within which "cybernetic feedback and control occur" (Walker 1990: 444) or the imaginary "space" on the other side of the computer screen (by analogy with the virtual space on the other side of a mirror).

Considered as a term, virtuality has the value of identifying an open boundary between the science-fictional imagination and various theoretical and philosophical discourses, a crossover potential exemplified by the well-known science-fictional origins of the term "cyberspace" in the work of William Gibson. This chapter will discuss some of the continuities and discontinuities between a French poststructuralist discourse on virtuality (e.g., Derrida 1994: 29–30), which has had considerable influence on recent theoretical work on new media, and an American discourse on interface design, and situate both in relation to sf narratives.

There is considerable debate about both the benefits and dangers of treating virtuality as a philosophical abstraction rather than a literal technology. Robert Markley warns against "the abstraction of 'cyberspace'" and its "metaphysics"; as a result, he insists upon the need for a clear and consistent distinction between cyberspace and "virtual technologies" (Markley 1996: 2). Allucquère Rosanne Stone agrees with Markley on the problem of generalizing about the effects, qualities, or implications of these virtual technologies, even as she suggests that cyberspace is the more specific term, with "virtuality" possessing a broader range of reference and preceding both the internet and cyberpunk (Stone 1995: 35).

Elizabeth Grosz expands on this latter argument when she interprets technologies of "computer simulation" as merely a "reconceptualization" of a preexisting concept of virtuality (Grosz 2001: 87), and cautions against "too closely identifying" virtuality "with the invention of new technologies" (Grosz 2001: 78). On this basis, she argues against any strong distinction between virtual reality and real life, as well as between virtuality and cyberspace; for her, virtuality (rather than virtual reality or cyberspace technologies) refers to "the embeddedness, the nesting or interimplication … of the virtual and real within each other" (Grosz 2001: 89).

The identification of these points of interimplication or feedback between the virtual and the material are necessary for virtual experiences to function critically rather than as escapism, for the virtual to have real effects. As Markley suggests, however, the philosophical deconstruction of the physical/virtual distinction often seems to lapse into metaphysical vagueness, precisely because the refusal to make virtuality dependent upon a particular technology tends to slide into a refusal to consider how the experience of virtuality is mediated – that is, a refusal to consider the specificities of different media and the different kinds of virtualities they might enable. Instead, this philosophical discourse places the emphasis on the demystifying effect that experiences of virtuality are presumed to have on a naïve concept of empirical reality as a given. The philosophical discourse on virtuality therefore tends to use this term to name a general insight into the mediated nature of our relation to ourselves and our experiences, no matter who has those experiences or exactly how they are produced, rather than attending to the effects of how different users engage with specific technologies. This metaphysics of virtuality asserts that "the virtual reality of computer space is fundamentally no different from the virtual reality of writing, reading, drawing, or even thinking" (Grosz 2001: 78). The virtual can therefore be defined by Grosz as "the space of emergence of the new, the unthought, the unrealized" (Grosz 2001: 78) or as an "idea of open-endedness" (Grosz 2001: 89). As Mark Hansen puts it, "far from being a synonym of the digital, the virtual must be understood as that capacity, so fundamental to human existence, to be in excess of one's actual state" (Hansen 2004: 50–1). This formulation in particular demonstrates how virtuality can be used both as a critique of essentialist ideas about a general human nature, which virtuality shows to be mediated or artificial, and paradoxically as a means of reuniversalizing and dehistoricizing that critique of a universalized and transhistorical concept of human identity, whose whole point is to redefine the "human" as fundamentally indeterminate, multiple, or open to change and futurity (see Harper 1994: 193). While virtuality is associated with plurality, open-endedness, and resistance to definition, considered abstractly, apart from specific technological infrastructures or material conditions of use, virtuality functions precisely as a defining feature of the "human."

In Gwyneth Jones's *North Wind* (1994), the narrator defines two different takes on virtual gaming. In one, the users "played for the experience alone and behaved as if the laws of the game were immutable as those of reality," while in the other "the lucid dreamers" or "trapdoor spiders" realized "that fairyland is a place where magic works" (Jones 1994: 211). "Magic" is Jones's term for what is sometimes called "reality hacking," the specific way that the critique of empirical self-evidence, or what Grosz calls "open-endedness" and Hansen "being in excess," is represented in many narratives of virtual technologies of computer simulation. However, this magical form of free agency in virtual space is clearly dependent, not upon some universalized concept of human creativity or force of will, but upon what hackers call an exploit (Jones's "trapdoor") – that is, an unexpected, emergent feature of the system or program's complexity, which allows a user with the requisite technical knowledge to make the system do something it was not intended to do. In contrast, the philosophical emphasis on virtuality as naming a fundamental human capacity to transcend limitations or external determinations (Hansen's "one's actual state") recalls nothing more vividly than the *Matrix* films (Wachowski brothers 1999–2003), specifically the pseudo-theological rhetoric of Neo as "the One," who possesses an innate capacity to perceive and manipulate through sheer force of will or personal charisma the computer simulation within which humanity finds itself trapped. Neo embodies the paradox that often informs the philosophical discourse on a general condition of virtuality, as distinct from specific technological infrastructures: the desire for a direct, unmediated relation to the underlying structure of mediation itself, to the material institutions and conceptual forms that produce and distort any view of "reality" (see Foster 2006). From this point of view, a focus on the actual media through which we apprehend virtuality becomes crucial.

The specific association of the term "virtuality" with computer interfaces originates with Theodore Nelson (Clute and Nicholls 1993: 1285). Defining virtuality in relation to the computer's emulation capacity, Nelson points out that "in computerdom there is a word which is the opposite of 'real.' That word is virtual. It means **as-if**" (Nelson 1987: 69; emboldening original). Defining "virtuality" as "the way things *seem to be*, as distinct from how they really are," Nelson's example is a "something ... not stored as a file," but which "behaves as if it were a file" (Nelson 1987: 69; original emphasis).

Nelson then associates virtuality with the production of an effect that cannot be assumed to derive directly from the cause that we would normally assume it to have, file-like behavior with no file (Nelson 1987: 68; see also Wilbur 2000: 47). Virtuality here describes a basic ontological uncertainty and a breakdown of accepted relations between representation and its presumed referent, in effect a version of the critique of empiricism that in philosophy is referred to as anti-foundationalism. Nelson here defines his main point of intersection with poststructuralist theories, and this overlap perhaps explains the semantic inflation the term "virtual" has undergone. "Virtual" often seems to function primarily to designate the ungrounding of various phenomena from any empirical base, their denaturalization or deterritorialization, imagined as the precondition for greater openness, mutability, and availability to change and becoming.

Damien Broderick has been credited with the first use of the term virtual reality in sf, in *The Judas Mandala* (1982) (see Clute and Nicholls 1993: 1285). In passages soon echoed in Gibson's *Neuromancer* (1984), which defines cyberspace as "the consensual hallucination that was the matrix" (Gibson 1984: 5), Broderick's virtual realities are stabilized "by consensus," including "sophisticated social compulsions as well as ... phylogenetic deep structures" (Broderick 1982: 29). At the same time, however, we are told that "ontology's plastic" in virtual reality (Broderick 1982: 119). Here, the virtual is already associated with a critique of naturalized, unchanging foundational realities, as it will be in the philosophical discourse on virtuality. However, Broderick's novel also expresses skepticism toward the assumption that such denaturalizing operations and ontological critiques are necessarily liberating in a positive way; without some form of constraint, or compulsion, some aspect of experience that cannot be modified at will, the user might end up a "mad god in a closed universe" (Broderick 1982: 29).

This definition of virtual reality as consensual hallucination implies an explicit recognition of the social mediation of any relation to the real and therefore the artificiality of social worlds and identities. One of the early designers of VR hardware, Jaron Lanier, claims that "In Virtual Reality, there's no question that your reality is created by you. *You* made it. Or somebody else did whom you know. There's no sense of it being handed to you on a platter"; when the interviewer comments, "That may be the actual case anywhere," Lanier replies, "Well it is, but in Virtual Reality, it's so explicit" (Lanier 1990: 49).

The popular association of virtual reality with the sensibility of the reality hackers, or Jones's "lucid dreamers," emphasizes the technology's potential to produce a crisis in ideological legitimation strategies (especially what Hall calls ideology's "naturalization effect" (Hall 1996: 33)), so that the emergence of reality's consensual or social aspects is imagined as the basis for new forms of political dissent. Reality hacking presumes that the experience of virtuality can make people aware of the ways in which "reality" masks the contingency of the world that seems to confront us as given. From this perspective, virtuality refers to a perception of the world as a product of human labor and creative effort. This sensibility finds a more concrete realization today in the open source computing movement. In general contrast to that movement, the concept of reality hacking assumes that the potential accessibility and manipulability of computer programming languages can be translated back into the material world. However, reality hacking often seems actually to exaggerate the differences between VR and RL (Real Life).

Discussing the desire for "magic in cyberspace," Michael Benedikt argues that "in patently unreal and artificial realities such as cyberspace, the principles of ordinary space and time, can, in principle (!), be violated with impunity"; "after all," he writes, "why have cyberspace if we cannot (apparently) bend nature's rules there?" (Benedikt 1991a: 128). But the seeming paradox Benedikt remarks, that one of the basic principles of virtual reality is that the principles that seem to govern the simulation can be violated or hacked, actually demonstrates the way in which technological skill, an understanding of the codes or principles that make the simulation possible, is necessary in order to intervene in it, and not just self-awareness of the simulated or mediated nature of the experience. An assumption that self-consciousness about virtual mediation is sufficient to give users power over it, to break the immersive effect, without the aid of an interface or the skills needed to use it, often informs ideas of reality hacking. However, this assumption represents a questionable application to VR of avant-garde claims about the positive effects of abandoning aesthetic realism for "patently unreal" data environments, conflated with assumptions about the progressive political effects of denaturalization derived from theories of ideology critique, especially as influenced by structuralism (see John Varley's "Overdrawn at the Memory Bank" (1978) for an example of this assumption). This version of reality hacking, popularized by *The Matrix*, moves beyond the desire to define how VR can promote critical reflection on real life, to imagine that virtual experiences have direct and immediate transformative effects on the real (see Manovich's critique (Manovich 2001: 58–9) of Lanier 1990: 49, and Bolter 1996: 257). The philosophical discourse on virtuality, which probably has its origins in Deleuze (1994), shares this tendency to interpret it as an extension, literalization, or lesson in ideological denaturalization and skepticism toward the empirical.

In contrast to this tradition, Broderick's *The Judas Mandala* defines virtuality as "a heuristic for the discovery that the world is neither illusory Maya nor insistent Fact" (Broderick 1982: 129). Virtual reality is here defined as a third space, one that is neither to be simply accepted as such nor manipulated at will, a space that is neither inertly natural nor just a social construct (see also Benedikt 1991b: 3). One of the most important questions concerning the concept of virtuality is whether it can sustain this ambivalence, or whether virtuality collapses into either mimetic realism or megalomaniacal, solipsistic fantasies of control and freedom (see Benedikt 1991a: 179). In turn, this question depends upon the extent to which cyberspace or virtuality is understood as a mode of social communication and interaction.

The most famous passages defining the cyberspace metaphor are found in Gibson's *Neuromancer*, where it appears as "a graphic representation of data abstracted from the banks of every computer in the human system," with its "roots in primitive arcade games ... in early graphics programs, and military experimentation with cranial jacks" (Gibson 1984: 51) or direct neural interfaces that "project" the user's point of view into the imaginary or simulated "space" of the network. Computer developer John Walker, at Autodesk, Inc., read Gibson's cyberspace metaphor back into the history of actual interface design, to argue current interactive technologies were informed by the metaphor of conversation with the computer in ways that were limiting, since when "interacting with a computer" we might better imagine that we are "exploring another world," not "conversing with another person" (Walker 1990: 443, 445). Around the same time, in the early 1980s, Jaron Lanier's company VPL Research began to develop and market virtual reality peripherals, including: head-mounted display devices, with the single computer monitor replaced by two small screens directly in front of the user's eyes, both producing a stereoscopic effect and, more importantly, filling the user's entire field of vision, so that the distance between viewer and screen is eliminated and the user experiences the illusion of entering the graphic environment "inside" the virtual space of computer screen; tracking devices to allow the computer to rotate the simulation to match the movements of the user's head; and the Dataglove, used to map the movements of a hand into the simulation, to create a kind of 3D cursor.

This specific kind of interface technology raises a basic question about the status of users' bodies within virtual reality, and how the experience of embodiment is reproduced, transformed, or, in some conceptions, eliminated; within a more philosophical tradition, the question becomes how this technology transforms or reproduces the Cartesian mind/body dualism (Bolter and Grusin 2000: 248–53). This question is foregrounded in *Neuromancer*, which imagines the projection of a "disembodied consciousness into the consensual hallucination that was the matrix" (Gibson 1984: 5). In the hacker subculture the novel depicts, "the elite stance involved a certain relaxed contempt for the flesh. The body was meat" (Gibson 1984: 56). These passages certainly seem to echo Descartes's devaluation of the body as mere vehicle for the rational mind, and virtual reality technologies can be read as a fantasy of techno-logically literalizing and intensifying the separation between mind and body and the organization of this dualism into a hierarchy that privileges the mind's ability to transcend the materiality and particularity of embodiment.

N. Katherine Hayles provides the most trenchant critique of this kind of dualistic thinking, as it continues to inform the representation, design, and use of new digital and interface technologies. Hayles argues that the privileging of information over materiality, message over medium, signal over noise, results in the narration of cyberspace as a process of disembodiment, what *Neuromancer* calls the "elite stance" of "contempt for the flesh" (Gibson 1984: 6; see also Nelson 1987: 68). For Hayles, this formulation exemplifies the anachronistic persistence of ideas derived from an early moment in the history of information theory and cybernetics (Hayles 1999: 17), but which continue to inform what Hayles calls the contemporary "condition of virtuality."

Hayles defines virtuality as "the cultural perception that material objects are interpenetrated by information patterns" (Hayles 1999: 13). The question left open is the precise nature of the relation between materiality and information, or, more importantly, the *range* of possible relations. Hayles goes on to emphasize a dominant "condition of virtuality" that assumes first of all that materiality is not really inter-penetrated by information, but that the two constitute a "duality" or dichotomy (Hayles 1999: 14); furthermore, this dichotomy is not a neutral distinction but is organized into a value hierarchy that privileges information (Hayles 1999: 18).

Hayles ties the devaluation of material embodiment to social constructionist theories, or the "contemporary belief ... that the body is primarily, if not entirely, a linguistic and discursive construction" (Hayles 1999: 192). Hayles's goal is to displace the opposition between essentialist theories, which define social differences as a function of biological differences, and constructionist ones, in order to find "a way of talking about the body responsive to its construction as discourse/information and yet not trapped within it," or a "more flexible framework in which to think about embod-iment in an age of virtuality" (Hayles 1999: 193). Broderick's novel suggested how virtual reality might provide such a framework. Hayles, however, usefully connects this rethinking of essentialism and constructionism, nature and culture, with feminist political concerns, when she argues that embodiment must be put "back into the picture" without allowing a normative idea of *the* body to secure "the univocality of gender" or "human identity" in general (Hayles 1999: xiv).

In contrast to Hayles, Allucquère Rosanne Stone emphasizes the need to critique this univocality, over the danger of disembodiment. Stone characterizes the "virtual age" in terms of a "gradual change that has come over the relationship between sense of self and body," a transformation defined as "virtual because the accustomed grounding of social interaction in the physical facticity of human bodies is changing" (Stone 1995: 17). While acknowledging that the interactions that result from these changes can still be "racially differentiated and gendered, stereotypical and Cartesian" (Stone

1995: 36), Stone's primary target of critique is not the devaluation of the physical, but the cultural insistence on a one-to-one relation between body and self, or between female embodiment and cultural norms of femininity. This normative relation is disrupted, Stone argues, when the self is experienced as inhabiting a network and therefore moving "in a spatiality from which the body is excluded" (Stone 1995: 92). The one-to-one relation between body and social identity becomes normative by assuming that social identity is an *expression* of bodily particularity, so that the natural expressions of female embodiment are feminine behaviors and appearances. For Stone, virtual systems are defined by the ways in which they disarticulate the components linked by this expressive interpretation of identity, so that Stone is led to make the rather startling assertion that "in cyberspace the transgendered body is the natural body" (Stone 1995: 180).

Where Hayles emphasizes the mapping of the information/materiality distinction onto Descartes's mind/body dualism, Stone insists that "the physical/virtual distinction is *not* a mind/body distinction" (Stone 1995: 40). Stone's claim that virtual interactions can displace familiar dualistic assumptions emerges as a function of her definition of the role of virtual technologies in the production of the "socially apprehensible citizen," and especially her definition of this model of citizenship in terms of theories of performativity that cut across the physical/virtual distinction and define a specific basis for theorizing both the material effects of virtual experiences and actions and the already "virtual" aspects of physical embodiment (as Jaron Lanier puts it, "in Virtual Reality, even your body looks like you did it"; Lanier 1990: 49). In other words, Stone offers a more concrete way of defining how the virtual feeds back into the physical than does *Matrix*-style reality hacking, as well as suggesting how some idea of the virtual can be understood as preceding the invention of virtual reality computer interfaces or cybernetics more generally.

Another approach to the status of embodiment in virtual systems is suggested by Walker's definition of cyberspace as "a three-dimensional domain in which cybernetic feedback and control occur," with the user "inside a world rather than observing an image" (Walker 1990: 444). The model of cybernetic feedback and control Walker describes requires the implication of the user who is spliced into the system in ways that do not just enable the user to control the system, but also require the user to be acted upon, to become vulnerable to change and transformation. Hayles suggests that Norbert Wiener's original cybernetic vision, of a pattern-identity continually produced and reproduced through informational processes of homeostatic self-regulation (Wiener 1954: 95), also implies both a fundamental instability (similar to the emphasis on iteration in theories of performativity) and a transformation of body boundaries, as the self-contained individual becomes spliced into feedback loops and entangled with his or her environment, in ways that make it difficult to sharply distinguish the two (Hayles 1999: 2, 10, 84).

Hayles's analysis here implies a redefinition of subjectivity and its boundaries, as well as embodiment. Scott Bukatman tends to emphasize a concept of virtual subjectivity as agency, and therefore to emphasize an interpretation of virtual reality interfaces as minimizing the differences between cyberspace and physical space in order to translate network topologies into more familiar physical and phenomenological terms (Bukatman 1993: 200). Far from decentering or transforming the individual subject, for Bukatman virtual reality recenters the human within virtual space, since projecting "the human into the nonvisible spaces within the computer" transforms the space of the network into a more familiar type of space, "a dramatic arena" (Bukatman 1993: 201). In contrast, Manuel Castells makes a much sharper distinction between what he calls "the space of places" and "the space of flows" or information networks; for Castells, the latter are strictly speaking uninhabitable, since the "structural schizo-phrenia" that separates these two spaces also sharply distinguishes function, power, and knowledge, located in the space of flows, from experience or meaning, located in the space of places (Castells 1996: 378, 428). In this context, it makes perfect sense that cyberspace would have been invented as a narrative device within sf prior to the development of virtual reality technologies, since such technologies only extend and literalize the desire to imagine computer networks as narratable, as phenomena that can be experienced subjectively, if only through the physical metaphors of informa-tional "space" or "moving" icons on a desktop.

Theorists of social space might argue that this critique is misleading, since space is always in part a metaphor or construct, never simply empirical. If Bukatman is right, and VR turns a non-phenomenological type of space into one that can be experienced subjectively and dramatically, how different is that from what we do in the physical world? This question has been addressed by theorists who situate virtual reality technologies within the more general context of new media. Lev Manovich points out that, instead of situating users within virtual space, virtual reality technologies might be understood as making "the two spaces – the real, physical space and the virtual, simulated space – coincide" (Manovich 2001: 97; see also Hansen 2004: 167). One effect of this layering or coupling of the physical and the virtual is to open "a newly mobilized point of view" within virtual simulations to formal manipulation (Hayles 1999: 37–8; Bolter and Grusin 2000: 243). This new mobility is often imagined to make possible new practices of boundary-crossing, alternately understood either as liberating forms of identity play, as in Stone's reference to the transgendered body as the natural body in cyberspace, as part of a "multicultural or transnational pedagogy" (Shohat and Stam 1996: 166), or as practices of identity tourism (Nakamura 2002: 13–14).

Stone's formulation, in which the transgendered body becomes "natural" or normative in virtual spaces, might also point toward a critique of the assumption that utilizing the mobility and plasticity of point of view in such spaces is necessarily liberating or even educating, a point Nakamura has explored in relation to repre-sentations of racial difference in online contexts and speculative fictions about VR and cyberspace. Maureen McHugh's "A Coney Island of the Mind" (1993) offers a balanced assessment of this debate, by distinguishing relatively superficial forms of online gender and sexual drag or role-playing from more critical and transgressive forms (see Foster 2005: 119–22).

McHugh's story, like Stone's comment on the naturalness of the trans*gendered* body in cyberspace, also dramatizes the problem of the asymmetry between gender or sexual performances of cross-identification and histories of racialization or ethnic formation. This asymmetry or resistance to understanding race as amenable to virtual redefinition can be explained in terms of the persistence of biologizing forms of racism, and the visual regimes of difference or raciology Paul Gilroy (2000) critiques, and perhaps because the redefinition of race as virtual style evokes anxieties about eugenics and genocide in ways that the virtualization of gender and sexuality does not. On the other hand, this same resistance offers a useful critical perspective on the tendency to think of sexuality and gender merely as transitive styles or plastic social constructs (see Hayles 1999: 5). Lisa Nakamura's work on racialized forms of online identity performance or "cybertypes" offers a critique of how race can be denaturalized, understood as a set of artificial representational conventions, without losing its normative power to define what kinds of performances are acceptable as "black" or "Asian" (Nakamura 2002: 36–7, 43).

Richard Morgan's *Altered Carbon* (2002) makes it clearer how denaturalization and the critique of ontological foundations have become normative in narratives about virtual reality. This novel imagines an implant technology, the "cortical stack," that stores human personalities in digital form (Morgan 2006: 69). Not only does a culture organized around such technologies demystify belief in an "essential person" or unchanging "core personality" (Morgan 2006: 354), but it goes further to characterize any resistance to or critique of the technology as "paranoid essentialism with its back to the wall" (Morgan 2006: 234). I cite this example because its appropriation of the language of academic critique supports Hayles's point about the tendency for constructivist or anti-essentialist theories to slide into and become assimilated to a dominant discourse of technological transcendence and disembodiment; one of Hayles's main points is that this transcendence of mind over matter actually produces the instrumentalization of the body that it purports to escape. Morgan's novel, however, also dramatizes the implications of this shift to a normative denaturalization or anti-essentialism for traditions of representing racial and sexual differences. One character in the novel is described as realizing the full potential of virtual systems for freeing users from "conventional perceptions of the physical" (Morgan 2006: 228). Referred to as the Patchwork Man, his virtual avatar is multiracial and transgendered. His "frame was that of a Caucasian Nordic," but his face contradicts that impression by beginning "African, broad and deep ebony," with the color ending "like a mask under the eyes" and "the lower half divided" into "pale copper on the left" and "corpse white on the right"; he has "impossibly full" breasts on an "overmuscled torso" (Morgan 2006: 227).

The recent emergence of models of embedded or ubiquitous computing, what Bruce Sterling calls the "internet of things" (Sterling 2005: 91), makes the question of the relation between virtuality and materiality (here represented by gender and racial formations) even more urgent. In sf, cyberpunk conventions are increasingly being reimagined in terms of the layering of virtual and physical spaces rather than the definition of a distinct cyberspace into which users project themselves. In this context, it seems more important than ever to realize the possibility that abstract patterns of information might finally be able to "capture the embodied actuality" by rendering themselves "as prolix and noisy as the body" (Hayles 1999: 23). But, as I have tried to show, this possibility always resided within the various discourses on virtuality

Bibliography

Benedikt, M. (1991a) "Cyberspace: some proposals," in *Cyberspace: first steps*, Cambridge, MA: MIT Press.

—— (1991b) "Introduction," in *Cyberspace: first steps*, Cambridge, MA: MIT Press.

Bolter, J.D. (1996) "Ekphrasis, Virtual Reality, and the Future of Writing," in G. Nunberg (ed.) *The Future of the Book*, Berkeley: University of California Press.

Bolter, J.D. and Grusin, R. (2000) *Remediation: understanding new media*, Cambridge, MA: MIT Press.

Broderick, D. (1982) *The Judas Mandala*, New York: Timescape/Pocket Books.

Bukatman, S. (1993) *Terminal Identity: the virtual subject in postmodern science fiction*, Durham, NC and London: Duke University Press.

Castells, M. (1996) *The Rise of the Network Society*, Cambridge, MA: Blackwell.

Clute, J. and Nicholls, P. (eds) (1993) *The Encyclopedia of Science Fiction*, London: Orbit.

Deleuze, G. (1994) *Difference and Repetition*, 1968, trans. P. Patton, New York: Columbia University Press.

Derrida, J. (1994) "The Deconstruction of Actuality: an interview with Jacques Derrida," *Radical Philosophy*, 68: 28–41.

Foster, T. (2005) *The Souls of Cyberfolk: posthumanism as vernacular theory*, Minneapolis: University of Minnesota Press.

—— (2006) "The Transparency of the Interface: reality hacking and fantasies of resistance," in S. Gillis (ed.) *Cyberpunk Reloaded: the Matrix trilogy*, New York: Wallflower Press.

Gibson, W. (1984) *Neuromancer*, New York: Ace.

Gilroy, P. (2000) *Against Race: imagining political culture beyond the color line*, Cambridge, MA: Harvard University Press.

Grosz, E. (2001) *Architecture from the Outside: essays on virtual and real space*, Cambridge, MA: MIT Press.

Hall, S. (1996) *Stuart Hall: critical dialogues in cultural studies*, ed. D. Morley and K. Chen, New York: Routledge.

Hansen, M.B.N. (2004) *New Philosophy for New Media*, Cambridge, MA: MIT Press.

Harper, P.B. (1994) *Framing the Margins: the social logic of postmodern culture*, New York: Oxford University Press.

Hayles, N.K. (1999) *How We Became Posthuman: virtual bodies in cybernetics, literature and informatics*, Chicago and London: University of Chicago Press.

Jones, G. (1994) *North Wind*, London: Gollancz.

Lanier, J. (1990) "Life in the Datacloud: scratching your eyes back in – Jaron Lanier interview by John Perry Barlow," *Mondo 2000*, 2: 44–51.

Manovich, L. (2001) *The Language of New Media*, Cambridge, MA: MIT Press.

Markley, R. (1996) "Introduction: history, theory, and virtual reality," in *Virtual Realities and Their Discontents*, Baltimore, MD: Johns Hopkins University Press.

Morgan, R. (2006) *Altered Carbon*, 2002, New York: Del Rey.

Nakamura, L. (2002) *Cybertypes: race, ethnicity, and identity on the internet*, New York: Routledge.

Nelson, T. (1980) "Interactive Systems and the Design of Virtuality," *Creative Computing*, 6(11 and 12): 94–106.

—— (1987) *Computer Lib/Dream Machines*, Redmond, WA: Tempus Books of Microsoft Press.

Shohat, E. and Stam, R. (1996) "From the Imperial Family to the Transnational Imaginary: media spectatorship in the age of globalization," in R. Wilson and W. Dissanayke (eds) *Cultural Production and the Transnational Imaginary*, Durham, NC: Duke University Press.

Sterling, B. (2005) *Shaping Things*, Cambridge, MA: MIT Press.

Stone, A.R. (1995) *The War of Desire and Technology at the Close of the Mechanical Age*, Cambridge, MA: MIT Press.

Walker, J. (1990) "Through the Looking Glass," in B. Laurel (ed.) *The Art of Human–Computer Interface Design*, Reading, MA: Addison Wesley.

Wiener, N. (1954) *The Human Use of Human Beings: cybernetics and society*, New York: Da Capo.

Wilbur, S.P. (2000) "An Archaeology of Cyberspaces: virtuality, community, identity," in D. Bell and B.M. Kennedy (eds) *The Cybercultures Reader*, New York: Routledge.

Part III

ISSUES AND CHALLENGES

33
ANIMAL STUDIES
Joan Gordon

Animal studies are scientific experiments using animal subjects to demonstrate hypotheses, but animal studies is also a growing field that uses the interdisciplinary range of cultural studies to examine the relationship between human beings and other animals; the latter is the kind of animal studies with which this chapter is concerned. Among many other things, this kind of animal studies questions the ethical complexities of the other kind of animal studies. Indeed, ethical concerns about our treatment and use of animals form an important strand of animal studies and are part of the long tradition of philosophical and religious consideration of human and animal. Other strands, with connections to the social sciences, consider the extent to which humans and animals are related evolutionarily (using the field of evolutionary development) or psychologically (using evolutionary psychology), or they consider the implications of animal behavior (ethology), animal psychology, and even animal culture: these strands might be grouped under the heading of sociobiology, a field established by E.O. Wilson. Further strands explore the nature of consciousness to consider the human/animal interface, the impact of the environment on human/animal interaction, and the varying attitudes in different human cultures toward animals. Feminist thought has become increasingly imbricated with animal studies. In all cases, animal studies problematizes the clear division between human and other animals, and probes the cultural implications of either making or erasing that division. It can be used to examine every kind of cultural product, from art, drama, film, and television to theme parks, political campaigns, and clothing design.

Sf, the literature of change (Landon 1997) and "cognitive estrangement" (Suvin 1979), is particularly well suited as an exploratory site for animal studies: evolution is a science of change, concerned with the developing relationships among different species, while ethology and the study of consciousness examine animal and human cognition. Estrangement allows one to step outside one's own form of cognition or place in the world and look at the change this alteration makes, or to consider one's own position as another might, or another's position as if it were one's own. Sf literalizes metaphor through its speculative situations, allowing one to write from the point of view of an animal or an alien consciousness, for instance, or to imagine the ability to communicate with another consciousness, or to consider how one's consciousness might change if one were differently embodied or in a radically different environment.

If one uses this science-fictional shift in perception, one can imagine the relation-ships of humans with other animals as evolution, ethology, and consciousness studies suggest, using sociobiology, for instance, to lend plausibility to one's speculation, and the philosophical arguments of animal studies to deepen the discussion. Sf dealing with alien contact, animal intellectual transcendence, hybrid creatures, human evolution or devolution, machine and other alternative sentience, wars between the sexes, economic and class struggle, and even ecodisaster, provides rich explorations of the concerns of animal studies. It is not surprising, then, that animal studies often feels quite "science-fictional."

The range of sf tropes for which animal studies is relevant forms an accurate measure of the topics with which the present age grapples: struggles over extinc-tions, extreme weather, climate change, and other indications of the ecological deterioration of the biome or ecosystem, and between relativistic and fundamentalist ideologies, nationalism and globalization, first and third worlds, and the organic and the technological. For these reasons, animal studies will continue to grow, and because all of these anxieties concern the future of our planet, sf will continue to be a vital method of exploration.

Historical overview

The central question of animal studies, what is often called the animal question, is that of the relationship between humans and other animals. Are we related? Are we superior? Can we exchange understanding? Do we have ethical obligations toward one another? Most Western philosophy, from Aristotle to René Descartes to Martin Heidegger, and Western monotheistic religion, from Judaism to Islam, emphasizes the superior moral worth of human beings over animals. For Aristotle, although animals have perception and memory, they lack reason and therefore do not have the same moral status as humans. Aristotle also ranked women below men, humans of lower intellect below those of higher, and extended this hierarchical organization to kinds of animals as well. Christianity, too, has traditionally seen the relationship of humans to animals as one of dominance, with hierarchical relationships between humans and animals in the great chain of being. Such thinking about the biome remains an important component of Western religious, moral, political, and scientific thought, explored in sf from Mary Shelley's *Frankenstein* (1818) and H.G. Wells's *The Island of Doctor Moreau* (1896) on. Hierarchies, in the wake of the revolutionary movements of Shelley's time, and the evolutionary theory and imperialist colonization of Wells's, demand questioning.

Descartes famously claimed that animals were organic machines, lacking not only reason but feelings, and thus we could use them as we saw fit without any moral qualm. His view, justified by and arising out of Christianity's claims of human dominion over nature, has been examined in sf, most purposefully in Philip K. Dick's *Do Androids Dream of Electric Sheep?* (1968). The protagonist is named Deckard; pronunciation with the emphasis on the second syllable instead of the first results in a phonetic rendering of Descartes. Deckard's job is to retire (kill) androids which (who) are defined as organic machines. He can do so only as long as he can convince himself that the androids have no feelings, no empathy. Once the Cartesian claim becomes untenable, Deckard must retire (in the conventional way) from his profession. The novel's references to the androids as servants in the nostalgic tradition of the old south demonstrate how Descartes's argument was used to claim the innate superiority of certain human "races" over others, while reminding us of how Darwin's evolutionary theory, which joined us to the rest of the animal world, was employed in social Darwinism and eugenics to reaffirm hierarchical thinking.

In the twentieth century, Heidegger saw animals as "poor in the world" and as clearly separate from human beings. The first point, that the animal is limited in its ability to act upon the world, is explored in sf stories from the 1940s through the 1960s that imagine the emergence of a new sentience in already existing species, such as Olaf Stapledon's *Sirius* (1944), in which a dog is given human intelligence, Cordwainer Smith's *Instrumentality of Mankind* stories (1950–75), with their hybrid animal underclass, and Clifford Simak's *City* (1952), in which dogs become the new sentient species. In many of these works, the predicament of animals parallels that of subjected peoples. The second point, our clear separation from other animal species, is questioned by current writers, such as Sheri S. Tepper in *Six Moon Dance* (1998) and other novels, and Karen Traviss, in her *Wess'har Wars* series beginning with *City of Pearl* (2004): for these writers, the animal's situation is both a metaphor for that of subjected peoples, including women, and a claim for the rights of animals.

A counter-view has existed in Western philosophy all along, although it has not dominated. Pythagoras saw animals as reincarnated human beings. Jeremy Bentham and Arthur Schopenhauer recognized that the ability of animals to suffer obligated human compassion. In Eastern religions such as Buddhism and Hinduism, the role of the animal is not separate from the human because of the belief in reincarnation, and the idea of human domination is not central. The twentieth century, with its genocides and extinctions, saw philosophical positions that acknowledge the moral worth of animals, questioning a hierarchical ordering of utility or moral value, in the ascendant, although this trend was, until recently, more prominent in Anglo-American than in Continental philosophy. In Christianity, thought began to be given to the human role as steward to animals, a more benign despotism than the earlier emphasis on domination. As more Westerners learned about Eastern religions, and as East and West became increasingly interdependent, the traditional monotheistic stand on the strict division between human and animal worth also began to waver. Thoughtful overviews of twentieth-century philosophical and religious attitudes toward the animal can be found in Erica Fudge (2002) and David DeGrazia (2002), while Peter Atterton and Matthew Calarco (2004) introduce Continental approaches to the animal question.

Once the division between human and animal begins to blur, it becomes more difficult to ignore the status of animals. As treatment of farm animals has become harsher with factory production, and as wild animals become increasingly endangered, the animal rights movement has grown to be another important impetus for animal studies. In 1975 Peter Singer brought animal rights into wide awareness, and made prominent the concept of "speciesism": "a prejudice or attitude of bias in favor of the interests of members of one's own species and against those of members of other species" (Singer 2002: 6). Most animal studies thinkers exhibit concern for animal rights, including the use of animals as tools for human purposes.

By the late 1980s, animal studies, combining philosophy, ethics, and sociobiology, evolved, and a number of philosophers, Continental and Anglo-American, began considering the animal in more dynamic and interconnected ways. Donna Haraway (1989, 1991) examines our cultural construction of nature by examining race, sex, and class, presenting foundational arguments for the emergent field. A number of texts by women make clear the connection between feminism and animal studies, including Lynda Birke (1994). Gilles Deleuze and Félix Guattari (1987) gave us the useful concepts of being and becoming human or animal as a way to confound the traditional divisions; and, questioning Sigmund Freud's and Jacques Lacan's hierarchical views of the human subject, preferred "nomad thought" instead. Jacques Derrida (2003) also critiques Lacan (2006). In the 1990s, developments in our understandings of genetics and DNA resulted in sociobiological speculations which added scientific support to these philosophers' nomadic thinking about the relationship between humans and animals, as well as to what, in both human and animal behavior, is conscious or unconscious.

In the new century, Derrida (2003) and Giorgio Agamben make clear that Continental philosophers are rethinking their position, and that of animals, no longer pleading the case for human exceptionalism but for "the central emptiness, the hiatus that – within man – separates man and animal, and to risk ourselves in this emptiness" (Agamben 2004: 92). Curiously, perhaps tellingly, Agamben uses the male pronoun, rebuilding one wall while tearing down another. Haraway (2003) continues her examination of the relationship between human beings and animals, telling dog stories to illustrate not only how species coevolve in often symbiotic ways but how the stories we tell of their relationships both describe and determine what those relationships are (see also Haraway 2007). Cary Wolfe (2003) gathers arguments on speciesism and how its discourse permits the violence that is perpetrated on any being categorized as the other, whether human or animal. Like Haraway, Derrida, and Agamben, he questions the notion that humans, however defined, are the only beings who can stand in the position of the subject. Once we allow other beings subjectivity, their position as tools is problematized, and this occurs not only as we question the traditional use of animals for labor and food, but as we extend their use as experimental objects and as spare parts (see Fudge 2002; Haraway 1997). Akira Mizuta Lippit suggests a further use for animals: noting concern for animals rising as their presence in the world diminishes in the modern era, he sees them functioning as "an ambiguous excess upon whose elimination human identity consolidates itself" (Lippit 2000: 9), so that the animal's disappearance threatens our sense of what it means to be human.

Animal studies and sf

Animal studies, in the twenty-first century, dismantles subject positions in positively science-fictional ways. It is growing fast, and with it the cross-fertilization between animal studies and sf. Of the theorists discussed above, only Haraway addresses sf specifically, although Wolfe uses Michael Crichton's *Congo* (1980), sf in fact if not in marketing. That situation is changing. Ursula Heise (2003) has written on Dick, and Sherryl Vint on Octavia Butler (2005), H.G. Wells and David Brin (2007a), and Dick (2007b). The next decade in sf criticism should catch up with both the burgeoning theoretical field and the rich sources for examination in sf. Here I would like to sketch a broad picture of how animal studies enriches sf and vice versa by considering the ideas of Haraway in particular, and of several other theorists more briefly, in relation to Carol Emshwiller's *The Mount* (2002). By restricting the discussion in this way, I do not want to imply that either animal studies or sf is so narrowly limited; rather, these few texts are metonymic of a much larger and broader cross-fertilization.

The Mount imagines humanity subjected and colonized by an alien species called the Hoots, non-primate "prey" beings that define superior intelligence according to their own sharper sight, hearing, and smell, their speed, and their imported technology. They treat humans as chattel, their "mounts," whom they use as transport and to race. The novel is primarily from the point of view of a young human boy, Charley, coming of age as a mount, who at first unquestioningly accepts his submissive role and inferior status, but who gradually awakens to the gratuitousness of the alien hierarchy when he joins his father's outlaw band. Charley is the mount of a young Hoot, Little Master, destined to take over command of the Hoots. In the course of the novel, a community of Hoots is overtaken by the human outlaws, the humans are imprisoned by the Hoots and then freed by other humans, and the Hoots are forced to compromise their status. Charley and Little Master learn to cooperate as equals and offer a new model for coexistence to both humans and Hoots. This summary emphasizes how sf uses human–alien relations to illustrate the implications of unequal power between different groups of humans or between humans and other animals. Although short, and sometimes marketed as a young adult novel, *The Mount* – which puts humans in the place of animals, describes cross-species communications, and literalizes its metaphors with great liveliness – is open to complex animal studies readings.

If Mary Shelley can be considered a founder of sf because she imagined a nonhuman consciousness returning the human view with its own alien one in *Frankenstein*, Donna Haraway can be considered a founder of animal studies for very similar reasons as she posits non-hegemonic views of science and culture in her work. Haraway (1989) concludes with a compelling reading of Butler's *Xenogenesis* sf series (1987–9). Later, Haraway illustrated her examination of the multiple subjectivities of the human/ animal relationship with stories of dogs, but her insistence on "the implosion of nature and culture in the relentlessly historically specific, joint lives of dogs and people, who are bonded in significant otherness" (Haraway 2003: 16) provides a compelling model for multiple species "who shape each other throughout the still ongoing story of co-evolution" (Haraway 2003: 29). All of Haraway's work is informed by both kinds of animal studies, scientific and philosophical, and by many strands of cultural considerations about animals. She also makes clear the connection between animal studies and feminist theory. Her ideas continue to be a primary influence on animal studies and so I will develop them in some detail.

Haraway moves "from reading primatology as science fiction to ... reading science fiction as primatology" (Haraway 1989: 376) to "facilitate revisionings of fundamental, persistent western narratives about difference, especially racial and sexual difference; about reproduction, especially in terms of the multiplicities of generators and offspring; and about survival, especially survival imagined in the boundary conditions of both the origins and ends of history" (Haraway 1989: 377). *The Mount* illustrates this project in its comparison of the human descendants of primates with aliens whose very different narratives about difference valorize the qualities of prey animals. Emshwiller references attitudes toward race and sex in the Hoots' stereotypical thinking about the humans upon whom they practice selective breeding, echoing treatment of women by men, of the colonized by colonizers, of nonwhites by whites in Western culture. She makes clear that the only way in which both Hoots and humans will survive will be to cast off domination of either one by the other and instead to evolve a new cooperative model. This echoes Haraway's strategy of "telling and retelling stories in the attempt to shift the webs of intertextuality and to facilitate perhaps new possibilities for the meanings of difference, reproduction, and survival ... on both sides of the bio-political and cultural divide between human and animal" (Haraway 1989: 377). Sf becomes the storyteller's way to make clear that science is also a narrative with its own biopolitical and cultural bias.

Haraway explores the relationship between humans and domestic animals, specifically with dogs. Considering how humans and companion animals have coevolved, she declares that "there are no pre-constituted subjects and objects" (Haraway 2003: 6), but that "subjects, objects, kinds, races, species, genres, and genders are the products of their relating" (Haraway 2003: 7). She goes on to describe the relational subjectivities of humans and other species as "relations of significant otherness" (Haraway 2003: 8). In *The Mount's* Charley and Little Master, the two species coevolve, through their cohabitation, to acknowledge each other's subjectivities and form "relations of significant otherness," moving beyond the limits of the human subject to more liminal ways of being both human and animal, offering this hybrid state as a utopian potential. Charley is not merely animal as machine, a form of transportation, and Little Master is not merely a domineering subject or a helpless victim; both become agents of their own and one another's well-being, subjects that disintegrate "the bio-political and cultural divide between human and animal." Stapledon's *Sirius* exemplifies much of what Haraway (2003) discusses. The protagonist of the novel is a dog bred for sheepherding but given human intelligence, who struggles to be taken seriously as a thinking and working partner, while his human companions struggle to see him in his full capacity, not as a work tool but as a working colleague.

Haraway "insist[s] on the embodied nature of all vision" (Haraway 1991: 188) and warns us against "the god-trick of seeing everything from nowhere" (Haraway 1991: 189) which is the gaze that "signifies the unmarked positions of Man and

White" (Haraway 1991: 188). *The Mount* puts the Hoots in the unmarked positions and we struggle, as does Charley, to see things otherwise. Since the novel develops a cooperative model rather than a new form of dominance, it reflects Haraway's goal of "feminist objectivity [which] is about limited location and situated knowledge, not about transcendence and splitting of subject and object" (Haraway 1991: 190). Human and Hoot knowledges will each offer situational ways of understanding rather than the "splitting of subject and object" that they had offered in the past. Traviss's *City of Pearl* and its sequels also show multiple sentient species struggling to recognize how radically different embodiments affect situated and localized knowledges.

Haraway's two books (1991 and 2003) both work toward an acknowledgment that communication is reciprocal, that when we look at the other, the other looks back, thinking its own thoughts as we think ours, however differently those thoughts and perspectives are embodied. *The Mount* insists on the exchange of perspectives, recognizing that each consciousness, influenced by its embodiment and its culture, observes and interprets the other. Emshwiller carefully dismantles gender assumptions in the two species. Charley is a typical budding heterosexual 13-year-old by the end of the novel, but Little Master's sexuality is opaque to his human partner. Because Little Master is the alien other, is small, more prey than predator, it is to some extent coded as female, but because it is also dominant, often patronizing, it is also coded as male for a Western human witness. Thus, the novel plays with many of the feminist speculations of Haraway's theoretical work, calling into question the "humane" ways in which we manipulate the lives of pets while ignoring their selfhood, and offering a more satisfying relationship of significant otherness.

Since Haraway's groundbreaking work, others have explored the relationships among science, feminism, and the animal, notably Lynda Birke, who points out "two ways in which the human/animal distinction is evident in feminist writing ... in the context of environmental concerns" and in reinscribing the biological differences between human and animal, thus separating us from nature (Birke 1994: 4–5). She also points to the power of naming that science brings. By naming women according to their biology, or by naming animals according to species, the scientist erases individuality and stresses only commonality. Again, *The Mount* shows humans and Hoots thinking of one another and of themselves in generalized ways rather than in individuating ones: all humans behave in certain ways, all Hoots behave in certain other ways, predetermined by their biology. That thinking blocks consideration of similarity and mutual communication or ethical value, as well as of individual variation. Pat Murphy's "Rachel in Love" (1987), by imagining a chimpanzee with the memories of a human girl, erases the human/animal distinction while examining subjectivity and the ethics of animal experimentation.

Deleuze and Guattari (1987) offer what becomes for animal studies a very useful distinction between being and becoming. If one sees the world in terms of being, one sees it as clearly divided into immutable categories: male or female, human or animal. If one sees it in terms of becoming, one sees everything in a dynamic state moving in flows, inhabiting zones without boundaries, so male and female exist along a continuum and human and animal are not divisible into separate categories. *The*

Mount engenders a sexual becoming by imagining the Hoots' alien and impossible to determine (for the humans) sexuality; the novel literalizes species becoming by showing two sentient species each making ethical claims to its own subjectivity, and by showing those species come to some acknowledgment of each other's claims.

In the new millennium, animal studies has continued to emphasize similarity over difference, describing the relationship of humans to other animals as a continuum rather than a division, echoing the discussions in sociobiology that ascribe "animal-istic" traits in humans and traits previously associated only with humans, such as tool-use, language, cultural and psychological variety, to animals. Cary Wolfe synthe-sizes the theoretical work of Haraway and others, including Deleuze and Guattari, as he makes his argument against speciesism: "as long as it is ... all right to systemati-cally exploit and kill nonhuman animals ... then the humanist discourse of species will always be available for use ... to countenance violence against the social other of *whatever* species" (Wolfe 2003: 8). He combines the arguments of animal rights with those of cultural theorists to question the definition and subjectivity of the human. Emshwiller makes it clear that members of the human and Hoot "races" are using such discourses when they seek to dominate or destroy one another (see also Paul Park's *Coelestis* (1995) and Mary Doria Russell's *The Sparrow* (1996)).

Jacques Derrida – best known for his theory of deconstruction, which treats texts as fluid sites for interpretation rather than as sites of fixed meaning, with ideas opposing one another in dynamical feedback loops – dismantled and reconstructed the Bible, Descartes, Heidegger, Levinas, and Lacan, among others, to suggest a fluid and inter-active view of animals in his 1997 lectures at the Cerisy-la-Salle conference (see Derrida 2002, 2003). Among his contributions in these lectures are the term "animot" and a recognition that, however we theorize *the* animal, observe *the* animal, gaze upon and consider *the* animal, animals themselves are looking back.

"Animot" is a singular version of the plural "animals" in French, intended to avoid the monolithic depersonalization of "*the* animal" as a generalizing term for nonhuman beings. Animal studies struggles with the problem of referring to nonhuman beings as both biologically separate from and ethically similar to human beings and "animot" is one way to deal with this problem. In *The Mount*, each species thinks of the other in the monolithic way – the human, the Hoot – and thus misses the more complex and fluid relationships between them. Only at the end do they perhaps see one another in more individuated ways. "Animot" goes some way to allow this individuated sense of the other to be expressed.

Derrida's discussion of how the animal looks back is extremely important in moving the ideas of animal studies forward. He announces that "I move from 'the ends of man,' that is the confines of man, to 'the crossing of borders' between man and animal" so that when "we can say that the animal has been looking at us" we acknowledge that our theorizing is not all our own, we are not the only subjects in the relationship between human and other (Derrida 2002: 372). Herein lies the inevitable paradox of animal studies. We study animals to acknowledge their subject-status, but must treat them as the objects of our inquiry. We can acknowledge that they too have their worldviews (their *Ümvelts*) but we cannot know what they are. Derrida, like Agamben, uses the "universal" term "man" instead of the more inclusive human, underlining how difficult it is to give up the subject-position. But his deconstructive interpretation of our relationship with (other) animals, with the other, is a flexible and fluid way of both recognizing and acknowledging the paradox. *The Mount* allows us to see into the minds of both humans and Hoots, both adults and children of each species, and lets these Ümvelts interrogate one another.

A conclusion

Animal studies, then, stimulates growth in understanding sf, just as sf nurtures the ideas and connections of animal studies. We can expect increasing scholarship recognizing this symbiotic relationship; feminist, eco-critical, postcolonial, and posthuman discourses add to its hybrid vigor. All fields of inquiry that question the role of the subject and the role of the other, that contemplate what it means to be alien or alienated, to exist beyond the protection of the "humane," will be invigorated by this fertile hybridization of theory and literary practice.

Bibliography

Agamben, G. (2004) *The Open: man and animal*, 2002, trans K. Attele, Stanford, CA: Stanford University Press.

Atterton, P. and Calarco, M. (2004) *Animal Philosophy: ethics and identity*, New York: Continuum.

Birke, L. (1994) *Feminism, Animals and Science: the naming of the shrew*, Philadelphia: Open University Press.

DeGrazia, D. (2002) *Animal Rights: a very short introduction*, New York: Oxford University Press.

Deleuze, G. and Guattari, F. (1987) *A Thousand Plateaus: capitalism and schizophrenia*, 1980, trans. B. Massumi, Minneapolis: University of Minnesota Press.

Derrida, J. (2002) "The Animal That Therefore I Am (More to Follow)," *Critical Inquiry*, 28(2): 369–419.

—— (2003) "And Say the Animal Responded," in C. Wolfe (ed.) *Zoontologies: the question of the animal*, 1997, trans. D. Wills, Minneapolis: University of Minnesota Press.

Fudge, E. (2002) *Animal*, London: Reaktion.

Haraway, D. (1989) *Primate Visions: gender, race, and nature in the world of modern science*, New York: Routledge.

—— (1991) *Simians, Cyborgs, and Women: the reinvention of nature*, New York and London: Routledge.

——(1997) *Modest_Witness@Second_Millennium.FemaleMan©_Meets_Onco Mouse™: feminism and technoscience*, London and New York: Routledge.

—— (2003) *The Companion Species Manifesto: dogs, people, and significant otherness*, Chicago: Prickly Paradigm Press.

—— (2007) *When Species Meet*, Minneapolis: University of Minnesota Press.

Heise, U.K. (2003) "From Extinction to Electronics: dead frogs, live dinosaurs, and electric sheep," in C. Wolfe (ed.) *Zoontologies: the question of the animal*, Minneapolis: University of Minnesota Press.

Lacan, J. (2006) "The Subversion of the Subject and the Dialectic of Desire in the Freudian Unconscious," in *Écrits*, 1966, trans. B. Fink, New York: Norton.

Landon, B. (1997) *Science Fiction after 1900: from the steam man to the stars*, New York: Twayne.

Lippit, A.M. (2000) *Electric Animal: toward a rhetoric of wildlife*, Minneapolis: University Minnesota Press.

Singer, P. (2002) *Animal Liberation*, 1975, New York: HarperCollins.

Suvin, D. (1979) *Metamorphoses of Science Fiction: on the poetics and history of a literary genre*, New Haven, CT: Yale University Press.

Vint, S. (2005) "Becoming Other: animals, kinship, and Butler's *Clay's Ark*," *Science Fiction Studies*, 32(2): 281–300.

—— (2007a) "Animals and Animality from the Island of Moreau to the Uplift Universe," *Yearbook of English Studies*, 37(2): 85–102.

—— (2007b) "Speciesism and Species Being in *Do Androids Dream of Electric Sheep?*," *Mosaic – A Journal for the Interdisciplinary Study of Literature*, 40(1): 111–26.

Wolfe, C. (2003) *Animal Rites: American culture, the discourse of species, and posthuman theory*, Chicago: University of Chicago Press.

34
DESIGN FOR SCREEN SF

Piers D. Britton

Sf film and television calls for an exceptionally high level of creative invention from those who realize the world of the "original" script for an audience – above all, perhaps, the designers of sets, costumes, and special effects. Annette Kuhn rightly emphasizes the centrality of the visual in sf film: "if science-fiction cinema possesses any distinctive generic traits, these … have to do in large measure with cinematographic technologies and with the ways in which these figure in the construction of diegetic and spectatorial spaces: while science-fiction films may certainly tell stories, narrative content and structure per se are rarely their most significant features" (Kuhn 1999: 11). Whether required to realize isolated artifacts and beings, as in *The X-Files* (1993–2002), or to evoke whole societies and topographies, as in *Star Trek* (1966–9), designers play a pivotal role in furnishing the "most significant features" of screen sf. Yet how may reflection on the role of design in sf film and television add to our understanding of these kinds of text?

To make any substantial claim about the significance of design for screen sf, we must first agree that there is, in visual and aural terms, something distinctive about the genre – something setting it apart from all others which use cinematic or televisual technologies to construct diegetic space. If there *is* a central and constant design imperative in screen sf, it can be best described as the principle of extended common sense. An sf diegesis must appear coextensive with "our" scientifically measurable and manageable world. Alien entities, however foreign or grotesque in bodily form, must *seem* as though they could operate within popularly understood laws of biology and physics; machines, however vast or advanced, must *seem* as though they could be engineered and successfully operated; and so on.

It is worth laboring the fact that the apparent, not theoretical, possibility of existence is the real concern of the sf designer. This is why I speak of extended *common sense*, rather than using the more scientifically skewed terms logic or reason. As numerous invectives against bad movie physics remind us, many of the sights and sounds of, say, starship battles in *Star Wars: Episode IV – A New Hope* (Lucas 1977) are quite contrary to physical laws, but they pass because they are common-sensical. In reality, the sounds of engines, missile fire, and detonations would not carry in the vacuum of space, and the incandescence of an explosion in the hull of a spacecraft would be limited by the paucity of available oxygen. Yet the bangs and booms, provided that they seem appropriate in scale and tone, will resonate believably for most members of an audience who are familiar with the nearest real-life technological cognates: jet air travel and aerial warfare.

Thus, in a strange and tendentious way, design for sf is strongly oriented toward verisimilitude (Barsacq 1976: 141). Nor should this be confused with mere illusionism, which is increasingly demanded of *all* fantastical screen fiction. For audiences to suspend their disbelief of flying scenes in the *Harry Potter* films (2001–), it is certainly true that the fantasy must be couched in terms of certain physical realities; for example, we expect Harry's hair to be ruffled or blown back in proportion to the velocity of his flight. Yet the conventions of magical fantasy do not call for the broomstick to be made into a credible flying machine. By contrast, when the Green Goblin takes flight on his Goblin Glider in *Spider-Man* (Raimi 2002), the designer's invention must seem airworthy, with a visible power source, balancing mechanisms, and so on – even if the design is actually, from an aeronautical perspective, no less fanciful than the broomstick. In short, then, screen sf privileges a very particular kind of "to-be-looked-at-ness": it is built primarily around visual phenomena which, while striking and novel, must appear to have a place in a contemporary common-sense worldview, informed by popular understanding of science.

But how can we proceed from these initial observations? The overarching claim for the importance of verisimilitude is of limited value in itself. An important corollary is that screen sf has always made an acute appeal to the viewer's sense of the tactile properties of unfamiliar phenomena. Consequently, among the classically defined elements of design, *texture* has always been paramount in sf, although the kind of surface detail generally favored by film- and program-makers has, over time, veered across the scale. This shifting taste is most obvious in the futuristic buildings, vehicles, weapons, and other machines which are arguably at the heart of the genre. Two distinct phases are identifiable. From the 1920s to the late 1960s, most designers leaned heavily upon modernist architectural and industrial design, above all in the idioms which emanated from the Bauhaus and the work of Le Corbusier. Sleek, streamlined forms, generally simple in profile and smooth in contour, and either shiny metallic or near-white were the norm: examples include Everytown in *Things to Come* (Menzies 1936), the lunar rocket in *Destination Moon* (Pichel 1950), and the Martian travel machines in *War of the Worlds* (Haskin 1953). Costume for everything except flesh-and-blood monsters tended to follow suit, with the apogee of this austere trend embodied in those of the alien Klaatu and his robot companion Gort in *The Day the Earth Stood Still* (Wise 1951). Such design was often juxtaposed with hyper-textured organic creatures, such as the eponymous protagonist of *The Creature from the Black Lagoon* (Arnold 1954).

After 1970, designers of screen sf rapidly and radically rejected streamlined modernism, and increasingly since then complex texturing has been prevalent. Part of the reason for this shift was undoubtedly the actual currency of spaceflight, which prior to the 1960s had been a central site of projective imagination in sf cinema. Both astronauts' garb and the craft in which they traveled were familiar sights in the mass media by the mid-1960s, but neither was a monument to sleek, seamless economy of line and contour. At the same time, confidence in the ideals of modernization and modernism was showing definite signs of disintegration, which began to express itself in contemporary architecture, industrial design, and fashion. Brutalist architects experimented with rough-hewn rather than smooth surfaces, while some mainstream early 1970s clothing, furnishing, and textile design had absorbed the "shaggy," ethnic-oriented tastes of the countercultural hippies.

Three massively influential films of the later 1970s and early 1980s, all now associated with the mainstream popularization of screen sf (and more specifically the sf blockbuster), represent the apogee of the new commitment to textural complexity and variety. These films – *Star Wars: Episode IV – A New Hope, Alien* (Scott 1979), *Blade Runner* (Scott 1982) – also epitomize a visual retreat from, or potent visual critique of, modernism. The opening shots of *Star Wars* and *Blade Runner* clearly signal to the audience that the films' fictive worlds, however remote in time or space, are as complex and nuanced as the world outside the theater. Both offer vistas of technology which combine gargantuan scale and power with a clear sense of the intricacy and untidiness of real-world spaces and artifacts. The riveted metal plating and tightly packed surface excrescences of battleship decks are vividly recalled in the treatment of the two spacecraft at the beginning of *Star Wars*, and the smog, floodlights, besmirched chimneys and gantries of contemporary heavy industry are amplified a thousand-fold in the aerial shot of the hellish 2019 Los Angeles in *Blade Runner*. Nor does the bombardment of evocative visual data let up in either movie. *Star Wars* was groundbreaking not only for the range of environments but also for the sheer density of "lived-in" realism which inflects each one. The surfaces of buildings, vehicles, machinery, and robots are scratched, oil-smeared and scorched; clothing and battle armor (even for the all-powerful Darth Vader) look used and scuffed rather than pristine; and the action periodically moves through spectacularly grim, disorderly environments, including a traveling scrapyard and a garbage sump. *Star Wars's* aesthetic evokes the mixture of flyblown shabbiness and dustily expansive natural grandeur which John Ford, Sergio Leone, and Henry Hathaway had rendered so picturesque in their Technicolor westerns.

The claustrophobic *Alien* extended the visceral meta-realism of *Star Wars*. Most of the film takes place on the massive, interstellar freighter *Nostromo*. Seen from without, the ship is a threatening, lumpen mass, emphatically unlike the austerely elegant craft of movies such as *Forbidden Planet* (Wilcox 1956) and television series such as *Star Trek*. Within, the *Nostromo* is a medley of eerily familiar-seeming environments, combining forms and palettes associated with industrial and clinical spaces. The darkness and drear of the ship's unimposing metal walkways and dingy, topically lit command center are punctuated by "white" spaces of the infirmary, lab, computer center, and cryogenic sleeping quarters. Yet the high-value notes offer nothing upbeat or reassuring, for these bright interiors are no less visually cluttered in their profiles and contours, and their harsh lighting belies comfort or optimism. Nor is there anything eye-catching, far less stylish, about the crew's costumes: studiedly unremarkable, neutral fatigues which might as well date from the Second World War as from the future. In other words, design for the *Nostromo* is deceptively spectacular, for in Scott's onscreen presentation it is made to affect dreariness.

The highly textured, visually complex design imagery typical of late 1970s sf accommodated wildly different filmic sensibilities, from the eclectic romanticism of *Star Wars* to the near *cinéma vérité* character of *Alien*. Both complex texturing (or in Ridley Scott's term, "layering") of design elements and the lived-in look continue to be used by designers in sf film and television as diverse as *Delicatessen* (Jeunet and Caro 1991), *Demolition Man* (Brambilla 1993), *Battlestar Galactica* (2004–), and *Torchwood* (2006–). Clearly these design sensibilities carry no special ethical or ideological valence. They are merely among those conventions which tend to accrue to any genre over time, and can be justified only in terms of filmmakers' and audiences' (perceived) expectations of what instances of that genre should look like.

The discovery of consistent stylistic concerns in screen sf does not really contribute much to our understanding of the genre's nuances. To pursue the ways in which design might generate meaning, it is necessary to move from the generic to the particular – to examine individual texts. Let me at once enter a caveat: it is not my intention in what follows to identify some kind of opposition between narrative and design. The idea that design imagery can potentially obscure, thwart, or block narrative, as more than one commentator has claimed, is based on a false premise (Affron and Affron 1995: 36–7; Tashiro 1998: 15–16, 21). Design is spatial: narrative is teleological; narrative is in part borne by, and in principle wholly reducible to, words; design is not (Britton and Barker 2003: 16–17). So rather than ask how design relates to narrative, as though the two had the potential to harmonize or quarrel, it is more productive to ask how design can operate within the whole imaginative and conceptual experience invoked by screen entertainment. In relation to sf, this overarching question begs more particularized ones. First, since design must tap into the viewer's common-sense response in order to uphold sf's meta-reality effect, by what means does it do so? And second, how much does design imagery excite reflection or speculation about the diegetic reality and the text's underlying ideas?

In addressing these questions, I will focus on *Blade Runner* and *Firefly* (2002–3) because the different role of design in each is heightened by the fact that they have certain baseline commonalities. Both exhibit that generic hybridity or "borrowing" which, at least since the 1970s, has been a standard modality of sf. *Blade Runner* draws heavily on the private-eye movie and film noir, involving as it does an attempt by a police detective to track down a group of killer androids. *Firefly* is a frontier saga in the manner of a western, following a gang of good-hearted thieves: it recalls not only historical facts of nineteenth-century America (such as a recent civil war) but also the manners, idiomatic speech, and other affectations of characters in screen westerns. In both texts, design is crucial to establishing the generic allegiance – and, of course, also necessarily a prime descriptor of the ways in which the worlds we see are *not* of the past but of the future.

One cannot discuss design in *Blade Runner* without acknowledging that this is a film with competing versions. The 1982 theatrical releases, with voiceover and happy ending, was largely supplanted by the 1991 "director's cut," from which both narration and the final sequence were omitted, but into which some excised footage – of an enigmatic reverie sequence – was reintegrated, with a 2007 "final cut" offering another version of the dream and, among other things, tidying up some continuity errors. Although the production design is powerfully evocative in all versions, it almost inevitably possesses more unconstrained potential for meaning in the later versions. The original version's voiceover tends to direct viewers' attention and inflect their responses, curbing some of the speculation and imaginative engagement for which the many protracted silences of the director's and final cuts open up a space. Consequently, I will focus on the latter versions. Without the Chandleresque monologue, the scene which introduces the protagonist, ex-"blade runner" Deckard, runs for over a minute with no substantive dialogue. The following sequence, in which Deckard's erstwhile colleague Gaff takes him to police headquarters in his flying "spinner," runs for almost as long with no diegetic sound except machine noise and the muted chatter of police radio communication. One could cite even longer dialogue-free scenes. With this kind of protracted exposure to nothing but bodies and objects in space, the suggestive power of design will almost inevitably loom large for the audience.

At a purely descriptive level, *Blade Runner*'s set design consistently affirms Scott's chosen aesthetic of a film set 40 years in the future but in the style of 40 years ago (Webb 1996: 44), for this is not only a noir city but also an almost oppressively art deco city. The "Mayan Revival" aesthetic of cast-concrete blocks used for the walls of Deckard's apartment is only the most oft-seen of an almost unceasing array of grooved, striated, and raised surfaces, most of which evoke the rich architectural ornament of the interwar period. Even the unequivocally futuristic exterior of the Police Headquarters building follows suit: the ridged roof of this essentially cylindrical building is subdivided into seven flared landing platforms which recall the stepped trapezoid motif so endemic to deco.

Costume is consonant with sets not only in that much of the dress evokes 1940s fashions – the square-shouldered suits and high-collared fur coats worn by the main female character, Rachael; Deckard's and Gaff's trench coats; the dinner jacket and octagonal glasses worn by android-manufacturer Tyrell – but also in the fact that most of the items have exceptionally rich surfaces. Deckard's broad trench-coat collar is wide-wale corduroy, his sports jacket of nubby tweed; one of Rachael's dresses is made up of broad horizontal strips of different silks, one of her coats consists of strips of faux-fur; and so on. Most remarkable of all is the correspondence between Tyrell's white matelassé dressing gown and the raised-lozenge panels of his bedroom doors, a detail which camera setups and editing provide ample opportunity to register.

This texturing of costume – together with the widespread use of muted, low-value palettes and multiple patterns – actually serves to defamiliarize the "vintage" forms, sidestepping the kind of nostalgia courted by the 1940s-esque visual world of *Batman* (Burton 1989). This defamiliarization is furthered by appositional contrast, such as the punk-influenced costumes and coiffures of the androids, especially their leader, Batty, and the high-tech modes of transport seen throughout (although the various road vehicles' shells actually have a sub-Cubist aesthetic not wholly inconsistent with the art deco norm). Conversely, the mass of accreted mechanical detail and quotidian flotsam in almost every scene – pipe-work, ducting, exhaust fans, fizzing fluorescent lights, uncollected trash piles, brazier fires, and so on – seems all too familiar, quite plausibly extending the grubby, retro-fitted mishmash of present-day high-density cities. Although *Blade Runner* speaks of interstellar travel beyond our current capabilities, its visual paraphernalia is compellingly credible as a common-sense image of the near future.

Beyond both evoking and complicating the noir benchmark, the film's saturation-level visual incident also plays powerfully into its larger conceptual concerns. As already implied, this is a movie so measured in pace as to be almost a montage of tableaux vivants and still-lifes: even the few action sequences are stately, balletic, and stylized. Attention to physical detail is oppressive, down to the lovingly photographed, minute swirl of blood in Deckard's shot glass as, after a fight, he drinks with lacerated lips. The film boasts a ceaseless pageant of fetishized phenomena, from the conventionally prized (Rachael's ultra-glossy hair, Gaff's and Batty's cool leather coats, the gorgeously rich "concrete textile" walls of Deckard's apartment) to the surreal, the sinister, and the sick (eyeballs floating in a tank of nutrients, Batty's pallid hand involuntarily clenched in the onset of his death throes). The consistent, mesmeric appeal to the sense of touch and the sensual foregrounding of manufactured artifacts in effect establish parity between inanimate objects and human bodies. How telling, in a text which is overtly concerned with distinguishing humans from their physically identical android counterparts, and with questions of how truth and identity are made.

Blade Runner begins with a tacit injunction to *look*: in the second shot, an eyeball fills the frame, reflecting the Los Angeles cityscape. Yet the unreliability of perception – in the metaphorical as well as literal sense – is stressed throughout, and special effects design plays a key, albeit subtle, part in this. Photographs are supposed to fix memories, to provide certitude. Yet when Rachael brings childhood snapshots to Deckard to prove to him that she is not an android, one of them briefly flickers into life in his hands as though making the fixed reality of the past fugitive. The effect is so deftly realized as to be almost subliminal. In summary, then, inasmuch as the relationships between memory, emotional experience, identity, and knowledge are central to the script of *Blade Runner*, the conception and deployment of design imagery establishes them as central to the construction of *Blade Runner* as a whole text – visual and aural.

Because of its smaller screen size and corresponding loss of definition, television cannot offer so sensuously absorbing an experience, nor so clearly defined a spectacle, as theatrically released films, even in the age of "home cinema." As a medium, television is therefore relatively ill-equipped to indulge the kind of intensely evocative pictorialism of directors such as Ridley Scott. If this is a general limitation, the television *series* as a form creates other, very specific problems for the designer – and these are greatly intensified for sf, given the constraints on budget and time. While a series is intended to command audience loyalty, it must remain "porous" enough to attract casual viewers. The onus of maintaining unity and continuity while effecting regular reintroductions and extensions of the diegetic world is considerable, especially for the designers who are responsible for settings (real or virtual).

In addition to these medium- and form-based difficulties, some of the design challenges in *Firefly* stemmed from the fact that its creator, Joss Whedon, so heavily exploited sf's capacity to hybridize. *Firefly* calls for the audience to believe in a very particular fusion of cultures and generic signifiers, even though the main components of this amalgam make slightly uneasy bedfellows. On the one hand, *Firefly's* projection of a would-be utopian Sino-American interplanetary alliance does not strain audience credulity: Pacific Rim sensibilities are now well entrenched in screen sf, so *Firefly's* images of cities and other spaces which amplify characteristics of Tokyo, Hong Kong, and Taipei could rest on generic precedent. On the other, the centrality of American Civil War and pioneer-era overtones had the potential seriously to upset the text's credibility if too strongly mirrored in design. Images of the "Old West," as that phrase implies, are expressive of an emphatically discrete, remote past, and consequently more difficult to project into a fictional future than, say, the machine-turned, crystalline motifs of art deco. This holds good even if we accept that *Firefly* is at some level a tongue-in-cheek twist on earlier science-fiction frontier narratives, such as the original *Star Trek*. Coarsely western-influenced design could easily have pushed such knife-edge playfulness into the realm of parody. The principle of extended common sense is upheld in *Firefly* by a variety of means, all of which tend to strengthen the series' distinctiveness and mute any potential "hokiness." In design terms, what yokes *Firefly's* various generic constituents together is the fact that they are tempered and melded by reference to aspects of the contemporary world which we take for granted. As noted above, for nearly a generation now this appeal to the "normal" has been a common conceit in screen sf design, but *Firefly's* designers went to unprecedented lengths in making an array of aspects of design self-effacing. A prime example is the use of conventional projectile weapons rather than laser guns. This not only makes sense in (and of) the quasi-western context but also renders the weaponry unremarkable.

The sophistication of the set and principal model design is that it hides its conceptual elegance in the seemingly familiar. Carey Meyer's exquisitely conceived and realized interiors for *Serenity*, the Firefly-class spaceship of the show's title, relate the ship to the unselfconscious forms of contemporary air and sea freighters: the studiedly workaday interior gives a strong impression of being ergonomically sound and for the most part baldly utilitarian. Lovely touches in the set dressing confirm that this is a domicile in which day-to-day problems have been solved in earthily reasonable ways. In the communal living space, for instance, shelves have netting guards strung in front of them to contain objects that might be displaced in a bumpy flight.

Utilitarian touches are overlaid with selective, unostentatious humanizing detail, such as the vine of foliate stenciling over the communal space's resolutely cheery, primary-color paint scheme, which sounds a touching note of domestic cosiness. Even on a 40-inch television screen, such detail is not rendered picturesque for the viewer; far less is it demanding of the gaze *à la Blade Runner*. It is in aggregate that shots of Meyer's sets offer a persuasive description of homely routine in rooms apparently designed to be livable rather than photogenic. Nothing, including most of the instrumentation, seems startlingly futuristic; but nor is it self-consciously retro. Thus, when we see the ship's captain, Mal Reynolds, eating with chopsticks while drinking from a pioneer-style tin mug, the potential anachronism of the latter has already been defused by the ethos of Meyer's set. We might well expect such cheaply available and crude wares to form part of the unpretentious hotchpotch of daily life so consistently avowed by this set.

Perhaps the most sensitive area of design in terms of both expressing and managing *Firefly*'s western aesthetic is costume. As a generality, the clothed body occupies rather more than half the screen on television, so any effect is likely to loom large – and potentially distract. Yet costume must also speak clearly to genre and character, especially in a text such as this, which for all its action set pieces is strongly character driven. Not merely the broad frontier/reconstruction narrative of *Firefly* but also the idiom of dialog itself seems to demand some kind of nod to "Old West" dress. Several of the protagonists speak in a Southern-inflected patois, and quasi-"western" collo-quialisms pervade the dialogue: the crew call *Serenity* a "boat," not a ship, say "'verse" for universe, use "conjure" where we would say "guess" or "suspect," and so on. Mal's clothing does indeed seem as though it might hail from the Civil War era, with suede duster, suspenders and knee-length boots, but in this respect he is alone. His costume is offset by the dress of the two other most overtly "Southern" characters, engineer Kaylee and tough-guy Jayne. Both are clothed in a manner which is, to all intents and purposes, present-day: Jayne wears athletic-fit T-shirts and combats, while Kaylee typically sports funkily colored, contemporary stretch shirts under her coveralls. Having said that, designers Jill Ohanneson and Shawna Trpcic sidestepped the danger of Mal's dress appearing at odds with his crew's through their handling of palette. Since warm, "earth" tones closely correspondent with Mal's dominate costumes for nearly the whole group, his outfit appears distinctive, even iconic, but not outré.

The other design strategy which encourages acceptance of Mal's dress, and simul-taneously cements the overall hybrid aesthetic of the *Firefly* 'verse, is the fact that his is not the only "heritage" costume. One of his companions, the courtesan Inara, dresses in garments variously redolent of the Chinese qipao and the Indian lehnga choli. Inara's are the series' most eye-catching outfits, by virtue both of their inherent sumptuousness and the fact that she has a new one for each episode. That she provides a visual counterweight to Mal's stately quasi-Victorian dress is especially apt, since the two characters question each other's values throughout, and there is unresolved sexual tension between them.

Just because *Firefly* is so strongly character driven, higher-order questions about the role of design yield answers as subtle, even reticent, as the designs themselves. While *Firefly* does not address philosophical matters relating to the nature of identity, it is oriented toward another frequent concern of sf. Many episodes deal with consequences of the invasive use of technology, in terms of both the manipulation of the individual and the problems of large-scale social engineering. To put this more broadly, the series addresses mutual responsibility at both the global and local levels. Consequently, quite apart from any other consideration of genre, medium or budget, *Firefly*'s primary focus on society and the "chosen family" of Mal's crew precludes a design aesthetic like *Blade Runner*'s, in which people and artifacts enjoy visual parity. Spectacle is an inevi-table constituent of screen sf, but in *Firefly* it was necessary to restrain it – to avoid a situation in which design compromised the plausibility of the text's fictional world, with costumes "drowning" the characters who wore them. Although it is touched upon in both case studies, I have given relatively little attention to the ways in which design imagery is mediated to the audience in the production process. This is not to undervalue the role of cameraman and lighting director, whose work crucially modifies the "raw materials" of costume and set design. But ultimately, for present purposes, I justify privileging materiality in this chapter by the fact that sf itself privileges materiality. Realized designs fundamentally dictate the conditions of their presentation: the smooth and sweeping *moderne* forms of the Aerospace Corporation headquarters in *Gattaca* (Niccol 1997) could never light like the baroque textures of the spaceship *Auriga* interiors in *Alien: Resurrection* (Jeunet 1997).

So, in conclusion, let me return to the notion of restraint. I hesitate to endorse, even by default, an image of design as some Kong-like beast, always seeking to break its bonds and run amok. Yet just because of its intrinsic generic tendencies, film- and program-makers working in sf undeniably need to calculate how much of the evocative potential of design they really want to "unleash" in any given text.

Bibliography

Affron, C. and Affron, M.J. (1995) *Sets in Motion: art direction and film narrative*, Brunswick, NJ: Rutgers University Press.

Barsacq, L. (1976) *Caligari's Cabinet and Other Grand Illusions: a history of film design*, Boston: New York Graphic Society.

Britton, P.D. and Barker, S.J. (2003) *Reading Between Designs: visual imagery and the generation of meaning in The Avengers, The Prisoner, and Doctor Who*, Austin: University of Texas Press.

Kuhn, A. (1999) "Introduction," in *Alien Zone II: the spaces of science-fiction cinema*, London and New York: Verso.

Tashiro, C.S. (1998) *Pretty Pictures: production design and the history film*, Austin: University of Texas Press.

Webb, M. (1996) "'Like Today, Only More So': the credible dystopia of *Blade Runner*," in D. Neumann (ed.) *Film Architecture: set designs from Metropolis to Blade Runner*, Munich and New York: Prestel.

35
DIGITAL GAMES

Tanya Krzywinska and Esther MacCallum-Stewart

Shooting regimented rows of insurgent pixilated aliens, speeding through dark tunnels inside an alien planet in a super-charged spacecraft to rescue kidnapped scientists, amassing and deploying resources to do battle with House Harkonnen, banding together to wage tactical war on the alien enemy, tracking down replicants, using cool moves to dance aliens to death ... One of the challenges for contemporary critical analysis is to understand the longstanding relationship between sf (themes, iconography, narratives) and digital games. This may be achieved by differentiating sf games in terms of genre, style, and narrative, and by exploring the potential gains and shortcomings of conceptualizing games in terms of the models used in the analysis of sf.

Table 1 lists a variety of landmark sf digital games. Unconstrained by the need for live-action performance and expensive sets, digital games have since their inception provided a ready location for sf. Like animation and computer-generated content, game technologies afford far greater flexibility for the creation of the impossible in terms of settings, physics, physicalities, point of view, and actions. The contemporary critic must also evaluate the simultaneous and contradictory claims that the new frontier of digital gaming has brought a new dimension to sf and that videogames less "boldly go" than "broadly follow."

Table 1 Sf digital games

Year	Game	Type
1962	*Space War* (Steve Russell *et al.*)	Space Shooter
1978	*Space Invaders* (Taito Corp)	Space Shooter
1979	*Asteroids* (Atari)	Space Shooter
1984	*The Hitchhiker's Guide to the Galaxy* (Infocom)	Text Adventure
	Elite (Acornsoft)	Trading Game/ Flight Simulator

Year	Game	Type
1992	*Dune II: The Battle for Arrakis* (Westwood Studios)	Real Time Strategy (RTS)
1993	*Doom* (id Software)	First Person Shooter (FPS)
1994	*Earthworm Jim* (Shiny Entertainment)	Platform Game
1995	*The Dig* (LucasArts)	Adventure
1997	*Oddworld: Abe's Oddysee* (Oddworld Inhabitants)	Platform Game
	Blade Runner (Westwood Studios)	Adventure
	Fallout (InterPlay, Black Isle Studios)	Role Playing Game (RPG)
	Turok (Iguana Entertainment)	FPS
1998	*Half Life* (Valve Software)	FPS/LAN enabled
	Starcraft (Blizzard Entertainment)	RTS
1999	*Sid Meier's Alpha Centauri* (Firaxis)	Management simulation – "God Game"
2000	*Space Channel 5* (Sega/UGA)	Rhythm Shooter
2001	*Halo: Combat Evolved* (Bungie Studios, Microsoft)	FPS/Single player/online/ co-op
	Uplink: Hacker Elite (Introversion)	PC Game
2002	*The Thing* (VU Games, Computer Artworks)	Action Adventure
2003	*EVE Online: The Second Genesis* (CCP)	MMORPG
2004	*Halo 2* (Bungie Studios, Microsoft Game Studio)	FPS/Single player/online/ co-op
2006	*Gears of War* (Epic Games)	FPS/Single player/online/ co-op
2007	*Halo 3* (Bungie Studios, Microsoft Game Studio)	FPS/Single player/online/ co-op

Central to understanding the ways that digital games use sf, and informing the challenge they present to intellectual investigation, are their media-specific formal properties. This includes the ongoing development of computing and other technologies used to produce increasingly detailed graphical environments, different types of gameplay, more nuanced control systems, and the ability to play games collectively over a network or the internet. Digital games are more centered upon player agency and participation than any other medium, yet simultaneously they are rule-based, grounded in computer-based systems of cause-and-effect, and designed in various ways to give the player a sense of progress (see Aarseth 1997; Juul 2005; King and Krzywinska 2006). This is what defines them as "games," as well as virtual spaces. It distinguishes the form from other media, and provides sf with new formal and structural dimensions, even though such games tend to follow established thematic and iconographic regimes. A medium that invites and responds to player participation and agency in new and more pervasive ways makes digital games more than just complex and involving entertainment. A further challenge for the critic is therefore to examine the implications of the new forms and modes of consumption that are emerging from games, whether in terms of new ways of learning and new ways of using technology in domestic arenas, or in terms of the way science and technology inform art and popular culture.

What conceptual tools do we need to understand digital games? Textual analysis, based on principles derived from semiotics and formalism, can be used to explore the ways in which games communicate meaning (through audio, visual style, narrative, movement, color, shape, spatial, and temporal organization) as well as a game's ludic aspects. Theories of interpretation and the active "reader," derived from cultural studies, hermeneutics, and reader-response theory, thereby come into play. How an individual reads the signifiers of a game is dependent on situational (social, cultural, epistemological, personal) factors, with different players' readings varying according to social, ludic, and narratological patterns. Therefore, the meaning of the game is far from fixed, regardless of designers' and artists' intentions. The nonlinear nature of many games – what one person encounters in their gameplay as a result of particular choices and actions will differ from any other player's experience – further complicates textual matters.

Games then have some textual features that differ from other media, largely because a player's choices are responded to in real time by the game's internal programming, but that does not mean that wholly new methodologies are required to understand that difference. Comparative analysis, a technique used by scholars seeking to understand the way that different types of media alter a particular narrative or a franchised fictional world, proves useful. Textual and comparative analysis, alongside approaches derived from sociology, audience studies, and participant observation, are established methodologies in sf studies. They similarly provide tools for understanding games as aesthetic and cultural artifacts as well as the complex relationship between videogame, text, and player. But without a close understanding of what it is to play a game, without a direct experience of how the ludic and aesthetic context shapes perception of meaning and narrative, and other situational contexts, any analysis will be lacking.

Not so many years ago, digital games seemed to confirm the notion that culture was becoming science-fictional, with gameplay providing an experience that resonated with the type of cyber-embodiment described in William Gibson's novels. But as games moved out of the "geek ghetto" and became integral to popular culture, working with increasingly sophisticated digital audio, visual, and communications technologies in an environment of media-convergence and cross-media franchising, what we expect from games has shifted enormously. While some nostalgically regard the way that the simple games of the early 1980s emphasized gameplay over graphics, high-budget sf games developed for the "next-gen" consoles capable of exploiting HD televisions are now largely informed by the audiovisual rhetoric of Hollywood spectacle. With the diversification of games onto multiple platforms, sf games have been increasingly made for those best suited to the production of detailed, diversely styled, graphical environments. For example, *Halo 2* (2004), the best-selling Xbox game to date, and *Gears of War* (2006) for the Xbox 360, easily outstrip rival products using similar gameplay but different generic references. At the same time, supported by internet rather than high-street distribution, there is a market for lower-budget puzzle games, such as the fiendish *Portal* (2007), which do not seek to please through the impressive graphics and "twitch" style gameplay of many sf games. As with most popular culture, there is a great deal of diversity within the field, presenting a further challenge for critical analysis. However, the formal properties and commercial context of games seem to have led to an emphasis on sf that privileges spectacle and action over contemplation, and in which speculation, clearly integral to the act of playing games, is not as radically realized as is possible. The "novum" (Suvin 1979: 63) of digital games lies not so much in content or theme, but in the way in which they are engaged with and through the technological means of their generation and display. Therefore, the analyst must balance any critique of the commercial imperatives that make games seem conservative or clichéd with an understanding of the ways that players make meaning from their gameplay that might not be immediately apparent. Theories developed for the analysis of popular culture, as well as paying due regard to the technical and formal innovations of digital games, aid in this endeavor.

Why sf?

The relatively primitive representational forms of early digital games – simple, largely abstract, graphics and limited movement – compelled designers to rely not on realism but on players' imaginative investment, fueled by generic knowledge to flesh out detail. Representing a space invader with a few carefully arranged pixels is easier than so depicting a human, and thus early sf games drew on what some regard as most valuable in sf novels: like prose fiction, and unlike later games, films, and television series, where everything is fully visualized, early games left room for imagination, despite the limited physical responses – "button bashing" – they offered.

The man-versus-alien premise of *Space Invaders* informed later sf games, including many of the most commercially successful, such as *Doom* (1993), *Quake* (1996), *Halo* (2001), and *Gears of War*. These fairly linear, map-based games use 3D graphical environments and are set in coherent worlds in which alien hordes threaten humanity. Players take on the role of tough, militarized heroes, furnished with an impressive armory to clear areas of aliens or their minions. The pace is fast and furious, requiring close attention and speedy responses. Controls and interface are kept to the bare essentials. The player–character is constantly on the move. These games promote a strong sense of immediacy and action, with agency grounded in fast reflexes and split-second decisions. Accordingly, pulp-sf narratives, distilled to a bare narrative minimum and posing no moral dilemmas, are ideally suited to rapid, twitch-based, adrenaline-fueled gameplay, itself contextualized by familiar generic iconography. In this regard, these games take from sf only what they need to create intense gameplay experiences. Sf serves the shoot'em-up genre exceedingly well, and these games bring technical and formal innovations and new pleasures to sf. However, some regard their simple narratives and central quick-draw action as juvenile in relation to more established forms (see Crawford 2003; Jenkins 2001) and lacking the philosophical scope, moral incertitude, and artistic sophistication of some sf literature and film. Yet the hands-on experience of such games, whether single or multiplayer, can present moral and problem-solving dilemmas to players, prompting later reflection.

It is easy for those unaccustomed to games to assume that they all follow the same pattern, but a great deal of diversity and genre splitting occur in the field. Genre formation is nebulous, protean, and contested, and as in most popular culture, genre hybrids are common. The *Resident Evil* cycle (1996–) merges horror with sf, the *Final Fantasy* series (1987–) mixes fantasy with sf, and even *Tomb Raider III* (1998) includes an *X-Files*-style alien-conspiracy theory in its treasure-hunting format. Complicating the issue still further, a game's "genre" is frequently defined on the basis of the viewpoint or the type of gameplay, rather than narrative type or setting. First Person Shooters (e.g., *Doom, Quake, Half Life* (2001), *Half Life 2* (2004), *Halo Combat Evolved* (2001), *Halo 2*) are regarded as a genre by players and categorized as such in reviews, as are Third Person games (*Unreal II* (2003), *Lego Star Wars* (2005), *Gears of War*), Real Time Strategy games (*Starcraft* (1998), *Emperor: Battle for Dune* (2001)), Role-Playing games (*Fallout* (1997)), and God/Management games (*Sid Meier's Alpha Centauri* (1999)). These may draw on sf narratives, themes, and iconography, but "sf" is rarely used to delineate a game's type. It is therefore useful in a games context to refer to "sf" as a "milieu" or "setting" found in diverse game genres.

Sf milieus have a number of advantages for game designers. They draw on familiar paradigms that sketch a game's context for the player. They also allow for all kinds of effects "magic" to be included as imagined technologies, such as the "teleport," which provides a contextualized way to move about worlds without having to take time away from a game's core activities to run a character to a desired location. In-game computers and other, more imaginary communication devices through which a player can be given information make sense in an sf milieu, such as that of *Doom 3* (2004), in which the player is required to access a mainframe through terminals dotted around the gamespace. In-game computers sometimes break the fourth wall. In the PC game *Blade Runner* (1997), when the player uses an "Esper" machine to examine photographs in close detail for clues, the machine fills the player's screen, making it synonymous with the diegetic screen. This is taken even further in *Uplink* (2001), a hacker game played as if the player's computer is the in-game computer, making for an uncanny sense that you are hacking into real-life systems.

An sf setting provides, therefore, the rationale for the stylistic coherence of in-game items – very often these take on a far more functional, practical iconography with an sf twist. The hyper-realized magic mushroom power-up of the *Mario* games (1983–) is replaced with health kits and given names (stimpack, medikit) that are linguistically stylized to suit an sf setting. Heads-Up Displays become part of a spacesuit (*Halo*, *Metroid Prime* (2002)). Guns become exaggerated, shoot spectacular bolts of neon blue light across the screen, graduating from mundane to monstrous, but still remaining within the bounds of the game's "science." In many shooter-based sf games, as the player progresses and becomes more powerful, guns get bigger and more fantastical – from handgun, to nail-gun, to Big Fucking Gun in *Doom*, for example.

Developments in filmic special effects technologies should also be considered when analyzing games' use of sf settings. The increasing popularity of blockbuster sf and dominance of franchising might be regarded as contributing to the race toward making games that look, in terms of their graphics, like movies and the servitude of games to brands established by films. These factors certainly contributed to the reversal of the trend toward games that were distinctive for their abstract styles and that required imaginative investment or, indeed, to the development of original intel- lectual property. The increasing connections between game-production houses and Hollywood have seen debates around the relationship between spectacle and other elements such as narrative extend into games studies. As with other popular cultural forms, this has led to concerns that games act as a social sedative, arresting the player's ability to think critically by providing the equivalent of highly calorific but nutri- tionally lacking junk food. Gamers' responses might illuminate the issue differently in terms of the symbolic, emotional, and psychological place games have in their lives.

Without succumbing to technological determinism, it must be noted that the varying graphical capabilities of available platforms, and the screen size of a console, PC, or handheld device, are also factors in the choice of fictional milieu. Games for consoles designed to be displayed on television screens and which have larger memories lean toward the cinematic; *Halo* for the Xbox and *Gears of War* and *Halo 3* for the Xbox 360 flaunt high-resolution graphics, and capitalize on the commercial success of widescreen televisions. This is also the case with PC-based games, where memory and graphics cards can easily be replaced to keep apace of new graphical developments. The PC's networked capabilities also make possible Massively Multiplayer Online Games (MMOGs), which take players into extensive social worlds that can easily be upgraded and patched to add new activities and spaces. Mobile platforms with smaller screens and memories tend to avoid sf precisely because they are far less able to create spectacle and large worlds, although they do provide a market for retro sf games (e.g., the Nintendo DS anthology title *Retro Atari* (2006) includes a version of *Asteroids* (1979)).

Originally almost the default choice in the production of games, sf must now fit specific markets. While many early games designers shared an interest in sf with their target audience of young male players, the gameplaying audience has expanded away from both this genre and demographic. For example, Japanese and MMOG players have a broader predilection for fantasy games, which has had a huge influence on the market in general, while games aimed at the family, casual gamers, and older users tend to opt for more prosaic themes. The recent success of *Dance Dance Revolution* (1998) and *Brain Training* games (2006–7) demonstrates how the market has successfully diversified.

Franchising culture: *The Matrix* vs *Star Wars*

It is important to understand the commercial context in which games are produced. They are the product of a large team of people with a range of different skills and it requires massive investment to make a triple-A game. Because of the risk involved, franchising is central to the industry. The *Mario* franchise is perhaps the best-known and commercially most successful, and following Miyamoto Shigeru's immensely popular platform games also come racing titles, puzzle games, and multiplayer games that take advantage of certain platforms. Franchising is also carried out on a smaller scale. Many films spin off a tie-in game relying on the title, rather than the quality or content of the game, for success. This can lead to rushed and flawed games nonetheless selling in large quantities (and being enjoyed by players seeking to partake in and extend their contact with the brand). A successful franchise is one that not only capitalizes on the product name, but also embraces the unique qualities of narrative and gameplay within digital games themselves.

Transmediality also has increasing pertinence in games (see Jenkins 2006; Klastrup and Tosca 2004), particularly as films, television series, urban myths, and literary texts all provide fertile narratives for game environments. Players often utilize their knowledge of these exterior texts to bring coherence to the gamescape itself (see Krzywinska 2004; MacCallum-Stewart and Parsler 2007). In the case of sf, designers have also tried to attune games with their media contemporaries more directly. *Enter the Matrix* (2003) was one of the first transmedial games, operating in tandem with a number of other media in order to produce a sustained whole, rather than remediation or adaptation. Along with *The Matrix Reloaded* (Wachowski brothers 2003) and a series of anime shorts, *The Animatrix* (2003), it attempted to provide a more cohesive whole, with overlapping segments and events. For example, in *The Animatrix*, the courier, Jue, dies when she delivers a message to the rebels after having discovered that the machines are approaching Zion; in *Enter the Matrix*, the player receives and must activate the codes; and in *The Matrix Reloaded*, the rebels meet to make plans around this information, commenting that Jue's ship, the *Osiris*, was lost in the attempt to deliver the information.

The later *Matrix* films were criticized for their lack of coherence and loose ends, suggesting that the potential for games to truly inform a large media event was not yet fulfilled. As Diane Carr (2005) observes in her examination of the game, to a viewer, the rebel leader Morpheus will always have more perceived power than the individual gamer, who is just one of many players enacting the same narrative. Thus, although the sf format might seem to lend itself to this type of cross-pollination, other factors – not least the fact that not all of the film's fans were gameplayers – interfered with the ability for full transmedial storytelling.

The extremely successful *Star Wars* game franchise takes a very different approach to making contemporaneous products that match the world-vision of *Star Wars* itself. The games vary enormously in scope and genre (see Table 2), developing alongside digital gaming in a way which suggests canny marketing and a shrewd eye for the potential of games platforms. *Star Wars* games are generally of high quality, providing excellent gameplay, but they do not follow the narrative of the films verbatim. The *Star Wars* universe is huge, with massive amounts of secondary narrative in books, comics, trading cards, toys, and merchandisng, all of which are strictly regulated to ensure the cohesiveness of its underlying principles and history. The games are no exception, and herein lies their strength – they can follow the ethos of the universe without necessarily repeating the action of the films. Very often, they play on a specific aspect of the films, and blend it with a developed games genre. This does not need to refer specifically to the plot or characters of the films, since the universe itself is not only populated by these people, but has frameworks for other races, laws, planets, and cultural systems. Thus, the *Star Wars* universe creates itself from a largely coherent bricolage of prior items.

Table 2 *Star Wars* digital games

1983	Star Wars (Atari)	Flight simulator/ shooter	Arcade
1992–4	Super Star Wars Super Star Wars: The Empire Strikes Back Super Star Wars: Return of the Jedi	Platform Games	Console (SNES)
1993–9	X-Wing Series	Flight Simulation/ dogfighting	PC
	Dark Forces/Rebel Assault	First Person Shooter	PC
1999–2002	Star Wars Racer Series	Racing Games	Consoles
2000–2	Galactic Battlegrounds	Real Time Strategy	
2003–	Star Wars Galaxies		PC/MMORPG
2005–7	Lego Star Wars	Beat'em-up/ adventure specifically aimed at child/new audience	Consoles

Star Wars Galaxies (2003–), the Massively Multiplayer Online Role-Playing Game (MMORPG), epitomizes the ability both to foresee successful game patterns and to appropriate the *Star Wars* universe successfully. Launched as MMORPGs were starting to gather momentum, it allows players to live, fight, and play within the *Star Wars* universe. Like most of the *Star Wars* game titles, it is not particularly original, and its success can be located in its ability to create good gameplay in a highly lucrative, preexisting world which does not clash too much with the established continuity of the films. Unlike the *Matrix* game, the players do not move through predetermined areas or follow set questing patterns but have the freedom to roam around and, to an extent, choose what they wish to do within a large-scale environment. Players can choose to follow the Alliance or the Empire, or simply enact developed characters who do not have to work toward predetermined goals.

Film-as-game/game-as-film exploitation can also be seen in the development of the racing games which immediately followed the release of *Star Wars: Episode I – The Phantom Menace* (Lucas 1999). The spectacular pod race which forms the film's centerpiece is clearly modeled on computer-game imagery and dynamics, owing as much to the sf racing game *Wipeout* (1995) as it does to *Ben Hur* (Niblo 1925, Wyler 1959). The pod race follows the pilots through narrow canyons and broad desert tundra, over obstacles and around packed stands. The camera privileges a cockpit view redolent of racing games, unless dramatic action (such as hijacking or crashing) is taking place. This creates what Roger Caillois (1961) calls "ilinx" in the broader context of play types – the sensation of speed and vertigo at the very edge of dizziness and fragmentation that games often seek to provide.

Speculation

Videogames present various challenges for the entertainment and engagement of players, often borrowing from sf to contextualize them. At the forefront of the so-called digital revolution, they also present challenges to those seeking to understand what videogames bring to sf. Although they offer features unavailable to other media, many of the methods and conceptual models developed in sf studies remain effective in understanding their form, meanings, and ramifications. However, new concepts tuned to the cybernetic and emergent features of digital games are also required.

While games have generally low cultural status relative to literature and cinema, the very nature of videogames challenges some of the fundamental semantic oppositions that both ground and produce meaning. Game media challenge the type of philo-sophical questions that have often informed the themes and concerns of sf literature about the nature of reality and consciousness. Videogames bind the real with the virtual and the imaginary in some very explicit and innovative ways, even in the case of the apparently most simple first-person shooter. This manifests most obviously in the way games demand real actions of a player to facilitate progress through the game, as well as in the real social dimensions at play in the context of multiplayer games. In addition, the interactive and algorithmic basis of videogames, where altering various parameters produces emergent outcomes, appears to offer a fruitful arena for speculative fiction. Because games are made of code, and are not subject to the laws of the material world, it is *possible* to create out of seemingly nothing persistent real-time virtual worlds, with speculative and often unpredicted emergent physics, physiques, economies, and societies. Therefore, some of the techniques and concepts used in the analysis of sf, as well as exploratory ideas found in sf, can also be applied to games.

Videogames draw on preexisting media (text, screen, audio), but their distinctive quality lies in the pervasively participatory nature afforded by computational technologies. While other media require participation mostly at the level of the imagination (and require for access nonspecialist skills, like reading or media literacy), videogames require more from the player. Videogames are cybernetic systems, where, in various ways, a game's programming and graphics respond to the player's moment-by-moment input and vice versa. Unlike other media, the player's actions have consequences within the context of the game in material and often narrative terms. It might be the case that the gamespace and what is done there is separated from other activities designated as "real," but it is also clear that the player is doing "real" things on a number of levels. Primarily, this is visible in the act of pressing buttons in response to events on screen. These physical responses are then amplified, extruded, and fictionalized "on-the-fly" and in close to real time by the game's internal programming into what is seen and heard on screen (or, with some handheld devices, even felt physically).

The player's choice of action in a given situation puts into play only *one* of many possible consequences. And, even if that choice is made in the apparent safety of a virtual, imaginary space where it is possible to manipulate diegetic time to turn back the clock, chains of varied consequence are still apparent to the player through a number of feedback mechanisms. It is in the fabric woven by these choices that the ludic and the narrative trajectories emerge and coalesce. While actions can be overturned by going back to a previous save point or restarting a game, this is not always the case (in *Eve Online* (2003), items that have taken months to acquire can be lost irredeemably in battle). The player's actions and choices might also have irreparable social or economic ramifications, particularly in the context of online games – another dimension in games in which the virtual is bonded inextricably to the real, disturbing thereby a foundational binary. Yet it is also the case (in what might be thought of as a hands-on experience of the many-worlds interpretation of quantum physics) that many possibilities can be explored – or, less mind-bogglingly, that we can go back into the past to correct an action and consequence through the knowledge afforded by hindsight. In the virtual, the real flickers, lures, and repels; it is there and not there. We might be able to go back in time to rectify failure, but game parameters still limit what a player can do, where the player can travel, in a very direct way. From a Lacanian perspective, this palpable limitation provides contact with the Real, even if the virtual frame and, where possible, the ability to go back softens that contact.

Intrinsic to game media are a number of the philosophical questions and themes that have often informed sf, including those about time, agency, reality, identity, space, aesthetics, causality, physics, metaphysics, "life, the universe, and everything." In many narrative-based games, the player's manipulation of the controller is translated into the actions of an onscreen avatar who represents the player in the gamespace. The player's progress can be made evident through new capabilities and attributes acquired by the avatar in response to the player's choices and actions. Unlike films and books, players have direct, if not total, control over their avatars, and a core activity of many games is learning effectively to use an avatar's programmed capabilities according to situation. The potential capabilities, as well as the situations that an avatar–player encounters, might be termed the "real" of the game; gaining such capabilities also provides the types of obstacles that Vladimir Propp (1968) argues have a structural role to play in the formation of narrative. The real of the game might also become manifest when a player is not yet sufficiently skilled to achieve a certain required feat of which they know the avatar is capable. While avatars have real dimensions within the game, they are coded often as imaginary beings through their appearance and in having powers that reach beyond those the player has in everyday life. This works extremely well for franchising established fantasy genre brands: a player is offered the possibility of acting temporarily and to some extent materially in the skin of an alien, cyborg, military hero, disco-dancing space cadet, or wookie. It is here that the virtual processes of the imagination that underlie our relationship with any fictional construct and which facilitate suspension of disbelief come into play, but in some very specific ways. In games, embodiment occurs at the level of both the real (in terms of what we can do in the game, the avatar as prosthesis) and the imaginary.

For these reasons, games can be regarded as emerging from two important aspects of fantasy: "I wish …" and "What if …?" The very nature of interactive games makes the latter personal, becoming "what if *I* …?" (see Atkins 2003). With their ability to engage the player actively in problem-solving and speculation, and to place the player at the motivational center of an emergent story, videogames have the potential to bring something new and innovative to sf. But in a risk-averse industry, where development times are quite prolonged, the costs of production high, and returns often low, games frequently tend to be derivative and conservative, relying on tried-and-tested commercial formulas. This situation is not helped by the fact that games are regarded as being for children, and have a relatively low cultural status. One of the challenges for the attentive critic is, then, to understand better the form of videogames, asking what is unique to them *as* games. Unlike cinema, they operate in dimensions other than mere representation. One of the challenges for the industry is not simply to replicate and remediate, but to make games that utilize the speculative qualities of the form.

Bibliography

Aarseth, E. (1997) *Cybertext: perspectives on ergodic literature*, Baltimore, MD: Johns Hopkins University Press.

Atkins, B. (2003) *More than a Game: the computer game as fictional form*, Manchester: Manchester University Press.

Caillois, R. (1961) *Man Play and Games*, 1958, trans M. Barash, New York: The Free Press of Glencoe.

Carr, D. (2005) "The Rules of the Game, the Burden of Narrative: enter the Matrix," in S. Gillis (ed.) *The Matrix Trilogy: cyberpunk reloaded*, London: Wallflower Press.

Crawford, C. (2003) *Chris Crawford on Game Design*, Berkeley, CA: Peachpit Press.

Jenkins, H. (2001) "The Game as Object of Study," paper presented at the *Game Cultures* Conference, Bristol, June.

—— (2006) *Convergence Culture: where old and new media collide*, New York and London: New York University Press.

Juul, J. (2005) *Half-Real: videogames between real rules and fictional worlds*, Cambridge, MA: MIT Press.

King, G. and Krzywinska, T. (2006) *Tomb Raiders and Space Invaders: forms and meanings of videogames*, London: I.B. Tauris.

Klastrup, L. and Tosca, S. (2004) "Transmedial worlds – rethinking cyberworld design," *Proceedings International Conference on Cyberworlds 2004*. Online. Available HTTP: <http://www.itu.dk/people/klastrup/klastruptosca_transworlds.pdf> (accessed 1 April 2008).

Krzywinska, T. (2004) "Demon Power Girls: regimes of form and force in videogames *Primal* and *Buffy the Vampire Slayer*". Online. Available HTTP: <http://www.lse.ac.uk/collections/newFemininities/Demon.pdf> (accessed 1 April 2008).

MacCallum-Stewart, E. and Parsler, J. (2007) "New Perspectives on Digital Literature: criticism and analysis," *Dichtung Digital*. Online. Available HTTP: <http://www.dichtung–digital.de> (accessed 1 April 2008).

Propp, V. (1968) *Morphology of the Folktale*, 1927, trans. L. Scott, Austin: University of Texas Press.

Suvin, D. (1979) *Metamorphoses of Science Fiction: on the poetics and history of a literary genre*, New Haven, CT: Yale University Press.

36

EMPIRE

Istvan Csicsery-Ronay Jr

Science fiction and technoscientific empire

Sf is gradually gaining acceptance as a significant arena of cultural mediation for the regime of globalizing hypermodernism. Throughout much of the twentieth century, Euro-American cultural elites considered the themes and icons that made up sf's megatext (the large and mutable body of references that most sf artists and audiences consider to be the shared subcultural thesaurus of the genre) embodied in literary fiction, visual art, cinema, comics, music, and games, as the obsessions of a small technophilic subculture on the periphery of mainstream humanism.

Looking back at the century, it has become difficult to sustain that view. Sf artists have played an important role in articulating some of the powerful trends that shaped the political and cultural consciousness of the age. Foremost among the literary genres, sf imagined the possibilities of radical historical transformations resulting from technological innovation applied to social life. It negotiated the relationships among these transformations and the ethical myths of earlier phases of Western culture. It simultaneously interpreted and shaped the ideology of technoscience, that is, of science in the service of the technological rationalization of every domain of material existence. For the political imagination, sf created tools with which audiences could imagine the steady consolidation of technoscientific hegemony, defined by the drive to construct a universal regime of technoscience – hyper-global, extending beyond the limits of known space and mortality, containing an infinite variety of sublime and grotesque possibilities, and guided by a transglobal technocratic elite with lax ties to traditional historical communities, for whom the technological transmutation of once-universally held human truths is an inexorable given. Sf has shaped the contours of a new social-political imaginary tied not to personal rulers, nations, and territories, but to the utopian vision of the consolidation of existence into one world, one polity, and one mode of awareness, through the expansion of technological rationalization: a technoscientific empire.

I would like to look at some contours of this mediation, considering four of its main intersecting concepts: the "air-mindedness" that attended the popular enthusiasm for heavier-than-air flight; the vision of a single, globe-uniting, technocentric "One State"; the dissolution of traditional being, human and others, breaching ontological boundaries about the notion of existence, and the production of new fusions of "cyborg" beings as a result of technoscientific redescriptions and splices; and, finally, the drive to escape from the limits of physical containment and mortality, from the personal body and species biology, by attaining "escape velocity" in the acceleration of technological transformation. These world-models, derived from visions of the future, have contributed significantly to the sense that political legitimacy is also derived from a future yet to be constructed by technoscientific solutions for which the present must pay forward.

Technology, imperialism, and empire

Discourse about the cultural dimensions of imperialism has undergone several changes. The classical sense that the term refers to the competitive global expansionism of European national powers that reached its formal end with the First World War, gave way to a looser conception that covered the continuing maintenance of colonial rule in the interwar and post-Second World War periods. As the perspective of anti-colonial movements gained authority after the Second World War, the term was further expanded to cover neo-colonial arrangements among the erstwhile national empires, based less on direct political control over colonies than on the manipulation of their economies via financial networks based in the former capitals. Distributed through a world-system of economic exploitation dominated by national military-industrial complexes, the neo-colonial sense of imperialism is complemented by, adapting Paul Virilio's phrase, "endocolonialism," the extension of the dominating network to the "home country" and its cities, and to the national subject itself (see Virilio 1995). In the work of Michael Hardt and Antonio Negri (2000), the concept of imperialism has been superseded by the notion of empire achieved – "imperialism" marking the historical stage of striving to achieve forms of international domination, "empire" marking its achievement as a transnational regime of finance capitalism controlling a far-flung network of biological resources (foremost among them human labor) through elaborate interlocking mechanisms of communication and weapons.

Until recently, surprisingly little attention was paid in this discussion to the invention, distribution, and legitimation of diverse, interlocking systems of technological innovation and organization. Yet the decline of the classically imperialist projects created the conditions for their succession by a new project of deterritorialized supranational dominance guided by a technocratic elite with stronger ties to post-Enlightenment technological development than to national histories. This regime has depended on the residues of political power of its imperialist predecessors. In the twentieth century nation-states came increasingly to depend on technological development to maintain their legitimacy, and to survive. Yet within the technoscientific elites there was no necessary commitment to pre-imperial national values or even ideological axioms. The ruling orders of this regime owe their loyalty to visions of a "post-historical" future, in which technological rationalization will solve the archaic concerns of scarcity and human disequilibrium. Their goal, and also their dwelling place, is a technological empire, whose systems of communication, commodification, and control infiltrate, and indeed saturate, all formerly "natural" relationships, from the institutional to the biological.

There can be no doubt that without constantly accelerating technological innovation imperialism could not have had the force it did, or progressed so rapidly. Without steamships and gunboats, repeating rifles and machine guns, submarine cables, telegraph lines, and anti-malarial medicines, the power of imperial adventurers would have been greatly limited, and perhaps not even possible (see Headrick 1981). But imperial technology was not only a set of tools for exploiting colonies. Imperial future shock blew back into the colonial center, consolidating a new idea of political power linked to technological momentum, essentially colonizing the homeland too, and at a speed that made resistance futile (see Arendt 1951: 136–8; Adas 1989: 365–6; Hughes 1994). Each global success brought power and money to technological projects, creating a logrolling effect that drove irrational political and economic exploitation in grand-scale uncontrolled social experiments. It also fueled ever more focused and complex momentum – until social conflicts, both within and beyond the national borders, could be seen as politically manageable only through technological means. With imperialism, politics became technological.

The suicidal exhaustion of the imperialist world-system in the First World War revealed the degree to which national political power had become a function of technology's power to correlate different domains of social existence. In Walter Rathenau's civil and military mobilization of Germany, modern political elites discerned how quickly and thoroughly industrial projects could be directed, managed, and synchronized; how invention and discovery could be institutionalized; how more and more aspects of social life could be brought under the umbrella of technosocial organization, at an ever-accelerating pace; and how the political charge of these processes could be concealed and sublimated into the ideology of technological development – all inspired, designed, and overseen by scientific knowledge directed toward large-scale technological applications. In sum, political technoscience (see Henderson 1951). The conversion of politics into matters of technique had begun with the need to find solutions to imperial problems, without challenging the political legitimacy of domination. This became a central aspect of all conceptions of the high modernist state.

In the process, technoscience consolidated into a semi-independent sphere connected to overtly political ideology. It did not matter ultimately to its institutions which form of government insured the penetration and transformation of material existence by scientific materialism, so long as its power was obeyed. Soviet Stakhanovism and the Five-Year Plans, civil defense and public works of the Nazi war economy, the New Deal and Marshall Plan reconstruction agendas, the Soviet and US space programs, all were alibis for hypermodernization. Indeed, technoscience developed as an envelope for political power in the twentieth century. Technoscience has inspired faith independent of partisan political commitments, preventing most critiques within political elites, indeed even the effort to find alternative terms of discourse. An invisible imaginary regime takes shape, one for which national borders are secondary obstacles. It is an Enlightened empire of shared commitments to instrumentality, justified by its promise of ever-greater rationality and material abundance in the future, a future in which new ideas consistently produce new realities that consistently produce new resources, managed by technoscientific means, stimulated by technoscientific innovation and discovery, sustained by technoscientific machinery, and heading off the potentially catastrophic consequences of its practices through internal critique, new invention, and new discovery – the actually existing sf of a technoscientific regime on the verge of global consolidation and expansion into space. It is a world in which technological problems require technological solutions – and all problems are technological.

This imaginary utopian regime, ostensibly nonpolitical and international in fact, has facilitated the extension of capitalism into its current global phase, in which the uneasy balance of nations and international institutions serves the interests of the heirs of earlier imperialism. Flexible boundaries and transnational flows – of capital, populations, techniques, and cultures – and the constant transformation of human bodies and subjectivities via world-scale experiments in technoscientific rationalization facilitate unfettered capitalism's inherently alienating and nonmaterialist dynamism. Perennial apocalypse and constant crisis (the most dependable of all generators of wealth for the few); an avalanche of nova and discordances; a maximum of sublime and grotesque fascinations to prevent routines, habits, and stable loyalties from taking root – all create a state of perpetual challenge that only yet-to-be-imagined techno-scientific solutions can address.

It is under these conditions that sf has become established as a popular, visionary genre of art. It emerged addressing a new elite, not the traditional "organic" ruling castes, nor the bourgeois intelligentsia and merchant-adventurers. It spoke to engineers, scientists, and technicians, many of them immigrants to the imperial city centers, many of them with no great allegiance to traditional systems of education and cultural privilege. "Science," in the 1920s, became the institution and sacred knowledge that could redeem the miserable failures of national projects. It is striking – especially after the technological barbarism of the First World War – how much quasi-religious fervor went into visions of technoscientific salvation in Europe and the US. These included dreams of scientific Marxism such as J.D. Bernal's future humanity, living in material and literal "ecstasy" in the form of modular cyborgs with superior perceptual mechanisms and literal telepathy via direct radio communication, brain to brain; the visions of German national redemption and revenge through rocket science (see Winter 1983: 35–54 and Fischer 1991); American fantasies of superweapons and utopian cities (see Franklin 1988); and Konstantin Tsiolkovsky's rocket mysticism, destined to realize humanity's purpose of expanding into the universe, the principles of Russian Cosmism (see Hagemseister 1997 and Lykin *et al.* 1995).

Air-mindedness

To the early twentieth century, mechanical flight seemed to offer a material means to overcome earthboundedness. Popular fascination with airships was manifest in glider clubs and rocket societies, airshows and air races, and highly publicized feats of speed and endurance. Flight was also quickly recognized by states and political parties as a political imperative; the development of more powerful and effective airships became interests of state and national pride.

Preconditions for these interests had been set already in the eighteenth century, as modernizing governments began to map their territories for the purposes of taxation and rationalized agriculture (see Scott 1998: 11–52). These maps enabled states to survey lands as if from the air, and to dominate them with imaginary surveillance. Balloon, glider, and Zeppelin technologies later added the popular charge of easy travel through the stratosphere. In the twentieth century, sf art, such as *Buck Rogers* comics (1929–67) and the pulp covers of Frank Paul, as well as films such as *Metropolis* (Lang 1927) and *Just Imagine* (Butler 1930), depicted future cities in which airplanes would be as plentiful and personalized as automobiles, and cities were constructed vertically to accommodate their three-dimensional traffic. In the Soviet Union, "air-mindedness" was expected to further the diffusion of communism through the vast agrarian and wilderness regions otherwise inaccessible to modernizing communications (see Palmer 2006: 79–159). Germans, in particular, came to associate their national identity with the technology of flight – "the flight of eagles" – that Hitler nurtured with enthusiasm and consummate propagandistic inventiveness (see Fritzsche 1992).

The most powerful impetus to air-mindedness, however, was war. Verne had imagined the destructive potentials of attacking cities from the air in his *The Master of the World* (1904). Wells in *The War in the Air* (1908) and *The World Set Free* (1914) predicted that such air-ground wars would be inevitable and cataclysmic. German and Russian governments were particularly moved by Wells's fiction to begin large-scale research and development programs to devise programs for managing air wars. The British transformed the RAF into an instrument for policing its restive colonies (see Omissi 1990). US imperial ambitions were stimulated by the dream of air command more than any other nation; the US based the military dimension of its post-Second World War *pax Americana* on air power and superweapons of mass destruction, "smart bombs," and scattered air bases with little connection to ground support, allowing it to extend military power far from the imperial center, without terrestrial lines of supply (see Press 2001; Sherry 1989; Pape 2004). Air-carried superweapons had been a staple of future-war sf throughout the century; indeed, sf had all but mandated their development in *The World Set Free*, in which Wells imagined airborne nuclear bombs dropped on European cities. Sf writers pursued their professional obligation to imagine diverse innovations by depicting bombs carrying germs, poison gases, mind-altering drugs, anti-matter, and nanophages.

Early sf made it clear that flight could be imaginatively extended to spaceflight with little effort. The experiences of air-ground wars – bombed cities, air-minded societies, dual-use combat/transport fleets – became models for concrete, detailed visions of political and social life for humanity as it expanded into outer space. Rocket societies of amateur aerodynamic engineers proliferated early in the twentieth century, in the US, France, Britain, Germany, and Russia. All advocated the application of state resources to the subvention of spaceflight, and all were influenced by imaginary models derived from sf – from Verne, in the case of the American Robert Goddard and the Russian Tsiolkovsky, from Kurd Lasswitz in the case of Willy Ley and Wernher von Braun. Sf's space stations and planetary colonies were modeled on forward military outposts evolving into imperial cities. The large body of sf works imagining human expansion into space was tied to the image of military/colonial settlements – either to escape from an ever-hungry terrestrial techno-political world-system, or precisely to serve such a power.

It is no wonder then that the counterforce has been imagined as itself coming from outer space. In this role, the alien appears either as a competitor for control over space and time, or as an enlightened obstacle to the sins of technologically facilitated expansion. In its techno-imperialist variant, the alien is the ultimate justification for technoscientific power – from *Flash Gordon* comics (1934–2003) to *Independence Day* (Emmerich 1996), sf has depicted the need of the human species to band together to protect itself against alien invaders or challengers of its colonial installations. In its anti-imperialist variants, aliens appear as life-saving obstacles to this process. In *The Day the Earth Stood Still* (Wise 1951), an enlightened extraterrestrial arrives with an ultimatum: either give up nuclear weapons or have a world-destroying robot, the consummate expression of the alien technological development, destroy the Earth itself. Sophisticated variants of this theme depict the alien invader from the skies as a metaphor for humanity's own technological development. In Wells's *The War of the Worlds* (1898) and its many successors, the air-ground war against human civilization is waged by versions of humanity's own hypertechnological descendants, as if they were attacking their own origins through time. Sf also depicts the self-destructive corruption of such war strategies, in works such as Joe Haldeman's *The Forever War* (1974), Orson Scott Card's *Ender's Game* (1985), Stanisław Lem's *Fiasco* (1986), Eleanor Arnason's *Ring of Swords* (1993), and the corrupting effect of developing alien resources for war in the *Alien* (1979–97) films.

These themes articulate the imaginary negotiation of technological development, not only in real terms, through the implications for social life of widespread air technology and spaceflight, but in their symbolic implications: the increasing distance of technologically mediated, technoscientifically defined, and electronically targeted social life observed at great speed from a great distance, as if from the windows, view-finders, and targeting scopes of air forces watching the ground.

The One State

In his great anti-utopian novel *We* (written 1920, translated into English 1924), Yevgeny Zamyatin named the oppressive, hyper-rationalized, totalitarian government blocking his protagonist's happiness "the One State." Sf had inherited the conception of a unitary world state from utopian fiction, but it came into its own as a plausible, ideal, able to be created in reality, with the technologies of mass-production and communications, Taylorized labor and pervasive surveillance. The utopian model took its emphatically technocentric turn in Edward Bellamy's *Looking Backward: 2000–1887* (1888) and Wells's *The World Set Free*, works of incomparable influence on Western imagination, but in Zamyatin's One State the irony of a utopia based on material control systems is foregrounded. Playing on the pun embedded in it, *We*'s One State embodies an ideal fusion of political and physical entropy.

Technology offered the airplane, the rocket, the radio, the superweapon, rationalized cities, and grand projects conquering brute nature as practical tools for extending the power of the state. Through the technological rationalization of labor of the Fordist and Taylorist regimes, the coalescence of the productive mechanism of the state and continual expansion into space could be guaranteed. Twentieth-century audiences were most familiar with the anti-utopian critiques of totalitarianism envisioned in *We*, Aldous Huxley's *Brave New World* (1932), and George Orwell's *Nineteen Eighty-four* (1949). But the One State was not only a myth of administrative monopoly. It represented an immanent momentum toward greater and greater intersections of political and economic institutions, and, in the second half of the century, the interlock of myriad communication and control systems required for the administration of institutions. A particularly sharp opposition is found in the conflict between Zamyatin and the Soviet Proletkult, an avant-garde movement that shared with constructivism the idealization of mechanism and a proletarian–Taylorist hive-mind (see Lewis and Weber 1988). For political sf, the One State represents not just the technological state (with its space programs and high-tech militarization), but a "social state," a technological condition of being, in which all aspects of life are mediated by intermeshing systems of technological rationalization.

Such a universalization of technical infrastructures is not necessarily a matter of state administration. It might just as easily derive from capitalist corporations, as in Frederik Pohl and C.M. Kornbluth's *The Space Merchants* (1953), or from the recon- solidation of diffuse cybernetic technologies into general control systems imagined in cyberpunk fiction such as William Gibson's *Neuromancer* (1984). Sf has also modeled avenues of resistance: the freelancing co-opters of technology who put the punk in cyber-bio-nanopunk, hacker anarchists, ecological saboteurs, surfers on the inevitable dissipative wave. Yet the One State remains as the stipulation of imperial techno- logical rationalization, the condition that must be addressed before freedom from it can be imagined.

The cyborg

Much has been written in recent years about the cyborg. Beginning with the real-world fighter pilot wired with sensors, electronically enhanced to operate his machinery faster than his own conscious decision-making will allow, to the machine-grafted human being kept alive or upgraded by cybernetic devices, to Donna Haraway's network beings who break down the ontological walls among machine, animal, human being, and information, the cyborg has evolved into a dominant science-fictional trope for technological empire (see Gray 1995). As Haraway's work and its great influence demonstrate, the cyborg is not limited to a particular bionic icon; it is rather a way of imagining relationships among domains in the technosocial world as interdependent and fluid. With the penetration of technoscience into the smallest regions of the body, the body of nature has become subject to transmutative manipulations. Sf has long operated in this world.

The earliest models of scientific rationalization pervading intimate social life were the robot and the lab-constructed monster. These figures first appeared in the Jewish Kabalistic tradition or in alchemical science, and were gradually naturalized by nineteenth-century German philosophy of nature (a tradition associated predominantly with Schelling) and Gothic sf, in works such as E.T.A. Hoffman's "The Sandman" (1816), Mary Shelley's *Frankenstein* (1818), August Villiers de L'Isle Adam's *Future Eve* (1886), and Wells's *The Island of Doctor Moreau* (1896). Such figures were brought fully into the politics of sf and empire by Karel Čapek's vision in *RUR* (1920) of the industrially produced slave robot labor. All these creatures of scientific myth embodied the intrusion of emerging technoscience into the most intimate matters of personal identity and origins. By placing among naturally evolved human beings humanoid beings made possible only through technoscientific creation, the imaginary empire could break down the notion of natural (i.e., extra-technological, extra-rational) identity, and pursue endocolonization, that is, the extension of the colonizing power networks into the imperial center at its base: human social consciousness.

The cyborg is the techno-imperial subject. Its condition of being is its fluidity, tactically reconstituting itself in innumerable configurations and constellations with other, similarly variable beings. The conditions for these quick adaptations are set by the network of technological possibilities of changing material existence itself. Although the name of the cybernetic organism implies a form of second-natural regulation equal to the natural (the difference between a cyborg on the one hand, and a mechanical or purely evolutionary prodigy on the other), it is impossible to be a cyborg outside the technological–informational matrix. Real scientific advances in digital analysis, transgenics, pharmacology, and micro-surgery have inspired a new conception that physical bodies are infinitely pliable local formations, no longer bound by oppressive general principles of natural generation. This is an imperial model, analogous to the goals of political empires to create new subjects no longer bound by their local traditions, nor forced to assimilate with the dominant power, but rather "free" to align with the imperial center and seek its mediation in managing local conflicts, all in the name of universal peace and wealth. The alternative is exclusion from community and overwhelmingly efficient violence.

In the techno-imperial sphere, resistance as well as dominance are possible only in the cyborg state, and much of contemporary oppositional politics occurs as contests over the technological control-system. The science-fictional image of the rebellious hacker codified in cyberpunk has profoundly influenced anti-establishment hacker saboteurs in the real world. Even deeply reactionary movements, like the Iranian Islamic revolution or Al Qaida, depend on elaborate electronic communications webs to gain and manage their power. And environmentalist resistance, in sf and reality alike, must negotiate with the need to face a world not only degraded by ecological plunder, but emptied of wilderness. In works such as George R. Stewart's *Earth Abides* (1949) and Ursula K. Le Guin's *Always Coming Home* (1985), only cataclysmic natural catastrophes, or, alternatively, as in Octavia Butler's *Dawn* (1987), only alien "gene-trading" technologists, can offer hope of restoring pre-imperial difference and wildness.

Escape velocity

In the first years of the twentieth century, Tsiolkovsky, the founder of Russian rocket science, profoundly influenced by Nikolai Fyodorov's early transhumanism and Verne's space-travel sf, proposed a program of rocket-assisted flight "by which human beings could escape the tyranny of earth's gravity and limited resources and eventually become the perfected, immortal beings" they were destined to become (Lykin *et al.* 1995: 370). The rocket's escape velocity was to be the literal human condition. Much of the history of technological innovation in the twentieth century can be viewed as a metaphorical extension of this dream of accelerating the transformations of every human faculty until it breaks from its biological, mortal, terrestrial weight, and radiates freely and powerfully through the universe. That universe may be the physical one that is opened up through enhanced spaceflight, begun with the space programs of the Soviet Union and the US, and continued through interplanetary travel, and even interstellar flight made possible by cryogenics, longevity chemistry, modular cyborg bodies, faster-than-light travel, warp drives – technologies still imaginary, but intimately familiar to a hypermodern culture pervaded by sf tropes. The super-seding universe may also be a virtual one of synthetic consciousness preserved or enhanced digitally, in more durable casings than the organic body, or infinitely pliable, distributed through space and time.

Many commentators on the hypermodern condition have noted this general acceleration of experience. For Virilio, it signifies the annihilation of space – and consequently all ties that bind human beings to earth – by sheer speed (see Virilio 1986 and 2000; see also Armitage and Graham 2001). Mark Dery has dubbed the ephemeralization of work, experience, and desire effected by perpetually accelerating digital technologies, the cherished theme of cyberpunk and posthumanist sf, as a drive to achieve escape velocity from history (Dery 1996: 3). Technological imperi-alism means leaving behind the local spacetimes of nation, gender, species, nature, mortality, and perhaps eventually body, animal, gene, life, and matter, as well. The velocity of experience in real social life has few mediating fictive images and themes from the past to draw on. (Notably, none of the classical categories of the sublime involved speed.) They come rather, properly, from sf's future.

Alan Shapiro has identified three science-fictional categories of escape-technologies in *Star Trek*, perhaps the most influential work of sf at the end of the century. There are the technologies of literal escape, such as the Holodeck, for people to escape from their own physical reality; the Transporter, to escape from their locations; warp-drive and managed wormholes, to escape from their physical spacetime; time-portals, to escape from their own ages; the Universal Translator, to escape from their local languages; and so on. These technologies of literal displacement figure the actual technologies of virtuality at the turn of the twenty-first century, which "clearly entail the 'leaving behind' of corporeal existence to enter an alternate reality, such as an android body or an online VR-environment" (Shapiro 2004: 20). Second, there are technologies through which human subjectivity escapes "into organ-substituting imaging apparatuses of television, cinema, VR and realtime communications" (Shapiro 2004: 20). Such prosthetic systems transform the sense of reality from one of fixed laws to a game of models, whose rules can be altered at will. In these technologies, the experienced world disappears into simulation. Finally, there is technologies' own self-liberation, through which they and their subjects are freed from their hyperrational determinations – the only resistance remaining against the empire.

The technological empire does not exist as a visible political entity. But it is not a phantom of conspiracy theorists. On the contrary, it is so pervasive a force of social gravitation that it feels like nature. Its power is negotiated by the traditional means of bourgeois mediation: journalism, education, advertising and propaganda, the entertainment industry, and by the daily transformations of everyday experience that occur when populations are compelled to depend on constantly and rapidly "upgraded" machines and communication networks simply to survive. Sf must be counted as the primary institution of art that makes this new regime habitable by the imagination.

Bibliography

Adas, M. (1989) *Machines as the Measure of Men: science, technology, and ideologies of Western dominance*, Ithaca, NY: University of Cornell Press.

Arendt, H. (1951) *The Origins of Totalitarianism*, New York: Meridian Books.

Armitage, J. and Graham, P. (2001) "Dromoeconomics: towards a political economy of speed," *Parallax*, 17(1): 111–23.

Bernal, J.D. (1969) *The World, the Flesh, and the Devil: an enquiry into the future of the three enemies of the rational soul*, 1929, 2nd edn, Bloomington: Indiana University Press.

Dery, M. (1996) *Escape Velocity: cyberculture at the end of the century*, New York: Grove.

Fischer, P.S. (1991) *Fantasy Politics: visions of the future in the Weimar Republic*, Madison: University of Wisconsin Press.

Franklin, H.B. (1988) *War Stars: the superweapon and the American imagination*, New York: Oxford University Press.

Fritzsche, P. (1992) *A Nation of Fliers: German aviation and the popular imagination*, Cambridge, MA: Harvard University Press.

Gray, C.H. (1995) "Science Fiction Becomes Military Fact," in C.H. Gray (ed.) *The Cyborg Handbook*, New York: Routledge.

Hagemseister, M. (1997) "Russian Cosmism in the 1920s and Today," in B.G. Ronsenthal (ed.) *The Occult in Russian and Soviet Culture*, New York: University of Cornell Press.

Haraway, D.J. (1991) "A Cyborg Manifesto: science technology, and socialist-feminism in the late twentieth century," in *Simians, Cyborgs, and Women: the reinvention of nature*, New York and London: Routledge.

Hardt, M. and Negri, A. (2000) *Empire*, Cambridge, MA: Harvard University Press.

Headrick, D.R. (1981) *The Tools of Empire: technology and European imperialism in the nineteenth century*, New York: Oxford University Press.

Henderson, W.O. (1951) "Walther Rathenau: a pioneer of the planned economy," *The Economic History Review*, New Series 4(1): 98–108.

Hughes, T.P. (1994) "Technological Momentum," in M.R. Smith and L. Marx (eds) *Does Technology Drive History? The dilemma of technological determinism*, Cambridge, MA: MIT Press.

Lewis, K. and Weber, H. (1988) "Zamyatin's *We*, the Proletarian Poets and Bogdanov's *Red Star*," in G. Kern (ed.) *Zamyatin's We: a collection of essays*, Ann Arbor, MI: Ardis.

Lykin, V. *et al.* (1995) "Tsiolkovsky, Russian Cosmism and Extraterrestrial Intelligence," *Quarterly Journal of the Royal Astronomical Society*, 36: 369–76.

Omissi, D.E. (1990) *Air Power and Colonial Control: the Royal Air Force, 1919–1939*, Manchester: Manchester University Press.

Palmer, S.W. (2006) *Dictatorship of the Air: aviation culture and the fate of modern Russia*, Cambridge: Cambridge University Press.

Pape, R.A. (2004) "The True Worth of Air Power," *Foreign Affairs*, 83(2): 116–30.

Press, D.G. (2001) "The Myth of Air Power in the Persian Gulf War and the Future of Warfare," *International Security*, 26(2): 5–44.

Scott, J.C. (1998) *Seeing Like a State: how certain schemes to improve the human condition have failed*, New Haven, CT: Yale University Press.

Shapiro, A.N. (2004) *Star Trek: technologies of disappearance*, Berlin: Avinus Verlag.

Sherry, M.S. (1989) *The Rise of American Air Power: the creation of Armageddon*, New Haven, CT: Yale University Press.

Virilio, P. (1986) *Speed and Politics: an essay on dromology*, 1977, trans. M. Polizzotti, New York: Semiotext(e).

—— (1995) *The Art of the Motor*, 1993, trans. J. Rose, Minneapolis: University of Minnesota Press.

—— (2000) *The Information Bomb*, 1998, trans. C. Turner, London: Verso.

Winter, F.W. (1983) *Prelude to the Space Age: the rocket societies: 1924–1940*, Washington, DC: Air and Space Museum/Smithsonian Institution.

37
ENVIRONMENTALISM
Patrick D. Murphy

What does the form of literary analysis based on environmental values, known as ecocriticism in the US and green studies in the UK, have to offer readers of sf? In turn, what does sf have to offer ecocriticism? A significant vein in the earliest sf, paralleling natural history, consisted of terrestrial voyages of discovery. Two ubiquitous questions appeared in both: what is nature? what is a human being? Sf's ethical dimension has long included a particular elaboration and method for addressing both questions: environmentalism, which in the public domain combines ethical theory and political activism.

Depending on definitions, one could consider novels by Mary Shelley, William Dean Howells, Jules Verne, and Charlotte Perkins Gilman, and short stories by Nathaniel Hawthorne and H.G. Wells as demonstrating at least a proto-environmentalist awareness, with several of these works overtly and obviously encouraging readers not only to think but also to act differently. It would be a mistake, however, to claim that because a significant portion of sf has an environmentalist orientation, the genre is intrinsically pro-nature. Different examples, such as Walter Miller Jr's *A Canticle for Leibowitz* (1959), Greg Bear's *Blood Music* (1985), Ian McDonald's *Chaga* (1995), and Michael Crichton's *State of Fear* (2004), could lead to the conclusion that sf is anti-environmentalist. While certain authors are self-consciously environmentalist in their literary politics, such as Ursula Le Guin, Kim Stanley Robinson, and Karen Traviss, I am not so interested in intent as in effect. Fictions can leave environmental or anti-environmental impressions in readers' minds often more as a result of the cultural and historical circumstances of their reception than as a result of their conditions or intentions of production.

Before proceeding, distinctions, which should be understood as relational differences rather than as antagonistic oppositions, must be drawn between *nature*, *environment*, and *ecology* (see Coupe 2000; Plumwood 2002). For heuristic purposes, let us define *nature* as the non-artificial or non-manufactured, material reality that provides the setting for a work of sf. It should not be perceived as external to the characters, since their *natural* physical makeup constitutes part of the non-artificial reality of the story. This recognition becomes particularly important in novels containing aliens. Not infrequently, these representations of the Other-as-alien both reflect back on the representations of the Self-as-alien and defamiliarize earthly animals as potentially anothers rather than others (see Wolfe 2003; Heise 2003), thereby blurring the common nature–human divide.

This non-artificial nature also should not be perceived as external or in opposition to culture and technology. Rather, culture and technology are designed and manufactured with, and on the basis of, nature. Even if humans posit an antagonistic relationship between a particular culture and nature, they do so on the basis of nature historically, physically, and biochemically preceding the period of historical viability of a culture and technology being synthesized from natural materials. Thus a cyborg represents a melding of the natural and the technological, an artificial construct that does not occur spontaneously as the result of genetic evolution or sexual reproduction, yet contains natural elements.

Let us limit the meaning of *environment* to the setting or locale surrounding characters that includes the natural, the cultural, and the artificial. Much sf is set in manufactured environments and some in natural environments, including the human body. The environment consists of the surroundings with and within which characters interact, but they themselves are usually represented as existing apart from that environment. Sometimes this environment becomes a nonhuman or non-individuated sentient character, such as the sentience-evolved planet in John Brunner's *The Dramaturges of Yan* (1972) or the "bio-mechanoid" ship in *Farscape* (1999–2003), but generally it remains a backdrop. Some eco-activists reject the use of the word "environment" precisely because it invokes the kind of limiting definition I use here (see Berg 1990: 23). While deep ecology and bioregionalism find it insufficiently systemic and global, those very limits make it useful for literary criticism because it facilitates an architectonic analysis of individual novels.

What then of *ecology*? It is generally defined in two related ways. First, as a field of knowledge: "the scientific study of the interaction of organisms with their environment, including the physical environment and other organisms living in it" (E.O. Wilson qtd in Thomashow 1996: 3). Second, as an existence: a natural system that undergoes, or can undergo, both autodynamic change and externally induced change and encompasses multiple interactive environments (local ecosystems). This system includes actants considered to have agency, in the sense that we usually reserve for human beings. In the case of sf, however, agency may be limited to biological entities or determined on the basis of manifestations of sentient behavior, thereby potentially including artificial persons and intelligent machines.

The relationship of climate, geology, flora, and fauna within a bioregion might constitute a valley, watershed, mountain, or desert ecology, with multiple levels of ecologies, from these local ones to the entire planetary biosphere as a macro-ecology (such relationships are the focus of Orr 1992). Living organisms invariably act as catalysts for change within ecologies, sometimes only to the degree of quantitative change and other times to the degree of qualitative change (see Merchant 1999). Organisms are either endogenous or exogenous to a specific ecology; the former are called native species or inhabitants while the latter are considered exotic species or aliens. Numerous sf stories rely on the reversal of self–other/resident–alien/domestic–exotic relationships.

But what about *environmentalism*? By its suffix, environmentalism is already represented as a philosophy or behavioral orientation. In literary production there are at least three differentially focused types of environmentalism (see Murphy 2000: 1–11). The first could be called *nature-oriented*: the literary work draws attention to particular aspects of a natural world (which need not exist in the reality we know, but may be a thought-experiment). To flesh out that place, the author describes various natural elements. Often these play a relatively minor role in the plot, which may be little more than a space western, as with *Firefly* (2002–3). In other cases, the flora or fauna play an important role, as with the oxygen-producing plants and the animals that eat them in Arthur C. Clarke's *The Sands of Mars* (1951), but an entire ecosystem is not mapped out.

The second form of environmentalism could be called *environmental writing*, and more narrowly *environmental justice writing*. In this type of sf, authors move beyond local color to make some kind of threat to an ecology or planet the key to the plot and the response to it a major theme. The 1950s saw a wide array of novels and films in which the environmental dangers of nuclear power and unsupervised biological and chemical experimentation disrupt natural processes and produce monstrous creatures and geological threats. These texts focus on a specific type of environmental insult or sudden natural imbalance that threatens human existence. Particularly in film, it is almost impossible to encompass the kind of detail needed for ecological environmentalism, and so viewers usually get agitational, single-threat environmental justice pleas. Often the threat arises not from accident or oversight, but from the connivance of corrupt individuals (see Alaimo 2001).

The third form of environmentalism could be called *ecological writing*. It tries to be systemic in scope, laying out an entire planet's biospheric activity, or educating readers about the interdependence of natural phenomena. While environmental writing can often be labeled as political, in the sense of wanting, predicting, or demonstrating a change in human social behavior, ecological writing is more likely to be seen as ethical and philosophical, asking fundamental questions about humanity's place, potential, or future. In terms of environmental politics, then, these come closest to deep ecology (see Naess 2003). Frequently, ecological plots take readers only to the point where a decision must be made, as in John Brunner's *The Shockwave Rider* (1975) or Whitley Strieber and James Kunetka's *Nature's End* (1986). In other cases, they go further, as in Joan Slonczewski's *Elysium* novels (1986–2000) and Robinson's *Science in the Capital* trilogy (2004–7), discussed below.

These provisional categories can help to organize our thinking about environmentalism and sf. Take Brunner's *Bedlam Planet* (1968) and *The Sheep Look Up* (1972), for example. In the former, a group of Earth colonists attempt to settle a new planet without coming to terms with its ecology. Their efforts fail until they recognize themselves as the aliens who can become inhabitants only through submitting to this new ecology. In order for the adaptive colonists to succeed they must find ways to turn off their rational minds so as to let the body instinctively engage the planet and thus break out of their alien mindset: "what sanity consists in is doing what *the planet you live on* will accept. And precisely because Asgard is not Earth, what is sane here may well seem crazy in earthly terms" (Brunner 1968: 171). This is an ecological novel, focused on ethics and philosophy that lead to a non-Earth-centered worldview. *The Sheep Look Up* is a more narrowly focused environmentalist novel. It details numerous assaults on Earth's biosphere and argues about ethical behavior in terms of politics and policies. Its focus encourages readers to take practical and immediate actions on any one of a number of fronts. Contemplating ecological sanity might seem a luxury in contrast to the practical actions of *The Sheep Look Up*'s eco-guerrillas, and many might find the later novel's stylistic sophistication and narrative complexity make for better reading. Deep ecologists, however, might argue that the less adept *Bedlam Planet* actually tackles more fundamental questions about ecological consciousness.

Many nature-oriented sf novels set on Earth use a post-apocalyptic situation to argue for a return to nature. Relying on a tremendous reduction of the human population, they are often not useful for readers who want to think their way through looming environmental crises. When virulently anti-technological, they promote a neo-primitive way of life, as with Jean Hegland's *Into the Forest* (1996), but when less intensely anti-technological they can encourage consideration of alternative structures for civilization, such as Ernest Callenbach's *Ecotopia* (1975) and Scott Russell Sanders's *Terrarium* (1985). The former focuses on how to live in a more nature-friendly way rather than on the potential ecological necessities for doing so, and thus promotes appreciation of nature while critiquing American consumerist lifestyles. In the latter, the claustrophobic enclosure that provides the initial anti-nature setting is represented as psychologically and physically unhealthy but not necessarily unsustainable. Late in the novel, several characters conclude that the urban enclosures have been necessary to protect the planet from environmentally destructive human behavior, one even conjecturing that the Earth itself orchestrated this as a self-protective measure. At the novel's end, Sanders indicates that people need to find their way back to an earlier nature-balance instinct in order, as he states in a 1995 afterword, "to build communities that are materially simple and spiritually complex, respectful of our places and of the creatures who share them with us" (Sanders 1995: 283). While metaphysically invoking a self-aware Gaia concept (see Lovelock 1987), Sanders encourages nature appreciation and a back-to-the-land movement that does not eschew all technology, but seeks to live akin to the goals of the simplicity movement (see Andrews 1997). His theme represents a nostalgic idealization of agrarian life that, like wilderness experience, can only be available to a statistical minority of the population.

I want to mention one other nature-oriented novel that differs significantly from the preceding ones, particularly because the publisher's packaging and mainstream reviewers downplayed its ecocritical and sf dimensions, while sf reviews downplayed its ecocritical dimensions: Jonathan Lethem's *Girl in Landscape* (1998). It opens with a heavily polluted earth, but this setting serves less to thematize environmental crises than to precipitate the 13-year-old Pella's family's departure from Earth to a colonizable planet. This space western has three intertwined plots: Pella's interaction with other colonists and the planet's various species; conflicts between educated *tenderfoot* newcomers and the established colonists' frontier mentality; and conflicts between colonists and native inhabitants. It criticizes both recently arrived and already established colonists in terms of the adults' inability to see the landscape and its natives intrinsically. Only the children seem able to develop new perceptual and conceptual paradigms in approaching the specific nature of their new home. They are nature-oriented precisely in the sense of trying to perceive this new reality in its uniqueness and show a potential for being remade into future inhabitants.

Environmental novels are issue-oriented. The crisis exists in the foreground, invariably providing the basis for the plot rather than merely its setting. Sometimes these novels function primarily as cautionary tales that call on readers to change current behaviors so as to avert impending catastrophe, such as nuclear disasters and wars. As early as the mid-1970s, novels with overtly environmental themes related to climate change appeared. Arthur Herzog's *Heat* (1977) presents the potential way that global warming might unfold. A dozen years before Bill McKibben published his nonfiction *The End of Nature* (1989), Herzog's protagonist becomes concerned about the buildup of CO_2 and a potential runaway greenhouse effect. As the novel progresses, weather conditions worsen and global temperatures rise. While Herzog's information could lead to labeling this book ecological, his emphasis on immediate technical solutions undercuts reader attention to a systemic view and focuses instead on what to do next in order to stop the earth from heating. Although disaster is finally averted by solar-deflecting arrays, Herzog does observe that a technical fix does not provide a long-term solution. Unfortunately, the necessity of developing an alternative way of life is quickly covered in a handful of pages. While *Heat* does educate readers about CO_2 concentrations, global warming, and a potential greenhouse effect, it tends to conceptualize them as environmental problems rather than fundamental nature–human tensions that require far-reaching systemic cultural and economic changes.

Whatever larger sense of ecology they might evoke, novels such as *Heat* fit relatively easily into the tradition of male-authored hard sf, with its frequent emphasis on physics, chemistry, and technology (and scant attention to the ecological systems through which they operate), and its preference for heroic, technological resolutions to crises (rather than the open-endedness and ongoing process that ecological plots might suggest or attention to the psychological–biophysical interactions that feminist sf often addresses). Other sf novels treating environmental themes, however, downplay *Heat*'s agitational emphasis in favor of more propagandistic and theoretical arguments which pay attention to symbiosis rather than competition in the human–nature interaction, and to cooperation and adaptation rather than conflict in the human–human interactions. Indeed, Lynn Margulis, author of *Symbiotic Planet* (1998), might serve as the patron saint of such sf, which is often set up to demonstrate a de-anthropocentric orientation that may ascribe intrinsic value to wild nature or extol environmental resilience in contrast to the ephemerality of civilization. Consider two novels written and published within a few years of each other: George R. Stewart's *Earth Abides* (1949) and Clarke's *The Sands of Mars*.

Two aspects of Stewart's novel, which thematically echoes the inhumanist philosophy elaborated in Robinson Jeffers's narrative poem "The Double Axe" (1948), are worth noting. First, its allusions to the verse from Ecclesiastes, "Men go and come, but earth abides." That is, humans depend on nature for their continuation, both individually and as a species, but the biosphere does not depend on human beings for its continuation: "We cannot put an end to nature; we can only pose a threat to ourselves" (Margulis 1998: 128). Second, the novel repeatedly emphasizes the limitations and errors of judgment of protagonist Ish. In this character, Stewart advances a quality of humility and sanity that leads away from the mindset of the civilization he has witnessed collapse. In contrast, *The Sands of Mars* is standard hard sf in its teleological, technocratic orientation, and fundamentally anti-ecological in its characters' attitudes. Many critics would note also its androcentrism, providing no significant roles for women on the new world. Clarke assumes that major technological interventions in the Martian biosphere can have utterly predictable results and no malignant unintended consequences. The first human colony on Mars is well established, expanding rapidly without having undertaken any systematic ecological mapping, and unconcerned that indigenous creatures might exist. Arrival on Mars is portrayed as a battle of conquest, and when an animal species is discovered, the colonizers only care about adapting it to terraforming, a process already underway with native flora. Treated as discrete entities, these animals and plants are portrayed as oddities rather than as living components of a biosphere. Indeed, an engineer dismisses the Martians: "What have *they* done except survive? It's always fatal to adapt oneself to one's surroundings. The thing to do is to alter your surroundings to suit you" (Clarke 1965: 453). Nothing in the novel contests this claim, although more recent scientific evidence increasingly indicates that such an approach on Earth could lead to the destruction of human civilization (see Kunstler 2006; Palumbi 2001). It is not simply that many people now know better than Clarke could have in the early 1950s, since *Earth Abides* directly contradicts his technophilia.

Stanisław Lem's *Solaris* (1961) is also worth contrasting to Clarke's vision. It contends that all of the human research combined is insufficient to make sense of another planet's ecology and to determine whether or not its biosphere contains any kind of sentience. If read as an allegory about inhabitation of Earth, Lem's novel complements Stewart's recommendation of humility and encourages a what-if approach to Lovelock's Gaia hypothesis. Other authors have emphasized the de-anthropocentric through sf fables about animal rights and evolution, as in Sheri S. Tepper's *Grass* (1989) and *The Family Tree* (1997) (see Heise 2001: 13). With Clarke and many other male writers of his generation, sf took a decidedly technophilic attitude toward crisis aversion, space exploration, and human development, but many contemporary sf writers, particularly women, take a different approach, emphasizing biology, biochemistry, ecology, genetics, and psychology, with frequent attention to ethics. Of this preeminent group of ecological sf writers, I will consider two: Amy Thomson and Joan Slonczewski.

Amy Thomson's *The Color of Distance* (1995) focuses on a human explorer marooned on another planet who can survive only because the primary sentient species, the Tendu, perform a biomolecular transformation of her body, including her immune system and skin. Thomson explores the very different approach these beings take to the biosphere they inhabit and how the protagonist must adjust not only her physical behavior but also her perceptions and ethics. *Through Alien Eyes* (1999) returns the protagonist to Earth with two aliens in tow. Readers then get to experience an ecological evaluation of Earth from their viewpoint. Perhaps most compelling in the second volume is the critique of white colonization and its destruction of indigenous lifestyles and peoples, and how that represents a threat to sentient beings on other planets.

Joan Slonczewski is a professor of biology, an expertise she combines in her novels with a strong feminist commitment and the promotion of nonviolent political action. *Door into Ocean* (1986), the first volume of her *Elysium* series, establishes a separatist feminist population on Shora, the ocean moon that circles Valedon, a planet of male-dominated societies under military government. Elysium is another planet in their loose confederation. Societies on Elysium and Shora make use of genetic manipulation. While on Elysium technologism dominates to fulfill the single goal of extending human life, on Shora the manipulation is biological rather than technological, driven by the goal of adapting as much as possible to the planet's watery biosphere. The plot, however, is not nearly as important as the society and the biomedical and ecological ethics these women develop. Slonczewski, like Thomson, recognizes that humans alter their environments just as other animals do, and that they must do so in order to evolve in response to the changing ecologies of any planet. The issue is not the simplistic "alter or don't alter" Clarke posited, but rather the ecological dimensions of the alterations and the ethical requirements for sustainability and the preservation of all species. *Daughter of Elysium* (1993) complicates the picture by addressing the potential for machines to achieve sentience and the rights they would have in what bioregionalists have termed a Council of All Beings (Seed 1990). In *The Children Star* (1998), Slonczewski writes an sf mystery as colonizers on another planet, Prokaryon, seek to discover whether or not a sentient species stands behind the seeming orderliness of its land-based ecology. Slonczewski's ecological ethic emphasizes two distinct issues: promoting the idea that colonists should be required to adapt their bodies, including their digestive and autoimmune systems, to settle a new planet; and exploring the possibility of sentient life at the microbial level, coordinating with host species physical modifications to meet their needs for survival. The discovery of such a species saves the planet from being ecologically razed and terraformed, enabling the adaptative colonists to remain. But, just as the colonists have taken up housekeeping on Prokaryon, the sentient species has taken up housekeeping within them.

I want to close with a focus on two other recent writers: Robinson and Traviss. Robinson's *Science in the Capital* trilogy presents a near-future vision of abrupt climate change resulting from global warming. *Forty Signs of Rain* (2004) focuses on rising sea levels, the slowing of the North Atlantic current, and the flooding of Washington, DC; *Fifty Degrees Below* (2005) on sudden severe temperature swings; and *Sixty Days and Counting* (2007) on scientific, economic, political, and personal responses to the changes. Agitational environmental literature, the trilogy reflects an interconnected world perspective about the global dimensions of the current climate-change crisis. But, because it focuses almost exclusively on relatively well-off American scientists, the long-term devastation and suffering that sea-level rises and extreme temperatures will cause are never brought to center stage even for poor and coastal American communities. Rather, it promotes what bioregionalists and others would label shallow or instrumentalist environmentalism. The *in medias res* conclusion implies that conditions will get worse, but that technology might rapidly mitigate the worst impacts. Robinson's optimism and hopefulness appear likely to undercut the urgency of his cautionary tale.

In contrast, although she sets her work some 200 years in the future, Karen Traviss creates a far more affective tale of ecological crisis and extreme remediation in her ongoing *Wess'har Wars* series (*City of Pearl* (2004), *Crossing the Line* (2004), *The World Before* (2005), *Matriarch* (2006), and *Ally* (2007)). Reminiscent of Le Guin's *The Dispossessed* (1974), Tepper's *The Gate to Women's Country* (1988) and *Grass*, and Slonczewski's *The Children Star* and *Brain Plague* (2000), the series also displays a unique female hero, Shan Frankland. Space does not permit a detailed analysis but it is important to emphasize the degree to which Traviss's fiction embodies a strategic ecofeminist philosophy akin to that of Val Plumwood. Plumwood argues that the "ecological crisis requires from us a new kind of culture" (Plumwood 2002: 4), and, like the Anarresti of Le Guin's *The Dispossessed*, Traviss's Wess'har exemplify an ecologically responsible culture, with a low-impact agrarian lifestyle backed by high-technology defenses. In addition to being matriarchal, they are also vegan and display a daily commitment to sustainability. Intriguingly, Traviss does not make them the only counterweight to our planet's ecologically destructive culture but also includes various human and alien communities that display a range of practices from extinction-causing absolutists to what Frankland labels "eco-jihadists." All of the action in the first five volumes takes place in another solar system, but the parallels Traviss develops affectively and intellectually emphasize the need for the bulk of Earth's societies to change their ways because the planet is already suffering massively destructive effects of global warming and threatens to share the fate of the badly overpopulated planet that forms part of the main setting. In line with Plumwood's emphasis that we need "better forms of reason" (Plumwood 2002: 14), the *Wess'har Wars* novels present an ongoing dialog about ethical behavior based on radically de-anthropocentric principles. Interestingly, the differences between Robinson's and Traviss's approaches echo those between the two novels by Brunner discussed earlier.

Attention to nature has always been a significant aspect of sf. In watching *War of the Worlds* (Spielberg 2005), many viewers who went to see Tom Cruise no doubt overlooked Wells's manifesto about how evolution adapts humans to survive on a planet filled with potentially deadly adversaries and symbiotes each seeking their own survival as well. Detailed depictions of nature abound in hard and soft sf, and there exists a significant body of environmental and ecological sf. Ecocriticism offers a method for engaging the particularities of such works and opportunities for exploring connections between feminist sf and ecocritical themes.

Bibliography

Alaimo, S. (2001) "Discomforting Creatures: monstrous natures in recent films," in K. Armbruster and K. Wallace (eds) *Beyond Nature Writing*, Charlottesville: University of Virginia Press.

Andrews, C. (1997) *The Circle of Simplicity: the return to the good life*, New York: HarperCollins.

Berg, S. (1990) "Bioregional and Wild! A New Cultural Image," in C. Plant and J. Plant (eds) *Turtle Talk: voices for a sustainable future*, Philadelphia: New Society Publishers.

Brunner, J. (1968) *Bedlam Planet*, New York: Ace.

Clarke, A.C. (1965) "The Sands of Mars," in *Prelude to Mars*, 1951, New York: Harcourt, Brace and World.

Coupe, L. (2000) "General Introduction," in *The Green Studies Reader*, London: Routledge.

Heise, U.K. (2001) "The Virtual Crowds," *ISLEI*, 8(1): 1–29.

—— (2003) "From Extinction to Electronics: dead frogs, live dinosaurs, and electric sheep," in C. Wolfe (ed.) *Zoontologies: the question of the animal*, Minneapolis: University of Minnesota Press.

Kunstler, J.H. (2006) *The Long Emergency: surviving the end of oil*, 2005, New York: Grove.

Lovelock, J.E. (1987) *Gaia: a new look at life on earth*, 1979, New York: Oxford University Press.

Margulis, L. (1998) *Symbiotic Planet: a new look at evolution*, New York: Basic Books.

Merchant, C. (ed.) (1999) *Ecology*, Amherst, NY: Humanity Books.

Murphy, P.D. (2000) *Farther Afield in the Study of Nature-Oriented Literature*, Charlottesville: University of Virginia Press.

Naess, A. (2003) *Ecology, Community and Lifestyles*, 1989, trans. D. Rothenberg, Cambridge: Cambridge University Press.

Orr, D.W. (1992) *Ecological Literacy: education and the transition to a postmodern world*, Albany, NY: SUNY Press.

Palumbi, S.R. (2001) *The Evolution Explosion: how humans cause rapid change*, New York: Norton.

Plumwood, V. (2002) *Environmental Culture: the ecological crisis of reason*, New York: Routledge.

Sanders, S.R. (1995) *Terrarium*, 1985, Bloomington: Indiana University Press.

Seed, J. (1990) "Deep Ecology Down Under," in C. Plant and J. Plant (eds) *Turtle Talk: voices for a sustainable future*, Philadelphia: New Society Publishers.

Thomashow, M. (1996) *Ecological Identity: becoming a reflective environmentalist*, 1995, Cambridge, MA: MIT Press.

Wolfe, C. (2003) "Introduction," *Zoontologies: the question of the animal*, Minneapolis: University of Minnesota Press.

38
ETHICS AND ALTERITY
Neil Easterbrook

In Arthur C. Clarke's *The City and the Stars* (1956), the young adventurer Alvin asks the godlike Central Computer of the city of Diaspar to unlock the memory, sealed by an ancient religious cult until the second coming of their gods, of a superannuated robot he has discovered. The Computer replies, "Your order involves two problems. One is moral, one technical" (Clarke 2001: 181), then tricks the robot with an illusion of the second coming. Resolving the technical problem renders the moral problem moot. This moment in a prime example of "Golden Age" sf concisely illustrates an essential tension within the genre: on the one hand, the pressure of technoscientific solutions to engineer the erasure of traditional human morality, and on the other, the persistence of questions concerning the causes and consequences of right action.

Such dynamic confusions are neither unique nor original to sf, and they come as no surprise, since ethics itself constitutes a highly contested discursive field. As a particular sort of discourse, it properly falls within the domain of philosophy, but it also plays a considerable role in religion, secular education, political theory, law, and all areas of humanistic study. Sometimes the word identifies morality, sometimes fraught situations, sometimes a person's essential character, and sometimes the advanced philosophical practice of investigating the very possibility of ethical discourse itself. Beginning with some basic distinctions can help, but it is in the very nature of ethical discourse to compel authentic, rigorously reflective questioning rather than to produce concise imperative algorithms that tell us how to act in every instance.

Ethics is the systematic and analytic treatment of human actions and their consequences, including considerations of character and motive. Historically, the philosophic study of ethics begins in Plato's *Republic* (c. 360 BC), in which Socrates asks not only "what is a moral life?" but also "why should we be moral?" Philosophy has since added further questions: What justifies my action? How are actions to be judged? Is my intent or the consequence of my action to be judged? Who will judge? What obligations do I have to others, and they to me? Must I be selfless, or may I be selfish? All of these questions revolve around matters of goodness, rights, and virtues. Philosophy has developed a dauntingly large technical vocabulary to deal with such questions (see Blackburn 2001; Singer 1990).

Generally, ethics may be subdivided into three areas: *normative ethics* attempts to develop moral maxims or rules; *applied ethics* studies the ways to solve individual ethical problems in practical contexts; and *meta-ethics* investigates the ontological and episte-mological conditions assumed by or needed for normative or applied ethics. Another name for normative ethics is morality; while morality and ethics are often thought synonymous, in one important sense they differ significantly. Externally codified and normative, moral codes set rules and establish conventions to guide conduct. Examples include religious indices, such as the Decalogue for Jew or Christian, Muslim or Mormon, and laws, which declare publicly what is and is not permissible. Consequently, morality is overdetermined: it designates preestablished behavioral and legal principles, as well as the less formal but "unwritten" rules of a culture – but these codes will differ, and conflict, from person to person and from place to place. (Recent attempts in evolutionary psychology or sociobiology to understand morality as a strictly evolutionary development, such as Hauser (2006), should be understood as moral, not ethical, discourse.) Ethics designates a radically underdetermined mode of discourse, in which we struggle to separate what *is* the case from what *ought* to be the case, setting aside all rules and maxims to rethink each situation anew.

Perhaps the best way to conceptualize ethics is as a discursive field, a particular way of thinking, deeply influenced by certain traditions and practices. Etymologically, the word derives from the Greek "ethos," which identifies a characteristic disposition or attitude of a person or practice. In rhetoric, "ethos" designates the particular qualities of an individual's character as expressed in argument. In either sense, ethics evokes the close analysis of character, and the elaborate complexities of situating relations to other people: "What is ethics? The answers to this simple inquiry are complexity itself, for they take us straight to the decentered center of ethics, its concern for 'the other'. Ethics is the arena in which claims of otherness – the moral law, the human other, cultural norms, the-good-in-itself, etc. – are articulated and negotiated" (Harpham 1999: 26). Establishing ethics as an account of the conditions and consequences of the self's relation to otherness (alterity) has had the most effect in literary study, especially in the past 40 years.

The study of alterity came to cultural criticism from European philosophy, which since the beginning of the nineteenth century has followed a slightly different trajectory than Anglo-American philosophy. One specific difference lies in how the individual human subject is conceived. The Anglo-American tradition took its cue from René Descartes, who thought the self ontologically singular and epistemologi-cally autonomous ("ontology" designates the study of existence, while "epistemology" designates the study of knowledge). After 1800, European philosophy increasingly followed G.W.F. Hegel's model, which understood human subjectivity as the dialec-tical relation of self and other, effectively questioning – or decentering – the Cartesian subject. In twentieth-century European thought, phenomenologists Edmund Husserl, Martin Heidegger, Jean-Paul Sartre, and Maurice Merleau-Ponty developed this Hegelian "social ontology" as the concept of "intersubjectivity." More or less simul-taneously, another movement in cultural criticism called "critical theory" emerged from the Frankfurt School led by Theodor Adorno and Max Horkheimer. Along with figures such as Frantz Fanon and Jacques Lacan in political theory or psychoanalysis, Luce Irigaray in feminism, or Emmanuel Levinas in theology, critical theory attempted to think through the genuine encounter with difference (alterity) without "reducing the other to categories of the self" (Nealon 1998: 32). Over the course of 60 or so years, these various schools and critiques coalesced as "poststructuralism," which in its most rigorous form the Anglophone world came to call "literary theory."

Whether in political or ontological contexts, foregrounding alterity reorients ethical discourse. Two of the most representative and influential theorists of the relation of ethics and alterity are Mikhail Bakhtin and Levinas, both of whom predicate their ethics on *intersubjectivity* – the social ontology of the human subject, "the social fact of otherness" (Nealon 1998: 35). Traditionally, Western philosophy understood ethics as concerning the relations that arise when an ontologically autonomous self meets an ontologically autonomous other, and hence that ethical relations privileged the ontological priority of the self to that of the other. Levinas argued for the reverse: that the self comes into being as the response to the other – "being for the other," in his phrase. Following arguments initiated by Hegel, Levinas envisioned the exchange with the other as requiring a response, one that was *responsive-to* and hence ethical. The self's very existence as a self comes into being in the obligation to the other, sacrificing self-contained identity for ethical reciprocity – the notion that self and other are ineluctably linked in mutual exchange, that in some paradoxical but profound sense the very origin of the self is its reciprocal response to the other. Levinas thus identifies an essential characteristic of ethical thought – since the self's authentic experience cannot reduce difference to one or another iteration of the same, the self requires an "opening" to alterity. Calling this relation *responsiveness* or *responsibility*, Levinas understood ethics as "first philosophy," the ground upon which all other aspects of philosophical discourse are to be developed. (Most of his argument is worked out in *Totality and Infinity: an essay on exteriority* (1961); a convenient short account can be found in Levinas (1989).)

Bakhtin's views are somewhat similar, arguing in his earliest work, *Toward a Philosophy of the Act* (1921)), that a definition of an individual human agent was a "non-alibi in Being" (Bakhtin 1993: 40). While Bakhtin retained the traditional sense of the ontological priority of the self, he no longer conceived it as wholly autonomous, largely since the self exists as a product *of* and *through* language, the medium of inter-subjectivity. One illustration of this assertion appears in *Marxism and the Philosophy of Language* (1929), probably written by Bakhtin under the name of his friend V.N. Vološinov:

> *A word is a two-sided act.* It is determined equally by *whose* word it is and *for whom* it is meant. As a word, it is precisely *the product of the reciprocal relationship between speaker and listener, addresser and addressee.* Each and every word expresses the "one" relationship to the "other". I give myself verbal shape from another's point of view, ultimately, from the point of view of the community to which I belong. A word is a bridge thrown between myself and another. If one end of the bridge depends on me, then the other depends on my addressee. A word is a territory shared by both addresser and addressee, by the speaker and his interlocutor.
>
> (Bakhtin 1973: 86)

This general language condition Bakhtin named "heteroglossia," which denotes the heterogeneous nature of our social condition; formed through the enormous inertia of history and previous use, its polysemic "multiaccentuality" (Bakhtin 1973: 23) makes even a single utterance simultaneously spin in several distinct directions. Within fiction, this empirical fact appears as the dialogic: "The chief characteristic" of the dialogic appears as "A plurality of independent and unmerged voices and consciousnesses, a genuine polyphony of fully valid voices," a "plurality of consciousness-centers not reduced to a single ideological common denominator" (Bakhtin 1984: 6, 17).

Bakhtin's ethics follow from this sense of the dialogic. "Because [several voices] all sound within a single consciousness, they become, as it were, *reciprocally permeable*. They are brought close to one another, made to overlap; they partially intersect one another, creating the corresponding interruptions in areas of intersection" (Bakhtin 1984: 239, my emphasis). Because "reciprocally permeable," the self's relation to alterity demands "answerability" and excludes the possibility of alibis. Bakhtin sees in these dynamics an unresolvable, *living* dialectic, one where each self is answerable to and must answer for the other. Like Levinas, Bakhtin insists "that ethics exists in an open and ongoing obligation to respond to the other, rather than a static march toward some philosophic end or conclusion" (Nealon 1998: 36). His notion that the dialogic produces an unresolved discourse, which "consequently makes the viewer also a participant" (Nealon 1998: 18), implies that in relation to literary texts, readers produce not a resolution but an aporia.

Judith Butler (2005) offers a short, accessible meditation on some of the consequences for an ethics that develops from the "social ontology" of philosophers such as Hegel, Merleau-Ponty, Levinas, and Bakhtin. (The parallel movement in Anglo-American ethics will be found in Putnam (2004) and Rorty (1999).) She begins with Adorno's 1963 lectures, *Problems of Moral Philosophy*, in which, as in much of his work after 1933, he focuses on the violence we do others in the name of value and ideology – even at those moments when we act on principle, thinking what we do just and good, and perhaps even insisting that what we do is good for the other, as well. Adorno worries that after the collapse of "collective ideas" (qtd in Butler 2005: 4) brought about – in very different ways – by such phenomena as Auschwitz or postindustrial globalization, any form of morality or "abstract universality" will be inherently violent, especially insofar as it refuses recognition of (and hence precludes responsibility for) "existing social conditions" (Butler 2005: 6). Under these conditions, Butler thinks, our accounts of ourselves invariably risk violence to others, and our self-narratives will invariably be little more than rationalizations or alibis that seek to disguise the necessarily flawed nature of our discourse about ourselves.

Take, for instance, the very problem of the self's format – narrative discourse and storytelling – in the context of causality; we do not know our own original causes or conditions, and these disrupt any conceit of *absolute* certainty for ethics. She remarks: "The singular body to which a narrative refers cannot be captured by full narration, not only because the body has a formative history that remains irrecoverable by reflection, but because primary relations are formative in ways that produce a necessary opacity in understandings of ourselves" (Butler 2005: 20–1). By the time her analysis finishes, she has compiled a list of five such "vexations in the effort to give a narrative account of oneself" (Butler 2005: 39). As one example: loss extends even to the words of the narratives themselves. For the accounts we give ourselves come in words that "are taken away as I give them" (Butler 2005: 36). This is the sort of aporia that emerges from modeling ethics hermeneutically (as an instance of the problems of interpretation) or phenomenologically (as an instance of the problems of immanent experience), and leads Butler toward her conclusion: "we must recognize that ethics requires us to risk ourselves precisely at moments of unknowingness, when what forms us diverges from what lies before us, when our willingness to become undone in relation to others constitutes our chance of becoming human" (Butler 2005: 136).

Like most works of literature, sf typically presents pithy moral apothegms rather than complex ethical dynamics. Most "anti-science" sf – Mary Shelley's *Frankenstein* (1818), Nathaniel Hawthorne's "The Birthmark" (1843), E.M. Forster's "The Machine Stops" (1909), Ray Bradbury's "There Will Come Soft Rains" (1950), James Tiptree Jr's "Houston, Houston Do You Read?" (1976), Marge Piercy's *He, She, and It* (1991), Margaret Atwood's *Oryx and Crake* (2003) – adopts this form. Such cautionary morality tales possess the subtlety of sledgehammers. But sf can also confront audiences with more difficult, ambiguous conclusions, as with Joanna Russ's *The Female Man* (1975): "Now the moral of this story is that all images, ideals, pictures, and fanciful representations tend to vanish sooner or later unless they have the great good luck to be exuded from within, like bodily secretions or the bloom on a grape" (Russ 1975: 154). Such notions need to be parsed, argued about, and discussed: confronted more than recited, interrogated more than memorized.

Sf offers hundreds of instances which foreground the ethical moment. Celebrated sf explorations of the dynamic relation of ethics and alterity, especially in encounters with the alien other, allegories of our estrangement from ourselves, include Octavia Butler's *Xenogenesis* trilogy (1987–9), which advocates embracing difference; China Miéville's *Bas-Lag* trilogy (2000–4), which struggles with the very attempt to define difference; Ursula K. Le Guin's *The Left Hand of Darkness* (1969), *The Dispossessed* (1974), or *The Telling* (2000); or Stanisław Lem's *Eden* (1959), *Solaris* (1961), *His Master's Voice* (1969), and *Fiasco* (1986). Just as often, sf presents scenarios where technological change alters the moral relationships and traditions. In Tom Godwin's "The Cold Equations" (1954), the empirical fact of mass ratios, available thrust, rations, and distance yet to travel must trump morality, with the human biological imperative to survive supplanting all argument – a strand of materialist determinism (as in Robert A. Heinlein's work) that would have us revise the humanistic ethics that thinks technology secondary to morality. Utopian and dystopian fiction often provides study examples, as in Yevgeny Zamyatin's *We* (written 1920, translated into English 1924), which critiques the attempt to apply to human society the utilitarian "moral calculus" advocated by Jeremy Bentham and embraced by Soviet-style totalitarianism. Books as various as Martin Amis's *Time's Arrow* (1991), Neal Stephenson's *The Diamond Age* (1995), Russell Hoban's *Riddley Walker* (1980), or Nancy Kress's *Probability Moon* (2000) all open serious engagements with the ethical.

One of the most important distinctions concerns writers who approach these questions as either moralists or ethicists. Heinlein provides a good example of a writer deeply concerned with interrogating conventional moral reasoning, but who consistently establishes a moral rather than ethical environment. In *Double Star* (1956), Lorenzo Smythe, a down-on-his-luck actor, is hired to impersonate a missing political leader. In chapter seven, Heinlein argues that if ethics are universal and transhistorical, they must apply to Martians, too. In the context of its publication, the Martians allegorize any oppressed, colonized, or disenfranchised race, though the immediate parallel concerns African-Americans. Heinlein's liberal humanism here is hardly innovative or progressive, but it does suggest that he had an honest concern for universal human rights. Of course, elsewhere he appears less sanguine about universal rights. In *Starship Troopers* (1959), Mr Dubois, protagonist Johnnie Rico's teacher of "History and Moral Philosophy," instructs a particularly hapless student that "moral sense" is "an elaboration of the human instinct to survive, and every aspect of our personalities derives from it. Anything that conflicts with the survival instinct acts sooner or later to eliminate the individual and thereby fails to show up in future generations. This truth is mathematically demonstrable, everywhere verifiable; it is the single eternal imperative controlling everything we do" (Heinlein 1987: 95). He goes on to say that we now have a "scientific theory of morals" – a brutal social Darwinism, derived more from Herbert Spencer's cultural politics than Darwin's evolutionary science – and "can solve any moral problem, on any level" (Heinlein 1987: 95). Resembling Edward O. Wilson more than Immanuel Kant, Dubois – Heinlein's typical authorial metonym – heralds a vaguely fascist polis justified by the baroque calculus of masculinist fantasy and never-ending war, and a morality based on a certain ideological conception of biology.

However infamous or exemplary *Starship Troopers* may be, *The Moon is a Harsh Mistress* (1966) provides, I think, the clearest example of Heinlein's moralistic but unethical environments. About three-quarters of the way through this novel, Manuel Garcia O'Kelley Davis worries if Professor Bernardo de la Paz, the authorial metonym, has not somehow committed unethical acts, such as stealing from the citizens of Luna and even deceiving Mannie about strategies and tactics. Mannie immediately says to himself, "I told conscience to go to sleep" (Heinlein 1997: 137), and that's that. To be sure, Prof's entire program stacks the deck; called "rational anarchism," the view posits two moral imperatives – one for society and one for the individual. Society should be bound by the individual's right to bargain in a free marketplace, and the individual should be bound by an undeniably absolute individual responsibility: "I am free because I know that I *alone* am morally responsible for everything I do" (Heinlein 1997: 85). Prof's proclamation conflates blame with obligation; one may be prohibited from blaming others, but it does not follow that one has no other ethical obligations. At a key late moment, when Wyoming Knott (the novel's Lysistrata) actually offers a challenge, she meets the same condescending response as the vapid ephebe in *Starship Troopers*: finally confronted with his hypocrisy, the meretricious Prof tries to present betrayal as universal, natural law (Heinlein 1997: 243).

Prof's "rational anarchism" flouts its own apodictic rule. It constitutes what philosophical ethics commonly labels "egoism": unarguably only personal preference produced by personal power. Note that Heinlein's authoritarian metonyms offer up their moral reasoning in the form of wholly unambiguous, already codified dogmas that preexist the human subject. Much sf operates in this mode because most of our culture operates in this mode, though perhaps Heinlein's false consciousness is especially appalling because of his claims to scientific fact and disinterested rationality. Heinlein's monologic didacticism closes down real ethical inquiry by transforming it into a series of patronizing screeds delivered by an exalted hierophant to his circle of credulous acolytes.

One characteristic of truly great literature involves its imaginative challenge to such orthodoxies. In the history of philosophy there have been several such orthodox metanarratives concerning the main purpose of philosophic discourse. Levinas's responsibility or Bakhtin's answerability seem to me to clarify the difference between new models of the ethical imagination and an older model, as in Heinlein, where a new orthodoxy is proffered to replace an old orthodoxy. This is best illustrated through the work of Philip K. Dick, who stands to Heinlein as Levinas stands to Plato.

Dick obsessed over what distinct qualities defined our human condition. An early story, "Human Is" (1955), provides the paradigm of Dick's definition. An astronaut travels to the distant stars, and upon returning acts decidedly differently; previously stern, intolerant, coldly stoic, he now behaves kindly, revels in quotidian pleasures, and opens himself emotionally to others, especially his wife. One day the security police arrive to tell his wife that they have discovered her husband is really an alien simulacrum, not a human being. "Terran ethics don't extend to them" (Dick 1987b: 265), they declare as they try to take the alien away, but his wife tells the police to bug off, metaphorically slams the door, and asks the alien if she can still call him "Lester," to which he agrees. They walk off into the sunset, arm in arm, smiling broadly. To Dick, *humanness*, then, is not a genetic code or species designation. Existence may precede essence, but essence is behavior, performance, action – ethics, not biology.

This understanding of human essence as ethical responsiveness dominates his fiction. In *The Man in the High Castle* (1962), each of the main characters moves toward an ethical moment that centers around a recognition of absolute alterity and empathic responsiveness to the other. Mr Tagomi, who seems the novel's Greek Chorus, appears at the nexus of much of the action, and provides a running commentary. Despite his status as a high-ranking civilian bureaucrat in the Japanese military occupation of San Francisco, Tagomi becomes physically ill when considering evil (Dick 1975: 83–4), something represented in the novel by Nazi genocide. Tagomi's illness builds until late in the book, where he says sotto voce that he "cannot face this dilemma ... That man should have to act in such moral ambiguity" (Dick 1975: 163); "we have entered a Moment when we are alone. We cannot get assistance, as before" (Dick 1975: 191), he eventually concludes. Tagomi's pessimistic existentialism finds its counterpart in Juliana, whose final circumstances remain more quietly optimistic. Having reached the High Castle and discovered that Hawthorne Abendsen is no unimpeachable hierophant of moral certitude, that he cannot provide objective assistance and resolve all ethical ambiguity, she returns to her world – "moving and bright and living" (Dick 1975: 259).

The novel in which Dick's position on responsiveness receives the most explicit exposition, *Do Androids Dream of Electric Sheep?* (1968), contains a religion called "Mercerism," first introduced in "The Little Black Box" (1964). The box is *an empathy box* – hold its handles, and you know empathy in the physical body. Commenting on the story, Dick observed that it identifies the *"concept of* caritas *(or* agape)[, which] shows up in my writing as the key to the authentic human"* (Dick 1987a: 389). *Caritas* means "charity" broadly construed: open altruistic friendship and unconstrained empathic care for others. It is occasionally used, especially in relation to medieval Christianity, as a synonym for "ethics," and is generally thought to combine aspects of *agape* and *eros*.

The novel's plot, and probably most of the thematic resonances, are well known – Deckard is a policeman tasked to kill rogue androids; he fails to love his wife; his experiences with the empathy box are not understood or incorporated into his life; the Voigt-Kampff test to identify androids is flawed; Rachael gets his goat; he has a false epiphany in the desert; and so on – and signal his misunderstanding of and failure to empathize. In this respect, he is more like the androids. For instance, he never learns that the toad (actually, a horned frog) is electric – only his wife and the reader learn this, and only we realize its significance. We also realize that Mercer turns out to be not Christ but a fraud, as revealed not by the empathy box but by its direct antithesis, television – via the androids' favorite spin doctor, Buster Friendly. The androids replace empathy with "friendly," the superficial appearance for the real, authentic thing, and that is the novel's central claim. That Mercerism is indeed ontologically bogus does not make it any less ethically useful.

The alternative notion would be that all we experience is illusory – but this is simply an alibi for Deckard's multiple failures (personal and cultural) to empathize, which the text works very hard to refute (despite its acknowledgment that we may be wrong, we may be delusional after all). Contrary to the pattern that marks most modern fictions, Dick refuses a *deus ex machina* resolution of ethical ambiguity, refuses to allow some mystical epiphany to redeem Deckard or, metonymically, to save his world. Deckard's wife Iran, obtusely, flattens out all affect, goes to the Penfield Mood Organ to dial 670, "long deserved peace" (Dick 1982: 215), then phones the pet service, requesting delivery of some electric insects for the electric toad, thereby missing the point in almost every pertinent respect. True epiphanies can *only* be experienced by readers, their hands erotically fastened upon the corporeal novel that is, truly, an empathy box.

In the practical sphere of daily life and quotidian struggles, both tedious and tumultuous, the central test of ethical reason is utter transparency. Dick passes, Heinlein fails. The second test is that in Dick's properly ethical understanding, there are no alibis – whereas in Heinlein, "prudence" demands that the self never take the rap. Heinlein follows the normative logic of morality; Dick follows the rhizomatic logic of ethics. For Heinlein, morality concerns articulated codes that legislate behavior, wherein people provide means to desired ends. For Dick, as for Kant and Levinas, other people are always already themselves ends.

For an example of a writer who, like Heinlein, projects and scripts a morality and

389

an ideological set of values, but who does engage the ethical mode, consider Greg Egan's hard-sf space opera, *Schild's Ladder* (2002). Set approximately 23,000 years into our future, it recounts a scientific experiment gone horribly wrong. Despite careful and rigorous precautions in an experiment that takes five years to conduct, a physicist attempting to capture the fundamental essence of reality beneath the Planck scale instead manages to instigate or "seed" another set of physical laws and constants, thereby creating a competing reality, dubbed the "novo vacuum," that proceeds toward a rapid and apparently unstoppable expansion. From our side of the apparently impassable boundary, we would call its advance destructive, since it transforms and absorbs everything in its path. Two sorts of response emerge: the Preservationists, who hope to reverse and destroy the new space–time, and the Yielders, who hope either to arrest its advance or resign to yielding (since the novo vacuum expands at less than the speed of light, much time remains to these posthumans). Eventually they penetrate the border, and the main characters find an improbable but miraculous universe, at 10^{-33} meters, teeming with improbably but miraculously intelligent life. *Schild's Ladder* represents a contact novel of the most basic sort: posthumanity seems threatened by the vast unknown, in all its sublime terror, and in making a crude sort of contact seeks a sort of teetering rapprochement between our vast, fearful ignorance and the possibility of progressive change: more knowledge, more inclusiveness, more love. Egan lifts both the novel's leitmotif and its theme from E.M. Forster's *Howards End* (1910) – "only connect": connecting to others and opening to difference.

Egan cleverly provides perfectly parallel accounts in both the novel's science and its plot. These he wraps rhizomatically in a web of parallel associations and connections. The novel's opening paragraph begins and ends: "In the beginning was a graph … the graph consisted only of the fact that some nodes were connected to others. This pattern of connections, repeated endlessly, was all there was" (Egan 2004: 3). The novel has two nova, the invented science called Quantum Graph Theory (QGT) and a technological device called the Qusp, a sort of Schrödinger's box that isolates its posthuman's autonomous individuality (the cat) from the implications of Everett's many-worlds hypothesis. The highly speculative QGT is what you might get if Gilles Deleuze and Félix Guattari had been physicists rather than speculative philosophers. On the other hand, the Qusp isolates human choice as singular, ensuring that each posthuman being remains a singularity rather than merely one of a nearly infinite number of potential iterations, each in its own endlessly bifurcating universe produced by the collapse of a single probability equation. But this Qusp itself proves the novel's crux, for "Nature had never had much imagination, but people had always found new ways to connect" (Egan 2004: 219). Connecting permits and presages real human progress. In *Schild's Ladder*, that progress turns out to be an escape from how the human imagination has imagined nature's limits, nature's boundaries: otherwise, we are trapped in "the old human nightmare: endless varieties of suffering, endless varieties of stupidity, endless varieties of banality" (Egan 2004: 29).

Caught in "their tangle of mutual interdependence" (Egan 2004: 125), the characters must continually open themselves to authentic difference. Then like any contact novel, this tale of posthuman contact with aliens provides an allegory of human with human contact, and not off in some unimaginably distant future but in the here and now, among readers holding the book and engaging its conceits. We should not be surprised to find a metonymic representation of readers. These "anachronauts" are the pre-posthuman remnants from 19,000 years before the novel's present; though this makes them members of our own future, the novel names them as holding nineteenth-century ideas and values. Using spaceships with slower-than-light drives and cryo-chambers, they sleep while traveling from star to star, their ships serving as time machines opening the posthuman future. They stop periodically, but only with the desire to witness their ancestors' destruction, devolution – as one posthuman says, "Dreaming of all the horrors they'd wished upon us, in the name of some crude, masochistic notion of humanity that must have been dying right in front of them before they'd even left Earth" (Egan 2004: 138).

Schild's Ladder places readers in the necessary position of self-interrogation brought about by seeing ourselves as other; a position without an alibi (metaphysical, religious, legal, psychological, linguistic, sociological) called "answerability." In the case of the anachronauts specifically, this opening happens by identifying one's ideology *as* ideology rather than the natural product of the natural world. Where Heinlein reinscribes the known, the traditional, the familiar, Egan embraces the other, the different, the unknown, almost as if he were following Butler's imperative "to risk ourselves precisely at moments of unknowingness, when what forms us diverges from what lies before us, when our willingness to become undone in relation to others constitutes our chance of becoming human" (Butler 2005: 136).

Since on television and in newspapers, in public forums and in literary criticism, the vast majority of invocations of ethics is little more than sanctimonious dismissal and ideological harangue, it is especially important that literary scholars and students learn the lessons of philosophical ethics. Reading in the tradition, from Plato to the present, brings increased rigor and greater clarity. It can help us realize what ethics is not: finger-pointing; the endorsement of a particular political ideology; the business practice of learning to skirt the difficult border between social etiquette and the profit motive; the materialist alibi named sociobiology that is really just moral Viagra for the status quo.

In turn, literature generally and sf specifically has much to teach philosophers. Art is not epiphenomenal to the formal philosophical study of ethics. Literature captures human life in its lived totality, something philosophy frequently forgets, or occasionally actively evades. Philosophical ethics tries to give apposite, syllogistic inferences that would freeze life as a set of abstractions, all for the sake of an understanding that might be called certain. However admirable and however desirable such an outcome may be, literature opens the risk of unknowing, the real difficulties of confronting lived contexts. Literature also demands a lived response. Literature can (and often does) provide something philosophy cannot: richly thick descriptions of the specific contexts wherein we struggle with philosophical problems. Indeed, this nexus between literary narrative and philosophy may itself be called ethics: "Ethics is ... the point at which literature interacts with [philosophical] theory, the point at which literature becomes conceptually interesting and theory becomes humanized" (Harpham 1999: 33).

This sense of ethics is "concussive: [it] shocks and lingers as 'traumatisms of astonishment'" (Levinas qtd in Newton 1995: 13). I think this moral estrangement is the special advantage of sf. Yes, the "literature of change" may be most superficially distinguished by its "sense of wonder"-producing engagement with the impact of science and technology on human life; but within the larger human project, it fosters a "sense of wondering" – not the sublime awe of space opera or the astonishment at the door that dilates, but the critical reflectiveness that opens us to the other, replaces notions of duty with notions of answerability, and leaves us always and everywhere subject to the obligations of ethics.

Bibliography

Bakhtin, M.M. as V.N. Vološinov (1973) *Marxism and the Philosophy of Language*, 1929, trans. L. Matejka and I.R. Titunik, Cambridge, MA: Harvard University Press.

Bakhtin, M.M. (1984) *Problems of Dostoevsky's Poetics*, trans. C. Emerson, Minneapolis: University of Minnesota Press.

—— (1993) *Toward a Philosophy of the Act*, 1921, trans. V. Liapunov, Austin: University of Texas Press.

Blackburn, S. (2001) *Being Good*, New York: Oxford University Press.

Butler, J. (2005) *Giving an Account of Oneself*, New York: Fordham University Press.

Clarke, A.C. (2001) *The City and the Stars and The Sands of Mars*, New York: Aspect.

Dick, P.K. (1975) *The Man in the High Castle*, 1962, London: Gollancz.

—— (1982) *Do Androids Dream of Electric Sheep?*, 1968, New York: Del Rey.

—— (1987a) *The Little Black Box: the collected stories of Philip K. Dick volume 5*, Novato, CA and Lancaster, PA: Underwood-Miller.

—— (1987b) *Second Variety: the collected stories of Philip K. Dick volume 2*, Novato, CA and Lancaster, PA: Underwood-Miller.

Egan, G. (2004) *Schild's Ladder*, 2002, New York: Eos.

Harpham, G.G. (1999) *Shadows of Ethics: criticism and the just society*, Durham, NC: Duke University Press.

Hauser, M.D. (2006) *Moral Minds*, New York: HarperCollins.

Heinlein, R.A. (1987) *Starship Troopers*, 1959, New York: Ace.

—— (1997) *The Moon is a Harsh Mistress*, 1966, New York: Orb.

Levinas, E. (1969) *Totality and Infinity*, 1961, trans. A. Lingis, Pittsburgh, PA: Duquesne University Press.

—— (1989) "Ethics as First Philosophy," in S. Hand (ed.) *The Levinas Reader*, 1984, trans. S. Hand and M. Temple, Oxford: Blackwell.

Nealon, J.T. (1998) *Alterity Politics: ethics and performative subjectivity*, Durham, NC: Duke University Press.

Newton, A.Z. (1995) *Narrative Ethics*, Cambridge, MA: Harvard University Press.

Putnam, H. (2004) *Ethics without Ontology*, Cambridge, MA: Harvard University Press.

Rorty, R. (1999) "Ethics without Principles," in *Philosophy and Social Hope*, New York: Penguin.

Russ, J. (1975) *The Female Man*, New York: Bantam.

Singer, P. (ed.) (1990) *A Companion to Ethics*, Oxford: Blackwell.

39
MUSIC
Ken McLeod

Cross-pollinations between sf and music encompass a rich variety of forms and media. These typically symbiotic relationships can be found among artists and songs that incorporate sf themes, in the importance of music in sf movies, television, and videogame soundtracks, and in the influence of futurism on musical styles, genres, and technology. However, despite the numerous musical works and artists inspired by sf and the significant role of music in sf, scholars have largely not recognized the importance of the relationship between these two modes of entertainment.

There are exceptions. John Corbett (1994) includes a chapter on "Brothers from Another Planet: the space madness of Lee 'Scratch' Perry, Sun Ra, and George Clinton." Timothy Taylor (2001) addresses the impact of postwar technology on music, particularly the rise of "futuristic" classical music and the role of technology in techno and electronica. Mark Dery (1996), Kodwo Eshun (1998), and Jeremy Gilbert and Ewan Pearson (1999) more directly address the impact of sf and technology on music and youth identity, as well as the impact of cyberculture on both music reception and production (see also Elms *et al.* 2006; Jakubowski 1993; Larson 1985; Lock 1999; McLeod 2003; Whittington 2007). Connecting the world of sf to music, Michael Luckman (2005) provides a somewhat less scholarly though nonetheless provocative study of the plethora of rock personalities, from Elvis and John Lennon to Jimi Hendrix and Michael Jackson, who have been influenced by real or imagined extraterrestrial encounters. Perhaps the most valuable contribution to the topic to date can be found in Philip Hayward (2004), a collection of essays that provides substantial and well-grounded analyses and critiques of many of the most influential sf soundtracks. Something of the increasing awareness of the importance of music and sf is evident in the panel "The Place of Music in Science Fiction and Fantasy" at the 2006 Annual Convention of the Modern Languages Association.

Classical music and sf

Allusions to sf in music prior to the twentieth century are relatively few and far between. One notable exception to this is Joseph Haydn's comic opera *The World on the Moon* (1777). In Carlo Goldini's libretto, the bumbling aristocrat Buonafede is obsessed with the relatively new science of astronomy. His servants and daughters trick him into believing that he has been transported to a world on the Moon, complete with extraterrestrial "moon people." While there, he permits his daughters to marry several suitors, none of whom he would have approved on Earth. Goldini's story proved to be extremely popular in the eighteenth century, with well-known composers such as Niccolò Piccinni, Leopold Gassmann, and Giovanni Paisiello also setting it to music. Other operas that involve sf include Jacques Offenbach's opéra bouffes, *The Voyage to the Moon* (1875) and *Doctor Ox* (1877), both adapted from fiction by Jules Verne.

Such operatic sf settings are rare. However, a number of twentieth-century classical composers were inspired by ideals stemming from scientific and technological advances and fascinated with concepts of utopian futurism and the exploration of sonic space. Following the Second World War, a technoscientific worldview began to impact on music-making and reception. While not directly inspired by sf, many of the musical innovations at this time evinced a similar notion of a futuristic utopianism that characterized much of the genre. The invention of magnetic tape, for example, engendered a new experimentalism in art music, particularly the electro-acoustic works of such European composers as Edgard Varèse, Pierre Schaeffer, Pierre Henry, and Karlheinz Stockhausen. The looping, tape effects, ambient electronic noises, and found sounds employed by these composers continued to be popular in modern art music, with later composers inspired by the appearance of even newer digital and computer sound-generation technologies. However, by the late 1970s this interest in musical futurism began to wane as many composers returned to more traditional musical values. The technoscientific approach to music nonetheless found a new voice in more popular styles, notably in the studio experimentation of the Beatles and of progressive rock artists such as Pink Floyd, Tangerine Dream, and Kraftwerk. In the 1990s many techno and rave DJs actively embraced the music of Schaeffer, Henry, and others in shaping their electronic dance mixes.

The interest in technology extended into the realm of consumer culture. The 1950s and 1960s, for example, saw the advent of new hi-fi and stereo sound systems which allowed consumers (particularly men) to simultaneously participate in notions of a futurist utopian lifestyle and to project a literal colonization of sonic space. As analogs to this fascination with music technologies, new genres of music arose that specifically catered to notions of gracious space-age living. Easy listening space-age pop albums, including Harry Revel's *Music Out of the Moon* (1947) and *Music from Outer Space* (1953), Les Baxter's *Space Escape* (1957), and Bobby Christian's *Strings for a Space Age* (1959), were purposely tailored for hi-fi and stereo audiophiles. Such albums often featured naked or scantily clad women on the cover, marking them as the alien "other" to male colonizers of exotic foreign worlds (Taylor 2001: 87–93), and typically included detailed technical information about the recording on the back of the sleeve. Together, space music and the audiophile fascination with playback technologies represented a domestication of the hopes and fears of the nuclear space age.

Forbidden sounds: sf movie soundtracks

Possibly the most public stage for the promotion of these technological dreams is to be found in sf films and the music that accompanied them. For example, the possibilities and threats of nuclear power were summed up by the alien Klaatu in *The Day the Earth Stood Still* (Wise 1951): "soon one of your nations will apply atomic energy to space ships. That will threaten the peace and security of other nations." Bernard Herrmann's score for the film avoided traditional core orchestral string and woodwind instruments, instead making extensive use of electronic instruments in combination with other orchestral instrumentation, including 30 brass instruments, four pianos, four harps, electric violin, and electric piano. The most prominent timbre employed in the film, however, was provided by two Theremins. Invented around 1920 by Léon Theremin, it generates a single high-register tone, the pitch and dynamic of which are controlled by the proximity of the player's hands to protruding antennae and wire loop. Creating an eerie high-pitched whine, almost an electric version of an operatic coloratura, it symbolizes the threat of alien technology. More generally, its unnatural tone was ideally suited for portraying other-worldly voices, and thus has often been employed in film and television representations of outer space and extraterrestrial creatures.

Forbidden Planet (Wilcox 1956), scored by Louis and Bebe Barron, is widely credited with being the first entirely electronically generated soundtrack. Using equations presented in Norbert Wiener (1948), the Barrons constructed numerous electronic circuits (ring modulators) that generated various synthesized sounds to which were later added effects such as reverb and delay. In the liner notes from the soundtrack album, the Barrons explained that they "created individual cybernetics circuits for particulars themes and leit motifs, rather than using standard sound generators … each circuit has a characteristic activity pattern" (Barron and Barron 1956). Rather than the predictable practice of accompanying humans with acoustic instruments and aliens with electronic music, they used a variety of unique circuits to create distinct electronic sound effects that set the mood of twenty-third-century technology and the disturbing atmosphere of the lethal planet.

Following the fears of technological annihilation inherent in the films of the 1950s, 1960s sf films began to embody issues of civil rights and other social concerns. *Planet of the Apes* (Schaffner 1968) portrayed a white human trapped in a world dominated by black apes, inverting the power structure experienced by African-Americans. Like many earlier sf films, its score is an example of high avant-garde modernism. Jerry Goldsmith's music subverts conventional expectations to reflect this world turned on its head, employing numerous unusual sounds, such as a ram's horn, tuned aluminum mixing bowls, and brass instruments played with inverted mouthpieces.

One of the most original and arresting scores of the era belongs to *2001: A Space Odyssey* (Kubrick 1968). In addition to its groundbreaking visual effects, it is equally notable for its use of previously composed music and, as such, moves away from the electronic representations of technology and space characteristic of earlier films. Kubrick set the soundtrack to music by a variety of late nineteenth- and twentieth-century art music composers, including Richard Strauss's tone poem *Thus Spoke*

Zarathustra (1896) for the striking opening montage and Johann Strauss II's *Blue Danube Waltz* (1867) for the space-docking sequence. Works by Aram Kachaturian and sound mass composer György Ligeti also play prominent roles. In using intact versions of previously composed music, Kubrick allows the music to set the mood while remaining detached from any real relationship to the drama. The large Romantic and twentieth-century orchestral works also suggested something of the sublime grandeur and timelessness of space. Kubrick also used classical quotation for *A Clockwork Orange* (Kubrick 1971), in which well-known musical works such as Beethoven's *Symphony No. 9* (1824), Rossini's Overture to *The Thieving Magpie* (1817), and a memorable rendition of "Singin' in the Rain" (1929) are dramatically juxtaposed with scenes of rape and violence. The film is also notable for its early use of the Moog Synthesizer and for some of its original music composed by Walter (Wendy) Carlos.

The late 1970s and early 1980s saw a number of important sf soundtracks. To some extent *Star Wars: Episode IV – A New Hope* (Lucas 1977), a self-conscious patchwork of clichés drawn from various film genres, also marked the beginning of a postmodern aesthetic in film music. It returned to elements typical of a classical movie score, with a large post-Romantic orchestra deploying the Wagnerian leitmotifs and thematic transformations that marked the techniques of earlier film composers such as Max Steiner and Erich Korngold. John Williams's score, consciously avoiding any reference to popular music, typically relies on imitating the style of other twentieth-century composers, particularly the American nationalist style of Aaron Copland. Although the film and its sequels – *Star Wars: Episode V – The Empire Strikes Back* (Kershner 1980) and *Star Wars: Episode VI – Return of the Jedi* (Marquand 1983), also scored by Williams – are full of strange worlds and fantastic alien characters, more often than not the music used in their support is familiar to audiences and thus supports the return to traditional values embodied in the narrative.

John Williams was, of course, responsible for scoring three other important sf films in this period. *Close Encounters of the Third Kind* (Spielberg 1977) is most notable for the enigmatic five-note theme that played a critical role in facilitating communication with the extraterrestrials, while for *Superman* (Donner 1978), as with *Star Wars*, Williams composed a recurring heroic theme for the main character. Williams's score for *E.T.: The Extra-Terrestrial* (Spielberg 1982) captures the childlike traits of the main character through gentle and delicate use of woodwinds, piccolo, harps, and celesta and unifies the work through a series of variations of the main five-note E.T. leitmotif. Williams's work was influential in the general trend toward a more extensive use of music in films and, in contrast to earlier technologically driven sf soundtracks, marked a return to the large-scale studio orchestra sound more typical of the 1940s and 1950s. A significant exception to this trend is found in the scores to *Star Trek: The Motion Picture* (Wise 1979) and its sequels. Jerry Goldsmith scored the first two films, and while a classical orchestra predominates, he made greater use of electronic instruments and sounds. James Horner scored the next two films, which notably quote the theme from the television show but overall are more influenced by Williams's post-Romantic approach.

Others took a more eclectic musical approach. For example, Vangelis's score for

Blade Runner (Scott 1982) relies heavily on a postmodern juxtaposition of ambient synthesized and electronic, romantic symphonic, jazz, popular, and pseudo ethnic Japanese and Arabic scoring to create a futuristic vision of the mechanistic world of 2019 while simultaneously evoking a nostalgia for the past. Many fantasy and comedy adventure films, such as *Back to the Future* (Zemickis 1985), *Ghost Busters* (Reitman 1984), and *Batman* (Burton 1989), took a similarly eclectic approach, mixing romantic symphonic music with rock and jazz styles. More recently, Don Davis's score for *The Matrix* (Wachowski brothers 1999) evokes a futuristic, machine-dominated world by juxtaposing minimalist art music with techno and heavy metal, using alternative rock band Rage Against the Machine's "Wake Up" at its conclusion to reiterate its dystopian warning.

It came from outer space: sf and the evolution of rock

Contemporaneous with the era of space exploration (and a concomitant sf boom) was the advent of rock 'n' roll, and in its earliest manifestations space was a popular subject. A leading candidate for the first ever rock 'n' roll record, Jackie Brenston's hot rod ode "Rocket 88" (1951), immediately linked space travel with teenage rebellion. The 1953 formation of Bill Haley and His Comets followed in this tradition, as did the DJ antics of Allan Freed broadcast in the mid-1950s via his radio show, *Moon Dog Rock'n'Roll House Party*.

Indeed, space, alien, and sf themes can be found throughout rock's history and has impacted on nearly all its stylistic manifestations, particularly blossoming in popular music following the 1969 moon landing. This period was also marked by the socio-political tumult evident in protests against the Vietnam War and against institutional racial and gender discrimination. Consequently many influential artists used space and extraterrestrial themes to represent political and sexual liberation and also to evoke the freedom associated with mind-expanding drugs. Perhaps the best-known exponent of this trend was David Bowie's alter ego Ziggy Stardust, who, in Bowie's own words, was a "Martian messiah who twanged a guitar." *The Rise and Fall of Ziggy Stardust and the Spiders from Mars* (1972) narrates the story of this bisexual alien rock superstar who ends up a victim of his own success and commits rock 'n' roll suicide. Bowie's fascination with outer space was already evident in "Space Oddity" (1969), inspired by the Apollo missions and *2001: A Space Odyssey*. In "Space Oddity" Bowie uses a series of atonal and rhythmically irregular tape effects and electronic squelches in combination with an ethereal string section to represent the defamiliarizing experience of space. The juxtaposition of avant-garde electronic sounds and instruments with familiar rock timbres (most notably a strummed acoustic guitar and military drum beat that sonically evoke the stability of home and tradition) provides a musical analogue for lyrics that warn of the dangers of technological nihilism and alienation in an increasingly dehumanized world. Bowie's conscious construction of an alien rock star was intended to shed light on the artificiality of rock in general, but equally importantly Bowie's alien persona was emblematic of his bisexual alienation from the heterosexual male-dominated world of rock music. Bowie's use of alien and sf imagery and empowering bisexual and asexual symbolism influenced numerous artists in the late 1970s and early 1980s, such as Nina Hagen, Klaus Nomi, and Gary Numan (who, in songs such as "Listen to the Sirens" (1978), was particularly inspired by Philip K. Dick). As in Bowie's messianic Ziggy Stardust character, the use of alien and futuristic themes by these artists revolves around notions of a radical alienation from traditional belief systems and a concomitant quasi-religious significance attached to alien communication (McLeod 2003).

As with the technoscientific stream of classical music, 1970s progressive rock artists colonized technology to create numerous futuristic space soundscapes, as in Pink Floyd's *The Dark Side of the Moon* (1973), Hawkwind's *In Search of Space* (1971), King Crimson's *Earthbound* (1972), and Yes's "Starship Trooper" (1973). The impressive technological displays associated with progressive rock – the multiple banks of keyboards, the complex arrays of knobs and dials used in both keyboard and guitar effects – were analogous to the advanced technology of the actual NASA space program. Indeed, the technological obsession of 1970s US space-race militarism, associated with the war in Vietnam and the arms race with the USSR, was increasingly reflected in various aspects of the rock-music industry, including advances in studio recording and sound-reproduction technologies. The fetishization of technique, virtuosity, and musical complexity, which marked much of this music, was mirrored in the complexity of its instrumentation and technology. Often supplementing their live performances with exotic futuristic staging and lighting effects, many progressive rock groups effectively created fictional sonic worlds.

In the 1980s, the darker, synthesizer-driven work of artists such as Kraftwerk and Gary Numan influenced hip-hop and techno acts, including Afrika Bambaataa and Cybotron, as well as cyberpunk fiction's examination of human–machine interactions. Later cyberpunk, which also drew upon the anarchic imagery associated with punk rock, was manifested musically by the rise of techno-driven Gothic shock rockers, such as GWAR, Nine Inch Nails, and Marilyn Manson, who explored various apocalyptic millennial visions of man–machine mergers in the late twentieth and early twenty-first centuries.

Mothership connections: alien nations

The most prevalent manifestations of sf in film, classical art, and popular music have been the products of white Anglo-American men. Among the most vibrant use of extraterrestrial themes in contemporary popular music, however, occurs within the realm of "Afrofuturism" (Dery 1993: 736). The term refers to the African-American artistic use of and association with images of advanced technology and alien or prosthetically enhanced potentials. Afrofuturism is found in a variety of media, including the fiction of Samuel R. Delany, Octavia E. Butler, Steve Barnes, and Charles Saunders, films such as John Sayles's *The Brother from Another Planet* (1984) and the cyborg creations of New York Graffiti artist–theoretician Rammellzee. Such Afrofuturistic art is typically concerned with the creation of mythologies based on confrontations between historical prophetic imagination, such as Egyptian theories of the afterlife, and modern alienated black existence. As Dery observes "African-Americans are, in a very real sense, the descendents of alien abductees" (Dery 1993: 736). Black diasporic consciousness has often sought to return to an inaccessible homeland, and black artists found in sf tropes and the image of outer space a locus for this utopian potential.

One of the most influential strains of Afrofuturism is manifest by George Clinton and his band Parliament-Funkadelic. During the same period as Bowie's Ziggy Stardust persona, Clinton, in albums such as *Mothership Connection* (1975), assumed the alter ego of an alien named Starchild who was sent down from the mothership to bring Funk to earthlings. Starchild was an allegorical representation of freedom and positive energy – a potent and socially activist image of African-American society during the early 1970s. In creating his Afrofuturistic mythology, Clinton provided an empowering mixture of glib sf fantasy, street slang, and ancient black history. The Afro-nauts of Parliament-Funkadelic combined synthesizers, acoustic piano, brass, heavy funk bass, and wah wah effects to create highly layered, otherworldly grooves. Like Bowie, the mechanistic sound of various synthesizers and wah wah effects creates an exotic soundscape that simultaneously reflects and empowers the alienation (from mainstream white society) experienced by Clinton's primarily black audience. Parliament also supplemented their alien image through audacious live shows that were orgiastic celebrations of excess (including a strobe-lit, fog-belching flying saucer that lowered Clinton to the stage). Synthesizers and other electronic effects associated with the latest in musical technology, combined with Clinton's futuristic lyrical references, were compelling markers of the potential for African-American wealth and power – a futuristic vision in which the previously marginalized "aliens" assume control of the world.

The Afrofuturistic fusion of sf, space, techno-futurism, and magical/mystical African heritage can also be glimpsed in the experimental cosmological jazz of Sun Ra and his Intergalactic Jet-Set Arkestra (to give just one of the Arkestra's many astrologically variant names), a pioneer of synthesizers and African percussion. The techno-tribalism of Miles Davis's "On the Corner" (1972), Herbie Hancock's jazz-cyber funk "Future Shock" (1983), or Bernie Worrell's "Blacktronic Science" (1993) also resonate such concerns. In a similar fashion, Jimi Hendrix, in works such as "Third Stone from the Sun" (1967) and "Astro Man" (1970 but not officially released until 1997), employed a psychedelic mix of electric guitar and studio effects to sonically project a futuristic image of black creativity, exploration, and experimentation.

In addition to providing models of racial empowerment, alien and sf tropes have also inspired artists concerned with gender. While access to and control of technology, and the masculine coding of machine culture, are still areas of contestation and often replicate institutionalized masculine domination, many theorists, such as Donna Haraway (1985), have begun to examine the liberating power of technology for women. In popular music, several artists consciously evoke cyborg and sf imagery to contest orthodoxies of masculine technological power, as in Laurie Anderson's "O Superman" (1981). Similarly Missy Elliott adopts heavily futuristic personae, and dresses in futuristic gender-blurring spacesuits in her videos for "Sock it 2 Me" (1997) and "She's a Bitch" (1999). Nina Hagen, on the other hand, frequently talks about her real-life "alien" encounters and the influence of alien culture in her transgressive vocal style (ear-piercing screams, guttural snarls mixed with florid coloratura) that is supplemented by futuristic synthesized soundscapes. These female artists, however, touch on sf only tangentially, reflecting the historically masculinist gender bias of Western popular music.

Space stations: videogames and other media

Sf and futuristic iconography are a significant feature of innumerable music videos, album packaging, and other promotional materials. For example, Michael Jackson's video/film *Black or White* (1991) uses alien and space-travel themes, although his marketing and image are not typically defined by space–alien association or imagery. There is also a significant sf crossover in the liminal spaces in which much popular music is consumed, as in the desensitizing experience of the sound and lighting effects, and accompanying futuristic imagery, employed in disco clubs such as *Xenon* and *2001 Oddyssey* (sic). Science-fictional landscapes and futuristic staging, typically foregrounding technological spectacle, are also a common trope of many rock-concert experiences, from the blood-spurting aliens associated with GWAR to the post-apocalyptic imagery of many goth and heavy metal acts. Similarly the transitive rave aesthetic can, at least in part, be understood in terms of its underlying attempt to literally travel to and explore new sonic and experiential worlds.

Another increasingly important interconnection between sf and music is found in videogame soundtracks, from well-known early classics, such as *Space Invaders* (1978), *Asteroids* (1979), and *Pac-Man* (1980), to later favorites, such as *Final Fantasy* (1987), *The Legend of Zelda* (1987), *Doom* (1993), *Myst* (1993), *Quake* (1996), *Halo* (2001), *Gears of War* (2006), and their typically multiple sequels. Approaches to game music in the early 1980s usually involved using simple tone generation and/or frequency modulation synthesis, and was often limited to electronic beeps, squelches, and simple melodies. Nonetheless, the importance of music in these early games is evident in *Pac-Man*, likely the most significant game of all time in terms of its impact on pop-culture consciousness. The sound of Pac-Man's insatiable appetite for dots has become synonymous with the sound of consumerism run amok, just as the sound of Pac-Man dying has become a universally recognizable marker of defeat (the game's popularity subsequently inspired musicians Jerry Buckner and Gary Garcia to release a single "Pac-Man Fever" (1982), a spoof of Ted Nugent's 1977 "Cat Scratch Fever," which rose as high as number nine on the US singles chart). Likewise, a large part of the appeal of *Space Invaders* stems from the sonic tension induced by its menacing soundtrack in which electronic bass squelches accelerate in tempo as the enemy aliens draw nearer.

The mid-1980s saw increasingly sophisticated computer systems that made use of 8- and 16-bit digital sound synthesis and sampling. In 1985, Nintendo released *Super Mario Bros.*, which set a new standard for sound design in videogames. This is considered, alongside his work on *The Legend of Zelda*, to be composer Miyamoto Shigeru's masterpiece in sound design. The constantly shifting melodies and tones evolve to match the action on screen and create a synthesis between music and gameplaying. As such, this approach marked a significant move away from cinematic musical conventions and opened a new direction in soundtrack design unique to videogames. Uematsu Nobuo's soundtrack for *Final Fantasy VI* (1994), a postmodern collage of musical styles as well as character-specific leitmotifs that recur throughout the course of the game, is seen by many as the epitome of videogame music sophistication.

Even more powerful 64-bit systems were introduced in the mid-1990s, with a consequently improved soundtrack quality. Among other innovations was the incorporation of previously composed pieces into videogames. In 1996, for example, techno artists such as The Chemical Brothers and Future Sounds of London, who feature a heavily futuristic sound and image, contributed soundtracks for Playstation's *Wipeout XL*, also known as *Wipeout 2097*; the soundtrack was also released as an album. In 1998, *The Legend of Zelda Returns* became the first contemporary non-dance videogame to feature music as part of the actual gameplay. Players use an ocarina to teleport, open portals, or summon allies. There is also a musical puzzle in which the player must follow the bass line of a song.

Melodies and themes from many games have been incorporated into various other media. In 1986, the London Philharmonic released a live performance of Sugiyama Koichi's compositions from the *Dragon Quest* videogame series (1986–), for which they also recorded soundtracks. Many of these classically performed soundtracks and sheet music, like anime soundtracks, are marketed exclusively in Japan. North American interest has, however, been growing. In 2005, the Los Angeles Philharmonic held a Video Games concert at the Hollywood Bowl, performing music from a variety of videogames, from *Pong* (1972) to *Halo 2* (2004).

Games predicated on futuristic or post-apocalyptic themes have also recently impacted popular-music sales. Perhaps the best example of this intermedia phenomenon is provided by "Mad World." This haunting song, originally written and recorded by Tears for Fears in 1982, was covered by film composer Michael Andrews for *Donnie Darko* (Kelly 2001), becoming a worldwide hit. In late 2006, Andrews's version was used as the trailer for Xbox 360's *Gears of War* and, after the trailer was posted on YouTube, it subsequently reached number one in the Canadian singles chart and became the top iTunes download.

Long overlooked, the connections between sf and music are numerous and multi-faceted. Whether it is the considerable influence of sf on classical and popular music, or the important role of music in sf and videogame soundtracks, it is clear that these two modes of entertainment form a close and often symbiotic nexus of cultural production. In an increasingly alienated society that often seeks utopian visions of the future, the study of sf/music crossovers provides us with a more focused reflection not only of our current identities but also of who we might become.

Bibliography

Barron, L. and Barron, B. (1956). Sleeve notes. *Forbidden Planet*. Soundtrack album. Planet Records.

Corbett, J. (1994) *Extended Play: sounding off from John Cage to Dr Funkenstein*, Durham, NC: Duke University Press.

Dery, M. (1993) "Black to the Future: interviews with Samuel R. Delany, Greg Tate, and Tricia Rose," *South Atlantic Quarterly*, 92(4): 735–78.

—— (1996) *Escape Velocity: cyberculture at the end of the century*, New York: Grove.

Elms, A., Corbett, J., and Kapslis, T. (eds) (2006) *Pathways to Unknown Worlds: Sun Ra, El Saturn and Chicago's Afro-Futurist underground 1954–1968*, Chicago: University of Chicago Press.

Eshun, K. (1998) *More Brilliant than the Sun: adventures in sonic fiction*, London: Quartet Books.

Gilbert, J. and Pearson, E. (1999) *Discographies: dance music, culture and the politics of sound*, London: Routledge.

Haraway, D. (1985) "A Manifesto for Cyborgs: science, technology, and socialist feminism in the 1980s," *Socialist Review*, 80(2): 65–107.

Hayward, P. (ed.) (2004) *Off the Planet: music, sound and science fiction cinema*, Bloomington: Indiana University Press.

Jakubowski, M. (1993) "Music: science fiction in classical music," in J. Clute and P. Nicholls (eds) *The Encyclopedia of Science Fiction*, London: Orbit.

Larson, R. (1985) *Musique fantastique: a survey of film music in the fantastic cinema*, London: Scarecrow Press.

Lock, G. (1999) *Blutopia: visions of the future and revisions of the past in the work of Sun Ra, Duke Ellington, and Anthony Braxton*, Durham, NC: Duke University Press.

Luckman, M. (2005) *Alien Rock: the rock and roll extraterrestrial connection*, New York: Simon and Schuster.

McLeod, K. (2003) "Space Oddities: aliens, futurism and meaning in popular music," *Popular Music*, 23(2): 315–33.

Taylor, T. (2001) *Strange Sounds: music technology and culture*, New York: Routledge.

Wiener, N. (1948) *Cybernetics: or the control and communication in the animal and machine*, Cambridge, MA: MIT Press.

Whittington, W.B. (2007) *Sound Design and Science Fiction*, Austin: University of Texas Press.

40

PSEUDOSCIENCE

Roger Luckhurst

One of the enduring ways of defining sf and legitimating its intellectual weight is to argue that it is part of the scientific enlightenment. Sf is a literature of modernity in that it deploys the scientific method. It is secular, rationalist, and skeptical; its futures are rigorously extrapolated from known empirical data; it wages war on superstition, magical thinking, and any argument made from tradition or unexamined authority. The ideologues of Scientific Naturalism, like Thomas Huxley and John Tyndall, secured this model for the new profession of "scientist" in the nineteenth century. In the twentieth century, advocates of the genre of sf tried to make similar claims. In early editions of *Amazing Stories*, Hugo Gernsback emphasized the functional role of "scientifiction" in furthering the scientific and technical education of America. John Campbell's team of writers at *Astounding Science Fiction* (ASF) included Robert A. Heinlein and Isaac Asimov, trained scientists who aggressively distanced sf from the literary world they considered decadent and immoral in its ignorance of science. Heinlein also used scientific rigor to begin to mark out territory *within* the genre. Science fiction was contaminated with fantasy the moment there was a "violation of scientific fact, such as spaceship stories which ignore ballistics": "A man writing about rocket ships," Heinlein insisted, "is *morally obligated* to be up on rocket engineering" (Heinlein 1959: 19, 35).

Such arguments for scientific verisimilitude and rigorous extrapolation from known principles now tend to be associated with hard sf, but the view that the genre is part of an Enlightenment project underpins a lot of the ways in which sf continues to be conceptualized. For example, Darko Suvin (1979) defines sf as a literature of "cognitive estrangement," expanding the "cognitive" out from scientific skepticism and rationalism to include political critique, at least of a demythologizing, secular, and scientized Marxist kind. This cognitive element determines Suvin's ruthless demarcations between genres, so that fantasy, Gothic, and horror are all degraded forms because they refuse enlightened critique and indulge the very superstitions that modernity is meant to eradicate. Many other critics and historians have fought similar rearguard actions against the degrading of sf into fantasy, or, like John Sladek (1978) and Thomas Disch (1998), have denounced the efflorescence of pseudo-scientific New Age beliefs, UFOlogy, and religious cults that adopt science-fictional trappings. Although Edward James calls this the "lunatic fringe," it appears to have more cultural centrality than sf itself: "Sf has unwittingly given birth to a number of cult beliefs which have been accepted by an audience wider than the sf audience; sf's greatest impact on the twentieth-century world may be indirectly communicated by those people who present science-fictional ideas as fact" (James 1994: 148). In this fringe, "science" is always in questionable inverted commas and "depends on intuition and emotional response rather than scientific method" (James 1994: 149). The tiny band of properly scientific or cognitive sf is threatened on all sides by a mass culture drenched in supernaturalism and pseudoscience. These plucky survivors occupy the same redoubt as Carl Sagan's (1997) latter-day vision of science as a candle in the dark, as enlightened knowledge gutters in the gathering dusk of a new Dark Age.

The problem with this defense of sf is that it has to jettison much of the content of the genre, which has self-evidently reveled in the imaginative potentials of every modern pseudoscientific belief, from animal magnetism, ether, and degeneration theory to ESP, UFOlogy, or the Gaia hypothesis. Very little fiction can survive the strict protocols that determine a scientific statement without losing the essential playfulness of the fictive. This defense also has to falsify genre history by separating "proper" sf from the sort of Gothic and fantasy fictions with which it has always been entwined. And perhaps most fatally, it risks having an ahistorical conception of science, as if it were an unchanging territory with easily determinable borders guarded by something like a Maxwell demon, working tirelessly and unhesitatingly to separate legitimate scientific knowledge from illegitimate social belief. What the science theorist Bruno Latour (1993) calls "the Modern Constitution," an enlightenment project with scientific naturalism at its core, operates through these acts of purification and separation, defining its proper terrain by rigorous acts of exclusion and denunciation, erasing its own history behind it as it triumphally advances.

In this chapter, I want to suggest a different relationship between science and sf that is more properly attuned to the historical interaction of scientific knowledge and cultural forms and is thus more inclusive. I do not for a minute want to dethrone science, or dismiss enlightened thought like some postmodern nihilist dressed in black and mumbling about the end of everything as if it were 1988 and cyberpunk still cool. Instead, the aim is to regard sf and its allied genres as historically situated forms that constantly change shape and boundary as scientific and technological possibilities emerge, the genre seizing opportunistically on new anomalies or nascent states or breakthroughs, working proleptically to open up (or close down) their cultural and narrative possibilities. Such imaginative interventions can in turn influence the parameters of actual scientific research, perhaps most intensively when the boundaries of the human are thrown into flux. Cultural and humanist conceptions of the integrity of the body probably have wider influence than scientific conceptions, making things like genetic and reproductive research highly contentious, but also highly productive for Gothic, fantastic, and science-fictional narratives. It is less, then, that sf and its cognates are to be judged as inside or outside "proper" science but more that these fictions might be seen to occupy the temporary intervals when knowledge is controversial or in flux, in the phase-space between anomaly and normalization (to use the ancient terminology of Thomas Kuhn's *The Structure of Scientific Revolutions* (1962)).

Sf is located in the passing epoch of extraordinary science, where anomalies challenge the known paradigms of normal science and multiple explanations are still, for a time, in circulation: "both during pre-paradigm periods and during the crises that lead to large-scale changes of paradigm, scientists usually develop many speculative and unarticulated theories that can themselves point to discovery" (Kuhn 1970: 61). Once these phases are over, the history of science quietly erases all trace of the theories that were left behind. Yet sf might be regarded as the cultural record of these multiple, speculative possibilities – sometimes right, accurately predicting the trajectory of normal science in advance, but often gleefully, delightfully, gorgeously *wrong*. There is no shame in this, no error of faculty or cognition: the interval is sf's niche habitat.

This approach requires displacing the term pseudoscience. The prefix "pseudo" means false, counterfeit, pretended, or spurious. As a modifying adjectival prefix it has been used since the fifteenth century, although "pseudoscience" is an extremely late addition, appearing in the 1830s with the early professionalization of science and around the time "scientist" was first coined (by William Whewell in 1833). The term is thus part of an aggressive act of demarcation: "pseudoscience is embraced ... by exact proportion as real science is misunderstood" (Sagan 1997: 19). What the term hopes to hide are those passages of history where the boundaries between science and its others are impossible to determine, where experiments are leaky or inconclusive or where expertise proved difficult to police. Since it is in these interstitial places where sf and its cognates find their habitat, we need to explore these terrains without using a term that has already prejudged what is delimitable as true and false science. There are many resources from recent developments in the history of science that allow us to think about what Seymour Mauskopf (1990) suggests should be called "marginal sciences." After a brief introduction to these resources, I will show how sf has shifted historically in its use of the anomalous and contested evidence of ESP as one instance of the genre's opportunistic way of generating stories from the margins of the normal and the intervals of extraordinary science.

Michel Foucault long ago observed that the postwar history of science pioneered by figures like Georges Canguilhem had abandoned the model of science as a stately progress of truth emerging into the light from a pitiful vale of ignorance and misconception: "Error is not eliminated by the muffled force of a truth which gradually emerges from the shadow but by the formation of a new way of 'speaking true'" (Foucault 1991: 15). Scientific truth only appears to transcend history because scientific discourse undertakes "successive transformations" of its own disciplinary trajectories, so that they "continuously produce reshapings of their own history" (Foucault 1991: 16). Foucault's genealogical method hoped to remember all of those "subjugated knowledges" erased from the textbooks, that "whole series of knowledges that have been disqualified as nonconceptual ... insufficiently elaborated ... [or] below the required level of erudition or scientificity" (Foucault 2003: 7, 8). So, for instance, the understanding of evolutionary theory in the nineteenth century changes from one of Darwin's difficult and heroic lone struggle with a traditional society to accept the truth of natural selection toward a recognition of the many rival theories of evolution offered by figures like Jean-Baptiste Lamarck, Herbert Spencer, and Samuel Butler, of the "eclipse of Darwinism" after Darwin's death in 1882 (Bowler 1992), of the many accommodations and syntheses of Darwinism and theology (Moore 1979), and of the efflorescence of racial science, degeneration theory, social Darwinism and eugenics, all of which derived their explanatory power from evolutionary theory. Dismissed as pseudosciences and their traces erased, many of these discourses had scientific legitimacy and carried political and cultural import at the time. Genealogical criticism has recovered some of these discourses. The impact of degeneration theory on the literature of the Gothic, the Wellsian scientific romance, and canonical authors like Thomas Hardy and Joseph Conrad has now returned to visibility (Pick 1989; Greenslade 1994).

In England, sociologists of science reformulated the conceptual and historical understanding of "marginal" sciences in a cluster of important works that appeared around 1980. Steven Shapin observed that the social contexts of science traditionally only become significant when error needs to be explained. Religious anxiety contaminated those Victorian men of science who confirmed the evidence of spiritualism; communist ideology kept the spurious agricultural theories of Trofim Lysenko defiantly alive in the Soviet Union. Such explanations imply that pseudoscience can be defined by the intermingling of social and scientific factors that is always inappropriate, reinforcing the view that "proper" science is asocial, the laboratory safely sealed away from muddying factors like society, morality, politics, or culture. Shapin's work aimed to explode this false divide, and to regard all scientific practices through "the historically contingent connections between knowledge and the concerns of various social groups in their intellectual and social settings" (Shapin 1982: 164). Before his social history of Boyle's experiments and the early controversies of the Royal Society (Shapin and Schaffer 1985), Shapin suggested that so-called pseudosciences were a useful place to start: they not only expose "the processes by which statements of fact are accredited or rejected" (Shapin 1982: 163), but also foreground the shifting ways in which historical actors define what properly belongs to science. "There is no reason to expect that present demarcations ... will adequately describe any past context," he warned (Shapin 1982: 179). More polemically, Harry Collins and Trevor Pinch focused on contemporary controversies in science (such as biological psychology and cold fusion) in order to suggest that experiment alone, more and better equipment, could not resolve competing claims in science: "The problem with experiments is that they tell you nothing unless they are competently done, but in controversial science no-one can agree on a criterion of competence" (Collins and Pinch 1998: 3). Instead, Collins and Pinch suggested that scientists deployed contingent social factors (reputation, standing, blocking publication, gossip, and other extra-scientific modes) to counter claims. Their metaphor for science practice is the golem myth: a creature created out of hybrid messy elements and beliefs. In the 1979 anthology *On the Margins of Science*, historians and sociologists like Collins and Pinch turned to the contested claims of Mesmerism, phrenology, psychical research, and parapsychology to examine how orthodoxies of scientific naturalism were forged in part by the shedding of these uncontrollable and ill-disciplined marginal knowledges. Some of these anomalies have wavered uncertainly on the edges of science for centuries: Mesmerism was rejected by eighteenth-century scientific commissions only to return as a respected "hypnotism" in the 1880s (Crabtree 1993). Phrenology was successfully marginalized as a popular belief and practice of amateur quacks by the 1840s but in fact anticipated the localization of brain function in the 1860s (Cooter 1984). In these moments, Brian Wynne observes, "science is even more unsettled by *overt* conflict than most institutions, because a vital part of the external ideology which it projects in the process of its authority maintenance to society at large, is the belief that science 'naturally' produces consensus by the collective pursuit of 'the scientific method'" (Wynne 1979: 79).

This English sociology has fed into the work of the prolific science theorist Bruno Latour (see Luckhurst 2006). Latour proceeds in the same vein, overturning the artificial separation of science and society or nature and culture. He traces the inherently social process of formulating scientific statements, arguing that success is determined not by how pure and isolated a laboratory is, but by how connected or *networked* it is. Success is measured by what resources you can bind in to support your thesis: prior scientific authorities, other, more prestigious laboratories, expensive instruments, and newer technologies, funding bodies, but also the specialist press, governments, the nonspecialist media, popular opinion, and so on. Science is a process of creating *heterogeneous assemblages* that inevitably breach any sense of a strict quarantine between the inside or outside of scientific practice. Indeed, Latour argues that "the harder, the purer science is inside, the further outside the scientists have to go" (Latour 1987: 156), since these big projects have to rely on the military-industrial complex to support the work and are thus inevitably plugged in to larger political processes: "The truth of what scientists say no longer comes from their breaking away from society, connection, mediations, connections, but from the safety provided by the circulating references that cascade through a great number of transformations and translations" (Latour 1999: 97). Latour's later work tries to dismantle the metaphysics of the Modern Constitution that has quarantined scientific from social knowledge, and thus produced Science and Culture as mutually exclusive opposites. His view of the world after the dismantling of this divide is just a little science-fictional: "We shall always go from the mixed to the still more mixed, from the complicated to the still more complicated ... We no longer expect from the future that it will emancipate us all from our attachments; on the contrary, we expect that it will attach us with tighter bonds to the more numerous crowds of *aliens* who have become fully-fledged members of the collective" (Latour 2004: 191).

Such theories are often dismissed as relativist, disabling any ability to distinguish scientific truth from social belief, but they actually *sharpen up* the ability to make these discriminations. Richard Dawkins's furious invective, in books such as *Unweaving the Rainbow* (1998), against the cultural pervasion of superstitious belief over scientific rigor only retrenches ideological positions and perpetuates reductive and unwinnable debates. Scientific practice is far better served by retracing its complex, socially embedded place in shifting discursive constellations.

How does this help us to read sf? The genre need not be subsumed under the strict protocols of scientific truth, or texts be discarded if they generate fantasmatic versions of science (which of course they *always* do, even in the very hardest sf). Sf is an element in a heterogeneous assemblage, a hybrid form that loops together the material of science with mass cultural narrative, making it a fascinating social locus of conflict, cross-fertilization, and negotiation. In particular, the work of sf is often to process the proleptic cultural consequences of phases of extraordinary science. From these temporary intervals, the same anomaly or breakthrough might produce utopian, dystopian, Gothic, or fantastic narratives, which might be seen as different assemblages exploring different ethical and political scenarios. These will be altered as the spaces of proleptic possibility change, sf becoming a kind of historical trace of successive transformations.

Often, the most alluring proleptic knowledges are those that hover contentiously in the interstice of the natural and human sciences and that imply major cultural transformation if confirmed. To illustrate, let us briefly take two phases in the history of parapsychology, which Mauskopf considers "paradigmatic of marginal science" (Mauskopf 1990: 876). The Society for Psychical Research (SPR) was formed in 1882 in London strictly on the model of the scientific society to undertake "an organised and systematic attempt to investigate that large group of debatable phenomena designated by such terms as mesmeric, psychical or spiritualistic" (Society 1882–3: 3). The leading investigator of the SPR, Frederick Myers, coined "telepathy" as an allegedly neutral term to describe anomalous communications outside the recognized channels of sense, phenomena which included hypnotic rapport, messages mental mediums believed came from spirits, the sightings of doubles or ghosts (theorized as projections of psychic energy), as well as telepathic communication. The SPR set about conducting thousands of experiments to secure the empirical existence of this fugitive psychology, innovating double blind tests and statistical analyses of results subsequently widely used in normal science (see Hacking 1988). Although the SPR could never secure scientific consensus for its laboratory protocols, test subjects, data-gathering methods, or psycho-physical theories, it nevertheless ensured that telepathy would have a remarkable career as a quintessential marginal scientific object, lit up by periodic controversies for over 120 years (see Luckhurst 2002). The heyday of the SPR ended with Myers's death in 1901; the Society, almost inevitably, turned its energies to a lengthy investigation of whether his spirit was in communication with them. In its first decades, psychical research was coterminous with the new dynamic psychology of its day – indeed, many leading figures including William James, Pierre Janet, and Sigmund Freud undertook serious investigations. By the 1920s, the coining of *para*psychology suggested that the attempt to incorporate telepathy into normal psychology had failed. However, a new phase opened when J.B. Rhine opened the first academic laboratory in the field at Duke University and published the surprise bestseller *Extra-Sensory Perception* (1934). He organized a disparate field full of odd objects and eccentric amateur investigators into a rigorous experimental regime using the five thought-reading "Zener" cards and soon embedded these contested mental powers in American popular culture (see Mauskopf and McVaugh 1980).

Myers theorized telepathy as the first sign of a prospective evolutionary leap, and psychical researchers always held out that definitive proof was only a little way into the future. With this promissory note, the announcement of an interval of extraordinary science that would soon end, the concept of telepathy fostered a complex array of late Victorian scientific and Gothic romances. In Gothic fiction, the exercise of an occult hypnotic rapport at a distance conjured dangerous exotic Mesmerists who could overmaster the defenseless or weak-willed, as in Arthur Conan Doyle's "The Parasite" (1894), Richard Marsh's *The Beetle* (1897), or Bram Stoker's *Dracula* (1897). Stoker's Van Helsing explicitly instructed the materialist Dr Seward on the need to push his understanding beyond the confines of normal science: "tell me – for I am a student of the brain – how you accept the hypnotism and reject the thought-reading" (Stoker 1979: 230). Stoker's fiction is built from an array of marginal sciences, referencing the theorists of criminal degeneracy Cesare Lombroso and Max Nordau, the hypnotic experiments of Jean-Martin Charcot, new-fangled X-rays, and the work of the SPR. As David Glover observes, Stoker "starts from some contemporary branch of learning, a set of observations or a stray theory, and uses it to elaborate a blatantly phantasmagoric order of possibilities" (Glover 1996: 17). These are in the Gothic register, scientizing supernatural forces, but they are generated from the kind of interval opened by scientific and cultural controversies surrounding the then contested evidences of hypnosis and telepathy.

H.G. Wells has been used to inaugurate "proper" sf because his training under Thomas Huxley at the Normal School of Science ensured that his turn to fiction used "real science, and the questions and techniques of science, rather than the pseudo-science of his competitors" (Smith 1986: 56–7). Writing in *Nature*, the official organ of the new scientific establishment, Wells expressed profound skepticism about the experimental method of psychical research: "In no other field of inquiry is so much faith in personal character and intelligence demanded, or so little experimental verification possible" (Wells 1894a: 121). Elsewhere, as a science journalist, he was tempted to dismiss psychology as a whole, given the "peculiarities" of its "accepted method" that "not only put it apart from natural science, but render it relatively unproductive" (1894b: 715). In his fiction, Wells gently mocked what was called the Society for the Investigation of Abnormal Phenomena in "The Plattner Story" (1896) and in the frame to *The Time Machine* (1895) presents the Traveller's demonstration of his model time machine as "a trick – like the ghost you showed us last Christmas" (Wells 1995: 10), as if he were a debunker of Spiritualism like his teachers Huxley and Edwin Ray Lankester. The narrator of *When the Sleeper Wakes* (1899) satirically mentions in passing the survival into 2100 of Spook Worshippers and Furniture Worshippers (physical mediums were associated with so-called "table-turning" communications), but the same book also speaks of "practical psychologists with some very interesting developments in the art of hypnotism," noting that "William James, Myers and Gurney … bore a value now that would have astonished their contemporaries" (Wells 1994: 152). Wells announced in *The Discovery of the Future* that "We are in the beginning of the greatest change that humanity has ever undergone" (Wells 1902: 91), and hypnosis and psychical research frequently featured as promissory signs of this change in Wells's fiction. In fact, he delightedly exploited the claims of late Victorian marginal and occult sciences to generate fictions about clairvoyance ("The Remarkable Case of Davidson's Eyes" (1895)), astral travel ("The Plattner Story"), soul swapping ("The

Story of the Late Mr Elvesham" (1896)), crystal gazing ("The Crystal Egg" (1897)), and out of body experiences ("Under the Knife" (1896)). Moreau instills humanity in his spliced creatures through hypnotism, and telepathy is marked as an evolutionary advance in both *The War of the Worlds* (1898) and *The First Men in the Moon* (1901). Part of his dismissal of psychical research in *Nature* was his view that "the public mind is incapable of suspended judgment; it will not stop at telepathy. Any general recognition of the evidence of psychical research will be taken by the outside public to mean the recognition of ghosts, witchcraft, miracles" (Wells 1894a: 122). His popular fiction for the "outside public" precisely exploited this extension. His fiction was not the stuff of "real science," but neither was it always quite definitively "pseudoscience." His early work thrived in the fissures and lacunae of orthodox science, only deploying a different register to Stoker. An English Wellsian tradition in sf has continued to consider telepathy a proleptic science. In Arthur C. Clarke's *Childhood's End* (1953), it is not the discovery of nuclear power that brings the intervention of the Overmind, but the development of telepathy: "the physicists could only have ruined the earth; the paraphysicists could have spread havoc to the stars" (Clarke 2001: 176).

Golden Age American sf is also intrinsically bound up with the fate of parapsychology. In 1929, John W. Campbell failed his first year at MIT because he was too busy writing his first sf stories. His move to Duke University was fortuitous: he volunteered for Rhine's early experiments in ESP and became a lifelong convert to what he called "psionics." Campbell wrote to Rhine in 1953, claiming kindred aims. Against the inherent conservatism of scientific institutions, *ASF* was doing its part to advance the cause: "I am trying to use fiction to induce competent thinkers to attack such problems as the psi-effects," he told Rhine (Campbell 1985: 225). *ASF* published the early work of A.E. van Vogt and L. Ron Hubbard, both of whom used telepathy as an indicator of mental evolution in their fiction. Both also moved beyond fiction to develop full-scale psychological theories, replete with textbooks, institutions, and followers. Van Vogt's Nexialism was less successful than Hubbard's Dianetics, a theory of willed mental evolution first published in *ASF*, with Campbell's enthusiastic endorsement in 1950. "This article is *not* a hoax," Campbell assured his readers: "I am most anxious to publish articles in the field of the mind based on direct experiment" (Campbell 1950: 4, 5). This was the height of *ASF*'s influence, and Hubbard's book went on to sell millions in its first years. Campbell's support cooled after Hubbard converted the science of Dianetics to the religion of Scientology, but he was still supporting the case for ESP in his introduction to the anthology *14 Great Tales of ESP* (1969), all taken from his years as editor of *ASF*. In Campbell's vision, psionics was engineering applied to the mind. Simply extending the paradigm of an elite technocracy of mechanics and engineers into the hardwiring of the human brain, it completed his social vision of an anti-democratic, technocratic future. The marginal status of telepathy redoubled the abjected status of sf: the slogan "Fans are Slans" picked up from van Vogt's *Slan* (1946), in which telepathic mutants were persecuted by the dullard masses. The prolepsis of telepathy projected the eventual triumph of the rejected subculture of sf itself.

These sorts of interactions make it difficult to demarcate between scientific and pseudoscientific strands in sf without doing damage to the intricacies of genre history.

The Maxwell demon, manically sorting hot and cold particles, was only ever a thought-experiment. Perhaps the old means of legitimating sf by acts of exclusion, separation, and purification can now be retired as redundant thought-experiments too.

Bibliography

Bowler, P.J. (1992) *The Eclipse of Darwinism: anti-Darwinian evolution theories in the decades around 1900*, Baltimore, MD: Johns Hopkins University Press.

Campbell, J.W. (1950) "Concerning Dianetics," *Astounding Science Fiction*, May: 4–5.

—— (1985) *The John W. Campbell Letters*, ed. P. Chapdelaine, T. Chapdelaine, and G. Hay, Franklin, TN: AC Projects.

Clarke, A.C. (2001) *Childhood's End*, 1954, rev. edn, London: Pan.

Collins, H. and Pinch, T. (1998) *The Golem: what you should know about science*, 2nd edn, Cambridge: Canto Press.

Cooter, R. (1984) *The Cultural Meaning of Popular Science: phrenology and the organization of consent in nineteenth-century Britain*, Cambridge: Cambridge University Press.

Crabtree, A. (1993) *From Mesmer to Freud: magnetic sleep and the roots of psychological healing*, New Haven, CT: Yale University Press.

Dawkins, R. (1998) *Unweaving the Rainbow: science, delusion and the appetite for wonder*, London: Joseph Allen.

Disch, T.M. (1998) *The Dreams Our Stuff is Made of: how science fiction conquered the world*, New York: The Free Press.

Foucault, M. (1991) "Introduction," in G. Canguilhem (ed.) *The Normal and the Pathological*, trans. C. Fawcett, New York: Zone.

—— (2003) *"Society Must Be Defended": lectures at the Collège de France 1975–6*, trans. D. Macey, London: Allen Lane.

Glover, D. (1996) *Vampires, Mummies and Liberals: Bram Stoker and the politics of popular fiction*, Durham, NC: Duke University Press.

Greenslade, W. (1994) *Degeneration, Culture and the Novel 1880–1940*, Cambridge: Cambridge University Press.

Hacking, I. (1988) "Telepathy: origins of randomization in experimental design," *Isis*, 79(3): 427–51.

Heinlein, R.A. (1959) "Science Fiction: its nature, faults, and virtues," in B. Davenport (ed.) *The Science Fiction Novel: imagination and social criticism*, Chicago: Advent.

James, E. (1994) *Science Fiction in the 20th Century*, Oxford: Opus.

Kuhn, T. (1970) *The Structure of Scientific Revolutions*, 1962, 2nd edn, Chicago: University of Chicago Press.

Latour, B. (1987) *Science in Action: how to follow scientists and engineers through society*, Cambridge, MA: Harvard University Press.

—— (1993) *We Have Never Been Modern*, trans. C. Porter, Brighton: Harvester.

—— (1999) *Pandora's Hope: essays on the reality of science studies*, Cambridge, MA: Harvard University Press.

—— (2004) *Politics of Nature: how to bring sciences into democracy*, trans. C. Porter, Cambridge, MA: Harvard University Press.

Luckhurst, R. (2002) *The Invention of Telepathy, 1870–1901*, Oxford: Oxford University Press.

—— (2006) "Bruno Latour's Scientifiction: networks, assemblages, and tangled objects," *Science Fiction Studies*, 33(1): 4–17.

Mauskopf, S.H. (1990) "Marginal Science," in R.C. Olby, G.N. Cantor, J.R.R. Christie, and M.J.S. Hodge (eds) *Companion to the History of Modern Science*, London: Routledge.

Mauskopf, S.H. and McVaugh, M.R. (1980) *The Elusive Science: origins of experimental psychical research*, Baltimore, MD: Johns Hopkins University Press.

Moore, J.R. (1979) *The Post-Darwinian Controversies: a study of the protestant struggle to come to terms with Darwin in Great Britain and America 1870–1900*, Cambridge: Cambridge University Press.

Pick, D. (1989) *Faces of Degeneration: a European disorder c. 1848–c. 1918*, Cambridge: Cambridge University Press.

Sagan, C. (1997) *The Demon-Haunted World: science as a candle in the dark*, London: Headline.

Shapin, S. (1982) "History of Science and its Sociological Reconstructions," *History of Science*, 20: 157–211.

Shapin, S. and Schaffer, S. (1985) *The Leviathan and the Air-Pump: Hobbes, Boyle, and the experimental life*, Princeton, NJ: Princeton University Press.

Sladek, J. (1978) *The New Apocrypha: a guide to strange sciences and occult beliefs*, Frogmore, St Albans and London: Granada.

Smith, D.C. (1986) *H.G. Wells: desperately mortal*, New Haven, CT: Yale University Press.

Society for Psychical Research (1882–3) "Objects of the Society," *Proceedings of the Society for Psychical Research*, 1: 3–4.

Stoker, B. (1979) *Dracula*, 1897, Harmondsworth: Penguin.

Suvin, D. (1979) *Metamorphoses of Science Fiction: on the poetics and history of a literary genre*, New Haven, CT: Yale University Press.

Wells, H.G. (1894a) "The Peculiarities of Psychical Research," *Nature*, 5: 121–2.

—— (1894b) "The Position of Psychology," *Saturday Review*, 29 December: 715.

—— (1902) *The Discovery of the Future: a lecture delivered to the Royal Institution on January 24, 1902*, London: Fisher Unwin.

—— (1994) *When the Sleeper Wakes*, 1899, London: Dent.

—— (1995) *The Time Machine*, 1895, London: Dent.

Wynne, B. (1979) "Between Orthodoxy and Oblivion: the normalisation of deviance in science," in *On the Margins of Science: the social construction of rejected knowledge*, Sociological Review Monograph 27, Keele: University of Keele.

41
SCIENCE STUDIES

Sherryl Vint

The term "science studies" describes the work of a broad group of interdisciplinary scholars who vary in their premises, methods, or conclusions. However, they share an interest in the history, practice, and social consequences of developments in science and technology, ideas which are also of interest to writers and scholars of sf. Science studies tends to focus on what are sometimes called the "hard sciences" – disciplines such as biology, chemistry, and physics which investigate the physical world through experimental practice. Scholarship in the field falls into three broad classifications: studies of the *content* of science, including its historical development and its difference from other sorts of knowledge; studies of the *practice* of science, such as ethnographic analyses of scientific writing or lab cultures, or critiques of science's philosophical underpinnings; and analyses of *technoculture*, which focus on the social and ethical consequences of scientific "discoveries" and technological creations. Both science studies and sf define themselves via a relationship to the discourse and practice of science, and both vary enormously in how they define "science" and conceive of its interactions with culture.

The relationship between science and sf is sometimes considered as a defining characteristic of the genre, in terms of either the "long history" marked by the Copernican revolution or the more narrow usage of the term, growing out of Gernsback's "scientifiction." Hugo Gernsback argued for a predictive and practical link between science and sf, emphasizing that his ideal story would be read by inventors and scientists, and suggesting that such stories could inspire the material creation of the marvels they depicted (see Westfahl 1998). John W. Campbell, on the other hand, saw the relationship as more oppositional, contending that sf writers "did what scientists were not capable of doing" (Westfahl 1998: 194), namely providing an independent, critical perspective on the consequences of scientific progress which would "indicate wrong answers, and why they're wrong, as well as suggesting right answers and possibilities!" (qtd in Westfahl 1998: 195). Science studies provides a similar critique, and, like sf, might be considered as a bridge between the "two cultures" of science and the humanities.

Some sf scholars have explored these affinities. Constance Penley examines the cultural significance of exchanges between sf and the institutions of science, arguing "*Star Trek* is the theory, NASA the practice" (Penley: 1997: 19). Luckhurst (2002) similarly moves between science and sf to establish the discourse around telepathy as central to the *fin-de-siècle* culture and emerging modernism, and his special issue of *Science Fiction Studies* (March 2006) significantly expands interactions between sf and science studies scholars, bringing work by Bruno Latour, Manuel Castells, Michel Serres, and Friedrich Kittler into dialog with sf. Martin Willis (2006) explores the intersections of literary and scientific cultures in the nineteenth century, outlining contemporary scientific paradigms and revealing how sf texts reproduce and challenge them. Patrick Sharp (2007) uses Darwinian theory to understand the racist structure of sf narratives of future war. Jane Donawerth (1997) sees female scientists in sf by women in the early pulps as part of a contemporary feminist utopian project that sought to make women the subjects rather than objects of science, a goal consistent with feminist science studies, as Helen Merrick (2007) points out. This chapter will provide an overview of research in science studies and suggest further ways it and sf might interrelate.

The philosophy of science has contributed to science studies in three important ways. It has given us the understanding that observation is dependent on theory (because it defines how we cognitively distinguish the "thing" from surrounding sense data). It provides a method for distinguishing "pseudo" from "real" scientific claims via Karl Popper's falsifiability thesis which requires a theory to make testable predictions (although not all science studies scholars accept this distinction). Finally, philosophy of science has been a factor in producing a culture dominated by positivism, the belief that the only authentic knowledge is scientific knowledge arrived at through the experimental method. Thomas Kuhn radically transformed the study of science, arguing that science does not proceed according to the gradual accumulation of "better" knowledge but instead is shaped by shared models of the world – *paradigms* – which structure the observations of their adherents. When sufficiently significant anomalies contradict a paradigm, "normal" science is put into a crisis that is sometimes resolved by the shift to a new paradigm. Crucial to Kuhn's conclusions was the argument that "when paradigms change, the world itself changes with them" (Kuhn 1962: 111), illustrating a connection between the epistemology of science and our experience of the entire social world, an observation which has shaped the field of science studies, often beyond Kuhn's own intentions.

Sociology of Scientific Knowledge also makes an important contribution to the emergence of the interdisciplinary field of science studies. David Bloor (1991) argued for the principle of symmetry in explanations of scientific phenomena, by which he meant that one could not retrospectively use one set of criteria to explain "real" science and another to explain failed research. Arguing against a tendency to believe that "nature" or "truth" explained the results of successful science while "society" or "error" explained the failure of other lines of research, Bloor maintains "real" science is shaped by the wider social world, a source of tension with many scientists who insist on a vision of science as separate and purified from the contingencies of human values and choices. Robert Merton (1973) argued that science is a self-regulated system which is governed by the norms of universalism (results should be reproduced in all contexts), communalism (results belong to humanity), and disinterestedness (values and desires of individual scientists should not enter scientific practices), but Warren Hagstrom (1965) emphasized that competition for recognition, and thus independence and individualism, were norms more commonly found. The presumed uniqueness of scientific practice is contested by Thomas Gieryn (1999), who explores the way fields of knowledge are created, advocated, dismissed, or reinforced, thus separating science from other sorts of knowledge and creating sub-fields within science. David Hess (1993) looks at the historical contingency of what counts as science, an analysis that could also be used to understand the values that shape the portrayal of scientific communities in sf texts.

Questions about the authority and validity of scientific method and conclusions are common in science studies. Isabelle Stengers (1997) explores the relationship of science to truth, partly based on her collaboration with physicist Ilya Prigogine. Stengers argues that if we understand something as merely complicated, we acknowledge that we do not have enough information to fully understand it at present but leave open the ideal that, in the future, sufficient data will render it transparent and hence predictable; complexity, in contrast, conceives of the world as active beyond the limits of our models – of any model – and hence is continually able to show us something new. Stengers insists that we can distinguish "good" from "bad" science by focusing on a method's ability to interact with the material world. She considers experiments a "wager" with reality which includes *a priori* determination of what is considered significant data and what should be judged as insignificant noise, and reminds us of the importance of recalling the difference between the isolated and controlled conditions of the laboratory and the messy world beyond. For Stengers, Kepler rather than Copernicus revolutionized science, as the latter merely changed our model of the universe but still allowed his preconceived notion of the perfection of circles to shape his observations of orbits. Kepler, on the other hand, "transform[ed] the significance of the relation between mathematics and astronomy" by using "mathematics as a research tool, thereby arriving at a figure that was for him just one among others: the ellipse" (Stengers 1997: 21).

Kepler's greater attentiveness to the world's own voice makes his the superior science, because science must be a "dialogue with a nature that cannot be dominated by a theoretical gaze, but must be explored, with an open world to which we belong, in whose construction we participate" (Stengers 1997: 40). Michael Crichton's *The Andromeda Strain* (1969) shares some qualities with Stenger's model of scientific practice because it is only when the researchers give up their *a priori* assumption that the organism causing the disease is static, like a bacteria, that the scientists are able to understand the disease and prevent its spread. They thus hear the voice of the world, as Stengers advocates. The novel's conclusion, however, reestablishes what Stengers would call "bad" science because they feel able to control the organism once they have a new model to understand its operation.

Science studies also investigates the material practice of science through ethnography. Key works include Sharon Traweek (1988), Karin Knorr-Cetina (1999), and Latour (1987). The first, a study of high-energy particle physicists, emphasizes the degree to which career success is contingent on personality traits as well as research ability and describes how stories are used to pass appropriate cultural norms to students. Knorr-Cetina's work reveals that the "purified" culture of the laboratory, so important to the dominant ideology of science, is constructed *post facto* during the publication of results when unplanned-for contingencies – such as the escape of test animals or the contamination of samples – are removed from the public view of science. She uses the concept of indexicality, borrowed from linguistics and meaning the property of a referent to point to some state of affairs in the moment of utterance, to describe local variations in research-decision criteria. These works suggest that the tools of sf scholarship might be usefully deployed in science studies scholarship sensitive to nuances of language and narrative. Greg Egan's stories articulate anxieties about genetic research and about forcing data into ideologically pre-selected conclusions; for example, in "Mitochondrial Eve" (1998) the grounds for racism must be reinvented when mitochondrial DNA destroys the basis for the genetic determination of race.

Bruno Latour (1987) studies laboratory practice, developing a theory of science and society that goes beyond the particular conclusions of most ethnographies. He argues that we need to study science and technology as they are made, not once they have become "blackboxed" into accepted "facts," and sees significant social and political implications in his conclusions, particularly the need for better and more widely shared understandings of science and for public input on decisions regarding the implementation of science and technology. He argues that the dominant culture – which connects science with universal "truth" and nature and separates it from the contingent, human realm of power and politics – has produced incomplete and inadequate accounts of both nature and society (Latour 1993). His work tries to reconnect the two, insisting that objects are both material and semiotic, that is, both material, concrete things *and* shaped by cultural assumptions and values. Latour carefully traces the practices by which things in the material world are observed and transformed into data in scientific discourse, acknowledging that elements are changed through this process of translation from one medium to another. He insists, however, that in addition to loss at each stage of the transformation (of multiplicity, materiality, particularity) there are also gains (of standardization, calculation, ability to circulate data). Crucially, each stage in the chain of translations must be reversible, so that there is no unbridgeable gap between language and the material world.

Latour believes that our culture has separated the question "of how we can know the outside world" from our understanding of how we connect to this world through signifying systems such as language, and, more significantly, from "the political question of how we can keep order in society, and the moral question of how we can live a good life" (Latour 1999b: 310). This separation is the reason that Latour's analysis of science and society has implications beyond simply providing a better account of science and a better scientific account of the material world. He maintains that allowing "nature" (the outside world) to be an uncontested and presumably apolitical space of knowledge closes down democratic debate, and allows certain political activity to be justified by presenting it as natural and hence inevitable. Latour argues instead that we should understand our reality as a collective is made up of humans and nonhumans all of whom interact to produce the material (the physical world) and the semiotic (our systems of understanding and explaining the world). Latour's belief in the equal collaborative role of humans and nonhumans (which for him includes the organic and non-organic) distinguishes his work from more conservative models such as Bloor's symmetry. Although Bloor argues for the equal contributions of "nature" and "culture" in producing scientific knowledge, he insists that humans and nonhumans should not be treated in an equivalent manner. Latour's work thus has more affinity with sf because the genre can give voice to various sorts of nonhumans, from the cyborg questioning his destiny to be used as a weapon in Marge Piercy's *He, She, and It* (1991) to the complex political alliances among human and animal others imagined in Sheri Tepper's *The Companions* (2003).

Latour's study of Pasteur emphasizes that science is a process of making, not discovering, but Latour is adamant that fabrication does not imply a lack of reality. In Pasteur's experiments, he argues, "something happens *to the bacillus* that *never* happened before" (Latour 1999a: 260) because the laboratory conditions allow the bacillus to grow in quantities not found in nature and thus become visible to the scientist. Latour sees the resulting science as a negotiation not merely between Pasteur and the bacillus, but among Pasteur, the bacillus, the laboratory equipment, the farmers whose cattle he studied, those who funded his research, and beyond. Such extended networks are key to Latour's work, and he is one of the main contributors to actor-network theory (in his later work Latour distances himself from the label if not from the practice of tracing networks). For Latour, actor-network theory explains the impossibility of separating science from politics, although it is important to remember that he insists that acknowledging the social and contingent dimension of science makes for a better and more "realistic" science; he has no patience for those who suggest that he fails to account adequately for objective reality. Using the example of the environment and the question of whether it is a "real" or a "political" issue, Latour insists it is both: "The ozone hole is too social and too narrated to be truly natural; the strategy of industrial firms and heads of state is too full of chemical reactions to be reduced to power and interest; the discourse of the ecosphere is too real and too social to boil down to meaning effects" (Latour 1993: 6). Latour has even written his own sf novel of sorts, *Aramis* (1996), a fictionalized account of the failed development of a French train system which also serves as a primer in his theory (see Bould and Vint 2006).

Latour contends that networking practices convey authority upon the scientist who then becomes the spokesperson for the entity made visible by and engaged in the scientific practice (such as Pasteur's bacillus). This authority gives scientists political power to represent the world in a particular way and to become the voice for "reality"; Latour and others fear leaving this power in the hands of scientists alone. Similar concerns about the relationship among science, politics, and ethics are familiar themes in sf. For example, one might usefully contrast Walter M. Miller Jr's *A Canticle for Leibowitz* (1959) and its concern for the preservation of knowledge within a religious framework that emphasizes the evil of using intellect without a concept of social responsibility with Greg Bear's *Moving Mars* (1993). Bear's physicists discover that they can tweak the properties of particles and change the entire physical world, giving humans the power to alter fundamentally what we take to be the laws of science itself. Yet the only moral dilemma they face is a pragmatically political one about whether they must hold a plebiscite about their plan to move Mars physically away from Earth (they have declared independence). Miller's work, on the other hand, sees any use of science to control the physical world as an ethical issue. Comparable themes about responsibility for the destructive potential of invented technologies are also explored in Russell Hoban's similarly post-apocalyptic *Riddley Walker* (1980). Science studies encourages us to see the differences in these books in terms of the various networks traced by the scientific practice in each, and the separation of science from government accomplished by the rather heroic ending of *Moving Mars*, in which the scientists decide that political questions about the use of their technology are the responsibility of the elected representatives alone, would be seen as too easy.

Feminist critiques of science are concerned with the ethical implications of how we conceive of science, nature, and the relationship between the two. Evelyn Fox-Keller and Helen Longino have written extensively on gender and science, exploring the degree to which patriarchal culture has influenced the axioms of scientific practice; Longino (2001) argues for an alternative epistemology (theory of knowledge), pluralism, which would see science as the product of community rather than individual perception. Sandra Harding considers our need for a successor science emerging from feminist epistemologies, one which would "transcend the damaging subject–object, inner–outer, reason–emotion dualities of Enlightenment science" (Harding 1986: 155). The genetic engineers, Sharers, of Joan Slonczewski's *A Door into Ocean* (1986) might be considered as models for a successor science; Sharers do not use technology to make "nature" more productive for human profit – such as Monsanto canola or broiler chickens modified to live in factory farm conditions – but to keep the ecosystems of the planet in balance. Their practice of science reflects their epistemology: they do not have a concept of "power over" and take for granted an egalitarian world, shared with all life; in contrast, Western science emerged from a culture of hierarchy and is often defined as the power to control nature.

Donna Haraway's work on technoculture brings together the fields of sf and science studies. She situates her work at "the cultural space hinted by the intersections of science fiction, speculative futures, feminist and antiracist theory, and fictions of science" (Haraway 1991b: 24) and frequently uses sf examples in her critiques. She exposes the gendered and racial assumptions shaping primatology (1989), while "A Manifesto for Cyborgs" (1985, revised as "A Cyborg Manifesto" (1991b)) has arguably been the most influential essay for sf scholarship about new models of subjectivity. Haraway considers the gene, the fetus, and race as three of the most important objects of knowledge in current science practice and theory, and traces them through "knowledge-making practices, industry and commerce, popular culture, social struggles, psychoanalytic formations, bodily histories, human and nonhuman actions, local and global flows, inherited narratives, new stories ... and more" (Haraway 1997: 129). Her extensive engagement with popular culture among other discourses makes evident the importance of sf as part of the networks of scientific practice, suggesting a fresh perspective from which to view the claim that there is a correspondence between the inventions of sf (such as Heinlein's waldos) and material science culture. Philip

Kerr's *A Philosophical Investigation* (1992) depicts a world transformed by the sort of genetic determinism that Haraway finds in many popular representations. The novel links violence with the scientific discovery of a certain chemical in some male brains, thus defining people as criminals based on their biology, not their actions. Similarly, Nancy Kress's *Beggars* trilogy (1993–6) considers the problems of wealth and opportunity in a world in which some are genetically engineered to exist without sleep and are thus more productive than non-modified humans. Kress's engagement with the topic is consistent with the insights of feminist science studies which require us to recognize that science happens connected to a social world and has consequences in this world. Kress argues for the importance of sf to the culture of science precisely because it focuses on pragmatic, concrete examples rather than abstract theorizing. She concludes "science fiction is the dress rehearsal for social change" (Kress 2007: 207).

Karen Barad (2007) follows in this tradition of feminist science studies, but more radically argues the physical attributes of matter require that we rethink most of the binaries that have structured Western thought. Drawing on Niels Bohr's work on quantum complementarity, she argues for reconceptualizing our notions of both agency and identity, arguing that individuals do not preexist their entangled interactions and that agency cannot be understood as a property of individuals. Instead of understanding the basic unit of reality to be the thing with given properties, quantum theory reveals that the basic unit of matter is the phenomenon. Determinate properties do not precede any particular physical intra-action between agencies and objects of observation. Accepting what quantum theory has taught us about the nature of being produces

> an *ethico-onto-epistem-ology* – an appreciation for the intertwining of ethics, knowing and being – since each intra-action matters, since the possibilities for what the world may become call out in the pause that precedes each breath before a moment comes into being and the world is remade again, because the becoming of the world is a deeply ethical matter.
>
> (Barad 2007: 185)

The aliens in Nancy Kress's *Probability* series (2000–2) who live in a world of shared consensual reality suggest one of the ways that similar ideas have been explored in sf thought-experiments.

Work in the history of science enables us to understand modern science not simply as the neutral and inevitable expression of the rational investigation of nature, but instead as a social relation with nature, including other humans, that is marked by its moment of historical emergence. Steven Shapin and Simon Shaffer (1989) map out the requirements for being able to witness in the seventeenth century when only gentlemen were presumed free in their own conscience and hence able to witness honestly, while those paid to work the machines were considered fettered by this economic exchange. Thus we see that the very methods of modern science are shaped by a dialectical exchange with contingent social structures; objectivity had to be achieved through the promotion of standardized measurements and a division of labor practices to minimize skill and thus eliminate contingent differences between locations, as Lorraine Daston (1999) demonstrates. Gwyneth Jones's *Life* (2004), in which an untenured female scientist's groundbreaking work is delayed and then goes unnoticed for decades, explores similar issues about the supposed separation of science from society.

The interdependence between developments in science and technology and the wider culture is material as well as ideological, as Thomas Hughes (1983) makes clear in his study of the development of the electrical system in Western society. In order to invent electricity, Hughes argues, one needs to make institutions, political policies, and forms of life, as well as capacitors, generators, and power lines. Once invented, such organizational forms have inertia and can forestall shifts to new and perhaps better technologies, such as the survival of direct current for a time although alternating current had proved more reliable. Similarly, the protagonist in L. Sprague de Camp's *Lest Darkness Fall* (1941), transported back to sixth-century Rome, finds that he must invent institutions such as wage labor and stockholders in order to invent more clearly technological items such as the printing press. Changes in technology can also lead to changes in our experience of human subjectivity. Kittler (1999) traces the ways that psychoanalytic models of consciousness are embedded within a changing technology of recording and storing data. Much of Philip K. Dick's work is concerned with questions of the relationship between human subjectivity and the technology that surrounds us, such as "Service Call" (1955), in which a repairman shows up to repair a swibble before they are invented. As he tries to work out what the swibble does, the protagonist learns that the entire future society has been transformed by the invention of the device which sorts out those who sincerely believe in the common ideology from those who merely profess it, all of whom presumably were eliminated in the last "*scientific* war – none of that random pulverizing" (Dick 1987: 32). Thus the vision of the future the protagonist sees is one that makes literal Kittler's insight that our interactions with technology transform the experience of being human; in Dick's world, those who cannot adapt to the new technological mode of consciousness are physically eliminated. *Primer* (Carruth 2004) similarly narrates the mutual evolution of humanity and technology in its story of two friends who accidentally discover a time machine that duplicates selves in two times; the more often they enter the machine, the more the protagonists find themselves changed until they end up turning not only on one another but also on their other temporal selves.

The social and political consequences of new information technologies receive their most extensive exploration in Manuel Castells's three-volume *The Information Age* (1996–8), a cross-cultural study of what he terms network society, focused on the restructuring of the economy through global communications. Castells argues that it is impossible to understand network society apart from capitalism, and diagnoses as one of its most salient effects the timeless and borderless flow of capital across information networks while all but the most specialized labor is constrained by national boundaries. He identifies "black holes" of information society, areas cut off from communication with the global information infrastructure, "from which statistically speaking, there is no escape from the pain and destruction inflicted on the human condition." He emphasizes that such a fate is not technologically determined but is instead the result of "the laws that govern the universe of informational capitalism" which "unlike cosmic forces" can be changed by human action (Castells 2000a: 165). Castells's critique is echoed in Neal Stephenson's *Baroque* cycle (2003–4), set in the seventeenth century but connected through family lineages to the information-age-set *Cryptonomicon* (1999). The cycle links the rise of Enlightenment science to the introduction of the gold standard and the international circulation of currency, and anticipates the interdependence of financial networks and information networks. Like Castells, Stephenson reveals how systems we now often take to be unchangeable and inevitable are made by the reversible choices of human agency.

As this brief survey suggests, science studies offers many tools useful for understanding sf, and sf explores in fictional form topics of interest to science studies. Science, science studies, and sf all offer us new ways of thinking about the material world, ourselves, and our practices of making knowledge. If at its worst sf can be the literature of all the worst aspects of science – technocratism, singularity of vision, domination of nature, inserting a new gadget into the same world – then at its best it might be considered the literature of science studies – concerned with the social consequences of developments in science and technology, insisting on dialectical exchange between the novum and the larger social world, sensitive to the contingency of knowledge, and open to new ways of seeing and being.

Bibliography

Barad, Karen (2007) *Meeting the Universe Halfway: quantum physics and the entanglement of matter and meaning*, Durham, NC: Duke University Press.

Bloor, D. (1991) *Knowledge and Social Imagery*, 1976, 2nd edn, Chicago: University of Chicago Press.

Bould, M. and Vint, S. (2006) "Learning from the Little Engines that Couldn't: transported by Gernsback, Wells, and Latour," *Science Fiction Studies*, 33(1): 129–48.

Castells, M. (2000a) *End of Millennium*, 2nd edn, Cambridge, MA: Blackwell.

—— (2000b) *The Rise of the Network Society*, 2nd edn, Cambridge, MA: Blackwell.

—— (2004) *The Power of Identity*, 2nd edn, Cambridge, MA: Blackwell.

Daston, L. (1999) "Objectivity and the Escape from Perspective," in M. Biagioli (ed.) *The Science Studies Reader*, New York: Routledge.

Dick, P.K. (1987) "Service Call," in *The Minority Report and Other Classic Stories*, New York: Citadel Press.

Donawerth, J. (1997) *Frankenstein's Daughters: women writing science fiction*, Liverpool: Liverpool University Press.

Fox-Keller, E. (1985) *Reflections on Gender and Science*, New Haven, CT: Yale University Press.

Gieryn, T.F. (1999) *Cultural Boundaries of Science: credibility on the line*, Chicago: University of Chicago Press

Hagstrom, W. (1965) *The Scientific Community*, New York: Basic Books.

Haraway, D.J. (1989) *Primate Visions: gender, race, and nature in the world of modern science*, New York: Routledge.

—— (1991a) "The Actors Are Cyborg, Nature Is Coyote, and the Geography Is Elsewhere: postscript to 'Cyborgs at Large,'" in C. Penley and A. Ross (eds) *Technoculture*, Minneapolis: University of Minnesota Press.

—— (1991b) "A Cyborg Manifesto: science, technology, and socialist-feminism in the late twentieth century," in *Simians, Cyborgs and Women: the reinvention of nature*, London: Free Association.

—— (1997) *Modest_Witness@Second_Millennium.FemaleMan©_Meets_OncoMouse™: feminism and techno-science*, London and New York: Routledge.

Harding, S. (1986) *The Science Question in Feminism*, New York: Routledge.

Hess, D.J. (1993) *Science in the New Age*, Madison: University of Wisconsin Press.

Hughes, T. (1983) *Networks of Power: electrification of Western society 1880–1930*, Baltimore, MD: Johns Hopkins University Press.

Kittler, F.A. (1999) *Gramophone, Film, Typewriter*, 1986, trans. with an introduction by G. Winthrop-Young and M. Wutz, Stanford, CA: Stanford University Press.

Knorr-Cetina, K. (1999) *Epistemic Cultures: how the sciences make knowledge*, Cambridge, MA: Harvard University Press.

Kress, N. (2007) "Ethics, Science and Science Fiction," in M. Grebowicz (ed.) *SciFi in the Mind's Eye: reading science through science fiction*, Chicago: Open Court.

Kuhn, T. (1962) *The Structures of Scientific Revolution*, Chicago: University of Chicago Press.

Latour, B. (1987) *Science in Action: how to follow scientists and engineers through society*, Cambridge, MA: Harvard University Press.

——(1993) *We Have Never Been Modern*, trans. C. Porter, Brighton: Harvester.

—— (1999a) "Give Me a Laboratory and I Will Raise the World," in M. Biagioli (ed.) *The Science Studies Reader*, New York: Routledge.

—— (1999b) *Pandora's Hope: essays on the reality of science studies*, Cambridge, MA: Harvard University Press.

Longino, H. (2001) *The Fate of Knowledge*, Princeton, NJ: Princeton University Press.

Luckhurst, R. (2002) *The Invention of Telepathy, 1870–1901*, Oxford: Oxford University Press.

—— (2006) "Introduction," *Science Fiction Studies*, 33(1): 1–3.

Merrick, H. (2007) "Modest Witnesses?: feminist stories of science in fiction and theory," in M. Grebowicz (ed.) *SciFi in the Mind's Eye: reading science through science fiction*, Chicago: Open Court.

Merton, R. (1973) *The Sociology of Science*, Chicago: University of Chicago Press.

Penley, C. (1997) *NASA/Trek: popular science and sex in America*, New York: Verso.

Shapin, S. and Schaffer, S. (1989) *Leviathan and the Air-Pump: Hobbes, Boyle and the experimental life*, Princeton, NJ: Princeton University Press.

Sharp, P.B. (2007) *Savage Perils: racial frontiers of nuclear apocalypse in American culture*, Norman: University of Oklahoma Press.

Stengers, I. (1997) *Power and Invention: situating science*, Minneapolis: University of Minnesota Press.

Traweek, S.J. (1988) *Beamtimes and Lifetimes: the world of high energy physicists*, Cambridge, MA: Harvard University Press.

Westfahl, G. (1998) *The Mechanics of Wonder: the creation of the idea of science fiction*, Liverpool: Liverpool University Press.

Willis, M. (2006) *Mesmerists, Monsters and Machines: science fiction and the cultures of science in the nineteenth century*, Kent, OH: Kent State University Press.

42
SPACE

James Kneale

Stories have to happen somewhere, or perhaps, more accurately, stories have to produce somewhere in which to stage their happenings. Film and television represent a three-dimensional space on the screen, and written fictions usually have some sort of setting; it seems reasonable to assume that there must be spaces of sf. However, it is not easy to say what "space" is. It is often taken for granted as a category of existence or experience, and has received much less attention than time in philosophy, social theory, and textual criticism – although not in the discipline of geography. The word "geography" means "writing about the earth," so it might seem useless for the study of other worlds, fictional or otherwise, but this chapter will argue that thinking about space can benefit sf criticism. At the same time, taking sf seriously can help the critical study of space by making us think again about experience and representation.

This chapter sets out three key arguments. First, space is not natural, or abstract, or literally "there," but is relational, lived, and lively. Recent arguments in geography have rejected the idea that space is an inert backdrop or container for action, nothing more than the canvas onto which life is painted, or the stage on which it is acted out. In the 1960s and 1970s many geographers subscribed to a form of spatial fetishism, ignoring the ways in which space was constructed and instead granting it causal powers of its own. A city was shaped by the distance between it and its neighbors, its size, transport networks, or other "spatial" phenomena, rather than by social agents or relations like landlords, racism, and governments. We might now suggest that space and society produce each other, though there are of course many different ways of conceptualizing society. Second, texts are not mimetic representations (of space or anything else). Combining these arguments, Sheila Hones contends that the idea of literary "setting" relies on three erroneous assumptions: that it is possible to make a simple distinction between real and fictional places; that the real world possesses a "definitive and self-evident geography which is more authoritative than the geography of the text"; and that a real geography is "a collection of named places that are internally coherent and totally knowable" (Hones 2005: 1). Finally, all of this is complicated by the nature of sf, which may be written or read in such a way that it escapes mimesis and represents alterity. If sf is "fiction squared" (Suvin 1979: 117), then its textual spaces must also be doubly fictional: representations of places that do not or cannot exist.

After outlining contemporary thinking about space, this chapter concentrates on its textual representation and its significance for sf, concentrating on two particular authors: Kim Stanley Robinson and M. John Harrison. As this suggests, my emphasis is upon written fictions; visual sf presents us with a slightly different set of issues that I am unable to go into here, though the general argument still holds.

Space

Geographer Doreen Massey (2005) discusses her frustration with the dominant narrative about globalization, which presents it as an inevitable historical process, a single path down which all nations must pass. Massey sees this as symptomatic of the subordination of space to time in philosophy and social theory, which equates change with time and stasis with space. This allows globalization to be seen as a singular narrative of change that applies to all spaces. Spatial variation (e.g., the differences that exist between rich and poor nations) is explained away in terms of time, so that places move forward along the track of "development," evolving from "traditional" to "modern." Massey's response is to ask a rather science-fictional question: "what if?":

> What if we refuse to convene space into time? What if we open up the imagination of the single narrative to give space (literally) for a multiplicity of trajectories? What kinds of conceptualisation of time and space, and of their relation, might that give on to?
>
> (Massey 2005: 5)

Massey offers three alternative propositions about the nature of space, by which she means space–time, each with progressive political implications. (It is not difficult to think of sf parallels, and in fact one answer to Massey's question would be that we would arrive at thoroughly science-fictional conceptualizations of time and space. When sf critics explored the connections between postmodernism and sf, many of the central metaphors turned out to be spatial as much as science-fictional: Fredric Jameson's "cognitive mapping"; Donna Haraway's cyborg (hybrid subjects located at the intersection or borders of realms – nature/culture, human/machine – commonly thought to be separate); Jean Baudrillard's simulacra and "Disneyfication.")

First, space is *relational* – it is not anything in itself but derives its apparently natural characteristics from its relations with other places, people, and things. This argument is attractive for its anti-essentialism, challenging nationalist and racist assumptions. What we call "Britain" is the sum of a set of historical connections to the rest of the world, rather than a self-evident, closed, and fixed place. This anti-essentialism is also suspicious of the nature/culture opposition, and we might follow Haraway (1991) and Bruno Latour (1993) in arguing that humans are effectively constituted through networks of nonhuman agents. In sf, this anti-essentialism is sometimes explored through the cyborg, or in cyberpunk discussions of the end of the nation-state in an era of information flows. However, the cyborg can also crystallize fears of hybridity and dreams of purity, and the end of older geopolitical certainties does not necessarily lead to more progressive imaginings of place; in Neal Stephenson's *The Diamond Age* (1995) an essentialized "Chinese-ness" fills the vacuum left by communism (Longan and Oakes 2002). Better examples include Jeff Noon's slogan "pure is poor" from *Vurt* (1993), with its posthuman hybrids, and the suggestion in Kim Stanley Robinson's *Mars* trilogy (1992–6) that the terraforming of Mars would also entail the transformation of its colonists into Martians. Mary Louise Pratt (1992) suggests that imperialism involved a series of encounters in "the contact zone," where engagement leads to transformation on both sides, and this sense of open (although clearly not equal) encounter also runs through Robinson's *Years of Rice and Salt* (2002).

Second, space is *multiple and heterogeneous*. There are many different narratives within one place and many experiences of it; the cultural politics of identity and difference become spatial metaphors of "position." Drawing on the ideas of Ernesto Laclau and Chantal Mouffe, Massey argues that any real recognition of difference means putting these uneven and agonistic relations at the heart of all discussions of change. Utopias have always added to the meanings of ordinary spaces by contesting taken-for-granted assumptions about our place within them. The figure of the alien has also offered a highly productive fictional device for revealing the contingency and multiplicity of place.

Finally, space is *in process*, becoming rather than fixed. The agonistic relations between and within places ensure that their futures are always open, allowing us to resist teleological arguments and to derail apparently singular narratives (like globalization). There are always alternatives. There is a parallel here with the call of Jane Bennett (2001) to "re-enchant" our encounters with the world. Narratives of disenchantment, like Max Weber's iron cage, can produce fatalism, she argues, but recognizing that the world is enchanted and learning to look for moments of disconti-nuity and difference can counter it, insisting on possibility and encouraging a kind of everyday utopianism that resembles the spirit of progressive sf. The appeal of utopias and counterfactual histories is their refusal to accept that the past, present, or future must be singular. Alternative universes and parallel worlds give life to spaces that seem closed and finished, just as time travel gives places new histories and futures. However, it is the means rather than the ends that are enchanting, just as utopia is more about process than outcomes. Opening up to possibility is genuinely enchanting in a world where there seems to be no alternative, even if there is nothing inherently progressive about the results of change.

Taken together these three points offer an escape from the paralyzing assump-tions of many arguments about space: "What is needed … is to uproot 'space' from that constellation of concepts in which it has so unquestioningly so often been embedded (stasis; closure; representation) and to settle it among another set of ideas (heterogeneity; relationality; coevalness … liveliness indeed) where it releases a more challenging political landscape" (Massey 2005: 13).

Textual space

Representations of space can help us to reflect on these arguments. Robinson's *The Wild Shore* (1984), set in a post-disaster California, offers an excellent example. Halfway through the book, Henry, the narrator, returns to San Onofre, the tiny hamlet where he has spent almost all of his life, from San Diego, just down the coast. Despite the fact that the first quarter of the novel is set in San Onofre, it has not been extensively described until this point. Henry writes:

> Have I described the valley yet? It is in the shape of a cupped hand, and filled with trees. Down in the crease of the palm is the river winding to the sea, and the fields of corn and barley and potatoes. The heel of the hand is Basilone Hill, and up there is the Costas' place, and Addison's tower, and Rafael's rambling house and workshop. Across from that, the spiny forested fingers of Tom's ridge.
>
> (Robinson 1984: 151)

This is an entirely ordinary piece of topographical writing but it soon becomes something much more interesting:

> When I got to the river I sat gingerly and continued to look around at it all. I couldn't get enough of it. It all looked so familiar and yet so strange. Before my trip south Onofre was just home, a natural place, and the houses, the bridge and the paths, the fields and the latrines, they were all just as much a part of it as the cliffs and the river and the trees. But now I saw it all in a new way. The path. A broad swath of dusty dirt cutting through the weeds, curving here to get around the corner of the Simpsons' garden, narrowing there where rocks cramped it on both sides ... It went where it did because there had been agreement, when folks first moved to the valley, that this was the best way to the river from the meadows to the south. People's thinking made that path. I looked at the bridge – rough planks on steel struts, spanning the gap between the stone bases on each bank. People I knew had thought that bridge, and built it. And the same was true of every structure in the valley. I tried to look at the bridge in the old way, as part of things as they were, but it didn't work. When you've changed you can't go back. Nothing looks the same ever again.
>
> (Robinson 1984: 151–2)

At first Henry sees the valley afresh, describing it as an outsider might, but this immediately becomes a relational space of which he is part; he can no longer simply see "things as they were." There are two reasons for this. First, he now has somewhere else to compare it to, and his movement from a taken-for-granted San Onofre to San Diego and back to a newly unfamiliar valley is presented as an epiphany of sorts. Mikhail Bakhtin suggests that "On the road ... people who are normally kept separate by social and spatial distance can accidentally meet; any contrast may crop up, the most various fates may collide and interweave with each other," and that the road reveals "the sociohistorical heterogeneity of one's own country" (Bakhtin 1981: 243, 245). Henry's journey leads to a new understanding of who and where he is. Spaces are relational in the sense that they mean something only in contrast with each other, strung out along a road for example, but also in the way that the object of landscape and the subject that experiences it may both be changed by their encounter with each other.

Second, Henry no longer sees the valley as natural because he now recognizes the social relations that went into constructing it, the planning, negotiation, and building, the engagement with the physical landscape itself (the path avoids rocks as well as properties). The villagers work together to ensure their survival, but there are different interests within the valley and tensions are exacerbated by the arrival of the strangers from San Diego. The tiny space of the valley contains a heterogeneous group of actors, and is itself the outcome of many agreements and disagreements between them. This leads us to Massey's third point, that San Onofre is lively and open. Clearly textual spaces tend to experience dramatic events, but even if we ignore the momentous challenge that the community faces its future unfolds in unpredictable ways. Again it seems significant that Henry is a teenager maturing into a man, a self-conscious narrator only too happy to record his doubts and hopes about the future and his place in it; as the novel concludes he has grown up and his world has changed around him. San Onofre contains the future because of the interwoven actions of Henry and others, and that future is never closed.

Before leaving San Onofre, we might consider a wider point about this kind of landscape description. Many fictions of all kinds get by with few extended descriptions of space. Even visual media can treat setting as a mere backdrop; for every detailed future city like the Los Angeles of *Blade Runner* (Scott 1982) there are a hundred anonymous quarries or factories that stand in for alien environments. Why do different texts give varying amounts of weight to textual space? Denis Cosgrove (1984) argues that the modern sense of landscape is essentially an outsider's view; under capitalism the laborer is alienated from the land and the owner can only appreciate it as property. Landscape becomes the object of painting at precisely this moment and ceases to be an important focus when this relationship comes to be taken for granted. Similarly, Lennard Davis suggests that extended topographical descriptions in print from the eighteenth century onwards were part and parcel of colonial and capitalist conceptions of land: "locations are intertwined with ideological explanations for the possession of property" (Davis 1987: 54). The realist texts of Balzac or Dickens also mark the highpoint of literary descriptions of place. Davis suggests that "The difference between nineteenth- and twentieth-century descriptions of space … is that the historical and ideological justification for space has dropped out" (Davis 1987: 96). In Robinson's novel, what Henry sees is a working landscape where everything is defined by its use-value, but we should remember the general point that many texts do not rely on extended descriptions, which means that they are worth considering when they *are* present.

Space and sf

Without the wider context of Robinson's post-disaster novel, this example is a rather ordinary one – in fact, John Barrell makes a similar point about textual space in analyzing the geographies of Thomas Hardy's Wessex. His article begins:

> I have never been to Dorset … I make that confession, not to disqualify myself from writing this essay, but to indicate at the outset the sort of essay it will not be. It will not be concerned with the identification of place in the Wessex novels with their possible originals in Dorset and the neighbouring counties.
>
> (Barrell 1982: 347)

In the same spirit, I should admit that I have never been to Tatooine or an orbital habitat or a gas giant. Sf represents places that do not exist (yet), or that are still somehow mysterious. If "Wessex" is a fiction, sf places must be doubly fictional. While there are readers who will compare the represented place with what science tells us is possible, it makes little sense to compare Iain M. Banks's Orbitals with their referents, because they do not exist outside sf, futurology, and other fictions. This is one of the most interesting aspects of sf; not only does it encourage a subtler form of analysis than examining texts for "mistakes" or "bias" in their representations of places, but it questions the very *idea* of setting. If sf encourages us to look again at the taken-for-granted, then representations of impossible places constitute experiments in what can be said about place, new ways of thinking about our experience of being-in-the-world.

However, some sf places are more estranging than others; we might distinguish between extrapolative and speculative environments, between the close-to-home and the truly alien. The cyberpunk city is a good example of the former. *Blade Runner* and William Gibson's fictions might have offered remarkable visions of the future, but it was their plausibility that appealed to audiences and critics, from Bruce Sterling's declaration that "Gibson's extrapolations show, with exaggerated clarity, the hidden bulk of an iceberg of social change" (Sterling 1986: 10–11), to Fredric Jameson's suggestion that cyberpunk offered "the supreme *literary* expression if not of postmodernism then of late capitalism itself" (Jameson 1991: 419, original emphasis) and "a mapping of the new geopolitical Imaginary" (Jameson 2003: 107).

While it was cyberspace that received most attention at first, the cyberpunk city divided critics. Urbanist Mike Davis (1998) applauded Gibson's depiction of the privatization of public space, leading to a dialogue between the two writers (see Kitchin and Kneale 2001), while Claire Sponsler (1993) and others dismissed this vision of the city as a white gentrifiers' playground. We are left with two different critical responses to represented spaces; Davis sees Gibson's texts as dystopian, Sponsler as a utopia of the powerful. Extrapolated fictional spaces are often seen as thinly disguised versions of the present; the text is read symptomatically, as an expression of wider cultural developments. For example, much of the work on *Blade Runner* reflects in some way upon the city and postmodernity.

Even more exotic sf environments can be strangely familiar. As Stanisław Lem's *Solaris* (1961) puts it:

> We don't want to conquer the cosmos, we simply want to extend the boundaries of the Earth to the frontiers of the cosmos. For us, such and such a planet is as arid as the Sahara, another as frozen as the North Pole, yet another as lush as the Amazon basin … We are only seeking Man. We have no need of other worlds. We need mirrors.
>
> (Lem 1987: 72)

For example, the settings of the *Star Wars* films (1977–83, 1999–2005) are as much nineteenth-century adventure fiction and twentieth-century westerns as classic sf.

The plausibility or otherwise of science-fictional places rests on extrapolation from what we know, but with more unfamiliar or speculative environments this has to assume that physical laws and conditions are the same throughout the cosmos. The act of imagining new kinds of life and environments that are consistent with these laws is sometimes called "world building." Hal Clement's *Mission of Gravity* (1954) remains the classic example, its depiction of the massive, highly oblate world Mesklin resting on a careful working-through of the causes and consequences of its size, rapid rotation, and other factors (although its superstitious "primitives" are pure H. Rider Haggard). Clement published his notes and calculations, and invited others to set stories on Mesklin as long as they maintained "reasonable scientific standards." In a sense, this commitment to playing the game is more important than an exact account of the assumptions made, and many other authors have engaged with current scientific thinking to build fictional worlds. Anthropological "laws" have been used to construct alien cultures, perhaps most obviously in the work of Ursula Le Guin, while the development of xenobiology has greatly encouraged sf based on the life sciences since Frank Herbert's *Dune* (1965), by authors such as Greg Bear, Octavia E. Butler, Kathleen Ann Goonan, Paul McAuley, Joan Slonczewski, Brian Stableford, and Peter Watts (see Slonczewski and Levy 2003).

In all of these examples, fictional worlds are felt to be plausible because they are coherent and consistent with scientific principles. However, this discussion of plausibility seems at odds with Massey's conviction that space is lively, as well as with the argument that sf should be estranging.

The problem with world building

While the science in hard sf can evoke a "sense of wonder," when these worlds are described in the language of nineteenth-century realism lively space can become structured and contained by the formulas of world building. It might be impossible to experience true alterity, but maybe we can glimpse it in the way language and representation struggle to cope with the encounter with complex, relational places. In Philip K. Dick's *Galactic Pot-Healer* (1969), for example, Joe Fernwright, taking his first trip from Earth, steps out onto Plowman's Planet:

He smelled the air. Another world and another atmosphere. It feels strange, he decided.

"Don't say," Mali said, "that you find this place 'unearthly'. Please, for my sake."

(Dick 1972: 63)

But to what else can Joe compare it?

For some authors, the attempt to describe or build worlds is central to the imaginative impulse of the genre itself. My final example therefore concerns M. John Harrison's critical assault on the idea of "world building," something he has worried away at since at least 1971 (2005a). In his comments which begin "Every moment of a science fiction story must represent the triumph of writing over worldbuilding" (Harrison 2007), Harrison appears to be echoing Roland Barthes's distinction between *scriptible* texts, which encourage multiple readings, and *lisible* texts, in which the play of meaning is "traversed, intersected, stopped, plasticized by some singular system (Ideology, Genus, Criticism) which reduces the plurality of entrances, the opening of networks, the infinity of languages" (Barthes 1975: 5). Harrison seems to suggest that world building produces *lisible* texts: "Worldbuilding gives an unnecessary permission for acts of writing (indeed, for acts of reading). Worldbuilding numbs the reader's ability to fulfil their part of the bargain, because it believes that it has to do everything around here if anything is going to get done." Authors and readers subordinate their own imaginations to the rules of world-creation. He continues, "Above all, worldbuilding is not technically necessary ... It is the attempt to exhaustively survey a place that isn't there. A good writer would never try to do that, even with a place that is there" (Harrison 2007).

Despite this, Harrison's own fiction is centrally concerned with the desire for something or somewhere better. He describes his story "Egnaro" (1981), in which the narrator searches for a secret country, as an "exploration of the poisoned liminal," which we ourselves poison through "the colonization of the fantastic, the literalization of the improbable, the amazing made ordinary" (Harrison 2003a: 436). World building is the corruption of our desire to escape elsewhere, one of the ways in which "SF rigorously and systematically 'naturalizes' or 'domesticates' its displacements and discontinuities" (Malmgren 1991: 6). Reviewing a recent collection of Le Guin's stories, Harrison concluded that "one of the traps of science fiction is its open invitation to build sensible worlds, rather than to live in – and with – the real thing" (Harrison 2003b: 29).

At the same time Harrison is clearly committed to landscape writing, including the poisoned postindustrial wastes in *The Centauri Device* (1974) and the unpredictable, disorientating event site of *Nova Swing* (2006). His writerly landscape descriptions take the form of a series of glosses on something that never comes into clear view. These lively places are provisional, open rather than fixed, even when they seem utterly mundane: "The bus was full of old women who nodded and smiled and read out all the signs to one another as if they were constructing or rehearsing between them the landscape as they went through it" (Harrison 1985: 140). Harrison has argued that "what modernism can give you is a surprising sense of what it's like to be inside your own life. For a second you are encouraged to reinhabit yourself" (Harrison 2005b: 146). As a result he makes writing about place a central *problem*, one that can be better explored in sf and in avant-garde writing than in realist fiction. Other sf authors see world building as a tool for creating plausibility, and in doing so ignore the problems with "setting," thinking perhaps that the world is simply given to us, knowable and coherent.

One way of developing this insight is to recognize that sf can help us to explore how to write about the Earth. In Robinson's *The Wild Shore*, Henry tries and fails to describe a storm at sea, concluding, "The world pours in and overflows the heart till speech is useless, and that's a fact" (Robinson 1984: 327). When Henry starts to think about writing down the summer's events as a book, the novel we are reading, he becomes increasingly disappointed with his efforts:

> Here all those things had *happened*, they had changed us for life, and yet the miserable string of words sitting on the table didn't hold the half of it – the way it had looked, the way I *felt* about it all. It was like pissing to show what a storm was like. Why, there was no more of last summer in that book than there is of the tree in an old scrap of driftwood.
>
> (Robinson 1984: 336)

Despite this, Henry continues to observe and describe San Onofre's sea, sky, and landscapes, and the novel ends with "I'll stay right here and fill another book" (Robinson 1984: 343). Harrison and Robinson recognize that this effort is inevitable and necessary: we must engage with the world, and while writing about it is one way of doing this there is no way of getting it *right*. Despite sf's capacity to explore our engagement with place, the temptation to indulge in world building contains much of this potential. This suggests that the real problem lies not with constructing plausible worlds but in establishing what it is we are trying to do with our descriptions of place. It is not just that sf criticism needs to think about the importance of textual space, but also that sf should treat textual space as a problem rather than just another object.

Bibliography

Bakhtin M.M. (1981) "Forms of Time and of the Chronotope in the Novel," in *The Dialogic Imagination: four essays*, trans. V. Liapunov and K. Brostrom, Austin: University of Texas Press.

Barrell, J. (1982) "Geographies of Hardy's Wessex," *Journal of Historical Geography*, 8(4): 347–61.

Barthes, R. (1975) *S/Z*, 1970, trans. R. Miller, London: Cape.

Bennett, J. (2001) *The Enchantment of Modern Life: attachments, crossings and ethics*, Princeton, NJ and Oxford: Princeton University Press.

Cosgrove, D. (1984) *Social Formation and Symbolic Landscape*, London: Croom Helm.

Davis, L. (1987) *Resisting Novels: ideology and fiction*, New York and London: Methuen.

Davis, M. (1998) *Ecology of Fear: Los Angeles and the imagination of disaster*, New York: Metropolitan Books.

Dick, P.K. (1972) *Galactic Pot-Healer*, 1969, London: Pan.

Haraway, D.J. (1991) "A Cyborg Manifesto: science, technology, and socialist-feminism in the late twentieth century," in *Simians, Cyborgs, and Women: the reinvention of nature*, New York and London: Routledge.

Harrison, M.J. (1975) *The Centauri Device*, London: Panther.

—— (1985) "A Young Man's Journey to Viriconium," in *Viriconium Nights*, London: Gollancz.

—— (2003a) *Things that Never Happen*, San Francisco and Portland: Nightshade Books.

—— (2003b) "Worlds Apart: Ursula Le Guin's *The Birthday of the World*," *The Guardian*, 18 January: 29.

—— (2005a) "By Tennyson out of Disney," in M. Bould and M. Reid (eds) *Parietal Games: critical writings by and on M. John Harrison*, London: Science Fiction Foundation.

—— (2005b) "The Profession of Science Fiction, 40: the profession of fiction," in M. Bould and M. Reid (eds) *Parietal Games: critical writings by and on M. John Harrison*, London: Science Fiction Foundation.

—— (2006) *Nova Swing*, London: Gollancz.

—— (2007) "Very Afraid," *Uncle Zip's Window*, 27 January. Online. Available HTTP: <http://uzwi. wordpress.com/2007/01/27/very-afraid/> (accessed 1 April 2008).

Hones, S. (2005) "Spectral Geography and Fictional Setting," paper presented at the Royal Geographical Society/Institute of British Geographers Annual Conference, London, September.

Jameson, F. (1991) *Postmodernism, or, The Cultural Logic of Late Capitalism*, London and New York: Verso.

—— (2003) "Fear and Loathing in Globalization," *New Left Review*, 23: 105–45.

Kitchin, R. and Kneale, J. (2001) "Science Fiction or Future Fact? Exploring imaginative geographies of the new millennium," *Progress in Human Geography*, 25(1): 9–35.

—— (eds) (2002) *Lost in Space: geographies of science fiction*, London: Continuum.

Latour, B. (1993) *We Have Never Been Modern*, trans. C. Porter, Brighton: Harvester.

Lem, S. (1987) *Solaris*, 1961, trans. J. Kilmartin and S. Cox, London: Harcourt Brace Jovanovich.

Longan, M. and Oakes, T. (2002) "Geography's Conquest of History in *The Diamond Age*," in R. Kitchin and J. Kneale (eds) *Lost in Space: geographies of science fiction*, London and New York: Continuum.

Malmgren, C.D. (1991) *Worlds Apart: narratology of science fiction*, Bloomington and Indianapolis: Indiana University Press.

Massey, D. (2005) *For Space*, London, Thousand Oaks, and New Delhi: Sage.

Pratt, M.L. (1992) *Imperial Eyes: travel writing and transculturation*, London and New York: Routledge.

Robinson, K.S. (1984) *The Wild Shore*, London: HarperCollins.

Slonczewski, J.L. and Levy, M.M. (2003) "Science Fiction and the Life Sciences," in E. James and F. Mendlesohn (eds) *The Cambridge Companion to Science Fiction*, Cambridge: Cambridge University Press.

Sponsler, C. (1993) "Beyond the Ruins: the geopolitics of urban decay and cybernetic play," *Science Fiction Studies*, 20(2): 251–65.

Sterling, B. (1986) "Introduction," in W. Gibson, *Burning Chrome*, London: Gollancz.

Suvin, D. (1979) *Metamorphoses of Science Fiction: on the poetics and history of a literary genre*, New Haven, CT: Yale University Press.

43

TIME, POSSIBLE WORLDS, AND COUNTERFACTUALS

Matt Hills

Sf is often thought of as a literature of world building and extrapolation, so in a sense it is unsurprising that a branch of philosophy dealing with "possible worlds" has been strongly linked to the genre's endeavors.

Ruth Ronen (1994) distinguishes between three different branches of "possible worlds" theory, dubbing these "modal realism," "moderate realism," and "anti-realist". The first of these, which Ronen argues is displayed in the work of philosopher David Lewis (1973, 1986), holds that "all modal possibilities we might stipulate, as well as the actual world, are equally realized in some logical space where they possess a physical existence" (Ronen 1994: 21–2). Lewis's work on what he calls "counterfactuals," or alternative states of existence to those experienced in our real world (i.e., counter-to-the-facts of history and society), therefore amounts to an almost science-fictional exploration of the "parallel" or "many worlds" hypothesis. On this account, our own "actual" world is simply one of many possible sociohistorical outcomes, with each and every potential variant or pathway not taken nevertheless existing in some other space or parallel dimension. Modal realists are involved in a philosophy which closely resembles the speculative ontologies and narratives of much sf: "I would be the last to denounce decent science fiction as philosophically unsound. No; tales of viewing or visiting 'other worlds' are perfectly consistent" (Lewis 1986: 81). Modal realism is, if you like, a philosophical expression strongly akin to the "many worlds" hypothesis in quantum physics; both amount to philosophical speculation over the existence of variant worlds, where all possible branches and all possible differences in our empirical history will have occurred outside our accessible time–space, but with equal status to our reality.

In contrast, the "moderate realists" view alternative worlds or counterfactuals not as literally "out there" somewhere, but rather as abstract, hypothetical scenarios within our actual world. Here, possible worlds do not ontologically exist, but they can be imagined, dreamed up, speculated over. Again, this branch of modal philosophy can shed light on the activities of sf writers, who we might say are frequently engaged in precisely such speculations. The "anti-realists" refute the realism and relevance of "possible worlds" to the actual. If anything, this last view is contradicted by the "explanatory power" and critical energy that sf's counterfactuals can possess (Ronen 1994: 23). However, both moderate realists and anti-realists would not appear to subscribe to the many worlds hypothesis, as these philosophies do not assume that counterfactual worlds have any ontological essence or existence outside of our ability to imagine them.

Although possible worlds theory has often been used, or critiqued, to conceptualize the role and power of "fiction" *per se* (see Pavel 1986; Walton 1990), its application to sf specifically has also been debated (see Buckland 1999, 2001; Sellors 2000). Peter Stockwell highlights a major issue with attempting to accurately apply possible worlds modal philosophy to sf:

> there is a reflexive problem in applying a logical model to science fiction. Imagine a science fictional universe in which a different local physics and mathematics operate: one in which the square root of nine is an even number, or where the inhabitants are able to perceive time as we perceive space … [These] exist as "Flatland" and "Tralfamadore" … in science fiction. The problem is that the basis of traditional possible worlds theory – logic – is as amenable to alternativity as any other system.
>
> (Stockwell 2000: 144–5)

Arguments strongly defending the logic of possible worlds theory, or ruling sf as being outside its orbits, thus miss this point. Following Stockwell and Marie-Laure Ryan (1991), we can instead take a less rigid view of possible worlds philosophy, which allows that sf's what-ifs can, and do, give rise to meaningful discussion and analysis of counterfactuals.

Brian Stableford (1993a) argues that it was not until historiography developed the philosophical concept of alternate timelines and historical outcomes, in the likes of the essay collection *If It Had Happened Otherwise* (1931), edited by J.C. Squires, that pulp sf was able to routinely appropriate and co-opt the idea. In this sense, then, imaginative and speculative history can be seen as closely linked to the emergence and popularization of counterfactuals in sf, though we should be careful to note that historiography and sf have themselves made variant uses of counterfactuals. For historians, it has been primarily deployed as a device to illuminate the actual historical contingencies and factors operating in and on "the past" as we culturally understand it, while sf has both developed this aim and used counterfactuals for purposes of melodrama and narrative experimentation.

Stableford notes that Guy Dent's *Emperor of the If* (1926) was an important precursor of pulp sf's appropriation and popularization of historiographical ideas, with L. Sprague de Camp's "The Wheels of If" (1940) and Jack Williamson's *The Legion of Time* (1938) subsequently using historical what-ifs and rival timelines for, respectively, serious-minded and high-melodramatic purposes (Stableford 1993a: 23–5; see Schmunk 2008 for a detailed, annotated bibliography of alternate histories, and Hellekson's chapter below). It could reasonably be said that perhaps the most important single word in such types of counterfactual sf, its appearance in various titles being no coincidence, is quite simply "if."

The what-ifs of sf's possible worlds give rise to a certain aesthetic and cognitive effect, which is not merely estrangement – our "own" world or time being seen anew – but more precisely an ontological disruption and decentering. Indeed, Brian McHale (1987) links much sf, especially the work of Philip K. Dick, to theories of postmodernism, terming this an "ontological" literature in which rationality and ontological certainty can be eroded. However, Stockwell takes issue with this, arguing that sf also "raises questions of epistemology. The genre not only creates alternative universes, but it almost always sets up a dynamic narrative to explore what these are like and why. Narrative drive ... means that science fiction ... is holistically epistemological, ontological and kinetic" (Stockwell 2000: 104). While postmodern literary experiments may occasionally lack narrative energy and resolution, Stockwell evidently views sf's ontological shocks as more reader-friendly and thus far more open to cognitive and epistemological debate than postmodernism's sometime excesses. However, it is important to note that this binary of "postmodernism" versus "sf" is a highly problematic construction, as it can just as well be argued that "It has fallen to science fiction to repeatedly narrate a new subject that can somehow directly interface with – and master – the cybernetic technologies of the Information Age, an era in which, as Jean Baudrillard has observed, the subject has become a 'terminal of multiple networks'" (Bukatman 1993: 2). Likewise, Gibson argues that feminist sf is anti-essentialist and postmodern (Gibson 1996: 257).

Therefore, rather than being opposed to postmodern literary experimentation, sf and its counterfactuals frequently resonate with the definitions and thematics of postmodern literature. And the fusing of ontological, epistemological, and kinetic (pulp sf) lineages favored by Stockwell is evident in much cyberpunk – viewed by Fredric Jameson as exemplary postmodern literature (Jameson 1991: 38) – as well as in its alternative history or counterfactual relative, steampunk. For instance, William Gibson and Bruce Sterling's *The Difference Engine* (1991), "premised on the idea that Charles Babbage's attempt to create a steam-driven Analytical Engine between 1820 and 1832 was successful, thus producing a computer revolution 150 years early," provides an exercise in ontological disruption that remains a sensationalist, narrative one, while also cognitively and aesthetically illuminating "the traumatic speed of technology change" on and for society (Luckhurst 2005: 213). By twisting its version of Victorian London into bright counterfactual forms, *The Difference Engine* speaks to contemporary concerns and epistemologies regarding technological determinism.

Another frequently cited example of sf's ontological shocks and counterfactual disruptions is Dick's *The Man in the High Castle* (1962). This explores one of several perennially popular alternative histories: what if the Second World War had ended differently? Dick sets out a vision of North America divided between the Germans and the Japanese, but the ontology of his fictional world is more complex than simply representing a counterfactual what-if as it "implicates art in the construction of reality, featuring a novel-within-the-novel that presents a history that is much closer to our own than the alternate history of the frame novel" (Landon 1997: 113–14). *The Man in the High Castle* is therefore not just about the creation of an impressive fictional possible world. It is also metafictional, focusing on the very power of fiction to build counterfactual worlds in which readers can immerse themselves imaginatively and cognitively. Like much of Dick's work, it questions and doubts reality and history, as if they are just one world-construction among multiple possibilities and narratively imagined/real versions. Although Stockwell is undoubtedly right to challenge generalizations that link sf *per se* to ontological concerns, where possible worlds and counterfactuals become the genre's focal points then history-as-ontology or essence is characteristically displaced by ontological skepticism and contingency.

Barney Warf analyzes this sf approach to history in greater depth. He argues that although sf's counterfactuals have frequently been thought of as "alternate histories," such as "what if the Victorians had invented the computer?" or "what if the outcome of World War II had been different?," it is not only reimagined temporality that is crucial to the sf counterfactual. Geography and spatiality are also necessarily reconfigured by alternate histories, given that these are "inherently geographical, just as all histories, 'real' or otherwise, unfold spatially, for different temporal trajectories produce different maps of human behaviour" (Warf 2002: 32). Hence, though it seems to make sense for time to be the crucial concept and matter in relation to science-fictional and counterfactual histories, time *and* space – cultural history and geography – call for equal consideration. The importance of imagined geographies is readily apparent in *The Man in the High Castle*, for example, just as it is in more recent examples of counterfactual world building such as Jon Courtenay Grimwood's *Arabesk* sf thrillers (2001–3), in which the First World War did not happen and the German Reich and Ottoman Empire have become significant powers in the twenty-first century as a result. The *Arabesk* series is just as much about shifted Islamic cultural geographies as it is about alternate timelines.

The prioritization of time when thinking about sf's alternative versions of history comes, perhaps in part, from the fact that a specific moment of divergence from actual history frequently underpins these fictions. The imaginative extrapolation of a path not taken can often be traced back to particular decisions or events in the diegetic world:

> The classic image is that of John Barr, in Jack Williamson's sf novel *The Legion of Time* (1938), standing in a field; if he picks up a magnet, rather than a stone, the history of the galaxy will be transformed. Sf writers have come to call these decisive moments "Jonbar points"; they range from the non-arrival of the comet which caused the extinction of the dinosaurs (Harry Harrison's *West of Eden*, 1984) to the non-occurrence of the Protestant Reformation (Kingsley Amis's *The Alteration*, 1976).
>
> (James 1994: 113–14)

The implication is that at an infinite number of moments, time and history could have been otherwise. Sf therefore does not restrict itself to imagining different outcomes for world-historical events such as the Second World War, or different lives for the "Great Men" of history. As the Jonbar point makes clear, massive shifts between narrative timelines can hinge on seemingly minuscule, unimportant, almost meaningless actions and events. This democratizing viewpoint – that history belongs to the unintended stumblings of ordinary, everyday life as much as it does to world politics – probably finds its most elegant expression in Ray Bradbury's "A Sound of Thunder" (1953), where one man's trampling of a butterfly back in prehistoric times ultimately leads to vast changes in the diegetic world's present-day language and politics.

Sf's use of counterfactuals is hence one way in which it can destabilize ontological perspectives and compel readers to see the "real" historical world in different, perhaps more critical ways. Fredric Jameson, writing about Dick's use of simulated realities and histories in *Time Out of Joint* (1959), argues that sf "corresponds to the waning or the blockage of ... historicity, and, particularly in our own time, to its crisis and paralysis" (Jameson 1991: 284). That is, where post-Enlightenment faith in historical development, progress, and even historical awareness have all arguably been reduced or weakened, sf can operate via its narrative simulations of history to pursue an "experience of our present as past and as history" (Jameson 1991: 286). In his analysis of sf's world building, it is again a cultural sense of time and historicity which Jameson prioritizes, rather than examining the differential geographies and spaces implied and interrogated by what-if worlds.

When thinking about sf's counterfactuals it is analytically useful to distinguish between narratives such as "A Sound of Thunder" or *Time Out of Joint* – in which characters can move between and experience different timelines or cultural geographies – and those which seemingly proceed as if they are almost realist novels, but with the difference that they reimagine and proceed from a turning point in "actual" history. Stableford marks this distinction, referring to the first cases as examples of pluralized parallel worlds or world frames which can possibly interact/intersect (Stableford 1993a: 23; 1993b: 908), and the second as a variant type of imagined alternate world, or singular "account of Earth as it might have become in consequence of some hypothetical alteration in history" (Stableford 1993a: 23). The former use time travel and other sf devices, whereas in the latter the only imaginative change is historical difference itself. In both cases, the "novum" – the "novelty, innovation ... validated by cognitive logic" that distinguishes sf from other genres (Suvin 1979: 63) – creates:

> a new historical situation, different from the one that we know. In consequence, sf is usually just as much about history as it is about science. Sf writers have to construct new histories, of our world or of others, in order to set their novum ... in context and discuss its ... impact upon individuals and society as a whole.
>
> (James 1994: 109)

But where history itself *is* the novum, literature which might not otherwise be categorized as sf can be thought of as, at the very least, science-fictional, such as Len Deighton's *SS-GB* (1978) and Robert Harris's *Fatherland* (1998), both of which imagine counterfactual narrative worlds where the Allies lost the Second World War.

Tom Shippey points out that despite "almost all definitions" of sf implying that the genre is "irrevocably committed to the future" (Shippey 1981: 26), it can also be a literature which challenges history, decentering it, and rendering it critically contingent. In place of historical teleologies (the view that history inevitably moves in a specific progression or sequence), sf and associated speculative fictions can "teach us how our world came to be by illuminating how it did not become" (Warf 2002: 36–7). While frequently a literature of extrapolation into possible futures, sf can also step sideways, and extrapolate from altered pasts into alternate versions of the present. And by doing so, it can of course challenge "the politics of the contemporary" (Warf 2002: 37).

It can be suggested that parallel worlds, possible worlds, and alternate histories have found a place not just at the blurry edges of the genre, but also well outside its reaches. As Adam Roberts acutely argues, "the symbolic purchase of SF on contemporary living is so powerful, and speaks so directly to the realities of our accelerated culture, that it provides many of the conceptual templates of the modern Western world" (Roberts 2000: 35). And with regard to possible worlds and counterfactual what-ifs, sf has increasingly become a significant part of popular culture more generally and of narratives and trajectories of the self. Anthony Giddens argues that in the social contexts of late modernity, self-identity means that "we have no choice but to choose" (Giddens 1991: 81) self-reflexively between lifestyles, between alternative possibilities and risks. In such post-traditional and consumer-cultural contexts, identity may not become wholly malleable or perfor-mative, but it is opened to a radical degree of contingency and self-consciousness with regards to possible future outcomes and pathways. Increasingly, it could thus be said that we practice quantum self-identities, living as if we are occupying one possible world among others, and self-reflexively monitoring the potential branching points in our Giddensian "life plans" (Giddens 1991: 80). Jameson also views this as characteristic of postmodern society, where "the incorporation of 'futurology' into our everyday lives, the modification of our perception of things to include their 'tendency' and ... our reading of time to approximate a scanning of complex probabilities" (Jameson 1991: 285) are all potentially normalized. Films such as *Run, Lola, Run* (Tykwer 1998) and *Sliding Doors* (Howitt 1998) can be taken to reflect the more general symbolic purchase of such science-fictional concepts. Similarly, "ergodic" literature – that which branches between different possible narrative outcomes – has found a place in "cybertext" (see Aarseth 1997) or hypertext narratives. However, these branching new media narrative strategies are sometimes seen as unsatisfactory:

> Our experience of reading hypertext works is often far from the liberating, empowering experience we might expect ... On the contrary, we often find ourselves positioned in particular pathways, unable to see beyond the next link, revisiting the same nodes over and over in loops ... In fact, the book is already a perfect random access system.
>
> (Lister *et al.* 2003: 29)

With this in mind, we should take care not to restrict the notion of branching narrative – in which different fictional possible worlds can be explored – to its new media iterations, for it has also found a rather more old-fashioned home in "Choose Your Own Adventure" or "Decide Your Destiny" style books, where the reader selects different options and so moves through a branched narrative with various conclusions. Indeed, Kim Newman adopted this "ergodic" style of fiction for *Life's Lottery* (1999) which begins with the reader having to choose between identifying as a *Star Trek* or *Doctor Who* fan. And in the arena of computer/videogaming, ergodicity is a crucial concept, allowing the player to branch between different game-world possibilities. For example, Barry Atkins (2003: 102–8) analyzes how wargames can allow their players to participate in the creation of sf's counterfactual staples, such as a world in which the Second World War turns out differently. Taken together, these examples can lead us to consider whether sf's symbolic centrality to contemporary culture is a matter not just of its cyberpunk-ish or technological imaginings, but also of its alternate world buildings.

Media sf has used the ergodic device of parallel worlds in distinctive ways. Both *Star Trek* (1966–9) and *Star Trek: Deep Space Nine* (1993–9) have represented a "mirror universe," while the long-running *Doctor Who*, in its "classic" and "new" incarnations (1963–89, 2005–), has shown its characters moving between parallel Earths, in "Inferno" (1970) and "Rise of the Cybermen" and "Age of Steel" (2006). The difference in sf television's use of parallel worlds is that they tend to be deployed primarily in order to produce character variation – turning our heroes into dictatorial villains, say – or in order to allow for narrative possibilities which an ongoing series format would not usually permit, such as the Doctor's failure to save the parallel Earth of "Inferno." The interrogation of specific historical turning points, or the detailed realization of alternate histories and worlds is thus typically restricted here in favor of exploring alternate characterizations, though the US series *Sliders* (1995–2000) used possible worlds and counterfactuals as a more integral part of its own format.

Sf's relationship to counterfactuals has not been restricted to its own diegetic constructions. Stanisław Lem's *A Perfect Vacuum* (1971) playfully explores the notion by reviewing books that do not, in fact, exist in the "actual" world. As Peter Swirski says, this "single work … epitomizes Lem's language-centered type of self-reflexivity" via its "sophisticated use of thought-experiments [and] counterfactual scenarios" (Swirski 2000: 75, 76). And this conceptual playfulness has been extended by, for instance, Angela Hague and David Lavery's edited collection *Teleparody: predicting/preventing the TV discourse of tomorrow* (2002), a series of critiques of nonexistent academic studies of television.

It is also worth noting that some sf writers have produced counterfactual tales in a highly unusual way, namely by creating fictions which represent rereadings of previous fictional worlds. Kim Newman has done this repeatedly in books such as *Anno Dracula* (1993), in which, rather than being defeated, Dracula becomes the head of the British Empire. Brian Stableford's *The Empire of Fear* (1988) creates a hard-sf vampiric alternate history, while Brian Aldiss's *Frankenstein Unbound* (1973) also revisits the masterworks of Gothic sf. However, in Newman's rereading and rewriting of Gothic tales such as Robert Louis Stevenson's *Strange Case of Dr Jekyll and Mr Hyde* (1886) and Bram Stoker's *Dracula* (1897) as sf, we are presented with alternate versions of these diegetic worlds: in "A Drug on the Market" (2002), Jekyll's potion is mass-produced and marketed, while the queered "Further Developments in the Strange Case of Jekyll and Hyde" (2000) suggests that Jekyll and Hyde were, perhaps, two different people after all, rather than two sides of the same personality. These clever pastiches of the originals create alternate possible worlds, but by doing so they reread and even critique Stevenson's and Stoker's stories for their ideological limits and their subtexts. The type of possible world put forward is distinctive in that it amounts to a counterfactual version not of our own world's history or geography, but rather of an established diegetic world. These "alternate story stories" (Byrne 2000: 6) produce "counterfictional" worlds (see Hills 2003). Despite this spin on sf counterfactuality, such alternate story stories work in similar ways to other possible worlds, in that they again compel us to see familiar events (this time, narrative rather than historical) in a radically new light. Aesthetically and cognitively, such fictions again provide the thoughtful thrill of "ontological shock" (Hills 2005: 39–44) while also frequently amounting to versions of literary or critical theory, whether they are self-consciously queering Stevenson's novella or challenging the imperialist ideology which marks Stoker's Dracula as foreign, exotic, and "Other."

Despite some writers' misgivings over the applicability of philosophies of modal logic to sf (e.g., Sellors 2000), thinking of sf as the creation of counterfactual "possible worlds" – alternate histories and stories – can illuminate its use of a novum and its critical, decentering, and creatively questioning stance in relation to the "actual" world. By dreaming up other possible worlds – even worlds approximating more to science fantasy which may not follow established logics, mathematics, or scientific paradigms – sf is able to imagine the present as future history, and approach the past as if it were an unwritten future. Shifted temporalities and timelines are obviously important to this process, but so too are projected cultural geographies. And, perhaps above all, sf's interest in possible worlds is one which resonates with life in late modernity, where post-traditional consumer lifestyles represent one choice or pathway among others, and where risks are variously calculated, projected, and themselves managed as counterfactuals. As such, it should come as no surprise to writers and readers of sf that possible worlds and alternate histories have found a home and an appeal far outside its usual generic boundaries and classifications. Our contemporary cultural realities are, in significant ways, science-fictional exercises in possibility and counterfactuality.

Bibliography

Aarseth, E. (1997) *Cybertext: perspectives on Ergodic literature*, Baltimore, MD: Johns Hopkins University Press.

Atkins, B. (2003) *More Than a Game: the computer game as fictional form*, Manchester: Manchester University Press.

Buckland, W. (1999) "Between Science Fact and Science Fiction: Spielberg's digital dinosaurs, possible worlds, and the new aesthetic realism," *Screen*, 40(2): 177–92.

—— (2001) "A Reply to Sellors's 'Mindless' Approach to Possible Worlds," *Screen*, 42(2): 222–6.

Bukatman, S. (1993) *Terminal Identity: the virtual subject in postmodern science fiction*, Durham, NC and London: Duke University Press.

Byrne, E. (2000) "Introduction," in K. Newman, *Unforgivable Stories*, London: Simon and Schuster.

Gibson, A. (1996) *Towards a Postmodern Theory of Narrative*, Edinburgh: Edinburgh University Press.

Giddens, A. (1991) *Modernity and Self-Identity: self and society in the late modern age*, Cambridge: Polity Press.

Hague, A. and Lavery, D. (eds) (2002) *Teleparody: predicting/preventing the TV discourse of tomorrow*, London: Wallflower Books.

Hills, M. (2003) "Counterfictions in the Work of Kim Newman: rewriting Gothic sf as 'alternate-story stories,'" *Science Fiction Studies*, 30(3): 436–55.

—— (2005) *The Pleasures of Horror*, London and New York: Continuum.

James, E. (1994) *Science Fiction in the 20th Century*, Oxford: Opus.

Jameson, F. (1991) *Postmodernism, or, The Cultural Logic of Late Capitalism*, London and New York: Verso.

Landon, B. (1997) *Science Fiction after 1900: from the steam man to the stars*, New York: Twayne.

Lewis, D. (1973) *Counterfactuals*, Oxford: Blackwell.

—— (1986) *On the Plurality of Worlds*, Oxford: Blackwell.

Lister, M., Dovey, J., Gidding, S., Grant, I., and Kelly, K. (2003) *New Media: a critical introduction*, London and New York: Routledge.

Luckhurst, R. (2005) *Science Fiction*, London: Polity.

McHale, B. (1987) *Postmodernist Fiction*, London and New York: Methuen.

Pavel, T.G. (1986) *Fictional Worlds*, London: Harvard University Press.

Roberts, A. (2000) *Science Fiction*, London: Routledge.

Ronen, R. (1994) *Possible Worlds in Literary Theory*, Cambridge: Cambridge University Press.

Ryan, M.-L. (1991) *Possible Worlds: artificial intelligence and narrative theory*, Bloomington and Indianapolis: Indiana University Press.

Schmunk, R. (2008) *Uchronia: the alternate history list*. Online. Available HTTP: <http://www.uchronia.net/> (accessed 1 April 2008).

Sellors, P. (2000) "The Impossibility of Science Fiction: against Buckland's possible worlds," *Screen*, 41(2): 203–16.

Shippey, T. (1981) "History in SF," in P. Nicholls (ed.) *The Encyclopedia of Science Fiction*, St Albans: Granada.

Stableford, B. (1993a) "Alternate Worlds," in J. Clute and P. Nicholls (eds) *The Encyclopedia of Science Fiction*, London: Orbit.

—— (1993b) "Parallel Worlds," in J. Clute and P. Nicholls (eds) *The Encyclopedia of Science Fiction*, London: Orbit.

Stockwell, P. (2000) *The Poetics of Science Fiction*, London: Longman.

Suvin, D. (1979) *Metamorphoses of Science Fiction: on the poetics and history of a literary genre*, New Haven, CT: Yale University Press.

Swirski, P. (2000) *Between Literature and Science: Poe, Lem and explorations in aesthetics, cognitive science, and literary knowledge*, Liverpool: Liverpool University Press.

Walton, K.L. (1990) *Mimesis as Make-Believe: on the foundations of the representational arts*, London: Harvard University Press.

Warf, B. (2002) "The Way it Wasn't: alternative histories, contingent geographies," in R. Kitchin and J. Kneale (eds) *Lost in Space: geographies of science fiction*, London and New York: Continuum.

44

YOUNG ADULT SF

Joe Sutliff Sanders

Given the old shibboleth about the Golden Age of sf being not a particular era but the age of adolescence, why is there not more scholarship on young adult science fiction (YASF)? Even some novels by Ursula K. Le Guin, on whose other work there is no shortage of commentary, have received limited critical attention because they "are considered adolescent fiction first and foremost, and that isn't a genre of interest for most of the critics who study [her]" (Cadden 2006: 428). C.W. Sullivan has suggested that it is "too risky" to research in a field whose residence in the academic gutter is guaranteed by its attention to fiction that is both juvenile (YA) and popular (sf) (Sullivan 1993b: xiv). When crossovers between the study of YA literature and sf do take place, it is often with an ignorance of the obligations and assumptions of one field or the other. Therefore, this chapter will outline for readers primarily interested in sf from the perspective of YA scholars, whose academic home is in the broader field of children's literature. By focusing on the central tenet of YA scholarship – that any fiction called "young adult fiction" must successfully address the experiences and needs of young adult readers – this chapter will introduce some of the ways YA and sf scholarship can complement (or frustrate) each other.

Defining the literature and the scholarship

The most obvious way to classify YASF is as "sf read by young adults," but even that definition quickly proves useless. Sullivan warns that YA "readers do not confine themselves to the books written specifically for them" and that young sf fans can "move indiscriminately between young adult and adult science fiction" (Sullivan 1999a: 25–6). Furthermore, because so many adult readers of sf began reading the genre as adolescents, "it is difficult to delineate those works written specifically for young people" (Reid 1998: 10–11). Therefore, YASF must instead refer to fiction with a certain agenda: in addition to satisfying whatever criteria are necessary for the text to be called "sf," it must also address the real needs and experiences of adolescent and teen readers. This is not to say that it must deal only with the mundane realities of youth culture, but it must make itself thematically and structurally relevant to the young adults of its period (for example, "plots centered on coming of age themes"

(Reid 1998: 11) or books "written to appeal to the rebellious and resurgent nature of youth" (Bailey and Sawyer 1999: 97)).

YASF's most reliable traits are its format and structure. Because young adults are not usually fully adept at reading – neither the physical act nor the mental exercise – savvy authors will build their stories so as to help readers navigate both the material book and the story. This is why YA novels more often feature frequent chapter breaks: these provide opportunities for rest, clear divisions between the story's structural segments, and manageable goals for a reading session. YA literature also often features a larger font and more generous spacing between lines of text than adult novels, giving readers the reward of turning pages faster but also recognizing that the development of the fine ocular musculature required for reading dense print is still developing until the age of physical maturity. In these and other ways, the material characteristics of a YA book must fit the actual needs of the young adults for whom it is intended.

Excellent YASF invariably pays attention to the developing reader's needs in its narrative elements, too. For example, the plot of John Christopher's *The White Mountains* (1967) stops from time to time as the book explains its premises and plans to the reader. Although experienced sf readers, particularly adults, will already have deduced the nature of the post-catastrophe setting and of the "Capping" ceremony, Christopher explains them in great detail over a five-page question-and-answer session and then sketches out the basic shape of the plot in the subsequent three pages. Both gestures provide a boost for readers who have not yet mastered the subtleties of fiction. Similarly, characters in Jeanne DuPrau's *The City of Ember* (2003) frequently stop to explain to each other the discoveries readers have already seen them make and to draw out connections that might have been apparent to an adult reader (and young readers who do not need this extra help are rewarded with confirmation of their interpretation of the text). When this is done well, as it is in DuPrau's novel, such scenes also advance the plot and character development.

YA scholarship is always interested in the skill with which an adolescent audience is addressed, praising a book for having the perfect plot for the young reader (Sullivan 1993a: 25) or defending dated books because they were well attuned to "the interests and needs of the generation of children who read [them]" (Sands and Frank 1999: 106). But if its relevance to its audience can be assumed, the text may then be read from a wide variety of theoretical positions. For example, Don Palumbo (1999) reads superhero comics through genre theory so as to articulate an argument about the boundaries between sf and fantasy. M. Sarah Smedman (1993) reads Madeleine L'Engle's YASF through biographical criticism, and J.R. Wytenbroek (1993) theorizes about technology and ecology in contemporary culture by working through the interplay of those themes in Monica Hughes's sf for young readers. Raymond E. Jones (1993) traces the archetypal resonances of Monica Hughes's *The Keeper of the Isis Light* (1980), and elsewhere compares it to *Frankenstein* (1818) and Wordsworth through gender theory (1999). Michael Levy (1999) considers YASF according to the structural form of the *Bildungsroman*, but he has also theorized about patterns of consumption in recent YASF by switching deftly between Jean Baudrillard, Abraham

Maslow, and adult sf by William Gibson, Frederik Pohl, Robert Sheckley, Somtow Sucharitkul, and Geoff Ryman (Levy 2006). Therefore no rigorous approach to YASF is inherently off-limits from a children's literature perspective – as long as the literature under consideration is relevant to young readers' real experiences.

The major figure: Robert A. Heinlein

There is no figure so important to YASF, particularly for scholars, as Robert A. Heinlein. One can analyze individual authors or specific texts without referring to him, but the larger the scope of an argument, the more likely it must eventually touch on him. Beginning in 1947 and continuing through the 1950s, "Robert Heinlein was primarily an author of science fiction aimed at the 'juvenile' market" (Franklin 1980: 73). The Heinlein juveniles, as they are usually called, made clear the financial viability of YASF and provided its touchstone texts. Certainly there had been earlier sf aimed at young adults, but the popularity of Heinlein's novels and the skill with which he addressed the genre's audience proved to be crucial to subsequent generations of YASF.

We can therefore identify in Heinlein's juveniles many of the ideas that would become central to YASF – and privileged by its scholarship – over the coming decades. For example, Sullivan (1993a) lists six themes Heinlein articulated in his juveniles that would become key ideas for subsequent YASF. Consider, for example, the alien pet motif, all but invented in *Red Planet* (1949), which echoes down through the ages, appearing in *E.T.: The Extra-Terrestrial* (Spielberg 1982) as well as in popular YASF by Andre Norton (a similarly key figure in the origins of the field) and contemporary YASF, such as *Siberia* (2005) by Ann Halam (Gwyneth Jones). Too, Heinlein's admiration for the frontier culture that space exploration promised resurfaces at least as late as Charles Sheffield and Jerry Pournelle's *Higher Education* (1996), as when one character praises the rough self-reliance of space travelers over the mollycoddling laws of home.

More important than these surface tropes are the consistent attempts Heinlein made to render his YASF relevant to the readers to whom the books were marketed. As Franklin says, *Red Planet* "is about growing up. Jim becomes a man. Willis prepares to metamorphose into a mature Martian. The colony issues a Proclamation of Autonomy modeled on the Declaration of Independence. Human society itself seems youthful compared with that of the Martians, who outgrew space travel millions of years ago" (Franklin 1980: 78). But encoding his books with such themes was hardly Heinlein's only strategy for making his books speak to young readers. *Rocket Ship Galileo* (1947), the first of the juveniles, demonstrates a respect for its readers that would define quality YASF for decades to come. *Galileo* is consistently impressed with the abilities of its teenage boys, and its plot is enabled by the conceit that a world-class scientist all but begs a group of boys to join him in high science. In frequent incidents, too, the book is respectful of teenagers' ability to understand science, as in the long discussions of how to test the rocket ship, demand evidence through observation, determine latitude and longitude through geometry, and handle key ratios of rocket fuel mass to thrust. In these scenes, Heinlein is respectful of not only his imaginary teens, but also his teen readers, trusting them to follow difficult explanations of math and science.

Consequently, key components of contemporary YASF are Heinleinian. The tropes and themes popular throughout the genre are often borrowed directly from the juveniles, and because they sold so well, their general attitude of respect toward young readers became standard. New writers and editors of YASF found it impossible to ignore Heinlein. Similarly, YASF scholarship compulsively turns toward Heinlein. This is often necessary when making a point about the history of the genre: Sands and Frank note the invigorating effect *Rocket Ship Galileo* had on the industry (Sands and Frank 1999: 1–2), Sullivan (1999a) uses the date of *Galileo*'s publication as a starting point for a chapter of the history of the category in America, and Francis J. Molson goes as far as to argue that *Tom Swift*, one of the juveniles' few clear predecessors, experienced a rebirth because of *Rocket Ship Galileo* (Molson 1993: 10). In arguing a history of Australian science fiction for young readers, John Foster must first grapple with the perception that YASF did not exist at all prior to Heinlein (Foster 1999: 85). Even analyses of the role of YASF in education often turn to Heinlein for examples, as when Fred Erisman (1991) explains how the juveniles teach cultural literacy or Sullivan extends an argument about the juveniles to argue that "Science fiction readers are the least likely to become calcified adults" (Sullivan 1999b: 3).

To contemporary scholarship, Heinlein is the most important figure in YASF, but in focusing on him the field has arguably minimized the importance of Andre Norton. Historically, her most important YASF is slightly predated by Heinlein's juveniles, and her contributions to the field clearly draw on his work, but she brings a significantly different emphasis to the genre. Conceiving of YASF as organized around Norton, a female writer who chose a gender-ambiguous name because of her predominantly male audience, could provoke interesting gender readings of the field. Similarly provocative is Norton's use of animals, a major characteristic of nearly all her work. Norton tends to imagine animals as comrades, rather than pets, of her central characters, sometimes with a bond between the two so deep that the division between human and animal becomes hazy. Again and again in Norton's YASF, these often telepathic companionships offer a profound way to reconceptualize the relationship between species. Seen with Norton as a central influence, the child–animal relationships that abound in YASF take on new significance. It is likely that this trope is only the first of many that would need to be reconsidered, were the history of YASF reconfigured around her.

Overlap and tensions between YA and sf scholarship

There are many reasons that scholarship written from a children's literature perspective will fundamentally differ from that written from an sf studies perspective. There are, for instance, theories about the history of children's literature that force questions that sf scholarship is not situated to notice. Consider, for example, Franklin's classic study of Heinlein, written from an sf perspective. In tracing Heinlein's reading history, Franklin notes that "Heinlein was an avid reader of the Frank Reade, Jr., and Tom Swift science-fiction dime novels, and there are still copies of them in his library.

His reading gradually moved on to authors with deep ties to this literature, including Verne, Edgar Rice Burroughs, and H.G. Wells, as well as the science fiction and other works of Mark Twain, Rudyard Kipling, and Jack London" (Franklin 1980: 11–12). This passage describes how Heinlein fits into the history of sf, correctly and insightfully linking him to various figures important to the history of the fantastic, but because Franklin is intent on telling that history, he does not pursue the influences *within the history of children's literature* that helped Heinlein conceive of YASF in its current form.

From a children's literature perspective, even the brief list Franklin gives offers provocative hints about the relationship between the Heinlein juveniles and literature for young readers in the first half of the twentieth century. Burroughs, Twain, Kipling, London, and the dime novels Franklin mentions were all key figures in a period of the history of children's literature that saw a deep divide forming between fiction marketed for boys and fiction marketed for girls. The influences Franklin mentions clearly fell on the masculine side of that divide, and children's literature scholarship has thought extensively about the implications of such a division. Put in this context, Heinlein's repeated linking to the pattern embraced by early twentieth-century stories for boys becomes striking: strapping young lads light out for the territories, dodging the feminizing effects of domesticity in favor of the deadly but free society that forges – so the story goes – manhood. This is evident throughout the juveniles, particularly in *Red Planet*: in the boys' successful and formative adventure fleeing from the headmaster who would make them gentlemen, in the men's and boys' frustration with women, in the casual insult "pantywaist," and elsewhere. From a children's literature perspective, then, it quickly becomes obvious that the series that shaped YASF for decades to come was itself patterned after stories which sought to produce manly men through anti-domestic boys.

Just as YA perspectives yield insights that sf scholarship has missed, sf scholarship provides perspectives not otherwise available. YASF often uses themes or conceits that appear tired to an sf reader, prompting sf scholars to comment on YASF in ways that YA scholars would not consider. Take, for example, Monica Hughes's *The Keeper of the Isis Light*, whose teenage female protagonist has two pivotal problems: the devastating loneliness of space and the relative nature of beauty. Raymond E. Jones reads Hughes's classic YASF novel as a profound analysis of "a female ethic" (Jones 1999: 15), but sf scholars would have a difficult time praising the novel because its two central problems are so familiar as to have become clichéd. No doubt many children's literature scholars recognize this, but from their perspective it is a minor problem: clichés can be excused if they produce a text useful to young readers, and "a female ethic" certainly fits that bill. Consequently, even the highest quality YASF is free to return again and again to the trough of outworn sf tropes. This frees children's literature scholars to ignore the familiarity of the themes that invigorate extraordinary YASF novels such as *The Keeper of the Isis Light*, but it also provides sf scholars with opportunities to explain the rich literary heritage of those themes.

Another fundamental difference between children's literature scholarship and sf scholarship is that the former is often inclined toward reader-response theory. This tendency creates two problems for new scholars in the field, namely that they often either ignore the inclination or comply with it too hastily. In the latter (and more visible) case, new scholars tend to insist that children's literature must be inoffensive. The reasoning behind this is obvious: if children's literature scholarship is concerned about the effect of the literature on the child reading it, one assumes that the literature must be judged according to its offensiveness. For such writers, the word "inappropriate" – meaning tinged by knowledge of sex, violence, or vulgar language – enables a quick dismissal of books that actually speak quite well to the experience of young readers. Children's literature scholarship does regularly use the word "inappropriate" to condemn a book, but only if it uses formatting, narrative strategies, or subtleties that do not match up with the abilities of readers of the age for which the book is intended. Therefore, children's literature specialists might question the appropriateness of Peter Dickinson's *Eva* (1988) for adolescent readers: they would do so because it uses a small, closely packed font, introduces its premise after readers have already formed their basic understanding of the story, and ignores long periods of time, all of which can frustrate an apprentice reader. The fact that the protagonist destroys property, conspires to steal, and copulates with multiple partners, however, does not constitute inappropriateness, at least from the perspective of children's literature scholarship. Indeed, from a YA perspective, *Eva* does not deal *enough* with the protagonist's sexuality, but treats it clinically and with nothing like the nervous excitement typical of actual teen reactions to sexual maturity.

But it is also true that scholars new to the field of children's literature have a tendency to under-deploy sensitivity to what is "appropriate" to young readers. In children's literature scholarship, the relationship between the literature and its ideal reader is a common topic. It does not precisely draw from reader-response theory, almost never quoting theorists, but it is always aware of how young readers can be affected by and interact with the literature. This should not be surprising: this is one of the few fields of literature named after its reading audience, so the presence of the reader is always felt in children's literature scholarship. Because there is an enormous amount of information available on what children and readers of early ages can understand, what they often prefer and what their cognitive needs and inabilities are, there is excellent research on which to draw in thinking about how children's literature and its primary readers interact. Therefore, the boundary between traditional literary analysis (whether close reading, application of literary theory, or historical contextualization) and reader-response has become quite porous. For example, Michael Levy's analysis of representations of consumer culture in YASF makes an extended series of comparisons between two YASF stories (Jennifer Armstrong and Nancy Butcher's *Fire-Us* trilogy (2002–3) and M.T. Anderson's *Feed* (2002)) and adult sf. Following immediately upon the heels of this genre analysis, Levy observes that Butcher provides a fairly concrete ending, but that the same is not true of Anderson: "*Feed*, however, perhaps because it was written for older teenagers who can presumably deal with a bit more ambiguity, closes with no real resolution" (Levy 2006: 12). Similarly, John Stephens (2006) slips confidently between theories of performativity and actual children's gendered behavior in his reading of children's literature. For this field, then, literary analyses do not require justification in terms of how readers will react to texts, but they can always make easy use of that knowledge.

As I have demonstrated, there are important points of overlap and potential benefit between the perspectives of YA and sf scholarship. However, when weighing the importance of traditional traits of sf in YASF, fundamental differences, even incompatibilities, emerge between these perspectives. At times, they seem less than profound, as when Sands and Frank complain that humor in YASF poses a danger "of producing faulty scientific notions in young readers" (Sands and Frank 1999: 59). While this might seem merely a version of an sf reader's insistence that the genre must contain accurate science, they are actually reiterating the by-now familiar argument that children's literature must be responsible to the young readers consuming it: science itself is not sacred, but an adolescent's consumption of it is, and therefore a children's literature scholar might be (incidentally) concerned about the accuracy of a text's science. Thom Dunn and Karl Hiller (1993), on the other hand, express the inverse of this complaint from an sf perspective. Their article on H.M. Hoover opens with an expression of frustration that children's and young adult sf does not adequately observe genre rules, blending sf and fantasy at will. But the uncomfortable truth is that less-than-rigorous science and casual disregard of genre boundaries within the fantastic do not appear as major problems to children's literature scholars, certainly not in the same way that they are to many sf scholars. Instead, the primary concern is always the relevance of the fiction to the readers, which is why when Sands and Frank worry about the science, they are really expressing a concern that humorous sf might accidentally *teach* inaccurate science.

There is some sense that YASF has profoundly different aims from those of adult sf. Writing in *The New York Review of Science Fiction*, Farah Mendlesohn complains that YASF's "growing tendency" to turn inward "closes down the universe for children, reducing sf to either metaphor or to a means to resolve personal problems"; she also accuses YASF of badly flubbing its science, failing to "reflect the values of sf", and producing "novels of manners with sf scenery" (Mendlesohn 2004: 10). She singles out one novel that has received a great deal of praise from children's literature critics: "A recent such horror perpetrated on the market is Jeanne DuPrau's *City of Ember*. The book is very well written, and the characters are vivid, but the scientific and technological premises of the book are so flawed that it would never have made it off an sf editor's slushpile" (Mendlesohn 2004: 10). This brief analysis makes clear two related points. First, from an sf perspective, good writing and vivid characters are nice, but flawed science is damning (and, as Mendlesohn implies, YASF such as DuPrau's does in fact frequently wink at scientific rigor and sf's "outward-bound" tendencies). Second, because children's literature scholars have praised the book so fully, this major criterion by which sf scholarship judges sf is evidently of limited importance to work published in children's literature journals.

Indeed, the mission of YASF might be so different from the mission of sf that there is no reconciling the two. Mike Cadden writes that "while science fiction tends to give us more or less complete characters reacting to a world or universe in dramatic flux, young adult literature gives us the constant in the form of the wide world and shows the dynamism in the developing character in response to that world" (Cadden 2006: 430). This generalization resonates strongly with Mendlesohn's complaint that YASF transforms the "values of sf" into "a means to resolve personal problems." As we have already seen, the primary criterion in analyzing YASF from a children's literature perspective is the relevance of the fiction to the reader, and children's literature in general has shown a tendency toward the analysis of interior issues, at least since the publication of J.D. Salinger's *Catcher in the Rye* (1951). To put it plainly, children's literature scholars are interested in whether YASF obeys genre rules, but that interest is dwarfed by the scholarship's fascination with the relevance of the literature to young readers, a relevance often signaled by a text's attention to exactly the personal problems Mendlesohn mentions. In order to examine the psychological realism of YASF's young protagonists, the genre will focus on, as Cadden puts it, a static world and a "developing character in response to that world." Therefore, if the science, outward-bound nature, and other values of sf that are of utmost importance to sf scholarship come into conflict with the mission of exploring the emotional engagement of young adults, children's literature scholarship is willing to sacrifice the former in the name of the latter.

Bibliography

Bailey, K.V. and Sawyer, A. (1999) "The Janus Perspective: science fiction and the young adult reader in Britain," in C.W. Sullivan III (ed.) *Young Adult Science Fiction*, Westport, CT: Greenwood Press.

Cadden, M. (2006) "Taking Different Roads to the City: the development of Ursula K. Le Guin's young adult novels," *Extrapolation*, 47(3): 427–44.

Dunn, T. and Hiller, K. (1993) "Growing Home: the triumph of youth in the novels of H.M. Hoover," in C.W. Sullivan III (ed.) *Science Fiction for Young Readers*, Westport, CT: Greenwood Press.

Erisman, F. (1991) "Robert Heinlein, the Scribner Juveniles, and Cultural Literacy," *Extrapolation*, 32(1): 45–53.

Foster, J. (1999) "Australian Science Fiction for Children and Adolescents: 1940–1990," in C.W. Sullivan III (ed.) *Young Adult Science Fiction*, Westport, CT: Greenwood Press.

Franklin, H.B. (1980) *Robert A. Heinlein: America as science fiction*, New York: Oxford University Press.

Jones, R.E. (1993) "'True Myth': female archetypes in Monica Hughes's *The Keeper of the Isis Light*," in C.W. Sullivan III (ed.) *Science Fiction for Young Readers*, Westport, CT: Greenwood Press.

—— (1999) "Re-Visioning *Frankenstein*: *The Keeper of the Isis Light* as theodicy," *Canadian Children's Literature/Littérature Canadienne pour la Jeunesse*, 25(1): 6–19.

Levy, M.M. (1999) "The Young Adult Science Fiction Novel as *Bildungsroman*," in C.W. Sullivan III (ed.) *Young Adult Science Fiction*, Westport, CT: Greenwood Press.

—— (2006) "'The Sublimation of Real Life': malls, shopping, and advertising in recent young adult sf," *New York Review of Science Fiction*, 18(7): 10–12.

Mendlesohn, F. (2004) "Does Ontogeny Recapitulate Phylogeny? Cognitive development, science fiction and science fiction for children," *New York Review of Science Fiction*, 16(11): 1, 6–11.

Molson, F.J. (1993) "The Tom Swift Books," in C.W. Sullivan III (ed.) *Science Fiction for Young Readers*, Westport, CT: Greenwood Press.

Palumbo, D. (1999) "Science Fiction in Comic Books: science fiction colonizes a fantasy medium," in C.W. Sullivan III (ed.) *Young Adult Science Fiction*, Westport, CT: Greenwood Press.

Reid, S.N. (1998) *Presenting Young Adult Science Fiction*, New York: Twayne Publishers.

Sands, K. and Frank, M. (1999) *Back in the Spaceship Again: juvenile science fiction series since 1945*, Westport, CT: Greenwood Press.

Smedman, M.S. (1993) "The 'Terrible Journey' Past 'Dragons in the Waters' to a 'House Like a Lotus':

faces of love in the fiction of Madeleine L'Engle," in C.W. Sullivan III (ed.) *Science Fiction for Young Readers*, Westport, CT: Greenwood Press.

Stephens, J. (2006) "Performativity and the Child Who May Not Be a Child," *Papers: Explorations into Children's Literature*, 16(1): 5–13.

Sullivan III, C.W. (1993a) "Heinlein's Juveniles: growing up in outer space," in *Science Fiction for Young Readers*, Westport, CT: Greenwood Press.

—— (1993b) "Introduction," in *Science Fiction for Young Readers*, Westport, CT: Greenwood Press.

—— (1999a) "American Young Adult Science Fiction Since 1947," in *Young Adult Science Fiction*, Westport, CT: Greenwood Press.

—— (1999b) "Introduction: extrapolation and the young adult reader," in *Young Adult Science Fiction*, Westport, CT: Greenwood Press.

Wytenbroek, J.R. (1993) "The Debate Continues: technology or nature – a study of Monica Hughes's science fiction novels," in C.W. Sullivan III (ed.) *Science Fiction for Young Readers*, Westport, CT: Greenwood Press.

Part IV
SUBGENRES

45
ALTERNATE HISTORY
Karen Hellekson

The alternate history (also known as alternative history, alternate universe, allohistory, uchronia, and parahistory) is that branch of nonrealistic literature that concerns itself with history turning out differently than we know to be the case. Although alternate histories were published in the 1700s, and although historians write such "counterfactuals" or "subjunctive conditionals" as thought-experiments with which to study causality, the alternate history has become chiefly associated with sf for two reasons: many sf writers are drawn to this subgenre and it provides one way of posing sf's fundamental question, "What if the world were different?" In the alternate history, a historical moment (a "nexus point" or "Jonbar hinge," the latter coined in Jack Williamson's *The Legion of Time* (1938)) is altered and the author explores the consequences of this divergence. The alternate history asks questions about time, linearity, determinism, and the implicit link between past and present. It considers the individual's role in making history, and it foregrounds the constructedness and narrativity of history. Typically, the nexus point refers to "our" world, but in some instances authors instead create an entirely different world or push the action so far into the past or future that tracing the effect of the changed nexus point becomes difficult or impossible – for example, Brian Aldiss's *The Malacia Tapestry* (1976) relies on a Jonbar hinge in which intelligent life descends from dinosaurs, yet results in a world strikingly like that of Renaissance Italy.

In the first novel-length alternate history, Louis-Napoléon Geoffroy-Chateau's *Napoléon and the Conquest of the World, 1812–1832* (1836), Napoleon crushes all opposition and becomes emperor of the known world until his death in 1832. Another important early text, Charles Renouvier's *Uchronie* (*L'utopie dans l'histoire*) (1857, revised 1876), coined "uchronie," meaning "utopia in history," although this sense has been lost, with the term becoming synonymous with "alternate history" (and the source for the English "uchronia"). The idea of utopia is retained in uchronia insofar as many alternate history plots involve time-travelers trying to improve the world by altering its history.

The first known alternate history in English is Isaac d'Israeli's "Of a History of Events which have not happened" (1824). J.C. Squire's important *If It Had Happened Otherwise: lapses into imaginary history* (1931) comprises essays written by important figures in the belles-lettres, including Hilaire Belloc, G.K. Chesterton, and Winston

Churchill. These historical counterfactuals imagined specific events turning out differently, although writers played with genre constraints: Churchill's "If Lee had not Won the Battle of Gettysburg" is written as if a historian in another timestream were trying to imagine our history. Several of the essays present made-up primary texts – telegrams, newspaper clippings, footnoted extracts from articles and books – that force the reader to infer a history from these fragments. As readers do this, they, like the author, share in the effort of creating meaning. The reader becomes the historian, piecing together historical traces, with the payoff being the recognition of specific points of divergence. Such readerly activity also emphasizes the constructed nature of history: it is not found in these traces, but crafted by an active mind that seeks to make meaning from historical artifacts. Indeed, this activity makes up the alternate history's primary message.

Continuing this belles-lettres tradition are: Niall Ferguson's *Virtual History: alternatives and counterfactuals* (1997); Robert Cowley's *What If? The world's foremost military historians imagine what might have been* (1999); Eric B. Henriet's *Revisited History: panorama of all forms of uchronia* (1999, rev. 2004), a French book-length essay which presents about 500 examples of alternate histories in many genres; and many of Peter G. Tsouras's edited volumes, including *Rising Sun Victorious: an alternate history of the Pacific War* (2007). These kinds of essayistic counterfactuals are concerned with questions particularly relevant to the historian: Who brings about history? Is the historian a transcriber of facts or a site of synthesis? Can anyone involved with making history be disinterested? What can be inferred from information? The counterfactual seeks to explore these ideas through the genre of the historical text, and the fictional texts so created read like history, not fiction.

Writers quickly applied fiction-writing techniques to the counterfactual thought-experiment. The earliest short story in the genre is Nathaniel Hawthorne's "P.'s Correspondence" (1845), with Mark Twain's *A Connecticut Yankee in King Arthur's Court* following in 1889. Murray Leinster's "Sidewise in Time" (1934) is generally recognized as the first alternate history in genre sf. The Sidewise Award for alternate histories (instituted 1995) is named after this important text, in which a natural upheaval of possible timelines occurs and an intrepid schoolteacher and his students negotiate a constantly changing landscape.

Many texts create rich alternate worlds that result, years later, from an effect following a point of divergence. Philip K. Dick's *The Man in the High Castle* (1962) explores the US 20 years after it lost the Second World War, leading to occupation by the Nazis and the Japanese. Dick focuses on conceiving of the world as something constructed by an individual mind, thereby linking history with ontological concerns. Dick's characters furtively pass around a banned alternate history, *The Grasshopper Lies Heavy*, which posits yet another possible reality, one in which the Axis Powers lose the war, thanks to the US fleet being removed from Pearl Harbor. In addition to the three histories the reader must track – the novel's reality, the reality within *Grasshopper*, and the reader's own reality, against which the other realities are judged – another text, the *I Ching*, further destabilizes cause and effect and its relationship to reality, as both Dick himself and the fictional author of *Grasshopper* use it to divine what comes next as they write their texts. Random chance sits uneasily next to three realities, emphasizing that many realities may coexist, that perhaps there is no single "right" reality but only the one we can experience. The metahistorical discourse permitted by an alternate history within an alternate history is also used in Kingsley Amis's *The Alteration* (1976) and Terry Bisson's *Fire on the Mountain* (1988), further emphasizing the constructedness and artificiality of history-making.

In mystery writer Len Deighton's moody whodunit, *SS-GB* (1978), a police officer has to solve a murder while traversing the political minefield of Nazi-occupied Britain in 1941. Vladimir Nabokov's *Ada or Ardor: a family chronicle* (1969), a study of incest, takes place within an alternate North America partly settled by czarist Russia. In *It's a Wonderful Life* (Capra 1946), a man learns what the world would be like if he had never been born. *Sliding Doors* (Howitt 1998) follows two possible outcomes – whether or not a woman catches a train – to their simultaneous, individual conclusions. The intensely personal is well treated in Philip Roth's moving *The Plot Against America* (2004), in which Charles Lindbergh defeats Roosevelt in his third bid for the presidency, leading to heightened oppression. Roth explores the effect of larger historical forces on an individual, and the decision to make the story an alternate history destabilizes the happy ending (Nazism's defeat) that we thought we knew was to come.

A great number of alternate histories focus on warcraft and battles, often centering on pivotal battles during major wars, such as the Second World War or the US Civil War, granting great influence to the Jonbar hinges of specific battles. The authors most associated with this subgenre include Harry Turtledove (*Great War* multiseries (1997–2003)), Harry Harrison (*Stars and Stripes* trilogy (1998–2001)), and Newt Gingrich and William R. Forstchen (*Civil War* trilogy (2003–5)). These meticulously researched and historically accurate texts focus on the nexus event itself, rather than on the consequences years later. Steeped in the historical moment, they usually posit a different outcome to a crucial battle while fetishizing the components important to warcraft: leaders, technology, bureaucracy, chain of command, and strategy. They explore the work that must be done by many players in order to bring about an event, detailing the sheer multiplicity of converging factors necessary to create what we call "history" and so emphasizing its contingency. All these texts are studies of a single world created from a nexus event, pushing it to a logical conclusion and estranging history in such a way as to throw open the possibility of interpretation and critique.

Alternate histories that deal with time travel provide insight into both the nature of the history-making process in terms of the event and the importance of a single individual in bringing about events. The first sf story to develop and sustain a single alternate world was also a time-travel adventure: L. Sprague de Camp's *Lest Darkness Fall* (1941). A lightning strike sends historian Martin Padway back in time to sixth-century Italy. He realizes that he is at a crucial juncture of history, so he decides to do what he can to keep the Roman Empire from falling, and he single-handedly brings about an altered reality. In *Bring the Jubilee* (1953), Ward Moore writes the memoir of a historian who time travels to the past to witness a crucial Civil War battle and inadvertently changes his history, bringing about our own. The narrator agonizes about what he has done, fully aware that his single action has wiped out his entire world;

themes include time as arrow and time as endlessly repeated cycle. The historian fears he is doomed to endlessly replicate the events that wiped out his reality. In the *Star Trek* episode "The City on the Edge of Forever" (1967), time travel permits a change to be made in the 1930s that leads to a Nazi victory in the Second World War, and things must be set right so history can follow its established course, causing agony for Kirk, who must *not* save the woman he loves from death.

Alternate histories that use time travel highlight the possibility (or, conversely, the ineffectuality) of individuals' impact on history. With time travel, an informed agent has the opportunity to act; he or she is in a position of power, with knowledge of the future and often, as in Poul Anderson's *Time Patrol* stories (1955–95), in possession of gadgets that help them carry out their mission. The individual thus becomes a tool bent to history's great task: the agent actively attempts to bring about events. The idea of a time corps policing the timelines to ensure history happens as it should is a common one. In *Voyagers* (1982–3), a boy joins such a time-traveler, lending his excellent grasp of history to his companion's time-traveling device. In Isaac Asimov's *The End of Eternity* (1955), the Eternals, who live outside time, seek to alter history via Reality Changes, ostensibly to minimize human suffering. In *Quantum Leap* (1989–93), Sam Beckett leaps from body to body, temporarily taking it over so he can bring about a change to set history back on the "right" path.

Many texts explore the notion of changing the past to change the future. In *Back to the Future* (Zemeckis 1985), Marty McFly has to get his parents together after accidentally driving them apart so as to ensure that he will be born. In *The 4400* (2004–), people from the future kidnap people from the past and imbue them with special powers before returning them all at once, the better to alter the world and forestall its destruction. In *Seven Days* (1998–2001), a branch of US intelligence sends an agent back seven days in order to avert specific catastrophes. In *Timequest* (Dyke 2002), a man goes back in time to prevent John F. Kennedy's assassination. And in Gregory Benford's *Timescape* (1980), scientists send messages to themselves in the past to avoid future ecodisaster. Foreknowledge provides the impetus for bringing about a desired event. Humans, these texts imply, have the capacity to act and thereby affect the world; humans, not some faceless force, create history by their actions, just as they later construct histories by examining the traces left by the past.

Simultaneous alternate histories, or parallel worlds stories, posit the existence of a number of simultaneously existing alternate worlds, known as the "multiverse." H. Beam Piper's *Paratime Police* or *Lord Kalvan* stories (1948–65) describe a civilization that exploits the resources of parallel realities. In *Charlie Jade* (2005), a transworld accident sends a detective from one reality to another, with no way to get back, even as its repercussions echo through three universes. Joanna Russ's feminist polemic, *The Female Man* (1975), posits four different realities, none of them "ours," each with a very different woman whose name starts with J, made up of the same genetic material, each in a world where women have different social status, emphasizing that women's status relies on what men give them – or on there being no men at all. In *Sliders* (1995–2000), people slide from one universe to another, trying to find the way home, meeting other versions of themselves and discovering worlds with clearly discernible historical nexus points. The *Star Trek* franchise has repeatedly visited its Mirror Universe, first in "Mirror, Mirror" (1967). In this alternate reality, the benevolent Federation has been replaced by the evil Empire, thanks to humans killing the alien ambassador who was to make first contact. *Star Trek: The Next Generation* (1987–94), *Star Trek: Deep Space Nine* (1993–9), and *Enterprise* (2001–5) all revisit the Empire, as do several *Star Trek* novels, with characters meeting their evil analogs.

In addition to cause and effect, these texts query nature versus nurture: the exact same genetic material results in different individuals, depending on the milieu in which they live. These texts conclude that humans have no individual essential nature but rather are beings constructed by the forces of their world. Just as history is constructed, so is the individual. Parallel worlds stories assume that history can change at almost any point, even if seemingly insignificant, with every choice resulting in a new universe splitting off. This provides great power to the individual while simultaneously indicating that because everything literally happens, there is no moral imperative.

46

APOCALYPTIC SF

Aris Mousoutzanis

Sf is often considered to be the dominant twentieth-century site for the expression of visions of apocalypse and catastrophe, something that might seem paradoxical for a genre originally associated with ideas of scientific progress and technological utopianism. And yet, this transmutation may be interpreted precisely by focusing on the significance of modern ideas of "progress" for sf as well as on its status as "the expression of, or reflection upon, the terrors and delights of technologized modernity" (Luckhurst 2005: 170). As Walter Benjamin (1939) argues, the "concept of progress" has always been "grounded in the idea of catastrophe," and "That things 'just go on' *is* the catastrophe" (Benjamin 1985: 50). Progress implies the destruction of an existing state of affairs so that it can be replaced by a new one (etymologically, "catastrophe" – from the Greek *kata* (over) and *strephein* (turn) – means an "overturning of a given situation" (Doane 1990: 228)). Furthermore, during the modern period, catastrophe became increasingly associated with technology, since new means of transportation, such as the railway, increased the potential for accidents (see Schivelbusch 1977). Therefore, catastrophe "is, through its association with industrialization and the advance of technology, ineluctably linked with the idea of Progress" (Doane 1990: 230). The convergence of sf and catastrophe may therefore be interpreted in terms of their shared relationship to modern conceptions of progress and technology. Tracing the trajectory of catastrophe fiction may elucidate the ways in which technological modernity developed during the past two centuries.

From this perspective, it seems hardly coincidental that the earliest examples of futuristic narratives now considered to be precursors of apocalyptic sf appear at a crucial cultural moment for the project of modernity, the late eighteenth century. The publication of the anonymous *Reign of King George VI* (1763) and Louis-Sébastien Mercier's *The Year 2440* (1771) marks "the beginnings of a vast new literature of anticipation, which has been characteristic of the industrialized nations" (Clarke 1979: 2) and should be seen as indebted to the future-oriented narrative of progress. The same period, however, witnessed the production of a number of texts whose outlook was anything but utopian and optimistic. Mercier's Enlightenment optimism was countered by narratives such as Jean-Baptiste Cousin de Grainville's epic poem *The Last Man* (1805), whose theme was adopted by Mary Shelley in her *The Last Man* (1826). The first "last man" novel published in English, Shelley's text, which staged the extinction of the human race by a plague, anticipated the "viral apocalypse" subgenre that was to figure prominently in later texts such as Edgar Allan Poe's "The Masque of the Red Death" (1842), Jack London's *The Scarlet Plague* (1912), Richard Matheson's *I Am Legend* (1954), Michael Crichton's *The Andromeda Strain* (1969), Neal Stephenson's *Snow Crash* (1992), and Margaret Atwood's *Oryx and Crake* (2003), as well as sf "zombie" movies, from *Night of the Living Dead* (Romero 1968) and *Shivers* (Cronenberg 1975) to *28 Days Later* (Boyle 2002) and the videogame-derived *Resident Evil* (Anderson 2002).

Shelley's *The Last Man* has been described as the "grandparent to an entire genre of elegiac British disaster stories, more directly fathered by Richard Jefferies' *After London* (1885)" (Stableford 2003: 19). In creating a landscape where nature has aggressively reasserted its dominance over civilization after some unspecified catastrophe, *After London* introduces a mode of writing that would later evolve into the post-holocaust novel of survival, as well as later narratives of natural disaster, such as J.G. Ballard's *The Drowned World* (1962), Kim Stanley Robinson's *Three Californias* trilogy (1984–90), and *The Day after Tomorrow* (Emmerich 2004). Texts like these represent the apocalypse as the result of either a lack of sensitivity to the planet's ecology or the inability of social systems to respond to environmental needs. Furthermore, *After London*'s depiction of quasi-medieval communities set the tone for later texts, such as John Christopher's *The Prince in Waiting* (1970), which represent the future as the return of the past. From literary narratives (e.g., H.G. Wells's *The Time Machine* (1895)) to blockbuster movies (e.g., the *Mad Max* trilogy (Miller 1979, 1981; Miller and Ogilvie 1985), and popular television series (e.g., *Planet of the Apes* (1974)), the post-apocalyptic future is often envisioned as the resurgence of a pre-modern, pre-industrial past. This is not unrelated to the status of catastrophe as the uncanny, repressed aspect of progress, as "the effaced signal of something which only takes on its value in the future" – the apocalypse, to paraphrase Jacques Lacan, "*will have been*" (Lacan 1988: 159). Because of this peculiar relationship to temporality, apocalyptic sf often flirts with time travel, as in the *Terminator* films (1984–) and *Twelve Monkeys* (Gilliam 1995). This is characteristic of some apocalyptic narratives that endlessly circle around but insistently deny the traumatic moment of total annihilation, which is never represented but only talked about or hinted at.

Stableford argues that, after such early nineteenth-century narratives as those by Grainville and Shelley, there was no significant production of disaster fiction before the last quarter of the century. The reason for this delay becomes evident when one considers as an alternative "father" of British disaster fiction Lieutenant-Colonel George Chesney's *The Battle of Dorking* (1871), the story of a successful German invasion of England. Published in the same year as Germany's victory in the Franco-Prussian War, the story was enormously popular and generated numerous imitations within months. This subgenre of "invasion scare" would persist throughout the period of a more aggressive and fiercely competitive "New Imperialism" (*c.* 1870–1914), as if to confirm Frank Kermode's suggestion that "the mythology of Empire and Apocalypse are very closely related" (Kermode 1967: 10). Strong feelings of confidence and jingoistic patriotism were then accompanied by a sense of guilt and anxiety about the prospect of impending disaster. This mood "underlay the popular literature" of the time and "simultaneously produced anxiety at the thought of invasion and confidence in England's capacity to defeat an enemy" (Beckson 1992: 364).

These mixed attitudes surrounding the invasion-scare novel help explain the fact that its most popular example is simultaneously highly representative and very atypical. Wells's *The War of the Worlds* (1898) follows the quasi-documentary format characteristic of the subgenre, as his narrator describes the Martians' destruction of specific southeast English towns in an "intensely visual fashion" that "frequently anticipated cinematic techniques" (Bergonzi 1961: 126), such as those later employed in such disaster movies as *Independence Day* (Emmerich 1996), *Armageddon* (Bay 1998), and *Deep Impact* (Leder 1998), as well as Steven Spielberg's *War of the Worlds* (2005). In contrast to the tradition established by Jefferies, these examples demonstrate an almost sadistic fascination with representing massive destruction in minute detail. Wells's novel is also typical in that it is clearly didactic. However, unlike most invasion-scare novels, its message is not propagandistic but anti-imperialist. The Martian invasion is continuously compared to British imperialist practices and there is a strong sense that the British deserve what they suffer. The complexity of this text, however, lies mostly in Wells's translation of imperial conflict into a Darwinian struggle for the "survival of the fittest," as his evolutionarily advanced Martians are defeated not by humans but by bacteria. Wells placed Darwinism at the center of his apocalyptic vision of the future, something that became a recurring motif in catastrophe writing, often associated with the idea of the apocalypse as transcendence and revelation in narratives such as Olaf Stapledon's *Last and First Men* (1930) and *Last Men in London* (1932), and Greg Bear's "Blood Music" (1983).

The New Imperialism period also witnessed the first fictional references to atomic power. In Robert Cromie's *The Crack of Doom* (1895), the leader of a group of evil scientists invents a device which may set off a reaction that will "etherize" the Earth by disintegrating the atoms of a drop of water. But the first novel to mention an "atomic bomb" was Wells's *The World Set Free* (1914), inspired by Frederick Soddy's *Interpretation of Radium* (1909), and inspiring Leo Szilard, who read it in German in 1932 and, two years later, applied for a patent to cover his method of setting up a nuclear chain reaction. A rather peculiar relationship between science, fiction, and reality can thus be found at the very start of the Nuclear Age, which became typical of nuclear catastrophe fiction, most of which condemns nuclear war but also gains an awkward legitimacy from it. Many sf narratives suddenly began to appear more plausible and realistic, and the atomic bomb served as a starting point for many sf classics. These either described the irreversible total extinction of the human race in the aftermath of a nuclear war, such as Nevil Shute's *On the Beach* (1957), or focused on the possibilities for rebirth and revelation in a much more distant future, as in Walter M. Miller Jr's *A Canticle for Leibowitz* (1959).

Catastrophe fiction has often been criticized for being sexist, an argument made for example by Maria Minich Brewer who, pointing to Russell Hoban's *Riddley Walker* (1980) and Denis Johnson's *Fiskadoro* (1985), notes that "the narrative of the Oedipal quest of male desire survives intact, continuing to dictate its laws of male identification and rivalry" (Brewer 1987). However, this argument seems to ignore the ways in which the apocalyptic sf discourse has been appropriated, reworked, or subverted by female writers, especially during the rise of feminist sf in the late 1960s and 1970s. Toxic wastes and mad scientists were combined with sex changes and gender benders in Angela Carter's post-apocalyptic *Heroes and Villains* (1969) and *The Passion of New Eve* (1977). Doris Lessing's *Memoirs of a Survivor* (1974), an abstract first-person narrative, hovers between autobiography, fable, and allegory as its initially unidentifiable narrator observes from her window a post-apocalyptic society ridden with anarchy and chaos. Marge Piercy's *Woman on the Edge of Time* (1976) relies on sf motifs such as time travel and utopia in order to create a feminist future as an alternative to a dystopian technological present. "What is fragmentation of identity to apocalyptic thinkers," narratives like these seem to testify, "may be an exhilarating experience of personal coming-to-voice for others" (Quinby 1994: 47).

An exemplary text in the tradition of feminist apocalypse is Octavia Butler's *Xenogenesis* trilogy (1987–9), which stages the arrival of the gene-splicing alien Oankali, who comes to rescue humanity – on the verge of extinction following a nuclear holocaust – through a project of hybridization that will create posthuman "constructs." While the trilogy has been praised for the ways in which it uses sf motifs to explore ideas of gender and racial otherness, it is also significant as a feminist alternative to contemporary cyberpunk, whose ambiguous gender politics generated critical debate. Cyberpunk's proponents, however, presented the subgenre itself as an alternative, as a movement against the hip apocalypticism of the late twentieth century: cyberpunk's distinguishing feature was "its boredom with the Apocalypse" (Sterling 1986: 12). Next to the accumulating narratives of nuclear catastrophe, there were novels such as William Gibson's *Neuromancer* (1984), whose setting is the post-apocalyptic cityscape of the Sprawl, whose cyberspace resembles a technological New Jerusalem where "death shall be no more," and whose main plot about the fusion of two AIs into a godlike entity leads to a final anticlimax: "Things aren't different. Things are things" (Gibson 1984: 270). For cyberpunks, the catastrophe had already happened, after the advent of cyberculture and consumer culture – those aspects of the postwar West that were at the heart of contemporary critical debates on postmodernism, with which cyberpunk has often been compared. *Neuromancer* represented an "inverted millenarianism in which premonitions of the future, catastrophic or redemptive, have been replaced by the senses of the end of this or that" (Jameson 1991: 1). That the perceived crisis of modernity suggested by postmodernists was narrativized in popular sf in post-apocalyptic terms further testifies to catastrophe's status as the uncanny underside of modernity and progress.

The appeal of the apocalypse might have been expected to subside after the year 2000. And yet, in the post-9/11 era, catastrophe fiction has hardly lost its popularity – in 2007, Cormac McCarthy's post-apocalyptic novel, *The Road* (2006), was awarded the Pulitzer Prize for Fiction, while Kim Stanley Robinson's *Science in the Capital* trilogy (2004–7) concluded with ecocatastrophe held, just barely and temporarily, at bay; the sun threatened to die in *Sunshine* (Boyle 2007), while viral apocalypse loomed in *The Invasion* (Hirschbiegel 2007), *Resident Evil: Extinction* (Mulcahy 2007), and *28*

Weeks Later (Fresnadillo 2007); the post-nuclear story of *Jericho* (2006–) continued, while *The Terminator: The Sarah Connor Chronicles* (2008–) was in production. The question is: would we really like to see the "end" of catastrophe fiction? For some, this would signify that political conflicts had ended, and social ills been cured; for others, it would mean that society has stagnated into a static, one-dimensional utopia. The continued imagination of the apocalypse suggests that it might not have happened yet.

Bibliography

Beckson, K. (1992) *London in the 1890s: a cultural history*, New York and London: W.W. Norton & Company.

Benjamin, W. (1985) "Central Park," 1939, trans. L. Spencer and M. Harrington, *New German Critique*, 34: 32–58.

Bergonzi, B. (1961) *The Early H.G. Wells: a study of the scientific romances*, Manchester: Manchester University Press.

Brewer, M.M. (1987) "Surviving Fictions: gender and difference in postmodern and postnuclear narrative," *Discourse*, 9: 37–52.

Clarke, I.F. (1979) *The Pattern of Expectation 1644–2001*, London: Jonathan Cape.

Doane, M.A. (1990) "Information, Crisis, Catastrophe," in P. Mellencamp (ed.) *Logics of Television: essays in cultural criticism*, Bloomington: Indiana University Press.

Gibson, W. (1984) *Neuromancer*, New York: Ace.

Jameson, F. (1991) *Postmodernism, or, The Cultural Logic of Late Capitalism*, London and New York: Verso.

Kermode, F. (1967) *The Sense of an Ending: studies in the theory of fiction*, Oxford: Oxford University Press.

Lacan, J. (1988) *The Seminar of Jacques Lacan, Book 1: Freud's papers on technique 1953–1954*, ed. Jacques-Alain Miller, trans. J. Forrester, Cambridge: Cambridge University Press.

Luckhurst, R. (2005) *Science Fiction*, Cambridge: Polity.

Quinby, L. (1994) *Anti-Apocalypse: essays in genealogical criticism*, Minneapolis: University of Minnesota Press.

Schivelbusch, W. (1977) *The Railway Journey: the industrialization of time and space in the 19th century*, Leamington Spa: Berg.

Stableford, B. (2003) "Science Fiction Before the Genre," in E. James and F. Mendlesohn (eds) *The Cambridge Companion to Science Fiction*, Cambridge: Cambridge University Press.

Sterling, B. (1986) "Introduction," in W. Gibson, *Burning Chrome*, London: Gollancz.

47
ARTHOUSE SF FILM
Stacey Abbott

In 1968, Stanley Kubrick's *2001: A Space Odyssey* encapsulated the two new directions facing sf cinema. On the one hand, its large budget and cutting-edge special effects, created by Douglas Trumbull, removed the sf film from the realm of the comparatively low-budget B-Movie of the 1950s and situated it clearly within big-budget Hollywood cinema. On the other hand, in its slow pace, poetic visual imagery, and narrative ambiguity, it had far more in common with arthouse cinema (or art film) than with previous Hollywood output. Arthouse cinema, originally associated with European cinema in the 1940s–1960s but now considered to range much more widely, refers to a type of filmmaking that exists in opposition to the Hollywood mainstream, and is defined as much by the means of distribution and exhibition as by a set of textual characteristics. Traditionally distributed by small independent companies, arthouse films are aimed at cineaste audiences and screened in alternative venues, such as independent or repertory cinemas, cinematheques, and galleries. As such, they are often associated with "culture" and "high art," rather than "entertainment." Having said this, independent and cult films that are often associated with "entertainment," and which similarly exist outside the mainstream, also often find a home in arthouse cinemas and have much in common with the art film. Both largely emerged in opposition to the classical Hollywood system, which had come to dominate filmmaking practice, and the art film in particular enabled other national cinemas to establish their own indigenous style of filmmaking distinct from Hollywood (Bordwell 1979; Neale 1981). The one factor that scholars and industry practitioners agree on is that "art films are *not* mainstream Hollywood films" (Wilinsky 2001: 15).

Arthouse sf, therefore, refers to films made beyond mainstream Hollywood. As a result this category can apply equally to films made outside of the US, such as *Solaris* (Tarkovsky 1972) and *Cube* (Natali 1997), within the American independent sector such as *Pi* (Aronofsky 1998) and *Primer* (Carruth 2004), and as part of underground cult cinema such as *Night of the Living Dead* (Romero 1968), *The Rocky Horror Picture Show* (Sharman 1975), and *Repo Man* (Cox 1984). Furthermore, it is not necessarily distinguished by its narratives, for it can include many of the same types of sf story as are found in more mainstream fare, from space travel to dystopias. Instead, it integrates sf's established narrative or thematic preoccupations with the stylistic and artistic approaches of the art film. As Geoff King and Tanya Krzywinska point out, "Films such as *2001: A Space Odyssey*, *Solaris*, *La Jetée* (1963), *Alphaville* (1965) and *Born in Flames* (1983) use science fiction to explore existential and/or political questions that were implicit in some of the films of the 1950s" (King and Krzywinska 2000: 6). Rather than embed such typical concerns within a seemingly spectacular and action-oriented filmmaking style, art cinema sf overtly explores the narrative complexities of and philosophical questions raised by the genre.

One of the key elements of art cinema is realism (real locations, problems, sexuality, and characterization) (Bordwell 1979: 57). While the genre is by its very nature speculative and often explores futuristic and/or fantasy narratives, such as time travel, space exploration, or alien visitation/invasion, arthouse sf's association with concepts of realism distinguishes it from more mainstream examples of the genre. The use of real locations is often mixed with realistically presented futuristic sets, creating a believable and recognizable environment in which to set the narrative. In so doing, arthouse sf often fosters a sense of genuine scientific speculation. For instance, while imagining what space travel might be like in the future, *2001* grounds its presentation within real experience. The journey to the orbiting lunar station is presented as a spaceflight, replete with attendants wearing Pan Am uniforms, serving refreshments, and defying the weightlessness of their environment through their gravity shoes. Presenting the future as a "realistic" or believable extension of the present provides the film with a sense of plausibility. This might be what the future will be like.

More significantly, arthouse sf draws from the art film its preference for psychologically complex characters and narrative ambiguity by emphasizing psychological motivation over cause-and-effect plot construction. As David Bordwell explains, "art cinema is less concerned with action than reaction" (Bordwell 1979: 58). For instance, *Solaris* begins on Earth in a recognizable country home as the scientist Kelvin prepares to leave his family and go on his mission to the eponymous planet. Other than a videophone, the house is unencumbered with the gadgets and technology often central to sf *mise en scène*. The pacing of this sequence is slow, with little narrative action: Kelvin simply wanders his surroundings, contemplating thoughts about the journey and his family that remain unexpressed. The film, therefore, focuses its attention not upon its space-travel narrative but rather upon the character. In fact, it takes 41 minutes for Kelvin to get into space – a stark contrast to more mainstream films, such as *Aliens* (Cameron 1986). When he arrives at the space station orbiting Solaris, he finds a lived-in environment, not overly laden with technology and scientific apparatus but rather cluttered with debris and rubbish, reflecting the disoriented psychological state of the cosmonauts. The *mise en scène* is more concerned with inner psychology than an imagined future.

In *The Man Who Fell to Earth* (Roeg 1976), the alien Thomas Newton poses as a human in order to recover water for his dying planet and more importantly to save his own family. But rather than tracking him step by step as he amasses a fortune and builds the rocket ship necessary for him to return home, the film focuses on the impact of human existence upon his alien sensibilities. He is regularly physically overwhelmed by the speed and the violence of modern society, passing out as a result of the motion of an elevator and having to leave a Japanese restaurant because he is disturbed by the ferocity of a Kabuki performance. The violence of this sequence is enhanced by Nicolas Roeg's decision to intercut the performance with an aggressive sex scene, reinforcing the image of modern humanity as a hostile race. Finally, it is through the corruption and downfall of the alien, as he becomes desensitized to the world around him and addicted to both alcohol and the stimulus of modern media, that Roeg offers his most convincing commentary on what it means to be human.

Similarly, Tarkovsky uses *Solaris*'s first-contact narrative to explore questions about memory, guilt, and remorse. Rather than develop an overt first-contact story as seen in many Hollywood films from *The Day the Earth Stood Still* (Wise 1951) to *Star Trek: First Contact* (Frakes 1996), which present the first encounter between humans and aliens as either a direct meeting or an alien invasion, *Solaris*'s first contact is metaphysical. Following experiments upon the oceans of Solaris, the crew of the station are haunted by corporeal visitations of people from their past. The scientists speculate that the planet's ocean is alive and has read their dreams in order to produce living specters from their past, including Kelvin's dead wife Hari, as a means of communication. In this manner, the film is less interested in the encounter with the "aliens" than in the psychological impact of the "visitors" upon the cosmonauts. As Steve Neale points out, the art film is often categorized by the "interiorisation of dramatic conflict" (Neale 1981: 13). In *Solaris*, this is manifested in the muted and introspective Kelvin. His initial reaction to the impossible sight of his dead wife is one of fear and revulsion, conveyed not through histrionics but rather his decision to eject her into space. However, when she reappears the next day he becomes increasingly preoccupied by her, but does not question how and why she can be there. Through her, he explores his own remorse for his role in the demise of their relationship and her subsequent suicide. Furthermore, as she becomes aware that she is not the real Hari, the film also focuses upon questions of humanity and the nature of being. If she is not Hari, then who is she? As with most arthouse sf, *Solaris* does not provide any clear answers to the many questions it poses, but instead uses the genre as a means of exploring these existential themes.

Arthouse sf is further identified by its visual aesthetics. Neale suggests that in the art film, there is a "stress on visual style," but not the "institutionalised spectacle" we associate with the Hollywood mainstream, but rather a personal form of creative expression (Neale 1981: 13). This can be seen in a more reflective and minimalist visual style than is found in blockbuster sf. The pacing is usually slow, the camera is observational, and the images do not necessarily progress the plot but instead often emphasize a certain poetic beauty. This approach often highlights the wondrous aspects of the genre and the artistic sensibilities of the director, as moments of spectacle or design are showcased. In *2001*, Kubrick privileges artistic spectacle for its own sake as the minor plot point about one ship docking at a space station is transformed into a cinematic ballet. In this sequence, the narrative pauses as the ship's circling of the station, accompanied by Johann Strauss's *Blue Danube*, is visually presented as a waltz. In George Lucas's *THX 1138* (1971), it is the art direction that conveys the director's minimalist vision for his dystopian future, while the "characters are at times reduced to dark silhouettes picked out against a blinding white background suggestive of a sterile, undifferentiated world in which individuality and love are suppressed" (King and Krzywinska 2000: 76). In *Alphaville*, Jean-Luc Godard uses jumpcuts and a disjunctive editing style, consistent with his French New Wave origins, alongside the graphic composition of modern architecture, set design, and expressionist chiaroscuro to convey his vision of an emotionally detached, technologically governed society.

This more contemplative style also encourages the audience to reflect upon the images that they see and to consider their meaning. Gone, for the most part, are the cinematic indicators that highlight significant elements so as to facilitate a clear understanding of the narrative. Instead, "audience members must work to keep up and figure out what is happening in such films" (Wilinsky 2001: 19). This approach to sf opens the genre to metaphysical speculation rather than the more grounded scientific rationale. This is best exemplified in the experimental time-travel film *La Jetée* (Marker 1963). Structured as a photomontage, the film is composed almost exclusively of still images of a man so haunted by an image of a woman from his childhood that he is able to escape from an apocalyptic future and into the past to meet her. While the broad strokes of the plot are clearly conveyed in the film's narration, little exposition is given to the science of time travel and the film's meaning is left to the audience to unravel by contemplating the juxtaposition of this series of still images. Capturing in its form the fleeting experience of time and memory, *La Jetée* haunts the audience with glimpses of the future and the past and leaves the significance of the film's one moving image unexplained. Like *Solaris*, it is to the subjective experience of memory that arthouse sf turns.

In contrast to the conventional approach to visuals used by the art film, independent and cult films frequently offer a more gritty and confrontational aesthetic that serves to undermine the high-art associations of the genre and as such appeal to a youth audience. The low-budget special effects and documentary filmmaking techniques of George Romero's *Night of the Living Dead* create a vision of an apocalypse in which the dead, resuscitated through nuclear radiation, return to feed off the living. Alex Cox, on the other hand, presents his comic tale of a radioactive car in *Repo Man* with a punk, irreverent sensibility through his use of contemporary music, fluorescent colors, cartoonish special effects, and a dead-pan performance style that reinforces the film's opposition to mainstream cinema and the art film. Tsukamoto Shinya's cyberpunk *Tetsuo* (1989) uses fast and disjunctive editing, grainy film stock, and discordant sound effects and music to explore the physical horror and violence of cyborg existence, while Darren Aronofsky's *Pi* adopts a similar style to offer a glimpse into the mind of a mathematician. The visuals may be different but these films, as well as the low-budget time-travel film *Primer*, share with more classical examples of arthouse sf the preoccupation with using the genre to convey a subjective perception of the world, science, and technology. In so doing, they remind us that this subgenre is constantly evolving and changing, in terms of both aesthetic and narrative conventions, even as sf's central preoccupations persist. What binds all of these films together is that they explore what it means to be a human in a scientifically and technologically determined world and they do so, not by creating advanced imagined cities or communities – although they can do that as well – but by conveying the subjective experience of a world in which our understanding of humanity is changing every day.

Bibliography

Bordwell, D. (1979) "The Art Cinema as a Mode of Film Practice," *Film Criticism*, 4(1): 56–63.

King, G. and Krzywinska, T. (2000) *Science Fiction Cinema: from outerspace to cyberspace*, London: Wallflower Press.

Neale, S. (1981) "Art Cinema as Institution," *Screen*, 22(1): 11–39.

Wilinsky, B. (2001) *Sureseaters: the emergence of art house cinema*, Minneapolis: University of Minnesota Press.

48

BLOCKBUSTER SF FILM

Stacey Abbott

A long shot of deep space; a small spaceship appears from the bottom of the screen, bombarded by laser fire and racing into the distance. Seconds later, another much larger ship enters the top of the frame and fills the screen as it passes overhead. This is the oft-described, iconic opening shot of George Lucas's *Star Wars: Episode IV – A New Hope* (1977) and it establishes many of the characteristics of the blockbuster sf film (see Bukatman 1998). It is made up entirely of special effects; the second ship, enhanced by the framing of the image, is presented as excessively big; and the sequence is driven by the kinetic pursuit of the smaller ship. Arguably, with this shot, blockbuster sf was born.

Richard Maltby defines the blockbuster, or "event film," in terms of a filmmaking practice that emerged in the 1950s and 1960s and produced "lavish and spectacular features" (Maltby 2003: 580). Sheldon Hall argues that the term applies to any "film that is extraordinarily successful in financial terms" *and* "which needs to be this successful in order to have a chance of returning a profit on [its] equally extraordinary production costs" (Hall 2002: 11). It is part of a Hollywood strategy to make fewer films but ones that are designed to generate huge box-office returns in a short period of time. They are generally expected to earn 90 percent of their box-office gross by their fifth week in the cinemas, with the opening weekend the most significant period in their release (Maltby 2003: 200–1). To generate this level of income, the blockbuster needs to appeal to as wide an audience as possible and thus is usually associated with entertainment and spectacle. With the increasing importance placed upon young audiences in the 1970s and 1980s, and following the success of films such as *Star Wars*, *Close Encounters of the Third Kind* (Spielberg 1977), and *Star Trek: The Motion Picture* (Wise 1979), sf came to replace the religious epic as the genre most associated with the blockbuster.

Merging with the blockbuster introduced certain characteristics into sf film. The most recognizable conventions of the blockbuster are its "enhanced production values," "large-scale story material and [a] display of technical virtuosity," and it has often been used to showcase developments in new cinema technologies such as sound, widescreen, and digital effects (Allen 2003: 101). Julian Stringer notes that blockbusters, primarily due to their large budgets, are characterized by size, excess, and the promise of something that "will excite you, expose you to something never before experienced, ... prick up your ears and make your eyes bulge out in awe" (Stringer 2003: 5). It is important to note that these elements are not exclusive to blockbuster sf, for the genre has always been characterized by spectacle and the display of technical wizardry. Films from *A Trip to the Moon* (Méliès 1902) to *Bride of Frankenstein* (Whale 1935) to *The Incredible Shrinking Man* (Arnold 1957) used sf's preoccupation with science and technology to showcase new developments in cinematic special effects, while the genre has always been predicated upon the promise of showing new and unimagined things, from alien spaceships to futuristic cities, from giant spiders to cyborgs. In fact, it is precisely because of this predilection for spectacle and technology that the sf film has become one of the primary forms of the blockbuster since *Star Wars'* phenomenal success.

While sf prior to the modern blockbuster period is traditionally perceived as a low-budget genre, such films as *Metropolis* (Lang 1927), *Things to Come* (Menzies 1936), *The War of the Worlds* (Haskin 1953), and *Forbidden Planet* (Wilcox 1956) married the genre's philosophical and social preoccupations with cutting-edge special effects and spectacular set design in order to bring their futuristic visions to the screen. Similarly, Stanley Kubrick's *2001: A Space Odyssey* (1968) combined its sophisticated special effects and big-budget production values with a deeply intellectual – even religious, according to some – narrative about human evolution. In contrast, *Star Wars* blended its big-budget special effects with more action-oriented generic elements, introducing the conventions of the western as well as the kinetic narrative drive of Saturday matinée serials, such as *Flash Gordon* (Stephani 1936) and *King of the Rocket Men* (Brannon 1949). These characteristics are all now intrinsically part of the genre.

Furthermore, while the sf film always bears a degree of hybridity in its makeup, often crossing lines between fantasy and horror, blockbuster sf is an inherently hybrid form – best exemplified through the regular casting of action or comedy stars, such as Arnold Schwarzenegger and Will Smith. This has led to the common perception that sf has been emptied of meaning through its association with a mode of filmmaking often described as "lowest common denominator" (Stringer 2003: 1), and the dispersal of its generic conventions through intermixing with such genres as the action/ adventure film, the disaster film, or the family melodrama. However, the sf film is "a cohering genre that is best able to articulate contemporary fears, such as those that presently exist over genetic engineering and nuclear war; and to play out ideological tensions around class, race, gender and sexuality" (Redmond 2004: x), and this is equally applicable to its less respectable contemporary form. As the exploration of climate change in *The Day after Tomorrow* (Emmerich 2004) demonstrates, meaning remains within the matrix of blockbuster sf. It is, however, often suffused beneath the action and expressed through the *mise en scène*.

So what are the conventions and preoccupations of blockbuster sf? It engages with a wide range of sf themes and cultural preoccupations, including time travel (*Terminator 2: Judgment Day* (Cameron 1991)), space travel (*Star Trek: The Motion Picture*), alien first-contact (*Close Encounters of the Third Kind*), alien invasion (*Transformers* (Bay 2007)), future cities and technologies (*I, Robot* (Proyas 2004)), scientific developments

(*Jurassic Park* (Spielberg 1993)), and dystopian visions (*The Matrix* (Wachowski brothers 1999)), and therefore is not easily distinguished from other forms of sf which share such traditional generic iconography and narrative. However, elements of other genres often compete with or diffuse the sf narrative. For instance, *War of the Worlds* (Spielberg 2005) reimagines the alien invasion narrative through the lens of family melodrama as the film's hero attempts to escape and later destroy the marauding aliens in order to protect his children and keep his family together. Other blockbuster sf films such as *Mars Attacks!* (Burton 1996) or *Men in Black* (Sonnenfeld 1997) introduce comedy into the genre by parodying the alien encounter/invasion narratives, while *Independence Day* (Emmerich 1996) and *Armageddon* (Bay 1998) combine sf with the disaster film. Blockbuster sf is heavily marked by hybridity.

The most significant characteristic that unifies blockbuster sf films is the manner in which they put their special effects on display. They feature the most cutting-edge effects innovations and have played an intrinsic role in fostering developments in computer-generated effects, such as "morphing" in *The Abyss* (Cameron 1989) and "bullet time" in *The Matrix* (see Abbott 2006). Each of these effects is showcased within the film for its spectacular value – a fundamental pleasure of the genre. The film will often deliberately pause to allow the audience to enjoy the dramatic reveal of both the object of wonder and the special effects that created it, such as the first appearance of the giant tripod alien invaders in *War of the Worlds*. In a moment of stasis following a series of devastating lightning strikes and earth tremors, a group of bystanders pause in anticipation of further destruction before the aliens finally burst from the ground, emerging from a cloud of dust and towering over the community. Through this dramatic revelation, the special effects encapsulate the "two key dimensions of the genre": "spectacle and speculation" (King and Krzywinska 2000: 7).

In addition to their function as spectacle, special effects are also intrinsically intertwined with the film's sf narrative. In *The Matrix*, the ability of effects artists to slow down and manipulate motion through computer technology is the basis for the film's dystopian vision of a future in which the world around us is a construct of a computer program and where the mind can control the program, bending it to its needs. So the opening fight scene, when the film's heroine Trinity escapes arrest by leaping in the air and hovering above the police officers before knocking them both unconscious, is a demonstration both of the artificiality of this simulated world *and* of the skills of the effects team to produce visuals that had never been seen before. Similarly in *Terminator 2*, the T-1000, an advanced form of cyborg killing machine sent to the past to murder John Connor, is a product of new developments in computer morphing. The T-1000's ability to transform into any person or object with which it comes into contact provides a space for the special effects team to showcase the wonders of their own technology, creating a series of spectacular and seamless metamorphoses from the actor into the cyborg's liquid metal form as well as into a series of other characters and artifacts. These effects, however, also serve the narrative in their portrayal of an unstoppable, technologically sophisticated cyborg. As such, they are integrated into the narrative and the genre. *Transformers* is a further example of this synergy between sf and special effects. The film's ability to tell the story of a technologically advanced alien race that can transform from giant alien robots into very familiar cars, trucks, and planes is entirely predicated upon the ability of special effects convincingly to represent this transformation.

Special effects are, however, not used purely to portray spectacular metamorphosis but play an absolutely vital role in creating the visions of alternative, future, or imagined worlds that are intrinsic to the sf film. The genre often utilizes special effects to bring alternative universes to life, as evidenced by the complex solar systems created for the *Star Wars* saga (1977–2005). They can also be used to imagine futuristic versions of our own world, taking familiar objects and technological devices and speculating upon how they might operate in a future society. For instance, *Minority Report* (Spielberg 2002) replaces America's freeway systems with automated circulation on a series of smooth conveyor belts. This abandonment of the traditional sf flying car grounds the futuristic image within a more plausible contemporary reality, something further evidenced by the diegetic presence of familiar brand-name products – as when, in an amusing synergy between product placement and futuristic vision, protagonist John Anderton is greeted by a hologram from Gap which reads his identity through retinal scans and politely asks if he liked the clothes he bought last time. Likewise in *I, Robot*, protagonist Del Spooner drives and eventually destroys a recently unveiled Audi concept car. Not only do these moments anchor the films within recognizable reality, but of course they also serve to fulfill the blockbuster's product-placement ambitions.

This use of technology within the diegesis, however, also brings to blockbuster sf another significant and yet paradoxical characteristic. While technology is itself glorified through its presentation, it is often critiqued through the narrative. While the image of a city populated by robots, convincingly created through cutting-edge computer-generated imagery, is wondrous, *I, Robot*'s depiction of the dangers of over-reliance upon automation is clearly articulated when the machines turn on their human masters – a narrative shared by *The Matrix*. *Minority Report* paints an equally stark warning about the perils of assuming that a scientifically engineered policing system is without flaw. In this film, the technology used by the Pre-Crime Unit to analyze and investigate visions of future crimes is conveyed through digital compositing of live-action and digital footage. Anderton's examination of the precognitive vision, accompanied by classical music, is presented as a graceful ballet as he shifts and maneuvers various elements of the image around the transparent screens that surround him. The presentation of these methods is an elegant display, but Anderton soon discovers the fallibility of the system when he is accused of a future murder.

Finally, it is important to remember when discussing blockbuster sf that the film itself does not exist in isolation but is just one element in a synergistic confluence of marketing, product placement, and merchandizing. Sf films in particular lend themselves to the demand for synergy, since narratives of alternative or dystopian worlds are often easily extended into ancillary products and sequels. For instance, *The Matrix* was followed by two sequels – *The Matrix Reloaded* (Wachowski brothers 2003) and *The Matrix Revolutions* (Wachowski brothers 2003) – and videogames, and *The Animatrix* series of animated films that prefigured the release of the final film. The

Star Wars saga is the most effective illustration of an sf universe that has fostered a merchandizing empire by reproducing the characters, sets, and props from its narrative universe as toys and collectibles. *Transformers* marks a reverse form of synergy as these transforming robots began as toys and spawned several successful comics and animated series before eventually becoming a big-budget summer spectacular. Blockbuster sf, therefore, often critiques or espouses our fears of the modern technological world but contradictorily remains a product of the technological and economic system of contemporary Hollywood.

Bibliography

Abbott, S. (2006) "Final Frontiers: computer-generated imagery and the science fiction film," *Science Fiction Studies*, 33(1): 89–108.

Allen, M. (2003) "Talking About a Revolution: the blockbuster as industrial advertisement," in J. Stringer (ed.) *Movie Blockbusters*, London: Routledge.

Bukatman, S. (1998) "Zooming Out: the end of offscreen space," in J. Lewis (ed.) *The New American Cinema*, Durham, NC: Duke University Press.

Hall, S. (2002) "Tall Revenue Features," in S. Neale (ed.) *Genre and Contemporary Hollywood*, London: BFI.

King, G. and Krzywinska, T. (2000) *Science Fiction Cinema: from outerspace to cyberspace*, London: Wallflower Press.

Maltby, R. (2003) *Hollywood Cinema*, 2nd edn, Oxford: Blackwell.

Redmond, S. (ed.) (2004) *Liquid Metal: the science fiction film reader*, London: Wallflower Press.

Stringer, J. (2003) "Introduction," in *Movie Blockbusters*, London: Routledge.

49
DYSTOPIA
Graham J. Murphy

Dystopia, the negative utopia, is "a non-existent society described in considerable detail and normally located in time and space that the author intended a contemporaneous reader to view as considerably worse than the society in which the reader lived" (Sargent 1994: 9). It is not the evacuation of eutopian hope (that belongs to the anti-utopia, which "has steadily attacked and refused Utopia and all that its authors claim for it" (Moylan 2000: 122)), but rather "draws on the more detailed systemic accounts of utopian narratives by way of an inversion that focuses on the terrors rather than the hopes of history" (Moylan 2000: 111) and works "*not* to undermine Utopia but rather to make room for its reconsideration and refunctioning in even the worst of times" (Moylan 2000: 133).

This dystopian inversion did appear in the late nineteenth century – in Jules Verne's *The Begum's Millions* (1879), H.C. Marriott-Watson's *Erchomenon* (1879), Walter Besant's *The Revolt of Man* (1882) and *The Inner House* (1888), H.G. Wells's "A Story of Days to Come" (1897) and *When the Sleeper Wakes* (1899) (Stableford 1993: 360) – and some might nowadays view the social collectivism of eutopias such as Thomas More's *Utopia* (1516) or Edward Bellamy's *Looking Backward: 2000–1887* (1888) as dystopian. However, E.M. Forster's "The Machine Stops" (1909), in which humanity has retreated to vast subterranean cities run by the Machine, has the strongest claim to being dystopia's originary text. Its depiction of "a totalizing administration that 'mechanizes' every dimension of daily life (from the organization of nature and industry to the standardization of the person) ... develops an abstract yet critical account of the new social spacetime of the twentieth century" (Moylan 2000: 111). It opens with Vashti, listening to music and breathing fresh air pumped into her room. The opening lines – "Imagine, if you can, a small room, hexagonal in shape, like the cell of a bee" (Forster 1988: 41) – evoke both the dehumanization of living like an insect and the confinement of a (jail) cell. Vashti is a "swaddled lump of flesh" with a "face as white as a fungus" (Forster 1988: 41). Although "[i]t is to her that the little room belongs" (Forster 1988: 41), it becomes apparent that she belongs to it.

Reluctantly visiting her son Kuno, she is perpetually shocked by the "horror of direct experience" (Forster 1988: 46). Kuno, however, longs for such experience and clandestinely visits the Earth's surface, where he discovers that the Machine has been lying about the planet's inhospitability: it is habitable and there are surface-dwelling humans. Kuno concludes "it is we who are dying, and that down here the only thing that really lives is the Machine" (Forster 1988: 54). When the Machine begins to break down, humanity is left suffocating, buried alive underneath modernity's technological detritus. The real hope in this dystopian nightmare about technological dependency, dehumanization, and the sacrifice of ideas, resides not in those humans living on the surface but with the *reader*. It compels the reader to prevent its realization.

Key early dystopias include Yevgeny Zamyatin's critique of totalitarian rationalization in *We* (written 1920, translated into English 1924), Aldous Huxley's condemnation of consumer capitalism in *Brave New World* (1932), and George Orwell's censure of nightmarish government power in *Nineteen Eighty-four* (1949). Despite their differing political foci, parallels among these classic dystopias abound: wars facilitate dystopia's ascendancy; protagonists endure some trial of their newfound beliefs; women, love, and carnal desire motivate resistance; language is both an oppressive and liberating tool; quasi-religious rituals are prominent; and utopianism is pushed to the very brink of darkness. *We* depicts the One State as a wondrous glass metropolis that has eliminated privacy. Names have been replaced by numbers, and in that reduction "people lose their identity and are no longer unique or irreplaceable: in the world created by and for the machine, human beings become redundant" (Gottlieb 2001: 57). D-503, a mathematician, is predicated on logic and equations but haunted by uncertainty: the wonders of spring interfere "to some extent with the flow of logical thought" (Zamyatin 1972: 3); and, "in the eyes, or in the eyebrows" of 0–90, a contracted sexual partner, he finds "a certain strange, irritating X, which [he] could not capture, could not define in figures" (Zamyatin 1972: 6). *We* "pulls no punches in pessimistically describing the extensive power of the One State to put down individual and collective resistance" (Moylan 2000: 160); but various narrative strategies – such as casting the novel as D-503's diary, which survives beyond the One State's political control – signal a "strong ... *utopian* stance" (Moylan 2000: 161).

Brave New World likewise pulls no punches in its critique of consumer capitalism, Fordism, and Taylorism. The World State, *c.* 2540 or After Ford 632, maintains social stability through strict eugenics and class hierarchy, the abolition of private property and independence, systematic consumption of the drug *soma*, and mandatory participation in sexual exhaustion and other distractions. But resistance bubbles forth. Bernard Marx, an Alpha Plus "eight centimetres short of the standard Alpha height" (Huxley 1994: 57), suffers from alienation and loneliness, while Helmholtz Watson is equally alienated because of a "mental excess" (Huxley 1994: 60) and a poetic spirit that defies logic. John the Savage, a child raised on a "primitive" Reservation and on a diet of Shakespearean drama that repeatedly frames his experiences, returns to the World State only to resist its seductions. Ultimately, Marx and Watson are exiled and John, in an act of despair and defiance, hangs himself. Nevertheless, it is these poetic and alienated sensibilities that form the crux of Huxley's critique of unrestrained capitalism.

Nineteen Eighty-four, in its "indictment of the deep tendency of modern, technologically sophisticated governments to manage reality, and as a further devastating assault upon the actual situation of the USSR in 1948," remains "unmatched" in its pessimism that is "both distressing and salutary. Its understanding of the nightmare of power – when wielded by representatives of a species which had evolved beyond the constraints of mercy – was definitive" (Clute 1993: 896). The inhabitants of Oceania are under constant observation or threat of observation by Big Brother, leaving protagonist Winston Smith nothing of himself but the interiority of his own mind. The ubiquitous sloganeering professing Big Brother's benevolence, the perpetual surveillance which requires one to avoid committing "facecrime" and "thoughtcrime" and to learn "doublethink," and even the threat posed by one's own children make those few centimeters a central battlefield. Oceania's citizens are repressed by a calcified and hierarchically organized regime. Smith is employed to purge factual evidence that contradicts Big Brother's official accounts of history or social policy: he drops such traces down a memory hole to be "whirled away on a current of warm air to the enormous furnaces which were hidden somewhere in the recesses of the building" (Orwell 1990: 40). Smith faces a similar fate: at the end of the novel, after his rebellious streak is excised through torture and brainwashing, he sits at the Chestnut Tree Café contemplating the wonders of Big Brother, but the reader knows this is merely the final stop before Big Brother drops Smith down its own memory hole. Nonetheless, *Nineteen Eighty-four* ends with a slim glimmer of hope: an appendix, "The Principles of Newspeak," which seems to have been written *after* the end of Big Brother (Margaret Atwood deploys a similar tactic in *The Handmaid's Tale* (1985)).

After the Second World War, the distinctions between utopian and sf texts collapsed as "the dystopian sensibility found a larger and more diffuse scope in the popular form of sf" and as sf "worked within an increasing enclosure of the lived moment and drew upon the dystopian sensibility even when its stories and novels were not fully cast in the classical dystopian form" (Moylan 2000: 166, 168). Moylan points to Ray Bradbury's *Fahrenheit 451* (1953), Kurt Vonnegut's *Player Piano* (1952), Bernard Wolfe's *Limbo* (1952), and Anthony Burgess's *A Clockwork Orange* (1962) as sf texts that were distinctly dystopian, and to J.G. Ballard, Philip K. Dick, and John Brunner as authors who worked "loosely with the spirit of the dystopia and produced tales of social nightmares that cannot be reduced to the strict parameters of dystopian narrative" (Moylan 2000: 168).

By the end of the twentieth century, this shared literary terrain coalesced into the critical dystopia, which tends "to be less driven by extremes of celebration or despair, more open to complexities and ambiguities, and more encouraging of new riffs of personal and political maneuvers" (Moylan 2000: 182). While using dystopia's traditional tropes, they "go on to explore ways to change the present system so that ... culturally and economically marginalized peoples not only survive but also try to move toward creating a social reality that is shaped by an impulse to human self-determination and ecological health rather than one constricted by the narrow and destructive logic of a system intent only on enhancing competition in order to gain more profit for a select few" (Moylan 2000: 189). Such critical dystopias include Kim Stanley Robinson's *The Gold Coast* (1988), Marge Piercy's *He, She, and It* (1991), and Octavia E. Butler's *Parable of the Sower* (1993) and *Parable of the Talents* (1998), Samuel Delany's *Dhalgren* (1975), Pat Cadigan's *Mindplayers* (1987) and *Synners* (1991), and Ursula K. Le Guin's *The Telling* (2000).

He, She, and It locates resistance in Tikva, an enclave (albeit a dangerous one under constant threat of attack) away from the dystopian cities of the multis and the disease-ridden Glop. Tikva reaches "back to the models of early American town hall government, New Left participatory democracy, feminist principles of equity and self-criticism, and the socialism of early Zionism ... Valuing optimal freedom for everyone, the citizens practice a total democracy that requires endless meetings ... and community duties such as town labor and reforestation work" (Moylan 2000: 253–4). Against this backdrop, *He, She, and It* is cast as a family narrative: there is a love story between Shira and Yod, an android clandestinely built by Gadi, Shira's former lover, to protect Tikva from aggressive corporate raids; the elderly matriarch Malkah uses the story of the golem of Prague to educate Yod; and, from out of the irradiated lands of Palestine, Riva, Shira's outlaw data pirate mother (and Malkah's daughter), returns to Tikva with her cyborg lover, Nili. Moylan concludes that in "Piercy's critical dystopia, the present social order is unflinchingly portrayed through the distancing lens of its imagined alternative, but in this case the story of the people who stand up to the corporate order leads to the possibility of an eventual utopian transformation of that order ... The social and aesthetic value of such a text therefore lies in the emphasis it places on the process of reaching toward Utopia and on the values and policies required for that process to move in a progressive direction" (Moylan 2000: 272).

The dystopian sensibility is also prevalent in comic books and graphic novels. Alan Moore has been at the forefront of the utopian graphic novel with *V for Vendetta* (1982–5, 1988), *Marvelman* (aka *Miracleman*; 1982) and *Watchmen* (1986–7). (Also of interest are: Mark Gruenwald's *Squadron Supreme* (1985–6); Frank Miller's *The Dark Knight Returns* (1986) and *The Dark Knight Strikes Again* (2001–2); Enki Bilal's *Nikopol* trilogy (1980–92); Warren Ellis and Darick Robertson's *Transmetropolitan* (1997–2003); Warren Ellis and Mark Millar's *The Authority* (1999–2002); Robert Venditti and Brett Weldele's *The Surrogates* (2006); and Justin Gray, Jimmy Palmiotti, and Daniel Acuña's *Uncle Sam and the Freedom Fighters* (2006–7).) *Watchmen* exemplifies the narrative possibilities and the types of critique comics can stage vis-à-vis utopian studies. Set in a Cold War era alternative US, five minutes from humanity's nuclear midnight, it follows past and present superheroes as they untangle the complicated plot surrounding the murder of one of their own, the violent and at times sadistic Comedian. Ultimately, Rorschach, Nite-Owl, Dr Manhattan, and Silk Spectre discover that his death was simply an accidental by-product of a plot by another superhero, Ozymandias, who has decided to solve the dystopian terrors of his age by precipitating (e)utopia. When his fabricated alien invasion destroys half of New York, the world's citizens ignore their differences and reverse the Doomsday Clock. "I did it!," he proclaims, "I saved Earth from hell. Next, I'll help her towards Utopia" (Moore and Gibbons 1987, no. 12: 19–20). Alongside the psychology of superheroism, *Watchmen* effectively explores the antinomies of dystopia and eutopia; yet, its dystopian darkness gets *so* dark that it eventually moves from dystopia to anti-utopia, wherein utopia and utopianism in general are more destructive to people's lives than nuclear Armageddon or alien invasion.

Dystopia has also proven popular in film. In addition to adaptations of *Fahrenheit 451*

(Truffaut 1966), *Nineteen Eighty-four* (Anderson 1956, Radford 1984), *The Handmaid's Tale* (Schlöndorff 1990), *V for Vendetta* (McTeigue 2005), and *Watchmen* (Snyder 2009), other notable films include *Metropolis* (Lang 1927), *Logan's Run* (Anderson 1976), *Blade Runner* (Scott 1982), *Brazil* (Gilliam 1985), *RoboCop* (Verhoeven 1987), *Akira* (Ôtomo 1988), *Gattaca* (Niccol 1997), *The Matrix* (Wachowski brothers 1999), *Equilibrium* (Wimmer 2002), *Æon Flux* (Kusama 2005), and *Children of Men* (Cuarón 2006). Dystopian worlds can also be seen in such television series as *The Prisoner* (1967–8), *Blakes 7* (1978–81), *Max Headroom* (1987), and *Dark Angel* (2000–2).

While it is too early to predict the resilience of the dystopia in the twenty-first century or whether a new dystopian form awaits over the horizon, there can be little doubt that the dystopia thrived in the twentieth century and continues to show its health in the new millennium. It continues to embody utopianism by kicking the darkness until it bleeds daylight and to critique timely political issues while also locating hope in perhaps unexpected places: sites of resistance both within the narrative and, perhaps more importantly, within those readers who heed its warnings.

Bibliography

Clute, J. (1993) "Orwell, George," in J. Clute and P. Nicholls (eds) *The Encyclopedia of Science Fiction*, London: Orbit.

Forster, E. (1988) "The Machine Stops," in P.S. Warrick, C.G. Waugh, and M.H. Greenberg (eds) *Science Fiction: the Science Fiction Research Association anthology*, New York: Harper & Row.

Gottlieb, E. (2001) *Dystopian Fiction East and West: universe of terror and trial*, Montreal and Kingston: McGill-Queen's University Press.

Huxley, A. (1994) *Brave New World*, London: Flamingo.

Moore, A. and Gibbons, D. (1987) *Watchmen*, New York: DC Comics.

Moylan, T. (2000) *Scraps of the Untainted Sky: science fiction, utopia, dystopia*, Boulder, CO: Westview.

Orwell, G. (1990) *Nineteen Eighty-Four*, New York: Penguin.

Sargent, L.T. (1994) "The Three Faces of Utopianism Revisited," *Utopian Studies*, 5(1): 1–37.

Stableford, B. (1993) "Dystopias," in J. Clute and P. Nicholls (eds) *The Encyclopedia of Science Fiction*, London: Orbit.

Zamyatin, Y. (1972) *We*, trans. Mirra Ginsburg, New York: EOS.

50
EUTOPIA
Graham J. Murphy

The literary eutopia, or positive utopia, is "a non-existent society described in considerable detail and normally located in time and space that the author intended a
contemporaneous reader to view as considerably better than the society in which the
reader lived" (Sargent 1994: 9). "Eutopia," a pun on "*eu*" (good) + "*topos*" (place)
as well as "*ou*" (no) + "*topos*" (place), is not, nor was it ever intended to be, an
identifiable place. Indeed, vagueness about location is a common strategy in narratives about these alternative communities. For example, in Thomas More's *Utopia*
(1516), although Raphael Hythloday describes the geographical features of the
crescent-shaped eponymous isle, he never explicitly *locates* it. Geographic isolation
and distance have since then become mainstays of eutopian narratives. This is perhaps
not surprising; after all, the

> "discovery" of the non-European continents and islands provided visionaries
> of the fifteenth and sixteenth centuries with actual and imaginary space in
> which to create both practicing and literary experiments. The new space
> in the world reinforced the sensibility found in the landscape painting and
> pastoral poetry of the time that effused the presence of an arcadian locale in
> which dreams could be lived.
>
> (Moylan 1986: 3)

Francis Bacon's *New Atlantis* (1627) deploys similar arcadian tactics. Bacon's band
of travelers, having set sail from Peru for China and Japan, quickly lose all sense
of direction, are buffeted by powerful winds, and eventually traverse the "greatest
wilderness of waters in the world" (Bacon 1999: 152) to find Bensalem, a scientifically advanced eutopia that remains hidden from the world while monitoring other
societies' social and technological progress.

Having deposited their fictional travelers in alternative social communities, authors
then critique their own society by offering social, political, legal, and ethical contrasts
with these idealized, unattainable alternatives. Book One of More's *Utopia*, for
example, is a dialogue among Hythloday, Giles, and More about the "ills of England"
(Bruce 1999: xviii) in the sixteenth century, covering such topics as unjust land
appropriation, political posturing, monarchical manipulation of currency, counterfeit

pleasures, and the social causes of brothels, taverns, alehouses, and thievery (and the hanging of thieves). Hythloday then provides a contrast in his description of the Isle of Utopia and its social justice, founded chiefly on the elimination of private property, the egalitarian division of labor, and beneficial spin-off social changes.

The extent to which More is to be read as satire or blueprint is an argument that continues to fuel utopian scholars, but there is little doubt that *Utopia* is "a rebuke to contemporary European societies, which he rightly saw as appallingly unjust" (Wertheim 2002: 218). It "seems important to insist that it is equally mistaken to understand the text solely as a joke. It is not self-evidently true that Utopia's subordination of individual choice and happiness to the good of the community is a misguided ideal," and while "Utopia may appear authoritarian, perhaps even totalitarian, it is worth remembering that it is not nearly so repressive as early modern England" in the limitations placed on freedom of speech, poverty's circumscription of people's future, the torturing of suspected traitors, and the capital punishment of petty thieves (Bruce 1999: xxvi).

Later literary eutopias – Bacon's *New Atlantis*, Tommaso Campanella's *The City of the Sun* (1602), Margaret Cavendish's *The Description of a New World, Called the Blazing-World* (1666) – took their cue from More's *Utopia* and offered social and political commentary couched in the dynamics of eutopian enclaves. For example, Bacon was keenly interested in codifying and systematizing "scientific enquiry" while also writing on "moral qualities … such as truth, envy, and love, or political matters, such as sedition, empire, and kingdoms" (Bruce 1999: xxviii). He depicts Bensalem's social dynamics and its scientific foundation, focusing on the scientist-priests of Salomon's House, a research institute "dedicated to the study of the Works and Creatures of God" (Bacon 1999: 167), whose scientific endeavors include experiments in coagulation, refrigeration, conservation of bodies, the artificial production of natural minerals and metals, the curing of disease, the prolongation of life, insulation, meteorology, conservation, water filtration, geometry, astronomy, and harmonics. Bensalem also sends Merchants of Light to the outside world "whose errand was only to give us knowledge of the affairs and states of those countries to which they were designed, and especially of the sciences, arts, manufactures, and inventions of all the world; and withal to bring unto us books, instruments, and patterns in every kind" (Bacon 1999: 167–8). Although the "epitome of Renaissance utopianism," there is "nothing communistic" in Bensalem: it "heralds a return to orthodoxy" where men and women alike know "their place in the social order" (Wertheim 2002: 217, 223).

The literary eutopia came under increasing pressure from the industrialized social conditions of the eighteenth and nineteenth centuries. After 1850, the systematic utopia that imagined structurally different social communities was replaced with the heuristic utopia, which "offered a strength of vision that sought to subvert or at least reform the modern economic and political arrangement from within" (Moylan 1986: 6). Tellingly, literary eutopias became increasingly science-fictional as the new century beckoned. Samuel Butler's anagrammatic *Erewhon, or Over the Range* (1872) is a utopian satire. It depicts the trials and tribulations of Mr Nosnibor as he finds and tries to understand the eponymous eutopian enclave. For sf readers, the most compelling part of *Erewhon* is probably "The Book of the Machines," which explores the implications of Darwin's *On the Origin of Species* (1859) for technology and progress. It offers "a serious perspective on the evolving world" and serves as a "shocking challenge to our ideas about the continuity or discontinuity existing between man and machines" (Mazlish 2002: 239, 238).

Edward Bellamy's *Looking Backward: 2000–1887* (1888) is perhaps the most important eutopia of the late nineteenth century. When it opens in 1887, protagonist Julian West is afflicted by labor disruptions that repeatedly delay the completion of his Boston residence and thus his marriage to Edith Bartlett. An insomniac, he sleeps in a subterranean vault that ensures absolute darkness and pure silence. One evening, he undergoes hypnosis to achieve sleep and an ensuing series of unfortunate circumstances leave him to awaken 113 years later when his bedroom is accidentally excavated. Having effectively time-traveled, he must acclimatize himself to this wonderful new – and explicitly eutopian – world. With the great-granddaughter of his former fiancée at his side, conveniently named Edith, and with whom he will eventually fall in love, West meticulously details the social dynamics of twenty-first-century Boston.

Looking Backward was immensely successful: it "sold in the millions, and it went global in more than twenty translations. Historians credit it with inspiring some forty or more other Utopian works, some … in direct" reply (Miller 2000: v). This is perhaps unsurprising. The US has, after all, a history of intentional utopian communities: the Shakers (United Society of Believers in Christ's Second Appearing), a "celibate millenarian group that established communal settlements in the United States in the 18th century," deriving social and spiritual direction from the "revelations of Ann Lee and her vision of the heavenly kingdom to come" (*Encyclopædia Britannica*); Brook Farm (1841–7), a 175-acre communal farm in Massachusetts partly influenced by Charles Fourier's utopian socialism and attracting interest from Nathaniel Hawthorne, Ralph Waldo Emerson, and Margaret Fuller; or, those social communities inspired by B.F. Skinner's *Walden Two* (1948). Bellamy's fictional eutopia itself translated into effective real-world politics: enthusiasts "organized more than 162 Bellamy Clubs in the States alone … dedicated to transferring Bellamy's Utopia from fiction to fact" (Miller 2000: v–vi), contributing to the rise of the Nationalist Party, including two major magazines (*The Nationalist, The New Nation*), 50 other periodicals that were aligned with Nationalism, and "[i]n 1892, with Nationalist aid, Populists polled more than one million votes for president and elected three governors and several state legislators" (Miller 2000: vi).

Charlotte Perkins Gilman, who would later pen the feminist eutopia *Herland* (1915), "was drawn to Bellamy's emphasis on political, social, and economic equality and quickly became a convert to Nationalism … Gilman was particularly attracted by the novel's emphasis on women's rights and began actively advocating such social reforms as economic independence, the restructuring of the home and child-care practices" (Knight 1999: xi–xii). *Herland* deploys a familiar pattern: a group of male travelers "discover" (and *name*) the all-female Herland nestled in the mountains. While learning about new social dynamics – family is completely reconstructed since women reproduce through parthenogenesis – the men also struggle (with various consequences) with Herland's divorce from heteronormative gender codes. Yet, unlike many eutopian predecessors, Gilman's utopia strives to break its isolation by reincorporating men into their social system, albeit without adopting patriarchal gender-coding. Like a merchant of light, Ellador eventually leaves Herland with one of the men, Vandyck Jennings, to explore the outside world and report back on its social conditions, itself a depressing report. In *With Her in Ourland* (1916), Ellador and Van "travel the world during the Great War. At the conclusion of the novel, the disillusioned pair returns to the utopian Herland, which offers a sanctuary from the disease-infested, poverty-stricken, and decidedly inequitable masculine world" (Knight 1999: xv). Thus, if assessments of literary utopias have "to focus on the identification the reader is invited to make with the protagonist/narrator" (Varsam 2003: 205), there is little doubt about Gilman's eutopianism.

In the twentieth century, the positive utopia was overshadowed by the rising popularity and political efficacy of the dystopia (negative utopia), although eutopia's tropes did reappear in the feminist critical utopias of the 1960s and 1970s, exemplified by Ursula K. Le Guin's *The Dispossessed: an ambiguous utopia* (1974), Joanna Russ's *The Female Man* (1975), Marge Piercy's *Woman on the Edge of Time* (1976), Samuel Delany's *Triton* (1976), Suzy McKee Charnas's *Motherlines* (1978), and Sally Miller Gearhart's *Wanderground: stories of the hill women* (1980). Unlike the eutopia, the critical utopia retains "difficult problems that the described society may or may not be able to solve and which takes a critical view of the utopian genre" (Sargent 1994: 9). For example, *Woman on the Edge of Time* depicts Consuelo "Connie" Ramos as a welfare-dependent New York City Chicana whose prior history of child abuse (a solitary incident brought on by extremity rather than psychopathology) lands her back in a mental institution when, following a defensive assault on her pregnant niece's pimp-boyfriend, she is judged to be suffering from an ongoing mental instability. Connie is apparently visited by Luciente, a citizen of the future utopia, Mattapoisett, and learns how to travel there, although her body remains locked in Rockover State Psychiatric Hospital. Her travels entail a complete restructuring of her formative principles. She is repeatedly challenged by alternative economics, gender relations, sexuality, reproduction and childrearing practices, democracy, medicine, and even pronouns ("per" has replaced "he" and "she"). The most troubling aspect for Connie is the divesting of pregnancy and reproduction from the female body. Profoundly upset by the "brooders," technological interventions into the reproductive process, she is initially mortified by the consequences: "She felt angry. Yes, how dare any man share that pleasure. These women thought they had won, but they had abandoned to men the last refuge of women. What was special about being a woman here? They had given it all up, they had let men steal from them the last remnants of ancient power, those sealed in blood and in milk" (Piercy 1976: 134). Connie's uncertainty highlights Piercy's avoidance of "a simplistic, élitist image of utopian perfection and links utopia more closely with the uncertainties of history" (Moylan 1986: 152). It is never clear whether this near-future village is a "real" non-place or a figment of Connie's imagination, one that Connie must actively bring to fruition. For example, when she involuntarily undergoes the surgical implantation of a dialytrode to monitor and control her behavior, she loses contact with Mattapoisett and accesses a nightmarish near-future New York City controlled by multinational corporations and saturated with drugs, abuse, prostitution and women who are nothing more than a "cartoon of femininity" (Piercy 1976: 288). When the dialytrode is removed, she ends up in another alternate near-future, this time united with her Mattapoisett compatriots in a battle against enemies who appear as:

> all the caseworkers and doctors and landlords and cops, the psychiatrists and judges and child guidance counselors, the informants and attendants and orderlies, the legal aid lawyers copping pleas, the matrons and EEG technicians, and all the other flacks of power who had pushed her back and turned her off and locked her up and medicated her and tranquilized her and punished her and condemned her. They were all closing in, guns blazing.
>
> (Piercy 1976: 336)

Juxtaposed with the future New York and this nightmarish battlefront, Mattapoisett, in spite of its internal conflicts, evokes eutopia: "democratic, anarchist, communist, environmentalist, feminist, non-racist – where freedom and responsibility are balanced in a steady-state economy and non-repressive value system" (Moylan 1986: 134).

From More's *Utopia* to Piercy's *Woman on the Edge of Time* and into the twenty-first century, the eutopia has had a long and varied career, its popularity ebbing and flowing with social changes and political dynamics but never entirely slipping into obsolescence. This may be because utopian authors and their literary texts assert "the power of desire as a mechanism of the collective human subject that cannot be totally denied or coopted, as an anticipation and practice of what could be as the current historical situation is negated" (Moylan 1986: 155). Just as the shape of political and social (in)justice has changed since More's groundbreaking *Utopia*, so eutopia has responded to and, more importantly, advocated change, catering "to our ability to dream, to recognize that things are not quite what they should be, and to assert that improvement is possible" (Sargent 1994: 26).

Bibliography

Bacon, F. (1999) "New Atlantis," 1627, in S. Bruce (ed.) *Three Early Modern Utopias*, Oxford: Oxford University Press.

Bruce, S. (1999) "Introduction [to *Utopia*]," in S. Bruce (ed.) *Three Early Modern Utopias*, Oxford: Oxford University Press.

Encyclopædia Britannica, (2007) "Shaker," in *Encyclopædia Britannica*. Online. Available HTTP: <http://www.search.eb.com/article-9067086> (accessed 1 April 2008).

Knight, D.D. (1999) "Introduction," in D.D. Knight (ed.) *Herland*, 1915, New York: Penguin.

Mazlish, B. (2002) "Butler's Brainstorm," in D. Tofts, A. Jonson, and A. Cavallaro (eds) *Prefiguring Cyberculture: an intellectual history*, Cambridge, MA: MIT Press.

Miller, W.J. (2000) "The Future of Futurism: an introduction to *Looking Backward*," in E. Bellamy *Looking Backward: 2000–1887*, New York: Signet Classic.

Moylan, T. (1986) *Demand the Impossible: science fiction and the utopian imagination*, London and New York: Methuen.

Piercy, M. (1976) *Woman on the Edge of Time*, New York: Fawcett Crest.

Sargent, L.T. (1994) "The Three Faces of Utopianism Revisited," *Utopian Studies*, 5(1): 1–37.

Varsam, M. (2003) "Concrete Dystopia: slavery and its others," in R. Baccolini and T. Moylan (eds) *Dark Horizons: science fiction and the dystopian imagination*, New York: Routledge.

Wertheim, M. (2002) "Internet Dreams: a utopia for all seasons," in D. Tofts, A. Jonson, and A. Cavallaro (eds) *Prefiguring Cyberculture: an intellectual history*, Cambridge, MA: MIT Press.

51
FEMINIST SF
Gwyneth Jones

What is feminist science fiction? In 1666, when Margaret Lucas Cavendish, Duchess of Newcastle, published her world-building fantasy *The Description of a New World, Called the Blazing-World*, she had clear goals, recognizable today. She was claiming a space for women in the new enterprise of writing about science. Equally, she satirized the scientific establishment: the men who blocked her way, and who were guilty, in her eyes, of having too much faith in their gadgets, too little trust in observation and intuition. Mary Shelley's *Frankenstein, or The Modern Prometheus* (1818), credited by Aldiss (1973) as the first true sf novel, established a different pathway: fusing anxiety about science and a layperson's direct interest in contemporary science (Galvanism) with the emotional charge and grotesque invention of the Gothic novel.

Although Shelley's material was extremely daring for a young woman of her time, and *Frankenstein* can be analyzed for its feminist implications, it has nothing overt to say about the rights of women. Margaret Cavendish, however, belongs to "a continuous literary tradition [of Utopias and science fictions by women] in the West, from the seventeenth century to the present day" (Donawerth and Kolmerten 1994: 1). Typically, these writers use the device of an imaginary domain to assert that women, deprived of civil rights in the real world, are fully capable of governance; and to demonstrate, with wit and ingenuity, that a world ruled by women would be a far more pleasant, peaceable, and ethical state. The public feminism of the late nineteenth and early twentieth centuries produced many variations on this theme. *Herland* (1915), by US feminist and social reformer Charlotte Perkins Gilman, probably the most readily available of these fictions today, still bears discussion, although the story, in which three young male explorers stumble on a country where men have been unknown for 2,000 years, provides little more than the naked description of a "feminine" but sexless and doctrinaire totalitarian state.

Justine Larbalestier, who has examined the significant and early contribution made by women to American sf pulps, argues that "women have been writing science fiction for as long as science fiction has been around" (Larbalestier 2006: xviii), and describes a level of engagement that remained stable for decades. Women writers and fans were a disproportionately effective minority group, often hiding behind initials or male pseudonyms; always "invisible" to the perception of sf as an exclusively male activity. C.L. Moore's original woman warrior, Jirel of Joiry, thrilled both male and female readers, who may not have known that the initials stood for "Catherine Lucille." Judith Merril, later a political activist and a highly influential US editor, offered one of the memorable sf images of the 1940s in "That Only a Mother" (1948), which asserts the moral superiority of women in the face of the catastrophic consequences of male-ordered science: a child born without limbs, victim of nuclear fallout, yet joyously intelligent, is the little girl that only a mother could love. Naomi Mitchison's *Memoirs of a Spacewoman* (1962) endures as an entertaining and insightful fiction about science featuring female scientists and explorers who are by no means second-class males. Later in the 1960s, Josephine Saxton and Pamela Zoline – associates of British New Wave writers whose "experimental" approach arguably opened the way for equally unorthodox feminists – published stylish stories touching on women's liberation issues in *New Worlds*; notably Zoline's "The Heat Death of the Universe" (1967), a memorable fusion of hard science and domestic chaos.

But while Moore, Merril, and Mitchison have the same pro-feminine agenda that can be found in feminine sf today – praising and valuing women's traditional roles, or offering the escapism of privileged women warriors, in an sf context – the women's liberation movement of the 1960s and 1970s had a more ambitious program. The emergence of *feminist* sf, which embraced the political "sexual revolution," uncovered the genre's ingrained sexism, and challenged male supremacy throughout time and space, was a difficult transition for both writers and fans. Veteran practitioners Leigh Brackett and Betty Ballantine were reluctant to accept a feminist reading of their experience. They "had made peace with the male dominated field [and] said that women had suffered no discrimination" (Merrick and Williams 1999: 126). Joanna Russ, creator of Alyx, a high-tech, time-traveling descendant of Jirel, describes her own rather different feelings: "I had turned from writing love stories about women in which women were losers, and adventure stories about men in which men were winners, to writing adventure stories about a woman in which the woman won. It was one of the hardest things I ever did" (Green and Lefanu 1985: 5).

Some vital texts of the feminist years (roughly, the 1970s) – Monique Wittig's *The Guerillères* (1969), Russ's *The Female Man* (1975) – were, and remain, difficult fare for the average sf reader, male or female: complex, elliptical, dense in ideas, minimalist in exposition. Others were greeted with enthusiasm, honored by the genre's highest awards, and became the influential novels and stories of their day. Ursula Le Guin's *The Left Hand of Darkness* (1969), another Hugo- and Nebula-winner and undoubtedly the most widely read of all the feminist sf canon, is set on a planet whose humanoid inhabitants take on male or female gender for sexual transactions, remaining uncondi- tioned *persons* the rest of the time (thus permitting Le Guin's startling first line, "The King was pregnant"). Frederik Pohl's remarkable Hugo- and Nebula-winner *Gateway* (1977) observes the feminist creed. John Varley, in several books and stories (notably *Titan* (1979)), embraced the new religion exuberantly. In *Walk to the End of the World* (1974), Suzy McKee Charnas examined the ultra-masculine culture of a devastated future US where women (fems) are kept like animals. Her harsh vision of male-on- male society, seen through the eyes of Alldera, a young female slave struggling toward personhood, was acclaimed by male critics, including William S. Burroughs.

Another writer, crucially a *male* writer, was James Tiptree Jr. His accomplished short stories (most readily available today in *Her Smoke Rose Up Forever* (1990)) offered an analysis of human sexuality and of male attitudes to women that was at once clinical, playful, and quite brutal. But the roles could be reversed. In the Hugo- and Nebula-winning "Houston, Houston, Do You Read?" (1976), three astronauts, returning to Earth after a long voyage, find a changed, future world of women (comparisons can be made with Gilman's *Herland*). They expect a rapturous welcome, but are regarded as relics of a contemptible past.

Role-reversal was a recurrent motif: sometimes positing the gentle "feminine" virtues as largely dependent on social context, and the subordination of one sex by the other as arbitrary; sometimes played for laughs. In Gerd Brantenberg's very funny *Daughters of Egalia* (1977), a male adolescent suffers agonies of shyness – and hopeless rebellion – when he is fitted for his first penis-sheath. He dreads having to walk past teams of crude, muscular builders, all claiming to have the biggest, wettest hole he ever saw.

More often, destructive value systems (subjection of women, global capitalism, exploitation of the Third World, despoliation of the natural world, organized violence) are seen as inherently male and irredeemable. In Sally Miller Gearhart's sentimental *The Wanderground: stories of the hill women* (1980), Earth herself has in some inexplicable way trapped men in their dying cities, while the Free Women live in nests in the woods, talking to animals, cultivating magical powers, and confidently awaiting the Goddess's final solution. The same worldview is offered, with equal conviction and far greater power and literary merit, by Charnas, Tiptree, and, later, in Le Guin's *Always Coming Home* (1985). The world as it is, run by men, is heading for disaster. Patriarchy is a structure that must be demolished before it poisons the earth beyond repair.

The catastrophe that wipes out most of the population, allowing a writer to reimagine society in a new pattern, is a venerable sf device. Feminist writers favored a mysterious plague that has selectively killed all the men: a motif used in Russ's "When it Changed" (1972) and *The Female Man*, Tiptree's "Houston, Houston, Do You Read?," and Nicola Griffith's *Ammonite* (1993). In *Ammonite*, the surviving (female) colonists of extra-solar planet Jeep break the bounds of *science* fiction by reverting to Bronze Age matriarchy. Russ's Whileaway is a true sf utopia: a planet where the "surviving female colonists" – squabbling passionately but never going to war, reproducing by fused-ova IVF – have developed stunning technologies and (relatively) ideal libertarian governance. "The Screwfly Solution" (1976), by a novice writer called Racoona Sheldon (later revealed to be a Tiptree pseudonym), provided a chilling variation on the theme. When every man on Earth suddenly turns femicidal, it transpires that prospective alien colonists are using a virus to get rid of humans, by making a *minor* adjustment to the natural drives of the human male. But although some writers, like Gearhart, could be ruthless about getting rid of the men, feminist writers who were seriously trying to change the world had a different attitude. In *The Female Man*, in a complex reworking of her earlier women-only utopia from "When it Changed," Russ suggests that the all-female planet is actually one possible future Earth. The men were killed off not by a virus but by a "genocidal" war, a guilty secret which has been erased from the records of peaceful "Whileaway." When she knows the truth, Janet, the utopian character, rejects this solution utterly, though this could mean wiping herself and her whole world out of existence.

The multiverse hypothesis – time seen as a twisted braid of possibilities – is another recurring device: proposed in *The Female Man* and powerfully employed in Marge Piercy's *Woman on the Edge of Time* (1976), it recently reappeared in Kathleen Ann Goonan's *In War Times* (2007). *The Female Man* offers readers four variants of the same character (implicitly Russ herself at varying stages of self-realization) inhabiting different possible timelines. Piercy, a feminist novelist who has made successful forays into sf, gives Connie Ramos, a poor Chicana woman in 1960s inner-city America, access to the daydream-like (it's only a possibility) future community of Mattapoisett, where women, men, and shades between, live as equals: sharing lust, love, work, and play; bringing up babies, tending their gardens, and struggling against the rearguard of the destructive, male-ordered past. Our heroine, unlike most self-identifying feminists of the time, is by no means an affluent middle-class white: victim of her menfolk and of the system, she has little chance of survival. But in this engrossing novel of ideas, our hope for the future depends, quite literally, on Connie's liberation.

In 1976, "James Tiptree Jr" was unmasked as a woman: Alice Sheldon (whose extraordinary life is revealed in Phillips (2006)). The effect of this revelation can be exaggerated. Feminist novels and stories, including Tiptree's, continued to be honored until the end of the decade, when Vonda McIntyre's *Dreamsnake* (1979) won the last "feminist sf" Hugo and Nebula double. But the fact that one of its central figures was believed to be male had been vital to the status of feminist sf. *As a man*, Alice Sheldon had been acclaimed, and acknowledged as a master of the genre. When the truth was known, Tiptree's reputation went into steep decline, and mainstream sf's interest in the feminist agenda quickly faded. Soon Bruce Sterling (1986), herald of the new cutting edge, could dismiss the 1970s as a blank in genre history (to the indignation of fan activist Jeanne Gomoll (1987)). Like the New Wave, the cyberpunks were a group of male radicals, acknowledging one or two female associates (notably Pat Cadigan) who could not hope for the same attention as the male stars. Sf's normal service had been resumed.

Feminist sf, however, was not dead. On the contrary, it had just been born. The careers of many feminist sf writers (Eleanor Arnason, Octavia E. Butler, Candas Jane Dorsey, Carol Emshwiller, Karen Joy Fowler, Kathleen Ann Goonan, Suzette Haden Elgin, Nalo Hopkinson, Gwyneth Jones, Pat Murphy, Melissa Scott, Joan Slonczewksi, Sheri Tepper, Lisa Tuttle, and others) began or developed in the 1980s and 1990s. Other women felt able, as Mary Gentle puts it, to take "a feminist background for granted, and [go] on from there" (Green and Lefanu 1985: 5). Thus, in her splendid *Golden Witchbreed* (1983), and its darker sequel, *Ancient Light* (1987), there is no discussion of sexual politics: the "Ortheans," male and female, are simply equal persons. In the same vein, Carolyn Janice Cherry, writing under the name C.J. Cherryh, became a much-honored popular sf writer, always playing subversive games with sex roles but not taking an overtly feminist stance. In her series beginning with *The Pride of Chanur* (1981), the females of the catlike Chanur run an interplanetary trading empire, while the emotionally volatile males stay at home. And finally, in February 1991, Karen Fowler and Pat Murphy initiated the James Tiptree Jr Award "for science fiction or fantasy that explores or expands our understanding of gender." Never intended as a feminist institution, the prize, often controversial, has become a coveted honor. It has been awarded to radical feminists, to essentialists, to women, men, and shades between; in fitting utopian, egalitarian style.

Here in the first decade of the twenty-first century, sf (like the human world) is as gendered as ever, and masculine sf commands the mainstream of the genre. Yet both feminine and feminist sf are flourishing in a way that would have been unthinkable before the 1970s, and the genre continues to be enriched by the alternative narratives of feminism: uncovering the inconvenient truth about patriarchy, tracing adventures of justice and peace instead of embracing permanent warfare; imagining humane future societies, rather than improved designs for planet-destruction. In concentrating on the "feminist decade" of the 1970s, it may seem that I have recounted the story of feminism as a passing fad. But the heyday of any artistic movement is brief (as the cyberpunks were swiftly to discover). The best of them do not vanish, they are assimi- lated: secretly propagating through the body of the art form, changing it forever.

Bibliography

Aldiss, B. (1973) *Billion Year Spree: the history of science fiction*, London: Weidenfeld and Nicolson.

Donawerth, J.L. and Kolmerten, C.A. (eds) (1994) *Utopian and Science Fiction by Women: worlds of difference*, Liverpool: Liverpool University Press.

Gomoll, J. (1987) *An Open Letter to Joanna Russ*. Online. Available HTTP: <http://www.geocities.com/Athens/8720/letter.htm> (accessed 1 April 2008).

Green, J. and Lefanu, S. (eds) (1985) *Despatches from the Frontier of the Female Mind*, London: The Women's Press.

Larbalestier, J. (ed.) (2006) *Daughters of Earth: feminist science fiction in the twentieth century*, Middletown, CT: Wesleyan University Press.

Merrick, H. and Williams, T. (eds) (1999) *Women of Other Worlds: excursions through science fiction and feminism*, Nedlands, WA: University of Western Australia Press.

Phillips, J. (2006) *James Tiptree, Jr: the double life of Alice B. Sheldon*, New York: St Martin's Press.

Sterling, B. (1986) "Introduction," in W. Gibson, *Burning Chrome*, London: Gollancz.

52
FUTURE HISTORY
Andy Sawyer

Despite some notable precursors, such as Mary Shelley's *The Last Man* (1826) and Jane Webb Loudon's *The Mummy!* (1827), the imagination of fictional futures only begins to become commonplace toward the end of the nineteenth century as sf crystallizes out of post-Romantic secular apocalypses and utopian speculations. It is as if the great narrative sweeps of history had to be composed before authors could consider the future not just as teleology but as narrative. Following the irrevocable changes of the American and French Revolutions, Darwinism and Marxism suggested that the flow of events moves beyond the present to a mysterious, often ineffable future. Just as the nineteenth-century historical novel made the past an imaginative territory in which to examine what we have become, so stories of the future increasingly turned to the exploration of possibility and the hopes and fears of what we *might* become.

In 1871, George Chesney's *The Battle of Dorking* and Edward Bulwer-Lytton's *The Coming Race* suggested the threat of national and racial overtaking. H.G. Wells's and George Griffith's apocalyptic futures extrapolated the threat and promise of as yet unachieved heavier-than-air flight from the known technology of ballooning. Moreover, Wells's *The War of the Worlds* (1898), *When the Sleeper Wakes* (1899), "A Story of the Days to Come" (1897), and "A Dream of Armageddon" (1901) share elements that might imply that they are part of a common future history – one that may simply have coalesced (as many do) through the feeling that imagining the settings for one story allows enough useful material to be reused elsewhere.

Wells, however, was fascinated with history. In "The Discovery of the Future" (1902), he suggested that the example of the way physical sciences use data to forecast results might enable social sciences to depict a picture of the future "that will be just as certain … and perhaps just as detailed as the picture that has been built up within the last hundred years of the geological past" (Wells 1989: 28). In Isaac Asimov's *Foundation* series (1942–50), such a calculus of probability became the science of "psychohistory," which could predict future "trends." Wells believed that such future developments as the World State were inevitable (or rather, without such developments the future of the human race would be chaotic and short), but his question "Why should things cease at man?" (Wells 1989: 35) can be taken to be as much uneasily contingent as transcendent. Out of this uneasy dynamic between destiny and randomness, Wells concludes that humanity can (if the collective will is strong enough) shape its own future, although its exact form remains unforeseeable. *The Shape of Things to Come* (1933) offered a possible version of this process. Perhaps the most influential future history, Olaf Stapledon's *Last and First Men* (1930), explores the dynamic between the intellectual and the passionate ideals of human (or rather, Western) culture as it plays out through 18 separate species of humanity over 40 billion years of "huge fluctuations of joy and woe" (Stapledon 1930: 2). Like Wells, Stapledon was influenced by Hegelian/Marxist notions of history as both cause and effect. His novel, cast as an account telepathically dictated by a member of the far-future Eighteenth Men to a contemporary writer, underlines the smallness of our place in the historical account.

As writers began to conceive of the possible future as a venue both for genuine speculation about its nature and for commentary upon the present, a sense that the future might have a history of its own developed. Rudyard Kipling's "With the Night Mail" (1905) and "As Easy as A.B.C." (1912) are simply story and sequel, but they suggest a development in the history playfully charted in the correspondence, answers to queries, adverts, and reviews appended to the first story. "With the Night Mail" implies the span of years between the reader in the early 1900s and its implied reader a hundred or more years hence – we see, in what we are told about the development of the Aerial Board of Control, history in action. (From the sequel, we can infer a less benevolent dictatorship, especially if we ask how deliberate was the omission of the words "of both sexes" from the description of the makeup of the A.B.C.) But the sense that the future has a history of its own is perhaps more suited to the long story-cycle or novel.

Robert A. Heinlein claimed that the timeline establishing the background to the stories later collected in *The Past Through Tomorrow* (1967) was produced in late 1939 as an *aide-mémoire*, while Ursula Le Guin considers her *Hainish* sequence (1964–2000) to be revealed like voyages of exploration as the stories come to her, rather than part of an overall plan. Frank Herbert's *Dune* sequence (1963–85), continued by Brian Herbert and Kevin J. Anderson (1999–2007), is more powered by reader-demand than authorial playfulness, although both processes are linked by the propensity to *imagine* historically. Neither Le Guin nor Herbert have fully charted their universes (Le Guin admits on her website to "forgetting planets"), although fans have attempted to construct future histories for them. Le Guin's chronology in particular is archaeological in its vagueness – a reference in one story may increase what we "know" about a period of time far distant to it, but constructing a timeline is difficult.

On the other hand, Cordwainer Smith's *Instrumentality of Mankind* sequence (1950–75) was developed according to a chronology and a framework in a (lost) notebook, although it is not always easy to tell which stories belong when and "the saga was never conceived as a seamless whole" (Pierce 1993: xi). Nevertheless, there is a core myth of the Rediscovery of Man and the liberation of the Underpeople in such stories as "Alpha Ralpha Boulevard" (1961), "The Ballad of Lost C'mell" (1962), and "The Dead Lady of Clown Town" (1964) – a grand teleological sweep informed by Smith's Christianity – that is counterpointed by a more secular history in some stories concerning the progress of China and the descendants of the VomAcht family. This series of multiple narratives illuminates the idea of process.

Much sf takes place in a charted history. Many of C.J. Cherryh's novels, such as *Downbelow Station* (1981) and *Cyteen* (1988), take place within the context of the "Union–Alliance" rivalry for which a fan website has produced a chronology. Likewise, various websites chart Lois McMaster Bujold's *Miles Vorkosigan* series (1986–2002) which is set within a loose future-history context, but as any sf series *has* to take place over a period of time it can be argued that all sf series are "future histories." However, we may choose to claim the term for those, such as Cherryh's, in which the processes of historical change are as important as the characters' stories.

Behind the future history is a theory of history itself: "Could Asimov have written as he did without the ground-breaking theories of Malthus and his many successors, down to A.J. Toynbee?" (Shippey 1973: 18; see also James 1985). While it has been strongly denied that the apparent patterns of history outlined in Toynbee's description of the rise and fall of civilizations and Oswald Spengler's more cyclical model of birth–adolescence–maturity–decay (drawn upon in James Blish's *Cities in Flight* sequence (1950–62) (see Mullen 1981)) have any explanatory power, the mythic element in these structures offers a mixture of familiarity and strangeness attractive to the sf writer: the *assumption* that our own civilization is only temporary opens up speculations about the future. Asimov's *Foundation* series shows history as process which, despite psychohistory's premises, can be fought against and possibly shaped. Such narratives might actually represent a "denial" of history: "by claiming that all times, like all heaps of sand, are basically the same, [Wells] denies the possibility of different eras with different contours," John Huntington argues, before critiquing Asimov's justification – history repeats itself – for "retelling" moments from Roman and Judaic history (Huntington 1989: 139–42). Asimov himself pointed to Toynbee's more sophisticated version of repetition (Asimov 1977: 48), but it is hard to refute Huntington's claim that this ignores sociological and political complexities. Nevertheless, its use of viewpoint, while perhaps not very good history, is effective myth.

Smith's stories are tales, fables, and histories looked back on from a far future. Asimov's are similarly retrospective but, instead of Smith's more flexible but less specific oral narratives, extracts from the *Encyclopedia Galactica* introduce individuals and events, providing not only snippets of important information but also a more *formal* context. Smith's distancing offers a more ironic version of this formality, allowing a sense of Stapledon's cosmic history to leak into the narrative. Doris Lessing acknowledges the influence of Stapledon's vast sweeps on her *Canopus in Argos* series (1979–83), but as myth rather than history. In *The Four-Gated City* (1969), Lessing brings Martha Quest, the protagonist of her *Children of Violence* series (1952–69), into an apocalyptic future by means of an appendix of documents dated between 1995 and 2000, describing the collapse of the British Isles and the hegemony of the Mongolian National Area. As her realistic *Bildungsroman* moves into a different key, the lives of individuals become a counterpoint to the lives of cultures. Octavia E. Butler's *Patternist* sequence (1976–84) begins in the past and extends into the future (although Butler deals most explicitly and movingly with history in *Kindred* (1979), in which time travel allows comparisons between past and present African-American experience).

This dynamic is also evident in those novels which comment more implicitly upon their own "presence" in history. The appendix to George Orwell's *Nineteen Eighty-four* (1949) concerning Newspeak raises questions about the diegetic history because it assumes that the world of the novel is situated in a past upon which voices from even further in the future might comment. In the appendix to Margaret Atwood's *The Handmaid's Tale* (1985), the narrator's account becomes the subject of future-scholars' attempts to tease out its relationship to their world. This device is not new – Arthur C. Clarke's "History Lesson" (1949) ironically reveals that the image of humanity constructed by a far-future race comes from a Mickey Mouse cartoon – but Atwood's confrontation of the events she has described through "scholarly" discourse allows us to ponder uneasily about how scholars construct models of history rather than describe or empathize with past events.

Such mild metafictionality is taken further in mock-historical fictions that weave future histories out of sf itself. R.C. Churchill's *A Short History of the Future* (1955) pretends that various accounts of the future charted by Ray Bradbury, Charles Chilton, Robert Graves, Aldous Huxley, George Orwell, Nevil Shute, and Kurt Vonnegut, among others, are textbook accounts of one time span. Like genuine historical sources, they are of course often at wild variance with each other, and Churchill has much fun in attempting to reconcile them. A more modern version, less in debt to specific works but clearly written with an eye to the sort of futures imagined in Arthur C. Clarke's fiction and nonfiction, is Brian Stableford and David Langford's *The Third Millennium (a history of the world: AD 2000–3000)* (1985), in which disaster (nuclear war in Latin America, volcanoes and earthquakes ripping Japan apart, greenhouse-effect flooding) goes hand in hand with technological progress (cheap power from nuclear fusion, genetically improved animals).

The sf future history exists in an uneasy relationship with teleology, often secularizing religious apotheosis as humans transcend physical limitations. Fictions set at the literal end of History itself – William Hope Hodgson's *The Night Land* (1912), Jack Vance's *The Dying Earth* (1950), Michael Moorcock's *Dancers at the End of Time* sequence (1972–6), Gene Wolfe's *Book of the New Sun* (1980–3) – look backwards at the past from a standpoint of racial or cultural decadence (although Wolfe's complex, ambiguous saga suggests that new cycles may spring from the old). The linking text in Brian Aldiss's *The Canopy of Time* (1959) weaves together stories to produce the Stapledonian vision that the "galaxy is nothing more than a gigantic laboratory for the blind experiments of nature" (Aldiss 1959: 222). Among other posthuman futures, Iain M. Banks's *Culture* (1987–) and John Varley's *Eight Worlds* (1974–) future histories include bodily modification or gender transference, while William Gibson's *Neuromancer* (1984) and Greg Egan's *Diaspora* (1997) imagine a transcendence out of the flesh and into software. The "Spike" or "Singularity" (the hypothetical moment at which progress zooms off at dazzling speed, usually involving artificial intelligence or the uploading of consciousness from flesh to machine, or out of the physical universe altogether), imagined in such fiction as Charles Stross's *Accelerando* (2005), has been dubbed, by Ken MacLeod, "the rapture for the nerds" (MacLeod 1998: 90).

These processes of decadence or apotheosis are, however, by no means part of the more traditional, carefully mapped future history, such as that of the *Star Trek* (1966–) franchise. The care given to the "history" of its universe, and how different series relate to each other, has as much to do with a desire for consistency as a fascination with the possibilities and process of history, but the detail of the franchise's universe is both rigorously charted and often imaginatively suggestive. This history exists in several forms (see "Memory Alpha" and "Memory Beta") which use information from both "canonical" and "noncanonical" sources to develop a timeline covering almost 14 billion years. While Huntington's criticism of Asimov's historical repetition could as easily be made of *Star Trek* (for example, "A Private Little War" (1968) replayed the then-current Vietnam War), much of the appeal of at least the first series was precisely in observing the present and the recent past played out on a larger canvas.

Whether a path to apotheosis or decadence, or simply an extra dimension of sf world building, the future history, even if it starts off as *aides-mémoire* or series Bibles, reminds us that history itself is a narrative, pieced together out of competing discourses.

Bibliography

Aldiss, B.W. (1959) *The Canopy of Time*, London: Faber & Faber.

Asimov, I. (1977) "Social Science Fiction," in D. Knight (ed.) *Turning Points: essays on the art of science fiction*, 1953, New York: Harper & Row.

Huntington, J. (1989) *Rationalizing Genius: ideological strategies in the classic American science fiction short story*, New Brunswick, NJ: Rutgers University Press.

James, E. (1985) "The Historian and SF," *Foundation*, 35: 5–13.

MacLeod, K. (1998) *The Cassini Division*, London: Orbit.

Memory Alpha (n.d.) Online. Available HTTP: <http://www.memory-alpha.org> (accessed April 2008).

Memory Beta (n.d.) Online. Available HTTP: <http://startrek.wikia.com> (accessed April 2008).

Mullen, R.D. (1981) "The Earthmanist Culture: *Cities in Flight* as a Spenglerian history," in J. Blish, *Cities in Flight*, London: Arrow.

Pierce, J.J. (1993) "Introduction," in C. Smith, *The Rediscovery of Man: the complete short science fiction of Cordwainer Smith*, ed. J.A. Mann, Framingham, MA: NESFA Press.

Shippey, T. (1973) "Science Fiction and the Idea of History," *Foundation*, 4: 4–19.

Stapledon, W.O (1930) *Last and First Men: a story of the near and far future*, London: Methuen.

Wells, H.G. (1989) "The Discovery of the Future," in P. Parrinder (ed.) *The Discovery of the Future with The Common-sense of World Peace and The Human Adventure*, 1902, London: PNL Press.

53
HARD SF
David N. Samuelson

Hard sf is the black hole around which the sf universe revolves, but whose identifying features are always in dispute. Stories most clearly drawn by its gravitational pull differ from other fantasy, but the genuine article is a logical impossibility. Most simply characterized as "getting the science right," hard sf seeks to avoid contradicting the contemporary state of scientific knowledge, something never completely realized. Less a category than a tendency, it is only loosely modeled on scientific practice. Hard science relies on mathematics usually inaccessible to most readers without translation into expository prose with practical applications. Drawing more on popularized versions than laboratory reports or theoretical papers, verbal sf transforms them into narrative. Only elements of spectacle translate well into visual media, as in the Stanley Kubrick and Arthur C. Clarke film and novel, *2001: A Space Odyssey* (1968). Guaranteeing no aesthetic quality beyond "local color," hard sf is distinguished by literary as well as scientific characteristics.

All sf requires some relationship to modern science and technology, including expectations of technological change. Hard sf ties much of its credibility to scientific rules and probability, enough that some readers define it simply as "hard" to read. Its "hardness" varies, however, as the sciences themselves differ in rigor from hard sciences (physics, astronomy, geology, chemistry, meteorology) to life sciences (biology, ecology) to softer behavioral sciences (though psychology, sociology, anthropology, linguistics, and semiotics have some hard components). Pseudosciences (creationism, spiritualism, ESP) and exploded theories (ether, phlogiston, humors, hollow Earth) are usually only pastiched, but esoteric speculation in physics, although impossible to verify or disprove, may belong. Projecting unknown rather than disproven developments also admits more subjective "postmodern" sciences, like molecular biology, psychochemistry, and interactive technology.

A paucity of published attempts suggests rigorous scientific investigation is too boring for popular or even literary fiction, but hard sf can summarize or allude to it, in part as an attitude of mind. It approaches the minimally or vastly unknown via hypotheses plausibly extending the here and now into imagined past and future, Earthly and off-world settings; it is no accident that so much hard sf involves alien worlds and beings, challenging both scientific and aesthetic knowledge and skills. Underpinned by facts and theory, both commonly superseded and reinterpreted, hard sf reflects scientific interpretations of reality. Wedded to empiricism, determinism, and relativism, scientists respect material evidence, causality, and context, seeking what should always take place, rather than simply what is known or believed to have happened, and experimenting to correct or improve theories. Rigorously controlled environments, however, seldom obtain outside laboratories strictly monitored by observers who let events overcome predilections.

Sf visions also require connections to the here and now. Like other fantasy, hard sf can use literary connections like allegory, satire, inversion, and myth, but the "what if?" most distinctive to it depends on speculation related to limits of science and technology, commonly by means of extrapolation and transformation. Extending "natural laws" in space and historical trends in time, extrapolation is the clearest way to evoke plausibility for the scientifically knowledgeable. Working from theories that stretch or even transcend existing paradigms, transformation may be no less scientific, but less likely to be proven. Successful paradigm shifts are more common in fiction than in science.

Readers less educated in science may miss the fudging, but hard-sf writers typically know, and seek to generate plausibility by manipulating words, characters, and even some elements of the cosmos. Stories put theory into action, display processes common to engineering, and portray the overcoming of obstacles much more easily in fiction than could be achieved in real science. Readers also need involvement in the action, a sense that it will make life easier or more complicated, perhaps even threatening human existence or identity. Elements of presentation given a scientific twist include setting, props, actions, characters, and narrative style, which can create an illusion of reality even for the impossible.

All extraterrestrial settings need some justification, but only hard sf often provides details of a spaceship, an alien artifact, a planet, or a solar system not just as a stage set but to generate motivation and narrative action. Future settings and actions require changes closely tied to historical trends or parallels. While future fashion or taste is unpredictable, changes in materials and design can be extrapolated. Technological forecasting, moreover, projects habitats, including laboratory setups, means of transport and communication, and electronic and other equipment, within feasible rather than miraculous or whimsical limits.

Characters displaying scientific knowledge and attitude serve as a conduit for the reader. "Nonhuman" characters like robots, computers, and their biological variants (androids, clones, modified animals, alien beings) are built on rational grounds related to context and evolution. Even the conduct of war, business, or romance involves exploration and discovery, requiring and even enabling technical solutions to problems. Habitual readers expect some jargon and neologisms, but many find highly suspect those "explanations" which only sound scientific. Narrative style tends to be more expository than dramatic, more transparent than opaque, factually exact, even flirting with mathematics, and broadly didactic, extending or confirming a reader's education and typically favoring unfettered application of scientific thought and actions. Though relying on these features, no self-respecting hard-sf writer would restrict a story to them, risking stereotype and self-parody. The centrality of hard sf lies in its relative credibility, and its discoveries and inventions often spread into the genre as a whole.

Much sf only uses science minimally, as a launching platform for social satire or psychological fables, with aesthetic complications. Poetic license even permits wholesale abrogation of contemporary scientific laws and theories. J.G. Ballard, Philip K. Dick, Ray Bradbury, Harlan Ellison, and Kurt Vonnegut Jr often have disregarded the science of their day. Some genre purists, however, try to limit themselves to H.G. Wells's claim of only one impossibility per story. Gary Westfahl (1996) argues that single-issue puzzle stories typically establish a hard-sf writer's bona fides, making experienced readers more willing to suspend disbelief in conceptually high-flown longer works. Perfect fidelity to science, however, is not always required, even by writers of hard sf. Indeed, sf judged both aesthetically and commercially successful often mixes hard science with mysticism, as in Clarke's *Childhood's End* (1953) and Frank Herbert's *Dune* (1965).

If science describes a true state of affairs in the material universe (a proposition by no means universally accepted), then sf presents some imaginary constructs that cannot be verified. Even when the core invention or discovery conforms to existing science, and some of its social and psychological effects are carefully projected, elements from previous literature, myth, and folklore dominate narrative. What is sound science is open to debate, especially in retrospect, and many hard-sf projections morph into fantasy (e.g., habitable worlds in an atomic "solar system") or a loose approximation of history (e.g., near-space travel). The rare story highlighting a good prediction or projection (early tales of atomic energy) becomes little more than hollow realism, lacking confirming historical detail; near-future projections more often become alternate history, betrayed by actuality (e.g., *Destination Moon* (Pichel 1950)).

Some stories from before the 1920s possess characteristics associated with hard sf. Johannes Kepler's mystical moon voyage (*A Dream, or Lunar Astronomy* (1634; written *c*. 1600)) used gravitational pull (as had Dante Alighieri's epic poem *Paradise* (*c*. 1307–21)). Exaggerating the nascent science of electricity, Mary Shelley's *Frankenstein* (1818) is driven by a heretical quest for the unknown. Edgar Allan Poe introduced medical characters and scientific reasoning to lend verisimilitude to fantastical tales, but also a "hollow earth" theory already discredited. Both on and beyond Earth, Jules Verne larded exploration tales with research by contemporary naturalists. Actually educated in science teaching, Wells exhibited in *The Time Machine* (1895) a dialectic of hypothesis and experiment and an awareness of how both living and nonliving matter evolve.

US magazine stories of the 1920s and 1930s seldom embodied pioneer editor Hugo Gernsback's claims of scientific "fact" and coherence. In the "Golden Age" of John W. Campbell's *Astounding Science Fiction*, more measured presentations of scientific details and rationale deferred to social consequences and storytelling, and popular *Astounding* writers like E.E. "Doc" Smith and A.E. van Vogt often paid scant heed to scientific limits or plausibility in surmounting them. Magazine letter columns show readers and writers "playing the game" of catching or excusing fudged science, but only when the late 1950s emphasized social and psychological issues did the "hard sf" label gradually emerge around 1957, in *Astounding* reviews by P. Schuyler Miller (see Westfahl 1996). Presupposing a time when a larger proportion of a smaller field of writers and readers were well versed in science and engineering, the term implied an imagined purity sounder than the growing reliance on the soft sciences. It also reflected a growing sense in a technological society that the natural world has essential coherence and that forecasts or projections should account for consequences and parallel trends.

Everybody fudges, however. Sf stories need at least one element that is not yet a recognizable part of the world known to educated readers in its era, commonly a new invention (gadget), locale (extraterrestrial world or vehicle), time frame (the future), or discovery. What does not exist empirical science may not sanction, but hard sf does use hypothetical possibilities supported (or not disproven) by contemporary scientific theory. Present-day unknowns, such as dark matter and dark energy, are no more subject to empirical disproof or narrative structures than string theory and multiple universes, however fascinating they may be. Fanciful devices like hyperspace and wormholes, tenuously underwritten by theory, serve a narrative need for stories set outside our solar system. Writers rarely justify such genre mythology, including time machines, extrasensory perception, extraterrestrial planets whose chemistry supports human life, and easy communication between cultures and species.

Devices more apparently obedient to Einstein's speed limit include Ursula K. Le Guin's ansible, which in several stories permits faster-than-light communication (although information still must be carried by matter), and Gregory Benford's tachyons which can only travel faster than light, but somehow permit in *Timescape* (1980) one-way communication between otherwise undetectable multiple universes. As with gravitational imbalances on the planet Mesklin in Hal Clement's *Mission of Gravity* (1954) and on Larry Niven's *Ringworld* (1970), hard-sf writers sometimes confess their errors and even try to rectify their violations.

Scientists fight a longstanding battle with subjectivity, particularly threatening to research in biology, medicine, and social science, where our image of ourselves is at stake. The scientist's exactitude regularly yields, however, to the writer's fascination with potential consequences of intriguing hypotheses. Research into interactive technology, virtual reality and virtual life, genetic engineering and brain research (psychobiology, psychochemistry, psychophysics) has spurred a recent upsurge in hard sf. Relying as it does on subjects' expressed reactions usually in a near-future setting, such "postmodern" science is a boon for fiction, despite a lack of objective verifiability for reputed changes in mental states and the purely metaphorical existence of "cyberspace."

Whether hard sf is a category or a tendency, debate rages among writers and fans over who or what most clearly belongs. Recognition by one's peers may matter most, as Kathryn Cramer (2003) argues, but that can also deteriorate into a popularity contest. A degree or profession in science or technology, publication of scientific papers, and even an explanation of the homework and sources involved implies plausibility, albeit outside a story's literary parameters. Even so, few writers outside English-speaking nations are recognized, not even from the Russian tradition of "Technological Fantasy," and women seem to have been conspicuously absent.

With women's presence growing in the hard sciences and in sf, their continuing relative absence begs an explanation. Hardwired or not, males seem statistically more fascinated with looking under the hood and taking mechanisms apart. Early male social conditioning also emphasizes the "hardness" of making and enforcing laws and assuming wartime footing against a cruel universe. Self-selection may be how gender bias works in this case, as many women writers show little interest or satisfaction in writing they call overly mechanical and unconcerned with human values. C.J. Cherryh's space operas are one exception; more typical is Le Guin's use of "soft" anthropology shading into folklore. "Getting it right" in postmodern science, however, qualifies Nicola Griffith's *Slow River* (1995), Joan Slonczewski's *Brain Plague* (2001), and Gwyneth Jones's *Life* (2004). Hardness is no index of literary quality, of course, only an illusory measure of conformity with the material universe, and simply using real science cannot make a story interesting.

Relatively few writers really qualify for hard sf. After the term was coined, Robert A. Heinlein's earlier fiction was retrospectively included in the subgenre, but it was not a major weapon in his arsenal. Seldom using his Ph.D. in biochemistry in fiction, Isaac Asimov wrote enormous amounts of popular science, one hard-sf novel, *The Gods Themselves* (1972), and six pre-Space Age juvenile novels which explored the solar system. Clarke also earned a science degree and wrote plenty of nonfiction, as well as numerous near-future novels and stories based solidly in scientific extrapolation, much of it now outdated. His *A Fall of Moondust* (1961) is a model solution for a problem (vehicles sinking into lunar dust) that later proved to be nonexistent. Clement, a high-school science teacher, has written little else but hard sf, teaching science in virtually every scene or chapter. For the epic odyssey of interspecies cooperation in *Mission of Gravity*, he created an alien world from the ground up, explaining the process in a supplementary essay accompanying the book's first serial publication.

Renowned for how planetary ecology figures (albeit incompletely) in *Dune*, Herbert established his credentials earlier with a closely extrapolated future submarine in *The Dragon in the Sea* (1956). *Tau Zero* (1970), often credited as hard sf though it offends contemporary cosmology, is one of many Poul Anderson stories of adventure and social commentary with a major role for science. The best-established recent hard-sf writer is Gregory Benford, a practicing physicist who has complemented his six-volume *Galactic Center* series (1976–95) with meticulous attention to scientific practice past and future in the award-winning *Timescape* and with many deftly turned short stories and nonfiction papers.

Writing hard sf is an attempt to make the not-impossible seem reasonable, so it is not surprising to see the frontier moving as the formerly far out becomes mundane, at least in fiction. The subjectivity and uncertainty of the postmodern era follows by at least a half-century the course of science itself since their introduction by Heisenberg in physics and Saussure in linguistics. Future developments of this tempting and problematic sort will undoubtedly stimulate more of the frustrating and fruitful quest for the Philosopher's Stone of hard sf.

Bibliography

Cramer, K. (2003) "Hard Science Fiction," in E. James and F. Mendlesohn (eds) *The Cambridge Companion to Science Fiction*, Cambridge: Cambridge University Press.

Westfahl, G. (1996) *Cosmic Engineers: a study of hard science fiction*, Westport, CT: Greenwood.

54

SLIPSTREAM

Victoria de Zwaan

The story of "the slipstream" is not hard to tell. It has a well-known history, so far book-ended by two documents: Bruce Sterling's 1989 *Science Fiction Eye* essay "Slipstream," and *Feeling Very Strange: the slipstream anthology* (2006), edited by James Patrick Kelly and John Kessel. I will discuss both of these documents and their critical reception below, but it should perhaps first be said that the most notable element of the continuing story of the slipstream is the apparent indeterminacy of the meaning of the term. Two fairly typical comments come from Jed Hartman, who calls the term "an ill-defined hodgepodge of several overlapping concepts" (Hartman 2005), and Greg Johnson, who says "there's some agreement that there's something different going on out there, and it may as well be called slipstream, but nobody's quite sure what it is" (Johnson 2006).

At its most interesting, slipstream discourse addresses the possible fluidity of the boundary between sf and non-sf; at its most problematic, it highlights an anxiety about the legitimacy or what Sterling calls the "worthiness" of sf. (See Luckhurst 1994 and Westfahl 2000 for analyses of the anxiety of legitimation that haunts sf criticism.) Put more broadly, however, as a new theoretical category, the term "slipstream" addresses the pressing problem of how the postmodernization of sf can be described without entirely undermining what has made and continues to make sf such a fertile genre on one side for writerly experimentation and innovation and on the other for a range of genre-specific readerly pleasures.

In 1989, cyberpunk writer and theorist/propagandist Bruce Sterling introduced the term "slipstream" to denote what he thought was an "emerging genre" on the borderlines between sf and "mainstream fiction," in which sf techniques – no longer able to service what Sterling called the "coherent social vision" of genre sf – were adapted by non-sf writers to produce more imaginative, estranging, counter-realist, and innovative works than sf proper could produce. Sterling suggested that "it is a contemporary kind of writing which has set its face against consensual reality," and which "simply makes you feel very strange; the way that living in the late twentieth century makes you feel, if you are a person of a certain sensibility" (Sterling 1989: 78). He closed his essay with an argument that "rack space" in bookstores should designate a shelf for "Novels of Postmodern Sensibility," which would sell better with the more catchy label of "slipstream fiction." His alphabetical list of slipstream texts included works by such diverse writers as Kathy Acker, Isabel Allende, Donald Barthelme, William Burroughs, Thomas Disch, Lawrence Durrell, Raymond Federman, Marge Piercy, Thomas Pynchon, Muriel Spark, and D.M. Thomas (of whom only Burroughs, Disch, and Piercy have been habitually associated with sf, in Burroughs's case more as a strong influence than a practitioner; and indeed there are very few established genre sf writers in Sterling's list). A closer examination of this selection of authors might reveal the criteria for inclusion as slipstream fiction. Burroughs's *The Naked Lunch* (1959) and *The Soft Machine* (1961), Pynchon's *Gravity's Rainbow* (1973), and Acker's *Empire of the Senseless* (1988) stand out from the list as texts that engage with scientific and technological themes in general and the human–machine interface in particular. Indeed, cyberpunk and other sf writers often cite Pynchon and Burroughs as two of their precursors; and Acker's book plays with motifs central to cyberpunk. It is clear, however, that a thematic connection with sf is not in itself a sufficient condition to garner Sterling's designation of a text as slipstream: there also needs to be an estranging and anti-realist element, either in subject matter or in form.

For example, Pynchon's overt engagement with science and technology in *Gravity's Rainbow* has at its root an absurd enigma, a sort of "hoax" typical of experimental fictions and perhaps an anathema in sf, having to do with an ostensible relationship between the sexual conquests of one Tyrone Slothrop and the pattern of the German bombings of London in the Second World War. Slothrop's personal quest, alongside the investigation by different schools of scientists into this "connection," opens up numerous intertwining metaphors which raise ontological and epistemological possibilities about the nature of reality but without any resolution (see de Zwaan 2002). Indeed, Slothrop disappears from the text long before its conclusion, undermining the realist idea that stories have beginnings, middles, and ends, and thwarting the readerly desire for closure that is rewarded by realist novels, whether these are mainstream or sf. The fact that Sterling mentions two other novels by Pynchon, *V.* (1963) and *The Crying of Lot 49* (1966), both of which are about quests that open up a dizzying array of possible answers but without resolution, confirms that it is the counter-realism of these texts that make them slipstream, especially as they do not have science as a central motif, except for a meditation on entropy that is sustained throughout both novels, though more overtly in *Lot 49* than in *V.*

Acker's *Empire of the Senseless* is even less "scientific" than *Gravity's Rainbow*. Adopting her usual strategy of lifting from other texts rather than making up her own stories, Acker uses aspects of William Gibson's breakout cyberpunk novel *Neuromancer* (1984) for the first section of her book. Though there are recognizable scenes and motifs, even whole passages from *Neuromancer*, there are subtle alterations that serve to eliminate cyberspace in particular and science in general, in order to redirect attention onto the death instinct that drives Gibson's Case, who (alongside a number of other male protagonists, including Mark Twain's Huckleberry Finn) provides a prototype for her own male protagonist, Thivai (see de Zwaan 1997). In this case, then, as with Pynchon, the designation of the text as slipstream has to do with the overtly disruptive, experimental, and counter-realist surface of the text, which amalgamates hundreds of different texts into something that carries Acker's own signature prose but never allows for ontological solidity or epistemological closure. Her style is of course influenced by the cut-up techniques of Burroughs as well as the metafictional/surfictionist experiments of such writers as Federman and Barthelme, who also make it into Sterling's list, precisely for their counter-realist experiments with narrative form.

The inclusion of novels by Piercy and Disch, and other sf writers such as Kurt Vonnegut, raises a slightly different set of considerations. The particular books Sterling mentions reveal to some extent the aesthetic sensibility that creates the list in the first place. Piercy's *Woman on the Edge of Time* (1976), for example, is a futurist/utopian fiction in which technology is a central theme, and which uses one of the staple features of genre sf, time travel. What presumably qualifies this text as "slipstream" is not so much the idea of time-shift or time travel but its pervasive meditation on madness. Reminiscent of Ken Kesey's *One Flew Over the Cuckoo's Nest* (1962) and Henry James's *The Turn of the Screw* (1898), Piercy's novel undermines the idea of a solid, knowable, "consensual" reality.

Others in my selection from Sterling's list have little or no connection with the themes or motifs of sf, but they do to different extents share in anti-realism and formal experimentation. Of these, perhaps the most intriguing choice is Isabel Allende's *The House of the Spirits* (1982), a novel about three generations of women in a South American family, written from two viewpoints, and often thought of as a *roman à clef*. Rather than disturbing the ontological ground of the novel's world, it offers some measure of beginning–middle–end as well as narrative closure to its reader, so Sterling presumably included it because of its magic realism.

Of course, it is not clear how considered each of these choices was, or if Sterling meant them to be taken so seriously, but the term "slipstream" caught on in sf criticism to designate those sf books that play with and undermine the conventions of the genre, as well as those apparently non-sf books and writers that could be discussed as sf because of their themes or techniques of estrangement. The vagueness of the term allows logical and heuristic slippage. Is slipstream an sf subgenre or a new genre outside sf? Is it genre fiction or literary fiction? Is slipstream sf part of mainstream literature or is mainstream literature being parasitical on sf? Is it a type of writing or a sensibility? Is it a genre or a marketing strategy? Such slippages allow a widening of the materials to be included in critical discourse around sf, fantasy, and utopian fiction, and obliterate the high/low culture divide of mainstream/genre fiction. Niall Harrison, recognizing the extent to which the term "slipstream" addresses the issue of literary legitimacy in sf criticism, calls this critical move "a land-grab by the ghetto" (Harrison 2006).

The term "slipstream" has continued to be of interest to sf theorists, despite its heuristic weaknesses, because it designates a development in sf toward anti-realism while simultaneously offering a potentially liberating expansion in the choice of objects that belong to the sf scholarly community. Since 1989, the term is to be found ubiquitously in sf blogs, encyclopedias, and critical essays. In blogs, sf fans swap recommendations for "the list," including such names as Jorge Luis Borges, Douglas Copeland, and Franz Kafka, as well as a range of contemporary films, even while voicing deep skepticism about the term itself (see, especially, Moles 2005). In the self-confessedly incomplete *Wikipedia* entry on the term, *Memento* (Nolan 2000), a film about time, memory, and witnessing that plays with the narrative conventions of the medium, is cited as an example because it falls into the category of "the fiction of strangeness." James Kelly and John Kessel, trying to come to grips with the term in order to justify their choices for inclusion in their anthology, carefully steer away from the idea of genre and focus instead on the literary effect of "feeling very strange" (Kelly and Kessel 2006). Johnson (2006), Harrison (2006) and Soyka (2006) are unconvinced that this approach brings clarity to the designation of these stories as slipstream.

In his original essay, Sterling claimed that "once the notion of slipstream is vaguely explained, almost all SF readers can recite a quick list of books that belong there by right" (Sterling 1989: 78); and indeed what emerges out of all this debate and discussion is a series of wonderful reading lists and potential anthologies that do not stay inside the boundaries of any single genre, but rather focus on literary affect and aesthetic taste. Similar lists might well be and often are generated with other starting points, some of which already have established usage and heuristic specificity, such as "magical realism," "anti-realism," "postmodern," "experimental," "surreal," or "fabulation." If the word "slipstream" is to continue to have staying power inside the sf community, or to develop heuristic power outside it either in other scholarly communities or in the wider cultural world – that is, if it is to have a meaningful impact on literary scholarship and the ongoing definition of "schools" of art – it will likely be in recognition of a type of writing that crosses boundaries, that has experimentalist roots but can become a series of conventional techniques and stylistic devices, and that can designate a sub-category or subgenre within any genre, including sf.

Bibliography

de Zwaan, V. (1997) "Rethinking the Slipstream: Kathy Acker reads *Neuromancer*," *Science Fiction Studies*, 24(3): 459–70.

—— (2002) *Interpreting Radical Metaphor in the Experimental Fictions of Donald Barthelme, Thomas Pynchon, and Kathy Acker*, Lewiston, NY: Edwin Mellen Press.

Harrison, N. (2006) Review of J.P. Kelly and J. Kessel (eds) *Feeling Very Strange*, *Strange Horizons*. Online. Available HTTP: <http://www.strangehorizons.com/reviews/2006/09/feeling_v-comments.shtml> (accessed 1 April 2008).

Hartman, J. (2005) Comment in response to D. Moles, "I Want My 20th Century Schizoid Art," *Chronautic Log*, 5 May. Online. Available HTTP: <http://www.discontent.com/log/archives/000547.html> (accessed 1 April 2008), reprinted in J.P. Kelly and J. Kessel (eds) (2006) *Feeling Very Strange*, San Francisco: Tachyon.

Johnson, G. (2006) Review of *Feeling Very Strange*, ed. J.P. Kelly and J. Kessel. *SFSite*. Online. Available HTTP: <http://www.sfsite.com/10a/fs233.htm>.

Kelly, J.P. and Kessel, J. (eds) (2006) *Feeling Very Strange: the slipstream anthology*, San Francisco: Tachyon.

Luckhurst, R. (1994) "The Many Deaths of Science Fiction: a polemic," *Science Fiction Studies*, 21(1): 358–66.

Moles, D. (2005) "I Want My 20th Century Schizoid Art," *Chronautic Log*, 3 May. Online. Available HTTP: <http://www.discontent.com/log/archives/000547.html> (accessed 1 April 2008), reprinted in J.P. Kelly and J. Kessel (eds) (2006) *Feeling Very Strange*, San Francisco: Tachyon.

Soyka, D. (2006) Review of J.P. Kelly and J. Kessel (eds), *Feeling Very Strange, SF Site*. Online. Available HTTP: <http://www.sfsite.com/08b/fv230.htm> (accessed 1 April 2008).

Sterling, B. (1989) "Slipstream," *SF Eye*, 5: 77–80.

Westfahl, G. (2000) "Who Governs Science Fiction?," *Extrapolation*, 41(1): 63–72.

Wikipedia (2007) "Slipstream." Online. Available HTTP: <http://en.wikipedia.org/wiki/Slipstream> (accessed 1 April 2008).

55

SPACE OPERA

Andy Sawyer

"Space opera" means different things depending upon when it is said and by whom. Wilson Tucker coined the term in 1941 for the "hacky, grinding, stinking, outworn, spaceship yarn," but like "soap opera," it lost its negative implications as fans started to use the term for stories that they liked rather than despised. First attached to such 1930s star-busting pulp epics as Edmond Hamilton's *Interstellar Patrol* (1929–30), Jack Williamson's *Legion of Space* (1934–9), and E.E. "Doc" Smith's *Lensman* (1934–48) series, it seems to have become a term for referring to material the reader has outgrown but still regards with affection. Stereotyped space opera has minimal characterization, and vast settings of interstellar conflicts between clearly defined "good" and "bad" sides (typically human and alien, respectively, although Smith was careful to emphasize that not all aliens are "bad"). Its orchestrated set-piece scenes of massive destruction, as in Hamilton's "The Universe Wreckers" (1930), are parodied in Harry Harrison's *Star Smashers of the Galaxy Rangers* (1973). Yet an increasingly vivid romanticism brought color and a sense of baroque sophistication to the mode (Stableford 1993), perhaps nowhere more clearly than in Leigh Brackett's space operas, published in *Planet Stories* and elsewhere from 1940 to the 1950s. These aspects perhaps culminated in *Star Wars: Episode IV – A New Hope* (Lucas 1977), in which pastiche of space-operatic tropes presented with state-of-the-art special effects brought knowing pleasure to older fans and created a vast new audience for the mode among younger ones. (Significantly, Brackett wrote a draft of the screenplay for its sequel, *Star Wars: Episode V – The Empire Strikes Back* (Kershner 1980).)

After its coining (quickly, according to Stableford (2006), slowly, according to David Hartwell and Kathryn Cramer (2006)), the term became less condemnatory, more a set of shared assumptions which defined stories with particular settings, effects, and literary goals. Patricia Monk (1992), Gary Westfahl (1994, 2003), David Pringle (2000), Hartwell (2006a, 2006b, 2006c), and *Locus*'s 2003 "New Space Opera" symposium have focused attention on the fact that space opera has never gone away. The term now describes a kind of story, or its effect, rather than judging it.

Not all fictions involving space travel, conflict, huge vistas, and Big Dumb Objects are space opera, which is committed to action and adventure, focused upon the heroic, and frequently takes a series or serial form which allows for either a sense of escalation or constant variations on a comparatively narrow set of themes. *Buck Rogers,* originating in Philip Francis Nowlan's "Armageddon 2419" (1928) (and adapted in various media, including comic strips, a radio series, a movie serial and two television series; see Nicholls 1993), and *Flash Gordon*, created in 1934 by Alex Raymond as a rival comic strip (also adapted for radio, movie serials, two live-action and three cartoon television versions and a film; see Nicholls and Brosnan 1993), are space opera by this definition, and probably what many readers understood by the term – as is the German *Perry Rhodan* epic, probably the longest-running sf series, created in 1961 by K.H. Scheer and Clark Darlton and issued weekly. Isaac Asimov's *Foundation* series (1942–50), which attempts to eschew the heroic in favor of a more collective view of history, is not, despite its galaxy-wide setting and cosmic melodrama.

In 1952, James Blish described a C.M. Kornbluth story – essentially an everyday satire translated into sf by a futuristic setting – as space opera (Blish 1973: 27), alluding to the way in which early action-adventure sf reworked westerns or the lost-race stories with, for instance, aliens taking the place of Indians. He assumes that his readership will understand this metaphorical, rather than taxonomic, use of the term. John Wyndham divides the genre into various categories, including space opera, which he defines as mixing the scientific "gimmicks" from the invention-stories of such sf pioneers as Jules Verne with adventure fiction (westerns, war-stories, sea-stories) relocated in space. In contrast to sf centered on science or a scientific problem and to extrapolative/speculative fiction which explores the implications of a particular technological or sociological change, space opera is "the wild riot of pointless imaginings" (Wyndham 1965) in which regard for the laws of science or narrative plausibility are cheerfully broken if there is any danger of their obser-vation alienating the reader. It is, essentially, a mode for adolescents, particularly American adolescents, from which Wyndham is of course attempting to distance his own Wellsian "logical fantasy" (although, as John Beynon Harris, he wrote for the American pulps in the 1930s).

While space opera may be "a wild riot of ... imaginings," its pointlessness is debatable. The galactic conflict of Smith's *Lensman* series may be clumsily written, but (especially when revised for book publication) it offered a significant chorus to the increasingly tremendous conflicts of the twentieth century. Humans are pieces in a vast, Manichean struggle spanning an entire galaxy and billions of years. Unstoppable forces collide with immovable objects and superweapons are countered by even more super-defenses, cheered on by characters whose language and emotional development is barely advanced from the lowest level of sanitized, unchallenging children's fiction. Yet the sense of layers behind layers, and incremental revelations about the scale of the conflict and the hierarchical structure of the contending forces, still offers a sense of the infinite sublime which is at the heart of sf's "sense of wonder." Wish-fulfillment power-fantasy and reductive dialectic the series may be, but it encouraged its readers to look for big ideas.

Sf's epic aspects were also catered for by other subgenres – the Galactic Empire story, the planetary romance, and those future histories which incorporated the conquest of space into an all-encompassing narrative of the human race – and individual writers took what they needed from the store of situations being built up. As the term space opera became increasingly descriptive of a particular *kind* of space story, so the space story itself became more complex and its possibilities richer. Blish's *Cities in Flight* series (1950–62) involved technological gimmicks (the "spindizzy" which enabled Earth's cities to become cosmic hobos), conflict and adventure within a Stapledonian framework of historical speculation. James White's *Sector General* series (1957–99), set in a hospital space station run by a galactic federation whose main priority is to prevent war and encourage cooperation between species, undermined virtually every space opera cliché so effectively that its achievement can only be understood in the context of the kind of fiction he was deliberately *not* writing. Cordwainer Smith's "The Game of Rat and Dragon" (1955), in its darkness and fusion of individual adventure with epic background, further suggests that by the 1960s a once-clumsy tool was becoming capable of great flexibility. As Brian Aldiss pointed out, this colorfully inventive form was developing increasing affinities with the baroque (Aldiss 1964: v–vi).

Other writers, with various degrees of affection, satirized space opera. Jack Vance's *Space Opera* (1965) features a musical company touring space. Many British New Wave writers reacted vociferously against the poor writing and stereotyped situations of earlier sf, yet Barrington J. Bayley wrote identifiable, if dark, space operas and (somewhat against his will) M. John Harrison was instrumental in revisioning the field with his "disgruntled space opera" (Clute 1993: 547), *The Centauri Device* (1974), whose bleak and seedy setting was received by some as a model rather than a parody. Harrison is reported as disliking the book (Hartwell and Cramer 2006: 345), and certainly its irony seems heavy-handed and cynical compared with his later space operas *Light* (2002) and *Nova Swing* (2006). However, its subversive approach offered a way forward for writers such as Colin Greenland, whose *Take Back Plenty* (1990) helped to return sf to its space-operatic roots, adding a touch of contemporary grittiness to the saga of space-captain Tabitha Jute. In his neo-Victorian fantasia *Harm's Way* (1993), spaceships really *are* ships, battling the aether flux between the stars, and the solar system is largely a British Empire. Innocent Sophie Farthing, tied by the cords of drudgery and boredom to her wastrel father and his opium dreams, encounters an iron-jawed stranger who hints of knowing her dead mama, and thus embarks upon a voyage that mixes space opera with melodrama, swashbuckler and Victorian penny dreadful. Iain M. Banks made it respectable to set fiction in the far future, with bigger and better spaceships and inventive gadgetry, but his *Culture* novels, beginning with *Consider Phlebas* (1987), are less space opera than traditional character-based fiction. Focusing upon the moral dilemmas of a post-scarcity hedonistic utopia, they eschew the good-vs-evil dichotomy and, like Vernor Vinge's *A Fire Upon the Deep* (1992), suggest a deeper set of questions, such as the morality of moving beyond the "human" frame and "subliming" out of the physical realm altogether.

Such "New Space Opera" may owe much to the New Wave, but it is clearly also indebted to the variations made by Cordwainer Smith and James White, neither of whom had identifiable villains and whose distinctive settings suggested that more complex stories could be told within the bounds of spaceships-and-aliens fiction. C.J. Cherryh simply matured the form as she established the detailed historical background of her *Union–Alliance* universe where trade and political rivalries result in episodes like the Hugo-winning *Downbelow Station* (1981). Multiple Hugo-winner Lois McMaster Bujold's *Miles Vorkosigan* series used space opera as part of a remarkably skilful manipulation of various storytelling modes, as in *The Vor Game* (1990). Peter F. Hamilton's *Night's Dawn* trilogy (1996–9) explored the form's sense of vastness. Catharine Asaro's *Skolian Empire* series (1995–) combines the "Brackett tradition" of color and romance with a more generic version of "romance" as well as a sophisticated consideration of what these encounters mean in terms of gender issues (Hartwell and Cramer 2006). The "military" sf popularized by authors such as Jerry Pournelle, David Drake (the *Hammer's Slammers* series (1979–)), David Weber (whose *Honor Harrington* series (1993–) follows a female version of C.S. Forrester's Napoleonic-era Horatio Hornblower), and Elizabeth Moon (the *Serrano's Legacy* series (1993–5)) is essentially space opera whose earlier western tropes have been replaced by those of modern warfare.

Space opera also owes much to the popularization of sf's visual aspects by, say, the iconic images of *Star Trek*'s USS *Enterprise* (which takes part in numerous space opera-type battles) and the ingenious combat sequences of the *Star Wars* franchise. While George Lucas's use of spaceships, large-scale interstellar warfare, and easy moral divisions was largely unquestioning of such space opera images and stereotypes, J. Michael Straczynski's *Babylon Five* (1993–8), Josh Whedon's *Firefly* (2002–3), and Ronald D. Moore's *Battlestar Galactica* (2003–) parallel, in visual media, the revisionings writers like Asaro, Bujold, Hamilton, Alastair Reynolds, Scott Westerfeld, John C. Wright, and, especially, M. John Harrison had brought to print space opera. Each of these television series (like the various *Star Trek* series) echoed American politics, notably anxieties about democratic values in times of war and social crisis. In particular, *Firefly*, a deliberate "space western," returned to explicit frontier images. Terraformed worlds offer a space for analogies with the pioneering days of the American West, as settlers, petty criminals (like protagonist Malcolm Reynolds and his spaceship crew), and refugees struggle against hostile environments and not-always-appropriate technology in a future of hybrid American and Chinese languages and customs. Linguistically playful, it moves knowingly and effectively between different sets of clichés. In one episode, the *Serenity* crew actually rustle cattle. In the spin-off film, *Serenity* (Whedon 2005), the Reavers turn out to be not outlaws or "savages" but the terrible result of a misconceived technological experiment.

To those unfamiliar with sf, space opera perhaps seems synonymous with the genre. Its "operatic" elements have nothing to do with opera except as a tangential, ironic reference to a shared concern with spectacle and diversion rather than character or logic. While few traditional space operas possess analogous elements to the great compositions of musical opera, the neo-space operas of the past couple of decades have explored what Aldiss called the "wide-screen baroque" elements of the form to impressive effect. The use of space and space travel as a default location for an sf story, of large concepts and conflicts, and of increasing detail and scale – building up from rather than merely imitating earlier examples – seems to have created a subgenre which is by no means "outworn." Space opera has developed a kind of shared "otherworld" in which readers can share their familiarity with a megatext while they observe their own world's issues transformed. In Smith's *Lensman* series, the great moral metanarratives of Totalitarianism versus Democracy can be observed, while the status of the Underpeople in Cordwainer Smith's *Instrumentality of Mankind* stories (1950–75) reflects aspects of the 1960s struggle for racial equality in the US, though the more contemporary space opera of M. John Harrison tends to undermine the solidity of such metanarrative as it plays with a more subjective idea of story. Despite the changes and variations, there will undoubtedly come a time when the space-operatic future will become as fossilized and decadent as Marie Antoinette's aristocratic shepherdesses cavorting on the eve of the French Revolution. But not, perhaps, yet.

Bibliography

Aldiss, B. (1964) "Introduction," in C. Harness, *The Paradox Men*, London: Faber & Faber.

Blish, J., as W. Atheling Jr. (1973) *The Issue at Hand: studies in contemporary magazine science fiction*, Chicago: Advent.

Clute, J. (1993) "Harrison, M[ichael] John," in J. Clute and P. Nicholls (eds) *The Encyclopedia of Science Fiction*, London: Orbit.

Hartwell, D.G. (2006a) "New Ways of Looking at Space Operas: part 1," *New York Review of Science Fiction*, 216: 17–21.

—— (2006b) "New Ways of Looking at Space Operas: part 2," *New York Review of Science Fiction*, 217: 19–21.

—— (2006c) "New Ways of Looking at Space Operas: part 3," *New York Review of Science Fiction*, 218: 17–19.

Hartwell, D.G. and Cramer, K. (2006), *The Space Opera Renaissance*, New York: Tor.

Monk, P. (1992) "Not Just 'Cosmic Skullduggery': a partial reconsideration of space opera," *Extrapolation*, 33(4): 295–316.

Nicholls, P. (1993) "Buck Rogers in the 25th Century," in J. Clute and P. Nicholls (eds) *The Encyclopedia of Science Fiction*, London: Orbit.

Nicholls, P. and Brosnan, J. (1993) "Flash Gordon," in J. Clute and P. Nicholls (eds) *The Encyclopedia of Science Fiction*, London: Orbit.

Pringle, D. (2000) "What is this Thing Called Space Opera?," in G. Westfahl (ed.) *Space and Beyond: the frontier theme in science fiction*, Westport, CT: Greenwood Press.

Stableford, B. (1993) "Space Opera," in J. Clute and P. Nicholls (eds) *The Encyclopedia of Science Fiction*, London: Orbit.

—— (2006) Review of *The Space Opera Renaissance* edited by D.G. Hartwell and K. Cramer, *New York Review of Science Fiction*, 215: 1, 8–13.

Westfahl, G. (1994) "Beyond Logic and Literacy: the strange case of space opera," *Extrapolation*, 35(3): 176–85.

—— (2003) "Space Opera," in E. James and F. Mendlesohn (eds) *The Cambridge Companion to Science Fiction*, Cambridge: Cambridge University Press.

Wyndham, J. (1965) "Science Fiction and Space-Opera," *The Preparatory Schools Review*, Wyndham Archive 5/3/7.

56

WEIRD FICTION

China Miéville

If considered at all, Weird Fiction is usually, roughly, conceived of as a rather breathless and generically slippery macabre fiction, a dark fantastic ("horror" plus "fantasy") often featuring nontraditional alien monsters (thus plus "science fiction"). Though particularly associated with the pulp magazine *Weird Tales*, the stop-start existence of which began in 1923, classic Weird Fiction predates it: S.T. Joshi (1990) plausibly treats its high phase as 1880–1940. It has had a colossal impact across work in all media, with under-investigated generically problematizing implications. Indeed, Weird Fiction may serve as the bad conscience of the Gernsback/Campbell sf paradigm, and as rebuke to much theorizing that takes that paradigm's implicit self-conception as its starting point.

The para-canon of Weird includes those associated with or influential on the *Weird Tales* circle, and others with similar concerns (among many others Fritz Leiber, E.F. Benson, Robert Bloch, E.L. White, E.H. Visiak, Donald Wandrei, Frank Belknap Long, Robert Chambers, C.L. Moore, August Derleth, M.R. James, Carl Jacobi). The weird credentials of various authors such as H.G. Wells might be debated, but certain key names recur: among them Clark Ashton Smith, William Hope Hodgson, Algernon Blackwood, Arthur Machen, and, overwhelmingly the preeminent figure in the field, H.P. Lovecraft. It is this *locus classicus* of the subgenre, what we might consider "Haute Weird," that is considered here.

In his "Notes on Writing Weird Fiction" (1937), Lovecraft describes his desire to "escape from the prison-house of the known" (Lovecraft 1995: 113) and his fascination with "shattered natural law or cosmic alienage or 'outsideness'" (Lovecraft 1995: 113). The focus is on *awe*, and its undermining of the quotidian. This obsession with numinosity under the everyday is at the heart of Weird Fiction.

Lovecraft, a philosophical materialist, disavowed spirit, and in the absence of such supernature his world-saturating Weird means the strangeness of the physical world itself, as in his astonishing reference in "The Call of Cthulhu" (1928) to "an angle which was acute, but behaved as if it were obtuse" (Lovecraft 1999: 167). Other Weird writers express their cosmic awe differently. Algernon Blackwood in "The Willows" (1907) talks about the "awe and wonder" of "the personified elemental forces" (Blackwood 1973: 7, 18), Hodgson in *The House on the Borderland* (1908) of "commingled awe and curiosity" (Hodgson 2002: 177) in the face of the cosmos. The same concern is evident in Machen's religiosity, his obsession with "awe" and "ecstasy," his Gnostic vision in "The Great God Pan" (1894) that the perceived world is "but dreams and shadows … that hide the real world from our eyes" (Machen 2004: 58).

This permeating numinous bespeaks Weird's relation to the sublime, traditionally conceived as a sense of awe at vasty strangeness such as that of the Alps, the vistas of which provoke "enjoyment but with horror" (Kant 1991: 47). According to Edmund Burke and other theorists of the sublime, the beautiful and sublime are mutually exclusive: at a certain scale, enormity and unrepresentability – "the infinite cosmic spaces beyond the radius of our sight *and analysis*" (Lovecraft 1995: 113, emphasis added) – the sublime appears. The Weird, though, punctures the supposed membrane separating off the sublime, and allows swillage of that awe and horror from "beyond" back into the everyday – into angles, bushes, the touch of strange limbs, noises, etc. The Weird is a radicalized sublime backwash.

Machen, in his short story "N" (1936), pilfers the theological term "perichoresis" to describe the intertwining of the heavenly and the everyday, in Stoke Newington. More than the atheist Lovecraft, or spiritualistically maundering Blackwood, Machen brings out how Weird Fiction writers are in a lineage with those religious visionaries and ecstatics who perceive an unmediated relationship with numinosity – Godhead itself.

For many of those religious radicals this is an emancipatory/utopian revolt against a priestly class. However, Haute Weird Fiction performs a backhanded service in reminding that there is nothing intrinsically progressive about the everyday numinous. Indeed, a disproportionate number of its writers have distinctly reactionary aims. Lovecraft's awe, for example, is inextricable – as Michel Houellebecq (2005) brilliantly argues – from a racism so obsessive it is a hallucinogen; and Machen draws on agonized conceptions of a god whose ubiquity makes it totalitarian and/or predatory (as for example in Francis Thompson's astounding poem of devotional terror "Hound of Heaven" (*c.* 1889)), to depict a numinous so threatening that it operates not as liberation but as discipline, policed with acts of astonishing narratorial sadism.

It is not only in the content that estrangement from the supposedly quotidian is effected in Weird Fiction, but often in its form. Lovecraft's writing is a kind of purple poetry, notoriously parody-able. Of course such language can be done badly, and is not a necessary corollary of Weird Fiction (see, for example, the more robust register of Hodgson in many of his short stories, or Blackwood's melancholy ruminations). However, at its best Lovecraft's (and others') writing achieves affect because of, not despite, its prose, a crime against a certain *au courant* middlebrow minimalism, that will in passing extol barer prose as "spare," as if logo-parsimoniousness were a self-evident virtue; or, even more absurdly, as "precise," as if the word "table" is somehow *more like a table* than a prolix descriptive alternative. (Of course both lush and "spare" prose are words on a page, exactly equally unlike a table, a wooden thing upon which rests my tea.)

One can argue that the frenzied succession of adjectives in Lovecraft, alongside his regular insistence that whatever is being described is "undescribable," is, in its *hesitation*, its obsessive qualification and stalling of the noun, an aesthetic deferral according to which the world is always-already unrepresentable, and can only be approached by an asymptotic succession of subjective pronouncements. Thus the form of writing is a function of sublime backwash, these baroque stylings a philosophy of militant adjectivalism struggling against a nounism that implies, carelessly speaking of "dog" and "door" as if that were the end of the matter, that such unrepresentable Reals are containable in our inadequate symbolic system. This is not Promethean but myopic. By contrast the careful and precise hysteria of "Pulp Modernist" Weird Fiction looks like radical humility in the face of Weird ontology itself.

The abasement to the Weird that this prose represents is also visible in Lovecraft's narrative. He is largely uninterested in plot: "Atmosphere," he says, "not action, is the great desideratum of weird fiction" (Lovecraft 1995: 116). His stories are often little more than excuses for descriptions of Weird presences, and what narrative "revelations" there are are predictable. His is a surrender to the *ineluctability of the Weird*, again implying no irruption of strangeness into a status quo, but a Weird universe.

At its best this works as pulp bricolage, where texts concatenate out of scattered scraps, in what looks like a deliberate undermining of "plot." In Lovecraft's key work, "The Call of Cthulhu," there is no story, only the slow uncovering, from disjointed information and discarded papers, of the *fact* of the Weird, an ancient alien creature, Cthulhu, sojourning below the ocean. The story is explicit about its anti-narrative methodology, stressing that "all dread glimpses of truth" are "fleshed out from an accidental piecing together of separated things" (Lovecraft 1999: 140).

The unique physiology of Cthulhu, the famous "monster of vaguely anthropoid outline, but with an octopus-like head whose face was a mass of feelers, a scaly, rubbery-looking body, prodigious claws on hind and fore feet, and long narrow wings behind" (Lovecraft 1999: 148), is exemplary of Weird Fiction. One of the most distinct ways in which Lovecraft moots a Weird universe is in his revolutionary teratology. The monsters that inhabit his tales are a radical break with anything from a folkloric tradition. Rather than werewolves, vampires, or ghosts, Lovecraft's monsters are agglomerations of bubbles, barrels, cones, and corpses, patchworked from cephalopods, insects, crustaceans, and other fauna notable precisely for their absence from the traditional Western monstrous. Paradigmatic is Weird Fiction's obsession with the tentacle, a limb-type absent from European folklore and the traditional Gothic, and one which, after early proto-Weird iterations by Victor Hugo, Jules Verne, and H.G. Wells, viralled suddenly in Haute Weird Fiction until it is now, in the post-Weird debris of fantastic horror, the default monstrous limb-type.

Lovecraft repeatedly stresses that his creatures are extraterrestrial and have been hidden among us for eons. This retro-historicization notwithstanding, their alterity is radical, rather than aghastly remembered. The awe that Weird Fiction attempts to invoke is a function of *lack* of recognition, rather than any uncanny resurgence, guilt-function, the return of a repressed. It is thus as much a break from as an heir to traditional Gothic. In "The Willows," Blackwood stresses that the dread aroused by a serpentine pillar of huge figures "was no ordinary ghostly fear" (Blackwood 1973: 37); while Lovecraft's *Supernatural Horror in Literature* (1927) stresses that the "true weird tale" is characterized by "unexplainable dread of outer, unknown forces," rather than of any "bloody bones, or a sheeted form clanking chains according to rule" (Lovecraft 1973: 15). In its interest in the *implacably alien* Outer Monstrosities, Old Ones, and Great Cthulhu, rather than revenant ghosts, the Weird is in opposition to that category for thinking through the history-stained present that, after Derrida (1994), has become known as the "Hauntological." The Weird, rather, impregnates the present with a bleak, unthinkable novum.

Such a literary moment is an expression of upheaval and crisis. This cluster of works resembles an explosion in the timeline of (particularly Anglo-American) fiction. Where the wounds of Weird are discernible before 1880 we may find Weird Fiction *avant la lettre* (arguably, for example, in Sheridan Le Fanu), and after 1940, work which is post-Weird in more than just its dates. (A very few of the truly enormous number of relevant writers are Neil Gaiman, Caitlin Kiernan, Peter Straub, Stephen King, Poppy Z. Brite, Thomas Ligotti, Clive Barker, Katherine Dunn, Hal Duncan, Joyce Carol Oates, Robert Aickman, Grant Morrison, Ramsey Campbell, Michael Moorcock.) Between these outliers there is a sense of defining *trauma* at the heart of the field.

Each Weird Fiction writer has her or (more usually in the haute phase) his own particular mishigas. Machen's horror, for example, at democracy and the perceived vulgarities of modernity's "disenchantment" are allied to a prurient misogyny, as evidenced in the grotesque snuff-murder of Helen Vaughan, the awe-tainted sexually provocative woman, in "The Great God Pan." For Lovecraft, the horror of modernity is above all horror of "inferior" races, miscegenation, and cultural decline, expressed in his protean, fecund, seeping monsters. These particular concerns, though central to understanding particular writers' work, are expressions of a foundational underlying crisis.

Though Lovecraft's greatest period of work started around 1924, his story "Dagon" (1919) was key to ushering in his new paradigm, locating the "Lovecraft Event" (Noys 2007) as a postwar phenomenon. The great Weird Fiction writers are responding to capitalist modernity entering, in the late nineteenth and early twentieth centuries, a period of crisis in which its cruder nostrums of progressive bourgeois rationality are shattered. The heart of the crisis is the First World War, where mass carnage perpetrated by the most modern states made claims of a "rational" modern system a tasteless joke.

The fantastic has always been indispensable to think and unthink society, but traditional monsters were now profoundly inadequate, suddenly nostalgic in the epoch of modern war. Out of this crisis of traditional fantastic, the burgeoning sense that there is no stable status quo but a horror underlying the everyday, the global and absolute catastrophe implying poisonous totality, Weird Fiction's revolutionary teratology and oppressive numinous grows. This backwashed horror–sublime is investigated by scientists, doctors, engineers (Blackwood's John Silence, Hodgson's Carnacki, Lovecraft's survey team in *At the Mountains of Madness* (1936), the sadistic surgeons of Machen), and it is their very "rationality" that uncovers the radical and awesome monstrous. It is the war of 1914–18 that is the black box, the heart of Weird. In its malevolent Real, and protean new monsters, inconceivable and formless (though possessing meticulously itemized surplus specificity of form), Weird does not so much articulate the crisis as that the crisis cannot be articulated.

It is noticeable that when dealing overtly with the war, Machen in "The Bowmen" (1914), for example, moves away from his reactionary-ecstatic notion of an unknowable numinous to articulate not Weird but Agincourt archers *messire*ing for England, ghosts so unencumbered by historic angst they are embarrassments to hauntology. Elsewhere, as in "The Great God Pan," Machen conceives folkloric/traditional figures as ways of talking about something *unrepresentable*: whatever the politics of the Weird Fictioneers or their texts, there is in Weird an awareness of total crisis. This leeway for readings against the ideological grain is part of what makes Weird Fiction such an ongoingly fascinating field. When Machen wants to deploy supernature in the national interest, he articulates neither the radical bad-numinous of Weird nor the returned repressed of Gothic, but, in classic fascist mode, warmed-over mythic kitsch.

The war is bracketed by the Lovecraft Event on one side, and the neglected William Hope Hodgson on the other. His tentacle-riddled *The Boats of the Glen Carrig* (1907), cosmically awed *The House on the Borderland*, and flawed but astonishing post-apocalypse nihil-dream *The Night Land* (1912) are vivid explorations of the radical monstrous and bad-numinous. It is even arguable that in Hodgson's relative lack of particularizing obsessions (even *The Night Land*'s bumbling S&M fantasy is inoffensive, more like a seaside postcard than like Machen's misogyny), and in his relative lack of prose facility – absent Lovecraft's strange but expert purple prose – Hodgson provides a uniquely *uncluttered* insight into Weird Fiction as the literature of crisis. His work cannot be understood without reference to the war in which he died fighting: it is, in John Clute's phrase, "pre-Aftermath fiction" (J. Clute personal communication, 2006).

Hodgson's expressions of patriotism were heartfelt but somewhat rote, and unlike Machen, even his war writing never flinched from the insights of Weird, giving his work a different political valence. In the outstanding "The Baumoff Explosive" (1919), written and set during the war and published, poignantly, after Hodgson's death at the front, the German protagonist is no evil Hun but a saintly man trying to tap into absolute goodness, who is entered instead by what Hodgson, in one of the absolutely key phrases in Weird Fiction, has his narrator suppose is "some Christ-apeing monster of the Void." As no such entities have been mooted at any point up to or after this supposed "explanation," the true horror of the story lies in the implication that there is no mummery involved, that it is the Christ itself that speaks with monstrous voice, that Godhead, in the midst of cataclysm, is malevolent. Here is the purest and most affecting humanist expression of Weird Fiction traditional awed horror (far from, say, Machen's reactionary ecstasy).

In a deeply moving letter from the front, Hodgson refers to his own sunless end-times landscape of *The Night Land*. Nowhere is the constitutive relationship between the war and the Weird made more clear. The piece serves as epitaph not only to Hodgson, but, preemptively, to Weird Fiction itself because this, the field's single most astonishing evocation of the bad-numinous, engages with and moves beyond Hodgson's own fiction into *nonfiction*. Formlessness, so brilliantly abstracted and teratologized in Lovecraft, is here something that was *done*, by humans, and more terrible for that. There is no Weird so Weird as the backwashed bad sublime called Passchendaele.

> What a sense of desolation, the heaved-up mud rimming ten thousand shell craters as far as the sight could reach, north and south and east and west. My God, what a Desolation! And here and there standing like mute, muddled rocks – somehow terrible in their significant grim bashed formlessness – an old concrete blockhouse, with the earth torn up around them in monstrous craters and, in some cases, surged in great waves of earth against the sides of the blockhouses. The sun was pretty low as I came back, and far off across that Desolation, here and there they showed – just formless, squarish, cornerless masses erected by man against the Infernal Storm that seeps for ever, night and day, day and night, across that most atrocious Plain of Destruction. My God! Talk about a lost World – talk about the END of the World; talk about the "NightLand" – it is all here, not more than two hundred odd miles from where you sit infinitely remote.
>
> (Hodgson 2005: 384)

Bibliography

Blackwood, A. (1973) "The Willows," 1907 in E.F. Bleiler (ed.) *Best Ghost Stories of Algernon Blackwood*, New York: Dover.

Derrida, J. (1994) *Specters of Marx: the state of the debt, the work of mourning and the new international*, ed. B. Magnus and S. Cullenberg, trans. P. Kamuf, New York and London: Routledge.

Hodgson, W.H. (1919) "The Baumoff Explosive," *Nash's Magazine* (20 September).

—— (2002) *The House on the Borderland*, 1908, in *The House on the Borderland and Other Novels*, London: Gollancz.

—— (2005) *Wandering Soul*, Hornsea, E. Yorks: PS Publishing/Tartarus Press.

Houellebecq, M. (2005) *H.P. Lovecraft: against the world, against life*, 1999, trans. D. Khazeni, New York: Believer Books.

Joshi, S.T. (1990) *The Weird Tale*, Holicong, PA: Wildside Press.

Kant, I. (1991) *Observations on the Feeling of the Beautiful and the Sublime*, 1764, trans. J.T. Goldthwait, Berkeley: University of California Press.

Lovecraft, H.P. (1973) *Supernatural Horror in Literature*, 1927, New York: Dover.

—— (1995) "Notes on Writing Weird Fiction," 1937, in S.T. Joshi (ed.) *Miscellaneous Writings*, Sauk City, WI: Arkham House.

—— (1999) *The Call of Cthulhu and Other Weird Stories*, London: Penguin.

Machen, A. (2004) "The Great God Pan," 1894, in *Tales of Horror and the Supernatural*, Leyburn, Lancs.: Tartarus Press.

Noys, B. (2007) "The Lovecraft Event," paper presented at the *Weird Realism: Lovecraft and theory* Conference, Goldsmith College, London, April.

INDEX